www.wadsworth.com

wadsworth.com is the World Wide Web site for Wadsworth and is your direct source to dozens of online resources.

At wadsworth.com you can find out about supplements, demonstration software, and student resources. You can also send email to many of our authors and preview new publications and exciting new technologies.

wadsworth.com
Changing the way the world learns®

FIFTH EDITION

Community-Based Corrections

Paul F. Cromwell
Witchita State University

Rolando V. del Carmen
Sam Houston State University

Leanne Fiftal Alarid
University of Missouri—Kansas City

WADSWORTH

THOMSON LEARNING

Australia • Canada • Mexico • Singapore • Spain • United Kingdom • United States

WADSWORTH

THOMSON LEARNING ™

Executive Editor, Criminal Justice: Sabra Horne
Criminal Justice Editor: Shelley Murphy
Development Editor: Terri Edwards
Assistant Editor: Dawn Mesa
Editorial Assistant: Lee McCracken
Marketing Manager: Jennifer Somerville
Marketing Assistant: Karyl Davis
Project Manager, Editorial Production: Jennie Redwitz
Technology Project Manager: Susan DeVanna
Print/Media Buyer: April Vanderbilt
Permissions Editor: Joohee Lee

Production Service: Vicki Moran
Text Designer: Adriane Bosworth
Photo Researcher: Laura Murray
Copy Editor: Colleen McGuiness
Illustrator: Lotus Art
Cover Designer: Yvo Riezebos
Cover Image: © Photo Disc
Cover Printer: R. R. Donnelley, Willard
Compositor: TBH Typecast, Inc.
Printer: R. R. Donnelley, Willard

ExamView® and ExamView Pro® are registered trademarks of FSCreations, Inc. Windows is a registered trademark of the Microsoft Corporation used herein under license. Macintosh and Power Macintosh are registered trademarks of Apple Computer, Inc. Used herein under license.

Library of Congress Cataloging-in-Publication Data
Cromwell, Paul F.
    Community-based corrections / Paul F. Cromwell,
Rolando V. del Carmen, Leanne Fiftal Alarid — 5th ed.
        p. cm.
    Includes bibliographical references and index.
    ISBN 0-534-55966-2
    1. Community-based corrections—United States.
2. Probation—United States.   3. Parole—United States.
I. Del Carmen, Rolando V.   II. Alarid, Leanne Fiftal.
II. Title.
HV9279.C76 2001
364.6'2'0973—dc21   2001026062

Wadsworth/Thomson Learning
10 Davis Drive
Belmont, CA 94002-3098
USA

For more information about our products, contact us:
Thomson Learning Academic Resource Center
1-800-423-0563
http://www.wadsworth.com

International Headquarters
Thomson Learning
International Division
290 Harbor Drive, 2nd Floor
Stamford, CT 06902-7477
USA

UK/Europe/Middle East/South Africa
Thomson Learning
Berkshire House
168-173 High Holborn
London WC1V 7AA
United Kingdom

Asia
Thomson Learning
60 Albert Street, #15-01
Albert Complex
Singapore 189969

Canada
Nelson Thomson Learning
1120 Birchmount Road
Toronto, Ontario M1K 5G4
Canada

Brief Contents

Contents

Preface

By 2000, the number of adults under some form of correctional supervision in the United States had reached an all-time high of 6.3 million persons. Of this total, more than 4 million offenders were being supervised by probation, parole, and other community-based correctional programs. Most offenders serve their sentences in the community, and even those who are incarcerated eventually return to the community, often on parole. This book examines these community-based methods of corrections.

The goal of this Fifth Edition of *Community-Based Corrections* is to provide students with comprehensive, up-to-date, objective knowledge of the procedures, practices, and personnel that constitute probation, parole, and other community-based sanctions. We have sought to present community-based correctional programs in their historical, philosophical, social, and legal contexts and to integrate theory and practice to the greatest extent possible.

Because we want this book to be of practical use, we have provided many examples of community-based programs, laws, and procedures from state and federal jurisdictions. In this edition, as in previous ones, we wrestled with the problem of using examples and laws from as many states as possible to make the materials relevant to a broad audience. However, the states' systems vary widely in their programs, laws, and sophistication. We decided we would not do students justice if we included laws and examples from only the large, populous states, and we could not possibly incorporate examples and laws from every jurisdiction. We therefore decided to use the federal system as our primary point of reference. We have cited state laws and programs throughout the book nonetheless.

NEW IN THE FIFTH EDITION

Community-Based Corrections, Fifth Edition, has undergone some changes from the previous edition.

At the end of some of the chapters we have added links to Web sites that provide more information on topics covered in that chapter.

We added case studies for ten chapters. These case studies were prepared for in-class discussion or for out-of-class written exercises to initiate critical thinking.

The Supplemental Readings we've selected for some of the chapters can now be found on the book-specific Web site. A supplemental reading reference appears at the end of appropriate chapters to lead the reader to the site. Chapter 1, "The State of Corrections Today: Why Community Corrections Is Important," is new. It provides students with an overview of the corrections system and describes some of the challenges the corrections system faces. This chapter also explains why the study of corrections in the community is important. Updated information on sentencing can be found in Chapter 3, "The Decision to Grant Probation." Updated information on mandatory release, decline in discretionary parole, and use of medical parole can be found in Chapter 9, "Development of Parole: From Its Origin to the Present." And updated information on parole assessment techniques can be found in Chapter 10, "The Parole Board and Parole Selection."

The Fourth Edition had only one chapter on intermediate sanctions. The Fifth Edition has divided intermediate sanctions into two chapters: Chapter 12, "Residential Intermediate Sanctions," covers boot camps, halfway houses, and therapeutic communities. Chapter 13, "Nonresidential Intermediate Sanctions," discusses house arrest, electronic monitoring, intensive supervision probation, day reporting centers, community service, restitution, and fines.

Chapter 14, "Juvenile Justice, Probation, and Aftercare," has been updated to include information on special courts for juveniles (teen courts, drug courts), the transfer of juveniles to adult court, the problem of youth gangs, the curfew program, and the issue of punishing parents for what their children do.

The Fourth Edition had a chapter entitled "The Effectiveness of Community-Based Corrections." The information in that chapter has been incorporated, where appropriate, throughout the Fifth Edition: The effectiveness of probation is examined in Chapter 8, the effectiveness of parole is covered in Chapter 11, and the effectiveness of intermediate sanctions is discussed in Chapters 12 and 13.

Chapter 15, "Direct and Collateral Consequences of Conviction," is updated, with a special section on registration and community notification of sex offenders.

ORGANIZATION OF THE BOOK

Chapter 1 provides an overall framework of where community corrections fits into the schemata of the corrections system, and why it is important for study. Following Chapter 1, the book is divided into three parts. Part I examines probation. Chapter 2 discusses the historical, social, and legal foundations of probation. Chapter 3 addresses sentencing and the decision to grant probation. Various forms of probation are discussed and analyzed. Chapter 4, "The Presentence Investigation Report," considers the purposes, contents, and legal issues of this important document. Examples of two types of presentence report are presented. Chapter 5 examines the terms and conditions of probation. Recent court decisions are discussed. Chapter 6 provides a review of the organization and administration of probation services. Chapter 7 is a comprehensive analysis of probation and parole supervision. Chapter 8 considers probation revocation and presents important court decisions.

Part II examines parole. Chapter 9 begins with a history of the concept and practice of parole, reviews the past and present controversies regarding the use of parole, and analyzes the issues currently being debated. Chapter 10 examines the parole board and parole decision making. Chapter 11 provides an overview of parole conditions and of the issues involved in parole revocation.

Part III is a review and analysis of intermediate sanctions and special issues. Chapter 12 has information about facilities where the offender lives, such as boot camps, halfway houses, and therapeutic communities. Chapter 13 discusses community programs in which offenders live at home while they periodically report or become involved in their sanction. We highlight house arrest, electronic monitoring, intensive supervision probation, day reporting centers, community service, restitution, and fines. Chapter 14 reviews the laws and practices of community-based corrections for juveniles.

Chapter 15 is unique for a textbook of probation, parole, and other community sanctions. It is a review of the collateral consequences of conviction. Probationers and parolees often face indirect, unanticipated sanctions: the loss of civil and political rights following conviction. The rights lost include not only basic citizenship rights such as the right to vote, but also more subtly the losses of "good character," of occupational and professional licenses, of the right to be bonded, and so on. These losses frequently work against the offender's efforts to put his or her life in order and to obtain and maintain employment. Chapter 16 examines the means by which the offender may regain some of these lost rights, taking a close look at pardons. We believe that the information presented in Chapters 15 and 16 can be of enormous benefit to probation and parole officers and the probationers and parolees under their supervision.

FEATURES AND LEARNING TOOLS

Each chapter begins with an outline, a list of key terms, and a brief statement of the learning objectives in the chapter. Key terms are defined in the margins of the text and in the glossary at the end of the book. Each chapter is followed by discussion questions that will encourage students to think critically about the materials presented in the chapter. These questions could also serve as written exercises in many cases or as topics for essays or research papers. Most chapters contain boxed features that amplify particular issues, events, and processes. The book contains many photographs, tables, and figures that will help students to visualize the phenomena and processes under discussion. An *Instructor's Manual with Test Bank* and a computerized *Test Bank* are also available. The following supplements are available for bundling to aid student comprehension:

- **Crime Scenes: An Interactive Criminal Justice CD ROM**—The first introductory criminal justice CD ROM available. This interactive CD ROM places students in various roles as they explore all aspects of the criminal justice system: policing and investigations, courts, sentencing, and corrections.
- **InfoTrac College Edition**—Gives students access to full-length articles from more than 600 scholarly and popular periodicals. Students can print complete articles or use the cut-and-paste and e-mail techniques. Includes readings from *U.S. News and World Report, Corrections Today, Prison Journal, American Criminal Law Review,* and much more.
- **Internet Investigator III**—Includes new criminal justice-related Web sites categorized by course for ease of use: policing, investigations, courts, corrections, research, juvenile delinquency, and much more. Save students money by bundling with the book.

ACKNOWLEDGMENTS

This book could not have been written without the generous assistance of many colleagues and corrections professionals. We wish to express our appreciation to Kent Sisson, parole director, Southern Parole Region, Kansas Department of Corrections, and Terri Sisson, deputy chief U.S. parole officer, District of Kansas, for preparing the case studies that follow some chapters and for their advice and consultation on many issues during the course of preparing this edition. Our thanks to Richard Russell, supervising U.S. probation officer (retired), Western District of Texas, for his contribution, "A Day in the Life of a Federal Probation Officer." Specific recognition goes to Shelley Morff, University of Missouri—Kansas City, for a fantastic job in creating the endnotes, obtaining articles from the library, and creating the tables that appear in this edition.

We would like to acknowledge the following colleagues who so kindly provided us with information and referrals to use in our text: William Barton, Indiana University; Dan Beto, director, Correctional Management Institute of Texas; John Byrd, chief U.S. pretrial services officer, Western District of Texas; Amy Craddock, Indiana State University; Alex Holsinger, University of Missouri—Kansas City; and Trey Williams, Prairie View A&M University. Thanks are also due to colleagues in the probation and parole field who have given Rolando V. del Carmen the necessary background in field training that has been invaluable in writing chapters in the book. Among those are Rick Faulkner, program specialist, National Institute of Corrections; Ron Corbett, deputy commissioner, Massachusetts Department of Probation; and Todd Jermstad, assistant legal counsel, Texas Department of Criminal Justice.

We leaned heavily on various documents published by the Bureau of Justice Statistics and the National Institute of Justice. These materials were essential to our effort.

In any undertaking of this sort, the extant literature in the field is relied upon for guidance and reference. In this regard we benefited from the work of Howard Abadinsky, Harry Allen, Peggy Burke, Dean Champion, Todd Clear, George Cole, Frank Cullen, Chris Eskridge, Burt Galaway, Ronald Jackson, Wesley Krause, Edward Latessa, Doris Layton MacKenzie, Belinda McCarthy, Bernard McCarthy, Norval Morris, Joan Petersilia, Edward Rhine, William R. Smith, John Ortiz Smykla, Michael Tonry, Larry Travis, and Gennaro Vito.

Shelley Murphy, criminal justice editor, and Vicki Moran, project editor, at Wadsworth were stalwart and supportive guides. They did a superb job of keeping us on track and on schedule and encouraging us when our energy and enthusiasm occasionally waned. Colleen McGuiness, our copy editor, significantly improved our book by her keen eye and attention to every detail.

We express our special appreciation to our colleagues who reviewed drafts of the book. Their insightful comments and suggestions proved invaluable. In particular, we appreciate the work of Lee Ayers, Southern Oregon University; Michael Brown, Ball State University; Dayton Hall, Tarleton State University; William Kroman, Kent State University; and Terry Miller, Valencia Community College.

Finally, Leanne Fiftal Alarid would like to personally thank the following individuals for their contribution to the text: Bob Goodson, Mike Hicks, Shawn Kelley, Jennifer Lager, Eric Myers, Dolly Owen, Jim Shriver, Don Turner, "Chopper" Dave Vargo, and Jim Wuster.

Paul F. Cromwell

Rolando V. del Carmen

Leanne Fiftal Alarid

About the Authors

Paul F. Cromwell is professor of criminal justice and director of the School of Community Affairs at Wichita State University. He received his Ph.D. in criminology from Florida State University in 1986. He also holds a B.A. in sociology and an M.A. in criminal justice from Sam Houston State University in Texas, as well as a master of public administration from Texas Christian University. He has previously taught at the University of Texas–Permian Basin and the University of Miami.

His extensive experience in the criminal justice system includes service as a U.S. probation and parole officer, chief juvenile probation officer, and commissioner and chairman of the Texas Board of Pardons and Paroles. His primary research interest is in corrections, criminal decision making, and crime prevention through environment design—a crime prevention methodology that stresses the manipulation of the physical environment (land use, roads, building design) to reduce opportunities for criminal activity.

Cromwell is author and editor of 16 books and 35 articles and book chapters in the academic literature in the fields of criminal justice and criminology, including *Breaking and Entering: An Ethnographic Analysis of Burglary, In Their Own Words: Criminals on Crime,* and *Crime and Justice in America.*

Rolando V. del Carmen is distinguished professor of criminal justice at the Criminal Justice Center, Sam Houston State University, in Huntsville, Texas. He holds a B.A. and a bachelor of laws degree from the Philippines; a master of comparative law from Southern Methodist University; a master of laws from the University of California at Berkeley; and a doctor of science of law from the University of Illinois.

Del Carmen was assistant dean and associate professor of a school of law in the Philippines and has held various administrative and academic positions in the United States. He has taught at various universities and has written extensively. His publications include more than ten books and numerous articles in several journals on law-related topics in criminal justice. His books include *Criminal Procedure: Law and Practice,* Fifth Edition, *Civil Liabilities of Law Enforcement Personnel, Texas Probation Law and Practice,* and *Potential Liabilities of Probation and Parole Officers.*

Del Carmen travels and lectures extensively and has served as a consultant to criminal justice agencies in a number of states. He was appointed to a six-year term to the Texas Commission on Jail Standards. In 1986, he won the Faculty Excellence in Research Award at Sam Houston State University, the first such award ever to be given by the university. The Academy of Criminal Justice Sciences named del Carmen as the recipient of the 1990 Academy Fellow Award during its national convention in Denver, Colorado. In 1996, he was the recipient of the Bruce Smith Award, given each year by the Academy of Criminal Justice Sciences, for his contributions to the field of criminal justice education.

Leanne Fiftal Alarid is assistant professor and program coordinator of criminal justice/criminology in the Department of Sociology/Criminal Justice and Criminology at the University of Missouri—Kansas City. She earned her M.A. in criminal justice/criminology and her Ph.D. in criminal justice, from Sam Houston State University in Huntsville, Texas. She graduated with honors as a double major in psychology and sociology from the University of Northern Colorado.

Alarid's areas of expertise are institutional and community corrections, women and crime, and criminal justice policy. She is the author of 15 journal articles and recently edited a book with Paul Cromwell entitled *Correctional Perspectives: Views from Academics, Practitioners, and Prisoners*. Alarid is currently coediting (with Scott Decker and Charles Katz) a book on controversial criminal justice issues.

Alarid has experience as an investigator for the public defender's office in Greeley, Colorado. She also worked as a counselor for a girls' group home and as a case manager at an adult halfway house, both in Denver, Colorado.

I

Probation

The idea behind community corrections programs is that most offenders can be effectively punished within their community of origin because most offenders are not violent. They do not pose a danger to themselves or to others in the community. Reintegration and rehabilitation are less difficult if offenders are allowed to maintain community ties and relationships. Furthermore, the community benefits for several reasons if nonviolent offenders are punished in the community.

First, the offender remains in the community where he or she has responsibilities. With legitimate employment, offenders can continue supporting themselves and their family of origin, and they will pay taxes. Second, offenders in the community are more likely than prison-bound offenders to compensate their victim through restitution or to pay back the community through community service. Finally, community corrections programs do not expose offenders to the subculture of violence in most jails and prisons.

Chapter 1 introduces the basic goals and programs of community corrections, and it provides justification for why the study of community corrections is important. Chapters 2 through 7 discuss probation—the most frequently used sentence in corrections. Chapter 2 provides the history of probation, and Chapter 3 covers factors that judges consider when they decide whether or not to grant offenders probation. Chapter 4 focuses on the presentence investigation report, a document prepared by probation officers to aid judges during sentencing. Probation conditions are discussed in Chapter 5. Chapter 6 pays particular attention to how probation departments are structured and how officers are selected and trained. Chapter 7 examines classification and probation officer supervision styles. Chapter 8 discusses probation revocation—the process that occurs when conditions of probation are not followed.

1

The State of Corrections Today: Why Community Corrections Is Important

Paul Conklin/Photo Edit

What You Will Learn in This Chapter

Correctional agencies and programs perform the function of carrying out the sentence imposed by a judge. Corrections is a social control mechanism for convicted offenders, and it also serves to keep others law abiding. You will learn about how more punitive sentencing policies have contributed to correctional growth in institutional and community-based corrections. Community corrections consists of two basic types of programs: (1) sanctions that serve as alternatives to incarceration and (2) programs that assist prisoners in community reentry after prison. You will learn, through an introduction to a variety of punishments, how the study of community corrections is important to an overall understanding of correctional policy and social control.

KEY TERMS

Indeterminate sentencing
Determinate sentencing
Community corrections
Institutional corrections
Restorative justice
Intermediate sanctions
Net widening
Recidivism

THE CORRECTIONAL DILEMMA

"Let's get tough on crime"
The "war on drugs"
"Three strikes and you're out"
"Lock 'em up and throw away the key"
"Juvenile offenders should be treated as adults"

These ideas relating to crime control reflect public sentiment and echo political rhetoric that have existed since the mid-1970s. U.S. society seems to be increasingly reliant on the criminal justice system, particularly on corrections, as a social control mechanism. These "get tough" public attitudes have resulted in staggering correctional growth, both in sheer numbers of people and correctional institutions as well as in budget allocations to support this expansion.

The United States currently has 6.3 million persons, or nearly 3 percent of the total adult population, under the supervision of the criminal justice system. According to the data in Table 1.1, about 3.7 million offenders are out in the community on probation, while those on parole totaled 712,713 by the end of 1999.[1]

In addition to those in the community, more than 2 million offenders are incarcerated in local, state, and federal institutions. This number includes juveniles held in juvenile facilities (105,790) and adults held in local jails (605,943), facilities on military bases (2,279), tribal territories (1,621), territorial prisons (18,394), and Immigration and Naturalization Service facilities (7,675).[2]

The recent rise in the state and federal prison population is directly related to a number of factors: (1) a change in sentencing laws and longer sentences for violent offenders, (2) differential police responses to drug offenses, (3) a decreased rate of release on discretionary parole, and (4) an increase of parole violators returning to prison. Drug offenders accounted for the largest percentage of the total growth in the federal system.[3]

Change in Sentencing Laws

From the 1930s to the mid-1970s, **indeterminate sentencing** was the primary sentencing philosophy in the United States. Under the indeterminate sentencing model, judges decided who went to prison, and parole boards decided when offenders were

INDETERMINATE SENTENCING

A sentencing philosophy that focuses on treatment and incorporates a broad sentencing range or undetermined amount of time served in prison or in the community, where release is reliant on offender rehabilitation or readiness to function prosocially.

TABLE 1.1 *Adults under Community Supervision or in Jail or Prison, 1980–99*

Year	Total Estimated Correctional Population[a]	COMMUNITY SUPERVISION		INCARCERATION	
		Probation	Parole	Jail	Prison
1980	1,840,400	1,118,097	220,438	182,288[b]	319,598
1981	2,006,600	1,225,934	225,539	195,085[b]	360,029
1982	2,192,600	1,357,264	224,604	207,853	402,914
1983	2,475,100	1,582,947	246,440	221,815	423,898
1984	2,689,200	1,740,948	266,992	233,018	448,264
1985	3,011,500	1,968,712	300,203	254,986	487,593
1986	3,239,400	2,114,621	325,638	272,735	526,436
1987	3,459,600	2,247,158	355,505	294,092	562,814
1988	3,714,100	2,356,483	407,977	341,893	607,766
1989	4,055,600	2,522,125	456,803	393,303	683,367
1990	4,348,000	2,670,234	531,407	403,019[c]	743,382
1991	4,535,600	2,728,472	590,442	424,129[c]	792,535
1992	4,762,600	2,811,611	658,601	441,781[c]	850,566
1993	4,944,000	2,903,061	676,100	455,500[c]	909,381
1994	5,141,300	2,981,022	690,371	479,800	990,147
1995	5,335,100	3,077,861	679,421	499,300	1,078,542
1996	5,482,700	3,164,996	679,733	510,400	1,127,528
1997	5,725,800	3,296,513	694,787	557,974	1,176,564
1998	6,126,300	3,670,591	696,385	584,372	1,224,469
1999	6,318,900	3,773,624[d]	712,713	596,485	1,284,894
Percentage change					
1998–99	2.8	2.8	2.1	3.2	2.3
1990–99	45.3	41.3	48.0	72.8	34.1

Note: Counts for probation, prison, and parole populations are for December 31 of each year except the 1999 prison count, which is June 30; jail population counts are for June 30 of each year. Counts of adults held in facilities for 1993–96 were estimated and rounded to the nearest 100. Data for jail and prison are for inmates under custody.
[a]A small number of individuals have multiple correctional statuses; consequently, the total number of persons under correctional supervision is an overestimate. The total is rounded to the nearest 100.
[b]Estimated.
[c]The estimated jail population for 1990–93 includes an unknown number of persons supervised outside jail facilities.
[d]Excludes 23,907 probationers in jail, 22,758 probationers in prison, and 2,163 probationers in an Immigration and Naturalization Service holding facility.
Source: U.S. Department of Justice, Bureau of Justice Statistics, *Correctional Populations in the United States, 1994,* NCJ–163916 (Washington, DC: U.S. Department of Justice, 1995), Table 1.1; and U.S. Department of Justice, Bureau of Justice Statistics, *Probation and Parole in 1999,* NCJ 183508 (Washington, DC: U.S. Department of Justice, July 2000), 3.

rehabilitated and ready for release on parole.[4] The release date was thus dependent upon how quickly the offender progressed toward rehabilitation, according to the judgment of the parole board. Parole could also be used as a backdoor strategy for controlling the prison population. When prisons became too crowded, the parole rate increased to make room for incoming prisoners. Under indeterminate sentencing, offenders who did not go to prison were, for the most part, placed on probation. Other than prison or probation, few other intermediate sentencing options existed, such as halfway houses and intensive probation. Furthermore, they were used infrequently.[5]

Support for indeterminate sentencing declined as people questioned whether prison rehabilitation worked and whether parole boards could determine when offenders were ready for release. Questions were also raised as to whether indeterminate sentencing was administered fairly. Because the release date was ambiguous, some offenders were spending many more years behind bars than their crime warranted, while others—who may have convinced the parole board that they were "cured"—were released after only a few years.

Maine in 1975 became the first state to return to a sentencing philosophy of **determinate sentencing.** In determinate sentencing, the sentence range is largely determined either by legislative statute or by a sentencing guideline matrix that listed the sentence the offender should receive based on the offender's prior criminal record and the current conviction.[6] In other words, sentence length is determined more by what the offender did than by how long it took for the offender to become rehabilitated behind bars. The slogan "you do the crime, you do the time" became more popular, while funding for prison treatment programs diminished. In determinate sentencing, judges lost most of their sentencing power and discretion, and prosecutors gained some discretionary power by being able to decide what crime with which the offender should be initially charged. Judges are sometimes able to deviate slightly (higher or lower) from the prescribed sentencing guidelines, but they must provide justification for doing so. This is to increase the certainty and severity of punishment as well as to decrease judicial sentencing disparity.

Many states have adopted mandatory minimum sentencing laws for certain types of offenses, such as violent crimes, carrying of firearms, narcotics, or repeat felony offenders. By 1983, 49 states had mandatory minimum prison terms for certain crimes. Mandatory minimum prison terms must be served before release can even be considered. "Truth in sentencing" laws became popular in the mid-1990s to refer to offenders who must serve at least 85 percent of the sentence length before becoming eligible for release.[7] To add to the problem of prison crowding, not only are offenders serving longer prison terms up front, but ten states have also abolished parole as a backdoor release strategy.[8]

The most controversial set of sentencing guidelines is at the federal level. Opponents say that the federal guidelines were developed with little thought as to how longer stipulated prison terms, particularly those for drug offenders, would affect burgeoning prison populations. Federal guidelines also seemed to almost completely ignore community corrections sanctions.[9] Furthermore, the 1984 Sentencing Reform Act abolished federal parole as an option to control federal prison crowding.[10] So, the only option was to build more federal prisons.

Sentencing guidelines at the state level have been more successful than at the federal level. State guidelines seem to provide for more judicial discretion and more viable alternatives to incarceration.[11] Evaluations of state sentencing guidelines have found that dispositional polices (whether offenders will or will not be incarcerated—the "in/out decision") have had a greater impact on prison population growth than a longer sentence length.[12] However, in the federal system for drug crimes, the reverse is true.[13]

Sentencing guidelines do not just stipulate imprisonment. Some states, such as North Carolina and Ohio, have incorporated intermediate sanctions into their sentencing guidelines for felonies and misdemeanors. This has been tried in a number of different ways: (1) by using "zones of discretion" in which the sentencing grid is divided into some offenses with confinement only and some offenses with an option of confinement or nonconfinement, (2) by establishing "categorical exception policies" that focus on the offender, and (3) by converting different sanctions into "punishment units" so that judges could impose any combination of sanctions that equaled a set number of punishment units. The goal of making intermediate sanctions an integral part of the sentencing guidelines is to further differentiate sentencing for violent versus nonviolent offenders, in which more nonviolent offenders are sentenced to community corrections programs and prison beds are reserved for individuals convicted of violent crimes.[14]

DETERMINATE SENTENCING

A sentencing philosophy that focuses on certainty and severity for the crime committed and incorporates an exact amount of time or narrow sentencing range of time to be served in prison or in the community. Amount of time served depends on the legislative statutes or the sentencing guidelines, which mandate how much time is to be served before the offender is eligible (if at all) for early release.

In general, the changes in sentencing philosophy since the mid-1970s, along with a decrease in parole rates and a greater tendency for probation and parole violators to proceed to prison (as discussed in Chapter 9), have all contributed to an increase of incarcerated individuals.

The Toughening of Juvenile Corrections

"Getting tough" with crime and changing sentencing laws have not been limited to adults. In the last decade, with the growing dissatisfaction with how juveniles are handled in the juvenile justice system, every state has changed its juvenile statutory laws to either more closely resemble the adult criminal justice system or create options for prosecutors to treat juveniles as adults for violent crimes. What this means is that some juveniles are tried and punished as an adult automatically by type of crime committed (such as murder) or by discretion of the prosecutor or the judge. Other key issues involved in the juvenile justice change vary by state. These issues include allowing juveniles to be fingerprinted, opening juvenile records, opening juvenile court proceedings to the public, allowing victims to attend juvenile court, making offenders pay victim restitution, and obligating parents to take responsibility for their children's actions.[15]

The juvenile justice system still exists as a separate entity from the adult criminal justice system. Since the juvenile justice system began more than 100 years ago, rehabilitation and diversion became the core mission. Because the vast majority of juvenile offenders are nonviolent, they are tried in juvenile courts under a private and more informal process than adult offenders. As discussed in Chapter 14, the juvenile justice system has recently begun to provide a wider variety of intermediate sanctions for nonviolent juveniles and has started to pay more attention to crime prevention through factors outside of the system, such as the family, peers, education, and the neighborhood.[16]

THE PARADOX

We are used to thinking of community safety as contingent upon who is allowed to live in the community. Justice seems separationist because formal justice processes remove offenders from everyday life for accusation and conviction ceremonies, and they often result in penal removal, as well. The idea that communities are made safe by eliminating unsafe residents is equally an ingrained idea in American traditions.[17]

Paradoxically, correctional policy shifts according to public perceptions, which are primarily influenced by the media, not by the realities of the corrections system. The media report a biased, sensationalist view of the criminal justice system, so the average American citizen is not well informed about the true nature of punishment and corrections. For example, as depicted in the quote above, the average American citizen believes that most criminals deserve to be incarcerated for long periods of time and that the corrections system is soft on crime. Americans have long held that view even though the United States has one of the highest rates of incarceration in the world.[18]

To support the current public sentiment, billions of dollars are spent annually to support the criminal justice system. In 1999 alone, a total of $32.7 billion dollars was spent on adult state and federal prison institutions, averaging $630.7 million per state. Out of the total amount, $3.3 billion was allocated for new prison construction or other building improvements.[19] This did not include the money spent to operate city and county jails. An additional $4.6 billion was spent just on probation and parole programs across the nation. The average probation department had a budget of $125.5 million dollars, and parole departments averaged almost $51 million.[20] Traditional incarceration is much more expensive than most community sanctions, including probation and parole.

Every year, state budgets must appropriate tax dollars for all social needs of the entire state. The problem with spending so much money on correctional growth is that a larger proportion of the state budget is being used to fund corrections, while money is being cut from programs such as education, public health, and the repair of roads and bridges.[21]

Even though new prison units are being built at an unprecedented rate, prison crowding remains a problem. Prison crowding contributes to an increase in physical and mental illnesses, an increase in violent incidents (assaults, suicides, murders inside prison, and so on), and unsafe conditions for prison staff. In addition, fewer treatment and recreational programs are available for inmates to better themselves while incarcerated.[22] Confinement neither significantly reduces the crime rate nor has any positive effect on recidivism.[23] Joan Petersilia made the argument that prisons have such a little overall effect on the crime rate for a number of reasons, including the fact that long prison terms are more often enforced on people who are already "aging out" of crime, while much of the predatory crime is committed by juveniles who are less likely to receive long prison terms or to receive any institutional time at all.[24]

The corrections system seems to have within it many contradictions that affect its goals and purposes. What are correctional agencies supposed to be doing?

THE PURPOSE OF CORRECTIONS

Correctional agencies and programs perform the function of carrying out the sentence imposed by a judge. At a basic level, corrections is a social control mechanism for convicted offenders, and it also keeps others law abiding through general deterrence. Corrections agencies are either institutional (jails and prisons) or community-based (probation, parole, electronic monitoring, and so on). We recognize the importance of keeping offenders incarcerated who are dangerous to the public or who have committed a violent crime so heinous that incarceration is a deserved punishment. However, we believe that the vast majority of offenders who commit a crime should not go to jail or prison, because the crime does not warrant imprisonment. Judges and prosecutors need a variety of punishments from which to choose, and community corrections offers them a diversity of sentencing options. This is why the United States has the most alternative community-based programs of any nation in the world.[25]

Community-Based Corrections

This text will focus exclusively on community-based corrections. **Community corrections** is defined as a nonincarcerative sanction in which offenders serve all or a portion of their sentence in the community. Community-based corrections consists of two basic types of supervision: (1) "front-end" sanctions, sentenced by judges, that serve as alternatives to incarceration; and (2) "back-end" programs, participants of whom are chosen by corrections officials, that assist prisoners in community reentry after prison.

COMMUNITY CORRECTIONS

A nonincarcerative sanction in which offenders serve all or a portion of their sentence in the community.

AN ALTERNATIVE TO INCARCERATION: As an alternative to incarceration, community-based corrections are sanctions imposed on offenders that allow them to remain in the community while participating in one or more programs aimed at controlling future criminal behavior. With these front-end programs, judges sentence offenders directly to one or more community punishments. The idea of community-based programs is not new. Traditional probation, the oldest and best-known program of community corrections, has been part of the criminal justice system since the mid-19th century. Chapter 2 provides a detailed discussion of the history of probation.

COMMUNITY REENTRY: As a backdoor program, community programs such as parole assist prisoners in community reentry after prison. Another type of backdoor program is when imprisoned offenders, who have already been sentenced to prison by a judge, are chosen by corrections officials and transferred to a different type of program that the offenders can complete in a shorter duration. Examples of these types of programs are boot camps and therapeutic communities that are located inside a prison, separate from the general prisoner population. The purpose of these back-end programs is to save money and prison space, while also providing program participants with a specialized treatment regimen.

HOW COMMUNITY CORRECTIONS FITS CORRECTIONAL GOALS

INSTITUTIONAL CORRECTIONS

An incarcerative sanction in which offenders serve their sentence away from the community in a jail or prison institution.

The goals of community corrections compliment the overall goals of **institutional corrections.** Community corrections attempts to punish offenders, while at the same time protect the public and prevent future criminal behavior through rehabilitation, community reintegration, and making amends.

Protection of the Public

Most offenders have shown by their offenses that they cannot easily conform to the norms of society. One of the goals of community-based corrections, therefore, is to help offenders conform to behavioral expectations and monitor their progress toward that goal. Perhaps the major criticism of traditional probation and parole has been their failure to protect the public from further criminal acts by individuals under supervision in the community. Crime control is currently a primary concern of community corrections administrators.[26] For probation or any other community-based program to be effective and accepted by policymakers and the public, it must first demonstrate that the offenders under supervision are adequately monitored and that the public has nothing to fear from their actions.

Control may be accomplished in a variety of ways. First, as discussed in Chapter 7, offenders should be assessed to determine the degree of risk posed by their participation in community programs. Community-based programs are not generally appropriate for violent offenders or those with extensive criminal records. Second, those who supervise offenders in community-based programs must accept responsibility to protect the public by monitoring compliance with court orders and conditions of release. Finally, violations of supervised conditions must be taken seriously. If the programs are to become credible sanctions, courts and paroling authorities must be willing to revoke probation or parole for those who cannot or will not comply with the conditions of release.[27] The procedures and reasons for violating probation and

BOX 1.1   *How Probation Fits Sentencing Goals*

Sentencing is in large part concerned with avoiding future crimes by helping the defendant to live productively in the community that he or she has offended. . . . [T]he best way to pursue this goal is to orient the criminal sanction toward the community setting in those cases where it is compatible with the other objectives of sentencing. Other things being equal, a given defendant is more likely to learn how to live successfully in the general community if he is dealt with in that community, rather than shipped off to the artificial, atypical environment of a correctional institution. Banishment from society, in a word, is not the way to integrate someone into society. Yet, imprisonment constitutes just such banishment—albeit a temporary one in most cases. This is of course not to say that probation [or other forms of community corrections] should be used in all cases, or that it will produce better results. There are many goals of sentencing, some of which may [range from] the imposition of a sentence to imprisonment in a given case. And, there are defendants for whom forced removal from the environment that may have contributed to their offense can be the best beginning to a constructive, useful life.

By the same token, however, probation is a good bit more than the "matter of grace" or "leniency" that characterizes the philosophy of the general public and many judges and legislatures. Probation is an affirmative correctional tool, a tool that is used not because it offers maximum benefit to the defendant (though, of course, this is an important side product), but because it offers maximum benefit to the public that is supposed to be served by the sentencing of criminals. The automatic response of many in the criminal justice system that imprisonment is the best sentence for crime unless particular reasons exist for "mitigating" the sentence is not a sound starting point in framing criminal sanctions. Quite the opposite ought to be the case; the automatic response in sentencing situations ought to be probation, unless particularly aggravating factors emerge in the case at hand. At least, if such aggravating factors cannot be advanced as the basis of a more repressive sentence, probation offers more hope than imprisonment that the defendant will not become part of the depressing cycle in which the gates of our prisons are more like revolving doors than barriers to crime.

. . . Too often a sentencing judge is faced with the "Hobson's choice" of sentencing the defendant to an overcrowded prison that almost guarantees that he will emerge a more dangerous person or to an essentially unsupervised probation that is little more than a release without sanction, and without incentive to avoid committing a new offense. Such a state of affairs represents a failure of the legislative process in the highest order. The U.S. criminal justice system has failed more for this reason than for any other; not enough attention has been paid to providing adequate correctional choices to those who must operate the system. An effective correctional system places great reliance on adequately funded and staffed probation services. Within such a context, probation can lead to significant improvement in the preventive effects of the criminal law at much lower cost than the typical prison sentence.

Source: American Bar Association Project on Minimum Standards and Goals, *Probation* (Chicago, n.d.).

parole are covered in Chapters 8 and 11. Box 1.1 explains how probation fits various sentencing goals, from protection of public safety to treatment and rehabilitation.

Rehabilitation

A second goal of community corrections programs is to correct some of the inadequacies of offenders that may be linked to their criminal behavior and their continued involvement in the criminal justice system. Some of these problems include, but are not limited to, drug or alcohol addiction, lack of emotional control, inadequate education or vocational training, lack of parenting skills, and mental illness or developmental disability.

Correctional treatment or "programming" is the means by which offenders can receive assistance for their problems to reduce further criminal behavior. The basis of effective rehabilitation is that the offender has to have the genuine desire to change and has to want to complete the mental, emotional, and sometimes spiritual work to promote this transformation. In his psychological practice working with antisocial personality individuals, Dr. Stanton E. Samenow firmly believed that offenders who do not have this basic desire cannot be rehabilitated.[28] This is an important point, because some offenders refuse to adequately respond to treatment. Offenders who pose a serious danger to society or to themselves should not be in a community corrections program. Instead, these offenders should remain incarcerated in prison (or sometimes in a mental health facility) until they have completed their sentence or until they are judged to be not dangerous to themselves or others.

Another point is that oftentimes offenders receive more treatment outside of prison than they do in prison. This results in part because, while in the community, offenders must pay for a portion or all of their treatment. William M. DiMascio writes that community-based sanctions

> provide a means for offenders who are not dangerous to repay their victim and their communities. Intermediate sanctions also promote rehabilitation—which most citizens want, but most prisons are no longer able to provide—and the reintegration of the offender into the community. And, once the programs are in place, they do this at a comparatively low cost.[29]

Most offenders can reduce their likelihood of future criminal behavior by changing other behaviors, such as abstaining from drugs or alcohol or controlling their emotions. Proponents of rehabilitation believe that for certain types of offenders, if the issues that are related to recidivism are addressed, the likelihood of future criminal behavior may be reduced between 10 percent and 60 percent. The Corrections Program Assessment Inventory (CPAI), designed by Don Andrews and Paul Gendreau, indicates that currently only 10–20 percent of all correctional rehabilitation programs were of "high quality."[30] A high-quality treatment program contained elements indicating that an effective correctional service was being provided.[31] Offenders are all different, and different treatment approaches must be used to address unique problems. Some advances have been made, and more is now known about what works (and what does not) with different types of offenders. The key is to replace ineffective programs with those that work and to fill the treatment programs with appropriate offenders who will respond to the type of treatment offered.[32]

Community Reintegration

Over thirty years ago the President's Commission on Law Enforcement and Administration of Justice introduced the term *reintegration*.[33] Its report stated,

> Institutions tend to isolate offenders from society, both physically and psychologically, cutting them off from schools, jobs, families, and other supportive influences and increasing the probability that the label of criminal will be indelibly impressed upon them. The goal of reintegration is likely to be furthered much more readily by working with offenders in the community than by incarceration.[34]

This statement still holds true today. The vast majority of prisoners behind bars will be released, and programs should be available to ease their reentry into society. Instead of clamoring for longer sentences, U.S. citizens should ask how best to aid in the reentry of large numbers of long-term offenders. Longer prison terms is not the answer.

Reintegration stresses adaptation to the community by requiring the offender to participate in programs that develop legitimate accomplishments and opportunities and allow the offender to use and refine those skills in a community setting.[35] The role of the community in providing needed services and opportunities is also emphasized. The commission called for mobilization and change of the community and its institutions. The commission said that communities must develop employment, recreation, and educational opportunities for all its citizens. Belinda McCarthy, Bernard McCarthy, and Matthew C. Leone conclude that to achieve the objectives of reintegration, community-based correctional programs must meet the following criteria:

- A location and interaction within a community that offers opportunities that fit an offender's needs
- A nonsecure environment—the offender's home, a surrogate home, or a communal residence in which the offender lives as a responsible person with minimal supervision
- Community-based education, training, counseling, and support services
- Opportunities to assume (or learn) the normal social roles as citizen, family member, student, or employee
- Opportunities for personal growth[36]

Community correctional workers, such as probation and parole officers, act as advocates and resource brokers, linking offenders to programs and monitoring their progress once the contact has been established (see Chapter 7 for a more detailed discussion of supervision as brokerage of services).

Restorative/Community Justice

Along with "get tough" retributive-style correctional policies, a different philosophy of justice has emerged in recent years. This alternative is known as **restorative justice** or community justice.[37] As shown in Table 1.2, this concept of justice is community-based and combines mainstream American criminal justice with indigenous justice practiced by Native Americans, long before European settlers colonized North America. In contrast to mainstream criminal justice that focuses on the punishment of the offender, restorative justice is centered on the victim throughout the whole process. Restorative justice emphasizes offender responsibility to repair the injustice and wrong he or she has caused the victim.

When a crime is committed, the offender harms both the individual victim as well as the community at large. Through shaming, mediation, and face-to-face meetings with the individual victim, restorative justice attempts to strengthen community life by drawing on the strengths of the offenders and the victim, instead of focusing on their deficits.[38] Local volunteers and the faith community agree to mentor or assist in the supervision of the offender's reparation. The offender must repair the damage by remaining in the community and performing community service, providing victim restitution, and participating in victim impact panels and other educational programs.

Restorative justice is most effective for property crimes, particularly those committed by juveniles or first-time adult felony offenders. This is because the victim is compensated for property losses. What many victims may not realize is that incarcerating offenders for property crime will provide a loss of temporary freedom, but the victim will rarely, if ever, be compensated. When given a choice between compensation and incarceration, 75 percent of respondents to a study conducted in Minnesota indicated that they would rather be compensated for a property crime

RESTORATIVE JUSTICE

The philosophy and sanction of allowing the offender to remain in the community with the responsibility of restoring the victim's losses.

TABLE 1.2 *Roots of Restorative Justice*

Mainstream American Justice	Indigenous Native American Justice
Imported from Anglo-American models	Indigenous, shared views of the community and victims*
Written codified laws, rules, procedures*	Unwritten or oral customs, traditions, practices
Law is applied*	Law is a way of life
Justice is administered*	Justice is part of the life process*
Offender is focal point; privilege against self-incrimination	Victim is focal point*; offender is obligated to verbalize accountability
Adversarial (fact-finding) process; victim and offender have no contact	Communal*; victim and offender are involved in the whole process and decide action jointly
Conflict settled in court	Conflict settled through mediation and repairing relationships*
Public defender or lawyer representation*	Extended family member representation
Retributive	Restorative or holistic; connects everyone involved*
Incarceration, so criminal can pay debt to society	Community service, restitution*
Criminals are bad and responsible for their actions; they deserve to be punished	Criminal acts are a part of natural human error, which requires correctional intervention on behalf of the community*
Church and state are separated	Spiritual realm is cohesive with justice*

* Applies to restorative justice.

than demand the offender be incarcerated.[39] Thus, community-based corrections programs are necessary and important to guide the restorative justice process. At this time, however, restorative justice is less likely to be endorsed for violent crimes. The information in Box 1.2 is a description of the restorative justice program in Vermont.

In sum, community corrections is important because the sanctions can provide many options for individuals who have committed a crime but do not pose a serious threat to community safety. Community-based corrections seeks to sanction offenders through punishment, while also attempting to improve individual life circumstances. Reintegration, rehabilitation, and restorative justice are important components in changing offenders' attitudes and behaviors, leading to the prevention of future criminal behavior. Other functions that community corrections serves is to ease institutional crowding in jails and prisons by drawing from the population of convicted offenders who are predicted to be less risky to the outside community.

TYPES OF COMMUNITY-BASED CORRECTIONS PROGRAMS

Community-based programs include traditional probation and parole as well as other noninstitutional sanctions such as intensive supervision probation, restitution, community service, fines, boot camps, house arrest, and others.

BOX 1.2 *Vermont's Reparative Probation: Upholding Standards of Community Behavior*

Vermont's Reparative Probation Program exemplifies how democratic community justice seeks to reaffirm norms and standards of acceptable conduct. Offenders and their victims come together in a forum in which the offender acknowledges his or her wrongdoing and has the opportunity to express remorse and make amends. Community Reparative Boards, consisting of citizens who have a stake in the outcome, represent the community as the custodian of behavioral norms.[1]

In what is essentially a community-based restorative justice program, more than 60 boards operating throughout the state handle the cases of people whom the courts have sentenced to reparative probation for non-violent offenses, including some property felonies. The sentence is conditioned on the offender's meeting with the board, which negotiates an agreement or contract specifying how the offender will repair the harm inflicted on the victim and the community. Victims meet with the board if they wish to do so, and all participants, including the victims, must agree to the terms of the contract.

The board works with the offender in three ways. First, it seeks to demonstrate to him or her the effects of the crime on the victim and the community; second, it identifies ways the offender can repair the damage; and third, it works with the offender to devise a strategy to reduce the likelihood of reoffending. With the victim, the board works to acknowledge the harm done, to listen to the victim's concerns, and to demonstrate that the community cares and will act on the victim's behalf.

The Community Reparative Boards of Vermont create a vital opportunity for citizen participation in the justice system. The boards do not establish guilt or innocence, but rather clarify, communicate, and enforce standards of acceptable behavior following the court's decision. By removing sanctioning from the courtroom to the informal problem-solving setting of the community, the process forces offenders to face their peers directly."[2]

[1] See John G. Perry and John F. Gorczyk, "Restructuring Corrections: Using Market Research in Vermont," *Corrections Management Quarterly* 1 (1997): 26–35.

[2] The success of Vermont's program led to its designation in 1998 as a winner in the prestigious innovations in American Government competition.

Source: Todd R. Clear and David R. Karp, "Toward the Ideal of Community Justice," *National Institute of Justice Journal* (October 2000): 24.

Probation

At one end of the continuum of sanctions lies probation, defined as the release of a convicted offender under conditions imposed by the court for a specified period during which the court retains authority to modify the conditions or to resentence the offender if he or she violates the conditions. Factors that influence judicial sentencing are examined in Chapter 3, and use of the presentence investigation report is discussed in Chapter 4. Probation is the most widely used punishment in the United States. Nearly 60 percent of all convicted offenders are under some form of probation supervision. Probation is most appropriate for nonviolent first offenders who do not represent a threat to the community but require structure, supervision, and assistance. The issues of classification, supervision, and risk management are considered in Chapter 7. Offenders sentenced to a term of probation are supervised by a probation officer, who enforces the conditions of release, reports violations of the conditions to the sentencing authority, and uses community resources to let the offender participate in self-improvement programs, including drug and alcohol treatment, job training, and educational opportunities. The conditions of probation are addressed in Chapter 5, and information about probation officer qualifications and training is presented in Chapter 6.

Parole

Parole is the discretionary release of an offender before the expiration of his or her sentence under conditions established by the paroling authority. Parole is in most ways like probation. Both involve supervised release in the community and the possibility of revocation should the parolee or probationer violate the conditions of release. While some technical differences do exist, the primary difference is that probation is supervision in the community instead of incarceration and parole is supervised release after a portion of the sentence in prison has been served. Chapter 9 covers the history of parole as well as the conditions that led to the current decreasing rate of release on discretionary parole. Chapter 10 explains the process of discretionary parole. And Chapter 11 reviews conditions of parole and discusses the increase of parole violators returning to prison.

Intermediate Sanctions

Because of the perceived failure of probation and parole to protect the public from further crimes by those under supervision, a continuum of community-based punishments called **intermediate sanctions** has been developed. These sanctions, which fall between probation and prison on a scale of severity and control, are most appropriately used on low-risk and nonviolent offenders. They offer graduated levels of supervision and harshness with simple probation at one end and prison at the other. In between are a variety of community-based options such as fines, day reporting centers, work release, community release centers, house arrest, and boot camps. Advocates of sentencing reform are increasingly calling for an expanded range of sentencing options that provide control but do not impose confinement for many offenses. For example, California, the state that originally passed the notorious "three strikes and you're out" law, also has a less publicized Community-Based Punishment Act. As of October 1995, this act provides for some nonviolent offenders convicted of a second or third felony to be placed in county-based community service, restitution, and electronic monitoring programs throughout the state.[40]

Different supervision levels and services along the continuum of sanctions are also important for a second reason: They provide options for judges and community corrections workers to reward positive behavior with increasing levels of responsibility by using "graduation points" for offenders when they achieve and maintain desired program outcomes.[41] However, other options should be available for community corrections offenders who violate conditions of their sentence. Jails and prisons do not have enough room to incarcerate all probation and parole violators. Thus, more restrictive community corrections options may be in order to increase the level of supervision, while the offender still remains in the community.

By developing these new sentencing alternatives, policymakers seek to

- make sentencing more just and effective
- enhance public safety
- control the growth of prison populations
- reduce costs

As one commentator explains,

> Using a sentencing scheme of this sort enables authorities to maintain expensive prison cells to incapacitate violent criminals. At the same time, less restrictive community-based programs and restitution-focused sentences punish nonviolent offend-

ers while teaching them accountability for their actions and heightening their chance for rehabilitation.[42]

This approach treats prison as the sentencing option of last resort instead of the sentencing option of choice. Intermediate sanctions impose much greater levels of surveillance, supervision, and monitoring than traditional probation, but less supervision than that provided in jail or prison. Intermediate sanction programs may require as many as 30 contacts per month between the supervising officer and the offender, his or her family and employer, and others. Most also require the offender to participate in treatment or educational programs, do unpaid community service, pay restitution, work, or attend school or vocational training. Some require the offender to wear electronic monitoring devices or to live under "house arrest," leaving home only to work.[43] A full range of sentencing options gives judges greater latitude to select punishments that more closely fit the circumstances of the crime and the offender.[44] Figure 1.1 illustrates the range of sanctions from probation at one end to incarceration at the other. The various types of intermediate sanctions are covered in greater detail in Chapters 12 and 13.

Intensive Supervision Probation

Intensive supervision probation (ISP) is a form of probation for offenders who require more structure and surveillance than ordinary probationers but for whom incarceration may be too severe a sanction. ISP involves considerable restrictions on offenders' freedom of movement and many other aspects of autonomy. ISP allows offenders to live at home under severe restrictions. They see their probation officers three to five times each week and may have to submit to curfews, drug and alcohol testing, and employment checks.

Intensive supervision probation emphasizes control. Offenders are supervised in small caseloads, sometimes by a team of two probation officers. A national survey reported that the average ISP caseload was 25 in 1998, compared with 124 for traditional probation.[45]

Restitution

Restitution is a monetary penalty paid to victims by offenders to compensate for their losses while teaching offenders responsibility for their actions. Restitution is one of the oldest punishments. The Code of Hammurabi (1792–1750 B.C.) established elaborate restitution schemes for crimes ranging from theft to murder. Today, 3,700 years later, restitution remains a mainstay among the range of punishments available to the courts. Restitution is the primary sanction for property crimes in the restorative justice philosophy. However, because most people still feel that restitution alone is insufficient punishment, it is frequently coupled with another penalty such as probation, ISP, or community service.

Restitution may be paid either directly to the victim or, as in some jurisdictions, to a state or federal restitution fund that passes the funds on to the victim. Some states have established secure facilities called rehabilitation centers or restitution centers, where offenders live until a restitution debt is paid. Residents work at a regular job and submit their pay directly to the center director, who deducts the amounts for room and board, support for dependents, supervision fees, and restitution to the victim. The remainder is returned to the resident upon release.

FIGURE 1.1   *A Continuum of Sanctions*

This figure has generalized descriptions of many sentencing options in use in jurisdictions across the country.

PROBATION
Offender reports to probation officer periodically, sometimes as frequently as several times a month or as infrequently as once a year, depending on the offense.

INTENSIVE SUPERVISION PROBATION
Offender sees probation officer three to five times a week. Probation officer also makes unscheduled visits to offender's home or workplace.

RESTITUTION AND FINES
Used alone or in conjunction with probation or intensive supervision and requires regular payments to crime victims or to the courts.

COMMUNITY SERVICE
Used alone or in conjunction with probation or intensive supervision and requires completion of set number of hours of work in and for the community.

SUBSTANCE ABUSE TREATMENT
Evaluation and referral services provided by private outside agencies and used alone or in conjunction with either simple probation or intensive probation.

Community Service

Community service, a form of symbolic restitution, is defined as unpaid service to the public to compensate society for some harm done by the criminal. It usually consists of work for a tax-supported or nonprofit agency such as a hospital or library, an antipoverty agency, or a public works program. It may involve picking up roadside litter or removing graffiti. In a more traditional model of justice, the offender repays the community he or she offended by performing some service instead of by earning money.

Like monetary restitution, community-service restitution is both punitive and rehabilitative. It is punitive in that offenders' time and freedom are restricted until the work is completed. It is rehabilitative in the same way as monetary restitution: It allows offenders to do something constructive, to increase their self-esteem, to reduce their isolation from society, and to benefit society through their efforts. Further, community service provides an alternative form of restitution both for offenders who are unable to make meaningful financial restitution and for those whose financial resources are so great that monetary restitution has no punitive or rehabilitative effect. As the search continues for less costly and more effective methods of dealing with offenders, community service is a productive and cost-effective sanction, yet it is the "most underused intermediate sanction in the United States."[46]

DAY REPORTING
Clients report to a central location every day where they file a daily schedule with their supervision officer showing how each hour will be spent—for example, at work, in class, at support group meetings.

HOUSE ARREST AND ELECTRONIC MONITORING
Used in conjunction with intensive supervision and restricts offender to home except when at work, school, or treatment.

HALFWAY HOUSE
Residential settings for selected inmates as a supplement to probation for those completing prison programs and for some probation or parole violators. Usually coupled with community service work or substance abuse treatment or both.

BOOT CAMP
Rigorous military-style regimen for younger offenders, designed to accelerate punishment while instilling discipline, often with an educational component.

PRISONS AND JAILS
More serious offenders serve their terms at state or federal prisons, while county jails are usually designed to hold inmates for shorter periods.

Source: William M. DiMascio, *Seeking Justice: Crime and Punishment in America* (New York: Edna McConnell Clark Foundation, 1997). Used with permission.

Fines and Day Fines

Monetary fines are routinely imposed for minor offenses ranging from traffic violations to misdemeanors. Well over an estimated $1 billion in fines are collected annually by courts across the country. Fines are used more extensively in lower courts (fines in 86 percent of cases) than in higher courts (fines in 42 percent of cases). However, higher courts are assessing fines more frequently in conjunction with other penalties, such as probation or imprisonment. The federal Comprehensive Crime Control Act of 1984, effective November 1, 1987, specifies that for every sentence of probation, the court must also order the defendant to "pay a fine, make restitution, and/or work in community service."[47] Presently, patterns in the use of fines vary widely, and judges have difficulty viewing fines as a meaningful alternative to incarceration.[48] Regions in the United States have been experimenting with day fines for misdemeanors.[49]

House Arrest and Electronic Monitoring

House arrest can be used either as a pretrial program for people not yet convicted or as a condition of probation. Electronic monitoring is a means of assuring that certain conditions of probation are met. Both have found acceptance in many jurisdictions because of their potential to satisfy the goals of imprisonment without the social and financial costs associated with incarceration.[50]

House arrest is viewed as an alternative to incarceration and a means of easing prison overcrowding. Programs vary, but most require that offenders remain within the confines of their home during specified hours, ranging from 24-hour-per-day confinement to imposition of late-night curfews only.

Electronic monitoring—a correctional technology, not a correctional program—provides verification of an offender's whereabouts. Electronic monitoring is useful at many points on the correctional continuum, from pretrial release to parole.[51]

Boot Camps

Recent innovations such as boot camps provide that convicted offenders reside in a correctional facility and participate in a program meant to instill discipline and responsibility. Most boot camp programs, designed for young, nonviolent offenders who have no prior incarcerations, provide an experience much like that of military basic training with intensive physical training, hard work, and little or no free time. After a specified period, typically 90–120 days, the probationer is released to regular probation supervision. Boot camps provide the court with an alternative disposition that is stricter and more structured than regular probation yet less severe than a prison sentence.

Boot camps have strong public appeal, and many new programs were opened in the 1990s in response to public sentiment.[52] Supporters of the concept cite evidence that the boot camp experience may be more positive than incarceration in traditional prisons. Moreover, they state, those who have completed such programs describe the experience as "difficult, but constructive." Others, however, have argued that boot camps hold potential for negative outcomes. Many boot camp environments are characterized by inconsistent standards, contrived stress, and leadership styles that are likely to reduce self-esteem, increase the potential for violence, and encourage the abuse of power.[53]

Despite the controversy, boot camps have the support of the public, the media, and most correctional policymakers. Although the opening of new programs has appeared to have tapered off since the year 2000, boot camp programs likely will continue to proliferate and will become an integral part of the correctional continuum of sanctions.

THE EFFECTIVENESS OF COMMUNITY-BASED CORRECTIONS

How effective are community-based sanctions? Evaluations of probation can be found in Chapter 8, parole evaluations in Chapter 11, and intermediate sanctions in Chapters 12 and 13. This section introduces an abbreviated history of the "what works?" debate and discusses how the effectiveness of community-based programs are measured.

What Works?

Community-based sanctions came under attack for failing to provide any assurance that released offenders will not continue their criminal activity while under supervision. This lack of confidence in correctional programming peaked in 1974 with

Robert Martinson's study of 231 correctional treatment programs across the nation. His study has been referred to as the "nothing works" research. Martinson concluded that, "with few and isolated exceptions, the rehabilitative efforts that have been reported so far had no appreciable effect on recidivism."[54] In the complete report published the next year, Douglas Lipton, Robert Martinson, and Judith Wilks concluded,

> While some treatment programs have had modest successes, it still must be concluded that the field of corrections has not as yet found satisfactory ways to reduce recidivism by significant amounts.[55]

These studies set off a national debate about the efficacy of corrections—both institutional and community-based—resulting in what one commentator called "a mixed and unsettled atmosphere regarding effectiveness."[56] Martinson's findings were poorly stated, and many criticisms were lodged against the methodology used in many of the earlier program evaluations. Martinson later modified his findings to accommodate the possibility that some treatment programs did work, but that much of the research may be invalid. Despite his recanted statements, the damage had already been done. People believed that no program would work to change offenders. Hubert G. Locke commented,

> Martinson's study was a prelude to one of the most conservative eras in American politics, one in which policy makers in many political jurisdictions were looking for reasons to repudiate the putative liberal policies of previous decades. The study confirmed what a cadre of reactionary policy makers wanted to hear, at a time in which the sentiments within the professional corrections community still ran toward a philosophy of rehabilitation rather than retribution. Currently, it is reactionary politics that still holds sway over the public policy process, at least in this nation and certainly regarding issues of crime and corrections.[57]

The issue was a question of methodology, or whether research was sophisticated and rigorous enough to determine what does and does not work. If the treatment does work, the research must be able to identify which type of offenders and under what conditions the treatment works the best. Although more is now known about what works, continuing to evaluate community-based programs and other offender treatment efforts is important.[58]

When evaluating the effectiveness of a program, it would be ideal to compare offenders who are randomly selected to receive the "treatment" (for example, the community corrections program) with matched "control" groups (those on regular probation, in prison, or both). Then, the groups can be compared on a number of outcome measures. This ideal situation is hard to come by in reality, because sentencing guidelines prevent it and many judges cannot be convinced to randomly assign offenders to programs.

Furthermore, many offenders are sentenced to multiple types of programs. Thus, it is difficult to isolate one treatment effect from another and to evaluate which program had the intended effect. It is also difficult to assess which of the program elements were responsible for positive or negative effects.

A final difficulty with evaluating the effectiveness of intermediate sanctions, in particular, is determining whether the sanction has participants that were diverted from probation (a front-end strategy) or prison (a back-end strategy). In other words, suppose that the only two sentencing choices were either probation or prison (control

NET WIDENING

Using an intermediate sanction as a stiffer punishment for offenders who would have ordinarily been sentenced to probation or other lesser sanction.

group). The intermediate sanction (the program to be measured) that targets criminals who would have gone to prison anyway but are being given one last chance is getting more serious offenders than if the intermediate sanction recruited offenders who were not prison-bound. Intermediate sanctions would be an increased penalty for offenders who would have been sentenced to probation had that intermediate sanction not existed. This is called **net widening** or "widening the net," and it usually results in a cost increase instead of a cost savings. Michael Tonry demonstrates how this works with the following example:

> [With] evaluations of community service, intensive supervision, and boot camps comes the consistent finding that offenders given intermediate sanctions have similar recidivism rates for new crimes as comparable offenders receiving other sentences. [These] findings may be interpreted as good or bad—good if the offenders involved have been diverted from prison and the new crimes are not very serious [and not so good for offenders recruited from standard probation]. Sentences to prison are much more expensive than [most intermediate sanctions] and if they are no less effective at reducing subsequent criminality, they can provide nearly comparable public safety at greatly reduced cost.[59]

However, intermediate sanctions cost more than traditional probation, so all evaluation results must be interpreted with these questions in mind.

How Is Effectiveness Measured?

RECIDIVISM

The repetition of or return to criminal behavior, variously defined in one of three ways: rearrest, reconviction, or reincarceration.

The most commonly used measure of program or treatment effectiveness is the rate of **recidivism.** Recidivism is defined as the repetition of or return to criminal behavior, measured in one of three ways: rearrest, reconviction, or reincarceration. Determining success or failure is difficult because recidivism is defined differently by different researchers, and no universally accepted means by which to measure it exists:

> Different studies have identified it variously as a new arrest, a new conviction, or a new sentence of imprisonment, depending on the kinds of data they had available or their project goals. As a result it is exceedingly difficult and complex to make comparisons about their results.[60]

Thus, the effectiveness of probation, parole, and other community-based corrections programs depends on

- how recidivism is defined
- whether recidivism is measured only during periods of supervision
- whether recidivism rates are compared with rates of offenders of similar age and criminal history or simply reported with no comparison group
- whether group assignment is random or quasi-experimental
- if offenders in the treatment group would have received probation (a lesser sanction) or prison (an increased sanction)

Strict reliance on arrests, convictions, or reimprisonment may not provide a valid measure of success or failure.

Other Outcome Measures for Evaluation

Recidivism as the primary or only measure of success has caused concern among criminal justice professionals, who suggest that one should look at other factors, including the contributions of those on probation to the overall crime problem. Joan Petersilia found that of all persons arrested and charged with felonies in 1992, 17 percent of them were on probation at the time of their arrest.[61] This suggests that probationers do not represent a disproportionate share of the crime in a community.

The American Probation and Parole Association (APPA) recommends to its members that they collect data on outcomes other than recidivism. APPA argues that factors such as the amount of restitution collected, the number of offenders employed, the amount of fines and fees collected, the number of community service hours, the number of probationers enrolled in school, and the number of drug-free days be considered as well.[62] We think that effectiveness should also be measured based on the impact that community corrections programs have in reducing the institutional crowding problem or on the total cost savings they incur. All of these important outcomes are usually ignored by policymakers and evaluators. Michael Tonry and Mary Lynch argue that "for offenders who do not present unacceptable risks of future violent (including sexual crimes) crimes, a punitive sanction that costs much less than prison to implement, that promises no higher reoffending rates, and that creates negligible risks of violence by those who would otherwise be confined has much to commend it."[63]

SUMMARY

The public demands correctional programs that satisfy both punishment and public safety objectives. Both the public and criminal justice policymakers must come to understand that not all criminals can be locked up. The cost in money and human potential of the unprecedented growth of the nation's prison population has caused policymakers to seek alternative solutions to control criminal behavior. For a majority of the more serious offenders—those who cannot be maintained safely under regular probation or parole supervision, yet for whom prison is too severe a sanction—a range of intermediate punishments may be safe and effective. While the public and policymakers tend to recognize that prisons and jails are expensive to build and maintain, they do not often factor in the human cost of incarceration in terms of the loss of human potentiation and stabilized families.[64]

Intermediate sanctions are a valuable resource to lessen these problems. They allow nonviolent offenders to repay their victims and the community and in doing so promote rehabilitation—all at a relatively low cost.[65] Providing a range of community-based sanctions allows the use of expensive prison beds to hold the most intractable and violent offenders while offering hope that others, less committed to a criminal lifestyle, may become useful citizens of the communities in which they live. This is the hope and promise of community corrections.

DISCUSSION QUESTIONS

1. What is the purpose of corrections?
2. What factors have contributed to correctional growth?
3. How does community corrections fit the general correctional goals?

4 How is restorative justice different from traditional justice approaches?

5 Using the restorative justice approach, what would you require as a sentence for a 17-year-old offender who forcefully broke a window to get into a house and stole property valued at $1,000 when the occupants were at work?

6 What does a "continuum of sanctions" mean in the sentencing process? If you were a judge, how would you apply this continuum?

7 How is effectiveness of community corrections measured? What other outcome measures could be used?

WEB SITES

U.S. Department of Justice, Bureau of Justice Statistics
Corrections statistics

> *http://www.ojp.usdoj.gov/bjs/correct.htm*

U.S. Bureau of Prisons, National Institute of Corrections

> *http://www.ojp.usdoj.gov/bjs/correct.htm*

RAND Corporation
Bibliography of areas in criminal justice

> *http://www.rand.org/areas/crim.toc.html*

U.S. Sentencing Commission
Information on federal sentencing laws

> *http://www.ussc.gov*

National Center on Institutions and Alternatives
Community-Based Alternative Initiative for dual diagnosed clients; publications on sentencing, death penalty, juveniles, rehabilitation, and the "war on drugs"

> *http://www.ncianet.org/ncia/cbai.html*

Families against Mandatory Minimums
Nonprofit group against the sentencing laws that require offenders to serve a mandatory number of years in prison before becoming eligible for release

> *http://www.famm.org*

New Jersey Chapter of the American Correctional Association
Article entitled "Community Corrections of Place" by Todd R. Clear and Ronald P. Corbett

> *http://www.corrections.com/njaca/Fact_Sheets/Fact_sheets_start.htm*

Fresno Pacific University's Center for Peacemaking and Conflict Studies
Web site links dealing with restorative justice

> *http://www.fresno.edu/pacs/links.html*

Restorative Justice

> *http://www.restorativejustice.org*

Restorative Justice

In the following scenarios, a condition of an offender's supervision requires community service that will enable a form of restorative justice to occur. For each of the following cases, discuss how restorative justice could be used to punish the offender.

Case A: An 18-year-old male with no prior record has been convicted of a "hate crime." He, along with two juveniles, burned a cross in the yard of a church and painted derogatory racial messages on the front door of the church. Most of the church's congregation is African American; the offender is a Caucasian who reports affiliation with a white supremacist organization. The offender states that he began his involvement with the organization only recently and committed the offense as a part of his initiation into the group.

Case B: A 40-year-old woman is convicted of a drug trafficking offense. She has little legitimate employment history and prior convictions for other offenses involving sales of illegal drugs. Despite her lack of legitimate earnings, this offender has acquired many assets. Most of the assets have been forfeited as the prosecutor has proven they were purchased with funds obtained in illegal activities. The offender denies illegal drug usage. She states that she was involved in the sale of illegal drugs for the money. She shows no remorse for her crime and has no understanding of the harm her criminal conduct has on society. In fact, she quickly states that she believes her sale of illegal drugs is a "victimless" crime.

Case C: A college professor has been granted diversion after an arrest for driving under the influence. (Diversion is a form of probation imposed before a plea of guilty that can result in dismissal of the charges if the conditions are successfully completed.) He states that he was taking a prescription medication and had three drinks at a colleague's home before driving home. The driver realized his judgment was impaired while he was driving and pulled to the shoulder of the road. Law enforcement observed him driving erratically and nearly driving in the ditch before bringing his vehicle to a stop on the shoulder of the road. Officers questioned him, and he admitted he had been drinking alcoholic beverages.

2

History and Legal Foundations of Probation

Colorado Historical Society

What You Will Learn in This Chapter

You will become familiar with the social and legal history of probation in both Europe and America. You will learn how probation grew out of early efforts by judges to mitigate the harsh punishments prescribed by law. You also will learn how distinctly American practices evolved, including the origins of both adult and juvenile probation.

INTRODUCTION

Probation, as it is known and practiced today, evolved out of ancient precedents in England and the United States devised to avoid the mechanical application of the harsh penal codes of the day.[1] Early British criminal law, which was dominated by the objectives of retribution and punishment, imposed rigid and severe penalties on offenders. The usual punishments were corporal: branding, flogging, mutilation, and execution. Capital punishment was commonly inflicted upon children and animals as well as men and women. At the time of Henry VIII, for instance, more than 200 crimes were punishable by death, many of them relatively minor offenses against property.

Methods used to determine guilt—what today is called *criminal procedure*—also put the accused in danger. Trial might be by combat between the accused and the accuser, or a person's innocence might be determined by whether he or she sank when bound and thrown into a deep pond—the theory being that the pure water would reject wrongdoers. Thus the choice was to drown as an innocent person or to survive the drowning only to be otherwise executed. Sometimes the offender could elect to be tried "by God," which involved undergoing some painful and frequently life-threatening ordeal, or "by country," a form of trial by jury for which the accused first had to pay an **amercement** to the king. The accepted premise was that the purpose of criminal law was not to deter or rehabilitate but to bring about justice for a past act deemed harmful to the society.

EARLY EFFORTS TO MITIGATE PUNISHMENT

The early Middle Ages saw efforts to mitigate the severity of punishment. Royal pardons, usually paid for by the accused, were sometimes granted. Judges could choose to interpret statutes narrowly or fail to apply them. Juries sometimes devalued stolen property so as to bring its value below that which required capital punishment. Prosecutors dismissed charges or charged offenders with lesser offenses. Devices such as "benefit of clergy" and "judicial reprieve" benefited some defendants, while "sanctuary" and "abjuration" enabled some criminals to gain immunity from punishment. Courts began to release certain offenders on good behavior for a temporary period, which allowed them time to seek a pardon or commutation of sentence. Gradually, an "inherent" power of certain courts to suspend sentences was recognized, although the existence and limits on that power were almost at once the subject of controversy.

Benefit of clergy was a privilege originally given to ordained clerics, monks, and nuns accused of crimes. Benefit of clergy required representatives of the church to be delivered to church authorities, instead of secular courts, for punishment. Although

KEY TERMS

Amercement
Benefit of clergy
Sanctuary
Abjuration
Judicial reprieve
Security for good behavior
Filing
Motion to quash
Recognizance
Suspended sentence
Peter Oxenbridge Thacher
Matthew Davenport Hill
John Augustus
Illinois Juvenile Court Act of 1899

AMERCEMENT

A monetary penalty imposed upon a person for some offense, he or she being in mercy for his or her conduct. It was imposed arbitrarily at the discretion of the court or the person's lord. *Black's Law Dictionary* distinguishes between fines and amercements in that fines are certain, are created by some statute, and can be assessed only by courts of record; amercements are arbitrarily imposed.

BENEFIT OF CLERGY

An exemption for members of the clergy that allowed them to avoid being subject to the jurisdiction of secular courts.

1. Have mercy upon me, O God, according to thy loving kindness: according unto the multitude of thy tender mercies blot out my transgressions.
2. Wash me thoroughly from mine iniquity, and cleanse me from my sin.
3. For I acknowledge my transgressions: and my sin is ever before me.
4. Against thee, thee only, have I sinned, and done this evil in thy sight: that thou mightest be justified when thou speakest, and be clear when thou judgest.
5. Behold, I was shapen in iniquity; and in sin did my mother conceive me.
6. Behold, thou desirest truth in the inward parts: and in the hidden part thou shalt make me to know wisdom.
7. Purge me with hyssop, and I shall be clean: wash me, and I shall be whiter than snow.
8. Make me to hear joy and gladness; that the bones which thou has broken may rejoice.
9. Hide thy face from my sins, and blot out all mine iniquities.
10. Create in me a clean heart, O God; and renew a right spirit within me.
11. Cast me not away from thy presence; and take not thy holy spirit from me.
12. Restore unto me the joy of thy salvation; and uphold me with thy free spirit.
13. Then will I teach transgressors thy ways; and sinners shall be converted unto thee.
14. Deliver me from blood guiltiness, O God, thou God of my salvation: and my tongue shall sing aloud of thy righteousness.
15. O Lord, open thou my lips; and my mouth shall shew forth thy praise.
16. For thou desirest not sacrifice; else would I give it: thou delightest not in burnt offering.
17. The sacrifices of God are a broken spirit: a broken and a contrite heart, O God, thou wilt not despise.
18. Do good in thy good pleasure unto Zion: build thou the walls of Jerusalem.
19. Then shalt thou be pleased with the sacrifices of righteousness, with burnt offering and whole burnt offering: then shall they offer bullocks upon thine altar.

the ecclesiastical courts had the power to imprison for life, they seldom exacted such severe punishment. Thus the benefit of clergy served to mitigate the harsh (frequently capital) punishments prescribed by English law. Benefit of clergy was later extended to protect ordinary citizens. Judges used the benefit as a means of exercising discretion when the prescribed punishment for a crime seemed too severe in particular cases. A person could qualify for benefit of clergy by demonstrating that he or she could read—a skill that only the clergy and some of the upper classes possessed. Over time the courts began to require these defendants to read in court the text of Psalm 51 as a test of their literacy. The psalm came to be known as the neck verse, and many criminals soon memorized it and pretended to read it in court, using its protection to escape being hanged (see Box 2.1). The benefit was practiced in the United States for a brief period, but the procedure became so technical and legalistic that it was almost unworkable. It was finally abolished in 1827.

Sanctuary referred to a place (usually a church or vestry) the king's soldiers were not permitted to enter for the purpose of taking an accused into custody. Offenders were accorded sanctuary until negotiations with the accusers could be accomplished or arrangements could be made to smuggle the accused out of the country. Offenders who confessed their crimes while in sanctuary were allowed **abjuration.** That is, they promised to leave England under pain of immediate punishment if they returned without the king's permission. One legal historian wrote, "For a man to take sanctuary, confess his crime, and abjure the realm was an everyday event. If the man who had taken sanctuary would neither confess to a crime nor submit to a trial, the state

SANCTUARY

In old English law, a consecrated place, such as a church or abbey, where offenders took refuge because they could not be arrested there.

ABJURATION

An oath to forsake the realm forever taken by an accused person who claimed sanctuary.

could do no more against him. It tried to teach the clergy that their duty was to starve him into submission, but the clergy resented this interference with holy things."[2]

Judicial reprieve (from *reprendre,* "to take back") was another method by which judges who recognized that not all offenders are dangerous, evil persons avoided imposing the prescribed punishment for crimes. Judicial reprieve amounted to a withdrawal of the sentence for some interval of time—similar to what today is called *suspension of sentence.* During the period of judicial reprieve the offender was at liberty, and the imposition of other criminal sanctions was postponed. At the expiration of the specified time, the accused could apply to the Crown for a pardon.

EARLY AMERICAN LAW

Recognition of the doctrine of benefit of clergy was never widespread in the American colonies. Instead, distinct American practices developed, such as "security for good behavior" and a practice known in Massachusetts as *filing.*[3] **Security for good behavior,** also known as *good abearance,* was a fee paid to the state as collateral for a promise of good behavior. Much like the modern practice of bail, security for good behavior allowed the accused to go free in certain cases either before or after conviction. Under **filing** the indictment was "laid on file" in cases in which justice did not require an immediate sentence. However, the court could impose certain conditions on the defendant. The effect was that the case was laid at rest without either dismissal or final judgment and without the necessity of asking for final continuances.

Massachusetts judges also often granted a **motion to quash** after judgment, using any minor technicality or the slightest error in the proceedings to free the defendant in cases in which they thought the statutory penalties inhumane. Some early forms of bail had the effect of suspending final action on a case, although the chief use of bail then (as now) was for the purpose of ensuring appearance for trial. Because the sureties "went bail" and became responsible for the action of the defendant, they assumed supervision of the defendant, at least to the extent of keeping track of his or her whereabouts. The continuous availability of the defendant for further action by the court was one of the conditions of liberty.

All of these methods had the common objective of mitigating punishment by relieving selected offenders from the full effects of the legally prescribed penalties that substantial segments of the community, including many judges, viewed as excessive and inappropriate to their offenses. They were precursors to probation as it is known today. The procedures most closely related to modern probation, however, are recognizance and the suspended sentence.

RECOGNIZANCE AND SUSPENDED SENTENCE

As early as 1830, Massachusetts courts had begun to release some offenders through the use of innovative and possibly extralegal procedures instead of imposing the prescribed punishments. In the 1830 case of *Commonwealth v. Chase,* often cited as an example of the early use of release on **recognizance** (from *recognocere,* "to call to mind"), Judge Peter Oxenbridge Thacher found the defendant (Jerusha Chase) guilty on her plea, suspended the imposition of sentence, and ruled that the defendant was permitted, "upon her recognizance for her appearance in this court whenever she should be called for, to go at large."[4] Recognizance came to be used often in Massachusetts as a means of avoiding a final conviction of young and minor offenders in

JUDICIAL REPRIEVE

Withdrawal of a sentence for an interval of time during which the offender was at liberty and imposition of other sanctions was postponed.

SECURITY FOR GOOD BEHAVIOR

A recognizance or bond given the court by a defendant before or after conviction conditioned on his or her being "on good behavior" or keeping the peace for a prescribed period.

FILING

A procedure under which an indictment was "laid on file," or held in abeyance, without either dismissal or final judgment in cases in which justice did not require an immediate sentence.

MOTION TO QUASH

An oral or written request that the court repeal, nullify, or overturn a decision, usually made during or after the trial.

RECOGNIZANCE

Originally a device of preventive justice that obliged persons suspected of future misbehavior to stipulate with and give full assurance to the court and the public that the apprehended offense would not occur. Recognizance was later used with convicted or arraigned offenders with conditions of release set. Recognizance was usually entered into for a specified period.

hope that they would avoid further criminal behavior. The main thrust of recognizance was to humanize criminal law and mitigate its harshness. Recognizance is used today to ensure a defendant's presence at court and is not a disposition in itself.

Suspended sentence is a court order, entered after a verdict, finding, or plea of guilty, that suspends or postpones the filing, imposition, or execution of sentence during the good behavior of the offender. Although suspension of sentence is, in a few jurisdictions, a form of disposition of the criminal offender that is separate from and in addition to probation, it is considered here chiefly in its close historical and legal relationship to probation.[5]

Where suspension of sentence exists independent of probation, it is distinguished from probation in that the offender is released without supervision. The only condition is the implicit, or sometimes explicit, imperative that the withholding or postponement of sentence will be revoked or terminated if the offender commits a new crime. As a disposition, suspension of sentence also differs from probation in that no term is specified. However, the period of suspension of sentence generally is limited by the maximum period of commitment permitted by statute for the offense.

Two Kinds of Suspended Sentence

There are two kinds of suspended sentence—suspension of *imposition* of sentence and suspension of *execution* of sentence. In the case of suspension of imposition of sentence, a verdict or plea and a judgment may be reached, but no sentence is pronounced. In the case of suspension of execution of sentence, the sentence is pronounced, but its execution is suspended. In other words, the defendant is not committed to a correctional institution or otherwise taken into custody. The form of the suspension—whether of imposition or of execution of sentence—has different legal consequences, and it directly impacts whether suspension of sentence is considered as a separate disposition of the offender or as the basis for or equivalent to probation. The distinction is critical and may affect such later issues as the following:

- Whether the offender has been convicted
- What civil rights he or she has forfeited
- The term for which he or she may be committed upon resentence after revocation of the suspension
- Whether probation is a part of the criminal prosecution
- Whether the probationer on revocation of probation is entitled to counsel under the holding in *Mempa v. Rhay* or the right to counsel rules announced in *Morrissey v. Brewer* and *Gagnon v. Scarpelli*[6]

The Power to Suspend Sentence

Several variables must be considered in discussions of the power to suspend sentence. For instance, it makes a difference whether

- the power is to withhold or delay sentencing indefinitely or is for only a temporary period or a specific purpose
- the power is inherent in the courts to suspend sentence or is granted to the courts by a legislative act
- the power is to suspend imposition of sentence or to suspend execution of sentence or both
- suspended sentence is a separate disposition or sentencing alternative or is connected with probation

- probation depends upon the existence of the power to suspend sentence or does not have the suspended sentence aspect
- probation is deemed to be a sentence

It is generally conceded that at common law the English courts had the power to suspend sentence for a limited period or for a specified purpose. This power was used, for example, in judicial reprieve, in which imposition or execution of sentence was temporarily suspended and the defendant—with neither the right of appeal nor the right to a new trial—could apply to the Crown for an absolute or conditional pardon.

Whether the common law recognized the inherent right of the courts to suspend sentence indefinitely is a matter of considerable dispute. Certain practices in both England and the American colonies support the view that such a right was recognized. Recognizance, in the 1830 Massachusetts case, permitted Jerusha Chase, "upon her own recognizance for her appearance in this court whenever she was called for, to go at large."[7] Judicial reprieve was also cited as proof of a court's inherent right to suspend sentence indefinitely, particularly because in some cases the temporary suspension became indefinite when the court subsequently refused or failed to proceed with the case.

As far as the United States is concerned, the matter was resolved in 1916 in the so-called *Killets* case, in which the Supreme Court held that the federal courts have no power to suspend indefinitely the imposition or execution of a sentence (see Box 2.2).[8] The Court—in *Ex parte United States*, 242 U.S. 27, which involved defendant John Killets—recognized that the temporary suspension of imposition or execution of sentence was frequently resorted to in both England and the colonies because errors in the trial or miscarriage of justice could not be corrected by granting a new trial or by appeal under the existing system. Many of these temporary suspensions became indefinite because of a court's failure to proceed further in a criminal case. The Supreme Court pointed out, however, that

> neither of these conditions serve to convert the mere exercise of a judicial discretion to temporarily suspend for the accomplishment of a purpose contemplated by law into the existence of an arbitrary judicial power to permanently refuse to enforce the law.[9]

The Court went on to hold that the practice was inconsistent with the Constitution because its exercise in the very nature of things amounts to a refusal by the judicial power to perform the duty resting on it, and, as a consequence thereof, to an interference with both the legislative and executive authority as fixed by the Constitution.[10]

Suspended Sentence and Probation

The Supreme Court indicated, somewhat inconsistently, that Congress had adequate power to authorize both temporary and indefinite suspension by statute. An earlier New York court had upheld the power of a court to suspend sentences indefinitely when this right had been conferred upon the court by statute.[11] The *Killets* case recognized the right of the legislative authority to grant the power of indefinite suspension to the courts by making probation as now defined and practiced in the United States largely a creature of statute.

The early controversy about the court's authority to suspend sentence has also resulted in differing ideas about the relationship between probation and suspended sentence. Depending upon the jurisdiction, four views are commonly held:

1. Probation may be granted on suspension of imposition of sentence.
2. Probation may be granted on suspension of imposition or of execution of sentence.
3. Suspended sentence is probation.
4. Probation does not have the suspended sentence aspect.

Supporting the fourth view, the *American Bar Association* states that probation should not involve or require suspension of any other sentence.[12] The matter is also complicated by the problem of whether probation itself is a sentence and by the varying definitions of "conviction." In 1984 the federal Sentencing Reform Act abolished the authority of U.S. courts to suspend the imposition or execution of sentence to impose a term of probation.[13] Instead, the act recognized probation as a sentence in itself.

Suspended Sentence as Conviction

Conviction has two definitions. By the narrow definition, which follows popular usage, conviction denotes a plea, finding, or verdict of guilt. By the broad definition, it is a plea, finding, or verdict of guilt followed by a final judgment of conviction and sentence. Conviction in the narrow sense is followed by the imposition of criminal sanctions, but a determination of guilt is not accompanied by loss of civil rights and privileges. Conviction in the broad sense is followed by the imposition of criminal sanctions and loss of civil rights and privileges.

Whether there is a conviction if sentence is suspended often turns on the question of what is suspended. A conviction is more likely reached if the execution—rather than the imposition—of sentence has been suspended, although this is not always true.

EARLY PROBATION

The increasing awareness that prisons were not accomplishing their stated purpose of reforming the offender and that suspension of sentence without supervision was not a satisfactory alternative brought about the development of probation as it is known today. Although judges such as **Peter Oxenbridge Thacher** in Massachusetts introduced probation-like practices such as recognizance and suspension of sentence

Colorado Historical Society

Early juvenile courts were informal proceedings focusing on rehabilitation rather than punishment.

in the early 19th century, the credit for founding probation is reserved for John Augustus, a Boston bootmaker, and Matthew Davenport Hill, an English lawyer who held the judicial position of recorder of Birmingham.

The development of probation in England has been traced to specialized practices for dealing with young offenders. Some judges sentenced youthful offenders to a term of one day on the condition that they return "to the care of their parents or master, to be by him more carefully watched and supervised in the future."[14] **Matthew Davenport Hill** had witnessed this practice as a young attorney, and when he became the recorder of Birmingham (a judicial post), he employed a similar practice when he perceived "that the individual was not wholly corrupt—when there was reasonable hope of reformation—and when there could be found persons to act as guardians kind enough to take charge of the young convict."[15] Under Hill's direction, police officers visited the guardians from time to time, "recording the progress of the offender and keeping a regular account."[16]

A probation law that authorized the use of recognizance for first offenders was not adopted in England until 1887. It did not provide for special conditions of probation or for supervision of those released.

It is generally agreed that the first true probation law was enacted in the United States in 1878. This legislation grew out of the work of **John Augustus,** the first person to apply the term *probation* to his new method. For this reason he is regarded as the "father of probation," and probation is said to be of U.S. origin.[17] Augustus was a member of the Washington Total Abstinence Society, an organization devoted to the promotion of temperance.[18] In August 1841 this interest led him to bail out a "common drunkard" by permission of the Boston Police Court. Augustus later wrote of this first "probationer" in his journal, which appeared in 1852:

He was ordered to appear for sentence in three weeks from that time. He signed the pledge and became a sober man; at the expiration of this period of probation, I accompanied him into the court room; his whole appearance was changed and no

MATTHEW DAVENPORT HILL

As recorder of Birmingham (England), he established probation-like practices with young offenders.

JOHN AUGUSTUS

The "father of probation."

one, not even the scrutinizing officers, could have believed that he was the same person who less than a month before had stood trembling on the prisoner's stand.[19]

Augustus viewed probation as a selective process, although his first probationer was selected on his behavior, his manner of speech, and his protestation of a "firm resolve to quit liquor." In his journal Augustus wrote the following:

> Great care was observed, of course, to ascertain whether the prisoners were promising subjects for probation, and to this end it was necessary to take into consideration the previous character of the person, his age, and the influences by which he would in [the] future be likely to be surrounded.[20]

John Augustus continued his work in the Boston courts for 18 years, during which he received some financial aid from other citizens of the community interested in the offender. His journal reports that of the first 1,100 probationers on whom he kept records, only one forfeited bond. As to reformation, he stated that if "only one-half of this number have become reformed, I have ample cause to be satisfied."[21]

As is true today, probation was not universally accepted. Augustus repeated over and over that "the object of the law is to reform criminals and to prevent crime, and not to punish maliciously or from a spirit of revenge," and he did not hesitate to castigate the police, the judges, and others who did not share his views.[22] As a result, a newspaper of the time described him as a "fellow who is called John Augustus" who "seems to have a great itching for notoriety, and dollars" and "hangs and loafs about the Police and Municipal Courts, almost every day, and takes more airs upon himself than all the judges and officers."[23] The newspaper continued:

> We know something about this Peter Funk Philanthropist, and peanut reformer, and unless he conducts himself henceforth with a great deal more propriety, we shall take it upon ourself to teach him decency.[24]

John Augustus and his immediate successors were not officials of the court and hence lacked official status, although Massachusetts had passed a law in 1689 that authorized an agent of the State Board of Charities to investigate cases of children tried before the criminal courts. In 1878, almost 20 years after the death of John Augustus, adult probation in Massachusetts was sanctified by statute. A law was passed authorizing the mayor of Boston to appoint a paid probation officer to serve in the Boston criminal courts as a member of the police force. For the first time the probation officer was recognized as an official agent of the court. The statute made probation available to "such persons as may reasonably be expected to be reformed without punishment." No other restrictions were inserted. Probation was thus available in the city of Boston to men and women, felons and misdemeanants, and juveniles and adults, regardless of the nature of the offense or the amount or kind of punishment assessed.

Early Probation Legislation—State

Statewide probation was first enacted in Massachusetts in 1891 with a provision that appears in many modern statutes: that the probation officer should not be an active member of the regular police force. Although this early legislation provided for probation officers, it did not specifically give courts the power to grant probation. Missouri in 1897 and Vermont in 1898 remedied this omission, although the Missouri statute was labeled "an Act relating to the parole of prisoners" and used the words *probation* and *parole* interchangeably.

Several other states passed probation laws in the late 19th and early 20th centuries. The statutes varied in their provisions. Illinois and Minnesota provided for juvenile probation only; Rhode Island placed restrictions on eligibility and excluded persons guilty of certain offenses. Some states provided for statewide probation, while others followed the example set by Vermont in adopting the county plan.[25]

Early Probation—Federal

The Supreme Court held in the 1916 *Killets* case that the federal courts had no inherent power to suspend indefinitely the imposition or execution of a sentence.[26] The Court indicated, however, that the power to suspend sentence could be given to the courts by statute.[27] Evidence shows that, as early as 1808, federal judges who thought that legislative penalties were too harsh suspended sentences in their courtrooms on an informal basis.[28]

Between 1916 and 1925, several attempts were made to pass laws authorizing federal judges to grant probation. In the closing days of the session in 1925, Congress enacted the National Probation Act, which authorized each federal district court, except in the District of Columbia, to appoint one salaried probation officer with an annual income of $2,600. By 1925 probation was authorized by statutes in 48 states and in the federal system.

Between 1927 and 1930, eight probation officers were required to pass the civil service examination. In 1930 judges were empowered to appoint without reference to the civil service list, and the limitation of one officer to each district was removed. Between 1930 and 1940, the federal probation system was administered by the Federal Bureau of Prisons (FBP), and the number of officers increased from 8 to 233 officers.[29] The objectives of the probation law were stated by Chief Justice William Howard Taft as follows:

> The great desideratum was the giving to young and new violators of law a chance to reform and to escape the contaminating influence of association with hardened or veteran criminals in the beginning of imprisonment. Probation is the attempted saving of a man who has taken one wrong step and whom the judge thinks to be a brand who can be plucked from the burning at the time of imposition of sentence.[30]

In 1940 the U.S. probation system had increased so dramatically that the administration of probation was moved from the FBP to the Administrative Office of the U.S. Courts. The era from 1940 to 1950 concentrated on initial qualifications, standardized manuals, and in-service training. The period between 1950 and the mid-1980s saw further expansion and innovative practices. In 1984 the Comprehensive Crime Control Act abolished federal parole and brought all supervised prison releases under the auspices of federal probation. The impact of this act will be discussed further in Chapter 9.

Early Probation—Juvenile

A tendency exists to think of juvenile probation only in connection with a juvenile court. Because the first juvenile court and apparently the use of the term *juvenile delinquency* were established in Illinois in 1899, some scholars trace the development of juvenile probation from that date. However, some English courts put into practice many of the principles, characteristics, and procedures that today are equated with juvenile courts long before any separate tribunals for the handling of juveniles were established in the United States.

As early as 1630 a guidebook that sanctioned special treatment of juveniles was prepared for justices of the peace in England. One provision read as follows:

> And yet if an infant shall commit larceny, and shall be found guilty thereof before the Justice of the Peace, it shall not be amiss for them to respite the judgment and so hath it often beene [sic] done by the Judges.[31]

A report of criminal trials from the Old Bailey Sessions in London, 1686–93, contains an account of the trial of Chollis Searl, "a little youth, aged about twelve years," who was acquitted of picking pockets in a proceeding that would be familiar in today's juvenile courts.[32] One of the justices of the peace for the county of Warwick, writing between 1820 and 1827, proposed the appointment of relatives acting as legal guardians to children without supervision.

Between 1866 and 1871 a boy's "beadle" or "persuader" was employed as an unofficial probation officer by the Reformatory and Refuge Union in London. In 1881 an article entitled "Massachusetts Method of Dealing with Juvenile Offenders," which advocated placing juvenile offenders on probation, was given wide publicity by the Howard Association of London.

Although the need for separate treatment of juveniles was recognized in the early 19th century in the United States, special children's institutions developed more rapidly than did special procedures and separate courts. Unfortunately, many of the special institutions came to be nothing more than children's prisons, and a system of contracting the labor of the children to private employers led to extremely harsh treatment and outright exploitation of children's labor. To protect children from this exploitation, late in the 19th century the New York Children's Aid Society shipped wholesale lots of Manhattan street urchins to farmers in the West. Otherwise, they would have been committed to the House of Refuge. In 1890 the Children's Aid Society of Pennsylvania offered to place in foster homes delinquents who would otherwise be sent to reform school. Known as *placing out,* this practice was an early form of juvenile probation.[33] The system of apprenticeship was another early form of probation of children. It was used chiefly to detach poor children from their parents and attach them to masters who would teach them a trade.

The First Juvenile Court

The **Illinois Juvenile Court Act of 1899** combined the Massachusetts and New York systems of probation with several New York laws to provide delinquents with special court sessions and separate detention facilities.[34] In an article that appeared in the *Harvard Law Review* in 1909, Julian W. Mack declared that juvenile court legislation

> has assumed two aspects. In Great Britain and in New York, and in a few other jurisdictions, the protection [of children] is accomplished by suspending sentence and releasing the child under probation, or, in case of removal from the home, sending it to school instead of to a jail or penitentiary. But in Illinois, and following the lead of Illinois, in most jurisdictions, the form of proceeding is totally different. Proceedings are brought to have a guardian or representative of the state appointed to look after the child, to have the state intervene between the natural parent and child because the child needs it, as evidenced by some of its acts, and because the parent is either unwilling or unable to train the child properly.[35]

Mack continued with an analysis of the main principles of juvenile court legislation. The first was that child offenders should be kept separate from adult criminals and should receive a treatment differentiated to suit their special needs. That is, the courts should be agencies for the rescue as well as the punishment of children. The second principle was that parents of offenders must be made to feel more responsible for their children's wrongdoing. The third was that, no matter what offense children have committed, placing them in the common jails was an unsuitable penalty. The fourth principle stated that removing children from their parents and sending them even to an industrial school should as far as possible be avoided, and

> that when it [a child] is allowed to return home it should be under probation, subject to the guidance and friendly interest of the probation officer, the representative of the court. To raise the age of criminal responsibility from seven or ten to sixteen or eighteen without providing for an efficient system of probation, would indeed be disastrous. Probation is, in fact, the keynote of juvenile court legislation.[36]

Mack further related,

> Whenever juvenile courts have been established, a system of probation has been provided for, and even where as yet the juvenile court system has not been fully developed, some steps have been taken to substitute probation for imprisonment of the juvenile offender. What they need, more than anything else, is kindly assistance; and the aim of the court, appointing a probation officer for the child, is to have the child and the parents feel, not so much the power, as the friendly interest of the state; to show them that the object of the court is to help them to train the child right, and therefore the probation officers must be men and women fitted for these tasks.[37]

A detailed discussion of the contemporary juvenile court and juvenile corrections can be found in Chapter 14.

SUMMARY

Probation grew out of efforts to mitigate the harsh punishments demanded by early English law. At the time of Henry VIII more than 200 offenses were punishable by death, many of them relatively minor offenses against property. Judges interpreted statutes narrowly or failed to apply them. Juries placed lower value on stolen property (to bring the value below that which required imposition of the death penalty). Prosecutors dismissed charges or charged offenders with lesser offenses. Devices such as benefit of clergy, judicial reprieve, banishment, and sanctuary reduced the otherwise unrelenting severity of the penal code.

In the American colonies, where English law prevailed, distinct American practices developed. Filing, security for good behavior, recognizance, and suspension of imposition of sentence were procedures by which American judges exercised discretion to reduce the severity of punishment in cases in which the circumstances of the crime or characteristics of the offender warranted leniency. These were the direct precursors of modern probation.

With the foundation laid by early judges in America and England, the later work of Matthew Davenport Hill, an English judge, and John Augustus, an American reformer, brought about the practice of probation as it is known today. The modern concept of probation depends on the power of the courts to suspend sentence. This power was the subject of much controversy in the early years of probation's use. The issue was eventually settled by the U.S. Supreme Court in the *Killets* case in 1916. The Court held that courts did not have an inherent power to suspend sentences indefinitely, but that power might be granted to the judiciary by the legislature. This aspect of the *Killets* case—recognition of legislative authority to grant the power of indefinite suspension to the courts—made probation as now defined and practiced in the United States largely statutory.

Although most researchers trace the origins of juvenile probation to the creation of the first American juvenile court in Chicago in 1899, English courts had put into practice many of its principles, characteristics, and procedures long before. As early as 1630 a guidebook for English justices of the peace recommended "respite of judgement" for crimes committed by "infants." Numerous accounts attest to procedures and practices of the 17th and 18th centuries that would be familiar to juvenile courts today. By 1899 the concept that crimes committed by children and those committed by adults should be dealt with differently, with special courts and special facilities for juveniles, was formalized by the creation of the first juvenile court in Illinois.

DISCUSSION QUESTIONS

1 How did the existence of extremely harsh penal laws in early England influence the evolution of probation?

2 Explain benefit of clergy. What was its original purpose, and how did it come to be used?

3 Why is Psalm 51 referred to as the neck verse?

4 What was judicial reprieve? How is it related to modern probation?

5 Explain the use of filing and security for good behavior in the American colonies.

6 What is the importance for probation of the ruling in *Commonwealth v. Chase*?

7 What are the two kinds of suspended sentence? Why is the distinction critical to an understanding of modern probation?

8 What is the *Killets* case? What was its impact on modern probation?

9 Distinguish between the narrow and broad definitions of conviction. What consequences arise from each?

10 Who were Matthew Davenport Hill and John Augustus? What did each contribute to modern criminal justice practices?

 **WEB SITES**

History of Federal Probation

   http://www.flmp.uscourts.gov/History/history.htm

History of U.S. Probation Office, District of New Mexico

   http://www.nmcourt.fed.us/pbdocs/history.html

Colorado Association of Probation Offices

   http://www.capo.net/index.html

History of New York Corrections, N.Y. Corrections Society

   http://www.correctionhistory.org/

American Probation and Parole Association (APPA)
History of the APPA

   http://www.appa-net.org/the_early_years.htm

American Probation and Parole Association
Publications on the labors of John Augustus

http://www.appa-net.org/publications%20and%20resources/areport.htm

Hampshire Probation Service, United Kingdom

http://probation.hants.gov.uk

Please go to the book-specific Web site for the Supplemental Reading related to the material in this chapter:
John Augustus: The First Probation Officer
http://www.wadsworth.com/product/0534559662s

3

The Decision to Grant Probation

James L. Schaffer/Photo Edit

What You Will Learn in This Chapter

You will learn the various types of probation, including regular probation, intensive supervision probation, deferred adjudication, and pretrial diversion. The factors that affect the decision to grant probation will be examined. Variations in sentencing policy will also be addressed in terms of their effect on the decision to grant or deny probation.

KEY TERMS

Nolo contendere

INTRODUCTION

In recent years the United States has responded to the public's fear of crime by incarcerating more offenders for longer periods. Prisoners are entering prisons and jails in record numbers. Every week more than 1,600 new prison beds are needed—the equivalent of 50 large, new prisons each year.[1] By June 1999 the nation's prison population had risen to 1.33 million, an increase of 5.8 annually since 1990. A report by the Edna McConnell Clark Foundation revealed that a greater percentage of convicted felons are being imprisoned than ever before in the nation's history and that, at the same time, budget limitations have made it impossible to build prisons fast enough to keep pace with the influx of new inmates.[2] The report concluded,

> Billions of taxpayer dollars are spent each year to support the burgeoning corrections industry, and yet, crime and the uncertainty of what to do with those who commit crime, remains. The problem is vexing and persistent.[3]

Many incorrectly assume that growth in prison populations will result in fewer persons under supervision in the community and that those remaining in the community will have become increasingly less serious and in need of less supervision. Unfortunately, this is not true.[4] The number of convicted offenders sentenced to probation or parole grew nearly as fast as the prison population, totaling 4.1 million on January 1, 1999.[5] Over one-half were on probation for a felony.

Judging by prior criminal records, current conviction crimes, and substance abuse histories, the crimes of the population of persons sentenced to probation supervision have become increasingly serious. The overall U.S. population has grown, more citizens are being convicted, and all correctional populations have increased precipitously. Even though over two-thirds of all convicted offenders are on probation or some other form of community corrections supervision, little attention or public discourse is directed at the community corrections process. Politicians and governmental officials find that it is more politically attractive to seek resources for prosecutors, police, and prisons than to appear to be "soft on crime" by proposing more support for community-based programs such as probation.[6] The data in Table 3.1 indicate the extent of community corrections programs across the United States.

The little attention that is focused on probation tends to be negative. Probation has been seriously criticized as lenient and as a threat to public safety. Some of these criticisms are warranted-not so much because of the lack of viability of probation as a correctional tool, but because the population of persons sentenced to probation is growing rapidly while resources and funding have not kept pace. Only 11 cents of every correctional dollar is directed to probation and parole, although over 70 percent of all persons under correctional supervision are on probation or parole. Because of a lack of funding, probation caseloads are high and continue to grow larger. While most correctional authorities agree that a probation officer should not

TABLE 3.1 *Community Corrrections among the States, Year-End 1998*

Ten States with the Largest 1998 Community Corrections Populations	Number Supervised	Ten States with the Largest Percent Increase	Percent Increase	Ten States with the Highest Rates of Supervision, 1998	Persons Supervised per 100,000 Adult U.S. Residents[a]	Ten States with the Lowest Rates of Supervision 1998	Persons Supervised per 100,000 Adult U.S. Residents[a]
Texas	443,758	Vermont	21.0	Washington	3,619	Kentucky	437
California	324,427	Idaho	20.6	Delaware	3,548	West Virginia	452
Florida	239,021	Arkansas	18.7	Texas	3,140	North Dakota	559
New York	190,518	New Mexico	17.5	Rhode Island	2,710	Mississippi	578
Michigan	172,147	Arizona	17.3	Georgia	2,702	New Hampshire	584
Washington	152,609	Alabama	13.8	Minnesota	2,625	Virginia	594
Georgia	151,865	Pennsylvania	11.9	Michigan	2,369	South Dakota	648
New Jersey	133,227	Illinois	10.4	Indiana	2,326	Utah	678
Illinois	131,850	Montana	9.6	Connecticut	2,316	Maine	730
Pennsylvania	121,094	Iowa	9.6	New Jersey	2,175	Montana	782

Note: The District of Columbia as a wholly urban jurisdiction is excluded.
[a]Rates are computed using the U.S. adult resident population on July 1, 1998.
Source: Thomas P. Bonczar and Lauren E. Glaze, *Probation and Parole in the United States, 1998* (Washington, DC: U.S. Department of Justice, Bureau of Justice Statistics, 1999).

supervise more than 50 probationers, national averages now exceed 115 cases per officer.

In some areas the number is even higher. Joan Petersilia reports that 60 percent of all Los Angeles probationers are tracked solely by computer and have no contact with officers.[7] Further, as prison populations swell to the bursting point, more serious and potentially dangerous offenders are placed on probation by judges who have few alternatives as a result of a lack of available prison beds.

The many problems faced by probation and other community-based correctional programs create a pressing need to focus on the role that community corrections can and should play in managing crime and criminal offenders. This chapter will examine various forms of probation and discuss how and when probation, instead of incarceration, is an appropriate sentence.

WHAT IS PROBATION?

Although no authoritative classifications exist by law, probation may be generally classified in four categories:[8]

1. Regular probation
2. Intensive supervision probation
3. Deferred adjudication probation
4. Pretrial diversion probation

Regular Probation

Regular probation can be defined as the release of a convicted offender under conditions imposed by the court for a specified period during which the court retains authority to modify the conditions of sentence or to resentence the offender if he or she violates the conditions. Regular probation is used in both misdemeanor and felony cases and is the type most often used, accounting for about 90 percent of all probation sentences.

Intensive Supervision Probation

Intensive supervision probation (ISP), for offenders who are too antisocial for the relative freedom afforded by regular probation yet not so seriously criminal as to require incarceration, has sprung up around the country since 1980.[9] Intensive supervision probation in some form had been adopted nationwide by 1990. Although ISP was originally designed to enhance rehabilitation and to ensure public safety by affording greater contact between probation officers and probationers, the purposes of newer programs include reducing costs and alleviating prison overcrowding. Intensive supervision programs are also seen as socially cost-effective in that they are less likely to contribute to the breakup of offenders' families than incarceration, they allow offenders to remain employed, and they lack the stigmatizing effects of prison. Although ISP programs vary between jurisdictions, most require multiple weekly contacts with probation officers, random night and weekend visits, unscheduled drug testing, and strict enforcement of probation conditions. Many require community service restitution and some form of electronic surveillance.

Probation officers who work with ISP clients generally have smaller caseloads than those with regular probation clients. Smaller caseloads allow for greater assistance to the probationer in his or her rehabilitation efforts and greater protection to the community through increased surveillance and control. One scholar has observed that ISP is what most communities want all probation to be.[10] A more detailed discussion of intensive supervision appears in Chapter 13.

Deferred Adjudication

Most states and the federal system also provide for deferred adjudication under the general probation statutes. In this form of probation, the court, after a plea of guilty or **nolo contendere,** defers further proceedings without entering an adjudication of guilt and places the defendant on probation, usually ordering some form of community service and restitution. Defendants who successfully complete the probation term have their charges dropped. Failure to comply with the terms of the deferred adjudication agreement may result in incarceration.

NOLO CONTENDERE

A plea option, available in a small number of states, that literally means "I do not wish to contend the charges."

Pretrial Diversion

Pretrial diversion is another form of probation authorized by most states and in the federal system. Criminal sanctions would be excessive for many persons who come to the attention of the criminal justice system because of their need for treatment or supervision. Programs that provide these needed services without the stigma of criminal prosecution have proved attractive. Pretrial diversion is like deferred adjudication in that there is no finding of guilt. The difference is that probation is imposed before a plea of guilty in pretrial diversion, whereas deferred adjudication is imposed after a plea of guilty or nolo contendere.[11] Pretrial diversion has been criticized based on research indicating that many persons who are diverted would not have been arrested or prosecuted in the first place were it not for the existence of a diversion program. Such net widening increases the number of persons involved in the criminal justice process.

FIGURE 3.1 *Typical Outcome of 100 Felony Arrests Brought by Police for Prosecution*

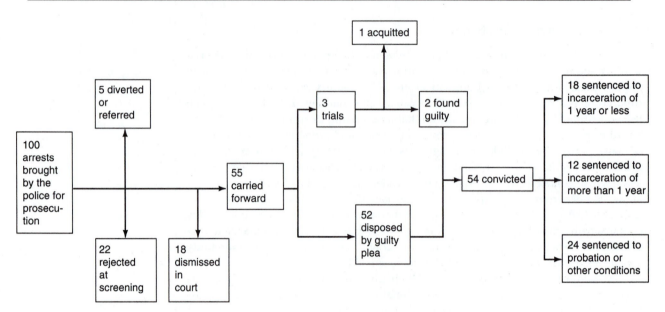

Source: U.S. Department of Justice; Bureau of Justice Statistics, *The Prosecution of Felony Arrests, 1986* (Washington, DC: U.S. Government Printing Office, June 1989), cover page.

THE DECISION TO GRANT PROBATION—SENTENCING

Sentencing has long been considered the most difficult decision in the criminal justice process. Sentencing can be defined as the postconviction stage of the criminal process in which the defendant is brought before the court for the imposition of a sentence. A sentence is the formal judgment pronounced by a court or a judge after conviction that imposes some degree of punishment. Problems abound when the issue of fair, just sentencing is addressed. Sentencing demands choosing among a number of alternatives. Figure 3.1 illustrates the typical outcomes of 100 felony arrests brought by police for prosecution. Probation is only one type of sentence that can be imposed by the court. The rest are death, imprisonment, fine, and intermediate punishment.

The death penalty has long been used in the United States, generally with public approval and, until recently, without much legal controversy. In *Furman v. Georgia*, 408 U.S. 238 (1972), the U.S. Supreme Court held that the death penalty was unconstitutional. Two out of the five justices who declared it unconstitutional said that it was per se a violation of the prohibition against cruel and unusual punishment; the other three justices said it violated the equal protection clause of the Constitution because the penalty was applied in a "freakish and wanton manner." After the *Furman* decision, states amended their laws to remove arbitrariness from their death penalty statutes. Four years later, in *Gregg v. Georgia*, the Court turned around and, in a 7–2 vote, declared the death penalty to be constitutional. Since then, and just about every year, the Court has resolved procedural issues involving the death penalty. The effort to resolve the legal issues on the death penalty will continue in the immediate future. In the meantime, the death penalty controversy has shifted to state legislatures. At present, 37 states and the federal government impose the death penalty for certain crimes. Texas currently leads the nation in the number of offenders executed by the state. Other states are reexamining their death penalty laws and one state, Illinois, has placed a moratorium on the death penalty.

Probation, in many cases, is a prelude to imprisonment. Jails and prisons are the places where society keeps individuals who are deprived of freedom. Jails are usually run by counties and hold offenders or detainees only for a short time, usually a maximum of one year. Prisons are run by the state and hold offenders for as long as life. The festering issue in jails and prisons is whether or not they are in compliance with minimum constitutional requirements. The usual allegation from inmates is that jails and prisons violate the Eighth Amendment against cruel and unusual punishment in a variety of ways. Among the most common allegations are that they are overcrowded, have bad food, give poor medical services, are unsafe, have no rehabilitative programs, and deprive inmates of their freedom of religion and right against unreasonable searches and seizures. Most cases brought by inmates do not succeed, but enough successes over the years have changed the landscape of prison operation so as to conform with court mandate. Although the basic constitutional rights of inmates have been laid out by the courts in a series of cases since the late sixties, supervision of jail and prison conditions will continue in the immediate future. The doors of the courts will always be open to inmates who allege a violation of constitutional and other rights.

A fine is a monetary punishment imposed by the court on a person convicted of a crime. The amount imposed is usually left to the discretion of the court, but with the maximum set by law. If an offender is indigent and cannot pay a fine, he or she cannot be sent to prison to work it off because such would violate the equal protection clause of the Constitution. To paraphrase a court decision, there can be no equal justice if the punishment imposed depends on whether or not a defendant is rich or poor. If, however, a person who can afford to pay refuses to pay, incarceration can result. A distinction must, therefore, be made between an offender who cannot pay and one who refuses to pay.

The term *intermediate punishments* can have a variety of meanings in different states. It can include such programs as community service, restitution, electronic monitoring, and forfeiture of proceeds of criminal activity. These programs may also be found in probation. Most probation departments also impose some form of intermediate punishments as a condition of probation.

A number of legal issues arise in sentencing, the most common focus on constitutional rights during sentencing and whether the sentence imposed is disproportionate to the offense as to constitute cruel and unusual punishment. Offenders have few constitutional rights during sentencing, but one constitutional right given is the right to counsel. Sentencing is considered a critical stage in a criminal proceeding, hence if an accused is indigent, he or she must be provided a lawyer by the state. Disproportionality of punishment is another legal issue often raised during sentencing. The legal question is whether the punishment imposed must be proportionate to the seriousness of the offense committed. The answer is that the Constitution does not require that the punishment be proportionate to the offense, with two exceptions. One is in death penalty cases in which the Court requires the taking of a life with malice (murder) as just about the only category of offense for which the death penalty can be imposed. It is hard to imagine a case, except treason, in which the Court would approve of the death penalty unless murder is committed. The second exception is that, in non-death penalty cases, the Court has hinted that a sentence that is grossly disproportionate to the offense will likely be declared unconstitutional. What is "grossly disproportionate," however, has not been defined by the courts. They are simply, in effect, saying, "Show us the circumstances and we will tell you whether the punishment is disproportionate or not." It can be assumed that life imprisonment for the crime of shoplifting will likely be considered disproportionate, but where does one draw the line as the severity of the punishment goes down and the severity of the offense goes up? That has not been answered with precision by the courts.

Factors That Affect the Probation Grant

The decision to grant probation to an individual offender must consider such factors as the following:

- the offender's eligibility for probation
- whether probation or incarceration is the preferred disposition
- the conditions of probation as fixed by statute
- the availability and quality of probation services
- the availability and quality of other sentencing dispositions
- the methods of developing sentencing information
- whether probation is appropriate for the offender

ELIGIBILITY FOR PROBATION: Courts have consistently held that probation is a privilege, not a right. The privilege theory considers probation a matter of grace and places the question of whether it should be granted in a particular instance entirely with the court. To phrase it differently, the decision to grant or withhold probation is a discretionary act of the trial court, and an offender has neither a constitutional nor a statutory right to probation. Statutes provide for probation, however, and an eligible offender has the right to be considered for it. When the statute provides that a class of offenders is to be considered for probation, the defendant is entitled to fair treatment and is not to be made the victim of whim or caprice. Thus a judge was found in error for considering probation only for defendants who pleaded guilty and for refusing to consider probation for a defendant who pleaded not guilty and stood trial. The court in the one case pointed out that there is nothing to bar the judge who entertains an application for probation from considering (among other things) whether the defendant pleaded guilty or stood trial, especially when the defendant has presented only a frivolous defense. The error occurred when the judge refused to consider as a class all defendants who had stood trial.[12] A judge who announced that he could "never grant probation to a drug pusher" committed a similar error.[13]

States sometimes legislate restrictions on the use of probation. Restrictions on eligibility tend to declare ineligible defendants convicted of certain specified offenses (usually crimes of violence), those upon whom a term longer than a specified number of years is assessed, and those with a prior felony conviction. New York, for example, precludes probation for anyone with a prior felony conviction. Minnesota sentencing guidelines, however, direct judges to grant probation for persons convicted of larceny regardless of their prior convictions and requires judges who depart from the guidelines to justify the sentence. Generally, probation is more likely to be granted to first-time offenders who have committed less serious offenses. A survey of felony convictions in 1988 in the nation's 75 largest counties found that 37 percent of defendants with no prior felony convictions received probation, compared with 15 percent of repeat offenders.[14] However, some observers have noted that more and more serious felony offenders are being placed on probation as a result of plea bargaining and because of prison overcrowding.[15]

Federal statutes provide that probation may be used as an alternative to incarceration when the terms and conditions of probation can be fashioned so as to meet fully the statutory purposes of sentencing, including promoting respect for law, providing just punishment for the offense, achieving general deterrence, and protecting the public from further crime by the defendant.

PROBATION AS THE PREFERRED DISPOSITION: In jurisdictions where the ordinary and expected disposition of the offender is commitment to an institution, the problem is to meet criteria for granting probation. In jurisdictions where probation is deemed to be the preferred and expected disposition of the offender, the problem is to meet criteria for denying probation. With regard to adult offenders, the former type of sentencing statute is more frequently found. However, model statutes and standards for probation emphasize the latter type of statute and recommend that sentencing statutes make probation preferable to incarceration, which should be ordered only when the welfare of the offender or the safety of society clearly demonstrates the need for withholding probation and sentencing imprisonment. The Model Adult Community Corrections Act, written and sponsored by the American Bar Association, makes the rebuttable presumption that a community-based sanction, such as probation, is the most appropriate penalty for individuals convicted of nonviolent felonies or misdemeanors. The act attempts to "foster the development of policies and funding for programs that encourage jurisdictions to minimize the use of incarceration where other sanctions are appropriate."[16]

The criteria for probation are often stated in general terms. The California statute, for example, provides that "[i]f the court shall determine that there are circumstances in mitigation of punishment prescribed by law, or that the ends of justice would be subserved by granting probation to the defendant, the court shall have the power in its discretion to place the defendant on probation as hereinafter provided."[17]

New York follows its general statement with more specific criteria. Probation is allowed if the court believes that institutional confinement of the defendant is not necessary for the protection of the public; the defendant is in need of guidance, training, or other assistance, which, in the defendant's case, can be effectively administered through probation; and such disposition is not inconsistent with the ends of justice.[18]

CONDITIONS OF PROBATION FIXED BY STATUTE: The conditions of probation as fixed by statute also must be considered in the probation-granting decision. If the presentence information about the defendant shows that he or she cannot meet the statutory conditions that must be imposed, then it is useless to grant probation. An example is the chronic alcoholic whose history indicates an inability to abstain from intoxicating beverages. Yet the nature of the crime may require as a condition of probation complete abstinence from the use of alcohol. Such a situation imposes both legal and practical dilemmas on the court. Has the court the right to assume that this time the defendant "won't make it" simply because he or she has been unable to abstain on previous occasions? Conversely, can the court ignore the intractable nature of alcoholism, the lack of treatment facilities, and the discouraging statistics about "cures"? In such a situation the court's duty is probably to take all the factors into consideration, to assign such weight to each factor as in its best judgment the situation seems to require, and then to grant or withhold probation accordingly.

To avoid confronting the court with dilemmas of this sort, many authorities recommend that statutes refrain from making specific conditions for probation, leaving the matter open for the judge based on the most up-to-date information that can be obtained by competent presentence investigations about the defendant and available treatment facilities and programs.

AVAILABILITY AND QUALITY OF PROBATION SERVICES: The decision to grant probation is also affected by the availability and quality of community and probation services. A judge may consider it useless to grant probation if no organized probation services are in the locality, if the probation department gives no supervision whatever to the misdemeanant placed on probation, or if the probation officers' caseloads are so large that meaningful and consistent supervision is not possible. However, efficient and effective probation services may be overused.

The organizational structure of probation services and the training and ability of the probation officers are important determinants of the availability and quality of probation services. In some states probation is part of the judicial branch of government, whereas in others it is part of the executive branch. Probation may be administered on a local or statewide basis and may or may not be combined with parole services. Juvenile and adult probation may be under a single administration, or they may be in separate departments. The trend seems to be toward establishing statewide probation departments in the executive branch of government. This structure provides greater uniformity of services statewide and allows for standardization of services, training, and probation officer qualifications.

Quality of probation service is also determined by the qualifications required of probation officers. These vary widely even when minimum qualifications are set out in the probation statute. The American Probation and Parole Association (APPA) recommends that all probation and parole officers have fully completed a baccalaureate degree at an accredited college or university supplemented by a year of graduate study or full-time field experience. The American Correctional Association requires entry-level probation officers to possess a minimum of a bachelor's degree. Edward J. Latessa and Harry E. Allen report that a majority of the jurisdictions in the United States now require a bachelor's degree or higher.[19] In addition, many require additional training or experience.

Unfortunately, neither statutory requirements nor recommended qualification standards for probation officers assure that adequate probation services will be available to the sentencing court. In some areas no probation department exists. Under such circumstances it is not uncommon for the judge to act as his or her own probation officer by setting up conditions and requiring that defendants report to the court at regular intervals. Police and prosecution officials are sometimes pressed into service as unofficial probation officers, although placing released persons in custody of police or prosecution officials is considered an unwise practice. The use of probation varies widely throughout the country and even within a single state. This is so partially because of the unavailability of probation services and also because of differing sentencing philosophies and differing degrees of community acceptance and involvement in probation.

A recent study of probation utilization showed that the southern states utilized probation to a greater extent than other areas.[20] The South reported 1,874 probationers per 100,000 adult residents. This ratio surpassed the Midwest (1,664), the West (1,576), and the Northeast (1,509). Delaware, Texas, and Washington all had more than 3,000 persons on probation per 100,000 persons in the population. States that utilize probation less generously include Kentucky, Mississippi, New Hampshire, North Dakota, Virginia, and West Virginia. This suggests that location can determine whether an offender will receive probation or a prison sentence.

OTHER AVAILABLE SENTENCING DISPOSITIONS: Granting probation also depends upon the availability and quality of other sentencing dispositions. State and federal statutes have provided a range of sentencing alternatives, including boot camps, restitution, community service, monitored home confinement, and intensive supervision programs. These intermediate sanctions have gained approval in the courts and have become popular adjuncts to regular probation. Where such programs exist, probation is more widely utilized. The court may also be influenced toward granting probation by its knowledge of overcrowding or deplorable conditions in the adult prison system or of lack of treatment in youth institutions. In addition, it may consider the fact that specialized facilities—such as those needed for sex offenders or narcotic addicts—are not available in the community or in state institutions. Juvenile dispositions are also influenced by the programs being offered in juvenile institutions and, even more, by the lack of juvenile probation services in some areas. The rate of commitment to state juvenile institutions is routinely higher from counties where commitment is the only viable disposition.

In its Model Adult Community Corrections Act (1992), the American Bar Association takes a strong stand in favor of increasing the dispositional alternatives available to the sentencing judge.[21] The act recommends that the sentencing court should be provided in all cases with a wide range of alternatives, with gradations of supervisory, supportive, and custodial facilities at its disposal so as to permit a sentence appropriate for each case.

Increased use of diversion strategies will tend to reduce the use of regular probation, but it may not reduce the need for probation services because many diversion programs involve probation-type supervision of the offender. Halfway houses, day care centers, and specialized institutions for the care of alcohol and drug abusers provide the sentencing authority with additional dispositional alternatives, which may tend to reduce the use of probation. However, making probation the preferred disposition places new burdens on probation services. The frequency with which probation and other sentencing dispositions are selected is changing as sentencing philosophy changes and other dispositional alternatives for the care and custody of offenders become available.

METHODS OF DEVELOPING SENTENCING INFORMATION: The information required to enable a judge to impose an appropriate sentence is developed in a post-conviction hearing or a presentence investigation. In the case of jury sentencing, the jury is furnished with information about the defendant's general reputation and character at a sentencing hearing.

If probation is one of the dispositions being considered, a particular need exists for accurate, complete information. Not all offenders can benefit from probation. Some offenders must be incarcerated, either for the public good or because they need specialized treatment that is not available with probation. In some cases the nature and circumstances of the crime dictate incarceration of the offender, especially if the public's ideas of fairness and justice in the criminal process are to be upheld and vindicated. Granting probation thus demands an investigative process that will inform the sentencing authority of the circumstances of the offense and the nature of the offender.

Of the three methods of obtaining sentencing information, the one most closely identified with the granting of probation is the presentence investigation report. The origins of the presentence investigation report can be traced to the use of probation as a disposition. Many states require a presentence investigation only when the offender is to be placed on probation. In such cases the statutory authority and requirements for the presentence investigation and report are contained in the proba-

TABLE 3.2   *Adults on Probation, 1998*

Region and Jurisdiction	Probation Population, Jan. 1, 1998	1998 Entries	1998 Exits	Probation Population Dec. 31, 1998	Percent Change in Probation Population during 1998	Number on Probation per 100,000 Adult Residents, Dec. 31, 1998
U.S. Total	3,296,513	1,672,910	1,555,762	3,417,613	3.7	1,705
Federal[a]	33,532	14,871	14,861	33,254	–0.8	17
State	3,262,981	1,658,039	1,540,901	3,384,359	3.7	1,688
Northeast	561,707	238,520	209,318	590,684	5.2	1,509
Connecticut	55,989	32,318	30,797	57,510	2.7	2,316
Maine[a]	7,178	:	:	6,953	–3.1	730
Massachusetts	46,430	40,165	40,028	46,567	0.3	993
New Hampshire	4,876	3,760	3,461	5,175	6.1	584
New Jersey[b]	130,565	58,200	55,538	133,227	2.0	2,175
New York	181,105	48,384	38,971	190,518	5.2	1,393
Pennsylvania[b]	108,230	43,091	30,227	121,094	11.9	1,325
Rhode Island[b]	19,648	7,099	6,404	20,343	3.5	2,710
Vermont	7,686	5,503	3,892	9,297	21.0	2,068
Midwest	746,286	441,239	416,898	774,455	3.8	1,664
Illinois	119,481	68,232	55,863	131,850	10.4	1,488
Indiana	96,752	84,946	79,798	101,900	5.3	2,326
Iowa	16,834	17,184	15,571	18,447	9.6	862
Kansas[c,d]	16,339	19,306	19,482	16,163	–1.1	837
Michigan[a,b,c]	165,449	61,755	58,729	172,147	4.0	2,369
Minnesota	94,920	54,671	58,618	90,973	–4.2	2,625
Missouri[b,e]	46,301	17,815	16,110	48,006	3.7	1,191
Nebraska	16,439	12,560	13,062	15,937	–3.1	1,309
North Dakota	2,700	1,622	1,664	2,658	–1.6	559
Ohio[a,b,e]	113,493	74,298	70,719	117,618	3.6	1,406
South Dakota[a,b,f]	3,730	4,098	3,958	3,480	–6.7	648
Wisconsin	53,848	24,752	23,324	55,276	2.7	1,427
South	1,306,375	658,788	638,146	1,327,705	1.6	1,874
Alabama[a,b,e]	38,720	17,279	15,626	44,047	13.8	1,348
Arkansas[g]	28,294	13,668	8,379	33,583	18.7	1,782
Delaware[b]	18,837	11,013	9,820	20,030	6.3	3,548
District of Columbia	10,043	9,840	9,278	10,605	5.6	2,524
Florida[a,b,e]	239,694	144,384	142,007	239,021	–0.3	2,101
Georgia[e]	149,963	60,206	58,304	151,865	1.3	2,702
Kentucky	12,093	6,554	5,755	12,892	6.6	437

tion statutes. In juvenile court the judge is routinely furnished with a social history report (also termed *predispositional report*) prior to the dispositional hearing.

Presentence reports are seldom required or used in misdemeanor probation. In some instances this is because no provision is made for misdemeanor probation. When a presentence report is prepared in a misdemeanor case, it is shorter and more summarized. In practice, the judge who sentences for a misdemeanor relies on the police officer for information about the defendant's criminal history and the circumstances of the offense. The defendant is usually given a right of allocution, a common-law privilege to speak to the question of sentencing. The defendant may also be given

TABLE 3.2 *Adults on Probation, 1998 (continued)*

Region and Jurisdiction	Probation Population, Jan. 1, 1998	1998 Entries	1998 Exits	Probation Population Dec. 31, 1998	Percent Change in Probation Population during 1998	Number on Probation per 100,000 Adult Residents, Dec. 31, 1998
Louisiana	35,453	16,136	18,561	33,028	–6.8	1,039
Maryland	74,612	40,179	36,740	78,051	4.6	2,029
Mississippi[c,d,h]	10,997	6,461	5,928	11,530	4.8	578
North Carolina	105,416	59,436	60,154	104,698	–0.7	1,861
Oklahoma[b,e]	28,790	13,912	13,760	28,942	0.5	1,173
South Carolina	43,095	15,280	17,066	41,309	–4.1	1,436
Tennessee[b,e]	35,836	23,368	21,796	37,408	4.4	913
Texas	438,232	196,385	190,859	443,758	1.3	3,140
Virginia	30,002	24,687	24,113	30,576	1.9	594
West Virginia[a,g]	6,298	:	:	6,362	1.0	452
West	648,613	319,492	276,539	691,515	6.6	1,576
Alaska[c,g]	4,212	1,745	1,501	4,456	5.8	1,057
Arizona[b,e]	44,813	28,944	21,177	52,580	17.3	1,544
California[g]	304,531	167,106	147,210	324,427	6.5	1,366
Colorado[a,b,e]	45,499	26,477	21,337	47,792	5.0	1,631
Hawaii	15,401	7,443	7,133	15,711	2.0	1,756
Idaho	6,367	3,138	1,828	7,677	20.6	875
Montana[a,g]	4,683	:	:	5,133	9.6	782
Nevada[b]	11,670	5,794	4,903	12,561	7.6	981
New Mexico[b,e]	8,905	8,926	7,371	10,460	17.5	849
Oregon	43,980	16,876	16,047	44,809	1.9	1,824
Utah	9,516	4,130	4,174	9,475	–0.6	678
Washington[a,b,e]	145,547	45,839	41,123	152,609	4.9	3,619
Wyoming	3,486	3,074	2,735	3,825	9.7	1,088

: = Not known.
[a]Because of incomplete data, the population on December 31, 1998, does not equal the population on January 1, 1998, plus entries, minus exits.
[b]Some data are estimated.
[c]Data do not include absconders.
[d]Data do not include out-of-state cases.
[e]Multiple agencies reporting.
[f]Data are for year beginning July 1, 1997, and ending June 30, 1998.
[g]All data are estimated.
[h]Data do not include inactive cases.
Source: Thomas P. Bonczar and Lauren F. Glaze, *Probation and Parole in the United States, 1998* (Washington, D.C.: U.S. Department of Justice, Bureau of Justice Statistics, 1999).

the right to submit a written memorandum that sets forth any information that may be pertinent to the question of sentence.

APPROPRIATENESS OF PROBATION: Probably the most important factor in the decision to grant probation is whether probation is an appropriate sentence for the particular offender. When probation is a statutory alternative, the decision to grant or deny it is seldom clear-cut. Individualized justice—that noble ideal of the criminal justice system—demands that the penalty fit the criminal as well as the crime. The needs of the offender, the protection of society, and the maintenance of social order must all be carefully weighed. This balancing of the best interests of both the offender and society is the crux of the probation decision process.

Such factors as the offender's age, criminal history, and potential for rehabilitation must be considered in probation decisions. The offender's history of substance abuse, potential for violence, community and family stability, and employment record also affect the judge's choice between prison and probation. Social and political attitudes in a community may affect the decision. The recommendations and advice of police, prosecutors, and victims can be significant considerations. Probation officer recommendations are frequently relied on. Seemingly extraneous factors such as overcrowded prison conditions may play a role. The defendant's attitude toward the offense and the existence or lack of remorse are often weighed in the decision. The judge's own biases, prejudices, and emotional responses toward the crime, the offender, and the victim(s) may affect the choice. In the final analysis, the decision is often subjective, and this has often led to sentencing disparity—markedly different sentences for individuals whose crimes and criminal history are similar.

SENTENCING GUIDELINES: In recent years the advent of sentencing guidelines has introduced a completely new variable into the decision whether to grant probation. Sentencing reformers have criticized current sentencing practices as abusive and as rooted in untenable assumptions. Although many different approaches have been suggested, none has yet satisfied the need to reduce or eliminate unjustifiable disparity in sentencing. Just what does constitute inequity or unjustified disparity in sentencing? The point is arguable, depending on one's philosophy. One scholar has stated,

> Inequity exists when significant differences in sentencing occur which cannot be justified on the basis of the severity of the crime, the defendant's prior criminal history, or characterological considerations which have a demonstrable bearing upon the appropriate penalty or disposition.[22]

According to this, it is not uniformity in sentencing that should be the goal, but a fair and rational approach to arriving at a sentence that allows for variability within a constantly applied framework.

Sentencing guidelines represent attempts to reduce sentencing disparity. Although guideline systems vary greatly from jurisdiction to jurisdiction, they generally establish an "appropriate" sentence based upon the severity of the offense and the offender's criminal history. In some jurisdictions the use of the guidelines is voluntary. Judges are not obligated to follow their recommendations. They merely provide the judge with information about the "usual" sentence for the offense and offender. Judges in some other jurisdictions—such as Minnesota, Pennsylvania, Washington, and the federal courts—have only limited discretion to sentence outside the ranges established by the guidelines. The federal sentencing guidelines, for example, state that if the minimum term of imprisonment specified by the guideline is more than six months, probation may not be granted. Minnesota's sentencing guidelines are shown in Figure 3.2. The range and form of the prescribed sentence can vary significantly from state to state, as the cases of Minnesota and Pennsylvania demonstrate. In Minnesota probation is the recommended sentence for most property crimes when the offender's criminal history is not extensive. Pennsylvania guidelines, in contrast, generally specify nonconfinement only for misdemeanor offenses when mitigating circumstances are involved. For normal misdemeanor cases, minimum ranges of 0 to 6 or 0 to 12 months are specified, regardless of offenders' prior records. Furthermore, Minnesota sentencing guidelines provide judges with a relatively narrow sentence range for a given severity level of offense and a given criminal history score. From

FIGURE 3.2 *Minnesota Sentencing Guidelines Grid*

Presumptive Prison Sentence Lengths in Months

LESS SERIOUS ◄──────────────────────► MORE SERIOUS

SEVERITY OF OFFENSE (Illustrative Offenses)	CRIMINAL HISTORY SCORE						
	0	**1**	**2**	**3**	**4**	**5**	**6 or more**
Sale of simulated controlled substance	12*	12*	12*	13	15	17	19 *18–20*
Theft-related crimes ($2,500 or less) Check forgery ($200–$2,500)	12*	12*	13	15	17	19	21 *20–22*
Theft crimes ($2,500 or less)	12*	13	15	17	19 *18–20*	22 *21–23*	25 *24–26*
Nonresidential burglary Theft crimes (over $2,500)	12*	15	18	21	25 *24–26*	32 *30–34*	41 *37–45*
Residential burglary Simple robbery	18	23	27	30 *29–31*	38 *36–40*	46 *43–49*	54 *50–58*
Criminal sexual conduct, 2nd degree	21	26	30	34 *33–35*	44 *42–46*	54 *50–58*	65 *60–70*
Aggravated robbery	48 *44–52*	58 *54–62*	68 *64–72*	78 *74–82*	88 *84–92*	98 *94–102*	108 *104–112*
Criminal sexual conduct, 1st degree Assault, 1st degree	86 *81–91*	98 *93–103*	110 *105–115*	122 *117–127*	134 *129–139*	146 *141–151*	158 *153–163*
Murder, 3rd degree Murder, 2nd degree (felony murder)	150 *144–156*	165 *159–171*	180 *174–186*	195 *189–201*	210 *204–216*	225 *219–231*	240 *234–246*
Murder, 2nd degree (with intent)	306 *299–313*	326 *319–333*	346 *339–353*	366 *359–373*	386 *379–393*	406 *399–413*	426 *419–433*

(Vertical axis: LESS SERIOUS ▲ / MORE SERIOUS ▼)

▨ At the discretion of the judge, up to a year in jail and/or other nonjail sanctions can be imposed instead of prison sentences as conditions of probation for most of these offenses. If prison is imposed, the presumptive sentence is the number of months shown.

☐ Presumptive commitment to state prison for all offenses.

Note: Criminal history score is based on offender's prior record and seriousness of prior offenses. Numbers in italics represent the range of months within which a judge may sentence without the sentence being deemed a departure from the guidelines. First-degree murder is excluded from the guidelines by law and carries a mandatory life sentence. Sentencing guidelines effective August 1, 1994.

* One year and one day.
Source: Minnesota Sentencing Guidelines Commission.

this range one fixed term is chosen. Pennsylvania sentencing guidelines, however, are broad, and they specify a minimum range, an aggravated minimum range, and a mitigated minimum range from which the judge chooses a minimum term (the maximum term being set by statute).

A sentencing commission in each jurisdiction monitors the use of the guidelines and departures from the recommended sentences by the judiciary. Written explanations are required from judges who depart from guidelines ranges. The Minnesota Sentencing Commission rules state that although the sentencing guidelines are advisory to the sentencing judge, departures from their established presumptive sentences should occur only when substantial, compelling circumstances exist. Pennsylvania sentencing guidelines stipulate that court failure to explain sentences deviating from the recommendations is grounds for vacating the sentence and resentencing the defendant. Furthermore, if the court does not consider the guidelines or if it inaccurately or inappropriately applies them, an imposed sentence may be vacated upon appeal to a higher court by either the defense or the prosecution.

SUMMARY

Since 1970 the number and rate of offenders sentenced to prison have increased alarmingly. As the nation's prisons have become critically overcrowded, courts have been forced to consider alternative sentences. Probation has emerged as a viable alternative. The number of persons sentenced to probation has expanded nearly as fast as the number sentenced to prison. Probation may generally be classified into four categories: regular probation, intensive supervision probation, deferred adjudication probation, and pretrial diversion probation. Each category of probation is regarded as appropriate for specific types of offenders. The decision to grant probation to an individual offender must consider many factors, one of the most critical being the jurisdiction's and the judge's philosophy of sentencing. Historically sentencing has been influenced by philosophical justifications based on retribution, incapacitation, deterrence, rehabilitation, and "just deserts." The extent to which probation is utilized in a jurisdiction is at least partially determined by these considerations. Other factors include the eligibility of the individual offender for probation as fixed by statute, whether probation or imprisonment is the preferred disposition, the conditions of probation as fixed by statute, the availability and quality of probation services, the availability and quality of other sentencing dispositions, the methods of developing sentencing information, and whether probation is appropriate for the particular offender. The use of sentencing guidelines is another variable recently introduced to reduce sentencing inequality and thus to ensure fairness.

DISCUSSION QUESTIONS

1. How do diversion and deferred adjudication differ? How are they alike?
2. Discuss net widening. How does it relate to pretrial diversion programs?
3. Discuss the "right" versus the "privilege" theory of probation.
4. What should be the purpose of sentencing—rehabilitation, deterrence, incapacitation, or retribution?
5. Is it more important that sentences be consistent or that they be individualized to the characteristics and needs of particular offenders?

6. What are sentencing guidelines? How might they affect the decision whether to grant probation?

7. What are the two positions with regard to criteria for granting or withholding probation? Which position is more prevalent in practice? Which position is recommended by both the Model Penal Code and the American Bar Association? Explain your position on this issue.

8. What major factors determine the availability and quality of probation services? How might the existence of highly professional services result in "overuse" of the justice system?

9. In your opinion, should probation services be administered on a local or a statewide basis? Should they be provided by the executive or judicial branch of government? Ask a judge or probation administrator in your area for his or her opinion on this issue.

10. How might the availability and quality of other sentencing dispositions affect the decision whether to grant probation? Give examples.

11. What are the three major methods by which a judge obtains sentencing information? Which do you believe is the most useful in establishing just and fair sentences? Why?

 WEB SITES

Florida Drug Courts as Pretrial Programs

http://www.fcc.state.fl.us/fcc/reports/courts/cttreat.html

Louisiana Pretrial Diversion Programs

http://www.grantda.org/pretrialdiversion.html

Monroe County Drug Court
Example of one pretrial diversion program

http://www.ihhsr.fsu.edu/Reports/1997%20-%209.htm

Minnesota Judge Offers Woman Second Chance
Article about factors affecting judicial decision to grant probation

http://www.familywatch.org/library/judge.htm

Please go to the book-specific Web site for the Supplemental Reading related to the material in this chapter:
American Probation and Parole Association: Position Statement—Probation
http://www.wadsworth.com/product/0534559662s

CHAPTER 3

CASE STUDY EXERCISE
The Decision to Grant Probation

This chapter discussed several factors that affect the decision to grant probation by a sentencing court. The following case examples are before the court, guilt has been determined, and you need to decide if probation should be granted.

Case A: Defendant Smith has been found guilty of involuntary manslaughter, the court may sentence the defendant to a prison term, or the court may or may not grant probation. The court has the following information to make a decision regarding probation.

Smith had been at a party with several friends. While at the party he and a friend, Jones, disagreed about the outcome of a football game. The disagreement grew in intensity. The two slapped at each other and even threw some punches. While they wrestled, Jones struck his head on a table when Smith pushed him down. Friends broke up the argument, no injuries seemed to have occurred, and the two made up. Later the same night, Jones slipped into a coma while sleeping and eventually died from a hemorrhaging injury to his brain. Medical personnel determined the injury occurred when Smith struck Jones and pushed him down, causing Jones's head to strike the table.

Smith has a criminal history—two convictions for misdemeanor theft. He had been placed on probation for those offenses and had successfully completed the probation period without any probation condition violations. Smith is employed as a laborer with a construction company. He has worked for the company for two years, except during a brief layoff period. He has a good work record with the company. He admits that he uses alcohol and had been drinking the night of the offense. Smith has used marijuana and cocaine, but he says that all of the usage has been in the past and not recent. The court has an anonymous letter indicating that Smith continues to use cocaine, but drug tests are negative for illegal drug use.

Smith lives by himself. He has never been married and has one child from a previous relationship. Smith is two months behind on his child support payments and does not see the child very often. Smith has never been in any form of mental health counseling or substance abuse treatment or counseling.

Smith proposes to the court that he be placed on probation, and he says that he will attend anger management counseling and substance abuse counseling classes. He proposes to continue living in his apartment and working for his current employer. The state's attorney is opposed to probation because of the death of the victim. He prefers that the court grant a midlevel prison sentence from the determinant sentencing grid. The law allows for a prison sentence or probation.

Case B: Defendant Thompson has been found guilty of throwing objects from an overpass, resulting in injury to a passenger of a vehicle. The court may sentence him to prison, or it may or may not grant him probation. The court has the following information to make a decision regarding probation.

Thompson is a 19-year-old college freshman. He and college friends had prepared shredded paper in their school colors for the homecoming football game. While walking across an overpass over the interstate highway, he and another student decided to throw some of the shredded paper onto some coming vehicles. The shredded paper was in plastic trash bags. They proceeded to cut open a bag and pour its contents down on the vehicles. When they cut into a second bag and poured the contents onto the passing vehicles, they were unaware that a brick had been put into the bag for weight. The brick struck the windshield of a vehicle, causing the windshield to break and chip. A piece of the glass flew into the eye of the victim causing permanent loss of vision.

The codefendant received probation in the case as he had no prior record, but because Thompson has a prior felony damage to property record, he can be sentenced to prison or placed on probation. Thompson was involved in some damage to a golf course when he and some friends drove onto it after drinking on his 18th birthday. Thompson completed a one-year probation term and worked weekends and evenings to pay restitution for the damages. He completed the probation term six months ago. He is not employed and is a full-time college student. He makes passing grades and has not had any student violations at the university. Thompson denies any illegal drug usage and admitted to drinking in the past, but he denies drinking at all since his prior arrest. Thompson has worked hard to avoid any illegal activity since his first arrest until this event occurred.

Thompson proposes to the court that he be placed on probation, that he will continue to attend school, and that he will participate in community service hours to the victim and her family by helping at their farm without pay. The state's attorney is opposed to probation, as this is Thompson's second felony and because of the seriousness of the victim's injuries.

4

The Presentence Investigation Report

AP/Wide World Photo

What You Will Learn in This Chapter

*Y*ou will learn the purposes of the presentence investigation report, how the presentence report is prepared, and what information goes into a presentence report. You will learn the difference between the "offender-based" report and "offense-based" presentence report. The process of writing a presentence investigation report is examined, with emphasis on the initial interview with the offender, the investigation and verification, and the evaluative summary. Legal issues and criticisms regarding the presentence investigation report are also considered.

INTRODUCTION

The **presentence investigation (PSI) report** has long been the major source of information on which courts base their sentence and is one of the major contributions of probation to the administration of criminal justice. This is especially true in indeterminate sentencing jurisdictions, where judges have considerable discretion in imposing sentence. The original function of presentence investigation reports was to assist the court in resolving the issue of whether to grant probation. Over the years, however, many other uses for the report's information have been found. The total use to which presentence reports are now put encompasses the entire range of correctional programs. The presentence report has changed with the shift in correctional philosophy from rehabilitation to punishment, and from indeterminate to determinate sentencing. Along the way, legal and philosophical issues have been raised concerning the PSI report.

PURPOSES OF THE PRESENTENCE REPORT

The primary purpose of the presentence investigation report is to provide the sentencing court with timely, relevant, and accurate data on which to base a rational sentencing decision. The PSI report also assists correctional institutions in their classification of inmates, institutional programming, and release planning. Paroling authorities use the PSI report to obtain information that is pertinent to considerations of parole. Probation and parole officers use it in their supervision efforts. The report may also serve as a source of information of research.[1]

CONTENTS OF THE PRESENTENCE REPORT

What are the essentials of a good presentence report? The philosophy guiding the preparation of presentence reports may be characterized as either primarily offender-based or primarily offense-based.

Offender-Based PSI Reports

Traditionally, presentence investigation reports have been offender-based. That is, probation officers have been guided in their **presentence investigation** by a philosophy that attempts to understand the causes of an offender's antisocial behavior and to

PRESENTENCE INVESTIGATION (PSI) REPORT

A report prepared from the presentence investigation and provided to the court before sentencing that serves a number of purposes.

PRESENTENCE INVESTIGATION

An investigation undertaken by a probation officer at the request of the court for the purpose of obtaining information about the defendant that may assist the court in arriving at a rational, fair sentence.

OFFENDER-BASED PRESENTENCE REPORT

A presentence investigation report that seeks to understand the offender and the circumstances of the offense and to evaluate the offender's potential as a law-abiding, productive citizen.

RECIDIVISM

The repetition of criminal behavior.

evaluate the offender's potential for change. One of the earliest references to the investigation states that its purpose is to learn the character and ability of the person under consideration, the influences that surround him, and those that may be brought to bear in the event of probation.[2] Another scholar asserted, "What the investigation seeks is a full understanding of the offender from the point of view of his possible *reintegration* into society as a self-sufficient and permanently useful member."[3] Another source states that a satisfactory PSI report

> describes a defendant's character and personality, evaluates his or her problems and needs, helps the reader understand the world in which the defendant lives, reveals the nature of his or her relationships with people, and discloses those factors which underline the defendant's specific offense and conduct in general. It suggests alternatives for sentencing and the supervision process.[4]

These statements make little or no reference to the nature of the offense. They are primarily centered on the offender.

Several excellent models exist on which a traditional (offender-based) presentence report might be based. We believe that the PSI report prepared by U.S. probation officers for the federal courts in the presentencing guidelines era (before 1984) was and is a model for jurisdictions with an offender-based sentencing philosophy. The format of a comprehensive **offender-based presentence report** is described in Box 4.1.[5]

A SHIFT FROM REHABILITATION TO PUNISHMENT: In the mid-1970s, the failure of the corrections system to curb rapidly growing crime rates or to reduce **recidivism** brought about public disillusionment with the existing emphasis on rehabilitation. One of the foundations of the "rehabilitative ideal" was an indeterminate sentencing structure. Under such a system, judges were authorized to impose a sentence from within a wide range, with a maximum sentence stated but release to be determined by a paroling authority based upon its determination of the offender's readiness to return to society. Richard Singer writes:

> This system was called indeterminate because the prisoner's actual time in prison would not be known, or determined, until release by a parole board. The system of indeterminate sentencing could be justified on a number of bases, but its primary theoretical rationale was that it permitted sentencing and parole release decisions to be individualized, often on the basis of an offender's rehabilitative progress or prospects.[6]

By the mid-1980s, the philosophy of rehabilitation and the **indeterminate sentence** were under heavy attack from advocates of a "get tough" approach to crime control. The rehabilitation and the indeterminate sentence were chief among the targets selected for abolition. Critics advocated the **determinate sentence**; that is, judges were given little discretion in sentencing options and offenders little opportunity to reduce their sentence through participation in prison programs. (A more detailed discussion of the "get tough on crime" movement is found in Chapter 9.)

With the emphasis on punishment, many courts no longer focused on the individual and the factors that may have led to criminal activity, but on the crime itself. In some jurisdictions judges' discretion in sentencing was limited by sentencing guidelines, which established a sentence based on the nature of the crime and the offender's criminal history. Personal and social variables, previously considered important in the sentencing decision, were no longer considered or played a very minor role in the sentence determination.

Offense-Based PSI Reports

In jurisdictions with determinate sentencing or sentencing guidelines—those in which the statutes specify a similar sentence for every offender convicted of a particular offense—the emphasis is on an **offense-based presentence report,** which is very different from the traditional document. Here also certain information about the offender is considered relevant (prior criminal record, employment history, family ties, health, and drug use), but the dominant focus is on the offense. The sentencing court is concerned with the offender's culpability in the offense, whether anyone was injured, whether a firearm was used, the extent of loss to the victim(s), and other aspects of the offense. In jurisdictions where the court uses sentencing guidelines to determine appropriate sentences, the emphasis of the PSI report is on applying the particular guidelines to the facts of the case.[7] In federal court, for example, the presentence report serves the major purpose of providing "solid, well-researched, verifiable information that will aid the court in selecting the proper guideline range."[8]

The *Federal Sentencing Guidelines Handbook* advises:

> Among the only offender characteristics taken into consideration by the [federal sentencing] *Guidelines* are the defendant's criminal record and criminal livelihood, which will enhance the sentencing range, and the defendant's acceptance of responsibility for the crime, which will lower the range.[9]

Although offender characteristics are not completely ignored, the crime, not the criminal, is the primary emphasis. Probation officers in some jurisdictions where sentencing guidelines are used no longer write presentence reports. They are responsible only for completing a guidelines worksheet and calculating the presumptive sentence.[10] This deprives other agencies of the criminal justice system of valuable information about the offender.

The current federal PSI report is offense-based, with primary emphasis upon providing the court with the necessary information to accurately apply the sentencing guidelines. Box 4.2 describes the format of the offense-based presentence report used in federal court. It addresses all the significant issues of the sentencing guidelines.[11]

Therefore, what constitutes a good presentence report depends to some extent on whether the jurisdiction utilized offender-based or offense-based sentencing. However, certain criteria apply to all types of presentence reports. All presentence reports should be factual, germane, precise, and succinct. Certainly, a concise report, fully

INDETERMINATE SENTENCE

A model of sentencing that encourages rehabilitation through the use of relatively unspecific sentences such as a prison term of 2 to 10 years with release to be determined by a parole board based upon its evaluation of the offender's readiness to return to society.

DETERMINATE SENTENCE

A sentencing model that establishes a specific punishment for a specific crime. Under such a model, all persons convicted of the same offense would receive essentially the same punishment.

OFFENSE-BASED PRESENTENCE REPORT

A presentence investigation report that focuses primarily on the offense committed, the offender's culpability, and the offender's criminal history.

BOX 4.2   *Contents of an Offense-Based Presentence Report*

1. Offense
   Charge(s) and conviction(s)
   Related cases
   Offense conduct
   Adjustment for obstruction of justice
   Adjustment for acceptance of responsibility
   Offense level computation
2. Defendant's criminal history
   Juvenile adjudications
   Criminal convictions
   Criminal history computation
   Other criminal conduct

   Pending charges (include if pertinent)
3. Sentencing options
   Custody
   Supervised released
   Probation
4. Offender characteristics
   Family ties, family responsibilities, and community ties
   Mental and emotional health
   Physical condition, including drug dependence and alcohol abuse

   Education and vocational skills
   Employment record
5. Fines and restitution
   Statutory provisions
   Guidelines provisions for fines
   Defendant's ability to pay
6. Factors that may warrant departure (from guidelines sentence)
7. Impact of plea agreement (if pertinent)
8. Sentencing recommendation

read, is more effective than a lengthy one that is not considered or used.[12] The effectiveness of a presentence report is directly related to the success with which the findings are communicated and the extent to which it is used. The report's length and content should be appropriate to the seriousness of the offense. The greater the consequences of a judgment, the more likely is the court or a subsequent decision-making body to need more information. Where an individual has committed a violent or potentially violent offense, consideration of release on probation, prison classification committee decisions, and parole release decisions will all require more knowledge of the individual than if the individual were a situational, nonviolent first offender. Above all other considerations, the PSI report must be objective and completely accurate.

Probation officers have often noted that judges frequently only skimmed their lengthy reports and considered only certain factors that they believed relevant. In response to this reality, some jurisdictions have moved to a shortened version that focuses only on certain relevant variables. In some cases these brief versions of the PSI report are presented to the court in a "fill-in-the blanks" format. This practice places a duty on the probation officer to present the most critical information in a concise, yet complete, manner.

Several aspects of the new PSI report are worthy of comment. In the 1984 Criminal Fine Enforcement Act, Congress cited the need to determine a defendant's ability to pay fines and restitution.[13] The federal presentence report and those of several states now include an analysis of the defendant's financial status for the purpose of imposing fines, ordering restitution, and assessing probation fees. The federal and some state presentence reports also require a **victim impact statement.** The use of victim impact statements stems from renewed interest in victim rights in the 1980s. Restoring the victim's wholeness has become an integral part of the sentencing process. The victim impact statement is to include "information about the impact of the offense conduct on identifiable victims or the community."[14] It assesses the financial, social, psychological, and medical impact upon, and cost to, any individual victim. An example of a victim impact statement in a presentence report is in Box 4.3.

VICTIM IMPACT STATEMENT

Information in a presentence investigation report about the impact of the offense on identifiable victims or the community.

A Typical Victim Impact Statement

Ms. Karen Mercer of Charlotte, North Carolina, was the victim in the instant offense in which the defendant hit her over the head and stole her purse. The purse contained $90, her driver's license, credit cards, and her car keys. The defendant also stole her car. The offense occurred at gunpoint outside Ms. Mercer's apartment. Ms. Mercer's 1995 Mazda Miata was discovered by local police a month later in damaged condition in New York City.

Although Ms. Mercer was covered by insurance, she was not compensated for the damage to her car by his insurance company, because her car was recovered and she did not have comprehensive coverage. Damages to her car included a broken windshield, two flat tires, and a smashed right front fender. Further, she had to travel to New York City, at her own expense, to pick up her car. Ms. Mercer was also hospitalized for a slight con-

cussion and, as a result, lost two weeks' work. Ms. Mercer certified by receipts (with the exception of the cash) that her total loss, because of the defendant's offense, was as follows:

Hospital bill (deductible costs)	$100.00
Bus ticket to New York	35.00
Gasoline (return trip)	18.50
Loss of two weeks' work at $6.70 per hr.	536.00
Two tires at $45 each	90.00
Windshield	150.00
Right front fender/ paint job	200.00
Cost of new driver's license	20.00
Cash loss (unable to verify)	90.00
Replacement of purse/keys	125.00
TOTAL	1,365

In addition to Ms. Mercer's loss, the hospital bill paid by International Casualty Insurance Co.

was $450. Ms. Mercer also stated that she now suffers from anxiety attacks when she considers leaving her apartment at night. She would like to attend counseling for this problem but presently does not have the money for this expense. It would not be covered by her health insurance. An estimate of the cost of such counseling is $60 per session. Ms. Mercer thought she might need as many as ten counseling sessions to clear up this anxiety problem.

Ms. Mercer has no savings, and even though she is employed, she is earning only $6.70 per hour. Thus, the probation officer's assessment of Ms. Mercer's financial situation is that she is in dire need of being compensated for her financial losses and of receiving the money for ten counseling sessions.

Source: Adapted and updated from Administrative Office of the U.S. Courts, *The Presentence Investigation Report*, monograph no. 105 (Washington, DC: Administrative Office of the U.S. Courts, 1965).

PREPARING THE PRESENTENCE REPORT

Preparing the PSI report is one of the most critical and imposing duties of a probation officer. Many probation officers also consider it their most interesting task. It requires many important skills, including interviewing, investigating, and writing. The probation officer's responsibility is to search out the facts about the offense and the offender, verify the information received, and present it in an organized and objective format.[15]

When Should the PSI Report Be Prepared?

The preferred practice is to conduct the presentence investigation and prepare the presentence report after adjudication of guilt. The American Bar Association's *Standards Relating to Sentencing Alternatives and Procedures* gives four reasons the presentence investigation should not be undertaken until after a finding of guilt.

1. The investigation represents an invasion of the defendant's privacy if he or she is later acquitted. The defendant's friends, employers, and relatives must be questioned, and potentially embarrassing questions must be asked.

A probation officer interviews a convicted offender to prepare the presentence investigation report before sentencing.

Leanne Fiftal Alarid

2. Certain information is sought from the defendant that can place him or her in an awkward position before the trial.
3. The material in the presentence report is not admissible at the trial on the question of guilt, and there is a chance that it may come to the attention of the court before guilt is determined.
4. It is economically unfeasible to compile a report that may never be used.[16]

Exceptions to this rule are allowed when the defendant's attorney consents that the preparation of the report may begin before conviction and plea. This recognized the fact that, under certain circumstances, prompt preparation of the report is advantageous to the defendant. In many cases the presentence investigation report is prepared before the defendant pleads or is found guilty by the court. In such cases, the report may be more accurately referred to as the pretrial/plea investigation report.

THE PRETRIAL/PLEA INVESTIGATION REPORT: The pretrial/plea report is most common in the case of a plea bargain. Many cases are settled not with a trial, but through negotiation between the prosecution and defense. In many jurisdictions, the plea bargain specifies an agreed-upon sentence. This has led, in some jurisdictions, to a pretrial/preplea investigation report. Judges may require a pretrial investigation before agreeing to the plea and sentence negotiated by the parties. In some areas, the pretrial investigation report is more common than the traditional PSI report. These pretrial reports, of necessity, are short-form reports that contain information about the defendant's prior criminal record, details about the circumstances attendant to the offense for which he or she is being sentenced, and some facts about the defendant's present social, employment, family, and economic circumstances.

THE POSTSENTENCE INVESTIGATION REPORT: Occasionally a court will order a postsentence report to be written. This usually occurs whenever the defendant has pled guilty and waived the presentence report, and the court proceeds directly to sentencing in accordance with the plea agreement. In such cases, the post-sentence report serves to aid the probation or parole officer in supervision efforts during probation or parole or supervised release and to assist the prison system in classification, programming, and release planning.

The Initial Interview

The first task in preparing the PSI report is to interview the newly convicted offender. This meeting usually occurs in the probation officer's office or, if the defendant has not been released on bail, in jail. In some cases the initial interview takes place at the defendant's home, which provides the officer the opportunity to observe the offender's home environment and thus offers an additional dimension to his or her understanding of the defendant. The home visit may also allow the probation officer to verify information gained from the offender with family members. The officer may also assess the offender's standard of living and relationships with family members.

The initial interview, wherever conducted, is usually devoted to completing a worksheet that elicits information about the offender, his or her criminal history, education, employment, physical and emotional health, family, and other relevant data. The officer also uses this time to develop some initial sense of the offender's character, personality, needs, and problems.

Investigation and Verification

Following the initial interview, the probation officer begins the task of investigating and verifying information supplied by the offender and obtaining employment, military, education, and criminal history records from local, state, and federal agencies. Many of these records are protected by state and federal privacy laws, and obtaining them may require the defendant's written permission. Friends, family, and employers are also excellent sources of information, and they are frequently contacted to assist in developing a well-rounded, accurate depiction of the offender. The probation officer is interested in information that might influence the sentencing decision but which is omitted during the trial, particularly any aggravating or mitigating circumstances. When obtaining information from any source—particularly from relatives, friends, acquaintances, and employers—the probation officer must be careful to distinguish between facts and conclusions. Much of the information given to the probation officer during the investigation will be opinions and conclusions that may have little basis in fact. As a general rule, the report should contain only information the probation officer knows to be accurate. In some cases, information may be presented that the officer has been unable to verify. When that is necessary, the information should be clearly denoted as "unconfirmed" or "unverified."

The Evaluative Summary

Writing the evaluative summary is perhaps the most difficult and painstaking task in preparing the presentence report—particularly in offender-based reports—as this has a significant bearing on the future course of the defendant's life. In writing the evaluative summary, probation officers call into play their analytical ability, diagnostic skills, and understanding of human behavior. They must bring into focus the kind of person that is before the court, the basic factors that brought the person into trouble, and the special assistance the defendant needs for resolving those difficulties.

The Sentence Recommendation

Some critics argue that judges place too much weight on the PSI report in sentencing, which effectively shifts the sentencing decision from the court to the probation officer. Many studies have shown a high correlation between the PSI report sentence recommendation and the actual sentence imposed by the court. A study by the American Justice Institute, for example, demonstrated that the probation officer's recommendation was adopted by the sentencing judge in 66 to 95 percent of the cases.[17] Among the factors that might explain this high correlation is that probation officers may make their recommendations in anticipation of what the judge desires. One of the authors of this book served as a U.S. probation officer for several years. He suggests that probation officers who work with judges for a period of time come to know the judges' biases and predispositions regarding offenses and offenders. They know, for example, that Judge X always sentences drug-sale defendants to the maximum allowable penalty and that Judge Y almost always grants probation to first offenders. After a while, the officers' recommendations come to reflect the inevitability of the situation. A federal judge once told this author, "Never give me a recommendation for probation in a drug case. I don't want to see it."

Other studies have suggested that prosecutors recommend a sentence to the probation officer after making a plea agreement with the defendant.[18] Florida State University criminology professor Eugene Czajkoski, himself a former U.S. probation officer, suggests that prosecuting attorneys often find a way to communicate the plea agreement to the probation officer, who responds with a conforming recommendation.[19] Czajkoski writes:

> Like the judge's role, the probation officer's role in sentencing is diminishing. If it has become the judicial role of the judge to simply certify the plea bargaining process, then the probation officer's role is quasi-judicial in that he does the same thing. . . . [T]he probation officer does a perfunctory presentence report and aims his recommendation toward what he already knows will be the plea bargaining sentence.[20]

However, judges vary widely in their reliance on the PSI report. Some judges do not read the report at all, and others utilize only certain parts of the report, such as the defendant's prior criminal record or drug abuse history or the defendant's degree of culpability in the current offense. Other judges discount the PSI report because of its hearsay nature.

LEGAL PROBLEMS CONCERNING THE PRESENTENCE REPORT

Several legal issues have been addressed by various courts concerning the PSI report. The most important questions raised are: Does the defendant have a constitutional right to disclosure of the PSI report? Are inaccuracies in the PSI report legal grounds for resentencing? Is hearsay information in the PSI report allowable? Does the exclusionary rule apply to the PSI report? Must the *Miranda* warnings be given when a defendant is asked questions by the probation officer for the PSI report? Does the defendant have a right to counsel during the PSI report interview?

Disclosure of the PSI Report

Should the defendant be permitted to see the presentence report—that is, be permitted **disclosure**—and have the opportunity to refute any statements contained therein? Compulsory disclosure has generally been opposed by judges and probation officers. The main argument against allowing disclosure is that persons having knowledge about the offender may refuse to give information if they know that they can be called into court and subjected to cross-examination and that the defendant will know they have given information about him or her. The concern is that disclosure of the presentence report to the defendant will dry up the sources of information. In the words of one court, the fear is that disclosure of the report "would have chilling effect on the willingness of various individuals to contribute information that would be incorporated into the report."[21] A second concern is that permitting the defendant to challenge the presentence report could unduly delay the proceedings. The defendant might challenge everything in the report and transform the sentencing procedure virtually into a new trial. A third concern is that it could be harmful to the defendant to have some of the report's information, such as the evaluation of a psychiatrist or even of the probation officer who is to be the defendant's probation supervisor. A fourth concern is protecting the confidential nature of the information in the report. Given all these concerns, some maintain that the report should be a completely private document; others would permit disclosure at the discretion of the trial judge.

The opposite view—advocating disclosure of the presentence report—is rooted in due process, meaning fundamental fairness. Because the PSI report might have a big influence on the type and length of sentence to be imposed, due process demands that convicted persons should have access to the information on which their sentence is to be based so that they can correct inaccuracies and challenge falsehoods. In jurisdictions where the accused has access to the reports, the sources of information have not dried up, nor have sentencing hearings turned into prolonged adversarial proceedings. Supporters of this position also argue that the defendants' attorneys cannot properly perform their constitutional duty to assure the accuracy of the information used in sentencing without access to the information on which judges are expected to act.

The U.S. Supreme Court has held that there is no denial of due process of law when a court considers a presentence investigation report without disclosing its contents to the defendant or giving the defendant an opportunity to rebut it.[22] A defendant may have such right, however, if disclosure is required by state law or court decisions in that jurisdiction.

There is a trend toward a middle position on the question of disclosure of the presentence report. Although the entire report—which contains the names of informants—is not disclosed to the defendant, it may be shown to his or her attorney. Also, the defendant and his or her attorney may be informed as to the nature of any adverse information in the report and given the opportunity to challenge its accuracy.

After an exhaustive consideration of the reasons for and against disclosure, the authors of the American Bar Association *Standards Relating to Sentencing Alternatives and Procedures* took a position in favor of disclosure.[23] The Model Penal Code would require that the court advise the defendant or the defendant's counsel of the factual contents and the conclusions of any presentence investigation of psychiatric examination and afford fair opportunity, if the defendant so requests, to controvert them. The sources of confidential information need not, however, be disclosed.[24]

In federal jurisdictions, Rule 32(c)(3) of the *Federal Rules of Criminal Procedure* requires that the PSI report be disclosed to the defendant and his or her counsel and to the attorney for the government, except in three instances:

1. When disclosure might disrupt rehabilitation of the defendant
2. When the information was obtained on a promise of confidentiality
3. When harm may result to the defendant or to any other person from such disclosure

The same rule also provides that should the accuracy of the presentence report be challenged by a defendant or the attorney, the court must either make a finding as to that allegation or conclude that such finding was unnecessary because the controverted matter would not be considered by the sentencing court.

When withheld information is used in determining sentence, the court must provide the defendant and counsel with a summary of the withheld information and give the defendant or counsel the opportunity to comment on such information.

The above federal rule represents an intermediate position between complete disclosure and complete secrecy. In those states practicing disclosure and in federal districts, the release of the presentence report has not resulted in the problems that have been anticipated by the opponents of the practice. Instead, it seems to have led the probation services to develop skills for analyzing the offense and the offender more objectively. With greater objectivity has come greater reliance on the reports by the courts and a resultant increase in the number of reports requested and persons granted probation. These analytical rather than judgmental presentence reports are not only more useful to the courts, but they are also more acceptable to the offender, for in them the offender may see that perhaps someone understands or at least attempts to understand his or her problems. This latter effect might result in a closer relationship between the offender and the probation officer. Further, disclosure is a requirement for fairness to the defendant. Thus, the presentence investigation report is an integral part of the correctional system and should be made available to the defendant or his or her counsel.

Are Inaccuracies in the PSI Report Grounds for Sentence Revocation?

Two federal circuit courts recently held that inaccuracies in the PSI report are not grounds for automatic revocation of the sentence imposed.[25] Both courts based their decisions on a determination of whether the inaccuracies are harmful or harmless, as determined by the appellate court. If the inaccuracies are harmful (meaning that the error would have affected the outcome of the sentencing proceeding), then there is reason for reversal. If the error is harmless, then reversal is not justified. Moreover, the defendant has the burden of establishing that the error was harmful. However, when a defendant is sentenced on the basis of a report that is materially false or unreliable, that person's due process rights are violated.[26] The usual remedy in these cases is vacating the sentence imposed and remanding the case to the trial court for resentencing.

Is Hearsay Admissible in a PSI Report?

Hearsay evidence is information offered as a truthful assertion that does not come from knowledge of the person giving the information, but from knowledge that person received from another. In general, hearsay is not admissible in trial because the truth of the facts asserted cannot be tested by cross-examination of the witness because the witness simply repeated what somebody else said. Decided cases are clear, however, that hearsay is not in and of itself constitutionally objectionable in a PSI report. The reason is that the purpose of the report is to help the judge determine an appropriate sentence for the defendant. It is important that the judge be given every opportunity to obtain relevant information during sentencing without rigid adherence to rules of evidence. Because the report is usually not compiled and written by a person with legal training, the judge must exercise proper and wise discretion as to the sources and types of information he or she might want to use. This does not vest the court with unlimited discretion, however. By state or case law, the defendant is usually given the opportunity to rebut information that is claimed to be false.

Does the Exclusionary Rule Apply to the PSI Report?

The **exclusionary rule** provides that evidence seized in violation of the Fourth Amendment prohibition against unreasonable searches and seizures is not admissible in a court of law. This rule does not apply, however, to PSI reports. Courts have consistently resisted efforts to extend the exclusionary rule to proceedings other than the trial itself and only in instances in which the misconduct was by the police. Some might argue that sentencing is so closely related to the trial that the use of illegally obtained evidence should not be allowed to influence the sentencing proceedings. Courts, however, have rejected this argument.

Another issue that has arisen is whether the exclusionary rule applies in cases in which the illegally obtained evidence is acquired by the probation officer or the police solely for use in a PSI report and not in connection with an investigation for a criminal act. Local courts likely will decide based on state rules rather than on a possible violation of a constitutional right. Evidence illegally seized cannot be used in the PSI report if its use is prohibited by state or case law.

Must the *Miranda* Warnings Be Given When the Defendant Is Interviewed for the PSI Report?

The Case of *Miranda v. Arizona* holds that warnings must be given whenever a suspect is under "custodial interrogation."[27] These warnings are as follows:

1. You have a right to remain silent.
2. Anything you say can be used against you in a court of law.
3. You have the right to the presence of an attorney.
4. If you cannot afford an attorney, one will be appointed for you prior to questioning.
5. You have the right to terminate this interview at any time.

Should the *Miranda* warnings be given by the probation officer when interviewing a defendant in connection with the PSI report? Courts say no, holding that the presentence investigation does not trigger the defendant's right to be free from self-incrimination even if the defendant is in custody and facing serious punishment.[28]

Is the Defendant Entitled to a Lawyer during Questioning for the PSI Report?

Courts have held that the defendant does not have a Sixth Amendment right to have an attorney present during the PSI report interview.[29] The reasons are that during the interview the probation officer acts as an agent of the court charged with assisting the court in arriving at a fair sentence, not as an agent of the prosecution. In most cases, guilt has already been determined; hence the adversarial situation that requires the assistance of a lawyer is absent. Moreover, the PSI interview is not considered by the courts as a "critical stage" of the criminal proceeding that requires the presence of a lawyer.

SUMMARY

The ultimate merit of probation as a correctional tool depends to a very great extent on the nature and quality of the presentence investigation report. Probation is in essence a method of individualization and is predicated on the proper selection of offenders to be accorded this community-based correctional treatment. Although the primary purpose of a presentence report is to examine and expose the factors that will mitigate for or against successful community adjustment in lieu of incarceration, use of the report should not be limited to the courts. It should also be made available to prison authorities for classification and treatment purposes and to the parole board to aid in the determination of parole grants and future aftercare needs of the offender.

DISCUSSION QUESTIONS

1. Discuss the importance of the presentence investigation report for the criminal justice system.
2. What is the primary purpose(s) of the PSI report? How might other agencies in the criminal justice system use it?
3. How has the introduction of sentencing guidelines affected the use and nature of the PSI report?
4. How do the PSI report prepared in a jurisdiction with offender-based sentencing and the PSI report prepared in an offense-based sentencing jurisdiction differ?
5. What is the purpose of the victim impact statement in a PSI report? What factors brought about the use of this statement?
6. What is the federal rule regarding disclosure of the PSI report? What are the arguments for and against disclosure? What is the middle-ground approach to disclosure?
7. Is hearsay evidence admissible in a presentence investigation report? Why or why not?
8. Is the probation officer required to give the *Miranda* warning to a defendant before the presentence investigation interview? Why or why not?

9 What factor(s) might explain why probation officers' recommendations are so highly correlated with actual sentences imposed by judges?

10 Discuss some of the other criticisms of the PSI report. Do you believe these criticisms are valid? Why or why not?

 ## WEB SITES

Sentencing Project
Resources and information for the media and citizens concerned with criminal justice sentencing issues

> *http://www.sentencingproject.org*

Bureau of Justice Statistics

> *http://www.ojp.usdoj.gov/bjs/pandp/htm*

Probation and parole statistics

Please go to the book-specific Web site for the Supplemental Reading related to the material in this chapter:
Presentence Investigation Report
http://www.wadsworth.com/product/0534559662s

5

Conditions, Modification, and Termination of Probation

A. Ramey/Photo Edit

What You Will Learn in This Chapter

The imposition of conditions is at the heart of probation because conditions are the means whereby the goals of probation are achieved. In this chapter you will learn that the court imposes the various types of conditions, but the court is limited in its ability to exercise this power. Conditions may be modified, but modification must also be done by the court and not by the probation officer. Most states have provisions for early termination of probation. This takes place when the court feels that the offender has behaved well and further supervision is unnecessary. You also will learn about the various special programs usually established to carry out the conditions imposed.

INTRODUCTION

Offenders are granted probation if they agree to abide by a set of rules or conditions for release. These conditions might apply to all persons released under supervision, or they may be tailored to the needs of particular offenders. Probation conditions determine the degree of freedom a probationer enjoys and are also the primary means by which societal objectives of control and rehabilitation are served.

The imposition of conditions can be a challenging function, particularly in jurisdictions where the prevailing sentencing philosophy is that conditions should fit the offender. The imposition of conditions varies greatly from state to state and even in jurisdictions within a state, in both theory and practice. Variations abound in the types of conditions imposed, whether these conditions are required by law or imposed by courts on their own, and the degree to which these conditions are enforced before revocation ensues.

This chapter looks at the role of the court in the imposition of conditions, the types of conditions imposed, and examples of conditions imposed. It looks at modification of conditions and discusses some of the common types of programs that carry out imposed conditions.

THE COURT IMPOSES CONDITIONS OF PROBATION

The power to impose conditions of probation is vested in the courts. In general, judges enjoy immense discretion when imposing conditions of probation, subject only to a few limitations. Although conditions are usually recommended by the probation officer, the judge has the final say as to which conditions are to be imposed on an offender, the justification being that judges are in a better position, by virtue of their authority and contact with the offender, to determine what conditions best serve the aims of probation (see Table 5.1).

Judges can be creative in imposing conditions because of the immense discretion usually given to them. For example, one judge required a man who beat up his wife to publicly apologize to her, with the wife's consent, in front of a dozen television cameras on the steps of the Houston City Hall during the lunch hour as a condition of probation.[1] Another judge ordered an offender with AIDS (acquired immune deficiency syndrome) to obtain written informed consent from all future sex partners as a condition of probation for a car theft conviction. That form read:

TABLE 5.1 *Conditions of Sentences of Adult Probations, by Severity of Offense, United States, 1995*

Condition of Sentence	Total	SEVERITY OF OFFENSE	
		Felony	Misdemeanor
Number of probationers	2,558,981	1,470,696	982,536
Any condition	98.6%	98.4%	98.9%
Fees, fines, court costs	84.3	84.2	85.1
Supervision fees	61.0	63.9	59.8
Fines	55.8	47.4	67.9
Court costs	54.5	56.4	54.5
Restitution to victim	30.3	39.7	17.6
Confinement and monitoring	10.1	12.9	6.3
Boot camp	0.5	0.8	0.1
Electronic monitoring	2.9	3.2	2.0
House arrest without electronic monitoring	0.8	1.1	0.5
Curfew	0.9	1.6	0.0
Restriction on movement	4.2	5.3	2.9
Restrictions	21.1	24.0	16.0
No contact with victim	10.4	11.8	8.2
Driving restrictions	5.3	4.3	5.8
Community service	25.7	27.3	24.0
Alcohol and drug restrictions	38.2	48.1	23.7
Mandatory drug testing	32.5	43.0	17.1
Remain alcohol- and drug-free	8.1	10.4	5.2
Substance abuse treatment	41.0	37.5	45.7
Alcohol	29.2	21.3	41.0
Drug	23.0	28.3	14.8
Other treatment	17.9	16.1	20.9
Sex offenders program	2.5	3.9	0.2
Psychiatric and psychological counseling	7.1	8.9	4.7
Other counseling	9.2	4.4	16.4
Employment and training	40.3	45.4	34.4
Employment	34.7	40.9	27.3
Education and training	15.0	15.5	15.1
Other special conditions	16.5	19.0	12.6

Source: U.S. Department of Justice, Bureau of Justice Statistics, *Characteristics of Adults on Probation, 1995,* Special Report NCJ-164267 (Washington, DC: U.S. Department of Justice, December 1997), 7, as cited in *Sourcebook of Criminal Justice Statistics 1998,* 470.

(Defendant's name) has advised me that he has been diagnosed as positive for the HIV virus in his body and may be symptomatic for the disease of acquired immune deficiency syndrome. Although I realize I am potentially risking my own life, I nonetheless desire to engage in sexual relations with the above named individual.[2]

In general, creative conditions, odd though they may be sometimes, are valid if they are reasonably related to the rehabilitation of the individual or the protection of society. Moreover, in case of doubt, the authority of the trial court to impose conditions is upheld by appellate courts.

In some states conditions imposed are set by the state legislature (see Box 5.1); in others they are imposed by the judge without legislative guidance. But even in states where some conditions are required by law, judges can usually set additional conditions as they see fit. In other states where conditions to be imposed are enumerated by law, judges are nonetheless given the discretion to impose all, some, or none of the conditions. In sum, except in rare cases in which their authority is specifically limited by the legislature, judges have vast discretion to do as they please when imposing conditions of probation, the assumption being that judges are in a position to individualize justice to fit the rehabilitative needs of the offender and the protection of society.

TYPES OF PROBATION CONDITIONS

Probation conditions may be further classified into two types: **standard conditions** and **special conditions.** Some writers classify conditions as required conditions and discretionary conditions. The terms *required* and *discretionary* can be confusing, however, because in most states the imposition of conditions is usually left to the discretion of the judge even if state law provides that certain conditions are required to be imposed. Given this practice, it is better to classify conditions as standard and special, as they are in this chapter.

STANDARD CONDITIONS

Conditions imposed on all offenders in all jurisdictions.

SPECIAL CONDITIONS

Conditions tailored to fit the needs of an offender.

Standard Conditions

Standard conditions are conditions imposed on all probationers in a jurisdiction, regardless of the nature of the offense committed. They are either prescribed by law or set by court or agency practice. Standard conditions usually require the probationer to

- commit no criminal offense
- work regularly and support dependents
- submit to drug testing
- not change residence or employment without first notifying or obtaining permission from the probation officer
- report regularly to the probation officer as directed
- not leave the jurisdiction without permission
- allow the probation officer to visit at any time
- not associate with persons who have criminal records

Special Conditions

Special conditions are tailored to fit the needs of an offender and therefore are imposed only on certain offenders (see Box 5.2). In many jurisdictions, special conditions are in addition to standard conditions. Judges are given much discretion in determining what conditions should be imposed so that the conditions can be individualized for a particular offender. Judges usually impose conditions based on their assessment in court of an offender's needs, or they rely on recommendations made by a probation officer, particularly in cases in which the probation officer prepared and submitted a presentence report. These conditions are suggested by law for certain offenses or are imposed by judges on their own.

Special conditions may require the probationer to

- attend counseling sessions for substance abusers
- attend literacy classes if the offender does not know how to read or write
- obtain a high school diploma
- serve time in jail if the offender needs exposure to the realities of incarceration
- participate in drug or alcohol treatment if the offender is addicted
- refrain from entering designated areas if the offense involves crimes against children
- pay restitution if damage was caused
- seek mental health treatment if the offender suffers from mental dysfunction
- obtain gainful employment if the offender is unemployed

LIMITATIONS ON THE POWER OF COURTS TO IMPOSE CONDITIONS

Courts generally enjoy wide discretion in imposing probation conditions. Unless certain conditions are clearly mandated by law, judges can be selective and impose any condition they deem proper. However, judges are subject to some limitations in their power to impose conditions. Based on decided cases, these limitations may be divided into four categories: the condition must be clear; the condition must be reasonable; the condition must protect society or rehabilitate the offender; and the condition must be constitutional.

The Condition Must Be Clear

Clear conditions are explicit, precise, and easily understood. Unclear conditions are invalid because they are unfair to the offender and therefore violate the offender's right to due process. For example, a condition saying that the probationer must not associate with "a person of disreputable character" would be unfair unless that phrase is defined and explained to the probationer—which is done in some jurisdictions. In one case a court said that the "probation condition must be sufficiently explicit so as to inform a reasonable person of the conduct to be avoided."[3] In another case a state court held that probation conditions must be "sufficiently precise and unambiguous to inform the probationer of the conduct that is essential so that he may retain his liberty."[4] In still another case a condition that the probationer not be within three blocks of a "high drug area" as defined by his probation officer was deemed too vague and was struck down because it could be violated by the probationer unintentionally.[5] Another court declared as too vague a condition that prohibited a probationer from residing in "Central Florida."[6] A condition that provided that the probationer "live honorably" was rejected on appeal by the court as vague and imprecise.[7] A condition that prohibited the probationer from "frequenting" establishments selling alcoholic drinks was declared unconstitutional because no evidence existed that the probationer understood what the term "frequenting" meant.[8]

The Condition Must Be Reasonable

Reasonable conditions can reasonably be complied with by the offender; conversely, unreasonable conditions are likely to fail because the probationer cannot possibly comply with them. What is reasonable or unreasonable depends on an offender's circumstances. For example, requiring a rich offender to pay $1,000 each week in restitution fees is reasonable, but the same condition would be unreasonable if imposed

CLEAR CONDITIONS

Conditions that are sufficiently explicit so as to inform a reasonable person of the conduct that is required or prohibited.

REASONABLE CONDITIONS

Probation conditions that can be reasonably complied with by the offender.

on an indigent probationer. A condition that prohibits a drug addict from using drugs might be challenged as unreasonable because chances are high that such a condition would fail. However, courts have upheld the validity of this condition because using drugs violates the law, and violation of the law by probationers in itself violates probation conditions. There is also the belief, right or wrong, that the use of drugs starts with the exercise of free will, hence is preventable, and that addiction can be cured if the offender submits to treatment and resolves to refrain from using drugs.

In one case, however, a defendant was placed on probation for five years on condition that he refrain from the use of all alcoholic beverages. His probation was revoked when he violated the condition. He appealed, alleging that a psychiatric examination would have shown that he was a chronic alcoholic and that he was not responsible at the time of the act. The appellate court sent the case back to the trial court on the ground that the district court may have imposed an impossible condition, particularly if psychiatric testimony established that his alcoholism had destroyed his power of volition and prevented his compliance with the condition.[9] This case appears to be the exception, however, not the rule. Most courts hold that alcohol or drug addiction does not deprive a person of free will.

What is reasonable or unreasonable cannot be defined with precision and usually depends on the perception of the appellate court that reviews the condition. What may be reasonable to one judge may appear unreasonable to another. Usually, appellate courts will consider a condition as reasonable and therefore valid, the benefit of the doubt being given to the trial court judge who imposed the condition. This explains why few conditions have been struck down on appeal as unreasonable.

The Condition Must Protect Society or Rehabilitate the Offender

Protection of society and rehabilitation of the offender are the two major goals of probation. Therefore, probation conditions must be reasonably related to these goals. In reality, these requirements for validity do not effectively limit the power of the judge because both goals are so broad as to include just about any condition that is not way out of line or clearly violative of basic constitutional rights. Nonetheless, appellate courts have limited what trial courts can set as conditions. For example, in a burglary case the court declared invalid two conditions that prohibited the defendant from living with a member of the opposite sex who was not a relative and from being in a certain area, saying that these conditions were not reasonably tailored to prevent future criminal conduct by the probationer.[10] In another case a state court invalidated a probation condition that imposed a 9:00 P.M. curfew on a defendant for five years, saying that the condition was not reasonably related to the defendant's rehabilitation.[11]

It is questionable whether a probationer who has never had a drinking problem and whose crime is unrelated to use of alcohol can be ordered to refrain from the use of alcoholic beverages.[12] The Federal Court of Appeals for the First Circuit has held, however, that the trial court could require that a defendant totally abstain from using alcohol during the defendant's three years of probation. In that case the defendant pleaded guilty to several counts of possession of stolen mail, theft of property used by the U.S. Postal Service, and other offenses resulting from a crime spree. The defendant later challenged the condition, saying that it was not related in any way to the circumstances of his offense. The court upheld the condition, saying that the defendant's family had an active history of alcohol abuse and that the defendant's record indicated that substance abuse was and continued to be a serious problem for him.[13]

In a 1997 case a defendant was placed on probation for tax-related offenses. One of the conditions imposed prohibited the defendant from leaving the judicial district without the permission of the court or the probation officer. The defendant thrice sought permission to travel to Russia; permission was denied. The Federal Court of Appeals for the Second Circuit concluded that the denial of the travel request was not reasonably related to the defendant's rehabilitation or the protection of the public and was therefore invalid.[14] And in a 1996 case the Federal Court of Appeals for the Tenth Circuit remanded a case to the district court to determine whether the condition prohibiting the defendant from contacting his son was reasonably related to the offense of making threatening telephone calls, saying that while a court enjoys broad discretion in setting conditions of supervised release, the condition must be reasonably related to the nature and circumstances of the offense and the history and characteristics of the defendant.[15]

A recent trend in sentencing is the imposition of conditions of supervised release that involve shaming an offender or notifying the community of the nature of the offender's conviction. Conditions of these types are better known as "scarlet letter" conditions. Over the last decade public notification laws have been enacted in many states seeking to inform the public of the residence of sex offenders. These laws vary from state to state, with some laws requiring information regarding the residence of a sex offender to be published in a local newspaper and others requiring residents living near a convicted sex offender to be individually notified of the residence of the offender. Although the legislative purpose of these laws is to protect the community by informing persons of potentially dangerous offenders living in their midst, these laws shame offenders because oftentimes the identify of these offenders, including their photograph, and a description of the crime committed are made public either through a newspaper or a Web site on the Internet.

A more controversial condition of probation is one that requires an offender to personally proclaim his or her guilt to the public. Appellate courts in the country are sharply divided on the validity of such a condition. Some jurisdictions have approved the imposition of scarlet letter conditions. For example, in *Goldschmitt v. State*, a trial court ordered a probationer, convicted of drunk driving, to place a bumper sticker on his car reading "Convicted D.U.I.—Restricted Licensee" as a condition of probation.[16] The appellate court upheld the imposition of this condition, stating that it served a sufficient rehabilitative purpose and that it did not constitute cruel and unusual punishment. In *Ballenger v. State*, a Georgia appellate court upheld the imposition of a condition requiring a probationer to wear a fluorescent pink plastic bracelet imprinted with the words "D.U.I. CONVICT."[17]

A number of jurisdictions, however, have disallowed the imposition of scarlet letter conditions. In *People v. Heckler*, the trial court imposed a condition on a probationer, convicted of shoplifting, that he wear a T-shirt bearing a bold, printed statement of his status as a felony theft probationer whenever he was outside his living quarters.[18] The appellate court, relying on state constitutional grounds, found that this condition impinged upon his inalienable right to privacy. The court further noted that this condition, which required him to wear this T-shirt whenever he was outside his home, would undermine certain other aims of his probation, such as procuring gainful employment and staying employed.

In another case, *People v. Meyer*, a trial court ordered a defendant to erect at his home a four foot by eight foot sign with eight-inch high lettering that read "Warning! A Violent Felon Lives Here. Enter at Your Own Risk!"[19] The Illinois Supreme Court found that the purpose of this sign was to inflict humiliation on the probationer. The court further noted that the statutory provisions for probation in Illinois did not include humiliation as a punishment. Thus, the court disallowed this condition. Finally, in *People v. Letterlough*, the New York Court of Appeals rejected the imposition of a condition that the defendant affix to the license plate of any vehicle he drove a fluorescent sign stating "convicted dwi" on the grounds that this condition was not reasonably related to the defendant's rehabilitation and only the legislature had the authority to create a new form of punishment, to wit: humiliation.[20]

The above cases indicate a split in court decisions. Courts that have disallowed the imposition of scarlet letter or shame conditions usually do so on the grounds that the trial court exceeded its statutory authority. They thus leave open the question of whether a state legislature can amend its laws and authorize a trial court to impose a scarlet letter condition. A California court, however, has disallowed the imposition of a scarlet letter condition on state, not federal, constitutional grounds. Challenging the constitutionality of scarlet letter or shaming conditions based on a violation of federal constitutional rights is more difficult and will likely fail.

Jurisdictions that have upheld scarlet letter or shaming conditions have done so on the grounds that the condition furthers the rehabilitation aims of probation by deterring the offender from committing future similar crimes. These courts have also held that shaming or scarlet letter conditions do not violate the Eighth Amendment prohibition against cruel and unusual punishment. The U.S. Supreme Court has yet to rule on this matter, so the issue has yet to be conclusively resolved.

The Condition Must Be Constitutional

Courts have invalidated conditions that violate constitutionally protected activity. Probationers, by virtue of a criminal conviction, have diminished constitutional rights, but they nonetheless enjoy some rights, particularly those considered basic and fundamental. When basic, fundamental rights are alleged to have been violated, courts are likely to hold that the condition is valid only if the government can establish a compelling state interest that would justify the condition. First Amendment rights are considered basic and fundamental and are therefore better protected by the courts than Fourth, Fifth, or Sixth Amendment rights. The burden of proof is on the government to establish that a compelling state interest exists. Again, however, that term is subjective, and its meaning may vary from one judge to another.

FREEDOM OF RELIGION: Freedom of religion is a First Amendment right that is highly protected by the courts. The First Amendment provides as follows:

> Congress shall make no law respecting an establishment of religion, or prohibiting the free exercise thereof; or abridging the freedom of speech, or of the press; or the right of people peaceably to assemble, and to petition the Government for a redress of grievances.

Based on this provision, the following are considered basic, fundamental rights that deserve protection by the courts:

1. Freedom of religion
2. Freedom of speech
3. Freedom of assembly
4. Freedom of the press
5. Freedom to petition the government for redress of grievances

In *Jones v. Commonwealth*, a Virginia court held that an order of a juvenile court requiring regular attendance at Sunday school and church was unconstitutional because "no civil authority has the right to require anyone to accept or reject any religious belief or to contribute any support thereto."[21] The Court of Appeals for the 11th Circuit has reviewed a condition requiring a probationer to participate in an "Emotional Maturity Instruction" program. The probationer claimed the condition violated his First Amendment freedom of religion because of the program's religious content. The court stated,

> A condition of probation which requires the probationer to adopt religion or adopt any particular religion would be unconstitutional. . . . It follows that a condition of probation which requires the probationer to submit himself to a course advocating the adoption of religion or a particular religion also transgresses the First Amendment.[22]

An issue related to freedom of religion is required participation in an Alcoholics Anonymous (A.A.) program. In one case a defendant pleaded guilty to a third alcohol-related driving offense within a one-year period. He was placed on probation on condition that he attend Alcoholics Anonymous at the direction of his probation officer. The probationer, an atheist, complained that A.A. was a religious program and therefore violated his freedom of religion. The court reviewed the Twelve-Step Program (for which A.A. has become famous) and concluded that the concept of a "higher power" is at the center of the 12 steps (see Box 5.3). Moreover, much of the literature of A.A. refers to God and encourages prayer, leading the court to conclude that the meetings tended to establish a form of religion. Therefore, requiring A.A. meeting attendance as a condition of probation was unconstitutional.[23]

Not all courts agree. Some courts have concluded that A.A., although bearing a religious flavor, is basically a secular treatment program that does not violate a probationer's freedom of religion. The issue has not been decided authoritatively by the U.S. Supreme Court and therefore disagreement among lower courts continues.

PRIVACY: The right to privacy is not found in any specific amendment. Instead, it is derived from, for example, the Fourth, Fifth, and the Ninth Amendments. Nonetheless, it is considered a fundamental right, particularly when applied to certain types of conditions. The right to privacy has been the basis of arguments challenging conditions that restrict relationships with family members, prohibit childbearing, and limit sexual intercourse.[24] A condition is usually not invalidated merely because it invades the fundamental right to privacy. Only where no compelling state interest exists to overcome the individual's right to privacy does the condition fail. The state therefore bears the burden of establishing that a compelling state interest justifies such a condition. This varies depending upon the offense involved. For example, a condition that prohibits childbearing would doubtless be unconstitutional if imposed for driving while intoxicated but would likely be constitutional if the crime were the killing of one's own infant child because in this case a compelling state interest (preserving the life of the child) justifies the condition.

PROCREATION: Although not found in any specific amendment, the right to procreation is considered fundamental and may be limited only if a compelling state interest exists to justify the limitation. In a California case, a probation condition prohibiting a woman, convicted of robbery, from becoming pregnant without being married was struck down.[25] The court said that there was no relationship between robbery and pregnancy.

In *Rodriguez v. State,* a Florida court placed a defendant convicted of aggravated child abuse on probation for ten years, provided she not have custody of her children, not become pregnant, and not marry without the consent of the court. The appellate court ruled that although trial courts have broad discretion to impose various conditions of probation, a special condition of probation cannot be imposed if it is so punitive as to be unrelated to rehabilitation. Applying these criteria to the case, the court held that a condition prohibiting custody of children has a clear relationship to the crime of child abuse and is therefore valid. However, probation conditions relating to marriage and pregnancy had no relationship to the crime of child abuse and were related to noncriminal conduct. The conditions prohibiting marriage and pregnancy did nothing to decrease the possibility of future child abuse or other criminality.[26]

THE RIGHT AGAINST UNREASONABLE SEARCHES AND SEIZURES: The Fourth Amendment right against unreasonable searches and seizures is not as highly protected by the courts as First Amendment rights. Several courts have held that conditions of probation that required probationers to submit to searches with or without a warrant were valid. In *People v. Mason,* the court ruled that the waiver of Fourth Amendment rights can be a probation condition and that by such waiver a probationer has no reasonable expectation of privacy.[27] The reasonableness standard of the Fourth Amendment has generally been held to apply, however, and probation and parole officers must have reasonable grounds to believe that searches are necessary to the performance of their duties relating to the probationer or parolee.[28]

In *Griffin v. Wisconsin,* the U.S. Supreme Court addressed the issue of searches by probation officers. In *Griffin,* a probation officer searched the home of a probationer under his supervision without obtaining a search warrant from the court. The probation officer had received a tip from a police officer that guns might be found in the probationer's home. A gun was found, and the probationer was subsequently convicted on a firearms charge. At his trial the probationer moved to suppress the gun evidence, saying that the search was a violation of his Fourth Amendment protection from unreasonable searches and seizures. The motion was denied, and the conviction was later affirmed by the Wisconsin Supreme Court. In making the search, the probation officer relied on a Wisconsin probation regulation that allows the search of a probationer's home without a warrant but with the approval of a supervisor. The regulation also required that there be reasonable grounds (which is lower in certainty than probable cause) to believe contraband is present in violation of the conditions of probation. Declaring the search valid, the U.S. Supreme Court described probation as a form of punishment, like incarceration, and said warrant requirements are impractical because of the necessity for quick decisions. The Court also found that the regulation permitting the search, on which the probation officer had relied, was consistent with the Fourth Amendment's "reasonableness" requirement and was therefore valid.[29]

THE PRIVILEGE AGAINST SELF-INCRIMINATION: The Fifth Amendment guarantees the privilege against self-incrimination. Does a probation condition that compromises this right violate the Constitution? The answer is uncertain. In a 1996 case the Vermont Supreme Court held that a condition requiring a probationer to admit guilt as part of a sex offender therapy program violated the probationer's right to be free from self-incrimination. The court added that a person in a probation setting cannot be forced to incriminate himself without first receiving immunity from criminal prosecution as a result of such admission.[30] The Montana Supreme Court has also ruled that the Fifth Amendment privilege against compelled self-incrimination bars a state from conditioning probation upon the probationer's successful completion of a therapy program in which the probationer would be required to admit responsibility for the criminal acts of which he was convicted.[31] The Alaska Supreme Court has held, however, that a probationer cannot validly invoke the privilege to be free from self-incrimination unless there is "real or substantial hazard of incrimination."[32] Various courts have decided this issue differently, so unless the U.S. Supreme Court resolves the issue, jurisdictions will continue to disagree as to its constitutionality.

The condition that the probationer "tell the truth" does not violate the right against self-incrimination, particularly if the evidence is used in a revocation proceeding and not in a subsequent criminal trial.

LENGTH OF PROBATION

The power to determine the length of probation is vested in the judge, although maximum and minimum limits are usually set by statute. These limits are sometimes similar to the terms fixed by statute for the offense if the offender were committed to a penal institution instead of placed on probation. The modern trend is to specify limits for probation that are less than the limits for commitment. In some states the court is empowered to extend the length of probation during the original term, but within a specified limit. For example, a five-year probation term may be extended but not exceed seven years.

Current standards for probation recommend that probation terms be fixed and relatively short and that the court be given authority to terminate the probation at any time during the probation period. Extended periods of probation are viewed negatively because they tend to be ineffective after a while and can be subject to abuse. In some jurisdictions that impose a probation fee, an extended period of probation without supervision may become a revenue-raising scheme instead of a genuine effort at rehabilitation or public protection. This is a concern because 17 states in 1997 charged probation fees ranging from a high of $45 a month to a low of $10.[33]

Short and more definite periods of probation are favored by many corrections groups. For example, the Model Penal Code suggests a probation of five years on conviction of a felony and of two years on conviction of a misdemeanor or petty misdemeanor.[34] The American Bar Association's *Standards Relating to Probation* provides that neither supervision nor the power to revoke it should be permitted to extend beyond a legislatively fixed time, which should in no event exceed two years for a misdemeanor and five years for a felony.[35] Section 3561 of the latest *Sentencing Reform*

Act, Sentencing Guidelines, and Parole for the federal government provides for the following terms of probation: for a felony, not less than one nor more than five years; for a misdemeanor, not more than five years; and for an infraction, not more than one year.

MODIFICATION OF CONDITIONS OF PROBATION

The length and conditions of probation may be modified in two ways: shortening the term or easing restrictions, and extending the term or imposing additional restrictions. Authority to modify the term of probation by decreasing the term and discharging the offender before completion of the term is also given to the court. The court can modify the conditions of probation on application of the probationer or the probation officer or on its own. The power to modify reinforces the need for flexibility of conditions as a correctional tool for rehabilitation.

The court can modify the term and conditions of probation in response to changing circumstances. Controversy sometimes arises over the technical issues of determining when a probation period has ended and the policy issues of what procedures should be required before the court can modify the original term and conditions of probation. This is particularly true if the modification is to extend the term or impose more restrictive conditions. Shorter and more favorable conditions are not challenged by the probationer and therefore do not raise legal concerns.

PROCEDURES FOR MODIFYING CONDITIONS AND LENGTH OF PROBATION

Some argue that the procedure for modifying the term or conditions of probation should be similar to those for revoking probation. However, such procedures may be impractical and unnecessary. For example, requiring an appearance of all parties before the court, together with a lawyer, to change the reporting day (say, from Friday to Wednesday) or to change a treatment program would be a waste of time and resources. Changes that impose longer, harsher, or more restrictive conditions on the offender might demand more formal procedures, but even these may not justify a full-blown hearing as in probation revocation cases.

The American Bar Association committee working with sentencing and probation standards distinguishes between modifications in probation conditions that may lead to defendant's confinement and those that would not. The standards recommend that, when necessary, there should be a review of the conditions and a formal or informal conference with the probationer to reemphasize the necessity of complying with the conditions of probation.[36] A request for clarification provides an avenue for resolving disputes between probationer and probation officer about the meaning of a condition. Such disputes are generally resolved without court intervention.[37]

Where a modification in the terms and conditions of probation may lead to confinement, procedures should correspond to those required for revocation of probation.[38] Whether this would include the "on-site hearing" demanded by *Gagnon v. Scarpelli* as well as the probation revocation hearing before the court is still an open question (see Chapter 8). If the suggested modifications are so extensive as to raise this question, the matter should probably be identified as a revocation hearing. Instead of the procedures for a modification of term or conditions, the revocation procedures would be followed.

ONLY THE JUDGE CAN MODIFY CONDITIONS AND LENGTH OF PROBATION

Setting and modifying the conditions and length of probation is a judicial function and cannot be performed by the probation officer. The only exception is if such authority is specifically given to the probation officer by law, which seldom happens. Neither can the judge delegate the power to set and modify conditions to the probation officer. The wording, usually at the end of the list of probation conditions, that the probationer is to "abide by any or other conditions as the probation officer may deem wise and proper to impose" is an outright delegation of authority by the judge and should be avoided unless such wording is authorized by law.

A distinction must be made, however, between setting conditions of probation and implementing conditions of probation. In the words of one court, a judge "can set general probation conditions and a probation officer can then set specific rules to implement the general condition."[39] For example, a judge may prescribe that the offender be required to submit to psychological treatment, the specific treatment to be determined by the probation officer. This is generally valid (unless specifically prohibited by state law) because it sets a condition but does not implement it. Similarly, a condition that sets restitution at a certain amount but leaves the method of payment to be determined by the probation officer would likely be valid because specifying the method of payment is implementation. The only possible exception is if this is specifically prohibited by state law. Leaving the restitution amount, however, to the discretion and final decision of the probation officer is likely to constitute an illegal delegation of judicial authority. In most jurisdictions the judge asks the probation officer to investigate and recommend a restitution amount, but the judge retains the authority to set the final amount. Collecting the restitution amount constitutes implementation of condition that can legally be delegated to the probation officer.

EARLY TERMINATION OF PROBATION

In many states the court is given authority to terminate probation at any time during the probation period or after some time has been served. For example, Texas state law provides that for felony offenses a probationer may apply for early termination after having satisfactorily served one-third of the probation term or two years, whichever is less.[40] Article 3564 of the Federal Rules of Criminal Procedure states that the court may "terminate a term of probation previously ordered and discharge the defendant at any time in the case of a misdemeanor or an infraction or at any time after the expiration of one year of probation in the case of a felony, if it is satisfied that such action is warranted by the conduct of the defendant and the interest of justice."[41]

The authority to terminate probation early is vested in the judge, who acts upon recommendation of the probation officer. **Early termination** is usually discretionary with the judge, who reviews the record of the probationer before granting or rejecting the request. Some states authorize early termination without providing statutory guidelines as to when the power should be exercised. A significantly larger number permit early termination upon the satisfaction of statutory criteria, such as good behavior during the period of probation. The motion for early termination can be initiated by the probationer or the probation officer.

Giving the court power to terminate probation early manifests legislative recognition that many probationers do not need probation services for the full term. It

EARLY TERMINATION

Termination of probation at any time during the probation period or after some time has been served.

Electronic monitoring can be a special condition of probation or a sentence by itself.

Corbis

removes from probation offenders whose reintegration into the community is complete or at least sufficiently acceptable to not warrant continued supervision.

SPECIAL PROGRAMS TO CARRY OUT PROBATION CONDITIONS

Probation conditions require that programs or arrangements be established to carry out the conditions imposed. Treatment-oriented conditions require the probationer to undergo treatment in-house or be referred to existing programs in the community. Control-oriented conditions may require the availability of programs that are not otherwise a part of regular probation. Some programs or arrangements available in many jurisdictions mentioned here are discussed in greater detail in Chapter 12 and 13.

Prison Time Prior to Probation

SHOCK PROBATION

A period of incaceration imposed as a condition of probation.

In some jurisdictions the court may order a brief period of incarceration as a condition of probation. Known in various states as **shock probation,** shock incarceration, or split sentencing, the practice is based on the assumption that if offenders are given a taste of prison (the "shock"), they will be less likely to violate the conditions of probation upon release. The federal probation statute allows the court to impose intermittent confinement as a condition of probation during the first year of probation.[42]

Combining a jail sentence with probation, in effect making a jail sentence a condition of probation, is used widely in various states. The Bureau of Justice Statistics reports that 16 percent of adults entering probation in 1999 did so with provision for incarceration, compared with 8 percent in 1990. The Model Penal Code permits a 30-day period of imprisonment in connection with a probated term for a person convicted of a felony or misdemeanor.[43] The American Bar Association's *Standards Relating to Sentencing Alternatives and Procedures* includes among the range of sentencing alternatives "[c]ommitment to an institution for a short, fixed period followed by automatic release under supervision."[44] It is worthy of note, however, that the commentary on this section recognizes widespread opposition to combining jail with probation. The National Advisory Commission recommended against the practice, arguing that the goal of probation should be to maintain in the community all persons who, with support, can perform there acceptably and to select for some type of confinement only those who cannot complete probation successfully, even with optimal support. Because of this, the commission recommended that the practice of commitment to an institution for the initial period of probation should be discontinued, saying that it defeats the purpose of probation. Those who reject jail as a condition of probation assert that short-term commitment subjects the probationer to the destructive effects of institutionalization, disrupts his or her life in the community, and stigmatizes the probationer for having been in jail.

The effectiveness of shock probation has not been conclusively established. Moreover, treatment-oriented critics see the practice as undermining the basic meaning and objective of probation. By contrast, others believe that an initial period of incarceration makes the offender more receptive to probation supervision and improves the person's chances of making successful community adjustment. In many cases the outcome may depend not so much on shock probation as it does on the offenders. Shock probation does not work for offenders familiar with detention systems or for those who commit crimes for reasons unrelated to free will. It may, however, be a deterrent for others.

Intensive Supervision

Intensive supervision is a form of probation in which the caseload is low and the probationer is supervised closely. Regular probation caseload may vary from 100 to 250 probationers for each probation officer. By contrast, the ideal intensive supervision caseload is 25. One or more probation officers are assigned to monitor a group, depending on how the system is structured. Intensive supervision differs from regular supervision mainly in the intensity of the supervision and the clientele involved. Probationers placed in intensive supervision are usually higher-risk offenders who would otherwise have been sent to jail or prison.

Two legal issues are raised in intensive supervision: possible violations of the constitutional rights to equal protection and the prohibition against cruel and unusual punishment. Equal protection requires that people be treated in the same manner unless treating them differently can be justified. Critics assert that placing some probationers in intensive supervision, while others are not as closely supervised, treats them differently in violation of the U.S. Constitution. They also allege that the Eighth Amendment ban on cruel and unusual punishment prohibits supervision that is overly intrusive on individual privacy. Both objections have been rejected by the courts, primarily because probationers have diminished constitutional rights and because offenders on intensive supervision would likely have been sent to prison anyway, where restrictions are more severe and privacy is virtually nonexistent. Besides, equality in supervision does not exist in probation because the treatment approach that undergirds many probation conditions requires individualized treatment based on what may best rehabilitate the offender.

The Corrections Yearbook: 1998 reports that there were 91,854 offenders on intensive probation (roughly 5.2 percent) out of a total adult probation population of 1,744,357.[45] Intensive supervision is more expensive than regular probation but is seen as better protective of society and is less expensive than incarceration.

Electronic Monitoring

Electronic monitoring has become popular as a condition of probation because it is efficient, is less expensive than intensive supervision or incarceration, and is definitely high-tech. It involves linking a monitor attached to the probationer's wrist or ankle to a home telephone, which is linked to a computer at the probation agency. This gives the probation officer greatly enhanced surveillance capacity. In most states electronic monitoring may be imposed by a judge as a special condition; in some states it is specifically provided for by law.

The Corrections Yearbook reports that 25 states and the federal government used electronic monitoring in 1999. The average number of devices used was 593, and the device was worn an average of 16 weeks.[46]

Fines

A fine is "a pecuniary (monetary) punishment imposed by lawful tribunal upon a person convicted of crime or misdemeanor."[47] Federal sentencing guidelines specifically state, "The amount of the fine should always be sufficient that the fine, taken together with the other sanctions imposed, is punitive."[48] Both federal and state court judges frequently impose fines as a condition of probation. The use of fines has been criticized as causing a greater burden on the poor than on the wealthy, so many of the laws regarding fines have been revised. Revisions are needed to ensure equality in the imposition of fines, although that may be an elusive goal primarily because circumstances surrounding offenses and offenders are never the same.

New York and some other jurisdictions have experimented with the European system of "day fines." Day fines are assessed as some multiple of the offender's daily wage, or "unit." For example, if an offender earns $100 per day and the fine is five units, the offender would be required to pay five times his or her daily wage, or $500. A day fine of five units imposed on an offender with an income of $1,000 a day would be $5,000. Failure to pay a fine imposed as a probation condition may result in revocation and incarceration. However, probation is seldom revoked for failure to pay fines alone.

In the 1983 case of *Bearden v. Georgia,* the U.S. Supreme Court held that probation cannot be revoked solely because of an offender's inability to pay a fine or restitution.[49] The Court said that such revocation based on indigency violates the equal protection clause of the Fourteenth Amendment. The Court distinguished, however, between indigency (inability) and unwillingness (refusal) to pay. Unwillingness to pay court-ordered restitution or fines, despite a probationer's ability to do so, may result in revocation. Statutes in most states and the federal system provide for allowing a flexible payment schedule if the defendant is unable to pay the entire fine immediately, modifying the sentence to reduce the fine, and in some cases forgoing the fine and imposing an alternative sanction.

The Seventh Circuit Court of Appeals held, in 1996, that the federal district court was not authorized to order the defendant to pay fines to private charities. The court could not require a defendant to pay a fine to private charities because fines are paid to the government, not to private parties.[50]

Restitution

Restitution is defined as "an equitable remedy under which a person is restored to his or her position prior to a loss or injury. . . . [It provides] compensation for the wrongful taking of property."[51] The main distinction between restitution and fines is that restitution is paid to the victim while fines are paid to the government. Restitution requires offenders to compensate their victims for damages or loss of property and may take the form of either direct monetary restitution to the victim or symbolic restitution, as in the case of community service. In recent years restitution has become widely accepted and popular as a condition of probation. However, it can be abused. John Ortiz Smykla warns that

> Restitution is not without its dangers. Because litigation has not contested its use, there is potential for abuse; the due process rights of probationers can be ignored in placing them in restitution programs, or they can be sentenced to prolonged periods of community service or to unfair amounts of restitution. For example, victims frequently exaggerate the amount of property damage inflicted upon them by offenders.[52]

Generally, however, restitution benefits the probationer, the victim, and society as a whole. In a National Institute of Justice report, Douglas McDonald writes, "Victim restitution . . . forces offenders to see firsthand the consequences of their deeds and thus may encourage the development of greater social responsibility and maturity."[53]

A 1992 Bureau of Justice Statistics study reported that in a sample of 79,000 probationers, 50 percent of all property offenders and 24 percent of all violent offenders were ordered restitution as a condition of probation. The average restitution ordered was $3,368. The study also reported that 60 percent of the offenders had completed their restitution by the time they completed their sentence.[54] A survey in Texas found that restitution was ordered in 49 percent of probation cases statewide.[55] Other studies have found that probationers receiving restitution orders have equal or lower recidivism rates than control groups receiving no restitution orders.[56]

The validity of restitution as a condition of probation has been upheld. In a recent case a defendant was convicted of criminally negligent homicide and was placed on probation. Among the conditions of probation was that the defendant was to "pay restitution to the victim, perform 100 hours of community service, and write a letter of apology to the victim's girlfriend and family." The state court of appeals held that "a trial court has discretion to order a probationer to pay restitution to the victim as a condition of probation, so long as the amount set by the court has a factual basis in the record and is just."[57] Another state court of appeals has held, however, that the court cannot delegate to the probation department the responsibility of determining the amounts of the loss and the restitution. This is a judicial function.[58]

Community Service

Community service is defined as the performance of unpaid work by the probationer for civic or nonprofit organizations. Many offenders on probation are poor and cannot reasonably be expected to pay monetary restitution. But even if the offender is able to pay, unpaid personal service by the offender is often a welcome form of restitution to the community and is a popular condition of probation. The offender is put to work for the public good. In a study of 79,000 sentenced felons, Patrick A. Langan

RESTITUTION

An equitable penalty under which an offender is required to restore the victim to his or her position prior to the loss.

COMMUNITY SERVICE

Performance of unpaid work for civic or nonprofit organizations as an alternative means of restitution.

and Mark Cunniff reported that 14 percent had a special condition requiring community service.[59] A survey in Texas shows that 59 percent of respondents said that community service was "always imposed" as a condition in felony cases, and 40 percent said that it was "always imposed" in misdemeanor cases.[60] Some states, by statute, require community service as a condition of probation for just about any offense. The number of hours of community service vary depending on the nature and seriousness of the offense. For example, one state provides for the following community service hours for probation:[61]

Punishment Range	Maximum Hours	Minimum Hours
First-degree felony	1,000	320
Second-degree felony	800	240
Third-degree felony	600	160
State jail felony	400	120
Class A misdemeanor	200	80
Class B misdemeanor	100	24
Class C misdemeanor	No range	No range

In *Higdon v. United States*, the Ninth Circuit Court of Appeals rejected a probation condition that required the probationer to do 6,200 hours of volunteer work over a three-year period. The court held that the condition, which was essentially full-time charity work, was "much harsher than necessary." The court reasoned as follows:

> First we consider the purpose for which the judge imposed the conditions. If the purposes are permissible, the second step is to consider whether the conditions are reasonably related to the purposes. In conducting the latter inquiry the court examines the impact . . . the conditions have on the probationer's rights. If the impact is substantially greater than is necessary to carry out the purposes, the conditions are impermissible.[62]

Drug Testing

Drug testing, usually in the form of urine testing, is widely used as a condition of probation to determine if an offender has used drugs. It is prescribed by law in some states and left to the discretion of the probation agency or probation officer in other states. A urine sample is obtained from the probationer, usually at random during an office visit, under the supervision of a probation officer. The sample is either tested in-house or sent to a laboratory for analysis. A survey in one state shows that drug testing was "always imposed" as a condition of probation in 78 percent of the departments surveyed. Among those departments, 92 percent conducted drug testing of probationers at random instead of on schedule.[63]

Drug testing offenders may be authorized by state law, by agency policy, or by agency practice, or it may be imposed by the judge even in the absence of any statutory authorization. Some courts have held that urine testing can be conducted by an officer even if it is not specifically prescribed as a condition of probation, because one of the required conditions of probation in practically all jurisdictions is that the offender not violate the law.[64] Because using drugs is a violation of law, urine tests are justified, said the court, even without being specifically prescribed as a condition.

Legal challenges have arisen concerning drug testing, among them the possible violation of the constitutional right to privacy, the right against unreasonable searches and seizures, the privilege against self-incrimination, the right to due process, and the right to equal protection. Courts, however, have consistently upheld drug testing against constitutional challenges, saying that these rights are not infringed because probationers have diminished constitutional rights anyway. Besides, these rights are waived when the probationer consents to drug testing as a condition of probation. Courts have generally required, however, that obtaining a sample not be unnecessarily humiliating and that the test used to determine the presence of drugs be accurate and reliable.[65]

SUMMARY

Probationers typically agree to abide by a set of rules or conditions of release. The power to fix these conditions lies with the court. Conditions may generally be classified into standard conditions and special conditions. Standard conditions are those imposed on all probationers in a jurisdiction, while special conditions are tailored to fit the needs of each offender and therefore vary.

Although courts have broad powers to impose other conditions of probation, there are nonetheless four limitations: Each condition must be clear, reasonable, related to the protection of society and the rehabilitation of the offender, and constitutional. Constitutional rights that might be violated by probation conditions are freedom of religion, privacy, the right to procreate, the right against unreasonable search and seizure, and the right against self-incrimination.

Courts have the power to modify the conditions and the term of probation. The power to set or modify conditions is exercised by a judge and cannot be delegated to a probation officer. Courts are also empowered in many jurisdictions to terminate probation early once it is determined that further supervision is no longer warranted.

Conditions imposed result in such special programs as prison time as part of the term of probation, intensive supervision, electronic monitoring, fines, restitution, community service, and drug testing. Each of these programs raises constitutional issues, but courts have generally upheld them.

DISCUSSION QUESTIONS

1. Discuss the extent of the power of the court to impose conditions. Can judges impose creative conditions? Give examples. Are creative conditions constitutional?

2. Argue that probation conditions should be left solely to the discretion of judges and should not be prescribed by law.

3. Argue that probation conditions should be prescribed by law and not left solely to the discretion of judges.

4. Distinguish between standard and special conditions of probation. Are there conditions that should be imposed on all probationers? Justify your answer in terms of the goals of probation.

5. What are the four limitations on the power of courts to impose conditions? What does each limitation mean?

6. Identify five constitutional rights that might be violated by probation conditions. Discuss each.

7. What are shaming or scarlet letter conditions? Are they constitutional?

8   Does a condition that requires attendance in an Alcoholics Anonymous program violate an offender's constitutional rights? Discuss your answer based on decided cases.

9   Does a condition that dictates participation in a treatment program that requires admission of guilt as a prerequisite violate a probationer's right against self-incrimination? Justify your answer.

10 "A probation officer has power to impose and modify conditions of probation." Is that statement true or false? Explain.

11 What is early termination of probation? When is it usually given and for what purpose?

12 Name five special programs and briefly discuss the essence of each.

13 What is restitution, and how does it differ from a fine?

14 What constitutional rights are usually alleged to be violated when drug testing offenders on probation? Will these alleged violations of constitutional rights succeed in court if raised? Explain.

Please go to the book-specific Web site for the Supplemental Reading related to the material in this chapter:
Court Decisions on Probation Conditions
http://www.wadsworth.com/product/0534559662s

Conditions and Length of Probation

This chapter provides examples of standard and special conditions of probation. It also discusses length of probation. The following case examples provide background the court would consider when imposing conditions of supervision. Discuss what conditions would be appropriate in the following cases and an appropriate length for the term of supervision.

Case A: Defendant Green devised a scheme to pass fictitious payroll checks. He recruited other individuals to pass the fictitious checks in exchange for money.

Green would open a bank account using a fictitious check he had produced. Green would then produce additional fictitious payroll checks using the bank's logo, routing number, and account number. He then would recruit, from homeless shelters, individuals who had valid identification. Upon receiving checks from Green, the individuals would go to area stores to pass the fictitious payroll checks. Green gave a portion of the money to the individual passing the check and kept the remainder.

When Green's residence was searched subsequent to his arrest for the offense, an electronic typewriter, 29 payroll checks matching those previously passed, a computer, marijuana, and drug paraphernalia were confiscated. Upon further examination of the computer, evidence of payroll check counterfeiting was discovered on the computer.

Nine retail stores were victimized in the offense as the stores had cashed the payroll checks. A total loss of $14,503 was determined through documentation and investigation.

Green's prior criminal history includes a conviction for misdemeanor possession of marijuana and disorderly conduct. He was raised in a two-parent home. Neither of his parents has a criminal record, and Green appears to have been provided appropriate structure and discipline by his parents. Green revealed he has used marijuana for the past 12 years. He is currently 28 years of age. He has a high school diploma and a sporadic work history. His personal finances reveal his only asset to be an automobile valued at $1,500. He has six credit accounts. Two of the accounts are current with combined balances of $470. The remaining four accounts are in collection status. Their balances total $2,210.

The defendant is eligible for not less than one nor more than five years of probation by statute.

Case B: Defendant Tuff was stopped by police officers after they observed his vehicle stopping and starting at an accelerated speed. He was subsequently arrested on several charges.

Police observed Tuff's vehicle accelerate at an unsafe speed after stopping at a yield sign. Tuff's vehicle had come to a stop at the yield sign although there was no traffic requiring the stop. Police stopped Tuff. They smelled the odor of alcohol on

Tuff, and a breath test showed Tuff had a blood alcohol content of .162. Tuff was arrested. Found on his person was a .38 caliber handgun and a small amount of marijuana. An open container of beer was inside the vehicle. Police reports reveal Tuff become angry and violent during the arrest. He had to be placed in restraints.

Tuff was convicted of driving under the influence, transporting an open container, and carrying a concealed weapon. All were misdemeanor charges. Tuff has a prior arrest for disorderly conduct. The prior offense involved police responding to a disturbance where shots had been fired. Upon arrival officers saw the defendant throw a pistol up onto a roof. He was chased and appeared to be intoxicated when apprehended. Tuff told officers he had called police because someone had shot at his home. Tuff was irate, shouting profanities and screaming he was going to kill someone. When attempts to calm him were unsuccessful, Tuff was taken into custody and charged with disorderly conduct.

Defendant Tuff is 21 years of age. His parents were divorced when he was born. At the age of six, he began living with his maternal grandparents because his mother worked nights at a tavern. When Tuff was 16 years old, he reports going to the Job Corps. He was terminated from the two-year program with the Job Corps after assaulting a security guard for not being allowed a pass into town. Tuff has been employed as a laborer for three different firms. The longest term of employment in any of the positions was eight months. He was terminated from two of the positions as a result of absenteeism. He states that he resigned from the third job because of personal problems with his spouse and a dispute with his employer over pay. Tuff completed one year of high school before the Job Corps. He completed his GED (general equivalency diploma) as a condition of a previous term of probation.

Tuff states that he was referred for anger management classes when in junior high school. He acknowledged he has had prior thoughts of suicide and, on one occasion, played Russian roulette. On another occasion he tried to shoot himself in the head. He pulled the trigger, but a friend pulled the gun away, causing the bullet to miss him. He states that he was "depressed with life" at the time. Tuff explains that he does not currently feel a desire to commit suicide and does not desire counseling. Tuff began using marijuana when he was in high school. He has also reported use of crack cocaine and methamphetamine. A urine specimen submitted by Tuff during the presentence phase revealed the use of marijuana.

The defendant was married two years ago. He has a daughter. The marriage lasted only a short period of time, and Tuff states that the couple has been separated for more than a year. He does not have contact with his wife or child and is court-ordered to pay $250 monthly in child support. His personal finances reveal his only reported asset to be a pickup he estimates to be valued at $3,000. His only outstanding debt is $1,600 in child support owed to the county in which his daughter resides.

The defendant is eligible for not more than five years of probation by statute.

6

Organization and Administration of Probation Services

Leanne Fiftal Alarid

What You Will Learn in This Chapter

Probation is both a disposition and a process. In this chapter you will learn about the process of probation—the way probation services are organized, administered, and delivered. You will review early probation organizational structures and consider modern organizational systems. The major organizational issues in the 21st century are whether probation should be administered at the state or local level and whether the judicial or executive branch of government should have operational control of probation services. You also will learn about the qualifications and appointment of probation officers, probation subsidy programs, and the Interstate Compact on Probation.

INTRODUCTION

The operation of a probation system is best understood when a distinction is made between probation as a disposition and probation as a process. The disposition of probation leads to granting and revocation of probation. The process of probation furnishes probation services. The two functions are closely related, and they frequently overlap. Different jurisdictions have different probation systems, and significantly less diversity is evident in probation as a disposition than in the way probation services are provided.

Probation as a Disposition

Probation as a disposition is court-related; that is, statutory limits laid down by the legislature place the power to grant it and to revoke it in a court. The federal government permits all courts having jurisdiction of the offenses for which probation may be used to place defendants on probation.[1] This is generally true in state jurisdictions also. Thus, if the state provides only for felony probation, **courts of general jurisdiction** with power to try felony cases have the authority to grant and revoke probation. If misdemeanor probation is provided for, **courts of limited jurisdiction** may grant and revoke misdemeanor probation. In a few states, the power to probate is limited to **courts of record.**

That the authority to grant probation resides with a court is not surprising, especially considering that probation developed out of the court's power to sentence criminal offenders and (depending on the point of view) from either its inherent or its legislatively granted power to suspend the imposition or execution of sentence. The power to revoke probation, logically, accompanies the power to grant it.

Opinions differ as to the exact nature of probation—whether, for example, probation is a sentence or a conviction. Another difference lies in whether it rests on suspension of imposition of sentence (SIS), suspension of execution of sentence (SES), or both. In Kansas City, Missouri, suspended imposition of sentence means that no criminal record will be kept if the sentence is completed, whereas suspended execution of sentence goes on an official record as a conviction and the offender serves time on probation. SES is also an option for SIS violators. Nonetheless, almost unanimous agreement exists that granting and revoking probation is a judicial responsibility.

COURT OF GENERAL JURISDICTION

A court having unlimited trial jurisdiction, both civil and criminal, though its judgments and decrees are subject to appellate review.

COURT OF LIMITED JURISDICTION

A criminal court in which the trial jurisdiction is restricted to hearing misdemeanor and petty cases.

COURT OF RECORD

A court that is required to make a record of its proceedings and that may fine or imprison.

Probation as a Process

The probation process encompasses the organization, administration, and delivery of probation services. The administration of probation services in the 50 states and the federal government differs in philosophy, organization, and procedures. In many cases, the differences have arisen more by historical accident than anything else.

EARLY PROBATION ORGANIZATION

As the states enacted probation legislation, they did not do so uniformly. They followed Vermont's local organizational pattern or Rhode Island's state organizational pattern. Some states combined adult and juvenile probation services, and some combined probation with parole services. States developed joint or separate agencies for felony and misdemeanor probation services. And they placed probation services in the executive branch or the judicial branch of the state government. Various organizational combinations were adopted. For example, Massachusetts enacted the nation's first probation statute in 1878, although the law related only to Suffolk County (Boston). The statute gave the power to appoint the probation officer to the mayor of Boston, subject to confirmation by the board of aldermen. It placed the officer under the general control of Boston's chief of police, although the officer was paid from the county treasury. The probation officer was considered an arm of the court, however, and had the power to investigate cases and recommend probation for "such persons as may reasonably be expected to reform without punishment."[2] Two years later, a law was enacted that permitted other cities and towns in Massachusetts to appoint probation officers. Statewide probation did not begin until 1891, when a statute transferred the power of appointment from the municipalities to the courts and made such appointment mandatory, instead of permissive.[3]

Vermont was the second state to pass a probation statute, adopting a county plan of organization in 1898. Each county judge was given the power to appoint a probation officer to serve all of the courts in the county.[4] Rhode Island in 1899 adopted a statewide and state-controlled probation system.[5] A state agency, the Board of Charities and Correction, was given the power to appoint a probation officer and assistants, with the requirement that at least one of the assistants be a woman.

California enacted a probation statute in 1903 following the Vermont pattern of county-based probation administration. The California law provided for adult as well as juvenile probation.[6]

In New York, probation began in 1901 under a law that empowered all justices of courts having original criminal jurisdiction in all cities to appoint officers to investigate and report cases to the courts that might deserve mitigation of punishment by probation. The first independent commission for supervising probation was established in 1907. By 1939, the probation system was made up of probation officers appointed by the local courts and paid by local governments, but under state supervision. Later, the Division of Probation in the charge of a director of probation was located in the Department of Correction. Subsequently, New York established a state Department of Correctional Services, which has as one of its divisions the Division of Probation.

The first juvenile court (and juvenile probation) statute was passed in Illinois in 1899. Illinois did not provide for adult probation until 1911, when the circuit and city courts were authorized to appoint probation officers and place adult offenders on probation. A state probation office was created in 1923, but it did not begin to function until 1929. In 1933 it was abolished.[7]

ORGANIZATION OF PROBATION SERVICES

The major arguments over the organization of probation services center on the issues of whether probation should be administered at the state or local level and whether the executive branch or the judicial branch of government should administer probation services.[8] Table 6.1 indicates the branch of government administering probation services in each state and whether probation is under state or local control in each state.

State versus Local Administration

Probation services in the United States are administered by more than 2,000 separate agencies. Adult probation is exclusively state-administered in 25 states. In an additional 11 states, a state-level agency is the primary but not the exclusive provider of probation services. Seventeen states have some form of mixed state and local administration.[9] In the states with a mixed state and local administration, the mix takes different forms. The National Institute of Corrections reports that larger cities may have municipal courts that provide their own probation services, primarily for misdemeanants, while the state-level agency handles all other cases.[10] Others are more complex. In Ohio, for example, 38 of the state's 88 counties have county probation departments. In 40 counties, probation services are provided contractually by the Ohio Adult Parole Authority, an agency of the state corrections department. The remaining 10 counties have a combination of county and state probation services. Municipal court agencies also provide adult misdemeanant supervision in 21 cities.

Arguments pro and con can be made for a statewide administration of probation services. The arguments in favor of state-administered probation contend that a state-administered system is free of local political considerations and can recommend new programs without approval by local political bodies. Furthermore, a state-administered system provides greater assurance that goals and objectives can be met, and uniform policies and procedures developed. Moreover, it allows more efficiency in the disposition of resources. County probation agencies also are arguably small and thus lack resources for providing staff training, research programs, and services to probationers.[11] The arguments against a state-administered probation system emphasize the need for local conditions and resources to be taken into account. The probationer remains in the local community and can be best supervised by a person thoroughly familiar with that community. A centralized administration is not likely to be in touch with the day-to-day field operations unique to a particular area.[12] Proponents also claim that local agencies are best equipped to experiment with new procedures and better methods. Because of their smaller size, mistakes are not so costly and far-reaching. They also argue that state policies are often rejected by local communities that then refuse to cooperate with the probation system, which undermines operational efficiency and success.[13] When probation is centralized at the state level under the department of corrections, probation administrators often decry what appears to be an emphasis on the institutional division to the detriment of the community corrections component. The president of the Texas Probation Association recently argued that community corrections in Texas should be deconsolidated from the Texas Department of Criminal Justice, which also oversees the vast institutional division. He wrote,

> In my opinion, this relationship has not been in the best interest of community corrections. . . . Under the direction of the prior agency, the Texas Adult Probation Commission, the State of Texas was at least sensitive to the needs of the local level, where the

TABLE 6.1 *State or Local Branch of Government Administering Primary Probation Services*

State	EXECUTIVE BRANCH		JUDICIAL BRANCH	
	State Level	Local Level	State Level	Local Level
Alabama	X			
Alaska	X			
Arizona				X
Arkansas				X
California		X		
Colorado			X	
Connecticut			X	
Delaware	X			
District of Columbia			X	
Florida	X			
Georgia	X			
Hawaii				X
Idaho	X			
Illinois				X
Indiana				X
Iowa		X		
Kansas			X	
Kentucky	X			
Louisiana	X			
Maine	X			
Maryland	X			
Massachusetts				X
Michigan	X[a]			
Minnesota		X		X[b]
Mississippi	X			
Missouri	X			
Montana	X			
Nebraska			X	
Nevada	X			
New Hampshire	X			
New Jersey				X
New Mexico	X			
New York		X		
North Carolina	X			
North Dakota	X			
Ohio				X
Oklahoma	X			
Oregon	X			X[b]
Pennsylvania				X
Rhode Island	X			
South Carolina	X			
South Dakota			X	
Tennessee	X			
Texas				X
Utah	X			
Vermont	X			
Virginia	X			
Washington	X			
West Virginia				X
Wisconsin	X			
Wyoming	X			
Total	30	4	6	13

[a] Felony.   [b] Community corrections act counties.

Source: LIS Inc., *State and Local Probation Systems in the United States: A Survey of Current Practice* (Longmont, CO: LIS Inc., 1995).

roots of our criminal justice system should be focused. Communication with our state agency was open and productive. The ideas we had were heard with open ears, and the frustrations we felt were shared. The current system, whose priority is justifiably centered about the Institutional Division of the Department of Criminal Justice, has not proven beneficial to our community corrections system, nor to our constituency.[14]

The American Bar Association does not favor any particular formula for allocating administrative authority for probation services between local and state governments. The association agreed with the National Council on Crime and Delinquency that adequate services can be developed through various approaches.[15]

The evidence on this issue appears to support state-administered probation services, in some form. Few states where probation is a local function have provided any leadership for probation services. Where probation is a local function, tremendous variations exist in the quantity and quality of services, the qualifications of probation personnel, and the emphasis on service to the court and probationers.[16]

State–County Shared Responsibility

In some jurisdictions, the system is said to be mixed; that is, the state and counties share responsibility for delivering probation services. The development of Community Corrections Acts, which provide state funding for increased local services, appears to have many advantages. This alternative arrangement usually involves a state executive branch agency with the authority to develop standards for local probation systems that provide for a minimum acceptable level of functioning. The state agency is also responsible for establishing policies, defining statewide goals, providing staff training, assisting in fiscal planning and implementation, collecting statistics and other data to monitor the operations of local probation agencies, and enforcing changes when necessary. This organizational structure recognizes the need for local control while allowing local governments to benefit from the greater revenue-generating capacity of state government.[17] Minimum standards of service delivery and the benefits of service uniformity may thus be established and enforced under threat of withdrawal of state funds.

Community Corrections Acts

For local government and citizens in the community to plan and deliver correctional services at the local level, community corrections acts were enacted to decentralize correctional sanctions so that they reflect community values and attitudes, which vary across the United States. The first community corrections act, or CCA, was enacted in Minnesota in 1973.[18] A **Community Corrections Act** is defined as a statewide mechanism through which funds are granted to local units of government to plan, develop, and deliver correctional sanctions and services. The overall purpose of this mechanism is to provide local sentencing options in lieu of imprisonment in state institutions.[19] In other words, state-run programs do not qualify as CCAs; only those that are operated through local government do. M. Kay Harris conducted an analysis of all CCAs and found that three primary CCA models exist, which all share the following characteristics:

- *Are legislatively authorized*: Statutes provide the framework and authority for the other defining features of CCAs.
- *Are authorized statewide*: CCAs mandate or authorize all localities, individually or in combination, to take advantage of the funds and authority granted.

- *Provide for citizen participation*: CCAs provide for citizen involvement and specify roles that citizens may play.
- *Define an intergovernmental structure*: CCAs delineate the roles to be performed and the power and authority to be exercised by involved state and local agencies or units of government.
- *Require local planning*: CCAs provide that local planning will precede and serve as the basis for the development, implementation, and modification of local correctional sanctions and services.
- *Provide for state funding*: CCAs provide for state subsidies to support local correctional programs and services.
- *Call for decentralized program design and delivery*: CCAs provide for local control of the processes employed to assess local needs, to establish local priorities, and to plan local programs.
- *Endorse locally determined sanctions and services*: CCAs provide resources and authority for sanctions and services to be developed and delivered at the local level.[20]

Harris also found that some CCAs integrate probation and parole, while others do not. Oregon's legislation is typical of a state that has unified probation, parole, and most of its local correctional programs. The act, which was revised on January 1, 1997, states:

> Because counties are in the best position for the management, oversight and administration of local criminal justice matters and for determining local resource priorities, it is declared to be the legislative priority of this state to establish an ongoing partnership between the state and counties and to finance with appropriations from the General Fund statewide community correction programs on a continuing basis. The intended purposes of this program are to:
> 1. Provide appropriate sentencing and sanctioning options including incarceration, community supervision and services;
> 2. Provide improved local services for persons charged with criminal offenses with the goal of reducing the occurrence of repeat criminal offenses;
> 3. Promote local control and management of community corrections programs;
> 4. Promote the use of the most effective criminal sanctions necessary to protect public safety, administer punishment to the offender and rehabilitate the offender;
> 5. Enhance, increase and support the state and county partnership in the management of offenders; and
> 6. Enhance, increase and encourage a greater role for local government and the local criminal justice system in the planning and implementation of local public safety measures.[21]

Between 1973 and 1996, 28 states passed CCA (or CCA-like) legislation.[22] In her assessment of these acts, Harris notes that there is no right way to structure a CCA because all communities have different needs. However, she emphasizes that in modifying CCAs, policymakers need to decide on the mission of the CCA—whether to reduce jail or prison population, to offer a wider array of intermediate sanctions between prison and probation, or both.

CCAs are constantly undergoing revision and modification, but very few CCAs have been evaluated. A statewide evaluation of Ohio's Community Corrections Act revealed that the act was successful in diverting appropriate offenders from prison at no increased risk to public safety.[23] Despite these positive evaluations, the majority of jurisdictions continue to operate either state or local probation services with few, if any, cooperative programs. Furthermore, the controversy over how probation services should be organized and administered ensues.

Judicial versus Executive Administration

Debate continues over whether probation would fare better in the judicial branch or the executive branch of government. Those who favor the judicial branch argue that placing responsibility for probation in the branch that holds responsibility for other human services and correctional services is a more rational alignment. Because federal probation is administered by the judicial branch and federal judges are appointed for life, the chain of command is less rigid and policies tend to remain more consistent than at the state level.[24] Probation would then be more responsive to the courts, to which it provides services, when it is administered by the judiciary. The courts, it is contended, are more aware of the resource needs of probation than the executive branch, and the relationship of probation staff to the courts provides automatic feedback on the effectiveness of probation services. When probation is in the executive branch, it is often a branch of the department of corrections, which includes institutional corrections (prisons and jails), which consumes over 90 percent of the budget. In this position, judicial proponents argue, probation services will have lower priority than when probation is part of the judiciary.[25]

Those who favor executive branch control point out that it allows program budgeting to be better coordinated because of that branch's greater ability to negotiate in the resource allocation process. Moreover, proponents claim that the executive branch facilitates a better coordinated continuum of services to offenders. Advocates of executive branch administration argue that judges are trained in law, not administration, and are thus not equipped to administer probation services. They fear that, under judicial authority, services to the court will have higher priority than services to persons. Finally, with respect to federal probation, the chief probation officers are appointed and dismissed by judges. Thus, some federal probation officers may attempt to satisfy judges before attending to the needs of their caseload or the community.[26]

Federal probation currently is administered by the judicial branch of the federal courts. State probation services are the responsibility of an executive branch agency at the state or local level in 34 states. All but four of these states administer probation services at the state level, making the state level and executive branch the most common administrative arrangement.[27]

Impact of Changing Concepts of Probation on Administration

The nature and objectives of probation have undergone considerable change, yet probation continues to be modified with the times. Regular probation is increasingly perceived as ineffective and as a threat to public safety. The public has had to redefine the role probation should play as a sanction for convicted felons. Increasingly, the response has been to develop intensive supervision programs that emphasize surveillance, control, and risk management. This shift of emphasis from "routine supervision" to "intensive surveillance" has implications for probation administration and organization. In their book *Between Prison and Probation*, Norval Morris and Michael Tonry discuss these organizational and philosophical issues.[28] Typically, they assert, the central questions are: To whom is the probation officer accountable? To whom does he or she look for promotion? And, thus, who has the power to influence his or her priorities?

When probation is a branch of the judiciary, the probation officer's duties are more likely to be preparing presentence reports than supervising probationers, because the officer's relationship with his or her superior—the judge—is centered on the presentence function. If, however, new duties such as intensive supervision and other risk-control responsibilities are assigned, the probation department and the individual officer will be forced to devote more time and higher priority to supervision. Under the control of the judiciary, the probation officer often has difficulty shifting priorities from servicing the court's presentencing needs to supervising the high-risk probationers. Even when the court supports and encourages the shift from service to the court to supervision, the judiciary seldom has the political clout to provide the necessary additional resources for such a change in priorities.

Placing probation administration under local executive branch administration seldom resolves the dilemma. Except in large, prosperous counties, few local communities can provide the additional resources necessary to supervise and control the type and volume of offenders being served if intermediate punishments are to be effective. The sheer volume of offenders overwhelms the resources of most communities.

In a state probation system, however, at least the possibility exists of allocating the staff and funding necessary for the task.[29] Such placement can facilitate a more rational allocation of probation staff services, increase interaction and administrative coordination with corrections and allied human services, increase access to the budget process and establishment of priorities, and remove from the courts an inappropriate responsibility.

THE SELECTION AND APPOINTMENT OF PROBATION OFFICERS

The selection of probation officers is similar to that used to select other public employees. Depending upon the particular laws and policies in a jurisdiction, one of three systems for employment of probation officers is employed; the appointment system, the merit system, or a combined system.[30]

Appointment System

Depending on the status of probation services in the judicial or executive branch of government, probation officers are appointed by the court or courts authorized to grant probation or by the director of the executive department or agency in which probation services are housed. If a county has only one felony trial court, the probation officer is selected by the judge that tries felony cases. Where two or more probation officers are needed, the usual pattern is that the judge or judicial body appoints a chief probation officer, who in turn selects assistants, subject to the approval of the advisory body. Salary scales are fixed, and broad policy matters are determined by the judicial body that holds the power to select the chief probation officer.

In the federal system, for example, the judges of each federal district court appoint a chief probation officer. The chief probation officer selects the subordinate probation officers who are all classified as law enforcement personnel.[31] Up until the mid-1990s, federal probation was administered by the Administrative Office of the

U.S. Courts. This meant that the administrative office dictated salary, minimum qualifications, budgets, and staffing. After federal probation was decentralized by President Bill Clinton in the latter part of the 1990s, each of the 94 districts is now responsible for all administrative decision making.[32]

Federal (U.S.) probation officers also supervise parolees. Parolees are assigned for supervision to the appropriate chief probation officer by the U.S. Parole Commission, the Justice Department agency that is responsible for administering the federal parole system.[33] The assignment is based primarily on geographic considerations. The chief probation officer assigns particular parolees to individual officers on the basis of each probationer or parolee's special needs and each officer's special skills, with due consideration to caseload, geographic location, and other matters. A U.S. probation officer also supervises offenders at liberty under supervised release (those not released on parole), as required by the Comprehensive Crime Control Act of 1984, and those on military parole.

In a state where probation services are locally administered and parole services are statewide, there are usually two sets of supervisory officers. Parole officers are appointed by an administrative department or the board that supervises the department. Power to appoint the chief probation officer is usually in the judiciary, although it may rest with the county governing body, the governor, a state board upon nomination by a judge, or the judiciary from a list supplied by a state agency.

Where juvenile and adult probation services are administered locally and separately, the chief probation officer for adult probationers may be chosen by the judge or judges of the criminal courts, and the chief probation officer for juveniles by the juvenile judge or a juvenile board. Sometimes the juvenile board has the additional authority to designate which court is to be the juvenile court for the particular geographic area.[34]

Merit System

Merit systems were developed to remove public employees from political patronage. In a merit system, applicants who meet minimum employment standards are required to pass a competitive exam. Persons who score above a specified minimum grade are placed on a ranked list. Candidates are selected from the list according to their order of rank. In some systems applicants are also graded on the basis of their education and employment history. The merit system is used in some states to determine promotions.[35] A merit or civil service system exam is required in four states (Delaware, Indiana, Rhode Island, and Wisconsin).

Combined System

Elements of both systems are used in some jurisdiction. Applicants are screened through an exam, and candidates are selected by the agency after a process similar to the appointment system.[36]

QUALIFICATION AND TRAINING OF PROBATION AND PAROLE OFFICERS

Probation and parole officers are required to have good oral and written communication skills. These skills are gained by education, experience, and training.

Education and Experience

The National Probation and Parole Association has recommended since 1959 that all probation and parole officers have a minimum of a baccalaureate degree. This requirement was reaffirmed by the American Correctional Association in 1981 for agencies to receive accreditation.[37] Traditionally, probation officers were recruited out of the social work and psychology areas. As the emphasis of probation has changed from that of treatment to public safety and control, a preference has emerged to recruit individuals with degrees in criminal justice, criminology, and sociology. Selection criteria for probation officers generally include education, experience, or a combination of the two.[38] Some jurisdictions may also require psychological evaluations, physical fitness tests, and drug screening. Some jurisdictions also specify that the baccalaureate degree must be in a social or behavioral science. Many states allow a combination of education and experience as a substitute for the bachelor's degree, while others require additional course work above the bachelor's degree. Seven states (California, Connecticut, Delaware, Idaho, Kansas, Minnesota, and Wisconsin) do not specify any particular educational background beyond high school as a prerequisite to selection as a probation officer.[39] One state (Hawaii) requires a master's degree, and others require graduate training or equivalent experience. Table 6.2 contains a state-by-state listing of selection and training requirements for probation officers. Most agencies are also including HIV (human immunodeficiency virus) and AIDS education and training so that probation officers can prevent themselves from on-the-job exposure and also for the purpose of providing prevention education to probationers.[40]

There is a debate as to whether college-educated officers, the majority of whom have undergone middle-class socialization, are able to sufficiently step into a role supervising streetwise individuals who come from primarily lower socioeconomic backgrounds.[41] One trend that has recently emerged in the United Kingdom (UK) is that the government has abolished the entry-level requirement that all probation officers hold a university degree. Instead, the UK government is replacing the degree requirement with on-the-job training for all probation officers in England and Wales. This change has caused much opposition, and its effects on recruitment and training remain to be seen.[42]

Preservice and In-Service Training

The federal probation system and all states except Connecticut and West Virginia require some preservice training before probation or parole officers assume their duties. Training "does not teach an individual to be a probation officer, rather the probation officer learns a role through exposure to the criminal justice system."[43] Preservice training requirements range from 32 hours in Indiana to 1,460 hours in Pennsylvania. The average preservice training requirement nationwide has increased steadily over the years to 246 hours.[44]

Nevada has a formal regimented Peace Officer State Training (POST) for its probation and parole officers that is modeled after training provided to law enforcement officers. POST topics include strategies of case supervision, record keeping, legal liability, professional ethics, arrest and detention procedures, firearms handling, defensive tactics, and stress reduction. Throughout his nonparticipatory research, John P. Crank found that POST training emphasized surveillance and enforcement as well as officer accountability and documentation. During the training process, POST instructors used metaphors and stories from their own field experiences that greatly influenced how new recruits perceived the organizational culture. In other words, Crank

TABLE 6.2 *Probation Officer Selection and Training Requirements*

| State | ENTRY-LEVEL REQUIREMENTS | | TRAINING REQUIREMENTS | |
	Bachelor's Degree	Other	Preservice Hours	In-Service Hours
Alabama	X		320	(Not indicated)
Alaska	X	Experience	40	40
Arizona	X		40	16
Arkansas	X	Experience	68	20
California		High school diploma; experience	200	40
Colorado	X		32	40
Connecticut		(Not specified)	200	20
Delaware		State Merit system test	160	(Not indicated)
District of Columbia	X	Experience, if candidate has an M.A., less experience required	(Not indicated)	40
Florida	X		380	(Not indicated)
Georgia	X		(Not indicated)	40
Hawaii		Master's degree plus experience	(Not specified)	(Not indicated)
Idaho		(No specific qualifications)	240	40
Illinois	X		40	20
Indiana	X	State merit system test	40	12
Iowa		Associate of arts degree	(Not specified)	0
Kansas		(Not specified)	(Not specified)	
Kentucky	X		40	40
Louisiana	X		(Not indicated)	40
Maine	X	Experience	(Not specified)	0
Maryland	X	May substitute experience or graduate work	209	20
Massachusetts	X	Experience	(Not specified)	(Not specified)
Michigan	X		440	40
Minnesota		(No statewide standards)	(Not specified)	0
Mississippi	X	May substitute experience	100	(Not specified)
Missouri	X	May substitute experience	160	0
Montana	X		80	16
Nebraska	X		(Not specified)	0
Nevada	X	May substitute combination of education and experience	200	40–60

found that trainers shaped the attitudes and values of the probation and parole officer subculture in addition to how new policies would be perceived.[45]

Forty-seven states and the federal system require probation officers to undergo annual in-service training. Probation officers are expected to keep current with new developments in the field, and in-service training offers an opportunity to accomplish this goal. Forty hours annually appears to be the most common requirement. While only three states do not require in-service training, such training has grown more popular over the past several years.

As with preservice training, officer in-service training seems to greatly influence whether a probation officer is oriented toward a control and enforcement role or more of a social support and assistance work role.[46] Probation officer training topics may include rational behavior training, which focuses on the officer using the principles of rationality to persuade the probationer to change old beliefs and attitudes. This training is particularly useful to influence a hostile offender to develop new beliefs, which are reinforced by the probation officer.[47] In San Luis Obispo County,

TABLE 6.2 *Probation Officer Selection and Training Requirements* (*continued*)

State	ENTRY-LEVEL REQUIREMENTS Bachelor's Degree	Other	TRAINING REQUIREMENTS Preservice Hours	In-Service Hours
New Hampshire	X		286	(Not indicated)
New Jersey	X		(Not specified)	0
New Mexico	X		40	40
New York	X		(Not specified)	0
North Carolina	X	Experience	0	0
North Dakota	X		440	(Not indicated)
Ohio	X	Experience and training	(Not specified)	0
Oklahoma	X		520	40
Oregon	X	Experience; may substitute experience for degree	160	64
Pennsylvania	X		(Not indicated)	40
Rhode Island	X	State merit system test	(Not indicated)	(Not indicated)
South Carolina	X		128	(Not indicated)
South Dakota	X	May substitute combination of experience and education	(Not indicated)	16
Tennessee	X	May substitute experience	(Not indicated)	0
Texas	X	State certification process	(Not indicated)	40
Utah	X	Experience (paid employment)	(Not indicated)	(Not indicated)
Vermont	X	Experience; may substitute education or experience for degree	40	(Not indicated)
Virginia	X	May substitute training and experience	80	40
Washington	X	Graduate training or experience	80	40
West Virginia	X		(Not indicated)	24–30
Wisconsin		State civil service examination	360	(Not indicated)
Wyoming	X	May substitute experience	80	40

Source: LIS Inc., *State and Local Probation Systems in the United States: A Survey of Current Practice* (Longmont, CO: LIS Inc., 1995).

California, new probation officers are exposed to empathy training, which aims to sensitize probation officers to what juvenile probationers endure during arrest and detention.[48]

SALARIES OF PROBATION AND PAROLE OFFICERS

As of January 1, 1999, for jurisdictions in which probation and parole services are performed by a single agency, starting salaries for probation and parole officers are the lowest, ranging from $17,964 in Kentucky to $38,732 in Rhode Island (see Table 6.3). The average starting salary nationwide for probation and parole officers was $25,662, and the average maximum salary was $44,173.

In states with separate probation and parole services, parole officers earned slightly more than probation officers. The average starting salary was $28,491 for

TABLE 6.3 *Probation and Parole Officers' Starting, Average, and Maximum Salaries on January 1, 1999*

State	Entry Salary	Average Salary	Highest Salary
Probation			
Arizona	$25,977	$32,333	$50,366
Colorado	30,348	47,225	57,204
Connecticut	37,314	58,000	66,838
District of Columbia	29,501	42,209	54,917
Georgia	22,800	32,000	41,800
Hawaii	32,544	a	46,356
Illinois[b]	25,500	32,000	48,000
Indiana	21,138	26,087	a
Kansas	24,523	a	34,507
Massachusetts	40,533	a	50,699
Nebraska	23,497	31,000	44,237
New Jersey	29,000	34,650	63,000
South Dakota	24,170	30,014	36,275
Tennessee	22,545	30,720	41,328
West Virginia	20,760	31,953	53,640
Federal	25,000	47,900	93,411
Average	$27,197	$36,622	$52,172
Parole			
Arizona	$23,876	$33,078	$40,561
California	43,644	54,000	64,212
Colorado	31,000	44,820	50,500
Connecticut	29,696	47,895	50,109
District of Columbia	29,500	a	54,900
Georgia	22,800	29,666	45,234
Hawaii[c]	30,756	38,142	49,104
Illinois	27,048	41,148	45,780
Indiana	24,076	27,850	34,325
Kansas	24,523	27,040	38,043
Massachusetts	38,068	47,915	48,735
Nebraska	23,156	31,068	39,620
New Jersey	36,644	51,226	62,362
New York[d]	42,053	47,034	52,015
South Dakota	21,902	23,600	28,766
Tennessee	20,412	a	a
Texas[e]	23,232	27,860	33,836
West Virginia	20,452	24,764	30,036
Average	$28,491	$37,319	$45,185

parole officers and $27,197 for probation officers. The highest beginning salary for parole officers was $43,644 in California, while the highest beginning salary for probation officers was $40,533 in Massachusetts.[49] One study found that entry-level probation officers employed by local governments exceeded state government probation salaries.[50] After some experience on the job, parole officers averaged $37,319 and probation officers $36,622. Probation and parole administrators earned considerably more than field officers. The average maximum salary for parole administrators was $76,904; for probation administrators, $89,038. For combined departments, probation and parole administrators could earn an average of $74,285.[51]

TABLE 6.3 *Probation and Parole Officers' Starting, Average, and Maximum Salaries . . .* *(continued)*

State	Entry Salary	Average Salary	Highest Salary
Probation and Parole			
Alabama	$24,645	$44,460	$68,458
Alaska	31,000	40,500	85,000
Arkansas	21,366	24,162	39,561
Delaware	27,246	31,200	40,880
Florida	27,170	31,814	49,150
Idaho	28,513	32,240	43,181
Iowa	29,702	38,000	43,971
Kentucky	17,964	26,256	34,568
Louisiana	20,088	30,000	45,644
Maine	24,627	27,914	33,426
Maryland	20,403	33,900	37,075
Michigan	29,390	a	49,774
Minnesota	26,768	34,932	49,402
Mississippi	20,537	a	30,305
Missouri	21,816	28,392	33,972
Montana	23,343	28,944	33,664
Nevada	33,375	45,569	49,613
New Hampshire	34,494	44,377	53,138
New Mexico[f]	25,438	31,100	38,150
North Carolina	21,600	27,584	39,666
North Dakota	23,520	30,528	43,800
Ohio	26,187	39,957	49,650
Oklahoma	22,221	30,811	32,116
Pennsylvania	30,746	45,868	53,296
Rhode Island	38,732	43,802	43,802
South Carolina	21,372	24,848	36,142
Utah	23,532	31,738	46,354
Vermont	28,000	36,000	45,000
Virginia	27,204	34,837	42,471
Washington	25,680	39,469	41,652
Wisconsin	23,053	34,745	47,215
Wyoming	21,456	26,400	33,444
Average	$25,662	$34,012	$44,173
Overall average	$26,806	$35,484	$46,317

[a]Data not provided. [b]This entry salary is an average. Depending on a department's salary schedule, starting salaries can range from $19,000 to $32,000 annually. [c]Salaries do not include supervisory positions. [d]Average salary figures are estimates. [e]Salaries include hazardous duty and longevity pay. [f]Entry salary is based on $12.55 per hour.
Source: Camille Graham Camp and George M. Camp, *The Corrections Yearbook: 1999* (Middletown, CT: Criminal Justice Institute 1999), 206. Reprinted with permission.

FIREARMS POLICIES FOR PROBATION AND PAROLE OFFICERS

Probation and parole officers are increasingly calling for the right to carry a firearm while on duty. In the past most probation and parole officers viewed themselves as therapeutic agents whose primary duties were oriented toward rehabilitation. Few officers thus carried firearms or wished to. The past two decades, however, have witnessed a shift from the medical model to a surveillance control orientation. As a result, many probation and parole officers now view their job and their role differently.[52] Also, the probation and parole caseloads include more dangerous offenders, and some evidence suggests that client violence against supervising officers is escalating. The hazards of probation and parole work are clearly illustrated in a 1993 study by the Federal Probation and Pretrial Officers Association.[53] This study revealed the following assaults or attempted assaults against probation, parole, and pretrial services officers nationwide between 1980 and 1993:

Murder or attempted murder	16
Rape or attempted rape	7
Other sexual assaults	100
Shot or wounded or attempts	32
Use or attempted use of blunt instrument or projectile	60
Slashed or stabbed attempt	28
Car used as weapon or attempt	12
Punched, kicked, choked	1,396
Use or attempted use of caustic substance	3
Use or attempted use of incendiary device	9
Abduction or attempt	3
Attempted or actual unspecified assaults	944
Total	2,610

Is it a good idea for probation and parole officers to carry a firearm while out in the field conducting home visits? Dean Champion argues that many officers will arm themselves anyway, regardless of law or agency policy. Our experience supports Champion's assertion. When surveyed, 59 percent of officers believed they should have the legal option to carry a firearm on the job. However, when asked if they would endorse a requirement to carry a firearm as a part of the job, 80 percent of the female and 69 percent of the male officers opposed such a requirement. Yet 80 percent of all officers said they would carry a firearm if required to do so.[54]

Those opposed to officers carrying a firearm argue that an officer's safety or life may be at greater risk if a probationer or parolee is carrying a weapon because a greater chance exists that the offender would use a gun against an armed officer than an unarmed officer. So far, no study has supported this contention. The key factor is whether or not probation and parole officers receive proper firearms training. Most agencies that allow community corrections officers to carry firearms use the same training, or one modeled after law enforcement.

Law and agency policy differs between jurisdictions, and it is difficult to determine which states allow probation and parole officers to arm themselves. One method of determining whether an officer has the legal right to carry a firearm is to examine the statutes to find whether probation and parole officers are considered peace officers under state law. Even this method is not foolproof because agency policy may prohibit carrying firearms even if state law defines the officer as a peace officer. As of January 1, 1999, a survey of state laws finds that probation officers are peace officers in 13 states, parole officers are peace officers in 9 states, and probation and parole officers are peace officers in 14 states.[55] In Missouri, the Department of Corrections provides its probation and parole officers with the firearms training, badge, and ammunition, but each individual employee is responsible for purchasing his or her own firearm and holster.[56]

The American Probation and Parole Association (APPA) neither supports nor opposes the carrying of weapons by probation and parole officers. The association argues that, should officers be authorized to carry weapons, decisions should be made within the framework of actual need and officer safety demands and must be consistent with laws and policies.[57]

The APPA has established guidelines for agencies implementing a decision to allow officers to carry weapons:

> In the event an agency determines that officers should carry a weapon or that specific job functions require that the officer be armed, it is mandatory that exceptional care be given to the implementation of such a decision. This decision to arm staff must be decisively made by the agency's leadership based on a clearly delineated and comprehensive plan responding to issues of staff safety. Once this decision is made, the agency must dictate all choices as to equipment, training, and procedures related to carrying a weapon. Nothing should be left to the discretion of individual officers except perhaps whether they want to accept an assignment which requires carrying a weapon. Standards must be established and monitored closely for compliance.[58]

The APPA also recommends clear policies, training in the handling of firearms, legal issues and liability, and selection procedures that minimally include a physical and psychological examination.[59]

INTERSTATE COMPACTS ON PROBATION

Consideration of probation administration would not be complete without a discussion of the interstate compacts for supervising adult and juvenile probationers and parolees. At one time a probationer or parolee could not be supervised outside the state where he or she was convicted, even though many transient offenders are arrested and convicted far from where they have relatives and community ties. As a result, the offender often could not be provided with supervision in the very place that would offer the best chance for success on probation or parole. Pursuant to the Crime Control Consent Act passed by Congress in 1936, a group of states entered into an agreement by which they would supervise probationers and parolees for each other. Known as the **Interstate Compact for the Supervision of Parolees and Probationers,** the agreement was originally signed by 25 states in 1937. By 1951, it had been ratified by all the states.

A similar agreement, the Interstate Compact on Juveniles, provides for return of juvenile runaways, escapees, and absconders as well as for cooperative supervision of juvenile probationers and parolees. An amendment to this compact provides for out-of-state confinement of juveniles. Each state enacts the compact as part of its state laws.[60]

The compacts identify the **sending state** (the state of conviction) and the **receiving state** (the state that undertakes the supervision). The receiving state informs the sending state on a quarterly basis of the probationer's progress, but the sending state retains ultimate authority. The offender must meet certain residence requirements of the receiving state. Ordinarily, the probationer or parolee must be a resident of the receiving state, have relatives there, or have employment there. The receiving state agrees to accept the offender and to provide the same supervision it accords other probationers or parolees in the state. The offender who obtains the benefits of out-of-state supervision waives extradition. The sending state may enter the receiving state to take custody of the probationer or parolee who has violated the terms of release without going through extradition proceedings, and a supplementary agreement permits the violator to be incarcerated in the receiving state at the expense of the sending state if both states agree.[61] During 1998, the average probation agency

INTERSTATE COMPACT FOR THE SUPERVISION OF PAROLEES AND PROBATIONERS

An agreement signed by all 50 states that allows for the supervision of parolees and probationers in a state other than the state of conviction.

SENDING STATE

Under the interstate compact, the state of conviction.

RECEIVING STATE

Under the interstate compact, the state that undertakes the supervision.

in each state received a total of 1,161 probationers from other states and sent 1,192 persons to other jurisdictions. In 1999, Texas was the most active sending state. There were 9,675 probation and parole offenders under supervision in other states. North Carolina was the most active receiving state with a total of 4,831 probationers and 1,833 parolees being supervised from other jurisdictions.[62]

Parole boards usually designate one member to be the interstate compact administrator. That person handles the details of arranging the supervision of parolees who are either sent out of the state for supervision or received into the state after conviction in another state. Where probation is locally administered, the compact does not work as smoothly for probation supervision as it does for parole supervision. Some exchanges take place, however, and probation supervision or detention and care of runaways and absconders are provided by the receiving state. For example, in 1999, after his release from a Maryland jail, professional boxer Mike Tyson was transferred via interstate compact to the Maricopa County Probation Department to finish his time in Phoenix, Arizona.[63]

Problems with Interstate Compacts

Under the interstate compacts, states agree to provide "courtesy supervision" of probationers and parolees from other states. Some requests are problematic and thus are not approved. Probation supervision styles vary from state to state. Each state has different thresholds and policies for when a probationer is considered to be in violation. For example, one state may consider a probationer to be in violation, while the other state will wish to continue supervision.[64] These differences sometimes need to be negotiated to maintain positive working relationships.

Furthermore, some probation and parole agencies have alleged that certain local departments and some states practiced "dumping"—transferring difficult cases to other states with little or no justification other than the desire to rid themselves of the problem individuals. In addition, some states are asked to accept far more interstate compact supervision cases than they send out. However, the vast majority of requests for transfer of supervision are legitimate, and when it appears that a case will not unreasonably burden the receiving department, the state usually complies.

SUMMARY

Probation is both a disposition and a process. As a disposition, probation is court-related; that is, the power to grant and to revoke it is vested in a court. As a process, it is the organization, administration, and delivery of probation services. Probation organizational patterns have little uniformity in the United States. Probation services may be combined with parole or kept separate. Adult and juvenile probation may be combined or entirely separate. Probation may be administered by the executive branch of government or by the judiciary. Probation services may be organized at the state level or at the local level. There are arguments for and against each of these organizational schemes. Generally, however, the evidence seems to support state executive branch control of probation services as the most effective and efficient approach. Recent developments such as Community Corrections Acts, which provide state funding to local probation agencies for enhancement of existing services and development of a wider range of sanction alternatives, appear to be increasing in use and interest. Issues continually evolving are the provisions for selecting probation officers, initial qualifications, preservice and in-service training, and whether probation and parole officers should be allowed to carry weapons. Interstate compact agreements for supervision foster probation administration in other states.

DISCUSSION QUESTIONS

1 Distinguish between probation as a disposition and as a process.

2 Early probation legislation followed one of the two existing organizational plans—that of Vermont or Rhode Island. How were these two organizational structures different?

3 What are the major patterns of administering probation services?

4 What are the advantages and disadvantages of placing responsibility for probation in the executive branch of government?

5 What are the advantages and disadvantages of administering probation services at the state level instead of the local level?

6 What is a mixed organizational structure, and what are its advantages?

7 According to Norval Morris and Michael Tonry, the trend in probation is toward the development of intermediate sanctions such as intensive supervision programs. How might this trend affect probation administration?

8 How are probation officers selected in your jurisdictions? What are some alternative methods?

9 What are Community Corrections Acts? What are the major advantages of such an organizational structure?

10 Discuss the various methods of probation and parole officer selection. What are some advantages of each? Disadvantages?

11 What are the issues regarding weapons being carried by probation and parole officers?

🌐 WEB SITES

Occupational Guide to Probation and Parole Officers in California

> *http://www.calmis.ca.gov/file/occguide/PROBOFF.HTM*

Job Description for Probation and Parole Officer in Australia

> *http://www.jobguide.thegoodguides.com.au/text/jobdetails.cfm?jobid=615*

Juvenile Probation Officer Job Description

> *http://www.hr.das.state.or.ush/rsd/class/6634.HTM*

Maine Probation and Parole Officer Duties

> *http://janus.state.me.us/legis/statutes/34/title34sec1502.html*

Probation Officer Qualifications and Expectations

> *http://www.fcpd.com/po_trn.htm*

Ohio Probation Officer Firearms Policy

> *http://ohioacts.avv.com/123/sb325/sec-1901.33.htm*

Arizona Probation Officer Firearms Policy

> *http://www.azleg.state.az.us/legtext/45leg/lr/bills/hb2350p.htm*

7

Supervision in Probation and Parole

Kevin Horan/Stock Boston

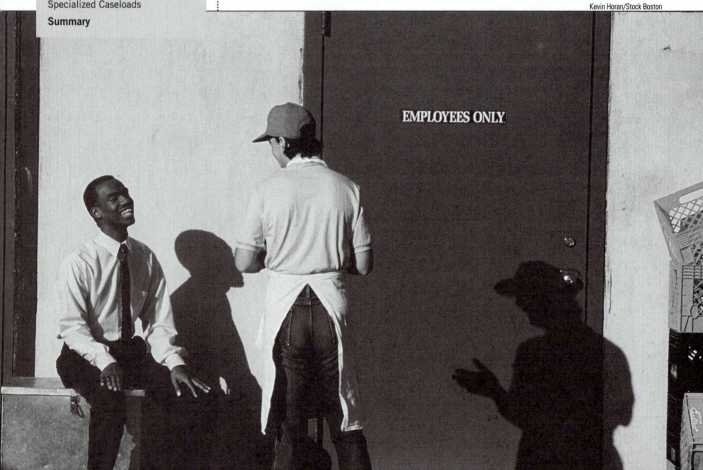

What You Will Learn in This Chapter

In this chapter you will learn how the philosophy and practice of probation and parole supervision have changed from an emphasis on casework (rehabilitation) to an emphasis on monitoring court orders and determining that the probationer or parolee is following the conditions of release (surveillance). You will then examine a middle-of-the-road approach to supervision, which we have labeled an "integrative approach to supervision." Probation and parole office roles and working styles will be explained. Caseload classification, risk assessment, and workload on issues are also discussed in detail.

KEY TERMS

Supervision
Casework model
Brokerage of services
Community resource management team (CRMT) model
Justice model
Integrated model
Classification
Risk assessment

INTRODUCTION

Supervision is the element that differentiates probation from suspended sentence and parole from other forms of early release. This chapter covers both probation and parole supervision, distinguishing between them when necessary. Some authorities believe that parole supervision requires more intense supervision, because parolees are more serious offenders in that they have been to prison. Furthermore, the transition from rigidly controlled prison life to life in the "free world" requires major living adjustments not usually faced by probationers.

Others, however, consider probationers and parolees essentially alike. Some probationers have been to prison as a result of earlier crimes. Others could have been sentenced to prison for their crimes, had they not plea-bargained (pleaded guilty in exchange for a reduced penalty). Further, parolees have had a "taste of prison" and may exert extra effort while on supervision to remain free. Accordingly, with some exceptions, the supervision process is identical. In many states and in the federal system, the same officers supervise both probationers and parolees.

In its simplest terms, **supervision** may be defined as an officer's oversight of those committed to his or her custody. However, supervision involves more than just watching and noting what offenders are doing. Few offenders can be expected to transform themselves into law-abiding citizens without some assistance. Moreover, probation or parole cannot be a constructive force in the administration of criminal justice if supervision amounts only to discipline directed toward holding in check antisocial tendencies during the period of supervision. Merely observing conditions of release or managing not to be arrested for a new offense does not indicate that an offender has been transformed. The element of constructive supervision distinguishes probation and parole from both leniency and punishment. The concept of supervision has undergone much change in the past 60 years.

SUPERVISION

The oversight that a probation or parole officer exercises over those in his or her custody.

CHANGING CONCEPTS OF SUPERVISION

The Casework Era

In 1939, the *Attorney General's Survey of Release Procedures* defined supervision as follows: "In the conventional attitudes of the criminal law, it is a form of punishment, but the purpose of it is reformative, reconstructive, and educational; to use a scientific term, it is therapeutic."[1] This philosophy of supervision flourished for the next 30 years. The supervision process was oriented toward *casework*, providing services to probationers or parolees (often referred to as *clients*) to assist them in living productively in the community. Probation and parole officers frequently viewed themselves as "caseworkers" and the term *agent of change* was a popular description of their role. The literature of probation and parole supervision during this period is replete with medical and psychiatric terminology, such as *treatment* and *diagnosis*. The National Advisory Commission on Criminal Justice Standards and Goals, reviewing the **casework model** era, stated: "The literature discussed the development of social work skills in interviewing, creating therapeutic relationships with clients, counseling, providing insight, and modifying behavior."[2] A leading textbook of the period, *Probation and Parole in Theory and Practice*, reflected this orientation with chapters entitled "Social Casework," "Case Study and Diagnosis," and "Casework as a Means of Treatment."[3] The probation officer was viewed as a social worker engaged in a therapeutic relationship with the probationer "client."

Supervision as Brokerage of Services

In the early 1970s the casework approach began to break down. The National Advisory Commission on Criminal Justice Standards and Goals reported in 1973 that probation had failed to realize many of its goals.[4] The commission pointed out that many services needed by probationers and parolees could be more readily and effectively provided by specialized community agencies that provide mental health, employment, housing, education, private welfare, and other services. The commission report stated: "Probation also has attempted to deal directly with such problems as alcoholism, drug addiction, and mental illness, which ought to be handled through community mental health and other specialized programs."[5] This alternative strategy for delivering probation and parole services is referred to as the **brokerage of services** approach. The "service broker" type of probation or parole officer does not consider himself or herself the primary agent of change as in the casework approach. Instead, he or she attempts to determine the needs of the probationer or parolee and locates and refers the client to the appropriate community agency. Thus, an unemployed parolee might be referred to vocational rehabilitation services, employment counseling, or the state employment office. Instead of attempting to counsel a probationer with emotional problems, the service broker officer would locate and refer the probationer to agencies whose staff were skilled in working with problems such as those faced by the probationer. In this supervision strategy, developing linkages between the clients and appropriate agencies is considered one of the probation or parole officer's most important tasks. Probation and parole officers were encouraged to differentiate between services that can be provided internally—by the probation officer—and those that need to be obtained from other social institutions. Under the brokerage model, the kinds of services that are provided directly to probationers through the probation system are those that:

- relate to the reasons the offender was brought into the probation system
- help him or her adjust to the status of probationer
- provide information and facilitate referral to needed community resources
- help create conditions permitting readjustment and reintegration into the community as an independent individual through full utilization of all available resources

Probationers' needs that are related to employment, training, housing, health, and so on are the responsibility of other social agencies and should be provided by them.[6] By the mid- to late 1970s the brokerage approach to probation and parole supervision was firmly entrenched.

Community Resource Management Team

Another approach to supervision, closely allied to the brokerage approach, is that of the **community resource management team (CRMT) model.** Using the CRTM strategy, individual probation and parole officers develop skills and linkages with community agencies in one or two areas only. One officer might be designated the drug abuse specialist, and another the employment specialist, while another develops expertise in family counseling. The CRTM concept recognizes that the diverse needs of the probation or parole caseload cannot be adequately satisfied by one individual. Thus the caseload is "pooled," and the probationer might be assisted by not one officer, but several officers. For example, Officer Mary Smith might assess the probationer's needs for drug treatment and refer him or her to the appropriate agency for assistance. Officer Sam Jones might work with him or her in obtaining job training and employment from other community social agencies. Each officer applies his or her particular skills and linkages in the community to serve the needs of the offender.

The Justice Model of Supervision

In recent years a new model of probation and parole supervision has come to dominate supervision philosophy. The **justice model** advocates an escalated system of sanctions corresponding to the social harm resulting from the offense and the offender's culpability. The justice model repudiates the idea that probation is a sanction designed to rehabilitate offenders in the community and, instead, regards a sentence of probation as a proportionate punishment that is to be lawfully administered for certain prescribed crimes.[7]

In the justice model of probation, the probationary term is not viewed as an alternative to imprisonment, but as a valid sanction in itself. The popular view that probation is an alternative to incarceration has led the public to regard probation as an expression of leniency, and the public often feels that the offender is "getting off." Justice and the community's welfare are best served when some offenders are imprisoned. But for the majority, who can safely remain in the community, the public must feel that appropriate penalties are imposed. Therefore, the justice philosophy regards probation as a separate, distinct sanction requiring penalties that are graduated in severity and duration corresponding to the seriousness of the crime.[8]

A justice model probation penalty has two major components—some degree of deprivation of personal liberty and reparation to the victim or the community.[9] Advocates of the justice model hold that practices of counseling, surveillance, and reporting accomplish very little and have minimal impact on recidivism. They favor probation that consists of monitoring court orders for victim restitution or community service and that ensures that the imposed deprivation of liberty is carried out.[10]

Justice model probation specifically gears offender assistance to helping probationers comply with the condition of their probation. Other services such as mental health counseling, alcohol and drug treatment, and so on should be available for probationers who express a need or desire for them. These services should be brokered through social agencies in the community. The primary responsibility of the probationer is to complete the conditions imposed by the court satisfactorily. Likewise, the

COMMUNITY RESOURCE MANAGEMENT TEAM (CRMT) MODEL

A supervision model in which probation or parole officers develop skills and linkages with community agencies in one or two areas only. Supervision under this model is a team effort, each officer utilizing his or her skills and linkages to assist the offender.

JUSTICE MODEL

A supervision model that specifically gears offender assistance to helping offenders comply with the conditions of probation.

BOX 7.1   *Supervision Objectives and Duties of Federal Probation Officers*

The primary objectives of supervision are to enforce compliance with the conditions of release, to minimize risk to the public, and to reintegrate the offender into a law-abiding lifestyle. To accomplish these objectives, the officer has the following specific responsibilities.

DISCHARGE STATUTORY DUTIES. To comply with the requirements of 18 U.S.C. section 3603, probation officers shall [see Ch. IV, A.1A]:

- instruct the person under supervision as to the conditions specified by the sentencing court and provide him or her with a written statement clearly setting forth all such conditions;
- keep informed concerning the compliance with any condition of supervision and report thereon to the court or Parole Commission;
- keep informed as to the conduct and condition of a person under supervision and report his or her conduct and condition to the sentencing court or Parole Commission;
- use all suitable methods, consistent with the conditions

specified by the court, to aid a person under supervision and to bring about improvements in his or her conduct and condition; and
- keep a record of the officers' work.

PROTECT THE COMMUNITY. To provide this most vital aspect of community supervision, the probation officer should [see Ch. IV.A.1B]:

- establish a plan of supervision consistent with the level of risk posed by the offender to the community;
- utilize risk control supervision activities including verification of employment and sources of income, financial investigation, monitoring of associates, record checks, urinalysis, and restrictions on travel;
- request modification of the conditions of supervision if necessary to reduce risk. Such modifications may include home detention, community confinement, provisions for search and seizure, and requirements for financial disclosure; and

- systematically review the conduct and condition of offenders and revise supervision plans in accordance with changes in risk levels.

ADDRESS RELEVANT PROBLEMS OF OFFENDERS. To assist the offender in becoming a law abiding and productive member of the community, the probation officer should [see Ch. IV.A.1C]:

- assess the relevant problems of the offender that are likely to be associated with further criminal conduct and develop a supervision plan to address those problems;
- utilize community resources to provide the offender with the opportunity to participate in substance abuse and/or mental-health treatment, employment assistance, and educational opportunities; and
- ensure that the offender's response to treatment is consistent with risk-control supervision.

Source: *Supervision of Federal Offenders*, monograph no 109 (Washington, DC: Administrative Offices of the U.S. Courts, Probation and Pretrial Services Division, June 1991).

primary task of the probation officer is to assist the probationer in satisfactorily completing the conditions. The probation agency, however, should be prepared to assist those individuals who voluntarily request rehabilitative assistance.[11]

Most probation and parole agencies in the United States now subscribe to the general tenets of the justice model (see Box 7.1). For example, the federal probation system supervision manual, *Supervision of Federal Offenders*, states: "The primary objectives of supervision are to enforce compliance with the conditions of release, to minimize risk to the public, and to reintegrate the offender into a law-abiding life style."[12]

The shift in philosophy in probation and parole systems throughout the country was obvious and abrupt. The primary impetus for this change can be traced to the philosophical and political movements of the late 1970s and early 1980s that placed

greater emphasis on punishment and the failure of corrections to live up to its promises to rehabilitate, reintegrate, and restore offenders to productive, law-abiding
lives.[13] One particular event contributed more than any other to the shift to a more
punitive role for probation and parole: the publication by Robert Martinson and his
associates of a national study of treatment programs. In this study, more than 200
correctional treatment programs were carefully evaluated and declared failures.[14]
The work was persuasive, and it was soon followed by other studies that reported
similar results.

The so-called medical model of corrections, which stressed diagnosis and treatment, ended with the "nothing works" findings by Martinson and others. Theirs was a
more conservative approach that stressed "deserved punishment," incapacitation,
and reparation to the victim.

Thus, at the beginning of the 21st century, the United States is in a conservative
era of criminal justice history. Probation and parole are at a crossroads, redefining
their mission and role from "therapeutic correctional treatment" toward control,
deserved punishment, and risk management.

AN INTEGRATED MODEL OF SUPERVISION

In practice, probation and parole supervision usually lies between the two extremes
of the casework approach and the justice model. Effective supervision has elements
of control and treatment; neither will suffice alone. The justice model of corrections
has been correctly described as "a solution . . . of despair, not hope."[15] Because treatment programs have not been shown to be successful in bringing about long-term
change in the offender, the assumption is that they have no value and that therefore a
strategy that emphasizes control and punishment is more efficacious. However,
research has not shown the justice model approach to be any more successful in
reducing recidivism than the approach it replaced.

Control and treatment are not mutually exclusive in supervision. An analogy can
be drawn to child-rearing practices. In their widely acclaimed book, *A General Theory
of Crime*, Michael R. Gottfredson and Travis Hirschi attribute crime to deficiencies in
self-control. They explored the nature and sources of self-control, locating it largely in
family child-rearing practices. They then went on to use self-control as the basis for a
general theory of crime.[16] They reported that low self-control tends to ensue in the
absence of nurturance, discipline, and training.[17] Good child-rearing practices—
which develop self-control—contain elements of all three. It is not too great an intel-
lectual step to move from child-rearing practices to probation and parole supervision
strategies. Many authorities have commented on the commonalities of behavior
between criminals and children; namely, the pursuit of immediate pleasures, lack of
ability to defer gratification, immature judgment, impulsiveness, and short attention
span. Discipline, nurturance, and training socialize the child and develop the self-
control and maturity of judgment necessary for successful integration into society. A
child who experiences only discipline is not likely to develop into a mature, contributing member of society. So, too, the child who is nurtured and trained, but not
disciplined, is equally unlikely to become a contributing member of society. Probation and parole supervision also must contain all three. Current philosophy does not
negate the nurturing and training elements. It merely assigns them much less priority
than the discipline (control) element.

The strategy we recommend involves an active treatment function (nurturing
and training) within a broad framework of control (discipline). This is referred to as

Residents of Delancey Street in San Francisco walk across the Gallery of the Delancey Street grounds. Delancey Street is a private organization that for the past 30 years has helped turn around the lives of ex-convicts, drug addicts, and the homeless.

AP/Wide World Photo

INTEGRATED MODEL

A supervision model that integrates a concern for control with a concern for treatment.

an **integrated model.** We recall an argument between the director of treatment and the director of security in a large state prison on the subject of the relative importance of rehabilitation and institutional security. The treatment director charged that the institution's security regulations undermined his efforts to treat and rehabilitate the inmates. The head of security, an assistant warden of many years' experience, drawled, "Doctor, no matter how good your programs are, you can't treat 'em if we can't keep 'em." It is in this context that we view probation and parole supervision.

The Surveillance Function in Supervision

Supervision must first involve surveillance, which is defined as "a watch kept over one or more persons."[18] Probation and parole are expected to provide a means of ascertaining whether those released live up to the conditions imposed by the court or the parole board. Failure to maintain proper surveillance can only bring the officer and the system into disrepute. Furthermore, an officer's failure to require the offender to adhere to the terms of release complicates the officer's task. Supervision cannot exist in a lax, haphazard manner without arousing the contempt of the offender. In addition, public support and cooperation are difficult to obtain for any probation or parole system that does not assure the community of at least minimum protection against renewed criminal activities by those under supervision.[19]

The Treatment Function in Supervision

The rehabilitative function of supervision includes both nurturing and training. Treatment-oriented supervision, conducted within a context of discipline and control, must be directed toward removing or reducing individual and social barriers that may result in recidivism. Carrying out a supervisory process that can accomplish this end is an extraordinarily difficult task. Offenders can be dealt with effectively only if on an individual basis and according to their special conditions and needs. Much of the effectiveness of supervision depends on the personal relationship between the officer and the offender. An honest, direct relationship between the officer and the offender is the most effective means of promoting change and ensuring successful completion of the term of probation. The authoritative nature of the relationship should be made clear to the offender, but the spirit of encouragement and helpfulness should also be apparent. Most probationers and parolees have problems they must overcome if they are to succeed in complying with the terms and conditions of release and remaining crime free. Among the most critical problems are employment and drug and alcohol abuse.

EMPLOYMENT SERVICES: It is not unreasonable to suggest that meaningful employment is the most important issue for most probationers and parolees. Not only does employment provide financial support for the offender and his or her family, but it is also crucial for establishing and maintaining self-esteem and personal dignity—qualities that are seen by most authorities as essential to successful reintegration into the community.[20] Joy Davidoff-Kroop, in a study of employment services provided by the New York State Division of Parole, concluded, "Two recent parole follow-up studies showed a high rate of unemployment amongst parolees returned to prison."[21] Experienced probation and parole officers know this to be true, and most probation and parole conditions require the offender to maintain employment during the period of supervision. However, finding and maintaining employment is not a simple task. Offenders are often the last to be hired and the first to be terminated. Many of them are unskilled, and many have poor work habits. Some are barred from employment in their chosen fields as a result of regulatory and licensing laws that preclude persons with a criminal conviction.

Because of the critical relationship between success on parole or probation supervision and meaningful employment, supervising officers must assess the employment status of each person under their supervision and work with him or her to locate a job. In many cases the probationer or parolee will require a vocational assessment to determine his or her employability, interests, capabilities, and any barriers to employment. Many will require vocational or job-readiness training before they can seek a job. Ideally, these services are obtained from external agencies and organizations such as state employment offices or vocational rehabilitation services. The probation or parole officer's job is to locate the existing service, refer the supervisee to the service, assist him or her in obtaining the service, and monitor progress and participation. Ideally, the probation or parole agency would have funds available for purchasing these services if they are not available otherwise.

DRUG AND ALCOHOL TREATMENT SERVICES: Drug and alcohol abuse have a negative effect on every aspect of an offender's life, contributing to unemployment, marital, and other personal and social problems. For many, if not most, substance abuse contributed directly or indirectly to the crime(s) that led to their conviction. Approximately 58 percent of all felony convictions in federal courts in the United

TABLE 7.1 *Federal Prison Population over Time, Drug Offenders*

Year	Total sentenced and unsentenced population	Total sentenced population	Total sentenced drug offenders	Percentage of sentenced prisoners who are drug offenders
1980	24,252	19,023	4,749	24.9
1981	26,195	19,765	5,076	25.6
1982	28,133	20,938	5,518	26.3
1983	30,214	26,027	7,201	27.6
1984	32,317	27,622	8,152	29.5
1985	36,042	27,623	9,491	34.3
1986	37,542	30,104	11,344	37.7
1987	41,609	33,246	13,897	41.8
1988	41,342	33,758	15,087	44.7
1989	47,568	37,758	18,852	49.9
1990	54,613	46,575	24,297	52.2
1991	61,026	52,176	29,667	56.9
1992	67,768	59,516	35,398	59.5
1993	76,531	68,183	41,393	60.7
1994	82,269	73,958	45,367	61.3
1995	85,865	76,947	46,669	60.7
1996	89,672	80,872	49,096	60.7
1997	95,513	87,294	52,059	59.6
1998	104,507	95,323	55,984	58.7
1999	115,024	104,500	60,399	57.8
August 2000	122,750	111,885	63,621	56.9

Source: Adapted from Federal Bureau of Prisons Data, September 30, 1999, www.bop.gov.

States in 1999 were for drug-related offenses (see Table 7.1). Table 7.2 illustrates recent findings from the Drug Use Monitoring program of the U.S. Department of Justice, which show that 50–75 percent of all newly arrested adult male offenders were positive for drug use on a urine test.[22] Most evidence today suggests that the majority of imprisoned offenders were using drugs or alcohol when they committed the offense for which they are serving time. Because these findings are obtained primarily from self-reports or from drug testing as much as 48 hours after arrest, they should be interpreted conservatively. The true figure is likely much higher.

In light of these data, probation and parole officers must consider drug and alcohol monitoring and treatment as a major aspect of their job. None of the goals of supervision can be met when the releasee is using and abusing alcohol or drugs. The federal probation manual, *The Supervision Process*, states:

> In the United States alcohol is the principal drug of abuse. Alcoholism represents a unique problem in the supervision of offenders in that often alcohol is not identified as a primary problem having a direct effect on all other aspects of an individual's life. A probation officer may address an offender's lack of employment, marital difficulties, or other social problems when, in fact, they are all secondary to the problem of alcoholism.[23]

It goes on to say: "One of the most important functions of the probation officer is the identification of drug abuse from available historical data, recognition of physical symptoms, and urinalysis."[24]

As in the case of employment problems, few probation and parole officers possess the expertise necessary to provide drug and alcohol assessment, urinalysis moni-

TABLE 7.2 *Drug-use Prevalence by Detained Arrestees in Selected Cities by Type of Drug*

City	Marijuana	Opiates	Cocaine	Amphet-amines	Benzodi-azepines	Methadone	Any Drug	Multiple Drugs
New York	33.5%	23.0%	50.4%	0.9%	6.5%	12.7%	70.4%	40.0%
Washington, D.C.	39.9	8.4	27.5	0.0	1.7	0.2	59.4	16.3
Portland	40.5	12.5	18.0	25.6	2.8	2.0	70.6	23.7
San Diego	47.1	9.4	12.5	44.3	5.0	1.3	75.9	37.1
Indianapolis	55.0	2.3	26.5	1.8	7.3	0.5	68.5	22.1
Houston	30.6	10.2	40.1	1.4	13.5	4.6	60.6	30.9
Ft. Lauderdale	42.0	4.5	43.7	0.0	11.7	0.0	70.0	28.4
Detroit	37.5	7.5	25.9	0.0	2.8	1.5	58.0	15.2
New Orleans	33.5	8.5	36.0	1.0	6.9	1.2	61.2	20.2
Phoenix	31.8	10.7	28.8	17.1	2.2	0.3	62.2	24.4
Chicago	54.9	16.9	50.3	0.3	4.7	0.3	78.2	36.9
Los Angeles	30.0	8.2	39.4	26.0	5.5	2.1	74.1	25.8
Dallas	44.2	8.0	24.9	3.4	4.0	0.2	61.4	18.8
Birmingham	40.2	6.7	30.2	1.5	12.5	1.5	65.3	20.3
Omaha	49.5	1.6	12.6	11.1	2.0	0.0	58.0	15.3
Philadelphia	33.7	16.1	30.8	2.6	14.0	0.9	59.4	29.5
Miami	47.2	1.5	41.7	0.0	4.7	0.0	69.7	22.5
Cleveland	31.7	4.4	30.3	0.0	7.2	0.6	53.9	16.5
San Antonio	36.9	9.4	30.4	3.2	4.4	1.7	56.3	22.5
St. Louis	51.3	7.8	35.2	0.8	4.1	1.3	72.1	22.3
San Jose	32.9	10.0	12.3	20.2	5.4	0.8	56.3	21.0
Denver	43.2	5.8	32.9	10.7	5.7	1.0	69.4	25.9
Atlanta	36.6	4.0	51.8	0.2	5.1	0.2	69.9	24.1

Source: Adapted from *Comparing Drug Use Rates of Detained Arrestees in the United States and England* (Washington, DC: U.S. Department of Justice, Office of Justice Programs, April 1999).

toring, and treatment. Once again, the releasee should have ready access to external agencies and organizations. To carry out his or her duties, the probation or parole officer helps the probationer or parolee obtain the needed services by assessing the needs, being aware of available community resources, contacting the appropriate resources, referring the probationer for services, and monitoring compliance.

A TYPOLOGY OF PROBATION OFFICER WORK STYLES

The broadest component of probation supervision is the role that officers set for themselves and the logic and rationale they develop to explain what they do or what they ought to do. Carl Klockars developed a typology of probation officers that defines four basic work styles on the "probation is not casework" versus "probation is casework" continuum: the law enforcer, the time-server, the therapeutic agent, and the synthetic officer.[25]

The Law Enforcer

At the "probation is not casework" pole are officers who stress the legal authority and enforcement aspects of the position. These officers' philosophies dictate firmness, authority, and rule-abidance as essentials of social life. Of prime importance to such officers are the court order, authority, and decision-making power.

The Time-Servers

Time-serving officers are nearly the functional equivalent of the law enforcers. They see their jobs as fulfilling certain requirements until their retirement, and they have little aspiration to improve their skills. Their conduct on the job is to abide by the rules, and they meet their job responsibilities minimally but methodically. Rules and regulations are upheld but unexamined. They do not make the rules; they just work there.

The Therapeutic Agent

At the other "probation is casework" pole are officers who consider themselves therapeutic agents. They see their role as administering a form of treatment, introducing the probationer or parolee to a better way of life, and motivating patterns of behavior that are constructive. They give guidance and support to those who are unable to solve their problems by themselves and provide them an opportunity to work through their ambivalent feelings. The philosophy of the therapeutic agent may be summarized as follows:

1. I take conscious pains in every contact with offenders to demonstrate my concern for them and my respect for them as human beings.
2. I seize every opportunity to help offenders come to understand the nature of the shared problem solving, aiding the process by actually experiencing it.
3. I recognize, bring into the open, and deal directly with offenders' negative attitudes toward me as the representative of social authority.
4. I partialize the total life problems confronting offenders.
5. I help individuals perceive the degree to which their behavior has and will result in their own unhappiness.

The Synthetic Officer

The fourth work style in Klockars' typology is distinguished by recognition of both the treatment and law enforcement components of probation officers' roles. These officers' attempts at supervision reflect their desire to balance the needs for therapy and law enforcement. Thus, they set for themselves the task of combining the paternal, authoritarian, and judgmental with the therapeutic. Theirs is a dilemma—combining treatment and control—that is found throughout the field of corrections.

From the foregoing, probation and parole supervision obviously is a multifaceted problem that depends not only on the quality of the particular administrative organization and the officers' education and experience, but also—and to a great degree, more important—upon the way in which the officers view their job and their role within the system.

CLASSIFICATION: THE FIRST STEP IN SUPERVISION

CLASSIFICATION

A procedure consisting of assessing the risks posed by the offender, identifying the supervision issues, and selecting the appropriate supervision strategy.

The first step in the supervision process is to classify the offender's case. **Classification** consists of assessing the risks posed by the offender, identifying the supervision issues, and selecting the appropriate supervision strategies. The resulting supervision plan serves as a blueprint for "enforcing the conditions of supervision, controlling the risk posed by the offender, and selecting the appropriate supervision strategies."[26]

The Supervision Planning Process—Federal Probation Model

The federal probation system manual, *Supervision of Federal Offenders*, emphasizes the need to create a strategy-based plan of action to address specific issues.[27] It requires that all supervision activities be structured to ensure compliance with the conditions of supervision, protection of the public, and correctional treatment. Such a supervision plan emphasizes what is accomplished by a particular supervision activity instead of the frequency of contacts.

Supervision planning is the initial phase of the supervision process. It begins with an initial assessment period during which the supervising officer obtains and evaluates information regarding the conditions of release, the degree and type of risk the offender poses to the community, and the traits of the offender that indicate a need for treatment. Based on these factors, the officer will identify as supervision issues those conditions of supervision and case problems that require direct action by the officer during the period and then select the supervision strategies necessary to address those problems.[28]

REVIEWING THE CONDITIONS OF PROBATION: The first stage of the planning process requires the officer to become familiar with the conditions of release and to understand their purpose. He or she must then develop a plan to ensure compliance with the conditions. Some offenders will have special conditions imposed, such as a requirement to participate in drug or alcohol treatment, or to avoid certain persons or places, or not to work in certain occupations. For example, a person convicted of violating Security and Exchange Commission regulations may not be allowed to work as a stockbroker or in investment banking.

ASSESSING RISK: **Risk assessment** provides a measure of the probationer or parolee's propensity to further criminal activity and indicates the level of officer intervention that will be required to deal with the problem. Most risk assessment instruments consider the degree of risk of recidivism posed by the offender and the amount of assistance the offender requires from the probation or parole agency. Together, these variables predict the level of supervision the offender needs.

> **RISK ASSESSMENT**
>
> A procedure that provides a measure of the offender's propensity to further criminal activity and indicates the level of officer intervention that will be required.

Most jurisdictions have developed some form of risk prediction scale to assist them in developing supervision plans and in caseload classification. These instruments differ in some respects, but all of them place offenders in groups with a known statistical probability of committing new crimes or violating the conditions of supervision. As illustrated in Figure 7.1, Pennsylvania assesses 11 risk variables to determine the level of supervision required by the offender. Pennsylvania also assesses 13 needs variables that provide a standardized means of discerning problem areas that should be addressed in the supervision process. The probationer is assigned to one of several levels of supervision on the basis of the two scores.

The federal probation system employs the Risk Prediction Scale (RPS-80) for classifying and developing supervision plans for probationers and the Salient Factor Score (SFS-81) for parolees. The RPS-80 is shown in Figure 7.2. (The SFS-81 for parolee risk assessment is found in Chapter 10.)

The RPS-80 and SFS-81 are based on variables that have been correlated empirically with probation and parole success or failure. For example, on the RSP-80, two variables have been found to predict a low level of required supervision. The probationer is automatically assigned to "low-activity" supervision if he or she has completed high school and has a history free of opiate usage. If the offender is not automatically assigned to low-activity supervision, the officer assigns points for the presence of five risk variables:

FIGURE 7.1 *Pennsylvania's Initial Client Assessment Form*

COMMONWEALTH OF PENNSYLVANIA
BOARD OF PROBATION AND PAROLE
PBPP-20 (1/85)

INITIAL CLIENT ASSESSMENT

CLIENT NAME (Last, First, Middle Initial)	PAROLE NO.	AGENT NAME	OFFICE	DATE

RISK ASSESSMENT

1. Age at First Conviction: (or juvenile adjudication)
- 24 or older 0
- 20-23 2
- 19 or Younger 4

2. Number of Prior Probation/Parole Revocations: (adult or juvenile)
- None 0
- One or more 4

3. Number of Prior Felony Convictions: (or juvenile adjudications)
- None 0
- One 2
- Two or more 4

4. Convictions or Juvenile Adjudications for:
(Select applicable and add for score. Do not exceed a total of 5. include current offense.)
- Burglary, theft, auto theft, or robbery...................2
- Worthless checks or forgery 3

5. Number of Prior Periods of Probation/Parole Supervision:
(Adult or Juvenile)
- None 0
- One or more 4

6. Conviction or Juvenile Adjudication for Assaultive Offense within Last Five Years: (An offense which involves the use of a weapon, physical force or the threat of force.)
- Yes 15
- No 0

7. Number of Address Changes in Last 12 Months:
(Prior to incarceration for parolees)
- None 0
- One 2
- Two or more 3

8. Percentage of Time Employed in Last 12 Months:
(Prior to incarceration for parolees)
- 60% or more 0
- 40%-50% 1
- Under 40% 2
- Not applicable 0

9. Alcohol Usage Problems: (Prior to incarceration for parolees)
- No interference with functioning 0
- Occasional abuse; some disruption of functioning 2
- Frequent abuse; serious disruption; needs treatment 4

10. Other Drug Usage Problems: (Prior to incarceration for parolees)
- No interference with functioning 0
- Occasional abuse; some disruption of functioning 1
- Frequent abuse; serious disruption; needs treatment 2

11. Attitude:
- Motivated to change; receptive to assistance 0
- Dependent or unwilling to accept responsibility 3
- Rationalizes behavior; negative; not motivated to change 5

TOTAL □

INITIAL ASSESSMENT SCALES

Risk Scale		Needs Scale
0-5.......................... Reduced Supervision		8-10
6-18.......................... Regular Supervision		1-10
19-30.........................Close Supervision		11-25
31 & above................... Intensive Supervision		26 & above

SCORING AND OVERRIDE

Score Based Supervision Level
- Intensive .... □   Regular .... □
- Close .... □   Reduced .... □

Score Override........... No .... □   Yes .... □
FINAL GRADE
OF SUPERVISION........... Intensive .... □   Regular .... □
                          Close .... □   Reduced .... □

Override Explanation:

NEEDS ASSESSMENT

1. Academic/Vocational Skills
- High school or above skill level ....−1
- Adequate skills; able to handle everyday requirements 0
- Low skill level causing minor adjustment problems ....+2
- Minimal skill level causing serious adjustment problems ....+4

2. Employment
- Satisfactory employment for one year or longer ....−1
- Secure employment; no difficulties reported; or homemaker, student or retired 0
- Unsatisfactory employment; or unemployed but has adequate job skills ....+3
- Unemployed and virtually unemployable; needs training ......+6

3. Financial Management
- Long-standing pattern of self-sufficiency; e.g., good credit rating ......−1
- No current difficulties ....−0
- Situational or minor difficulties ....+3
- Severe difficulties; may include garnishment, bad checks or bankruptcy ....+5

4. Marital/Family Relationships
- Relationships and support exceptionally strong ....−1
- Relatively stable relationships 0
- Some disorganization or stress but potential for improvement ......+3
- Major disorganization or stress ....+5

5. Companions
- Good support and influence ....−1
- No adverse relationships 0
- Associations with occasionally negative results ....+2
- Associations almost completely negative.................+4

6. Emotional Stability
- Exceptionally well adjusted; accepts responsibility for actions ....−2
- No symptoms of emotional instability; appropriate emotional responses 0
- Symptoms limit but do not prohibit adequate functioning; e.g., excessive anxiety ....+4
- Symptoms prohibit adequate functioning; e.g., lashes out or retreats into self ....+7

7. Alcohol Usage
- No interference with functioning 0
- Occasional abuse; some disruption of functioning ....+3
- Frequent abuse; serious disruption; needs treatment ....+6

8. Other Drug Usage
- No interference with functioning 0
- Occasional substance abuse; some disruption of functioning ....+3
- Frequent substance abuse; serious disruption; needs treatment ....+5

9. Mental Ability
- Able to function independently 0
- Some need for assistance; potential for adequate adjustment; mild retardation ....+3
- Deficiencies severely limit independent functioning; moderate retardation ....+6

10. Health
- Sound physical health; seldom ill 0
- Handicap or illness interferes with functioning on a recurring basis ......+1
- Serious handicap or chronic illness; needs frequent medical care ....+2

11. Sexual Behavior
- No apparent dysfunction 0
- Real or perceived situational or minor problems ....+3
- Real or perceived chronic or severe problems ....+5

12. Recreation/Hobby
- Constructive 0
- Some constructive activities ....+1
- No constructive leisure-time activities or hobbies ....+2

13. Agent's Impression of Client's Needs
- Minimum ....−1
- Low 0
- Medium ....+3
- Maximum ....+5

TOTAL □

Source: Commonwealth of Pennsylvania, Board of Probation and Parole.

FIGURE 7.2 *Risk Prediction Scale*

RISK PREDICTION SCALE (RPS 80)

NAME	PROBATION OFFICER	DATE

I. Automatic Assignment

    If "yes" is checked for both A and B, place in Low Activity Supervision.

A) Individual has completed high school education   YES ☐   NO ☐

B) Individual has history free of opiate usage   YES ☐   NO ☐

II. Risk Score Determination

    If not automatically assigned, use items C through G to determine risk score and supervision activity level.

C) Twenty-eight years or older at time of instant conviction...(7) ——

D) Arrest-free period of five (5) or more consecutive years..(4) ——

E) Few prior arrests (none, one, or two)...(10) ——

F) History free of opiate usage...(9) ——

G) At least four (4) months steady employment prior to arraignment for present offense.............(3) ——

                              SUM OF POINTS (33) ——

RISK SCORE RANGE

                                        SUPERVISION LEVEL

Automatic Assignment
or
20–33   ————————————————————→ Low Activity ☐

0–19   ————————————————————→ High Activity ☐

Source: Administrative Office of the U.S. Courts.

1. Twenty-eight years or older at time of instant offense; 7 points
2. Arrest-free for five or more consecutive years; 4 points
3. Few prior arrests (none, one, or two); 10 points.
4. History free of opiate use; 9 points
5. At least four months' steady employment prior to arraignment for present offense; 3 points

The maximum possible score is 33 points. An offender is automatically assigned to low-activity supervision if his or her score is 20–33 points. A score of 0–19 points places the offender in high activity supervision.

While objective, statistics-based devices such as the RPS-80 provide educated predictions of risk, the federal system uses an additional, subjective method to assist the probation officer in determining whether the risk posed by the offender is greater than that predicted by the risk prediction instrument. If the offender has already been identified as a risk, this subjective method helps to identify the type of risk involved. Such indications include:

- substance abuse related to criminal conduct
- current or prior violent behavior or use of weapons
- participation in continuing criminal conspiracies (for example, wholesale drug distribution or organized crime offenders)
- unexplained assets or current lifestyle incompatible with reported income
- pattern of similar criminal conduct
- serious mental health problems

The combination of the risk prediction score and the presence or absence of the risk indicators will assist the officer in determining which, if any, risk control factors must be addressed.

IDENTIFYING TREATMENT NEEDS: The officer must also identify those characteristics, conditions, or behavioral problems that limit the offender's motivation or ability to function within the conditions of supervision. Treatment activities are defined as actions taken by the supervising officer intended to bring about a change in the offender's conduct or condition for the purpose of rehabilitation and reintegration into the law-abiding community.[29]

Sources of information that may be used to identify treatment needs include the presentence report, prison records and the prerelease plan, physical or medical health evaluations, information from family or other collateral sources, records of drug or alcohol abuse and other related criminal conduct, financial history, and residential history. The importance of careful gathering and evaluation of the offender's history cannot be overstated, for past behavior is the best predictor of future behavior.[30]

Developing the Case Plan

After reviewing the conditions of probation, assessing the offender's risk, and determining treatment concerns, the officer may then identify specific supervision issues and select the appropriate strategies for addressing them. Supervision issues may involve any or all of the three areas—conditions, risk control, and treatment.

IDENTIFYING SUPERVISION ISSUES: A supervision issue is a condition or offender characteristic or pattern of conduct that requires intervention by the officer to correct or control. When an issue is identified, the officer should then develop a strategy to deal with or monitor that issue.

Levels of Supervision and Caseload Contacts

Although various names are used to differentiate the levels of supervision, most are essentially restatements of the traditional *maximum, medium,* and *minimum* supervision classes (see Box 7.2). Practically all classification systems specify contact requirements for each level. Unfortunately, these requirements are usually specified in terms of number of contacts per month or some other time interval, or by the type or location (that is, home, telephone, office, or collateral). Few specify the quality of content of the contact. The federal probation system requires that the

BOX 7.2   *Typical Contact Standards by Supervision Level*

MAXIMUM/INTENSIVE SUPERVISION

- One face-to-face contact and one collateral contact monthly.
- Monthly report; one home visit; one face-to-face (in addition to home) visit; one employment verification; one special condition.
- Two face-to-face contacts monthly; one collateral contact monthly; one home visit every 45 days.
- Four face-to-face contacts monthly; one collateral contact monthly; one home call within 30 days of placement on caseload and within two weeks after each reported move; verification of residence every three months; criminal history check after first year of supervision.
- Two face-to-face contacts monthly, one of which must be in the field; two collateral contacts per month.

MEDIUM/MODERATE SUPERVISION

- One face-to-face contact monthly and one collateral contact per quarter.

- One home visit per quarter; one monthly report; one residence verification; one face-to-face contact; one face-to-face contact; one employment verification; one special condition, if applicable.
- One face-to-face contact and one collateral contact monthly; one home visit every 90 days.
- Two face-to-face contacts monthly with unemployed offenders; one contact if verified full-time employment/training; one collateral contact per month; home call within 30 days of placement on caseload and within two weeks after each reported move; verification of residence every three months and employment/training monthly; criminal history check after first year of supervision.
- One face-to-face contact per month; one collateral contact monthly; one field visit every three months.

MINIMUM SUPERVISION

- One face-to-face semiannual contact and one collateral contact quarterly.
- One home visit, as needed; one monthly report; one face-to-face contact per quarter; one employment verification per quarter.
- One face-to-face contact monthly, unless quarterly reporting.
- One face-to-face contact monthly, verification of residence once every three months.
- Mail-in-report monthly; one face-to-face contact every three months; one collateral contact every three months.

Source: Edward E. Rhine, William R. Smith, and Ronald W. Jackson, *Paroling Authorities Recent History and Current Practice* (Laurel, Md.: American Correctional Association, 1991). Reprinted with permission of the American Correctional Association.

frequency, place, and nature of supervision contacts be determined by the supervision plan and be directly related to the supervision issues. The supervision manual states:

> If the primary purpose of a supervision contact is to secure information or verify compliance with a special condition or correctional treatment program, the officer should make such contact by phone, mail, or office visit. If personal observation is necessary to verify compliance with conditions or to control risk, the officer should make a field contact.

In most instances, the supervision plan optimistically looks toward gradual reduction of the level of supervision if the offender manages to avoid further transgressions of rules or laws. In many instances, the final, minimum level is that of no supervision or level of assistance other than that specifically requested by the client or necessitated by a new arrest.

Caseloads and Workloads

Traditionally, 35–50 cases have been considered the ideal caseload for a probation or parole officer. However, no empirical evidence shows that this range is ideal or that it is regarded as such any longer. In practice, caseloads vary widely. *The Corrections Yearbook: 1999* reported that the average caseload of adult probationers was 124. Caseloads ranged from 54 in Wyoming to 352 in Rhode Island. Intensive supervision probation caseloads averaged 25 offenders, ranging from 9 in Arizona to 51 in Rhode Island.[31] The report also said that the average face-to-face contacts between officer and probationer was 18 in 1998. Offenders under intensive supervision averaged 114 contact per year.[32]

The American Probation and Parole Association (APPA) argues that the issue is not one of numbers alone:

> Simply stated, not every offender needs the same type of amount of supervision to achieve the goals of probation or parole. There are a number of proven and accepted methods for determining the type and amount of supervision, but the key is that in order to be most effective and efficient, there must be varying amounts of supervision provided to offenders. This concept is crucial to the discussion of ideal caseload size because it states as a given that cases will be treated differently in terms of the amount and type of supervision they will receive. This means that the caseload officer will be expected to give differing amounts of time and types of attention to different cases.[33]

The APPA recommends a "workload standard" instead of a "caseload standard." It does not make sense, the APPA argues, to count every case as equal. A case requiring maximum supervision effort may require, for example, four hours of the probation or parole officer's time per month. A medium supervision case may require two hours per month to effectively supervise. A minimum supervision case may only require one hour or less per month of the probation or parole officer's time. Depending on the makeup of the caseload, the officer could effectively and efficiently supervise 30–40 maximum supervision cases, 60 minimum cases, and as many as 120 minimum cases. In practice, caseloads contain offenders at every level of supervision need. The ideal caseload, then, is calculated by determining how many hours are available to the officer and adjusting the caseload to account for the various supervision requirements of the persons being supervised.[34] The average caseload per officer by caseload type in 1998 is presented in Box 7.3.

Using workload instead of caseload allows for making time for duties other than supervision. Many probation officers have presentence report responsibilities as well as supervision duties. A workload computation method allows for the time required to complete a presentence investigation report. Other factors, such as geography, can also play a part in determining the number of cases an officer can effectively supervise. One of the authors of this book, while a U.S. probation officer in the Western District of Texas in the 1970s, supervised a caseload dispersed geographically from San Antonio to Midland, a distance of more than 300 miles. At the same time, one of his colleagues in New York City was able to visit his entire caseload within the confines of 12 city blocks.

No magic number can be set for the optimal caseload size.[35] However, development of a workload standard should be a goal for the future of community corrections. It would allow for comparison between jurisdictions, guide research in probation and parole effectiveness, and assist probation administrators in interpreting their work to legislators and other policymakers.

BOX 7.3   *Average Caseload per Officer during 1998 by Type*

Caseload: The number of individuals, or cases, for which one probation, parole, or probation and parole officer is responsible.

Face-to-Face Contact: Contact between an offender and a probation, parole, or probation and parole officer as required to properly supervise and counsel the offender.

Caseloads for probation officers ranged from 352 cases per officer in Rhode Island to 60 cases per officer in the District of Columbia. Among probation and parole officers, caseloads per officer ranged from 154 in Arkansas to 51 in Wisconsin. Parole officers' caseloads varied from 105 cases per officer in Minnesota to 40 per officer in Nebraska.

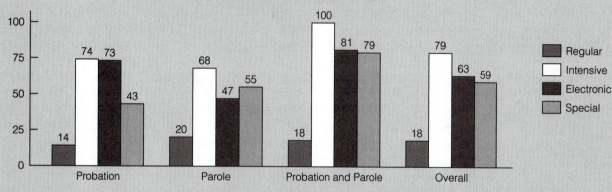

AVERAGE FACE-TO FACE CONTACTS BETWEEN OFFENDERS AND PROBATION AND PAROLE STAFF DURING 1998

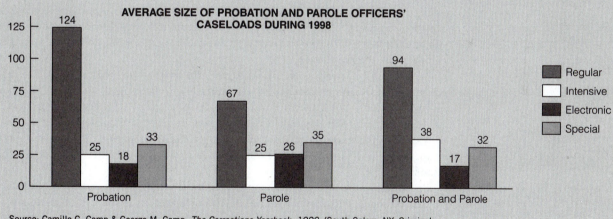

AVERAGE SIZE OF PROBATION AND PAROLE OFFICERS' CASELOADS DURING 1998

Source: Camille G. Camp & George M. Camp, *The Corrections Yearbook: 1999.* (South Salem, NY: Criminal Justice Institute, 1999), 177. Reprinted with permission.

Specialized Caseloads

The use of specialized caseloads has proven to be effective in improving supervision quality and effectiveness. Offenders with certain characteristics can often benefit from supervision by a specialist—a probation or parole officer who has specialized education, training, or experience in a certain area. These specialized caseloads are used with such groups as youthful offenders, drug addicts, alcoholics, dangerous offenders, sex offenders, and emotionally disturbed offenders.[36]

Edward E. Rhine, William R. Smith, and Ronald W. Jackson found that specialized parole caseloads were being used in 25 states by 1990. Fourteen states were using specialized caseloads for sex offenders, 12 for drug offenders; 10 for offenders with mental disabilities, 5 for "career criminals," and 2 for violent criminals.[37] Specialized caseloads for DWI (driving while intoxicated) offenders were established in Texas in 1983 and now exist in virtually every medium-to-large probation department in the nation. Although few empirical studies have been conducted of the efficacy of specialized caseloads, anecdotal evidence supports the concept.

SUMMARY

The most vital aspect of the probation and parole process in the criminal justice system is supervision. In its simplest terms, supervision is an officer's oversight of those who have been placed on probation and parole. A supervisory process that is highly individualized and purposefully reconstructive can meet the needs of most offenders and will advance the goals of a probation or parole system. The personality, training, and experience of the supervisory officer largely determine the adequacy of the process. Lax supervision and failure to deal firmly with those who persistently violate the terms of release can bring an entire system into disrepute. Adequate probation and parole supervision must deal with all phases of an offender's life including his or her family and the community in which he or she lives. Although probation and parole professionals may disagree on the value and propriety of many specific techniques of supervision, all recognize the need for a plan of supervision that is based on the needs, capacities, and limitations of each offender. The physical and mental health, the offender's home and family, his or her leisure time activities, education, vocational training, economic status, work habits, and capacity for discipline and self-control must all be considered by those who are attempting to help him or her become a law-abiding citizen.

To deal affirmatively with all aspects of the probationer or parolee's life that require aid, the officer cannot act entirely alone. The officer must, whenever possible, endeavor to secure the assistance and cooperation of community agencies and facilities. Responsibility for securing this assistance, and for monitoring and evaluating the results of these agencies, rests with the probation or parole officer. This is the indispensable part of the officer's duty. If it is neglected, the officer's work will be unsatisfactory.

Probation and parole supervision necessitates frequent and continuous contact with the offender. This contact should be characterized by a positive relationship of mutual respect and trust and the officer's willingness to see his or her role as multi-faceted, not as a singularly therapeutic or enforcement-oriented role.

Good probation service is not easily accomplished when officers are compelled to supervise too many cases. A supervision caseload of 35–50 offenders per officer has been suggested as desirable. Research has indicated, however, that the total work-load, based on a properly classified caseload, should determine the ratio of offender to officer.

Supervision in probation and parole may be summarized by paraphrasing from the American Bar Association Standards for Criminal Justice project, *Standards Relating to Probation:* "The basic idea underlying probation and parole is to help the offender learn to live productively in the community that has been offended."[38]

DISCUSSION QUESTIONS

1. Discuss how the concept of supervision has changed over the past half-century. What factors have brought about the change?
2. How do the "casework" and "brokerage of service" supervision models differ?
3. What are the probation or parole officer's major functions under the justice model?
4. What is case classification? What are the advantages?
5. Discuss the use of risk prediction scales. What is their purpose? How might they be used in case management?
6. Discuss the concept of caseload and workload computation. What is the traditional position? Why might workload be a better method of allocating probation or parole officer resources?
7. How does a specialized caseload differ from a traditional caseload?
8. Explain the analogy of child rearing to probation supervision.
9. Discuss Carl Klockars' typology of probation officers.
10. Why is it critical for probation or parole officers to assess a client's needs regarding substance abuse and employment? How are they related to the other needs and risks in probation supervision?
11. Differentiate between risk control and risk reduction. Give examples of each strategy.

 WEB SITES

Provides information on case management and risk assessment

http://www.justiceconcepts.com/

Presents RAND Corporation research on risk reduction

http://www.rand.org/areas/CRIM.Toc.html

Please go to the book-specific Web site for Supplemental Readings related to the material in this chapter:
A Day in the Life of a Federal Probation Officer
http://www.wadsworth.com/product/0-534-559662s

Supervision in Probation and Parole

A portion of this chapter discusses typology of probation officer work styles (law enforcer, time-server, therapeutic agent, synthetic officer). Case A provides examples of events occurring during an offender's term of supervision. In which category would you place the probation officer supervising these cases? What strategies would probation officers with the other three styles have used supervising this offender?

Classification of an offender under supervision is also explained in this chapter. Case B provides information available to the probation officer when supervision begins. Classify the offender's case by assessing the risks posed by the offender, identifying the supervision issues, and selecting the appropriate supervision strategy.

Case A: Thomas User was under supervision as a result of his conviction for possession of a chemical used in the manufacture of methamphetamine. He was released from prison to begin his supervision term on February 10. A standard condition of his supervision required that he not use or possess any illegal drugs. He also had a special condition requiring that he participate in substance abuse treatment.

On February 12 a urine specimen was taken from User. The specimen tested positive for methamphetamine. User admitted to his probation officer that he had used methamphetamine the day he was released from prison. The officer addressed the use of illegal substances by verbally reprimanding User. Because User had not begun his treatment at the time of the admitted use, he was referred to substance abuse counseling and the officer increased the number of urine specimens that would be taken from the offender. The probation officer made unscheduled contacts at User's residence. During the contacts, the officer walked throughout User's home and garage. In the contacts the officer did not observe any items that he considered related to drug usage or manufacture. User secured a job that his probation officer verified. He lived alone in a small house. He submitted his required monthly written report to his probation officer at the beginning of March and had not had any adverse contact with law enforcement. On March 22 User admitted to his counselor that he had relapsed. After the admission, results of urine specimens taken on March 18 and March 22 were received and were positive for methamphetamine. In response to the admission, his counselor and the probation officer implemented a plan for User to participate in intensive outpatient treatment. He was to attend three counseling sessions weekly in addition to four Narcotics Anonymous meetings each week. Urine collection was also increased, and User was placed on home confinement. He was to leave his home only for work, counseling sessions, and support group meetings. User was advised that further illegal drug usage would result in the probation officer recommending a more restrictive action.

A urine specimen taken on April 22 was positive for methamphetamine. When confronted by the probation officer, User became tearful and explained he had been using methamphetamine two to three times weekly. He had been surprised some of the other urine specimens taken from him were not positive for the drug. User said he had been attending all the support group meetings and sessions with his counselor. However, he recognized that he was addicted to the drug and needed more help. He denied involvement in manufacture of the illegal drug and said he had purchased it from an individual who was a codefendant in the case for which he was under supervision. His probation officer set up an intake assessment for an inpatient treatment facility and User was accepted to the facility. In addition to requiring satisfactory completion of the treatment, the probation officer imposed a special condition requiring placement in a treatment-oriented halfway house for up to 120 days following completion of the inpatient treatment.

Case B: Sue Steel was convicted of passing worthless checks. She is 52 years of age and has a history of criminal conduct. All her prior convictions involve some type of fraud or theft. At the time her supervision began, she had a pending misdemeanor case for "theft by deception." Steel received a sentence of 6 months' confinement. As she had been in detention prior to sentencing, she was given credit for 3 months and 22 days, and the sentencing court ordered that she serve the remainder of the 6 months on home confinement with electronic monitoring while under her 3-year term of supervision.

Steel was ordered to pay $975 in restitution. She had not made any payment toward the obligation at the beginning of her supervision term. She has employment at a janitorial service cleaning office buildings. Steel worked at this firm prior to detention in this case, and her employer was willing to rehire her upon her release from custody. Her employer is aware of her conviction and supervision. She is living with her daughter and son-in-law and their two children.

8

Probation Revocation

AP/Wide World Photo

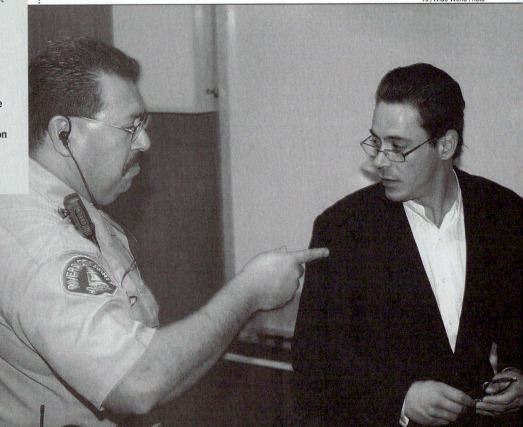

What You Will Learn in This Chapter

You will learn that the decision to revoke probation is significant but discretionary. Revocation has implications for the probationer, the probation officer, and the community. You will learn about the two types of violations and the procedure followed after the decision to revoke probation is made. The rights given to probationers during revocation are listed, and other issues related to revocation are explored. Alternatives to revocation are also discussed.

INTRODUCTION

Placing an offender on probation implies that, in the best judgment of the court, the probationer will respect and abide by the law and observe the conditions of release. Unfortunately, this is not true in many cases. Revocation rates are high. The Bureau of Justice Statistics reports that 14 percent of probationers nationwide were revoked in 1999 because of a rule violation or the commission of a new offense.[1] A study in one state shows that "50 percent of probationers did not comply with court-ordered terms of their probation; 50 percent of known violators went to jail or prison for their noncompliance."[2] A 1995 survey in Texas concludes that the revocation rates in that state's probation departments reached a maximum of 60 percent for felony probation and 78 percent for misdemeanor probation.[3] A more recent study of 2,000 felons in Arizona placed on probation shows that four years later:[4]

61 percent had completed their term of probation or were still "active" on probation
25 percent were subsequently sentenced to prison and did not complete probation
6 percent were unknown
4 percent had absconded
3 percent were discharged
1 percent were deported

When probation is unsuccessful, the court has the option to revoke probation or modify the conditions of supervision. Various issues are involved in probation revocation, including the authority to revoke probation, the types of probation violation, revocation procedures, rights during revocation, and other legal issues. Furthermore, various alternatives to revocation are available and situations arise under the interstate probation compact.

THE DECISION TO REVOKE

Probation release is conditional, meaning that the probationer's liberty is not absolute. Instead, it is subject to compliance with specified conditions. Violation of conditions can cause revocation of probation and incarceration of the offender. Revocation is a serious matter to the probationer because it denotes failure and loss of freedom. It is also important for the probation department and society because the offender will now serve time in jail or prison and become a financial drain on the public treasury.

Although a probationer is subject to court-imposed restrictions, the probationer's freedom is often similar to that enjoyed by persons who have not been charged with or convicted of an offense. The probationer continues to live in the community (although with some restrictions), can work at suitable employment, enjoys the association of family and friends, can participate in community activities, and partakes of the benefits enjoyed by nonoffending members of the community. In other words, the probationer can live basically the same kind of life as the other members of the community. The big difference comes when conditions are violated and the probationer is held accountable for failure to comply. The probationer's status after revocation changes dramatically, so revocation is not taken lightly by either the offender or the court.

Court Authority to Revoke Probation

Although the probation officer or the probation department may recommend revocation, only the court has authority to revoke probation. This authority remains with the court that granted probation unless the case has been transferred to another court that is given the same powers as the sentencing court.[5] The federal probation statute and all state statutes provide for transfer of jurisdiction in appropriate cases to allow the probationer, with the court's permission, to change residence. Transfer may be from one part of the state to another or, in the case of a federal offender, from one part of the country to another. Transfer of jurisdiction to another court is distinguished from the provision of interstate compacts for the transfer of responsibility for supervision to another state's probation department. When transfer occurs under the interstate compact, authority to modify the conditions of probation, revoke probation, or terminate probation remains with the court of the sending state.

Revocation Is Discretionary

The authority to revoke probation is discretionary, meaning that whether probation is revoked or not is solely up to the court. The only exception is if the law provides for mandatory revocation. Examples of discretionary and mandatory revocation are found in federal probation, where federal law provides for discretionary revocation as follows:

> If a defendant violates a condition of probation at any time prior to the expiration or termination of the term of probation, the court may, after a hearing pursuant to Rule 32.1 of the Federal Rules of Criminal Procedure, and after considering the factors set forth in section 3553(a) to the extent that they are applicable—(1) continue him on probation, with or without extending the term or modifying or enlarging the conditions; or (2) revoke the sentence of probation and resentence the defendant.[6]

This provision for discretionary revocation is followed by a provision for mandatory revocation, which states that revocation is mandatory for federal probationers in three types of violation: (1) if the probationer is found to possess a controlled substance, (2) if the probationer possesses a firearm, or (3) if the probationer refuses to comply with drug testing. In these cases the "court shall revoke the sentence of probation and resentence the defendant . . . to a sentence that includes a term of imprisonment."[7]

Some departments provide general guidelines for revocation, but these guidelines are seldom strictly followed because the probation department realizes that the court has the final decision. Even in cases in which the probationer is convicted of another crime, revocation is often optional unless state law provides otherwise, which is rare. Conversely, some jurisdictions simply revoke probation if the probationer commits a new crime instead of prosecuting the offender for the new crime. Revocation for the new crime is a more convenient option that achieves the same result, which is the incarceration of the offender and removal from society.

DIFFERING PERCEPTIONS OF REVOCATION BY PROBATION OFFICERS

Revocation of probation is a serious matter not only for the probationer and the public but also for the probation officer. The officer's supervision orientation often determines how he or she perceives the revocation.

The traditional probation officer is likely to view revocation as a "failure."[8] Before the officer-probationer relationship has deteriorated to the point where revocation is considered, the officer will have invested considerable time and effort to rehabilitate the probationer. Sometimes an officer develops a genuine interest in the probationer and becomes acquainted with his or her family. The officer may feel that imprisonment will impede instead of facilitate a probationer's rehabilitation and reintegration into society.

The community resource manager officer sees probation revocation as his or her own failure to identify and arrange for the probationer's needs or as the community's failure to provide the necessary resources. Revocation is further viewed as society's failure, not that of the offender. Often decision makers are blamed for not providing sufficient support to enable the probationer to succeed.

The justice model officer attributes the revocation decision to the probationer's failure to live up to the terms of the contract or agreement with the court. This officer knows that despite probation officers' efforts, a percentage of probationers will fail. These are not failures of the system, the community, or the probation officer, but the failure of probationers to respond positively to an opportunity to remain free and rehabilitate themselves.

REVOCATION AND THE COMMUNITY

Revocation raises serious concerns for the community. Incarcerating the offender increases the cost to the community because keeping an offender under probation supervision costs much less than providing care and treatment in a correctional institution. In Texas in 1999, the cost per day to keep an offender on probation was $1.92; to keep an offender in prison, $38.71.[9] The costs in most states are higher and will continue to climb.

Imprisoning offenders who otherwise would have been on probation may force their families to go on welfare or make greater demands on community resources. The offender ceases to be a contributing member of society and instead becomes dependent on the state. Revocation, however, protects the community from offenders who continue to commit criminal acts or fail to abide by conditions designed to rehabilitate. It is also needed so offenders will take the conditions imposed seriously, thus ensuring a higher likelihood of compliance. The public needs reassurance that persistent offenders are incapacitated by incarceration so they cannot continue to prey

BOX 8.1 *Examples of Results of Statistical Analysis of Violation Practice*

Length and Complexity of the Revocation Process

How long does it take to move from detection of a violation through court disposition?	Estimated average ranges from 44 to 64 days
Who is involved in the process?	Probation officer, supervisor, prosecutor, judge, law enforcement, jail administration, service providers
What mechanism is used to bring probationer into the violation process?	18% receive summons 82% have warrants issued against them

Dispositions of Motions to Revoke

DISPOSITION	NUMBER	PERCENTAGE OF DISPOSITIONS	PERCENTAGE OF TOTAL PROBATION POPULATION
Prison	94	36.0	2.5
Jail	8	3.0	.21
Jail with probation	56	21.0	1.5
Probation with conditions	4	1.5	.1
Probation	100	38.0	2.6
Incarcerative sanctions	158	60.0	4.2
Nonincarcerative sanctions	104	40.0	2.7

For What Violations Do Probation Officers File Motions to Revoke?

TYPES	PERCENTAGE
Positive urinalysis	27.0
Failure to participate in treatment	20.0
Abscond	18.5
New felony	12.0
Failure to report	10.0
New misdemeanor	4.0
All other technical	8.5

Source: Peggy B. Burke, *Policy-Driven Responses to Probation and Parole Violations* (National Institute of Corrections, March 1997), 12.

on society. Examples of the results of a statistical analysis of revocation are presented in Box 8.1.

TYPES OF PROBATION VIOLATION

LAW VIOLATIONS

Violations of probation or parole conditions that involve the commission of a crime.

TECHNICAL VIOLATIONS

Violations of the conditions of probation that do not involve law violations.

Revocation of probation is generally triggered in two ways: **law violations** and **technical violations.** A law violation occurs if a probationer commits another crime. Some states limit the condition to commissions of crimes within the state, but most states provide that a criminal act anywhere in the United States triggers revocation. By contrast, technical violations are infractions that do not involve law violations. Examples of technical violations are failure to report, violation of curfew, and association with criminals and disreputable characters.

Violation of the Condition to Obey the Laws

Most jurisdictions provide that the offender "commit no offense against the laws of this state or of any other state or of the United States."[10] In rare instances when this condition is not specified, it is usually deemed an unwritten condition of probation because law violation is a form of conduct society condemns. Even if the offender commits a new crime, however, revocation is not automatic. Instead, it is left to the discretion of the court. Most courts require the probation officer to report law violations and to make a recommendation regarding the issuance of a warrant and the initiation of revocation proceedings. But whether to revoke or not is for the court to determine.

The guidelines manual for federal probation classifies violations into three categories:[11]

1. Grade A Violations—conduct constituting a federal, state, or local offense punishable by a term of imprisonment exceeding one year that is a crime of violence, is a controlled substance offense, or involves possession of a firearm or destructive device . . . or any other federal, state, or local offense punishable by a term of imprisonment exceeding twenty years;
2. Grade B Violation—conduct constituting any other federal, state, or local offense punishable by a term of imprisonment exceeding one year;
3. Grade C Violations—conduct constituting a federal, state, or local offense punishable by a term of imprisonment of one year or less; or a violation of any other condition of supervision.

Conviction of an offense, particularly if the offense is a misdemeanor, does not necessarily lead to revocation. Even a felony conviction does not necessarily lead to revocation, particularly if the sentence for the second offense is lengthy and makes incarceration for the first offense unnecessary. However, acquittal for a new offense may nonetheless lead to revocation. This is because conviction of an offense requires guilt beyond reasonable doubt, while revocation usually needs only a preponderance of the evidence or even less—such as reasonable grounds or reasonable suspicion. What may not suffice for conviction may suffice for revocation. There is no double jeopardy because revocation is merely an administrative and not a criminal proceeding, although it results in incarceration.

Technical Violations

Most violations come under the category of technical violations, meaning they do not constitute criminal acts. They include violations of conditions that require the offender to report regularly to the probation or parole officer, not move from or leave the jurisdiction without obtaining permission, support dependents, refrain from excessive use of alcohol, work regularly at a lawful occupation, pay a fine or restitution, and other similar conditions. One jurisdiction reports that the three most commonly alleged technical violations are failure to report to the probation officer (89 percent), failure to pay probation fees (76 percent), and substance abuse (37 percent).[12]

Courts have upheld revocation for technical violations under a wide variety of circumstances. These are representative:

- Engaging in a scuffle with campus police during a demonstration in violation of the condition that the probationer not participate in demonstrations[13]
- Failure to pay off civil judgments for fraud although the probationer was able to pay[14]

A probation officer arrests one of her clients for violating his probation.

Raymond Alarid, Jr.

- Failure to make child support payments[15]
- Failure to report[16]
- Failure to pay supervision fees although financially able[17]
- Associating with persons who were not law-abiding[18]
- Driving a motor vehicle when condition specified license to drive was suspended[19]

As a general rule, probation is not revoked for occasional violations of technical conditions. Probation officers are instead urged to address these violations promptly and take whatever action is necessary to ensure compliance. In some cases, this results in reclassification for tighter supervision. Revocation, however, is the last resort for dealing with technical violations. Revocation policy in most jurisdictions is generally consistent with the federal guideline, which states:

> When a violation is detected, the officer is to respond with the least restrictive measures necessary to bring the offender into compliance in light of the seriousness of the violation, its implications for public safety, and the type and frequency of supervision strategies that were being employed at the time of the violation.[20]

BOX 8.2   *Sample Provision on Probation Revocation*

Section 23. Revocation. (a) If community supervision is revoked after a hearing under Section 21 of this article, the judge may proceed to dispose of the case as if there had been no community supervision, or if the judge determines that the best interests of society and the defendant would be served by a shorter term of confinement, reduce the term of confinement originally assessed to a term of confinement not less than the minimum prescribed for the offense of which the defendant was convicted. The judge shall enter the amount of restitution or reparation owed by the defendant on the date of revocation in the judgment in the case.

(b) No part of the time that the defendant is on community supervision shall be considered any part of the time that he shall be sentenced to serve. The right of the defendant to appeal for a review of the conviction and punishment, as provided by law, shall be accorded the defendant at the time he is placed on community supervision. When he is notified that his community supervision is revoked for violation of the conditions of community supervision and he is called on to serve sentence in a jail or in the institutional division of the Texas Department of Criminal Justice, he may appeal the revocation.

Source: Texas Code of Criminal Procedure, Article 41.12, sec. 23 (a) & (b).

The measures contemplated by the guideline range from a simple admonition from the probation officer to revocation and incarceration.

In many jurisdictions only repeated serious technical violations lead to revocation. The reasons are that revocation (in cases in which the violation is minor, simple, or occasional) may be a waste of time and resources. Moreover, revocation means incarceration and the high cost that goes with it. In jurisdictions where a probation fee is imposed, revocation means not collecting money from the probationer and the state having to support the offender while he or she is in jail or prison. For example, a probationer pays $30 a month for supervision. This income ceases for the county or agency upon revocation, and the county or state will now have to support the cost of incarcerating the offender. Because incarceration results in high costs, revocation is used only as a last resort in many states.

REVOCATION PROCEDURE

Revocation procedures are governed by a combination of constitutional rules, state law, and agency policy. Constitutional rights, such as the right to a hearing and basic due process, are required in all jurisdictions and must be afforded the probationer. Revocation procedures vary greatly from state to state or even from court to court within a state. Variations in procedures and rules are valid as long as they respect the basic constitutional rights of the probationer (see Box 8.2).

How It Begins

Revocation proceedings usually begin with a violation report. This report is prepared by the probation officer and becomes the basis for revocation. The decision to initiate revocation is usually made by the officer or, in some cases, by the probation chief or immediate supervisor. Jurisdictions differ as to who files the motion to revoke probation. A survey in one state shows that while the violation report is usually initiated by the probation officer (96 percent of the time), it can also be initiated by the officer's immediate supervisor or by the probation director.[21]

The prosecutor files the motion to revoke after reviewing the probation violation report. The prosecutor's authority to file a motion to revoke is discretionary, in that the prosecutor makes the final decision to file or not to file for revocation.

Most states have no guidelines for initiating a violation report. Whether to initiate revocation or not is a decision initially made by the probation officer or the department after a review of the alleged violation. No guidelines stipulate when a prosecutor should file the motion to revoke. Some judges set guidelines for probation officers to follow, but most judges do not. The discretionary nature of the revocation authority discourages the structuring of guidelines by which decisions to revoke or not to revoke are made. A study by Peggy B. Burke for the National Institute of Corrections, released in 1997, shows that probation officers nationwide file motions to revoke for the following violations:[22]

Types of Violation	Percentage
Positive urinalysis	27.0
Failure to participate in treatment	20.0
Abscond	18.5
New felony	12.0
Failure to report	10.0
New misdemeanor	4.0
All other technical violations	8.5

The Warrant to Revoke

In all states the warrant to revoke is issued by a court, usually the court that granted probation, and is served by law enforcement officers or by probation officers. Federal law has the following provision for federal probationers:

> If there is probable cause to believe that a probationer or a person on supervised release has violated a condition of his probation or release, he may be arrested, and upon arrest, shall be taken without unnecessary delay before the court having jurisdiction over him. A probation officer may make such an arrest wherever the probationer or releasee is found, and may make the arrest without a warrant.[23]

Other states have similar provisions, except that the level of certainty required for warrant issuance may vary. While probable cause is used in many states, a lower degree of certainty (such as reasonable grounds or reasonable suspicion) is allowed in others. The U.S. Supreme Court has not prescribed the minimum level of certainty required for revocation, hence variation among states exists.

The Power to Arrest Probationers

In some states probation officers are authorized to make an arrest with or without a warrant as long as the arrest is justified (see Box 8.3). In other states probation officers are expressly prohibited from making an arrest. In these states arrests are made by the police or other law enforcement officers. In still other states probation officers are authorized to make an arrest, but only under certain conditions, such as if a warrant has been issued by the court or if a general authorization empowering probation officers to make an arrest has been entered in the court docket.

These differences in the arrest powers of probation officers reflect the orientation of probation departments in the various states. Those with treatment orientation do not want their officers to be viewed as law enforcement agents because it lessens their effectiveness as treatment agents, so the power to arrest is denied. By contrast, states

§ 1205. COMMENCEMENT OF PROBATION
REVOCATION PROCEEDINGS BY ARREST

1. If a probation officer has probable cause to believe that a person on probation has violated a condition of that person's probation, that officer may arrest the person or cause the person to be arrested for the alleged violation. If the probation officer can not, with due diligence, locate the person, the officer shall file a written notice of this fact with the court that placed the person on probation. Upon the filing of that written notice, the court shall issue a warrant for the arrest of that person.

2. [1999, c. 246, §1 (rp).]

3. [1999, c. 246, §1 (rp).]

4. A person arrested pursuant to subsection 1, with or without a warrant, must be afforded a preliminary hearing as soon as reasonably possible, but not later than on the 3rd day after arrest, excluding Saturdays, Sundays, and holidays, in accordance with the procedures set forth in section 1205-A. A preliminary hearing may not be afforded if, within the 3-day period, the person is released on bail or is afforded an opportunity for a court hearing on the alleged violation. A preliminary hearing is not required if the person is charged with or convicted of a new offense and is incarcerated as a result of the pending charge or conviction. . . .

6. Whenever a person is entitled to a preliminary hearing, the failure to hold the hearing within the time period specified in subsection 4 is grounds for the person's release on personal recognizance pending further proceedings.

with a surveillance orientation believe that law enforcement is a necessary function of probation. In these states it is not unusual for probation officers to be armed and certified as law enforcement officers.

Proceedings after Arrest

After arrest, the probationer is taken to jail to await a court hearing. How long jail detention lasts varies from one state to another. Some states specify by law how long a probationer can be detained before a revocation hearing must be given. Other states prescribe no limitation or, if one is prescribed, there is no provision for automatic release if the limit is exceeded. This is usually because the probationer has already been convicted and could have been sent to prison at that time anyway. Bail prior to hearing is usually discretionary with the judge. A hearing must be held before the probationer is finally sent to prison to serve whatever incarceration term may have been originally imposed.

Time Served on Probation Is Not Credited

If probation is revoked, time served on probation is not credited as jail or prison time.[24] In essence, it is "wasted time" for the probationer. For example, Probationer X has served more than four years of probation for a five-year prison term that was suspended. If probation is revoked, Probationer X goes to prison for the original five years even if the revocation took place with a few months left to go on the five-year probation term.

The guidelines manual for federal probation provides as follows: "Upon revocation of probation, no credit shall be given (toward any sentence of imprisonment imposed) for any portion of the term of probation served prior to revocation."[25] In some states, however, judges may reduce the original sentence imposed, but the sentence cannot be increased.

Most offenders on probation either have been convicted of or have pleaded guilty to an offense. In some states, offenders may be placed on deferred adjudication or suspended sentence, which means that the finding of guilt is deferred and the offender is placed on probation just like those who have been found guilty. If the offender serves out the deferred adjudication period successfully, charges are dismissed and the finding of guilt is never made. It is as though the offender was never on probation, except that in some states the prior record of probation can be used to increase the sentence if the offender subsequently commits another offense.

REVOCATION RIGHTS OF PROBATIONERS

Offenders are entitled to some rights prior to probation being revoked. These rights were granted by the U.S. Supreme Court in the case of *Gagnon v. Scarpelli*, arguably the most important probation case ever to be decided by the Court.[26]

Gagnon v. Scarpelli—The Facts

Gerald Scarpelli was on probation for a felony when he was arrested for burglary. He admitted involvement in the burglary but later claimed that his admission was coerced and therefore invalid. His probation was revoked without a hearing and without a lawyer present. After serving three years of his sentence, Scarpelli sought release through a writ of habeas corpus. He claimed violations of two constitutional rights: the due process right to a hearing and the right to a lawyer during the hearing.

The Right to a Hearing

The right to a hearing prior to revocation was the more significant and far-reaching issue in the *Scarpelli* case. The Court held that probationers, like parolees, are entitled to a hearing prior to revocation. The Court said that, like parolees, probationers were entitled to a two-stage hearing consisting of a preliminary hearing and a final revocation hearing. More important, however, the Court ruled that probationers are entitled to the following due process rights during the hearings:

1. Written notice of the alleged probation violation
2. Disclosure to the probationer of the evidence of violation
3. The opportunity to be heard in person and to present evidence as well as witnesses
4. The right to confront and cross-examine adverse witnesses, unless good cause can be shown for not allowing this confrontation
5. The right to judgment by a detached and neutral hearing body
6. A written statement of the reasons for revoking probation, as well as of the evidence used in arriving at that decision

These due process rights are the same as those given to parolees in parole revocation proceedings in the case of *Morrissey v. Brewer*, decided by the Court one year earlier. The Court said in *Scarpelli* that there was no difference between probation and parole revocation because both of them resulted in loss of liberty. Therefore, rights in both revocation proceedings should be the same. The only exception is that while a two-stage hearing is still required in parole revocation, one hearing suffices in probation revocation.

Although *Gagnon v. Scarpelli* provides for preliminary and formal revocation hearings prior to revocation, as was mandated in *Morrissey v. Brewer* for parolees, most courts uphold as valid probation revocations after just a single hearing. This is because probation revocation usually involves an offender who is in the same city or county as the court, while parole revocation (done by the parole board through its agents) involves offenders who come from various places in the state and therefore deserve a preliminary hearing in the place where they are arrested.

Courts consider it important that the probationer be given a hearing. But even more important is that due process rights must be given to probationers in these hearings.

The Right to a Lawyer

Is a probationer constitutionally entitled to a court-appointed lawyer during revocation proceedings? The answer is no, but there are exceptions. The first case that addressed this issue was *Mempa v. Rhay,* decided in 1967.[27] In that case, the Court said that a defendant has a constitutional right to a lawyer during probation revocation that is followed by sentencing. However, the reason the Court required the presence of a lawyer in this case was not because of the probation revocation, but because the revocation was followed by sentencing—a practice in many states where the offender is placed on probation prior to the sentence being imposed. Sentencing is an important phase of a criminal trial and has always required the presence of a lawyer for the defendant.

Years later, in *Gagnon v. Scarpelli,* the Court said that the issue of whether a probationer is entitled to a lawyer during revocation proceedings should be decided on a need basis. The Court said that the introduction of counsel into every revocation proceeding will "alter significantly the nature of the proceeding" and make it "more akin to that of a judge at a trial, and less attuned to the rehabilitative needs of the individual probationer." Most states hold that although the state is not constitutionally obliged to provide counsel in all revocation cases, it should do so when the probationer is indigent and might have difficulty presenting his or her version of the facts to the court. Many states by law, however, routinely provide counsel to indigent probationers in revocation proceedings.

OTHER LEGAL ISSUES IN PROBATION REVOCATION

Gagnon v. Scarpelli is the leading case in probation revocation. It addressed two issues: the right to a hearing and the right to a lawyer during probation revocation. Lower courts have explored other issues not raised in that case.

Sufficiency of Notice

In accordance with heightened due process consciousness among probationers, recent cases are requiring an increasing degree of specificity in notices of intended revocation of probation. Allowing sufficient time for preparation of a defense is mandated. In a Texas case the defendant was served with notice of a motion to revoke probation on the day of the hearing and was told orally that one of the bases for the revocation would be "theft by false pretext" instead of "felony theft" as set out in the written notice. The court held that the defendant was denied due process by the court's failure to give him adequate and prior notice to prepare his defense.[28] In another case the state's motion to revoke probation alleged that the defendant had "violated paragraphs (a), (b), and (c) of his Conditions of Probation." The defendant claimed the pleadings were insufficient. The denial of his motion by the trial court was reversed on appeal. The appellate court stated that the state's pleadings were not sufficient to give the defendant fair notice of the conduct or acts for which the state intended to offer evidence to prove a violation of the conditions of probation.[29]

Nature of the Hearing

The requirements of minimum due process in a revocation hearing have not changed the basic character of the probation revocation hearing—which is that it is not a criminal trial. In *Morrissey v. Brewer*, the U.S. Supreme Court said, "We begin with the proposition that the revocation of parole is not part of a criminal prosecution, and thus the full panoply of rights due a defendant does not apply to parole revocation."[30] Similarly, a hearing on probation revocation is a hearing and not a trial. As such, it is not governed by the rules concerning formal criminal trials.[31] Not all technical provisions in criminal procedure are followed. The result of a probation hearing is not a conviction but a finding upon which the trial court may exercise discretion by revoking or continuing probation.[32] The defendant is not constitutionally entitled to a jury in revocation proceedings.[33] Some states, however, by law provide for a jury hearing, particularly in juvenile cases.

Level of Proof Required in Revocation Proceedings

What level of proof is needed to revoke probation? Is guilt beyond reasonable doubt the level used to convict criminal defendants? The standard varies widely among the states because this issue has not been decided by the U.S. Supreme Court. For example, Georgia requires only "slight evidence" for revocation, whereas Oklahoma requires that the decision be supported by a preponderance of evidence.[34] A Texas appellate court in 1996 also held that the state need only prove through a preponderance of the evidence that the terms of probation were violated.[35] Similarly, the Fifth Circuit Court of Appeals held in 1995 that a federal court may revoke probation if it finds by a preponderance of the evidence that a condition of release has been violated.[36] Most courts require preponderance of the evidence as the standard for revocation. Whether a lower level than preponderance of the evidence (such as reasonable grounds, reasonable suspicion, slight evidence, suspicion, or no evidence at all) would suffice for revocation has yet to be addressed by the Court. Even within a state the level needed to revoke probation may vary from one court to another. A "liberal" judge may require preponderance of the evidence, while a "conservative" judge might revoke even if the evidence merely amounts to reasonable suspicion. The level is the same within a state only if one standard is set by law or by a state supreme court decision, which not many states have done.

Kind of Evidence Required

Illinois has held that once a defendant has admitted violating probation, the admission eliminates the need on the part of the government to present proof of the violation.[37] Louisiana, meanwhile, has held revocation improper when the only evidence was the probationer's guilty plea without counsel.[38]

The testimony of the probation officer is often crucial at a revocation proceeding. Whether such testimony—unsupported by any other evidence—is sufficient to revoke varies. In Texas a court has held that revocation cannot be based merely on the statement of a probation officer that the probationer failed to report at least once a month as directed.[39] Oklahoma did not permit revocation based solely on an officer's testimony, without supporting evidence, that the defendant had moved to another state.[40] North Carolina reached the opposite result, holding that the uncontradicted testimony of a probation officer—that the defendant had been fired from his job and had not made payment toward his probation costs—was sufficient to support a revocation.[41] In Georgia (where only "slight evidence" is needed to revoke) probation revocation was upheld based solely on the testimony of an arresting officer that in his opinion the probationer was driving while intoxicated.[42] Most states admit hearsay evidence during revocation, other states do not. In sum, the kind of evidence required for revocation varies from one court to another.

The Exclusionary Rule Does Not Have to Apply

The **exclusionary rule** states that any evidence obtained by the government in violation of the Fourth Amendment guarantee against unreasonable searches and seizures is not admissible in a criminal prosecution to prove a defendant's guilt.[43] The main purpose of the exclusionary rule is to deter police misconduct, the assumption being that if evidence illegally seized is not admissible in court, then the police will be deterred from behaving illegally. This rule has been applied in federal courts since 1914 but was not extended to prosecutions in state courts until 1961.

For a while, state cases reflected uncertainty over the admissibility in revocation proceedings of evidence obtained in violation of the Fourth Amendment. A few states provided full Fourth Amendment protection, and the evidence obtained was excluded. In a Kansas case, for example, an appeals court applied the exclusionary rule and excluded the evidence during the revocation proceeding, saying that the law enforcement officer knew the subject was on probation and therefore may have had an incentive to carry out the illegal search because he knew that if the evidence obtained was not admissible in a criminal prosecution, it could still be used in a revocation hearing.[44] In most states, however, the exclusionary rule did not apply, so the evidence obtained was held admissible in probation revocation.[45]

The issue of whether evidence illegally obtained in violation of the constitutional rule against unreasonable searches and seizures is now considered settled by a 1998 U.S. Supreme Court decision in the case of *Pennsylvania Board of Probation and Parole v. Scott*.[46] In that case, the defendant pleaded "no contest" to the charge of third-degree murder and was sentenced to prison for ten to twenty years. Ten years later the defendant was released on parole. One of the conditions of the defendant's parole was that he refrain from "owning or possessing any firearms or other weapon." In addition the defendant signed a consent to allow agents of the Pennsylvania Board of Probation and Parole to conduct searches of his person, property, and residence.

Five months into the defendant's parole, he was arrested for several alleged violations of the conditions of his release. The parole agents subsequently conducted a search of parolee's residence, which was also the home of his mother. The agents found five firearms, a compound bow, and three arrows. Although the parolee objected to the introduction of the seized weapons at his revocation hearing, the evidence was nevertheless admitted at the hearing and his parole was revoked.

The defendant appealed the admission of this evidence to the Pennsylvania Supreme Court. The defendant argued that the evidence was seized in violation of his U.S. constitutional rights under the Fourth and Fourteenth Amendments. The Pennsylvania court agreed and held that the exclusionary rule applied to this case. The state appealed this ruling to the U.S. Supreme Court.

The U.S. Supreme Court noted that it had applied the exclusionary rule only when its deterrence benefits outweighed its "substantial social costs." The Court then examined the deterrence benefits versus the social costs in applying the exclusionary rule to a revocation proceeding. A majority of the Court concluded that

> the application of the exclusionary rule would both hinder the functioning of state parole systems and alter the traditionally flexible, administrative nature of parole evocation proceedings. The rule would provide only minimal deterrence benefits in this context, because application of the rule in the criminal trial context already provides significant deterrence of unconstitutional searches.

Therefore the Court held that the exclusionary rule did not prohibit the introduction at a parole revocation hearing of evidence seized in violation of a parolee's Fourth Amendment rights. In short, the Court held that the Constitution does not require the states to exclude illegally obtained evidence in revocation hearings. This means that a state can, at its discretion, admit or exclude illegally obtained evidence in revocation proceedings.

Although *Pennsylvania Board of Probation and Parole v. Scott* involved a parolee, there are strong reasons to believe it also applies to probation revocation proceedings.[47] Previous U.S. Supreme Court decisions have not made any distinction between the rights of probationers and parolees. What is given to parolees is also given to parolees; conversely, what is denied to parolees is also denied to probationers. There are more similarities than differences in probation and parole revocation proceedings such that courts do not distinguish between rights enjoyed by or denied to probationers and parolees.

Equal Protection

Can an indigent probationer be revoked and sent to prison if he or she is too poor to pay fine or restitution? The U.S. Supreme Court answers no. In *Bearden v. Georgia,* an offender pleaded guilty in a Georgia court to burglary and theft by receiving stolen property.[48] The court did not enter a judgment of guilt. Instead, it sentenced the petitioner to probation on condition that he pay a $500 fine and $250 in restitution, with $100 payable that day, $100 the next day, and the $550 balance within four months. The probationer borrowed money and paid the first $200, but a month later he was laid off from work and, despite repeated effort, was unable to find other work. Shortly before the $550 balance became due, he notified the probation office that his payment was going to be late. Thereafter, the state of Georgia filed a petition to revoke probation because the probationer had not paid the balance. The trial court, after a hearing, revoked probation, entered a conviction, and sentenced the probationer to prison. The record of the hearing disclosed that the probationer had been unable to find employment and had no assets or income.

On appeal, the U.S. Supreme Court held that a sentencing court cannot constitutionally revoke a defendant's probation for failure to pay a fine and make restitution, absent evidence and findings that he was somehow responsible for the failure or that alternative forms of punishment were inadequate to meet the state's interest in punishment and deterrence. To send an indigent offender to jail or prison because he or she is too poor to pay a fine discriminates against the poor and violates the equal protection clause of the Constitution.

The probationer, not the probation department, has the burden of proving indigency. This means that the state does not have to prove that the probationer can pay. The probationer must prove as a defense in a revocation proceeding that he or she cannot pay. A distinction must be made, however, between failure to pay because of indigency and refusal to pay. While failure to pay because of indigency cannot lead to revocation, refusal to pay can result in revocation or a possible contempt proceeding.

Due Process

Is the judge obliged to consider alternatives before revoking a probationer? The answer is no. In *Black v. Romano*, the offender pleaded guilty in a Missouri state court to several controlled substance offenses.[49] He was placed on probation and given suspended prison sentences. Two months later he was arrested for and subsequently charged with leaving the scene of an automobile accident, a felony under Missouri law. After a hearing the judge revoked his probation, and Romano was sent to prison. Romano appealed, saying that the judge violated his constitutional right to **due process** (meaning fundamental fairness) by revoking his probation without considering alternatives to incarceration. On appeal the U.S. Supreme Court held that the due process clause of the Fourteenth Amendment does not generally require a sentencing court to indicate that it has considered alternatives to incarceration before revoking probation. The procedures for revocation of probation, first laid out in *Morrissey v. Brewer* and then applied to probation cases in *Gagnon v. Scarpelli*, do not include an express statement by the fact finder that alternatives to incarceration were considered and rejected. The Court reiterated that the procedures specified in *Gagnon v. Scarpelli* adequately protect the probationer against unfair revocation.[50]

REVOCATION AFTER THE TERM OF PROBATION HAS EXPIRED

The general rule is that probation can be revoked only during the probation term. After that the court loses authority unless an extension is provided by law. In the absence of such authorization, the power of the court to revoke ends. For example, in a 1996 case an appellate court in Arkansas set aside an order of revocation, saying that "the general rule is that the trial court may revoke a defendant's suspension of sentence [probation] only prior to the expiration of the period of suspension." The court's ruling was based on Arkansas state law, which says that the court may revoke probation after the expiration of the probation period in only two instances: when the defendant is arrested for violation of probation or when a warrant is issued for the probationer's arrest before the period of probation expires.[51]

The exceptions in Arkansas law are also found in other state laws. Federal law also authorizes delayed revocation, saying that "the power of the court to revoke a sentence of probation for violation of a condition of probation, and to impose another sentence, extends beyond the expiration of the term of probation for any period reasonably necessary for the adjudication of matters arising before its expiration if, prior to its expiration, a warrant or summons has been issued on the basis of an allegation of such a violation."[52]

Probation may also be revoked after the term of probation has expired if the probationer evades supervision before completing the sentence. Probation statutes usually provide that the term of probation is "tolled" if the defendant is either charged with a violation of probation or flees the jurisdiction (or cannot be found) and a warrant is issued. To toll the running of a sentence or a period of time limitation is to interrupt it, to "stop the clock." The Illinois statute, for example, provides that when a petition is filed charging a violation of a probation condition, the court may order a summons for the offender to appear or a warrant for the offender's arrest:

The issuance of such warrant or summons shall toll the sentence of probation or of conditional discharge until the final determination of the charge, and the term of probation or conditional discharge shall not run so long as the offender has not answered the summons or warrant.[53]

ALTERNATIVES TO REVOCATION

Not every violation of probation conditions results in revocation. In fact, most violations do not. Most probation departments use alternative programs instead of outright revocation. These programs vary, but they usually take the form of more severe restrictions on the offender or a different type of treatment. The attitude in most probation departments is one of adjustment and accommodation, partly because of the high costs to the probationer and the state if probation is revoked.

A controversial alternative to revocation is jail therapy. This consists of placing a probationer in jail without holding a subsequent revocation hearing. The period of incarceration is usually short. The "therapy" has two purposes: (1) to impress upon the probationer the seriousness of the offense and the possible consequences of continued violation and (2) to provide a realistic comparison between life in the community and life in jail. Opponents of jail therapy reject it as punitive, saying it does not contribute to the probationer's rehabilitation. They also believe that the relationship between the probation officer and the probationer may be permanently damaged by such action.

Federal guidelines for reporting violations of probation conditions—which are similar to those in many states—require the probation officer (except for certain specified serious incidents) to "consider whether or not a modification of the conditions of supervision would bring the offender into compliance and serve the relevant purposes of sentencing."[54]

Sometimes the probation officer will tolerate a series of minor violations before taking the offender to court. While in court, the officer may recommend modifying the imposed conditions in hopes that a change in the conditions will increase the chance of successful adjustment. Some courts will hear a motion for revocation, postpone a violation finding, and continue probation. However, the next time the probationer violates another condition of probation, the probation is revoked without a hearing based on the earlier violation. This gives a probationer one more chance at probation but allows revocation without any further hearing (thus saving the court time) if another violation occurs.

Probation officers have discretion to deal with probation violations without referral to the court so long as the infractions do not develop into a pattern or threaten public safety. Carl Klockars suggests that much probation work is conducted by threats of revocation.[55] For most probationers a warning or admonition from the probation officer is sufficient. In some jurisdictions probationers are brought back to court to show cause why the probation should not be revoked. This return to court to face the judge has a more sobering effect on the defendant than a simple admonition in the probation officer's office.

In sum, probation departments use many alternatives to revocation courts. These vary from state to state and often from court to court within a state. Many states do not provide for automatic revocation, so judges can create innovative alternatives to use before revoking probation and sending the offender to jail or prison.

PROBATION REVOCATION AND THE INTERSTATE COMPACT

Special problems arise after a probationer is revoked while supervised in a state other than the state of conviction. The Interstate Compact for the Supervision of Parolees and Probationers provides that any state that has signed the compact will accept supervision of a parolee or probationer who meets the residence requirements set forth in the compact. That state will supervise the probationer at the same level of supervision that it gives to its own cases. The sending state may retake a person being supervised in another state simply by having its officer present appropriate credentials and proving the identity of the person to be retaken. When requesting and accepting out-of-state supervision, the probationer waives extradition prior to leaving the sending state, although formal extradition procedures may be resorted to if necessary.

The sending state can retake a probation violator being supervised under the compact without resorting to formal extradition procedures. The receiving state is obligated to surrender the probationer unless a criminal charge is pending against the individual in the receiving state. In such a case the probationer cannot be retaken without the receiving state's consent until he or she is discharged from prosecution or from any imprisonment for such offense. The effect is that the sending state cannot retake the probationer into custody until all local charges are disposed of. Some states admit a probationer to bail pending disposition of charges for revocation of probation. Other states hold that the right to bail does not apply to persons who have been tried and convicted.

The validity of extradition waivers has been upheld against a challenge that they violate an offender's constitutional rights and are invalid because they would not become operative until some future date. It is also generally held that the sending state alone has authority to determine upon what basis a violator may be returned. The reasons for return are not reviewable by the receiving state.[56]

THE EFFECTIVENESS OF PROBATION

Before the "get tough on crime" era, the public generally assumed that probation was reserved for less serious, nonviolent offenders. Unless some probationer committed a particularly shocking or violent crime, little attention was paid to him or her. However, as the flood of convicted felons began to overwhelm the prisons of most states, courts began to rely on probation as a disposition for greater numbers of individuals who had committed serious offenses. As probation utilization increased and more serious offenders were assigned to their caseloads, probation officers faced a crisis of quantity and quality. There were too many probationers and too few probation officers for the supervision to be effective. In the wake of these conditions, public confidence in probation and parole began to wane.

What do studies show about the successfulness of probation? Studies of probation outcomes demonstrate that the rate of success depends on the definitions of recidivism used by researchers. For example, Ralph W. England's study in 1955 found that about 18 percent of federal probationers received new convictions after they were placed on probation.[57]

More recently Patrick A. Langan and Mark A. Cuniff, in a Bureau of Justice Statistics study of 79,000 felons placed on probation in 17 states, found that 43 percent were rearrested for a felony within three years while still on probation. However, they also found that 46 percent of the probationers that had been sent to prison or jail had absconded within the three years. Further, 71 percent had either completed their probation or were still on probation three years later. Each of these figures is correct in context. The dilemma is to determine which figure represents the rate of recidivism. As they stand, these statistics could represent either success or failure of probation.[58]

The NILECJ Study

One of the earliest comprehensive evaluations of probation effectiveness was conducted in 1979 by the National Institute of Law Enforcement and Criminal Justice (NILECJ). The study analyzed the probation evaluation literature. The NILECJ researchers divided the literature into three groups: research that compared probation with other sentencing options, probation with no comparison, and studies that attempted to isolate the variables contributing to success on probation.[59] Research that compared probation with other sentencing options produced mixed results. However, probationers generally had lower recidivism rates than did a group of similar offenders who had been incarcerated and then paroled. One study, which included only female offenders, found no difference in recidivism between the two groups.

Studies that examined recidivism rates for probationers with no comparison group also produced no conclusive results because they were based on diverse groups, varied definitions of recidivism, and different follow-up periods.[60]

The NILECJ attempt to isolate factors that led to success on probation was limited by the same factors that led to the mixed results in the other studies. However, significant correlations were noted between recidivism and prior criminal history, unmarried younger offenders, unemployment, low income, drug and alcohol abuse, and limited education. The fewer of these variables, the more likely the probationer was to succeed on probation.[61]

The RAND Study

One of the most notable effectiveness studies was conducted by Joan Petersilia and associates for the RAND Corporation. To study probation recidivism rates, they selected a sample of 1,672 felony probationers sentenced in Los Angeles and Alameda counties in California in 1980. The researchers followed the probationers for 40 months, recording their arrests, convictions, and incarcerations. During that period, 65 percent of the probationers were rearrested, 51 percent were reconvicted, 18 percent were reconvicted of serious violent crimes, and 34 percent were reincarcerated. Moreover, they found that 75 percent of the official charges filed against the study population involved burglary or theft, robbery, and other violent crimes. Probationers who were like those imprisoned in terms of criminal history and seriousness of their crimes were 50 percent more likely to be rearrested than other probationers.[62]

Petersilia and associates then looked at the factors associated with failure on probation. They analyzed the data to determine which factors were associated with rearrest, reconviction, and success on probation.

The likelihood of rearrest was increased by the number of prior juvenile and adult convictions, an original sentence of jail plus probation, and living with parents. Black probationers were more likely to be rearrested than white or Hispanic probationers. Drug offenders living with their parents and those under 21 and over 30 were more likely to be rearrested.[63]

The probability of reconviction was increased by having prior juvenile and adult convictions. Property and violent offenders were more likely to be reconvicted than drug offenders.[64] The number of prior juvenile convictions was associated with reconviction for a violent crime. However, prior adult convictions were not correlated with reconviction for a violent crime.[65]

Property offenders were more likely to make a successful adjustment to probation supervision than drug or violent offenders. Older offenders and those with no prior adult or juvenile convictions were less likely to become recidivists. Those with no drug history, those who were employed, those who were high school graduates, and those who lived with their spouse or children were also less likely to become recidivists.

The RAND researchers found that the crimes and criminal records of about 25 percent of the offenders who were granted probation were indistinguishable from those of offenders who were sentenced to prison terms. They concluded that the courts have very limited ability to identify offenders who are likely to succeed on probation and that "given the information now routinely provided to the court," the ability to predict which felon will succeed on probation "probably cannot be vastly improved."[66]

Petersilia and her associates summarized, "In our opinion, felons granted probation present a serious threat to public safety."[67] They concluded that the criminal justice system needs an alternative intermediate punishment for serious felons—one that changes the current perception of probation as a "slap on the wrist."[68] They wrote,

> The core of such an alternative must be intensive surveillance, coupled with substantial community service and/or restitution. It must be structured to satisfy public demands that the punishment fit the crime, to show criminals that crime really doesn't pay, and to control potential recidivists.[69]

Petersilia and colleagues were referring to a type of alternative called intensive supervision probation, or ISP. A discussion and evaluation of ISP is presented in Chapter 12.

SUMMARY

The decision to revoke is important for the probationer, the probation officer, and the community. The authority to revoke lies with the court and is discretionary. There are two types of probation violation: violation of the condition to obey all laws and technical violation. Technical violations are violations of conditions other than the condition to obey the law.

The revocation procedure begins with a violation report filed by the probation officer. The motion to revoke is usually filed by the prosecutor. The court then issues the warrant to revoke. After arrest, the probationer is kept in detention pending a hearing. Time served on probation is not credited as jail or prison time if the probation is revoked.

The case of *Gagnon v. Scarpelli* provides that probationers must be given a hearing and certain due process rights prior to revocation. Other legal issues in probation revocation include sufficiency of notice, nature of the hearing, level of proof in revocation proceedings, the applicability of the exclusionary rule, and whether probationers have equal protection and due process rights prior to the final decision to revoke. The general rule is that probation can be revoked only during the probation term, not after it has expired. There are several alternatives to revocation, usually limited only by whatever arrangements the court might allow.

DISCUSSION QUESTIONS

1. Support the statement, "The decision to revoke is important." What are revocation's implications for the probationer, the probation officer, and the community?
2. "Revocation is discretionary." Discuss what that means.
3. What are the two types of probation violation? Discuss each.
4. Discuss the revocation procedure. How does it start and what are the steps?
5. Do probation officers have the power to arrest probationers? Discuss your answer.
6. What is the leading case on probation revocation? Discuss what that case says.
7. What are the six due process rights given to probationers during the revocation hearing?
8. There is no single level of proof prescribed by the U.S. Supreme Court in revocation proceedings. What standards are used in various jurisdictions?
9. What is the exclusionary rule? Does it apply in revocation proceedings?
10. What does the case of *Bearden v. Georgia* say?
11. "There is no way a probationer can be revoked after the probation term has expired." Is that statement true or false? Discuss.
12. Identify alternatives to revocation and discuss each.
13. Is probation effective? Discuss the findings in each of the different studies.

Probation Revocation

This chapter explains the probation revocation process and the types of violations that can result in revocation. In the following case, list the violations of probation known to the probation officer. Would you concur with the probation officer's recommendation for revocation of probation? If not, at what point would you consider recommending revocation in this case? Are there other alternatives you might have recommended?

Joe Conner was under supervision for possessing a destructive device. He has a history of some violent behavior (domestic violence, battery of a law enforcement officer). Special conditions of Conner's supervision require that he participate in mental health treatment and substance abuse treatment.

Shortly after Conner's supervision term begins, he tests positive for marijuana use. When confronted by his probation officer, he admits to using marijuana. However, Conner states that he uses the marijuana to self-medicate and he will commit violent acts if he ceases its usage. Conner concludes that his probation officer will be responsible for his violent acts toward others and himself as the officer is instructing him to cease the marijuana usage. The probation officer reminds Conner of the condition of supervision, which states that he is not to use or possess illegal drugs, and advises him that his use of illegal substances cannot be allowed and that the sentencing court will be advised of the violation.

Conner entered treatment at the beginning of his supervision term. As a result of Conner's response to the instruction to cease marijuana usage, the probation officer recommended to the court that Conner be referred for a psychiatric evaluation to see if he would benefit from psychotropic medications. The court concurred with the officer's recommendation, and Conner was referred for the evaluation. The psychiatrist diagnoses bipolar affective disorder, type II, and prescribes Depakote. This medication requires regular lab work to evaluate its effectiveness. Conner fails to attend his next appointment with the psychiatrist. Results of a urine specimen taken from Conner a week after his evaluation with the psychiatrist are received. The specimen reveals Conner has used both marijuana and amphetamine.

The probation officer petitions the court for a warrant to have Conner arrested and brought before the court for violations of his supervision.

II

Parole

Nearly all prisoners will be released from prison someday on either mandatory or discretionary parole release. Higher demands have been placed on parole agencies to supervise offenders following their prison terms. This has happened as a result of a change in sentencing philosophy; a decrease in prison rehabilitation programs; and less funding for release, which has led to higher caseloads and less supervision.

The structure of the discretionary paroling process—including the composition and selection of the parole board, caseloads, training, and authority of field staff and procedures used for the parole grant or revocation—varies considerably from jurisdiction to jurisdiction. The same is true for the use of parole. Some states continue to parole many adult prisoners, while legislative action in other states has abolished all discretionary parole release. Variations in the structure and use of the parole process, as well as the accompanying variations in sentencing structures from one jurisdiction to another, account in good part for the lack of agreement about the legal status of parole across the country.

The next three chapters focus on different methods of release from prison. The history and philosophy of parole are discussed in Chapter 9. Chapter 10 pays particular attention to how discretionary parole boards decide releases. Chapter 11 examines conditions and legal aspects of parole while offenders are on parole as well as what happens when these conditions are not met. It also reviews the effectiveness of parole.

9

The Development of Parole: From Its Origin to the Present

Raymond Alarid, Jr.

What You Will Learn in This Chapter

*I*n *this chapter you will learn how parole differs from probation and pardon. You will examine the history of parole, beginning with the work of Manuel Montesinos in Spain and Georg Michael Obermaier in Germany. The practices of transportation and ticket-of-leave and their influence on the development of parole will be discussed. Particular emphasis will be placed on the work of Alexander Maconochie on the penal colony of Norfolk Island, the subsequent implementation of parole by Walter Crofton in Ireland and by Zebulon R. Brockway in America. Finally, you will continue to trace parole into the modern era, examining the various attacks on parole and the role parole plays in the 21st century.*

INTRODUCTION

State and federal prisoners release nearly 600,000 prisoners to the community every year. Twenty percent of all felons receive no supervision whatsoever after they leave prison because they have served their full sentence in prison (otherwise known as "maxing out" or "killing your number"). Eighty percent of all prisoners are supervised in the community on some form of parole.[1] **Parole** is the conditional release, by an administrative act, of a convicted offender from a correctional institution, under the continued custody of the state, to serve the remainder of his or her sentence in the community under supervision.

Types of Release from Prison

Most prisoners enter the community either by mandatory release or discretionary parole (see Table 9.1).

MANDATORY RELEASE: Individuals on **mandatory release** (otherwise known as "postrelease supervision" or "supervised release") enter the community automatically at the expiration of their maximum term minus credited time off for good behavior. In other words, mandatory release is not decided by a parole board, but by legislative statute or good-time laws.

At the federal level, the Sentencing Reform Act (1987), which implemented sentencing guidelines that led to the abolition of parole, created a version of mandatory release called supervised release. Federal courts may impose a term of supervised community release in addition to the term of imprisonment. The conditions of supervised release are the same as those of discretionary parole.[2]

In many state jurisdictions where parole board authority has been abolished, most released prisoners return to the community via mandatory release for between one and three years. As with parole, mandatory release may be revoked for failure to comply with the conditions of release. Mandatory release is thus associated with a determinate sentencing philosophy, emergency releases, or good-time provisions.

DISCRETIONARY PAROLE: In contrast to mandatory release, individuals released on discretionary parole enter the community because members of the parole board have decided that the prisoner has earned the privilege to be released from prison while still remaining under supervision of an indeterminate sentence. (Chapter 10 focuses on the methods by which parole boards decide who should be

KEY TERMS

Parole
Mandatory release
Pardon
Parole d'honneur
Ticket-of-leave
Transportation
Ticket-of-leave man
Alexander Maconochie
Mark system
Norfolk Island
Sir Walter Crofton
The Irish system
Indeterminate sentence
Zebulon R. Brockway
Medical model
Just deserts
Justice model
Determinate sentence
Presumptive sentence
Split sentence
Good time
Medical Parole

PAROLE

Conditional release, by an administrative act, of a convicted offender from a penal or correctional institution, under the continual custody of the state, to serve the remainder of his or her sentence in the community under supervision.

MANDATORY RELEASE

Conditional release to the community that is automatic at the expiration of the maximum term of sentence minus any credited time off for good behavior.

TABLE 9.1 *Adults Entering Parole, by Type of Sentence, 1996*

Region and Jurisdiction	Total	NUMBER OF ADULTS ENTERING PAROLE			
		Discretionary[a]	Mandatory[b]	Reinstatement[c]	Other, Unknown, or Not Reported
U.S. total	421,055	194,138	199,103	17,615	10,199
Federal					
Federal	30,518	29,462	1,056	0	0
State	390,537	164,047	198,047	17,615	10,199
Northeast	74,605	66,847	5,565	1,360	833
Connecticut	1,505	1,502	0	3	0
Maine	2	0	0	2	0
Massachusetts[d]	3,889	3,666	0	223	0
New Hampshire[d]	854	0	639	123	92
New Jersey	13,530	12,576	0	954	0
New York	27,064	21,397	4,926	0	741
Pennsylvania	26,903	26,903	0	0	0
Rhode Island	532	477	...	55	0
Vermont	326	326	0	0	0
Midwest	60,401	27,053	29,467	1,336	2,545
Illinois	22,763	23	21,405	107	1,228
Indiana	4,382	84	3,510	99	689
Iowa	1,964	1,964	0	0	0
Kansas	4,074	3,578	191	104	201
Michigan	9,463	8,584	404	475	0
Minnesota[d]	2,698	8	2,490	0	200
Missouri	4,316	3,768	548	0	0
Nebraska	823	823	0	...	0
North Dakota	191	191	0	0	0
Ohio	4,785	4,015	0	543	227
South Dakota	614	606	0	8	0
Wisconsin	4,328	3,409	919	0	0
South	108,639	63,313	39,091	395	5,840
Alabama[d]	1,651	:	:	:	1,651
Arkansas[d]	5,551	4,388	:	:	1,163
Delaware[d]	:	:	:	:	0
District of Columbia	2,951	1,792	679	89	391
Florida[d]	3,984	3,781	0	203	0
Georgia	11,959	11,959	...	...	0

released.) Nearly as many people are released annually on discretionary parole as are on mandatory release. Parolees on mandatory release or discretionary parole are supervised by a parole officer and adhere to similar conditions. If these conditions are not followed, both types of releasees can be returned to prison.

Parole Distinguished from Probation

The general public sometimes confuses parole with probation and pardon. Whereas parole is a form of release granted to a prisoner who has served a portion of a sen-

TABLE 9.1 *Adults Entering Parole, by Type of Sentence, 1996* (continued)

Region and Jurisdiction	Total	NUMBER OF ADULTS ENTERING PAROLE			
		Discretionary[a]	Mandatory[b]	Reinstatement[c]	Other, Unknown, or Not Reported
South (*continued*)					
Kentucky	3,491	3,406	0	85	0
Louisiana	11,408	1,627	9,763	18	0
Maryland	11,080	3,918	7,162	0	0
Mississippi	1,107	:	:	:	1,107
North Carolina	10,544	10,544	:	:	0
Oklahoma	465	465	...	...	0
South Carolina	1,334	1,334	0	0	0
Tennessee	3,918	3,918	:	:	0
Texas[d]	28,149	11,910	16,153	0	86
Virginia[d]	10,479	3,703	5,334	0	1,442
West Virginia	568	568	0	0	0
West	146,892	7,463	123,924	14,524	981
Alaska	542	94	448	:	0
Arizona	5,314	1,224	3,622	162	306
California	126,506	200	112,001	14,305	0
Colorado	3,039	2,288	552	0	199
Hawaii	623	623	0	0	0
Idaho	469	469	0	0	0
Montana	:	:	:	:	0
Nevada	:	:	:	:	0
New Mexico	1,381	:	1,381	:	0
Oregon	6,893	609	5,920	57	307
Utah	1,914	1,914	0	0	0
Washington[d]	42	42	0	0	0
Wyoming	169	:	:	:	169

: Not known

... Not applicable

[a] Discretionary parole entries are persons entering because of a parole board decision.

[b] Mandatory parole entries are persons whose releases from prison were not decided by a parole board; includes those entering because of determinate sentencing statutes, good-time provisions, or emergency releases.

[c] Reinstatement entries are persons returned to parole after serving time in prison because of a parole violation.

[d] Detailed data are estimated for entries.

Source: U.S. Department of Justice, Bureau of Justice Statistics, *Correctional Population in the U.S., 1997* (Washington, DC: U.S. Department of Justice, 2000).

tence in a correctional institution, probation is granted to an offender without required incarceration. Parole is an administrative act of the executive or an executive agency, whereas probation is a judicial act of the court. Therefore, so-called bench parole—which is nothing more than a suspension of sentence without supervision—is not parole at all but a form of probation. The use of the word *parole* in this connection is improper and misleading and should thus be eliminated.

Parole Distinguished from Pardon

PARDON

An executive act of clemency that absolves an individual from the legal consequences of a crime and conviction. A pardon is an act of grace or a remission of guilt. A full pardon freely and unconditionally absolves the party from the consequences of the crime and conviction. A conditional pardon becomes operative when the grantee has performed some specified act, or it becomes void after the occurrence of some specified event, or it remits only a portion of the penalties that are the legal consequences of a crime and conviction.

Parole may be distinguished from pardon as follows: **Pardon** involves forgiveness. Parole does not. Pardon is a remission of punishment, while parole is an extension of punishment. Pardoned prisoners are free. Parolees may be arrested and reimprisoned without a trial. Pardon is an executive act of grace; parole is an administrative expedient.[3]

The distinction between parole and pardon was clearly drawn in an address before the American Prison Association in 1916:

> The whole question of parole is one of administration. A parole does not release the parolee from custody; it does not discharge or absolve him from the penal consequences of his act; it does not mitigate his punishment; it does not wash away the stain or remit the penalty; it does not reverse the judgment of the Court or declare him to have been innocent or affect the record against him. Unlike a pardon, it is not an act of grace or of mercy, of clemency or leniency. The granting of parole is merely permission to a prisoner to serve a portion of his sentence outside the walls of the prison. He continues to be in the custody of the authorities, both legally and actually, and is still under restraint. The sentence is in full force and at any time he does not comply with the conditions upon which he is released, or does not want to conduct himself properly, he may be returned, for his own good and in the public interest.[4]

No similarity exists between pardon and parole except that both involve release from an institution.[5] Release on parole is not based on any concept of clemency. Nor is it regarded as a lenient treatment of prisoners, even though they are released prior to the expiration of their sentences. Parole, as it functions today, is an integral part of the total correctional process. As such, it is a method of selectively releasing offenders from the institution and placing them under supervision in the community, whereby the community is afforded continuing protection while the offender is making adjustments and beginning to contribute to society.

THE ORIGINS OF PAROLE

PAROLE D'HONNEUR

French for "word of honor," from which the English word *parole* is derived.

The English word *parole* is derived from the French **parole d'honneur,** meaning "word of honor." This choice of word was unfortunate inasmuch as most people would distrust a released prisoner's word of honor. It is not surprising, therefore, that the French themselves prefer the term *conditional liberation* to the one borrowed from their language.

In penal philosophy parole is part of the general 19th-century trend in criminology from punishment to reformation. In 1791, during the French Revolution, the Comte de Mirabeau (Honore-Gabriel Rigueti) anticipated modern penal theories when he published a report based on the idea of reformation and emphasized the principles of labor, segregation, rewards under a mark system, conditional liberation, and aid on discharge.[6] Another Frenchman, Bonneville de Marsangy, public prosecutor of Versailles, published a book in 1847 in which he discussed a pardoning power, conditional liberation, police supervision of discharged convicts, aid upon discharge, and rehabilitation. This book was distributed by the government to the members of both chambers of Parliament. In 1864, in a further work on this subject, he used the following simile in his argument for what is now called parole:

> As a skillful physician gives or withholds remedial treatment according as the patient is or is not cured, so ought the expiatory treatment imposed by law upon the criminal

to cease when his amendment is complete; further his detention is inoperative for good, an act of inhumanity, and a needless burden to the state. Society should say to the prisoner, "Whenever you give satisfactory evidence of your genuine reformation, you will be tested, under the operation of a ticket of leave; thus the opportunity to abridge the term of your imprisonment is placed in your own hands."[7]

Parole as a practice originated almost simultaneously with three European prison administrators: a Spaniard, Manuel Montesinos; a German, Georg Michael Obermaier; and an Englishman, Alexander Maconochie.

Manuel Montesinos

In 1835 Col. Manuel Montesinos was appointed governor of the prison at Valencia, Spain, which held about 1,500 convicts. He organized the institution on the basis of semimilitary discipline and encouraged vocational training and primary education of the prisoners. The novelty of his plan was that there were practically no guards to watch the prisoners, who nevertheless made few, if any, attempts to escape. The main reason for this was probably that each prisoner could earn a one-third reduction in the term of his sentence by good behavior and positive accomplishments. The number of recommitments while Montesinos was governor fell from 35 percent to "a figure which it would be imprudent to name, lest it should not be believed."

The law that allowed this program was subsequently repealed, and the system collapsed. Montesinos resigned and, in a pamphlet published in 1846, drew the following conclusions from his experiment:

> What neither severity of punishment nor constancy in inflicting them can secure, the slightest personal interest will obtain. In different ways, therefore, during my command, I have applied this powerful stimulant; and the excellent results it has always yielded, and the powerful germs of reform which are constantly developed under its influence, have at length fully convinced me that the most inefficacious methods in the prison, the most pernicious and fatal to every chance of reform, are punishments carried to the length of harshness. The maxim should be constant and of universal application in such places, not to degrade further those who come to them already degraded by their crimes. Self-respect is one of the most powerful sentiments of the human mind, since it is the most personal; and he who will not condescend, in some degree, according to circumstances, to flattery of it, will never attain his object by any amount of chastisement; the effect of ill treatment being to irritate rather than to correct, and thus turn from reform instead of attracting to it. The moral object of penal establishments should not be so much to inflict punishment as to correct, to receive men idle and ill-intentioned and return them to society, if possible, honest and industrious citizens.[8]

Georg Michael Obermaier

When Georg Michael Obermaier became governor of a prison in Munich, Germany, in 1842, he found approximately 700 rebellious prisoners being kept in order by more than 100 soldiers.[9] In a short time he gained the men's confidence, removed their chains, discharged nearly all of their guards, and appointed one of them superintendent of each of the industrial shops. His success in reforming prisoners was so great that reportedly only 10 percent relapsed into crime after their discharge. He was aided by two favorable circumstances: Many of the men were sentenced to simple imprisonment with no fixed term, and discharged inmates were thoroughly supervised by numerous prison aid societies.

Alexander Maconochie and Walter Crofton

Chief credit for developing early parole systems, however, goes to Alexander Maconochie, who was in charge of the English penal colony at Norfolk Island, and to Sir Walter Crofton, who directed Ireland's prisons. Crofton refined the scheme originated by Maconochie into what is known today as the **ticket-of-leave,** or Irish system. Inasmuch as the earliest known plan of conditional liberation was used in the Australian convict colonies, and because present-day parole is closely linked to these experiments, their tragic history is worthy of consideration.

TRANSPORTATION AND TICKET-OF-LEAVE

The **transportation** of English criminals to the American colonies began in the early 17th century. The system evolved from a 1597 law that provided for the banishment of those who appeared to be dangerous. As early as 1617, reprieves and stays of execution were granted to persons convicted of robbery who were strong enough to work in the colonies. The government devised a plan to transport convicted felons to the American colonies as a partial solution to the labor shortage in the colonies and the poor economic conditions and widespread unemployment in England. The London, Virginia, and Massachusetts Companies and similar organizations supported the plan. The king approved the proposal to grant reprieves and stays of execution—pardons—to convicted felons who could physically be employed in the colonies.

Initially no specific conditions were imposed on those receiving pardons. Consequently many of them evaded transportation and returned to England before their terms expired, which made it necessary to impose certain restrictions on individuals who were granted pardons. About 1655 the form of pardon was amended to include specific conditions and to provide that the pardon would be nullified if the recipient failed to abide by the conditions.

Until 1717 the government had paid a fee to contractors for each prisoner transported. Under a new procedure adopted that year, the contractor was given "property in service," and the government took no interest in the welfare or behavior of the offender unless he or she violated the conditions of the pardon by returning to England before the sentence expired. Upon arrival in the colonies, the "services" of the prisoner were sold to the highest bidder, and thereafter the prisoner was an indentured servant.

The system of indenture dates to 1512, and it originally had no relation to persons convicted of crimes. It usually applied to the indenture of both apprentices and masters for a number of years. The indenture consisted of a contract stipulating the conditions of the relationship and was somewhat similar to the parole agreement of today.

The Revolutionary War brought an end to the practice of transporting criminals to America, but the transportation law was not repealed. Detention facilities in England became overcrowded, resulting in a more liberal granting of pardons. During a serious crime wave, the English public demanded enforcement of the transportation law, and Australia was designated as a convict settlement, with the first shipload arriving there in January 1788. Transportation to Australia differed from transportation to the American colonies in that the government incurred all expenses of transportation and maintenance, and the prisoners remained under government control instead of being indentured. The governor was given "the property and service" for the prisoners, and he assigned them to the free settlers, who assumed the property and service agreement. As early as 1790 the governor of New South Wales had the right to grant conditional pardons. He could set the convicts free and give them grants of land, afterward even assigning newly arrived convict laborers to them. Such was the original ticket-of-leave system that was regulated by statute in 1834. Originally there were no provisions for governmental supervision of **ticket-of-leave men.**

In 1811 a policy was adopted that required prisoners to serve specific periods of time before becoming eligible to receive ticket-of-leave. Strict enforcement of the policy was not seen until 1821, when an eligibility scale was formulated. Prisoners serving a sentence of 7 years became eligible for the ticket-of-leave after serving 4 years; those serving sentences of 14 years, after serving 6 years; and those serving life sentences, after 8 years.

In 1837 **Alexander Maconochie,** a former British naval captain and geographer, proposed to the House of Commons a system whereby the duration of the sentence would be determined not by time but by the prisoner's industry and good conduct. He proposed a **mark system** by which "marks" or credits would be allotted to the prisoner daily in accordance with the amount of labor performed and his or her conduct. His system saw the prisoners passing through a series of stages from strict imprisonment through conditional release to final and complete restoration of liberty, with promotions being based on marks accredited.

Maconochie was given the opportunity to test his mark system in 1840, when he was appointed governor of the notorious penal colony on **Norfolk Island,** a thousand miles off the eastern coast of Australia. Under his mark system there, prisoners were able to progress through stages of custody, each less restrictive than the previous one:

1. Strict custody
2. Labor in work gangs
3. Freedom in certain areas of the island
4. Conditional release-ticket-of-leave
5. Complete freedom

Vocal and powerful detractors in Australia and in England rallied against Maconochie's system. Many influential colonists in Australia, who believed that convicts should be kept in irons and not given any relief from their sentences, saw it as radical and too liberal. They lobbied the colonial governor of Van Dieman's Land (now Tasmania), who had appointed Maconochie to his post, for his dismissal. The governor was torn between his hope that Maconochie's experiment would succeed and his fear of the political power of the colonists who opposed the project. Finally, however, partly as a result of the controversy over his methods and partly because of pressure in England to cut the costs of the transportation system, Maconochie was dismissed in 1844, and the "noble experiment" came to an end.

As the free settlers in Australia increased in number, they protested the use of the country as a dumping ground for prisoners. In response to the protest, England initiated a selection system whereby prisoners would undergo an 18-month training program before being transported to Australia. The selection experiment failed, but it was the first use of trained, experienced individuals for selecting prisoners who have profited by a training program. Three prison commissioners were appointed to make the selections, which may well have set the precedent for the three-member parole boards later established by prison reformers in America. In 1867 transportation of prisoners to Australia was terminated.

TICKET-OF-LEAVE MAN

A convict who has obtained a ticket-of-leave.

ALEXANDER MACONOCHIE

A British naval captain who served as governor of the penal colony on Norfolk Island, who instituted a system of early release that was the forerunner of modern parole. Maconochie is known as the "father of parole."

MARK SYSTEM

Credits for good behavior and hard work. In Alexander Maconochie's mark system on Norfolk Island, convicts could use the credits or marks to purchase either goods or time (reduction in sentence). In this system the prisoner progressed through stages from strict imprisonment, through conditional release, to final and complete restoration of liberty, with promotion being based on the marks accredited. One of the historical foundations of parole.

NORFOLK ISLAND

The notorious British penal colony 1,000 miles off the coast of Australia.

England's Experience with Ticket-of-Leave

Although England did not stop transporting prisoners to Australia until 1867, the English Penal Servitude Act of 1853, pertaining to English and Irish prisoners, substituted imprisonment for transportation. In accordance with the act, prisoners sentenced to 14 years or less were committed to prison, but the judge was given the option of ordering transportation or imprisonment for prisoners with sentences of more than 14 years. The law also specified how long prisoners must remain incarcerated before becoming eligible for conditional release on ticket-of-leave. This act legalized the ticket-of-leave system.

Prisoners released on a ticket-of-leave in England were subject to three general conditions:

1. The power of revoking or altering the license of a convict will most certainly be exercised in the case of misconduct.
2. If, therefore, he wishes to retain the privilege, which by his good behavior under penal discipline he has obtained, he must prove by his subsequent conduct that he is worthy of Her Majesty's clemency.
3. To produce a forfeiture of the license, it is by no means necessary that the holder should be convicted of a new offense. If he associates with notoriously bad characters, leads an idle or dissolute life, or has no visible means of obtaining an honest livelihood, and so on, it will be assumed that he is about to relapse into crime, and he will at once be apprehended and recommitted to prison under his original release.[10]

The British policy assumed that the prison program would be reformative, that the prisoners released on ticket-of-leave would have responded positively to prison training programs, and that those released would be adequately supervised. Such was not the case. The three years following the enactment of the Penal Servitude Act saw an outbreak of serious crime attributed to a lack of supervision of the ticket-of-leave men. The British public thus came to regard the ticket-of-leave system as a menace to public safety and an absolute failure.

A series of prison riots in 1862, accompanied by another serious crime wave, again focused attention on prison administration and the ticket-of-leave system. A royal commission was appointed to investigate both areas. The commission's final report blamed poor training programs for the problems and gave the opinion that prisoners were released on ticket-of-leave without giving reliable evidence of their reformation. The royal commission's report resulted in policemen being given responsibility for supervising released prisoners. Later, a number of prisoners aid societies, supported in part by the government, were established. These agencies aligned their methods of supervision with the method that had proven effective in Ireland.

Sir Walter Crofton and the Irish System

SIR WALTER CROFTON

An Irish prison reformer who established an early system of parole based on Alexander Maconochie's experiments with the mark system on Norfolk Island.

Sir Walter Crofton, who had studied Maconochie's innovations on Norfolk Island, became the administrator of the Irish prison system in 1854, one year after the Penal Servitude Act was passed. He believed that the intent of the law was to make the penal institution more than just a house of incarceration. Crofton felt that prison programs should be directed more toward reformation and that tickets-of-leave should be awarded only to prisoners who had shown definite achievement and positive attitude changes.

Under Crofton's administration, **the Irish system** became renowned for its three classes of penal servitude: strict imprisonment, indeterminate sentence, and ticket-of-leave. Each prisoner's classification was determined by the marks he or she had earned for good conduct and achievement in industry and education, a concept borrowed from Maconochie's experience on Norfolk Island. So-called indeterminate sentences were employed, and institutional conditions for this class were made as near to normal as possible—the restraint exercised over the prisoner being no more than what was required to maintain order. The ticket-of-leave system was different from the one in England. The general written conditions of the Irish ticket-of-leave were supplemented with instructions designed for closer supervision and control and thus resembled the conditions of parole in the United States today.

Ticket-of-leave men and women residing in rural areas were under police supervision, but a civilian employee—called the inspector of released prisoners—supervised those living in Dublin. The inspector had the responsibility of securing employment for the ticket-of-leave person, visiting the residence, and verifying employment. The ticket-of-leave man or woman periodically reported to the inspector of released prisoners or a designated local police officer. The Irish system of ticket-of-leave had the confidence and support of the public and convicted criminals.

THE IRISH SYSTEM

Developed in Ireland by Sir Walter Crofton, the Irish system involved graduated levels of institutional control leading up to release under conditions similar to modern parole. The American reforms at Elmira Reformatory were partially based on the Irish system.

DEVELOPMENT OF PAROLE IN THE UNITED STATES

The procedure now known in the United States as parole was first tried in New York at Elmira Reformatory in 1876. Four concepts underlie the development of parole in the United States: (1) reduction in the length of incarceration as a reward for good conduct, (2) supervision of the parolee, (3) imposition of the indeterminate sentence, and (4) reduction in the rising cost of incarceration.

Reward for Good Conduct

Release as a result of a reduction in the time of imprisonment was always accompanied by a written agreement in which the prisoner would abide by the conditions specified by those authorizing the release. These documents would now be considered parole agreements. The agreement normally stipulated that any violation of the conditions would result in a return to the institution. The first legal recognition of shortening the term of imprisonment as a reward for good conduct in the United States was the 1817 good-time law in New York.

Postrelease Supervision

Volunteers originally supervised those released from prison. Members of prison societies were also among the first volunteer supervisors of adult offenders. The Philadelphia Society for Alleviating the Miseries of Public Prisons recognized the importance of caring for released prisoners as early as 1822. In 1851 the society appointed two agents to assist prisoners discharged from the Philadelphia County Prison and the penitentiary. The first public employees paid to assist released prisoners are believed to have been appointed by the state of Massachusetts in 1845.

Zebulon R. Brockway and the Indeterminate Sentence

By 1865 American penal reformers were well aware of the reforms achieved by conditional release programs in the European prison systems, particularly in the Irish system. As a result, an **indeterminate sentence** law was passed in Michigan in 1869 at the instigation of **Zebulon R. Brockway.** (This law was subsequently declared unconstitutional, however.) Brockway later became superintendent of the newly constructed Elmira Reformatory in New York, and he succeeded in getting an indeterminate sentence law adopted in that state in 1876. The first parole system in the United States had come into being.

The system established at Elmira included grading inmates on their conduct and achievement, compulsory education, and careful selection for parole. Volunteer citizens, known as guardians, supervised the parolees. A condition of parole was that parolees report to the guardian the first day of each month. Written reports became required and were submitted to the institution after being signed by the parolee's employer and guardian.

Parole legislation spread much more rapidly than did indeterminate sentence legislation. By 1901, 20 states had parole statutes, but only 11 had indeterminate sentence laws. By 1944, however, every U.S. jurisdiction had adopted some form of parole release, and indeterminate sentencing had become the rule rather than the exception.[11]

Reduce the Cost of Incarceration

Howard Abadinsky maintains that the idea of parole was initiated in the United States primarily due to economic reasons.[12] For about one century between the 1840s and 1940s, American prisons were self-supported entirely by convict labor. Many penitentiaries, particularly those in the South, turned a huge profit from convict labor by leasing out their convicts to private companies. The private companies benefited because they paid the prison less than they otherwise would have to pay nonincarcerated workers for hard labor such as building railroads, making goods to sell on the open market, and growing crops. The prisons pocketed the money, given that the prisoners did not get paid at all. Most prisoners worked long hours "under the gun" in remote prison camps miles away from the main prison unit.[13]

Private companies liked the idea of using convict labor so much that it began to affect the employment rate of "free world" people (who were not prisoners). Organized labor unions outside of prison began to apply pressure to limit private companies' use of convict labor. Legislation was finally passed to limit convict labor only to goods that could be sold to other government entities. Because of this legislation, prisoners in remote prison camps had to be relocated to a prison unit where they could be behind bars and work within the walls. This meant that more prisons had to be constructed to make space for these incoming prisoners. The profits decreased, and for the first time, taxpayers began to bear some of the cost of incarceration.[14] It was at this point that the idea of parole became more popular. Nearly every state had some form of release from discretionary prison by 1944—shortly after legislation that was passed limiting convict labor to behind the walls.

DEVELOPMENT OF FEDERAL PAROLE

Federal parole began in June 1910 because of legislation that established the first three federal penitentiaries. In 1930, a formalized federal parole board was created under the U.S. attorney general's office. In 1950, because of a larger prison population in the federal system, the parole board expanded and was placed under the Justice Department. The most significant change for federal parole occurred in 1984, when the U.S. Sentencing Commission recommended that federal parole be abolished and that parole be replaced by "supervised release" for offenders sentenced after November 1, 1987.[15] Offenders must now serve a period of prison time without eligibility for parole. Upon completion of the incarceration period, the second term is supervised release in the community. The Federal Probation Office is now responsible for all releases from prison, including parole, supervised release, mandatory release, and even military parole. Although federal parole was initially to be phased out by 1992, a current statute calls for cessation by the year 2002. The Parole Commission, however, retains jurisdiction over offenders who committed their offenses prior to November 1, 1987.[16]

THE MEDICAL MODEL: 1930s–1960s

Parole was seen as a major adjunct to the rehabilitation philosophy that dominated American corrections between the 1930s and the 1960s. This rehabilitative ideal, called the **medical model,** assumed that criminal behavior had its roots in environmental and psychosocial aspects of the offender's life and that corrections could correct it. This meant that every offender would be dealt with on an individual basis to determine the causes of his or her criminal behavior. In their book *Reaffirming Rehabilitation,* Francis T. Cullen and Karen E. Gilbert wrote,

> Since the life experiences of one offender will inevitably differ from the next, the source of crime in any given instance could be expected to vary. This meant that every lawbreaker would have to be processed on a case-by-case basis. It would be necessary to study the offender closely and then to diagnose the particular criminogenic condition—perhaps the sordid influence of a slum home, perhaps a mental conflict—responsible for the person's waywardness. Once the cause of the problem was discovered, then the offender would be subjected to a treatment program specifically designed to eliminate the abnormality giving rise to the criminal inclinations in question.[17]

Under the old punitive model of corrections, the question asked was: What did he do? Under the medical model, the relevant questions were: Who is he? How did he come to be the person he is? What can be done to ameliorate his condition? One early commentator wrote,

> There can be no intelligent treatment until more is known than the fact that a man did a certain thing. It is as important to know why he did it. Diagnosis is as necessary in the treatment of badness as it is in the treatment of illness.[18]

If prison staff could diagnose and treat "badness," then the lawbreaker should be released when "cured." The mechanisms for accomplishing this were the indeterminate sentence and parole. The theory held that the judge at the time of sentencing could tailor a sentence to the particular needs of the offender and provide, by means of an indeterminate sentence, an opportunity for release at the optimum time in the rehabilitative process. The release decision is thus shared between the court, which sets a minimum and a maximum period of incarceration, and the correctional system—typically a parole board. The parole board's responsibility is to determine, with the assistance of prison authorities, the optimal release moment; that is, the time at which the inmate is most ready to reenter the community as a responsible citizen.

MEDICAL MODEL

The concept that given proper care and treatment, criminals can be changed into productive, law-abiding citizens. This approach suggests that people commit crimes because of influences beyond their control, such as poverty, injustice, and racism. Also called the rehabilitation model.

In 1933 the American Parole Association stated that fitness for release under parole supervision should be determined by the answers to the following questions:

> Has the institution accomplished all that it can for him; is the offender's state of mind and attitude toward his own difficulties and problems such that further residence [in prison] will be harmful or beneficial; does a suitable environment await him on the outside; can the beneficial effect already accomplished be retained if he is held longer to allow a more suitable environment to be developed?[19]

This philosophy assumes that correctional specialists have the ability to diagnose an offender's problems and develop a means of curing those problems. Because one cannot know at the time of diagnosis how long it will take to effect a cure, the indeterminate sentence makes it possible, in theory at least, to confine an offender as long as is necessary and to follow up that confinement with community supervision.

Changing Public Opinion

Although parole has generally drawn support from many sources and has a history of consensual acceptance, it has occasionally been subject to vigorous criticism and reexamination. In the early 20th century, particularly after World War I, parole administration came under attack. Critics claimed that parole was not fulfilling its promise. Antiparole groups believed that parole release was used primarily as a means of controlling inmates and that it failed to produce the desired lasting changes in their behavior and attitudes. This was a severe criticism at a time of increasing acceptance of the rehabilitative ideal with its emphasis on treatment and cure in criminal corrections.[20] Other critics of the system pointed out that release was granted after only a cursory review of the inmates' records and that paroling authorities had no criteria by which to measure rehabilitation and on which to base release decisions.

These criticisms led to two major changes in parole administration and organization. First, more emphasis was placed on postrelease supervision, and the number of parole conditions was increased. Second, a shift occurred in parole authority from prison personnel to parole boards with independent authority and statewide jurisdiction.[21]

Attorney General's Survey of Release Procedures

By the mid-1930s the parole system's continuance as a viable part of the justice system again was being scrutinized. The *Attorney General's Survey of Release Procedures*, a monumental study of the correctional process, reviewed the efficacy of parole. The survey report stated,

> While there has never been a time when the functions and purpose of parole have been clearly understood, at no period has the entire institution been the object of so much controversy and attack or viewed with as much suspicion by the general public as it has been during the past four or five years.[22]

Mounting prison populations and rising recidivism rates aggravated the general uneasiness concerning early release via parole. Questions involving the value of rehabilitation as a goal of corrections arose, and without the philosophical underpinnings of reform and rehabilitation as purposes of punishment, parole has much less to offer the criminal justice system.

Both the concept of rehabilitation and the practice of parole survived the criticism, and in 1940 President Franklin D. Roosevelt declared, "We know from experience that parole, when it is honestly and expertly managed, provides better protection for society than does any other method of release from prison."[23]

Perhaps a bit optimistically, New York parole commissioner (later director of the U.S. Bureau of Prisons) Sanford Bates, in a 1941 speech entitled "The Next Hundred Years," stated,

> Parole, as a method of release, will soon have become an indispensable part of this correctional process. We shall speak more accurately of subjecting a prisoner to parole than of granting him parole. We shall learn to speak of recidivists not as parole failures, but as unreformed inmates. We shall not shrink from the word, parole, as something involving weakness or vulnerability, but shall recognize institution after-care and supervision as a necessary sequel to a prison term. Nevermore shall we talk about abolishing parole any more than about abolishing police or commitment or discipline.[24]

Thus the medical model of corrections was born during the early years of the 20th century and grew into prominence in the late 1930s and early 1940s. This rehabilitative ideal viewed corrections as corrective and reformative, as opposed to punitive.

The years between World War II and 1970 saw the advent and development of classification systems, vocational training, academic training, group and individual therapy, conjugal visitation in some prisons, work release, and numerous other reforms. By 1967 (at the height of the reformative era), a Harris Poll of a nationwide sample found that 77 percent of the population believed that prisons should be mainly corrective, while only 11 percent believed they should be mainly punitive.[25] The belief that criminals could be changed if they were given the opportunity and if sufficient skills, funds, and personnel were available was the central philosophy of the rehabilitative model of corrections. Parole was once again considered a viable and necessary aspect of the American system of corrections.

A PHILOSOPHICAL CHANGE

In the middle 1970s, with suddenness remarkable in social change, there was a dramatic turnabout. Individualism, rehabilitation, sentence indeterminacy, and parole all seemed to fall from grace and appeared to be on their way out.[26] By 1978 a Law Enforcement Assistance Administration publication stated, "One of the movements we are currently witnessing in the criminal justice field is the trend toward the establishment of determinate or 'fixed' sentencing of criminal offenders."[27]

The correctional system's failure to reduce the steadily increasing crime rate and its obvious inability to reduce recidivism, rehabilitate offenders, or make predictive judgments about offenders' future behavior brought about public disillusionment, disappointment, and resentment. Concern also arose that wide and unfair disparities existed in sentencing based on the offender's race, socioeconomic status, and place of conviction.[28] The pendulum began to swing, and by the late 1970s it seemed to have moved 180 degrees from the rehabilitative ideal to the "just deserts" approach to criminal correction.

In contrast to the rehabilitative ideal, the **just deserts** or **justice model** denies the efficacy of rehabilitation and changes the focus of the system from the offender to the offense. The September 1977 issue of *Corrections Magazine*, for example, was devoted to the debate regarding the justice model and determinate sentencing. Even a brief review of the contents of this journal indicates that liberals and conservatives alike embraced determinate sentencing and the abolition of parole.

JUST DESERTS

The concept that the goal of corrections should be to punish offenders because they deserve to be punished and that punishment should be commensurate with the seriousness of the offense.

JUSTICE MODEL

The correctional practice based on the concept of just deserts. The justice model calls for fairness in criminal sentencing, in that all persons convicted of a like offense will receive a like sentence. Prisons are viewed as a place of even-handed punishment, not rehabilitation. This model of corrections relies on determinate sentencing and abolition of parole.

Prison reformers and police chiefs seemed to agree almost completely. The Vietnam War, the Kent State shootings, and the Attica prison uprising convinced many liberals that the state could not be trusted to administer rehabilitation in a just and humane manner. Popular movies such as *A Clockwork Orange* and *One Flew over the Cuckoo's Nest* depicted a less than benevolent government and the potential oppressiveness of deviant institutions. Furthermore, contemporary research such as the "nothing works" study by Robert Martinson found that few correctional treatment programs were successful in reducing recidivism or drug and alcohol addiction, or in fostering personality and attitude change or community adjustment. Martinson concluded that "with few and isolated exceptions, the rehabilitative efforts which have been reported so far have had no appreciable effect on recidivism."[29] For liberals the indeterminate sentence was too vague and without due process protections to limit discretion. The just deserts approach was perceived as stressing fair punishment, which reduced the "more pernicious abuses that had arisen when state authorities were invested with the discretion 'to fit the punishment to the criminal.'"[30] For conservatives the indeterminate sentence, parole, and treatment programs were too "soft" on crime. They viewed determinate sentencing and the just deserts approach as consistent with their political and social agenda—a return to the "hard line" and a punishment-oriented correctional system.

The general aim of those favoring determinate sentencing was to abolish, or at least to tightly control, discretion. This included the discretion of the prosecutor to choose charges and plea-bargain, the discretion of judges to choose any sentence within a broad range of time, the discretion of prison administrators to decide what kind of treatment a prisoner needed to become law-abiding, and the discretion of parole boards to release prisoners without having to justify their decisions or render their decisions consistent. Determinate sentencing was the reformers' answer to this problem.[31] The proposals of the mid-1970s called for clear, certain, uniform penalties for all crimes, either through legislative action or the promulgation of guidelines to which prosecutors, judges, and parole boards would be required to adhere.

Origins of Modern Determinate Sentencing

DETERMINATE SENTENCE

A sentence to imprisonment for a fixed period of time as specified by statute. Also known as flat, fixed, or straight sentence.

Where did all this talk of the **determinate sentence** begin? John Irwin, an ex-prisoner and now an author and college professor, contends that inmates themselves, particularly inmates in California prisons in the 1960s, were the original advocates of determinacy.[32] The situation in California prisons prompted the formation of a working group of the American Friends Service Committee, which produced the book *Struggle for Justice* in 1971.[33] In it the group denounced the very existence of U.S. prisons as well as the rehabilitative model of corrections, declaring coercion of prisoners for any purpose to be immoral. Although *Struggle for Justice* said that all prisons should be shut down, it recognized that such a proposal was unrealistic. The book argued that the least that should be done was to repeal all indeterminate sentencing laws and design a system in which offenders convicted of similar crimes served roughly equal terms in prison.

The Justice Model

David Greenberg, one of the primary authors of *Struggle for Justice*, was also a member of a group called the Committee for the Study of Incarceration. Together with Andrew von Hirsch, the committee's executive director, Greenberg persuaded the committee that the most important subject to study was not the conditions of incarceration, but the haphazard and irrational manner in which some offenders ended up in prison, and the equally chaotic system of release. The committee's final report was published in 1976 under the title *Doing Justice: The Choice of Punishments.*[34] Written by von Hirsch, it was a heavily philosophical monograph whose thesis was that the motives underlying the treatment of criminal offenders at the time were all wrong.

The principal goals of the correctional system at the time were to rehabilitate and restrain offenders based on predictions of their future criminality or dangerousness. As a result, the sanctions prescribed for particular crimes had little to do with the severity of criminal behavior. In fact, large numbers of widely disparate crimes were often punished with the same indeterminate term, with the setting of a release date left to parole boards, which judged particular offenders' potential rehabilitation and dangerousness.

Doing Justice pointed out that the goal of sentencing should be to punish offenders, that it is proper to punish the criminal because he or she "deserves" to be punished, and that each punishment should be commensurate with the gravity of the last offense or series of offenses. The committee recommended the adoption of a **presumptive sentence** for each crime or category of crimes, with the presumptive sentences graded according to the severity of the crime. The severity of the crime would be graded on two scales: the harm done by the offense and the offender's culpability. The judgment of the degree of culpability would be based partly on the offender's prior record. The reasoning behind this was that a succession of criminal acts would imply calculation or deliberate defiance of the law, thus making the offender more culpable for the current offense.

Having proposed punishment as the main goal of sentencing, the committee then ruled out prison as the punishment for all but the most serious offenses, those in which bodily harm is threatened or done to the victim. The committee proposed alternatives such as periodic imprisonment, increased use of fines, and other lesser sanctions. In cases in which prison is deemed necessary, the committee recommended that no prison sentence exceed five years except in some murder cases.

At about the same time *Doing Justice* was making the academic rounds, another determinate sentencing model emerged. David Fogel, author of *". . . We Are the Living Proof . . .": The Justice Model for Corrections,* is considered by many to be the "father of determinate sentencing."[35] As early as 1970 he had actively urged a narrowing of sentencing and parole discretion and had been among the most influential determinate sentencing advocate in the drafting of legislation in various states.

One of the main goals of Fogel's sentencing reforms was to humanize the internal operation of correctional institutions by extending much more freedom to inmates and "unhooking" their release date from their progress or participation in programs. He advocated abolishing parole boards and establishing "flat-time" sentencing—a single sentence for each class of felonies that could be altered slightly for aggravating or mitigating circumstances.[36]

In June 1977, then University of Chicago Law School dean Norval Morris, speaking at a symposium on criminal sentencing, addressed the issues of determinacy and parole by asking, "Should the indeterminacy of parole discretion be preserved?" Morris questioned the ability of parole or the parole board to do the following:

1. Find the optimum moment for release
2. Provide an incentive for rehabilitation
3. Facilitate prison control and discipline
4. Share sentencing responsibility to maximize deterrence while reducing the time served
5. Control the size of the prison population
6. Rectify unjust disparity in sentencing[37]

PRESUMPTIVE SENTENCE

A statutorily determined sentence convicted offenders will presumably receive if convicted. Offenders convicted in a jurisdiction with presumptive sentences will be assessed this sentence unless mitigating or aggravating circumstances are found to exist.

Morris stated that the first justification, the parole board's ability to predict the optimum moment for release, has repeatedly failed to be proved empirically. The second justification, provision of an incentive for the offender's rehabilitation, has as its net effect the reliance on compulsory rehabilitation in the prison setting. "This type of coerced curing of crime is ineffective," Morris said, "and is wasteful of resources. We don't know enough to make that second purpose work." The third justification, facilitating prison control and discipline, is an important, latent, pragmatic justification of parole, but it is vulnerable to attack on grounds of injustice. The fourth justification, the sharing of sentencing responsibility between the court and the parole board to maximize deterrence, is a charade that is so well known that court systems compensate for it. Judges and juries (where jury sentencing is applicable) routinely take parole laws into consideration when handing down sentences, knowing that, in most cases, the offender will serve less time than the sentence publicly announced. There still exists the question, however, of whether the parole experience has increased or reduced times served in the United States. The fifth justification, the ability to control the prison population, has occasionally been useful. Generally speaking, however, in times of community anxiety about crime and the pressures for law and order, parole boards have been pressured to be more conservative in granting parole. When this has occurred, parole boards, instead of attempting to solve the problem by releasing more prisoners, have compounded the problem by tightening requirements for parole. To the last claimed justification of parole, rectifying unjust sentencing disparities, Morris responds as follows:

> In Illinois, and I believe the same is true in many states, crime for crime and criminal for criminal, sentences imposed by courts in Chicago are subsequently less severe than those imposed in downstate, small-town, and rural areas. The Illinois Parole Board, not incorrectly, in my view, exercises its releasing discretion so as to minimize the grosser disparities—it moves toward a regression to the mean.[38]

A question arises, however: Should other mechanisms be developed for serving that purpose in place of parole? Morris believes they should, and he views the ultimate abolition of parole as inevitable. What alternatives to parole are available?

Most people would answer this question by saying "prison should replace parole." The problem with this answer is that space does not exist for all these prisoners. Furthermore, most prisoners are not emerging out of prison with any skills and knowledge that will keep them out of prison for very long. Jeremy Travis, former director of the National Institute of Justice, believes that:

> The overarching goal of reentry, in my view, is to have returned to our midst an individual who has discharged his legal obligation to society by serving his sentence and has demonstrated an ability to live by society's rules. . . . [We should be] asking a different question—"How should we manage the reentry of large numbers of people who have been imprisoned for a long time?"[39]

A DECLINE IN THE USE OF DISCRETIONARY PAROLE

More than 70 percent of prisoners were released via a parole board in 1977. Two decades later, that number has declined to less than 30 percent.[40] As of 1999, 14 states have replaced discretionary parole with mandatory release by abolishing parole boards.[41] In response to public pressure, the legislature has limited the releasing power of the parole board in some jurisdictions by requiring that prisoners serve a

Charles Manson, in prison since 1971 for ordering the murders of eight people, has developed his own history with the parole board. Manson has been denied parole nine times since 1978 because he remains a societal threat. His next scheduled parole hearing is in 2002.

AP/Eric Risberg

flat minimum or some proportion of the maximum sentence before becoming eligible for parole. Other jurisdictions that have retained discretionary parole have established parole guidelines to reduce and structure release decision making. A small number of states have not only abolished parole, but also have no postrelease supervision for prisoners returning to the community.

Abolition of Parole

Because of the trend toward determinate sentencing, and the criticisms toward disparity in decision making, the policy of abolishing parole was first tried in 1976 by state correctional departments. Between 1976 and 1990, 12 states had placed severe restrictions or eliminated parole completely.[42] Some states abolished parole to appear "tough on crime" and to increase the level of public safety brought on by negative media attention toward a handful of parolees that committed violent crimes while on parole. Furthermore, the public was led to believe that prisoners would serve longer sentences. One recent study indicated that prisoners in states without discretionary parole served seven months less than states that retained parole boards.[43]

The American Probation and Parole Association and the Association of Paroling Authorities have been two leading agencies working to retain parole. A book published by these two agencies, and authored by Peggy B. Burke, is entitled *Abolishing Parole: Why the Emperor Has No Clothes*. In this book, Burke provides strong justification in favor of parole as an important correctional institution. Some of the arguments in favor of discretionary parole include:

- Parole boards can impose prisoner participation in treatment programs as incentives for release; with automatic release, there are no more incentives for prisoners to better themselves while behind bars.
- Parole boards have improved their techniques for more objective and open decision making through parole guidelines.
- Victims can attend parole board hearings to convince the board not to release their offender, but victims have no say in mandatory or automatic release situations.
- Release from prison is a right under automatic supervision, not a privilege under discretionary parole.
- Release decisions are made by computer under automatic release, not by a human parole board that can keep prisoners in prison if it feels the offender will remain a danger to society.
- Prisoners on postrelease supervision generated by automatic release can still commit crimes (for example, the brutal killing of Polly Klaas in California in 1993, by Richard Allen Davis, who had been on mandatory parole release. This case aided the passage of California's "three strikes" law).
- Abolishing discretionary parole does *not* mean that prisoners will serve their full sentence; it does *not* prevent prisoners from getting out, and it does *not* necessarily increase public safety.[44]

Many criminal justice practitioners strongly believe in some kind of aftercare or postrelease offender supervision. To illustrate the importance of postrelease supervision, one scholar points out that practitioners will even "legitimately go around" the system to sentence an offender to a sanction that they feel will be most beneficial. In states without any postrelease supervision (for example, Maine), many judges began sentencing large numbers of prisoners to split sentences. A **split sentence** is a term of jail or imprisonment to be followed by probation. The purpose of a split sentence is some assurance that inmates would not be released without some kind of supervision.[45]

SPLIT SENTENCE

A term of jail or imprisonment followed by a period of probation.

FUNCTIONS OF PAROLE TODAY

Parole is far from completely disappearing from the correctional scene. In most states today, a parole board or some similar body with a different name retains the power to alter the amount of time served in prison by releasing prisoners to community supervision before the completion of the maximum sentence. The parolee population nationwide as of December 31, 1999, totaled more than 712,000 prisoners, or 352 people per 100,000 adults in outside society (see Table 9.2).[46] Table 9.2 also provides the number of prisoners on parole in each state and in the federal system.

Ericka Watson/The Childress Index

Project RIO is a program that exists within the Texas Department of Criminal Justice to reduce recidivism through preparing prisoners and parolees for gainful employment upon release. Project RIO stands for "Re-Integration of Offenders," which remains one of the purposes of parole.

As of January 1, 1999, most parolees were men, but nearly 11 percent of offenders on parole were women (see Table 9.3). In terms of ethnic background, 20.5 percent of parolees were of Hispanic origin. The race category breakdowns were white, 44.9 percent; black, 43.9 percent; Asian or Native American, 0.9 percent; and "other," 10.3 percent.[47] However, note that Hispanic is not considered a separate race category. For example, Hispanics can be reported in official statistics as part of the white race or as "other."

The function of parole is arguably different now than it was traditionally. Parole used to serve as a more gradual, supervised transition from prison to the community to aid in reintegration and reduce recidivism. The ideal goal was to modify the situation from that of the law-abiding taxpayer supporting the offender to that of ex-offenders legitimately supporting themselves.

According to Frank P. Williams III, Marilyn D. McShane, and H. Michael Dolny, the function of parole has changed:

> [P]arole is tasked primarily with protecting the public from released offenders. This goal is accomplished in three general objectives: (1) by enforcing restrictions and controls on parolees in the community, (2) by providing services that help parolees integrate into a non-criminal lifestyle, and (3) by increasing the public's level of confidence in the effectiveness and responsiveness of parole services through the first two activities (i.e., in part a reduction in fear of crime).[48]

Bringing Back Parole Boards

After abolishing parole, some states were faced with burgeoning prison populations and were forced to reintroduce parole—usually by another name. California abolished parole and then introduced the Board of Prison Terms, which had almost identical responsibilities as the former parole board. Florida abolished the Parole Commission in 1983 and replaced it in 1990 with a Controlled Release Authority. Idaho adopted a hybrid scheme that permitted judges to impose either fixed sentences with no parole eligibility or indeterminate sentences, with the parole board

TABLE 9.2 *Adults on Parole under State and Federal Jurisdiction, 1999*

Region and Jurisdiction	Parole Population December 31, 1999	Percent Change in Parole Population during 1999	Number on Parole on December 31, 1999 per 100,000 Adult Residents
United States, total	712,713	2.3	352
Federal	71,020	5.7	35
State	641,693	2.0	317
Northeast	162,840	0.5	415
Connecticut	1,526	9.3	62
Maine	31	−6.1	3
Massachusetts[a]	4,304	−4.1	91
New Hampshire	1,146	0.4	128
New Jersey	12,968	−1.9	211
New York	57,956	−2.7	421
Pennsylvania	83,702	3.3	916
Rhode Island	413	−4.4	55
Vermont[a]	794	6.1	175
Midwest	100,021	6.3	213
Illinois	30,484	0.2	341
Indiana[a]	4,539	6.6	103
Iowa[a]	2,514	14.6	117
Kansas	5,909	−1.9	302
Michigan	15,541	1.4	213
Minnesota	3,151	5.2	90
Missouri	11,448	10.4	281
Nebraska[a]	612	−1.9	50
North Dakota	157	−9.8	33
Ohio[a]	15,776	39.6	188
South Dakota[a]	1,360	20.9	254
Wisconsin	8,530	−8.1	219
South	223,469	−0.2	312
Alabama[a]	5,005	−4.1	151
Arkansas	7,645	9.5	404
Delaware[a]	634	10.8	111
District of Columbia	5,103	b	1,204

setting release dates.[49] The U.S. Parole Commission was scheduled initially to be phased out by 1992 but was extended until 2002. In 1985 Colorado reinstated parole, six years after abolition, and Connecticut did the same in 1990. North Carolina, which had severely limited the use of parole, has since allowed more discretion.[50]

Prison Population Control

Parole boards have always been the "backdoor keeper" of America's prisons, often serving as the operators of safety valves to relieve crowded institutions.[51] Although this function is not consistent with the philosophy of parole as a tool of rehabilitation, and most paroling authorities do not believe that the management of prison populations is (or should be) their primary responsibility, it has become a de facto if

TABLE 9.2 *Adults on Parole under State and Federal Jurisdiction, 1999* (continued)

Region and Jurisdiction	Parole Population December 31, 1999	Percent Change in Parole Population during 1999	Number on Parole on December 31, 1999 per 100,000 Adult Residents
South (continued)			
Florida[a]	6,418	−1.1	56
Georgia	22,003	7.4	384
Kentucky[a]	4,868	8.0	163
Louisiana	21,904	16.8	688
Maryland[a]	15,007	−3.4	389
Mississippi	1,356	−8.9	67
North Carolina	4,389	−24.4	77
Oklahoma	1,527	−0.3	62
South Carolina	3,944	−10.4	135
Tennessee	7,338	−3.5	177
Texas	109,310	−0.5	763
Virginia	5,860	−12.5	113
West Virginia	1,158	18.8	83
West	155,363	4.1	348
Alaska[a]	493	3.1	117
Arizona[a]	3,742	−0.7	108
California[a]	114,046	5.2	471
Colorado[a]	5,263	1.1	176
Hawaii[a]	2,252	12.1	251
Idaho[a]	1,310	0.1	145
Montana[a]	549	−17.7	83
Nevada	3,893	−4.0	295
New Mexico	1,922	8.4	154
Oregon	17,874	3.5	718
Utah	3,388	−1.1	238
Washington	200	−46.7	5
Wyoming	458	2.2	130

[a] Data do not include parolees in one or more of the following categories: absconder, out of state, inactive, intensive supervision, or electronic monitoring.
[b] Comparable percentage could not be calculated.
Source: U.S. Department of Justice, Bureau of Justice Statistics, *Probation and Parole in 1999*, NCJ 183508 (Washington, DC: U.S. Department of Justice, July 2000), 5.

not a de jure function.[52] Recent years, however, have witnessed an institutionalization of this function.

Some states have given legislative authority and direction to their parole boards to control prison populations. Others have done so through informal agreements among the governor, the director of corrections, and the parole board. Boards in states such as Georgia, Michigan, and Texas have become actively involved in prison population management out of necessity. Prison populations in those states had risen to levels that threatened the correctional authorities' ability to maintain control of their institutions. In Georgia the governor cited an "atmosphere of tension, and potentially explosive violence."[53] Federal court orders established "caps" on the prison populations in Michigan and Texas. Through a variety of formal and informal methods, parole boards in each of these jurisdictions have been utilized in efforts to

TABLE 9.3 *Parolees under Active Supervision on January 1, 1999*

| State | Total Number | PERCENTAGE | | PERCENTAGE | | | | | |
		Male	Female	Black	White	Asian/ Pacific Islander	Native American/ Native Alaskan	Other	Hispanic
Alaska	630	79.0%	21.0%	9.5%	53.0%	0.6%	34.9%	1.9%	1.9%
Arizona	3,801	90.0	10.0	15.9	45.6	0.2	4.1	34.2	33.0
Arkansas	6,371	85.8	14.2	49.0	49.5	0.3	0.1	1.1	1.1
California	111,875	89.7	10.3	25.4	70.4	1.1	0.7	2.5	39.6
Colorado[a, b]	3,678	88 0.7	11.3	25.2	72.2	0.4	1.8	0.4	26.5
Connecticut	1,232	90.3	9.7	44.2	29.1	0.4	0.2	26.1	26.1
Delaware	572	94.4	5.6	57.5	38.6	0.0	0.2	3.7	3.7
District of Columbia	3,564	93.0	7.0	97.0	3.0	0.0	0.0	0.0	0.0
Florida	2,267	92.3	7.7	38.9	55.1	0.7	0.0	5.2	10.2
Georgia	21,223	89.2	10.8	66.5	33.5	0.0	0.0	0.0	0.0
Hawaii[c]	1,369	85.4	14.6	d	d	d	d	d	
Idaho[e]	1,165	90.0	10.0	1.1	79.3	0.9	2.1	16.5	16.3
Illinois[e]	30,704	90.6	9.4	67.9	23.9	0.1	0.1	7.9	7.9
Indiana	4,258	92.1	7.9	d	d	d	d	d	d
Iowa[e]	2,194	88.3	11.7	14.2	80.9	0.2	1.3	3.3	3.2
Kansas[f, g]	4,875	88.6	11.4	33.3	63.9	0.5	1.9	0.5	6.0
Louisiana	20,276	d	d	d	d	d	d	d	d
Maine	883	80.0	20.0	3.6	87.9	0.5	0.0	8.0	7.0
Maryland	15,528	92.0	8.0	75.4	24.4	0.2	0.1	0.2	0.0
Massachusetts	3,838	91.9	8.1	24.5	57.9	0.7	0.1	16.8	16.7
Michigan	12,096	d	d	d	d	d	d	d	d
Minnesota[h]	667	89.5	10.5	10.0	81.0	0.0	7.9	1.0	4.9
Mississippi	1,849	90 0.8	9.2	71.3	28.1	0.0	0.0	0.6	0.5
Missouri	10,366	90.3	9.7	39.8	59.7	0.1	0.1	0.2	0.0
Nebraska	684	87.3	12.7	22.4	74.3	0.6	2.8	0.0	8.6
Nevada	3,736	88.0	12.0	33.0	59.0	0.3	1.5	6.2	11.5
New Hampshire	883	80.0	20.0	3.6	87.9	0.5	0.0	8.0	7.0
New Jersey	14,557	89.0	11.0	71.1	28.5	0.4	0.0	0.0	20.5
New York[e]	52,887	90.8	9.2	50.2	15.8	0.0	0.0	34.0	31.9
North Carolina[i]	5,733	90.2	9.8	60.9	35.1	0.1	2.5	1.4	0.5

reduce and maintain the prison population, with varying and arguable degrees of success.

Most authorities agree, however, that it is not feasible, in the long term, to control prison populations by parole board action. The reductions achieved in those states that so use their paroling power are, at best, temporary—and have often achieved those results to the detriment of effective postrelease supervision because of escalating caseloads. Edward R. Rhine, William Smith, and Ronald W. Jackson concluded that when parole boards are used as the "back door" for overcrowded prisons, the population crisis is often simply transferred from the institutional component of corrections to the community component. They report that many jurisdictions have increased and expanded community correctional facilities—such as halfway houses, work release centers, house arrest, electronic monitoring, and intensive supervision—to monitor the offenders who are granted early release. Furthermore, in some states the continuing escalation in prison populations has had another, albeit unanticipated, effect on the ability of parole officers to revoke parole for anything other than serious criminal violations. In several states parole officers have experienced dif-

TABLE 9.3   *Parolees under Active Supervision on January 1, 1999 (continued)*

State	Total Number	PERCENTAGE		PERCENTAGE					
		Male	Female	Black	White	Asian/ Pacific Islander	Native American/ Native Alaskan	Other	Hispanic
North Dakota	212	84.4	15.6	3.3	83.5	0.0	13.2	0.0	3.8
Ohioj	8,685	92.7	7.3	56.5	39.5	0.0	0.0	4.0	1.8
Oklahoma	2,014	82.0	18.0	28.5	62.1	0.0	3.5	5.9	5.3
Oregon	10,589	88.6	11.4	11.6	79.5	0.8	1.7	6.3	6.3
Pennsylvania	16,762	91.4	8.6	49.8	42.1	0.1	0.0	7.9	7.8
Rhode Island	597	d	d	d	d	d	d	d	d
South Carolina	3,381	89.5	10.5	68.3	31.3	0.1	0.1	0.3	0.0
South Dakota	1,125	86.0	14.0	0.0	80.5	0.0	14.4	5.1	0.0
Tennessee	7,605	90.3	9.7	55.5	44.2	0.3	0.1 0.0	0.5	
Texase	76,988	86.5	13.5	44.3	33.6	0.1	0.1	21.9	21.8
Utah	3,839	90.3	9.7	6.0	88.7	1.6	2.5	1.2	20.2
Vermont	691	90.2	9.8	1.0	98.3	0.0	0.7	0.0	0.0
Virginia	6,700	89.6	10.4	63.3	35.9	0.0	0.0	0.8	0.4
West Virginia	975	90.8	9.2	18.3	81.7	0.0	0.0	0.0	0.4
Wisconsin	7,507	d	d	d	d	d	d	d	d
Wyoming	457	86.7	13.3	4.2	81.4	0.0	3.5	10.9	10.3
Federalk	6,000								
Total and average	**497,888**	**88.7%**	**11.3%**	**35.6%**	**55.5%**	**0.3%**	**2.6%**	**6.1%**	**9.1%**
Percentage of total		**89.4**	**10.6**	**43.9**	**44.9**	**0.4**	**0.5**	**10.3**	**20.5**

a Figures are estimates.   b Hispanic reported in white race.   c Racial breakdown data not available.   dData not provided.   e"Other" includes Hispanics.   fFigures do not include interstate compact supervision.   gUnknown included in "Other."   hMinnesota does not have parole but has supervised release under a sentencing guideline system. A parole system is in place for life-sentenced, first-degree murder inmates only.   iTotal includes absconders.   jFigures are for total population, active, and administrative (inactive).   kFigures as of January 1, 1997.
Source: Camille Graham Camp and George C. Camp, *The Corrections Yearbook: 1999* (Middletown, CT: Criminal Justice Institute, 1999).

ficulty in revoking parolees for technical violations of the conditions of supervision, even when indications exist of deteriorating behavior on the part of the parolee.

Good-Time Policies

In some jurisdictions, parole boards may handle good-time decisions. Most of the new laws, even the states without discretionary parole, have retained policies for **good time,** which award prisoners days off their minimum or maximum terms for maintaining good behavior or participating in various prison activities or programs. The amount of good time that can be accrued varies widely among states, ranging from 5 days to as much as 45 days per month off an inmate's time in prison. Because a good-time policy can greatly reduce sentenced terms, it can be a real incentive for cooperative behavior.

It is more common for good-time policies to be written into many states' statutes, but they may also be nonstatutory, systemwide correctional policies. Good time is typically awarded and administered by the state department of corrections. Typically

GOOD TIME

Reduction in sentence for institutional good conduct.

this credit is automatically awarded and subtracted from a prisoner's sentenced term at the time of prison entry and then rescinded in whole or in part for unsatisfactory behavior. In Oregon good-behavior credit is subtracted from the maximum sentence and does not affect a prisoner's parole eligibility date or actual time served unless the prisoner is not paroled and serves the maximum term. More typically, however, the minimum sentence is reduced by good time, so that good-time policies are a significant element in prison term length. This is particularly true in states that have eliminated discretionary parole release.

A few states award good-time credit in ways that do not reduce sentence length. In New Hampshire, for example, a number of disciplinary days are automatically added to the minimum term, and it is from this number that good-behavior days are subtracted. If the prisoner accrues all of his or her good time, the disciplinary days will cancel out, and the parole eligibility date will occur, as scheduled, on the completion of the minimum sentence. Otherwise the prisoner is penalized by a delay in the eligibility date.

Good-time reductions based on prisoners' positive actions are in effect in most states and the federal system. These reductions result from participating in various programs (such as work, school, rehabilitative counseling) or from meritorious conduct (including success under minimum security).

Parole Revocation

Parole boards in most jurisdictions continue to handle parole revocation decisions. Parole is revoked when one or more of the parole conditions are not met. Parole revocation is discussed in greater detail in Chapter 11.

Medical Parole

Parole can be a back-end release strategy for prisoners who pose minimal security risk and who would be better served in the community. One type of prisoner that would likely fall into this category would be prisoners with terminal illnesses, particularly those with full-blown AIDS (acquired immune deficiency syndrome).

Because prisons have experienced significant increases in inmates who have tested positive for HIV (human immunodeficiency virus) or who are dying of an infection as a result of AIDS, state correctional systems have recently created policies for medical parole. **Medical parole** is the conditional release from prison to the community for prisoners with a terminal illness who do not pose an undue risk to public safety. Many states (53 percent) and localities (29 percent) have a medical parole policy, but few states utilize this option.[54] Sixteen states that use medical parole, such as Missouri, New York, and South Carolina, do so sparingly, in a small number of cases.[55]

THE MARYLAND MEDICAL PAROLE PROGRAM: Every state has its own procedures for determining candidacy for medical parole and establishes for itself which parties (doctors, judges, parole boards, wardens, and governors) partake in the decision-making process. Newton E. Kendig and his colleagues conducted research on the medical parole program in Maryland.[56] Inmates were initially nominated by prison nurses and doctors who worked with terminally ill prisoners with a documented diagnosis and full medical evaluation. Once the inmates were medically eligible, a security evaluation of the level of risk that the inmate may pose in the community took place by the warden and a case management team. If the inmate posed a minimal risk, then an aftercare plan would be put together by a social worker. Inmates were candidates for this program if:

They "no longer jeopardized public safety if released" and at least one of the following three conditions existed:

1. A verifiable terminal medical condition
2. A medical condition that incapacitated the individual that imprisonment was not required to ensure public safety
3. A medical condition that could be more appropriately treated in a community treatment facility instead of a prison.[57]

Kendig and his colleagues describe the next level of scrutiny that these nominated cases undergo after they pass the inspection of prison unit employees:

These evaluations were reviewed by the DOC [Department of Corrections] medical director, the director of social work, and the assistant commissioner for inmate health care, who then recommended for or against medical parole to the commissioner of correction. Upon review of the relevant assessments and recommendations, the commissioner of correction either ruled against medical parole or forwarded his recommendation for medical parole to the Maryland Parole Commission. . . . Inmates with life sentences or parole-restricted sentences . . . were referred by the Maryland Parole Commission with a recommendation for parole to the governor for gubernatorial approval or denial.[58]

Kendig and his colleagues reviewed all 230 cases that were submitted for medical parole from 1991 to 1994. Of those cases, 144 (62 percent) were approved for parole, but only 120 were released (some prisoners died prior to being approved or released). The major findings by Kendig and his colleagues included a follow-up of the 120 released inmates at the end of 1994. They found that 60 inmates were still on parole in the community, 54 inmates died, 2 inmates had successfully completed their sentences (and were not on parole), and 4 inmates had failed parole and returned to prison. Three of the four inmates who had returned to prison committed technical violations (for example, verbally threatening staff, using illegal drugs, and moving to a new address without notifying the parole officer). One inmate violated parole by committing an armed robbery. After serving 12 months in prison for the robbery, this inmate was released and died two months later. The researchers concluded that "early release for inmates with terminal illnesses can be accomplished expeditiously and with minimal impact on public safety."[59]

Large-scale evaluations of medical parole have not yet been conducted, so its effectiveness in other areas on public safety and receiving treatment services in the community remain to be seen.

Other Parole Functions

Discretionary parole may also continue in these jurisdictions to a limited extent for three groups of offenders: (1) persons sentenced before the current structure went into effect (for example, before parole was abolished or after parole was reinstated); (2) persons sentenced to life imprisonment, and (3) youthful offenders with special circumstances.

SUMMARY

Parole is different from other forms of release and community supervision, but the term *parole* is often used interchangeably with *probation*, *pardon*, and *mandatory release*. The misunderstanding and misapprehensions about parole today to some extent stem from this semantic confusion.

Parole has origins in the work of penal reformers in Germany, Spain, and France and on Norfolk Island in the early decades of the 19th century. The Norfolk Island experiments with ticket-of-leave and the mark system by a former British naval officer, Alexander Maconochie, constitute the origins of parole as it is known in the United States. Walter Crofton, head of the Irish prison system, studied Maconochie's work on Norfolk Island and implemented his ideas in Ireland. U.S. prison reformer Zebulon R. Brockway noticed Crofton's efforts, and Brockway adopted them in 1876 at the Elmira Reformatory in New York. This program was the first to use parole in the United States.

Although the beginning of the 21st century finds corrections embroiled in controversy, engaged in self-examination, and subjected to scrutiny by the public and the courts, the issues involved—prison overcrowding, the efficacy of probation and parole, sentencing disparity, parole release decision making, and the continued existence of parole—are not new. Neither are the proposed solutions. The inertia of the criminal justice system is as great as is its failure to learn the lessons of history.

More than a century ago the leading penologists of the time met in Cincinnati to form the National Prison Association, now the American Correctional Association. The main objective of that first meeting in 1870 was to attempt to resolve the conflict between those who advocated the punishment-centered Pennsylvania and Auburn prison systems and those who advocated a progressive new system recently imported from Ireland. The new system, which appealed to progressive prison administrators, had three main factors: trade training, the indeterminate sentence, and parole.

What emerged was the remarkable "Declaration of Principles," a blueprint for the future of U.S. corrections. The concepts of vocational training, indeterminate sentencing, and parole were established and for the most part embraced by the leadership of the newly emerging discipline of corrections. Since that time these same issues have been scrutinized, rejected, embraced, modified, codified, outlawed, and reincarnated under new labels. Presidential commissions have recommended the extension of parole and indeterminacy of sentencing and the outright abolition of the same. The optimal solution is not yet at hand. History teaches that all too often the unanticipated and unintended consequences of reform have aggravated rather than mitigated the problems they sought to solve. Prudence in reform efforts is advisable, and such lessons as can be learned from past efforts should be carefully evaluated.

DISCUSSION QUESTIONS

1 How is parole different from probation and pardons?
2 Discuss the founders of parole and their contributions.
3 What is the mark system, and what is its relationship to the origins of parole?
4 What was a ticket-of-leave, and what is its relationship to the origins of parole?
5 What was transportation? What is the connection between transportation and parole?
6 What were the five stages in Alexander Maconochie's mark system? How did his system differ from the English practice of ticket-of-leave?
7 How did parole develop in the United States? Be sure to include discussions of the Irish system, Zebulon R. Brockway, and the indeterminate sentence in your explanation.
8 Why did the medical model fall out of favor? What factors were associated with this phenomenon?

9   What is the justice model of corrections? What factors were associated with its emergence in the 1970s?

10   What happened to parole under the justice model? Why?

11   What role does parole play in the 21st century?

12   What are the pros and cons of abolishing parole?

13   How do you feel about the use of medical parole?

WEB SITES

U.S. Parole Commission

http://www.usdoj.gov/uspc/parole.htm

U.S. Department of Justice
Parole statistics

http://www.ojp.usdoj.gov/bjs/pandp.htm

Parolee Services

http://www.cdc.state.ca.us/program/parole3.htm

History of Parole in Alabama

http://www.al.com/news/birmingham/Dec2000/18-history.html

History of Parole in Delaware

http://www.state.de.us/parole/history.htm

History of Parole in Texas

http://tdcj.state.tx.us/parole/parole-history.htm

History of Parole in Utah

http://www.cr.ex.state.ut.us/lawenforcement/bop/history.html

History of Parole in Canada

http://www.npb-cnlc.gc.ca/infocntr/parolec/phistore.htm

Please go to the book-specific Web site for Supplemental Readings related to the material in this chapter:
A Case Study of Abolishing Parole in Virginia
http://www.wadsworth.com/product/0-534-559662s

10

The Parole Board and Parole Selection

R. Ramey/Stock Boston

What You Will Learn in This Chapter

In this chapter you will learn about the characteristics of discretionary parole. You also will learn about the parole selection process, particularly traditional parole decision making and selection methods that rely on objective measures of potential risk. Special attention is paid to the question of due process in parole selection, with an emphasis on appellate court decisions addressing the issue.

INTRODUCTION

Both determinate and indeterminate sentencing policies allow the release of felony offenders from prison to parole or some other form of community supervision. In general, determinate sentencing has automatic or mandatory release, while a distinguishing characteristic of indeterminate sentencing is discretionary release by a **parole board.** A big difference exists, then, between parole boards and parole officers. All parole boards have four basic functions:

1. To decide which offenders should be released from prison
2. To determine the conditions of parole
3. To successfully discharge the parolee when the conditions have been met
4. To determine whether parole privileges should be revoked[1]

Some parole boards have additional functions, such as reviewing pardons and executive clemency decisions made by the governor, restoring civil rights to ex-offenders, and granting reprieves in death sentence cases. Each state establishes the extent of its own parole board's authority.

Once an offender is released on parole, parole officers (also called parole agents) enforce the conditions set by the parole board by supervising the parolee in the community. Offenders released in states without parole boards are still supervised on conditional release by parole officers.

The role of the discretionary parole board in the decision to release an offender from prison is examined in this chapter.

ORGANIZATIONAL MODELS OF PAROLE

Parole services are administered within the governmental structure that assures the most effective coordination with other prisons and with community-based correctional agencies such as probation, halfway houses, and drug and alcohol treatment agencies. Parole services are administered in one of three ways:

1. By a separate independent parole system (the autonomous model)
2. By the state correctional agency that administers both probation and institutional services (consolidation model)
3. By the department that administers the state correctional institutions (the institutional model)

In the **autonomous model,** both parole decision making and supervision are done by a completely independent authority. In other words, the parole board makes decisions on release and revocation as well as supervises people released on parole.

PAROLE BOARD

An administrative body (usually 3–18 members) empowered to decide whether inmates shall be conditionally released from prison before the completion of their sentence, to revoke parole, and to discharge from parole those who have satisfactorily completed their terms.

AUTONOMOUS MODEL

An organizational pattern in which parole decisions are made by an autonomous body not affiliated with other agencies of the criminal justice system. The most common pattern for adult paroling authorities.

Proponents of the autonomous model believe that it is more successful in gaining budgetary resources from the legislature and more effective in controlling for accountability.

In the **consolidation model,** parole decisions are made by a central authority that has independent powers, although the supervision of parolees is organizationally situated in the department of corrections. The parole board makes release and revocation decisions, but parolees are supervised by parole officers from the department of corrections. The consolidation model was developed later by states that wished to consolidate institutional (prison) and field (parole) programs into a single corrections department. Advocates of this model contend that it provides greater sensitivity to institutional programs. At the same time, the structural model separates parole decisions from the institution's immediate control, thereby giving appropriate weight to parole considerations beyond management of the institution.

The **institutional model,** most prevalent in juvenile corrections, centers parole decision making primarily in the institutions. Advocates of the institutional model believe that because the institutional staff is most familiar with offenders' response to institutional programs, they are most sensitive to the optimum time for release.

ELIGIBILITY FOR PAROLE

The first step in the parole process is that an offender must be eligible for parole consideration. Those permanently ineligible for parole include offenders on death row, offenders serving life without parole, and some habitual offenders sentenced under statutes such as "three strikes and you're out."

Time Sheets and Eligibility Dates

For the rest of the inmates, a computer keeps track of all good time earned and number of days served to determine a minimum eligibility date and a maximum eligibility date.[2] The **minimum eligibility date** is the shortest amount of time defined by statute, minus good time earned, that must be served before the offender can go before the parole board. Some states, such as Nebraska, are required to see offenders once per year, even if the minimum eligibility date has not yet been met.[3] The **maximum eligibility date** is the longest amount of time that can be served before the inmate must be released by law (where the offender has "maxed out" his or her sentence).

Good time (or "gain time") was originally introduced as an incentive by prison authorities for institutional good conduct. Good time reduces the period of sentence an inmate must serve before parole eligibility. Now, good time is automatically granted (in states that have it) unless the inmate commits a disciplinary infraction. That is, good time is lost for misbehavior, not awarded for good behavior. Good-time credits vary greatly from state to state, ranging from 5 days per month to as much as 45 days per month. In recent years large amounts of good time have been awarded (for example, 120 days for every month served) by correctional authorities who are forced to temporarily increase the good time to reduce prison overcrowding and avoid a lawsuit. When jail and prison crowding subsides, good time is decreased to the usual amount.

Typically, the case manager at each prison institution must submit good time earned (or in some cases, submit good time lost) to the parole board or the division within the department of corrections that prepares status or time sheets. Offenders receive an updated time sheet every six months to one year so they know when to expect their first parole hearing.

Prisoners generally become eligible for parole at the completion of their minimum sentence. The manner in which a **parole eligibility date** is established varies from state to state. Many states require an inmate to have served one-third of the imposed sentence to be eligible for consideration for parole. Thus, a 15-year sentence would require that 5 years be served before parole eligibility. However, most statutes allow further reductions in the eligibility date through credit for time served in jail before sentencing and good-time credits.

Some states credit good time to the inmate upon arrival in prison and calculate the eligibility date by subtracting credited good time from the maximum sentence. An inmate who is serving a 15-year sentence and receiving standard good time of 20 days per month (50 days' credit on his or her sentence for each 30 days served) would be eligible for parole consideration after 40 months.

As the first parole eligibility date approaches, institutional case managers (also called institutional parole officers in some states) prepare an individualized prerelease plan for the parole board. Leanne Fiftal Alarid, one of this book's coauthors, prepared prerelease plans and attended monthly parole board hearings with offenders on her caseload who were scheduled to see the board.

PAROLE ELIGIBILITY DATE

The point in a prisoner's sentence at which he or she becomes eligible to be considered for parole. If the offender is denied parole, a new parole eligibility date is scheduled in the future.

Prerelease Preparation within the Institution

Some states have hearing officers who interview the prisoners and report directly to the parole board with their recommendation. Other states submit written reports along with the case file. Having some form of prerelease plan prepared in advance of a scheduled parole hearing has two main advantages:

1. A prerelease plan increases an offender's chances of parole because it solidifies living arrangements and work opportunities.
2. A prerelease plan saves time during the parole board hearing.

An institutional case manager meets with the prisoner in an interview to document where the inmate will be living, including names of people and an exact address for the household. A different (local) field parole officer will check out the address and interview household members to ensure that the address is a valid and acceptable place for the offender to be living. Offenders are discouraged from paroling to "themselves," which means living and supporting oneself without any assistance. Because most offenders, at the time of release from prison, do not have the money required for rent and utility deposits, the vast majority must parole to an existing household of a friend or relative. In an effort to assist offenders in community reintegration, paroling some offenders to a halfway house or community residential center is helpful. Halfway houses can provide a graduated sanction that is less than prison, but more supervision than regular parole. This is ideal for offenders who are nearing the end of their sentences (so release is inevitable) but pose an increased risk to public safety.

The institutional case manager documents the amount of money the prisoner has in savings and any job leads or specific employment plans the prisoner has upon release. According to Joan Petersilia, most prisoners leave prison without any savings and few solid job prospects.[4] The case manager then summarizes any programs the offender has attended or completed (for example, general equivalency diploma courses) while in prison and then makes a list of all disciplinary infractions (write-ups) the prisoner received during the entire period of incarceration.

Essentially, the case manager brings together official data (for example, current conviction, current age, amount of time served for the current conviction, number of prior prison incarcerations, number and type of prior convictions) along with data about the offender's education level, employment history, and substance abuse history. All of the information is written and scored using a systematic, report-style for the parole board to interpret at the parole hearing. In other words, the institutional case manager prepares a report according to predefined state parole guidelines for the parole board to interpret, much like a probation officer prepares a presentence investigation for a judge to read at time of sentencing.

Time is saved during the parole board hearing because the parole board does not have to go searching through offender files (many of which are fairly thick) to find the factors that measure the risk level that the offender will pose when released. The parole board, however, did not always function in this manner.

THE PAROLE BOARD

The vast majority of state parole board members are full-time, salaried employees (see Table 10.1). In the states with both full-time and part-time members, the chair is usually full time and the other members serve on a part-time basis. Many authorities view the part-time board of parole, often found in smaller states, as one of the most severe problems in correctional release decisions. Able to give only a limited amount of time to the job because of their business or professional concerns, part-timers cannot participate effectively in correctional decision making. There has been a trend toward increasing the number of full-time boards.[5]

Table 10.1 also lists the size of parole boards in each state. Parole boards range from 3 to 59 members, with an average of 7 board members. Most felony cases do not require a "full board review"—when all members of the board review the case. If a full board review is specified in the state statute, it is usually for crimes of a violent or sexual nature. Illinois (12 members) and Indiana (5 members) are the only two states that require a full board approval to grant parole in all cases.[6]

In cases not involving a full board review, a panel of three or four representatives reviews the case. In general, the number of parole board members required to grant parole is a majority (two-thirds), but a vote of an average of two members is required to revoke parole.[7]

Term and Qualifications of the Parole Board

In most states, the governor appoints parole board members.[8] In all but six states (Georgia, Michigan, Minnesota, Ohio, West Virginia, and Wisconsin) parole board members are appointed for a specified term, typically four or six years.[9] Parole board members should be of such integrity, intelligence, and good judgment as to command respect and public confidence. Because of the importance of their quasi-judicial functions, they must possess the equivalent personal qualifications of a high judicial officer. They must be forthright, courageous, and independent. Board members should have sufficiently broad academic training and experience that qualifies them for professional practice in fields such as criminal justice, education, psychiatry, psychology, law, social work, and sociology. Each member must have the capacity and the desire to learn and understand legal processes, the dynamics of human behavior, and cultural conditions contributing to crime. Ideally, parole board members have previous professional experience that has given them intimate knowledge of the human experience—situations and problems confronting offenders.[10]

Statutes vary in the explicitness with which they specify the qualifications of a parole board member. A few require only that the member be of "good moral character." Edward E. Rhine and his associates reported that over half of the jurisdictions had no requirement that board members possess any special professional qualifications. In these states, the governor may nominate any person without regard for education, training, or experience. Others cite specific educational or special qualifications. For example, New York statutes require that each member of its board graduate from an accredited college or university with a degree in criminology, criminal justice, law enforcement, sociology, law, social work, psychology, psychiatry, or medicine, plus five or more years of experience in one of those fields. Montana requires that at least one board member have "particular knowledge of Indian culture and problems."[11]

A parole board should be entirely free from political control, manipulation, or influence from pressure groups. The American Correctional Association (ACA) recommends that parole board members be forbidden to participate in partisan political activities and that they be granted independence and security of tenure to resist interference successfully.[12]

THE PAROLE HEARING

The decision to grant parole is complicated, and the consequences of the decision are of the gravest importance both for society and for the inmate. In a classic study of parole board hearings, David T. Stanley concluded that parole board hearings are merely ceremonial in nature and that the real decisions are made in advance of the hearing, largely affected by institutional reports, such as that completed by correctional case managers.[13] The parole board makes a decision on each case out of three possible options: grant parole, deny parole, or defer to a later date. A decision to grant parole results in conditional release before the expiration of the maximum term of imprisonment. A denial results in continued imprisonment. A deferral means that the parole board has delayed their decision (to grant or deny) until a later time, somewhere between one and six months.[14] For indeterminate sentences, the parole release decision is often more important than the court's sentence in determining how long the prisoner spends incarcerated. Parole decisions involve the maximization of both public safety and offender rehabilitation.[15]

Under discretionary parole practice, the prisoner is given a first parole hearing shortly before completing the minimum term. The majority of parole hearings are held inside designated state prisons. The attending parole board members will have access to the entire offender case file with the summary report completed by the institutional case manager. Some states examine the case file only without interviewing the offender, while other parole boards have access to the case file and are able to interview the offender in person. Each state varies as to who can attend the hearing. Most states do not permit legal representation or the offender's family at parole hearings, but they will allow relatives or others associated with the offender to write letters

TABLE 10.1 *Paroling Authority Characteristics on January 1, 1999*

| State | PAROLE BOARD MEMBERS | | | NUMBER OF BOARD MEMBERS REQUIRED TO | | STAFF CONDUCT HEARINGS IN LIEU OF BOARD TO | |
	Full Time	Size	Salaried	Grant Parole	Revoke Parole	Grant Parole	Revoke Parole
Alabama	X	3	X	2	2	X	X
Alabama	X	3	X	2	2	X	X
Alaska		5		3	3		
Arizona[a]	X	5	X	2	2	X	X
Arkansas	X	7	X	5	0		
California[b]	X	59	X	3	1		
Colorado	X	7	X	1	1		
Connecticut				2	2		
Delaware[c]							
District of Columbia[d]	X	3	X	0	0	X	X
Florida[a]							
Georgia	X	5	X		1		
Hawaii	X	3	X	2	2		
Idaho		5		3	3	X	
Illinois	X	12	X	12	3		
Indiana	X	5	X	5	5		
Iowa	X	5	X	3			
Kansas	X	4	X	3	2		
Kentucky	X	7	X				
Louisiana	X	7	X	3	3		
Maine		5		3	3		
Maryland	X	8	X	2	1		
Massachusetts	X	7	X	3	3	X	X
Michigan	X	10	X	3	3		
Minnesota[c]							
Mississippi	X	5	X	3	3		
Missouri	X	6	X	1	1		
Montana		5		3	3		
Nebraska	X	5	X	3	3		
Nevada	X	7	X	3	3		
New Hampshire		7		3	3		

or submit any other pertinent information for use at the hearing. The vast majority of states do, however, allow victims to attend or to submit impact statements.

Victim Participation in Parole Hearings

One of the major changes in parole board hearings is the increased involvement and participation of crime victims in parole board hearings. Approximately 90 percent of parole boards provide victims with information about the parole process, and 70 percent allow victims to attend the parole hearing.[16] A **victim impact statement** mentions how the crime has taken a toll physically, emotionally, financially, or psychologically on the victim and the victim's family. Many victim impact statements cite how the victim continues to experience psychological, physical, or financial difficulties as a direct result of the actions of the offender.[17]

The majority of states allow victims to present written statements, oral statements, or both. However, "few state laws provide clear guidelines detailing the nature

VICTIM IMPACT STATEMENT

A written account by the victim(s) as to how the crime has taken a toll physically, emotionally, financially, or psychologically on the victim and the victim's family. Victim impact statements are considered by many states at time of sentencing and at parole board hearings.

TABLE 10.1 *Paroling Authority Characteristics on January 1, 1999* (continued)

State	PAROLE BOARD MEMBERS			NUMBER OF BOARD MEMBERS REQUIRED TO		STAFF CONDUCT HEARINGS IN LIEU OF BOARD TO	
	Full Time	Size	Salaried	Grant Parole	Revoke Parole	Grant Parole	Revoke Parole
New Jersey	X	9	X	2	2	X	X
New Mexico	X	3	X	2	2		
New York	X	19	X	2	1		X
North Carolina	X	3	X	2	2		
North Dakota		6		2	2		
Ohio	X	12	X	1	0	X	X
Oklahoma		5	X	3			X
Oregon	X	3	X				
Pennsylvania	X	9	X			X	X
Rhode Island							
South Carolina		7		5	3		
South Dakota		6					
Tennessee	X	7	X	4	2	X	X
Texas	X	18	X	3	3		
Utah	X	10	X	1	1	X	X
Vermont		7		3	4		
Virginia	X	5	X				
Washington	X	3	X	2	2		
West Virginia	X	5	X	3	3		
Wisconsin	X	6	X	1	0		
Wyoming		7		3	3		
Federal	X	3	X			X	X
Total or average	**36**	**360**	**37**	**3**	**2**	**11**	**11**

X = Yes.
[a] The parole board is a separate agency and not part of the department of corrections.   [b] The parole board includes 50 deputy commissioners and nine appointed members.   [c] Does not have a parole board.   [d] There are five positions under law. As of January 1, 1999, two were vacant.
Source: Camille Graham Camp and George M. Camp, *The Corrections Yearbook: 1999* (Middletown, CT: Criminal Justice Institute, 1999), 209.

and scope of victim statements, how and when victims are to be notified of their rights, and how parole authorities are to utilize such information."[18] For example, most states are unclear as to whether parole authorities are to keep victim impact statements confidential or if the offender has the right to read, and even respond to, a victim impact statement. States such as Alabama specify that impact statements should be confidential because of the concern that prisoners may attempt to further harm their victim(s) for opposing the offender's release.[19]

Only 17 states make mention in their state statutes that the parole board is to consider victim impact statements (if available) in the parole release decision. Arizona and Oklahoma allow victims to veto (refuse) a parole release decision if the victim requested notification of the hearing but was not given a chance to contribute their opinion.[20]

The effects of victim participation on parole hearings are noteworthy. One study in Pennsylvania found that victim testimony through impact statements was the most significant variable associated with parole refusal decisions.[21] Parole was refused in

43 percent of cases in which victim impact statements were present, but only 7 percent of cases were denied when victim statements were absent.[22]

A similar study conducted in Alabama examined all parole records for one year for violent offenses in which injury to the victim occurred (N = 763). Cases were screened at first based on such factors as offense seriousness, prior criminal history, time served on current conviction, prison disciplinary record, and participation in treatment programs. Once the cases were screened on those factors, victims were notified only in the cases that had a greater likelihood of parole (N = 316). During the parole decision-making process of the screened cases, victim input, especially victims who wrote a statement and attended the hearing, was a significant factor in the parole board's decision.[23]

Parole Deferrals

If the prisoner is not granted parole, another hearing is scheduled after some additional period. Consequently a prisoner may have several parole hearings before release. From the perspective of the traditional rehabilitative model, this practice is both necessary and desirable, because parole decisions are based primarily on rehabilitative concerns. The goal of the parole release authority is to identify the optimal time for release. Thus deferral of the release decision is necessary for monitoring the prisoner's rehabilitative progress.

THE PAROLE RELEASE DECISION

Statutes have typically directed parole boards to base their decisions on one or more of these criteria:

- The probability of recidivism
- The welfare of society
- The conduct of the offender while in the correctional institution
- The sufficiency of the parole plan

Such statutory language does not lend itself to workable decision making, so the parole boards have had to interpret and determine the best means by which to turn the legislative mandate into functioning administrative machinery. This broad discretion has brought criticism upon the paroling authority for making arbitrary, capricious, and disparate decisions. The lack of published standards to guide decision making, combined with the lack of written reasons for parole decisions, contributes to this perception.[24]

Parole Decision Making before the 1970s

Traditionally the hearing stage of parole decision making was thought to allow decision makers to speak with and observe the prospective parolee, to search for and intuit such indications of his or her rehabilitation as repentance, and to discern willingness to accept responsibility. Parole decisions were based not on formally articulated criteria or policies but on subjective intuition of individual decision makers.[25] The courts, to the extent that they were willing to review the parole decision at all, agreed with the contentions of paroling authorities that to impose even minimal due process constraints on the decision process would interfere with the fulfillment of their duty to engage in diagnosis and prognosis.

In 1970, in *Menechino v. Oswald,* the U.S. Court of Appeals held as follows:

> The Board has an identity of interest with [the inmate]. . . . It is seeking to encourage and foster his rehabilitation and readjustment to society. . . . In making this determination the Board is not restricted by rules of evidence developed for the purpose of determining legal or factual issues. It must consider many factors of a nonlegal nature [such as] medicine, psychiatry, criminology[,] . . . psychology and human relations.[26]

Since the 1970s, however, there has been a movement toward the use of objective guidelines in the release decision. The National Advisory Commission on Criminal Justice Standards and Goals suggested that parole decisions be made visible and that parole authorities be made accountable for their decisions through the use of explicit parole selection policies.[27] The American Correctional Association recommended: "The criteria which are employed by the parole authority in its decision making are available in written form and are specific enough to permit consistent application to individual cases."[28]

In his book *Conscience and Convenience,* David J. Rothman discussed the issue of discretionary decision making by parole boards. He reported that in the early 20th century parole boards considered primarily the seriousness of the crime in determining whether to release an inmate on parole. However, no consensus was reached on what constituted a serious crime. "Instead," Rothman wrote, "each member made his own decisions. The judgments were personal and therefore not subject to debate or reconsideration."[29]

Paul F. Cromwell, one of this book's coauthors, served on the Texas Board of Pardons and Paroles in the mid-1970s and observed situations in which board members' biases or preconceptions mitigated for or against a release decision—with little else factored in. One decision maker refused to vote to parole any person convicted of murder. Another member of the same paroling body regarded murder as a situational crime of passion and reminded his colleagues that "murderers have a very low recidivism rate." As Rothman states, "one man's nightmare case did not necessarily frighten another."[30] Another Texas board member looked only at the nature and seriousness of the offense in arriving at a release decision, and his colleague was primarily concerned with an inmate's adjustment and behavior since being incarcerated. She commented, "A person can't do anything about what he did to get here [in prison]. I look at what they have done to get their life in order." Growing recognition of the lack of fundamental fairness in such situations made obvious the need for research-based predictors of recidivism.

Development of Parole Guidelines

In an attempt to make parole selection decisions more rational and consistent, the U.S. Board of Parole established **parole guidelines** in 1972 that structure discretion.[31] By specifying the primary factors to be considered in parole selection and the weight to be assigned to each factor, the paroling authority gives judges, the public, and potential parolees a clearer idea of how it generally exercises its discretion.[32]

Research had shown that parole decisions could be predicted by using specific variables. Three variables were identified as explaining a large number of the board's decisions:

1. The seriousness of the offense
2. The risk posed by the inmate (probability of recidivism)
3. The inmate's institutional behavior (relatively less important than the first two)

PAROLE GUIDELINES

Guidelines to be followed in making parole release decisions. Most guidelines prescribe a presumptive term for each class of convicted inmate depending on both offense and offender characteristics.

The researchers produced a chart that related seriousness of offense and risk of recidivism to suggested terms of imprisonment. Based on this chart, the parole board constructed a matrix by placing the two dimensions—seriousness of offense and risk of recidivism—on the X and Y axes of a graph. Range of sentence length was then determined by plotting intersections of the dimensions on the graph.

The Salient Factor Score

This actuarial device has been continually validated and evaluated for years and was revised several times, the most recent in 1981. Known as the **Salient Factor Score** (SFS), it provides explicit guidelines for release decisions based on a determination of the potential risk of parole violation. The SFS measures six offender characteristics and assigns a score to each. Note in Figure 10.1 that the first offender characteristic considered in the Salient Factor Score calculation is prior convictions/adjudications. This offender characteristic has a score range of 0 to 3. Offenders with no prior convictions are assigned a score of 3; one prior conviction results in a score of 2; two to three prior convictions gives a score of 1; and so on. Each offender characteristic is scored in a similar manner, and the sum of the six items yields the predictive score. The higher the score (maximum of 10) the less likely is the probability of recidivism.[33]

Decision makers then use guidelines to determine the customary time to be served for a range of offenses, based on the severity of the offense (see Figure 10.2). Severity is based on eight categories, ranging from the least to the most severe. For example, an adult offender whose SFS/81 score was 5 and whose offense severity was rated in Category Two would be expected to serve 12–16 months before being paroled.

Although the SFS provided a method of summarizing research data on the relationship between offender characteristics and the likelihood of recidivism, its use with a guidelines system did not eliminate the need for clinical judgment. No prediction device can take into account all the variations in human behavior. Thus the decision maker was allowed to override the Salient Factor Score, but only for articulated, written reasons. If the decision maker chose to make a clinical judgment outside the guidelines, he or she was required to explain the specific factors considered in the decision to override the SFS.[34]

In his extensive study of the effectiveness of the SFS, Peter B. Hoffman concluded:

> The Salient Factor Score has retained predictive accuracy over the seventeen-year period in which the three samples were released. These findings add to the evidence that the Salient Factor Score is able to separate prisoners into categories having significantly different probabilities of recidivism, and that its predictive accuracy has not diminished over time.[35]

State Parole Guidelines

Following the lead of the federal parole system, many states adopted guidelines for use in release decision making. Some states adopted a matrix guideline system similar to the SFS, while others adopted different types of guidelines. Most of these other systems feature a list of factors to be considered in making release decisions. Rhine and associates refer to this second category of guidelines as guiding principles. Joan Petersilia and Susan Turner compiled a list of criteria used in both types of instruments—matrix and guiding principles (see Figure 10.3).[36]

Regardless of the form that parole release guidelines take, they structure the exercise of discretion. Parole boards are free to deviate from their guidelines, but they

FIGURE 10.1 *Salient Factor Score (SFS/81)*

Item A........PRIOR CONVICTIONS/ADJUDICATIONS (ADULT OR JUVENILE)..☐
.......................None..=3
.......................One..=2
.......................Two or three..=1
.......................Four or more...=0

Item B........PRIOR COMMITMENT(S) OF MORE THAN THIRTY DAYS (ADULT OR JUVENILE) ....☐
.......................None..=2
.......................One or two...=1
.......................Three or more..=0

Item C........AGE AT CURRENT OFFENSE / PRIOR COMMITMENTS...☐
.......................Age at commencement of the current offense:
...........................26 years of age or more.....................................=2*
...........................20–25 years of age...=1*
...........................19 years of age or less..=0
...................*EXCEPTION: If five or more prior commitments of more than
...................thirty days (adult or juvenile), place an "x" here _____ and
...................score this item..=0

Item D........RECENT COMMITMENT-FREE PERIOD (THREE YEARS)..☐
.......................No prior commitment of more than thirty days (adult or
.......................juvenile) or released to the community from last such
.......................commitment at least three years prior to the
.......................commencement of the current offense ....=1
.......................Otherwise ....=0

Item E........PROBATION/PAROLE/CONFINEMENT/ESCAPE STATUS VIOLATOR THIS TIME ....☐
.......................Neither on probation, parole, confinement, or escape
.......................status at the time of the current offense; nor committed
.......................as a probation, parole, confinement, or escape status
.......................violator this time ....=1
.......................Otherwise ....=0

Item F........HEROIN/OPIATE DEPENDENCE..☐
.......................No history of heroin/opiate dependence............................=1
.......................Otherwise ....=0

TOTAL SCORE ....☐

Source: United States Parole Commission, *Rules and Procedures Manual* (Washington, DC: U.S. Parole Commission, 1997).

generally must give reasons for doing so. Parole authorities are guided in decision making while retaining broad powers; deviations from these guides are held in check by the possibility of appeal.

Researchers have attempted to improve parole risk prediction instruments for adult parolees. Many current risk prediction instruments are based on factors that correlate with risk of male parolees. Because female parolees have lower recidivism

FIGURE 10.2 *Guidelines for Decision Making*

Offense Characteristics: Offense Severity (Some Crimes Eliminated or Summarized)	OFFENDER CHARACTERISTICS: PAROLE PROGNOSIS			
	Very Good	Good	Fair	Poor
Category One *Low:* possession of a small amount of marijuana; simple theft under $1,000	*Adult Range*			
	≤ 6 months	6–9 months	9–12 months	12–16 months
	Youth Range			
	≤ 6 months	6–9 months	9–12 months	12–16 months
Category Two *Low/Moderate:* income tax evasion less than $10,000; immigration law violations; embezzlement, fraud, forgery under $1,000	*Adult Range*			
	≤ 8 months	8–12 months	12–16 months	16–22 months
	Youth Range			
	≤ 8 months	8–12 months	12–16 months	16–20 months
Category Three *Moderate:* bribery; possession of 50 lb. or less of marijuana, with intent to sell; illegal firearms; income tax evasion $10,000 to $50,000; nonviolent property offenses $1,000 to $19,999; auto theft, not for resale	*Adult Range*			
	10–14 months	14–18 months	18–24 months	24–32 months
	Youth Range			
	8–12 months	12–16 months	16–20 months	20–26 months
Category Four *High:* counterfeiting; marijuana possession with intent to sell, 50 to 1,999 lb.; auto theft, for resale; nonviolent property offenses, $20,000 to $100,000	*Adult Range*			
	14–20 months	20–26 months	26–34 months	34–44 months
	Youth Range			
	12–16 months	16–20 months	20–26 months	26–32 months
Category Five *Very High:* robbery; breaking and entering bank or post office; extortion; marijuana possession with intent to sell, over 2,000 lb.; hard drugs possession with intent to sell, not more than $100,000; nonviolent property offenses over $100,000 but not exceeding $500,000	*Adult Range*			
	24–36 months	36–48 months	48–60 months	60–72 months
	Youth Range			
	20–26 months	26–32 months	32–40 months	40–48 months
Category Six *Greatest I:* explosive detonation; multiple robbery; aggravated felony (weapon fired—no serious injury); hard drugs, over $100,000; forcible rape	*Adult Range*			
	40–52 months	52–64 months	64–78 months	78–100 months
	Youth Range			
	30–40 months	40–50 months	50–60 months	60–76 months
Category Seven *Greatest II:* aircraft hijacking; espionage; kidnapping; homicide	*Adult Range*			
	52–80 months	64–92 months	78–110 months	100–148 months
	Youth Range			
	40–64 months	50–74 months	70–86 months	76–110 months
Category Eight	*Adult Range*			
	100+ months	120+ months	150+ months	180+ months
	Youth Range			
	80+ months	100+ months	120+ months	150+ months

Source: United States Parole Commission, 1997.

FIGURE 10.3 *Criteria Used in Parole Release Risk Instruments*

MOST COMMONLY USED ITEMS (5)
(found in over 75 percent of instruments identified)

Number of parole revocations
Number of adult or juvenile convictions
Number of prison terms served
Number of incarcerations served
Current crime involves violence

SECOND MOST COMMONLY USED ITEMS (11)
(found in 50–74 percent of instruments identified)

Number of prior convictions
Number of previous felony sentences
Number of juvenile incarcerations
Number of jail terms served
Age at first incarceration
Commitment-free period shown
On parole at arrest
Victim injured
Current age
Drug use
Prison infractions

THIRD MOST COMMONLY USED ITEMS (15)
(found in 25–49 percent of instruments identified)

Number of adult or juvenile arrests
Age at first conviction
Repeat of conviction types
Length of current term
Total years incarcerated
Current crime is property crime
Current crime involved weapon
Current crime involved forcible contact
Educational level
Employment history
Living arrangements
Alcohol use or abuse
Program participation in prison
Parole release plan formulated
Escape history

Source: Joan Petersilia and Susan Turner, "Guideline-Based Justice: Prediction and Racial Minorities," in *Prediction and Classification*, ed. D. Gottfredson and M. Tonry (Chicago: University of Chicago Press, 1987).

rates than male parolees, a group of researchers are examining the possibility of developing a risk prediction instrument for female parolees (see Box 10.1).

Research indicates that guidelines have performed one of their intended functions, that of smoothing obvious sentencing disparities so that prison time is more predictable. One study found that parole board decisions are much more automatic and correlate strongly with the institutional recommendation, suggesting that the parole process has more than one decision point.[37]

To further increase reliability of parole decisions, Victoria J. Palacios encourages the following three changes for all states: (1) allow both the offender and the department of corrections to present testimonial or documentary evidence during the hearing; (2) give offenders advance written notice of parole criteria; and (3) require the parole board to make written statements as to the reasons that cases were denied parole.[38]

PRISONERS' PERCEPTIONS OF PAROLE SELECTION

Whether the length of incarceration before parole is any more predictable in guide-line jurisdictions is still speculative. In the 1970s, research by John Irwin, a professor and ex-convict, found that prisoners had six different ideas for how they think parole is achieved:

- Parole is granted once the going rate of time has been served without regard to rehabilitation.
- Parole is decided not by the board, but by prison staff, such as psychologists and sociologists.
- Parole depends on the impression the prisoner made at the last board hearing.
- The most important factor is one's prior criminal record.
- Evidence of rehabilitation influences parole decisions.
- Evidence of participation in treatment programs is most important.[39]

Overall, prisoners at that time perceived parole decisions to be largely out of their control.[40]

James L. Beck compared prisoners' perceptions of parole decision making in the federal system and in Pennsylvania. The federal system used a "justice" guideline system, while Pennsylvania used a "rehabilitative" nonmatrix guideline system.[41] The Pennsylvania board was generally treatment-oriented and strongly considered institutional behavior, recommendations of institutional staff, and parole release plans. The federal system primarily considered offense severity and offender characteristics such as prior criminal history. Beck found no significant difference in the two groups' abilities to predict parole decisions, but he found that a significantly greater percentage of Pennsylvania inmates than federal inmates considered the parole procedure "basically fair" (48 percent of inmates as opposed to only 20 percent of the federal inmates). The major conclusion of the study was that the justice approach to parole does not result in greater perceived certainty for the offender, even though the criteria are made concrete and more sharply defined. The treatment model—based on institutional adjustment—allowed the offender a greater perceived influence over the parole decision and thus was viewed as basically more fair. Beck concluded that the justice approach to parole is still a useful tool for reducing sentence disparity and that the rehabilitation approach will remain suspect until some method of rehabilitating offenders has been proven effective. Offenders, however, seem to prefer the rehabilitation model of deciding when they should be released from prison.

Beck's findings are not surprising. While serving on the Texas Parole Board, Cromwell received hundreds of letters from inmates protesting the use of offense-related factors in making parole decisions. One such letter illustrates this point:

> I can't do nothing about what I did. I did it and I'm sorry I did. Now I'm trying to show you people that I've changed and can be trusted out in the free world but you keep setting me off [denying parole] because of "nature and seriousness of the offense." Tell me what I can do to make parole. Please.[42]

In a more recent study, Mika'il A. Muhammad interviewed 263 prisoners from the Eastern New York Correctional Facility concerning prisoners' attitudes toward the release process and strategies used to seek early release. Half of all prisoners believed the case appeal process was the most important thing to be working on to obtain release.[43] This is ironic because, as Muhammad points out, prisoners' chances of getting out on appeal are much more rare than release on parole. It appears, therefore, that lack of prisoner information about "what the board wants," especially for prisoners doing long sentences or those who have been denied by the parole board before, has contributed to a large number of prisoners who have completely disregarded "impressing the parole board" and who have turned instead to the courts.[44]

After appeal, maintaining good institutional conduct, recommendations from "important people," and educational improvement were viewed as the next three most important aids to release, especially for younger inmates. Older prisoners, especially those who have spent many years behind bars, see appeal as their most important remedy.[45]

One of the more interesting findings Muhammad reported was attitudes toward "contract parole." Sixty percent of inmates favored contract parole over all other release alternatives because it professed to decrease stress associated with ignorance and ambiguity. Contract parole is defined as "wherein the inmate negotiates with parole and correctional personnel at the beginning of the sentence a plan to address specific needs that, if met, would facilitate parole readiness and insure release on a specified date."[46] Contract parole is not used at this time, but reducing uncertainty about the parole process would likely decrease some prison stress.

Any system that totally ignores positive institutional behavior runs the risk of alienating offenders and increases the possibility of poor adjustment. Many, however, suggest that career criminals know how to do time; that is, they can manipulate the parole board by avoiding institutional violations and participating in rehabilitation programs that look good on their record when they are reviewed for parole. Research suggests that good behavior while in prison does not always mean that an inmate will obey the law if released early on parole.[47]

So despite criticisms leveled at the use of guidelines, this procedure appears to offer the greatest degree of fairness to the parole-granting process. By making explicit the primary factors that the board should consider in parole selection and the weight that should be given to each, the unfettered discretion traditionally allowed parole boards should, at the very least, be structured and more predictable.

DUE PROCESS DURING PAROLE HEARINGS

One of the most striking aspects of the traditional parole release process has been the virtual inability to review parole decisions.[48] In recent years courts have provided some procedural protections and articulated criteria for reviewing the conditions that parole boards have set on parolees' conduct and for revoking parole and returning parolees to prison. Until recently, federal and state courts almost invariably rejected claims that the denial of parole was subject to review because of procedural or substantive defects in the parole release decision process.[49]

In the late 1960s, courts have viewed parole as an act of grace or privilege, neither of which gives rise to rights or expectations in need of due process.[50] In addition to the **grace or privilege theory** rationales, another theory justifying judicial passivity in this area has been the continuing custody theory. **Continuing custody theory** views parole as simply a change in the nature of custody, which places the parole decision in the area of administrative decision making.[51]

Another rationale used to justify the vast and unreviewable discretion is that parole boards act as *parens patriae*, or substitute benevolent parents, with respect to the inmates. As such, the boards need be concerned only with promoting the inmates' rehabilitation through the exercise of their expert knowledge and judgment, which obviates any need for procedural protection.[52] This rationale reflects the pervasive view that release decisions are part of the rehabilitation process. In support of this view, courts have emphasized that parole boards possess an administrative expertise in evaluating "nonlegal" factors relevant to the release decision.[53] The courts acquiesced in the board's assertion that the proper moment for parole can be determined only after an inmate has been observed for a period of time and attempts have been made to treat the inmate within the rehabilitative institutional context.[54]

Menechino v. Oswald

In *Menechino v. Oswald*, a prisoner argued that the New York State Board of Parole's denial of his application for parole was illegal because he had not received a fair parole hearing.[55] In particular, he stated he did not receive any of the following: notice of the charges, the right to counsel, the right to cross-examine witnesses, the right to produce favorable witnesses, and the specification of the grounds and underlying facts upon which the denial was based. The court offered two reasons in holding that these due process rights did not apply to parole release hearings. First, the court ruled that the inmate had no legally cognizable "interest" in his parole grant, because he did not enjoy a status that was being threatened or taken away. Second, the parole board's interest in the proceeding was not adverse to that of the inmate because the

GRACE OR PRIVILEGE THEORY

The view that parole is a privilege and a matter of grace (mercy) by the executive. Under this theory parole confers no particular rights on the recipient and is subject to withdrawal at any time.

CONTINUING CUSTODY THEORY

The view that the parolee remains in custody of either the parole authorities or the prison and that his or her constitutional rights are limited. Release on parole is merely a change in the degree of custody.

PARENS PATRIAE

Latin for "parent of the country"; refers to the traditional role of the state as guardian of persons under legal disability, such as juveniles, the insane, and incarcerated persons. The assumption is that the state acts in the best interest of those over whom the *parens patriae* relationship exists.

board was "seeking to encourage and foster his rehabilitation and readjustment into society."[56]

Although the courts' prevailing view has been that of noninterference in parole release decisions, abuses of discretion have been judicially reviewed. Parole boards have been found abusing their discretion, committing capricious acts, and conducting practices contrary to the general notions of fairness.[57]

Greenholtz v. Inmates of the Nebraska Penal and Correctional Complex

In 1979 the U.S. Supreme Court directly addressed the issue of due process in parole release decision making. In *Greenholtz v. Inmates of the Nebraska Penal and Correctional Complex*, the inmates of a Nebraska prison brought an action alleging they had been unconstitutionally denied parole by the Nebraska Board of Parole.[58] The inmates also contested three other procedures: (1) the state's hearing process, (2) the board's practice of informing inmates when it denies parole, and (3) a notice procedure of informing inmates in advance of the month their parole hearing will be held. After the lower federal courts held in favor of the inmates, the U.S. Supreme Court reversed the decision of the court of appeals. The Court stated,

> Like most parole statutes, it [the Nebraska statute] vests broad discretion in the Board. No ideal, error-free way to make parole release decisions has been developed. The whole question has been, and will continue to be, the subject of experimentation involving analysis of psychological factors combined with fact evaluation guided by the practical experience of the actual parole decision makers in predicting future behavior.[59]

The Court continued the trend of past decisions by discussing the "ultimate purpose of parole[, which] is rehabilitation," and stated,

> The fact that anticipation and hopes for rehabilitation programs have fallen short of expectations of a generation ago need not lead states to abandon hopes for those objectives; states may adopt a balanced approach in making parole determinations, as in problems of administering the correctional systems.[60]

The Court refused to require a hearing in all cases for every inmate as prescribed by the court of appeals, holding that such a requirement would provide, at best, a negligible decrease in the risk of error. In sum, the Court held,

> The Nebraska procedure affords an opportunity to be heard, and when parole is denied it informs the inmate in what respect he falls short of qualifying for parole; this affords the process that is due under these circumstances. The Constitution does not require more.[61]

Although the *Greenholtz* case did not extend due process as far as desired by the plaintiffs, or as extensively as did the court of appeals, it did establish that some due process protections were available in the parole-granting process. The Court held that the methods provided for in the Nebraska statute—the right to an initial hearing, notice of the hearing, and articulation of the reasons for denial—were sufficient. It distinguished parole release decision making from parole revocation decision making and refused to apply the due process provisions of *Morrissey v. Brewer*, which prescribe a series of rights to a parolee in a revocation hearing. The Court concluded that parole release and parole revocation "are quite different" because "there is a . . . difference between losing what one has and not getting what one wants."[62] In summary, the *Greenholtz* decision appears to require reasonable notice of a parole hearing date (one month before the hearing is reasonable); an initial hearing wherein the prisoner is allowed to present the case; and, if parole is denied, a recitation of the reasons for denial. In addition, a formal parole hearing for all inmates is not required every year, but one parole hearing per year is constitutionally adequate.

State-Created Liberty Interest

LIBERTY INTEREST

Any interest recognized or protected by the due process clauses of state or federal constitutions.

Following the *Greenholtz* case, many state courts examined state parole statutes in cases brought forth by inmates, to determine whether the mandatory wording of some statutes created a constitutionally protected **liberty interest.** The courts decided that prison inmates do not have a protected liberty interest in parole unless the state creates that interest via mandatory wording in the state statute.

For example, in 1987, in *Board of Pardons v. Allen,* the U.S. Supreme Court held that the state of Montana had created a protected liberty interest in its parole statute.[63] The statute read:

> Subject to the following restrictions, the board shall release on parole . . . any person confined in the Montana state prison or the women's correction center . . . when in its opinion there is reasonable probability that the prisoner can be released without detriment to the prisoner or to the community.

The mandatory wording in the statute is "shall," and this word creates a liberty interest that triggers due process protections. If the mandatory wording was amended to discretionary language, no liberty interest would be at stake and thus no additional due process required, beyond that of *Greenholtz.*

The state of Missouri faced the same problem as Montana. To overcome the problem, Missouri replaced "shall" with "may in its discretion" to remedy the issue in another case.[64]

ACA Due Process Standards

The American Correctional Association standards require parole hearings to be conducted as fairly and equitably as possible with due process conditions maintained and all procedural safeguards assured.[65] Further, ACA standards require that decision-making criteria be written in enough detail to permit consistent application in individual cases and that the decision regarding parole release and the reasons for it be communicated to the prisoner orally and explained to agree with the written criteria. Applicants denied parole must be informed of an approximate future hearing date and must receive suggestions for improving their chances to receive parole by the time of the next hearing.

The ACA standards far exceed the due process requirements established by the courts, although the standards are not binding on any paroling authority. Instead, they are only guidelines or models.

Guarding against Arbitrary Parole Decisions

Victoria Palacios, a professor of law, suggests ways to increase fairness and consistency in parole board hearings, such as providing a copy of parole guidelines to prisoners before the parole board hearing, requiring reasons for denial of parole, and offering an opportunity for inmates to present relevant information. Palacios states:

> Another way to heighten the reliability of parole decisions is to allow the applicants to present evidence, either testimonial or documentary, that supports their petition.

The inmates have the greatest incentive to see that certain information is brought to the attention of the board. A system that relies only on the prison for information about offenders is pregnant with the potential for arbitrary, discriminatory action.[66]

IMPOSING PAROLE CONDITIONS

While the court sets conditions for probation, the parole board—a nonjudicial body that is usually part of the executive branch of government—sets parole conditions. Once the board sets conditions, supervision of parole is then left to field parole officers who work either for the parole board or for another government agency independent of the parole board, such as the parole division of a department of corrections. The function of the parole board is limited to deciding whether to release an inmate on parole. Once released, the parole division, which is independent of the parole board, supervises the parolee.[67]

As in the case of probation, in which conditions are imposed by judges, parole boards also enjoy vast discretion when imposing conditions of parole. Decided cases, however, set some limitations on what parole boards can do. These limitations are similar to those in probation:

- The condition must be clear.
- The condition must be reasonable.
- The condition must protect society or rehabilitate the offender.
- The condition must be constitutional.

Parole officers are responsible for enforcing parole conditions (see Chapter 11).

SUMMARY

The scope of a parole board's authority and the consequences of its actions are enormous. No other part of the criminal justice system concentrates such power into the hands of so few.[68] Parole boards select prisoners for parole and determine when revocation of parole and return to prison are necessary. In some states the parole board also supervises parolees in the community.

Because parole selection determines the character of the organization itself, the process of selection has serious consequences for the effectiveness, and perhaps even the survival, of the entire parole system. Despite its importance to the prisoner, society, and the justice system as a whole, however, the process is a confused procedure, with little consensus regarding the proper means by which decisions are made, the grounds for decisions, and whether minimal due process should be allowed.

From the intuitive approach of the rehabilitative parole board to the justice model system with its guidelines and parole matrices, the system has not yet evolved a consistent decision-making base. Even prisoners, who are at the complete mercy of the system, do not agree on which method they prefer. One study indicates that inmates may prefer mercy to justice, as they overwhelmingly favored the intuitive approach of the Pennsylvania parole system to the guideline approach of the federal system.

The courts, too, are at odds, although at present a consistent theme has emerged that due process, if allowed at all, will be minimal and determined by the statutes of the jurisdiction. It will not be protected by the Fourteenth Amendment and thus will not be a constitutional issue.

The ACA *Manual of Correctional Standards* perhaps summarizes the issue of due process at the release hearing as well as possible:

> To an even greater extent than in the case of imprisonment, probation and parole practice is determined by an administrative discretion that is largely uncontrolled by legal standards, protections, or remedies. Until statutory and case law are more fully developed, it is virtually important within all of the correctional field that there should be established and maintained reasonable norms and remedies against the sort of abuses that are likely to develop where men have great power over their fellows and where relationships may become both mechanical and arbitrary.[69]

DISCUSSION QUESTIONS

1. Compare and contrast the autonomous, institutional, and consolidation models of parole organization. What is the pattern in your state?
2. What are the major functions of a parole board?
3. What are the primary qualifications of a good parole board member? Why are these qualities important?
4. Why are good public relations necessary to parole's effectiveness?
5. How is parole eligibility typically determined?
6. What is good time, and what is its relationship to eligibility for parole consideration?
7. If you were a victim of a violent crime, would you take the time to write an impact statement or attend the parole board hearing?
8. Distinguish between the matrix guideline method and the guiding principal method.
9. Why is unstructured discretion unfair to the inmate? Give some examples.
10. What criteria do statutes typically establish for parole release decisions?
11. What was the ruling in *Menechino v. Oswald*? How did it affect parole decision making?
12. What issues arise when seriousness of the offense is considered in parole decisions? What do you think about this issue?
13. If you were a parole board member, what factors would you consider in attempting to arrive at a fair and just decision? Why?
14. If you were a prisoner, what method of release from prison would you prefer, discretionary or automatic? Why?
15. What were the issues and what was the decision in *Greenholtz v. Inmates of the Nebraska Penal and Correctional Complex*? In light of the conservative composition of the present Supreme Court, what do you think will be the result of future decisions on these issues?

 WEB SITES

Parole Watch
Keeps track of when high-profile violent offenders come up for parole

www.parolewatch.org

U.S. Parole Commission

http://www.usdoj.gov/uspc/parole.htm

Prison Legal News
Monthly magazine containing uncensored writings from the prisoner perspective

http://www.prisonlegalnews.org

CHAPTER 10

CASE STUDY EXERCISE

Parole Board and Parole Selection

Various systems are used to make release decisions for incarcerated offenders. Often with states where sentences are indeterminate, a paroling authority decides whether the offender should be released and when that release should occur. Sentencing laws may determine when an offender is eligible for release, but the offender is not granted a release until the parole authority approves the release.

In the following cases, the paroling authority must consider the offender cases and make a determination to release or not to release the offender to the community. Factors considered often involve probability of recidivism, victim impact, community impact, conduct of the offender in the institution, and release plan offered. Consider these cases and determine if the release has merit.

Case A: Offender Doe is serving a 10- to 25-year sentence for two counts of armed robbery. He has served the mandatory minimum of five years and is being considered for release for the first time. By statute, he can be held in custody for 13 years before he reaches a mandatory release date. Doe served a previous sentence for burglary and successfully completed the release period before he committed the current crimes. The victims in both robberies were elderly gas station attendants, and very small amounts of money were obtained from the robberies. The victims remain fearful of the offender, and both indicate their lives were significantly impacted by the experience. Both victims never returned to work out of fear of similar future events. While incarcerated Doe has completed substance abuse treatment for his cocaine dependence. The treatment summary calls for his attendance in facility, cocaine-anonymous meetings. He attends the meetings about half of the time they are offered. He has also completed an anger management program, has been assigned to several inmate jobs, and has had no rule violations while incarcerated. Doe would like to have gone to a work release facility but, because of a waiting list, he has never been able to enter this program prior to being considered for release. His community plan is to return to the same community where the crimes were committed, live with his elderly aunt, seek work as a construction laborer, and attend community substance abuse aftercare. He would be under the supervision of a parole officer upon his release if granted.

Case B: Offender Smith is serving a 5- to 15-year sentence for sexual assault of a minor. He has served seven and one-half years of his sentence, which is five years beyond the minimum time to be served. Because he has three prior convictions for similar offenses, he does not have to be released until he has served ten years of his sentence. Smith spent time in prison for two of three prior offenses against minors. Each time he was released he successfully completed the release period of parole supervision. All of his victims have been his grandchildren. Family members are strongly opposed to his release and feel he will commit similar acts upon release. Smith has completed a sexual offender treatment program during this incarceration. He always refused to participate in treatment during prior incarcerations. The prognosis by the treatment counselor is guarded but indicates Smith has worked hard on learning his offending triggers and knows what to avoid if released. He has not had any rule violations while incarcerated and has been employed in a private prison industry. He proposes a release to a community where none of his family resides, and he does not want to have contact with his family. He has been accepted into a halfway house program and plans on attending community-based sexual offender aftercare groups. If released he would be under the supervision of a parole officer.

11

Parole Conditions and Revocation

Spencer Grant/Stock Boston

What You Will Learn in This Chapter

You will learn that parole conditions imposed by parole boards are subject to the same limitations as probation conditions. Parole conditions vary from state to state, but common conditions can be found in most states. You will see that parolees have the same limitations as probationers and are also legally handicapped by diminished constitutional rights. Revocation is the ultimate sanction if parole is violated. It represents a loss of freedom. Therefore, parolees are guaranteed basic due process rights prior to revocation. You will become familiar with the case of Morrissey v. Brewer, *the leading case on parole revocation.*

INTRODUCTION

The factors and conditions that lead to the decision of discretionary prison release were discussed in Chapter 10. What it is like to be on parole is examined in this chapter. Parole is a form of community supervision of offenders. Therefore, as with probation, supervision conditions are an integral part of parole. **Parole conditions** imposed determine the amount of freedom versus restrictions a parolee has.

The main goal of parole is societal protection, which is accomplished by enforcing parolee restrictions and providing services that assist in community reintegration, while at the same time maintaining public confidence in parole.[1] Some believe the approaches to these goals are different and irreconcilable; others think they can be mixed and still get desired results. Whatever may be the primary goal behind parole release, conditions imposed play a big role in achieving that goal. They also often determine whether the parolee succeeds or fails.

The length of time spent on parole averages about two years, although the amount of time is longer for violent offenders and shorter for property and drug offenders.[2] The length of supervision largely depends on the laws of the state of conviction. For example, parole is limited to six months in Oregon and one year in Indiana regardless of the type of crime. Most states allow parolees to be discharged before the full term of their sentence.

Parole revocation follows parole supervision if the parolee violates the conditions of parole. As with probation, revocation is not automatic in that violations can result in lesser sanctions. Revocation is important for parolees to avoid because it means losing their freedom and being brought back to jail or prison to serve the remainder of their sentence. It represents a "grievous loss" of liberty, so parolees have been afforded constitutional rights by the courts prior to revocation. Revocation is also important to society because the parolee will once again be under the care and custody of the state, and with that comes the high cost of keeping an offender incarcerated. Much is at stake for the parolee and the state in parole revocation.

PRISONER PERSPECTIVES OF GETTING OUT

Few publications examine the prisoner perspective while on parole. Most researchers conduct studies about inmate life experiences inside prison, primarily because institutional prisoners make captive audiences. An exception to this is research conducted

PAROLE CONDITIONS

The rules under which a paroling authority releases an offender to community supervision.

with prisoners recently released from prison. Craig Hemmens supervised a research team that interviewed 775 former inmates as they were waiting for the bus within a few minutes to a few hours of release from prison. Hemmens found in his study of "ex-mates" that black and Hispanic prisoners are significantly more likely than white prisoners to agree that parole will be harder than prison.[3] Furthermore, as prisoners age, Hemmens found that they seem less apprehensive about reentry. Less reentry apprehension also applied to prisoners who served sentences of three years or less.[4] Because this study was cross-sectional, none of the prisoners was tracked to see if he did succeed. Prisoners generally have good intentions of staying out of prison. Many prisoners do attempt to live a legitimate life by finding employment after release, but prisoners experience a great deal of stress and disdain from the community.[5]

One such individual is Robert M. Grooms. Grooms writes about the perils of release from prison and why, despite all the advantages he had over most other convicts upon release, he was one of the ones who did not make it. Grooms found that when he was released, he had problems finding a job, had nothing in common with old friends, and was uncomfortable around "square-johns."[6] He writes:

> I had another problem common among recently released prisoners. I wanted to make up all at once for lost time. I wanted the things that others my age had worked years to achieve, and I wanted them right away.[7]

Grooms found that he could not "sit still" and he did not want to be alone, so he began to hang around places and people where he did feel comfortable. He found himself talking to ex-convicts in taverns, and they talked about what they all had in common: crime, the prison experience, and violence. Grooms concludes by saying:

> When he is released, a prisoner is in a real sense cast out into a totally alien society. Overnight he is expected to discard months and years of self-survival tactics, to change his values, to readjust to situations and circumstances that he had long forgotten, and to accept responsibility. More important, he has to overcome, in a society that rejects him, his lack of self-worth; he has to become accepted where he is not wanted. Is it any wonder that so many newly released prisoners feel out of their natural environment, that many first-time, petty offenders leave prison and find someone weak to prey on, or that the recidivism rate is so high?[8]

California Study

A classic study of parolee perspectives was completed in 1973 in California. A collaborative team of researchers, students, and ex-convicts was assembled to interview 60 parolees about their experiences as they first left prison.[9]

The researchers found that the reentry process was a negative experience for about half of all parolees, as most of them had experienced failure on parole many times before. While on parole, offenders felt pressure to obtain a job, money, food, clothes, and a place to stay. Many parolees relied more on friends and other ex-convicts for these basic needs than they did on their own family.[10] For example, Lloyd Nieman, age 36 with an eighth-grade education and convicted of forgery, was in the process of enrolling at a state college while on parole. Nieman explained:

> The first few days I was out were about the roughest days of this entire period. I've only been out a short time—five weeks—but the first three days were a hassle. . . . [N]o money, no transportation, no job, and no place to live. Now these things have a way of working themselves out in time, but you have to contact the right people, and sometimes it's hard to find the right people. . . . I was lucky that I had two friends here, too, that could help me. Nick [an ex-con] gave me a place to stay, because I was out of

money within four days. They [the prison] give you $60, and out of that you got to buy your own clothes.[11]

Shortly after his interview, Nieman absconded, leaving the state and never returning. A warrant was issued for his arrest. After one year, Nieman could not be located.

The researchers also found that many parolees were socially detached and many admitted to being lonely. For example, Anthony Mendez, age 46, spent the last 16 years in prison for possession of narcotics and had been out on parole for 3 months when interviewed. Mendez's experience is a bit different from Nieman's. Mendez has more financial assistance from his family in Los Angeles, but he was paroled to an area of San Diego where he does not know anyone. Mendez explains his experience:

> I was just kinda lost when I got out. If you've been in a while, so many things are new and different. . . . I've always gotten a lot of help [from family], so I think I've just been lucky; but I know there's a lot of other guys that didn't get the help I got. . . . I really couldn't talk to anybody, which is hard. . . . For the majority of fellows in the joint, they're so starved emotionally and so closed in, so shut off from any warmth, any friendship, that it takes a long time when you get out to break out of these bonds and be a normal person out here where you can talk to people. . . . I think that when a guy first gets out, it's a very important thing that that man go to work, if for no other reason than that eight hours is going to be occupied . . . and it's not going to let him dwell on how much he's missed and much he's missing again.[12]

One year after Mendez was interviewed, he was still on parole but had lost his job.

Through the interviews, parolees made suggestions ranging from increasing rehabilitation and vocational programs inside prison to increasing community resources on release. The lack of reentry resources has been a continual problem for parolees nationwide. For example, one parolee stated:

> It just doesn't seem fair to give the convict such a little money and tell him to make it. What regular citizen today can set out in the world, with less than a high school education, no job, $50, and no close ties or other resources, and make it? That is what we are asking the parolee to do, and we will not let him forget that he is an outsider.[13]

One of the most innovative suggestions made in some of the interviews was that everyone released from prison be assigned a mentor in his or her area. The mentor would be a successful ex-convict who has remained out of the system, and he or she would be available to deal with emotional and social problems the parolee faces. Even though this research was conducted 30 years ago, the needs and problems of parolees remain the same today.

Iowa Study

Stephen C. Richards and Richard S. Jones conducted a more recent study of the transition from prison to a correctional halfway house, and then to parole. They interviewed 30 men that were just released from prison and were sentenced to a halfway house as a form of graduated release.[14] The researchers found that the men had not been prepared for release from prison to an environment that required them to pay rent, look for employment, sustain a job, and pay for food. One prisoner explained the pressures of getting behind in rent upon his arrival at the halfway house:

> You leave the penitentiary on a Tuesday, you come here [to the halfway house], and you're broke for the whole week or two till they send your money from the penitentiary. What kind of shit is that? Ya know, I mean a man come home from the penitentiary they don't even give you gate money. They give you $5 [and] bus fare. . . . I owe

for [bed] sheets, owe for bus tokens, I owe for my rent. You're automatically 2 weeks behind in rent, see what I'm saying. . . . I didn't ask to come here and be put in the hole by your all program. Ya all know that when I come here it would take a while for me to find a job.[15]

One of the issues that likely affects success rate at the halfway house is financial pressures, which includes not only daily living expenses, but also setting aside money for paying court costs, fees, victim restitution, and back child support that accumulated while the prisoner was behind bars.[16]

In sum, then, the intent of parolee interview research is to determine parolee needs from their point of view, so that intervention programs could be designed to help address problems on parole that ultimately lead many to fail or to sabotage themselves while on parole. A parole failure leads to a revocation and can sometimes result in a return to jail or prison. Revocation rates of parolees have increased from previous years.

THE FIELD PAROLE OFFICER

A field parole officer enforces the conditions of parole that are mandated by the parole board. Parole officers manage caseloads of between 60 to 75 prisoners, while others have smaller, more specialized caseloads (numbering 25 to 50) of prisoners who need more intensive supervision. "Regular" supervision typically means about two 15-minute face-to-face contacts per month, with an annual cost of about $2,200 per parolee.[17]

Parole officers are expected to perform five main functions:

1. Carry out and enforce the conditions of parole through supervision and monitoring by means of home visits, employment checks, and meeting with the parolee at the office.
2. Refer parolees to drug and alcohol treatment, anger management programs, parenting classes, and so on.
3. Conduct investigations, write reports, and evaluate, interpret, and present data for the guidance of the court, the institution, reporting serious violations to the paroling authority.
4. Provide crime victims with information on the offender's living and working arrangements, parole conditions, and restitution payment schedule, if applicable.
5. Share applicable information with law enforcement personnel on a need-to-know basis.

To perform these functions a parole officer must possess certain basic qualifications and specialized knowledge. The minimum qualifications should be a working knowledge of the principles of human behavior, knowledge of the laws of the jurisdiction in which he or she will work and of the powers and limitations of the position, and familiarity with the operation of related law enforcement agencies in the particular jurisdiction.

The functions and responsibilities of parole officers are roughly the same as probation officers. The minimum standards for employment as a probation or parole officer typically include a bachelor's degree from a college or university with coursework in the social sciences, and many positions also require one year of paid full-time experience in employment for the welfare of others or one year of graduate work beyond the baccalaureate as well as good character and a well-balanced personality.

The Officer's Perspective

Mona Lynch conducted an ethnographic study on California parole officers to examine how officers manage competing job pressures. The first pressure is from the public to be tough on crime, while, at the same time, parole officers must satisfy the desire in California to use the new computerized method of tracking risk management by means of the California Parolee Information Network (CPIN).[18] CPIN is a new tracking system that requires parole officers to spend an enormous amount of time inputting accurate data into a computer, which would then assist them in determining the level of supervision each individual required. In addition, parole officers must maintain a specific number of contacts, have their parolees drop urine specimens within a specified time frame, and file reports and reviews, all within a specific time period.

Lynch found that parole officers came from a variety of backgrounds, but their "role identity" was similar in that they viewed parole more as an art than as a science. In other words, parole officers perceived that "keeping a pulse on their caseload"—knowing what their parolees were doing—through face-to-face interactions and monitoring was more important than the increased paperwork that resulted from using the computerized tracking records.

> The agents generally strove toward a very traditional law enforcement role, where they did not need to assess danger or risk or criminal activity by anything more than their own developed intuition and personal investigative skills.[19]

CONDITIONS OF PAROLE

As in the case of probation, parole conditions may also be classified into two types: **standard conditions** and **special conditions.** Standard conditions are imposed on all parolees in a jurisdiction, while special conditions are tailored to fit the needs of an offender and therefore vary between offenders. The parole conditions imposed in Massachusetts are typical of conditions imposed in other states. The Massachusetts parole conditions provide as follows:

- I will obey local, state, and federal laws and conduct myself in the manner of a responsible citizen.
- I will notify my parole officer in writing within 24 hours of any change in my employment or residence. I will notify my parole officer before applying for a license to marry. I will inform my parole officer within 24 hours if arrested.
- I will make an earnest effort to find and maintain legitimate employment unless engaged in some other program approved by my parole officer.
- I will not engage in a continuous pattern of association with persons I know to have a criminal record or who are known to be engaged in a violation of the law. This prohibition does not apply where such association is incidental to my place of residence or employment or connected with activities of bona fide political or social organizations. However, the Parole Board retains authority to impose

STANDARD CONDITIONS

Conditions imposed on all parolees in a jurisdiction.

SPECIAL CONDITIONS

Conditions tailored to fit the needs of a particular offender.

TABLE 11.1 *Selected Conditions of Parole in Effect in 51 Jurisdictions*

Condition of Parole	Number of Jurisdictions	Percentage
Obey all federal, state, and local laws	50	98.0
Report to the parole officer as directed and answer all reasonable inquiries by the parole officer	49	96.1
Refrain from possessing a firearm or other dangerous weapon unless granted written permission	47	92.2
Remain within the jurisdiction of the court and notify the parole officer of any change in residence	46	90.2
Permit the parole officer to visit the parolee at home or elsewhere	42	82.4
Obey all rules and regulations of the parole supervision agency	40	78.4
Maintain gainful employment	40	78.4
Abstain from association with persons with criminal records	31	60.8
Pay all court-ordered fines, restitution, or other financial penalties	27	52.9
Meet family responsibilities and support dependents	24	47.1
Undergo medical and psychiatric treatment and/or enter and remain in a specified institution, if so ordered by the court	23	45.1
Pay supervision fees	19	37.3
Attend a prescribed secular course of study or vocational training	9	17.6
Perform community service	7	13.7

Source: Edward E. Rhine, William R. Smith, and Ronald W. Jackson, *Paroling Authorities: Recent History and Current Practice* (Laurel, MD: American Correctional Association, 1991). Used with permission of the American Correctional Association.

limits to these latter activities as a special condition of parole where such associations are inconsistent with my approved home plan.

- I will not leave the State of Massachusetts for a period in excess of 24 hours without securing permission from my parole officer.

Examples of special parole conditions in various states may provide for the following:

- Prohibition against the use of a motor vehicle (for habitual DUI [driving under the influence] offenders)
- Payment of victim restitution (for property or violent offenders)
- Community service
- Residence in a community corrections center
- Prohibition from any contact with small children (in the case of sex offenders)

Table 11.1 presents various parole conditions and the extent to which they are imposed in selected jurisdictions. Parolees have many regulations to follow. One study found that the average number of standard conditions for a parolee was about 15.[20] Furthermore, parole boards are allowed to mandate that parolees enter drug or alcohol treatment programs. One research study found that coerced drug treatment is as successful as voluntary participation.[21]

This raises the question as to the level of realistic expectations of parole. Is the system of conditions so rigid and strict that the parolee is destined to fail?[22] The courts will generally uphold reasonable conditions but will strike down illegal conditions or those considered unreasonable because they are impossible to meet. As in probation, appellate courts generally allow parole boards immense discretion in imposing conditions of parole.

Legal Issues in Parole Conditions

Recent court cases have raised interesting legal issues involving parole conditions. For example, the Tenth Circuit Court of Appeals upheld a condition that paroled Colorado sex offenders provide blood and saliva samples to create a DNA (deoxyribonucleic acid) bank for easy identification should the parolee commit a similar offense.[23] The condition was challenged as violating parolees' right against unreasonable searches and seizures. The court held that this requirement was reasonable because of the significance of DNA evidence in solving sex offenses, the minimal intrusion on the inmate's right to privacy, and the inmate's diminished constitutional rights.

Similar cases have been decided in two other federal circuit courts of appeals.[24] Plaintiffs argued that they were unconstitutionally required to incriminate themselves with such samples; that they were being singled out as sex offenders, thus violating their right to equal protection; and that it denied them liberty interest under the Fourteenth Amendment. The courts held the tests constitutional, saying that parole is discretionary and may be conditioned on a requirement that is itself legal.

Legal issues have also been raised concerning requirements that offenders who are on parole for sex offenses register in communities where they reside, even if the registration law was passed after the offense was committed. Some states require registration and notification in the community of the presence of sex offenders on parole and even after they have completed their sentence (see Chapter 15). The validity of those statutes has been upheld, but higher courts have not yet decided the question as to whether the law should apply to convicted sex offenders before the law was passed.

The Seventh Circuit Court of Appeals has upheld submission to a penile plethysmograph as a parole condition for a Michigan inmate who was convicted in federal court of kidnapping and allegedly molesting a six-year-old boy before attempting to drown him.[25] The offender in this case objected to the condition, saying that it was fundamentally unfair and therefore denied him due process. His parole was revoked. On appeal, the Seventh Circuit ruled that "the Commission may impose or modify other conditions of parole so long as they are reasonably related to the nature of the circumstances of the offense and the history and characteristics of the parolee."

The American Correctional Association (ACA), in its *Standards for Adult Parole Authorities*, recommends that general conditions that apply to all parolees should require simply that a parolee observe the law, maintain appropriate contact with the parole system, and notify the parole officer of any change of residence. Special conditions, it states, should be added "only when they are clearly relevant to the parolee's compliance with the requirements of the criminal law." Conditions should not concern "the lifestyle of the offender, as such, but should be tested directly against the probability of serious criminal behavior by the individual parolee."[26] The ACA also recommends that parolees be encouraged to inform the paroling authority about their views concerning the conditions to be imposed and that they should have the opportunity to appeal any request of a parole officer to impose a new condition of parole. These ACA recommendations, however, do not have the force and effect of law and may be followed or ignored by paroling authorities in various states.

Rights of Parolees While on Parole

DIMINISHED CONSTITUTIONAL RIGHTS

Constitutional rights enjoyed by an offender on parole that are not as highly protected by the courts as the rights of nonoffenders.

PREFERRED RIGHTS

Rights more highly protected than other constitutional rights.

An offender on parole does not lose all constitutional rights. However, the rights enjoyed are **diminished,** meaning that they are not as highly protected by the courts as similar rights enjoyed by nonoffenders. Even First Amendment rights (which are considered **preferred rights** because they are more highly protected than other constitutional rights) can be limited if an offender is on parole or probation. For example, in a probation case (which could also apply to parole) a defendant was convicted for obstructing a federal court order arising from the defendant's antiabortion activities. The court imposed as a condition of probation that defendant was prohibited from "harassing, intimidating or picketing in front of any gynecological or abortion family planning services center."[27] The defendant challenged that condition, claiming it violated her rights under the First Amendment. On appeal, the Federal Court of Appeals for the Tenth Circuit held the condition valid, saying "conditions which restrict freedom of speech and association are valid if they are reasonably necessary to accomplish the essential needs of the State and public order." If First Amendment rights of parolees can be curtailed in this fashion, it follows that other constitutional rights that are not as highly protected may likewise be curtailed as long as proper justification is established by the state.

The parole officer, without a search warrant and without the parolee's consent, may usually search the place where a parolee lives. The only exception would be in states where warrantless searches are prohibited by agency rules. Some states require that the parolee, as a condition of parole, give blanket permission to search his or her place of residence. This condition has generally been upheld, although problems arise when evidence of a new crime is obtained as a result of the search. In a New York case a parole officer obtained a warrant charging a parolee with a violation and then went to the parolee's apartment. The officer charged the parolee with parole violation and conducted a two-and-a-half-hour search, which yielded narcotics. The parolee was convicted on the new charge, and the conviction was upheld. The court said, "Defendant appellant, as a parolee, was deprived of no constitutional rights by the search and seizure which was made under the circumstances of this case."[28]

In another New York case the court noted that the reasonableness standard for a search and seizure is not necessarily the same when applied to a parolee as when applied to a person whose rights are not similarly diminished, implying that Fourth Amendment protections are diminished when applied to parolees.[29]

Two recent cases from Pennsylvania, however, hold to the contrary. In 1993, a Pennsylvania court refused to admit drugs seized without a warrant in a new criminal case against a parolee.[30] The court said that the absence of a state regulation authorizing and governing warrantless searches of parolees by parole officers, coupled with the lack of consent by the parolee, violated the parolee's constitutional rights. The court concluded that because the evidence was to be used in a new criminal case and not in a parole revocation proceeding, parole officers were in effect acting as police officers when making the warrantless search and so were bound by the warrant rule.

In 1995 another Pennsylvania court suppressed evidence against a parolee that had been obtained by virtue of a parole condition that required the parolee to submit his person, property, and residence to warrantless searches by the agents of the Pennsylvania Board of Probation and Parole.[31] Although the parolee signed a search consent condition, the court said that "to allow a search of a parolee for no reason other than that the parolee accepted parole was tantamount to the parolee checking his or her Fourth Amendment rights at the door of the prison."

Note, however, that in a 1997 case the Pennsylvania Supreme Court in effect overruled the Pennsylvania lower court decision. The court held that a parolee's consent to warrantless searches by state parole agents, based on reasonable suspicion that the parolee had committed a parole violation as specified in the conditions of release, was proper under both the Fourth Amendment and the applicable provision of the Pennsylvania constitution.[32]

These decisions show clear disagreement about the extent of the Fourth Amendment rights of parolees. This area of law is uncertain. However, most courts tend to follow the New York cases, which severely limit a parolee's Fourth Amendment rights and allow warrantless searches by parole officers as long as the condition imposed can be justified.[33] This reiterates the dominant philosophy among courts that parolees do not have the same constitutional rights as the rest of the public.

The Power to Arrest a Parolee

Many states, by law or agency policy, give a parole officer the right to arrest a parolee without a warrant. Other states require that the parole board issue a warrant before a parole officer can make an arrest. In New York and Pennsylvania parole officers may arrest a parole violator without a warrant and receive authorization, a temporary detainer, by telephone immediately afterward. These temporary detainers must be replaced by an arrest warrant within 24 hours in Pennsylvania and 48 hours in New York. Federal probation officers, who also supervise federal parolees, may arrest a parolee without a warrant if there is probable cause to believe that the person being supervised has violated a condition of release.

Upon arrest the parolee must be taken before the court having jurisdiction over the offender or before the proper authority "without unnecessary delay."[34] Justification for these practices is found in the occasional need to take immediate action. Howard Abadinsky reports,

> When I was a parole officer in New York, it was not unusual to encounter parolees, unexpectedly, who were in serious violation of the conditions of their release. For example, heavily involved in abusing heroin (and obviously engaging in criminal acts to support the habit); prohibited from the use of alcohol (because of the dangerous nature of their behavior while under the influence) and intoxicated; child molesters found in the company of children. I could take such persons into custody immediately and use the telephone for detainer-warrant authorization.[35]

In other states, such as Texas, the parole officer must request in writing a warrant from the parole board, although emergency warrants may be obtained by telephone in limited circumstances.[36] Other states allow citations to be issued in different instances, such as:

- Requiring the parolee to appear for a hearing (Oregon)
- Ordering the parolee to appear before the parole agency supervisor for a case review (Wisconsin)
- Allowing the parole officer to arrest alleged violators, taking them before a magistrate to determine whether probable cause exists that the parole conditions have been violated and, if so, issue a warrant for arrest (Iowa)

ACA standards regard the arrest and detention of a parolee on violation charges as a serious act with profound implications for the parolee. The ACA therefore recommends that arrest be made only with a warrant issued by "the affirmative approval of a parole authority member or the statewide or regional director of parole supervision services." Standard 2–1107 provides as follows:

> Warrants for the arrest and detention of parolees are issued only upon adequate evidence which indicates a probable serious or repeated pattern of violation of parole

conditions and a compelling need for detention pending the parole authority's initial revocation decision.

PAROLE ABSCONDERS

While on community supervision, a parolee sometimes commits a series of technical violations or a new crime. A multitude of parole conditions can be violated either in a very short period of time or they can occur over an extended period of time. One of the more serious, and surprisingly frequent, types of technical violations resulting in parole failure involves parole absconders. An **absconder** is defined as an offender under community supervision who, without prior permission, escapes or flees the jurisdiction he or she is required to stay within. Different sources estimate that between 11 percent and 27 percent of all parolees abscond from supervision.[37] In some jurisdictions that have absconding from supervision listed as a criminal offense, a parole absconder can be charged with a new crime. For most parolees, leaving the area without notifying the parole officer is a violation of a parole condition.

Absconding from community supervision can be a politically sensitive issue because, technically, the offender's whereabouts are not known. It is, therefore, unknown whether absconders are active criminals, whether they threaten public safety, or whether they threaten the credibility of community supervision.[38]

Why Do Parolees Leave?

Very little research has been done on the reasons that parolees flee. From the available data, and from the experience of Leanne Fiftal Alarid, one of this book's coauthors, parolees who abscond do so to avoid having their parole revoked and possibly being sent back to prison. Many parolees are uncertain about what their parole officer will do once he or she discovers a violation, and that uncertainty translates into fear. This fear sometimes leads parolees to do anything to avoid a revocation hearing. Parole absconders fall into two main categories: benign and a possible threat to community safety.

TYPE I ABSCONDERS: Benign. The first and most common category is absconders who have committed technical violations and do not understand the system well enough to predict what the outcome of their actions will be. The uncertainty and fear gets the better of them, and in a highly emotional state, the offender drops all responsibilities and pressures that have been building up and leaves them without thinking about the more serious consequences of escape. The ironic part about this type of absconder is the reasons that led up to their escape are usually less serious than the escape label that will affect them for the remainder of their sentence and any future convictions. Reasons for absconding for this type of person range from drug use to financial difficulties, to leaving the state to visit a dying relative. Dale G. Parent substantiates the benign type of absconder by noting that "typical absconders are low-risk property offenders who remained in the community after they absconded. . . . [M]ost were not arrested for new crimes while on absconder status."[39]

TYPE II ABSCONDERS: Menace to Society. The second category of absconders is individuals who understand the system too well. These individuals constitute a very small percent of all absconders and have committed one or more new crimes (some of which are serious) while on community supervision. They know with certainty that they will return to prison anyway. If the recent criminal behavior is serious enough,

ABSCONDER

An offender under community supervision who, without prior permission, escapes or flees the jurisdiction he or she is required to stay within.

this type of absconder knows that they may never get out of prison again, so they take the chance of living out of prison until they are caught. This type of absconder is more likely than the first type to come to the attention of law enforcement officers and to be extradited (returned) to the original state of conviction. Type II absconders are the ones most likely to return to prison, as well as the ones prone to threaten community safety.

Locating and Apprehending Fugitives

Because budgets for fugitive units are low and most absconders are seen as benign, most states take a passive approach to locating and apprehending fugitives. When a parolee (or probationer) absconds from supervision, a warrant is filed with local, state, or national crime information systems. The parole officer will first contact the offender's family, friends, and employer to check the offender's whereabouts and inform them to call the parole office or police if they find out any information or see the offender again. Many absconders are caught from a routine check for a traffic violation, and some are arrested from detection on a new crime. Ironically, many absconders never leave the state and could later be located through searching public utility records or other applicable databases.[40]

Type II absconders are pursued through more aggressive tactics because they may pose a threat to community safety. Parent and his colleagues found that states that aggressively pursue an absconder use one of three methods:

1. Their own fugitive apprehension unit
2. Receiving assistance from the Federal Bureau of Investigation (FBI)
3. Contracting out with a private apprehension unit

Six states had enhanced fugitive units that operated in certain counties or statewide (Arizona, California, Massachusetts, Minnesota, Oklahoma, and Utah). One of these fugitive units, the Special Operations Unit in Massachusetts, is highlighted in Box 11.1.

The vast majority of states does not have their own fugitive units and must seek assistance from the FBI or a private contractor. In using the FBI, the U.S. attorney's office is made aware of the situation and agrees to extradite the absconder back to the original state of conviction from wherever the offender is captured. The state requesting the extradition must pay the extradition costs, which are about $4,000 per fugitive. The fugitive is usually accompanied by two federal officers and is transported (from long distances) by aircraft to designated airports used by the U.S. marshall's office. At that point, the fugitive is transported by car to the home state of conviction.[41]

A final option for states that wish to apprehend certain absconders would be to hire a private contractor. For a heftier price, one individual or an assembled team will attempt to actively locate and transport the absconder back to the original state of conviction to answer charges.

Predicting Absconding Behavior

The argument can be made that if absconding behavior can be predicted, then it can be prevented—or at least decreased. Only two known empirical studies of parole absconding behavior have been conducted in the last decade. Shawn Schwaner compared a sample of absconders (11 percent) with nonabsconders (89 pecent) in Ohio using two different data sets.[42] Using bivariate analyses, he found that the following variables were most predictive of absconding behavior:

- Juvenile and adult felony convictions
- Arrests within five years of the current crime
- A presence of previous adult incarcerations
- Presence of previous probation or parole revocations

Furthermore, the high-risk parole absconders were more likely to be apprehended than low-risk absconders.[43]

More recently, Frank Williams III, Marilyn D. McShane, and H. Michael Dolny collected data on 863 California parolees who absconded during their first time on parole, representing 21.3 percent of their entire sample of about 4,052 parolees. There were 186 parolees (4.6 percent of the sample) who absconded two or more times in one year.[44] The researchers found no gender differences in the absconding rate. However, individuals of Hispanic origin were less likely than persons of other race or ethnic groups to abscond. Using multivariate statistical techniques, the researchers ascertained that the following seven variables contributed significantly to prediction of absconding behavior (in order of higher to lower importance):

1. Unstable living arrangements
2. Frequent unemployment
3. Previous parole violator
4. Low stakes
5. Larger number of prior arrests
6. Single marital status
7. Previous felonies

Unstable living arrangements contributed 29 percent to the explanation, making it the most powerful predictor. The bottom four variables, collectively, contributed only

Former Seattle grade school teacher Mary Kay Letourneau, who had an affair with a 13-year-old boy and had his baby, was resentenced to 7.5 years in jail in 1998 for violating her parole by meeting with the youth.

Alan Berner/Seattle Times

half as much (14 percent) to the model. Another drawback, which the researchers themselves point out, is that about 27 percent of nonabsconders also fit the absconder profile (a false positive), and thus separating absconders from nonabsconders is difficult.[45] More work needs to be done to improve predicting absconder behavior.

To prevent absconding, parole officers must understand factors and situations leading up to an offender's decision to leave. Then, parole officers should "keep a pulse" on each person on their caseload, noting changes in behavior, to determine if a revocation pattern is occurring. Preventing absconding behavior will be more effective for the first, more benign type of absconders. The second, more serious type is more difficult to predict. Until more resources can be devoted to studying absconders, this behavior seems to be a casualty of community supervision.

Some jurisdictions, such as the District of Columbia with its Find and Fix program, have experimented with different methods of returning absconders to community supervision, with some changes in the parole conditions. In Minneapolis, Minnesota, absconders were offered a brief period of amnesty. Absconders could voluntarily turn themselves in and not be reimprisoned. These programs have reported significant success.[46]

PAROLE REVOCATION

The term **revocation** refers to the formal termination of a parolee's conditional freedom and (usually) the reinstatement of imprisonment. The violation process begins with the field parole officer who must discover the violation and who must obtain supervisor approval to issue either a citation to appear at the revocation hearing or a warrant for arrest. When a warrant is issued, the parolee is detained in the county jail until a preliminary hearing. When a citation is issued, the parolee remains in the

REVOCATION

The formal termination of a parolee's conditional freedom and the reinstatement of imprisonment.

community until a revocation hearing. The decision of whether or not to revoke resides with the parole board.

In the event parole conditions are not followed (a technical violation), or a new crime is committed while on parole, one of three options will likely occur:

1. The parolee will remain on parole with even more restrictions.
2. The parolee will be transferred to an intermediate sanction (for example, a halfway house or work release program) for a more intensive form of community supervision.
3. Parole will be revoked, and the offender will finish the sentence in jail or prison.

If the prisoner is convicted of a new crime, the time served may either be done at the same time as the original charge (concurrently) or after the original charge has been served (consecutively).[47]

Rate of Revocation

The rate of parole failure, or revocation rate, has increased.[48] In 1995, 12 percent of all state-level parolees were convicted of a new crime, 18 percent had their parole revoked for a technical violation, and 11 percent were returned to jail or prison "for other reasons."[49] A federal-level study indicates that 18.6 percent of all federal prisoners released in 1994 were returned to federal prison within three years.[50] This number does not include federal offenders who were reincarcerated for a state-level offense after discharge from the federal system. These numbers do not sound like much until one takes into consideration that recent prison growth has been largely affected by admissions for parole violations. In 1998, 206,751 offenders entering state prisons had violated parole in some manner. Parole violators now constitute 34 percent of all prison admissions—a number that has doubled since 1980.[51]

For 1997 alone, a total of 189,765 prisoners were returned to state and federal prisons for violating discretionary parole or some other form of conditional release (see Table 11.2). The vast majority of parole violators finished serving time for their current crime with no new sentence, while others received more time with a new sentence.

Of the 1997 state-level parolees who failed on parole, most did so as a result of the commission of a new crime:

- 59.5 percent committed a new crime
- 19.0 percent absconded or failed to report to their parole officer
- 13.7 percent had a drug-related violation (relapse, possession, or failure to attend treatment)
- 13.9 percent had other reasons (failure to secure employment, pay fines, possession of a gun, and so on)[52]

In a different study of the federal system, most parolees failed on parole for a technical violation:

- 60 percent returned to prison following a technical violation
- 30 percent committed a new crime
- 10 percent returned for "other violations"[53]

Reasons for Increased Revocation Rates

Being that the rates of violations have risen in recent years, studies have been undertaken to understand parole and probation revocations. Dale Parent and colleagues cited five reasons for this increase:

TABLE 11.2 *Sentenced Prisoners Admitted to State and Federal Institutions for Violation of Parole or Other Conditional Release, 1997*

Violation	JURISDICTION		
	State	Federal	Total
Parole			
New sentence			
Male	24,534	NA	24,534
Female	1,885	NA	1,885
No new sentence			
Male	33,714	1,137	34,851
Female	2,706	124	2,830
Total	62,839	1,261	64,100
Other conditional release			
New sentence			
Male	30,614	NA	30,614
Female	2,564	NA	2,564
No new sentence			
Male	82,656	1,714	84,370
Female	7,986	131	8,117
Total	123,820	1,845	125,665
Total	**186,659**	**3,106**	**189,765**

Note: NA = Not available.
Source: U.S. Department of Justice, Bureau of Justice Statistics, *Correctional Populations in the United States, 1997*, NCJ 177613 (Washington, DC: U.S. Department of Justice, 2000), Table 5.16.

1. A shift in the purposes of community supervision from treatment to control and punishment
2. An increase in the average number of offenders on each caseload
3. An increase in the number of parole and probation conditions
4. The use of improved technology to detect violations
5. Changes in the types of offenders[54]

With more emphasis placed on control and punishment, the threshold level is lowered for what behavior is tolerated before a revocation occurs. An increased caseload suggests that officers spend less quality time with offenders and more time on rule enforcement and paperwork. An increased number of conditions placed on offenders imply that offenders have more pressure to perform and try to meet all those conditions. Equally likely, with more conditions, more chances arise to violate those conditions. Finally, with the advances made in drug testing technology, more drug use will be detected. With the increased use of electronic monitoring in parole and probation, more hardened offenders tend to be placed in the community to avoid institutional overcrowding.[55]

When revocation rates increase, a number of other components in the criminal justice system experience hardships. For example, parole and probation officers must devote more of their time to revocation paperwork and less time to supervising other offenders on their caseload who are functioning satisfactorily. Furthermore, while probation and parole revocators are awaiting hearings, revocation drains court resources, parole board resources, and county jail bed space.[56]

Attitudes on Revocation

The frequency of parole revocation has generated controversy. Some feel there are too many parole revocations; others think more parolees ought to be revoked. Too many parole revocations lead to prison congestion, and too few revocations lead to public apprehension about safety from convicted offenders. The implication is that parole officials are reluctant to revoke if it means adding prisoners to an already over-crowded prison system. A balance must be achieved between reintegrating offenders into society and public protection.

The public tends to view the rate of parole violation as indicative of parole success or failure. Criminal justice practitioners, in contrast, recognize that what may appear to be good parole statistical results can, in light of the quality and extent of supervision, indicate just the opposite. One state may report a violation rate of 8 percent, but the only indicator the state may count as a "violation" is the conviction for a new crime. This violation rate does not mean much. Another state may report a much greater rate of violation, but it may practice close, intensive supervision and have a policy of strictly enforcing all parole rules. In neither practice does the reported violation rate accurately measure the success or failure of that jurisdiction's parole system. One of the more significant criticisms of parole revocations is when revocation hearings are used in place of criminal prosecution, particularly if the case is too weak to pass the burden of proof required for prosecution.[57]

LEGAL ISSUES OF PAROLE REVOCATION

A strictly legal perspective now controls the nature of parole revocation.

Morrissey v. Brewer: The Leading Case on Parole Revocation

The U.S. Supreme Court has given parole authorities specific guidance on certain legal aspects of parole revocation. The constitutional rights given to parolees in revocation proceedings are laid out by the Court in *Morrissey v. Brewer,* arguably the most important and best-known case in probation and parole.[58]

Morrissey pleaded guilty to and was convicted in 1967 of false drawing or uttering of checks. He was paroled from the Iowa State Penitentiary in 1968. Seven months later his parole was revoked for violating a series of parole conditions. Morrissey bought a car under an assumed name and drove it without permission, gave false statements to the police about his address and insurance company after a minor accident, obtained credit under an assumed name, and failed to report his residence to his parole officer. The parole officer's report also noted that Morrissey had been interviewed, had admitted to the violations, and could not explain why he had not contacted his parole officer. Morrissey's parole was revoked. He challenged the revocation, saying it was unconstitutional because there was no hearing and therefore he was deprived of due process rights. The issue brought to the U.S. Supreme Court on appeal was whether the due process clause of the Fourteenth Amendment affords a parolee certain rights before parole revocation.

TABLE 11.3 *Procedural Due Process Routinely Provided at Parole Revocation Hearings*

Due Process Protection	PRELIMINARY HEARING		FINAL HEARING	
	Number	Percent	Number	Percent
Written notice of alleged violation	45	88.2	51	100.0
Disclosure of evidence of violations	42	82.4	51	100.0
Opportunity to confront and cross-examine adverse witnesses	44	86.3	47	92.2
Representation by counsel	31	60.8	40	78.4
Opportunity to be heard in person and to present evidence and witnesses	43	84.3	51	100.0
Written statement of reasons for the decision	45	88.2	48	94.1

Source: Edward E. Rhine, William R. Smith, and Ronald W. Jackson, *Paroling Authorities: Recent History and Current Practice* (Laurel, MD: American Correctional Association, 1991), 128.

Five Basic Rights before Revocation

The U.S. Supreme Court held that revocation represents a **grievous loss** of liberty, and therefore a parolee is entitled to some due process rights prior to revocation. The Court described two important stages in the typical process of parole revocation: the **preliminary hearing** and the **revocation hearing.** The preliminary hearing requires that "some minimal inquiry be conducted at or reasonably near the place of the alleged parole violation or arrest and as promptly as convenient after arrest while information is fresh and sources are available." The revocation hearing "must be the basis for more than determining probable cause; it must lead to a final evaluation of any contested relevant facts and consideration of whether the facts as determined warrant revocation." In *Morrissey* the Court enumerated five rights that must be afforded the parolee before revocation as the minimum requirements of due process. These rights are:

1. A written notice of the claimed violations of parole
2. The disclosure to the parolee of evidence against him; the opportunity to be heard in person and to present witnesses and documentary evidence
3. The right to confront and cross-examine adverse witnesses (unless the hearing officer specifically finds good cause for not allowing confrontation)
4. A "neutral and detached" hearing body such as a traditional parole board, members of which need not be judicial officers or lawyers
5. A written statement by the fact finders as to the evidence relied on and the reasons for revoking parole

A survey by Edward E. Rhine, William R. Smith, and Ronald W. Jackson indicates that these due process rights are routinely provided at present by a great majority of states in parole revocation hearings (see Table 11.3). The survey shows that, at least in the revocation hearing, 100 percent of the states gave the parolee a written notice of the alleged violation, disclosed evidence of violations, and gave parolees an opportunity to be heard in person and to present evidence and witnesses. Over 90 percent of states gave parolees a written statement of the reason for the decision and allowed the parolee an opportunity to confront and cross-examine adverse witnesses. Less (78 percent) allowed representation by counsel.[59]

GRIEVOUS LOSS

Revoking parole is a grievous loss because it involves being sent back to prison.

PRELIMINARY HEARING

An inquiry conducted at or reasonably near the place of the alleged parole violation or arrest to determine if there is probable cause to believe that the parolee committed a parole violation.

REVOCATION HEARING

A due process hearing that must be conducted before parole can be revoked.

The Significance of *Morrissey v. Brewer*

Morrissey is arguably the most significant case ever to be decided by the U.S. Supreme Court on the issue of parole because for the first time the Court held that parolees are entitled to some form of due process, at least in the parole revocation process. Relying on previous nonparole cases, the Court said that "whether any procedural protections are due depends on the extent to which an individual will be 'condemned to suffer grievous loss.'" Revoking parole signifies a grievous loss because it means being sent back to prison, hence due process guarantees are needed.

Some scholars interpret *Morrissey* to mean that parolees are constitutionally entitled to the two-stage hearing process (the preliminary hearing and the revocation hearing) in addition to the five due process rights enumerated. Nothing in the *Morrissey* decision, however, indicates that two hearings are constitutionally required. The Court simply said "in analyzing what is due, we see two important stages in the typical process of parole revocation," referring to the two hearings. Nonetheless, a survey shows that 45 jurisdictions conduct preliminary hearings prior to the revocation hearings.[60] Although most states have a two-stage hearing process, some states merge these two proceedings into one, with the five due process rights being given during the merged proceeding. The U.S. Supreme Court has not addressed the constitutionality of a merged proceeding, hence most states play it safe and give two hearings.

Other Legal Issues in Parole Revocation

A number of court rulings address parolees' rights during special conditions, such as preparole, provisional release, and when the parole board changes its mind before approving early release of a prisoner.

THE CONSTITUTIONAL RIGHT TO COUNSEL: In *Morrissey v. Brewer*, the Court did not address the question of the parolee's right to the assistance of retained or appointed counsel at the preliminary and revocation hearings. The Court simply said, "We do not reach or decide the question whether the parolee is entitled to the assistance of retained or appointed counsel if he is indigent." One survey shows, however, that representation by counsel is provided for in 78.4 percent of the states surveyed.[61]

In one of the first cases decided after *Morrissey*, the California Supreme Court held that a probationer was entitled to representation by retained or appointed counsel at formal proceedings for the revocation of probation. The court held that a violation of a probation condition is often a matter of degree or quality of conduct, and the point where a violation occurs is often a matter of technical judgment. It then quoted from *Goldberg v. Kelly* that "trained counsel in such circumstances can help delineate the issues, present the factual contentions in an orderly manner, and generally safeguard the interests of [the] client."[62]

The California Supreme Court decision requiring counsel is at odds, however, with a decision of the U.S. Supreme Court on the same issue involving probation. In *Gagnon v. Scarpelli*, decided a year after *Morrissey*, the U.S. Supreme Court mandated a case-by-case determination of the need for counsel at probation and parole revocation hearings.[63] The determination of the need for counsel is to be left to the discretion of the state authority responsible for administering the probation and parole system. The Court stated that in cases in which a probationer's or parolee's version of a disputed issue can be fairly presented only by trained counsel, appointment of counsel for the indigent probationer or parolee should be made, "[a]lthough the presence and participation of counsel will probably be both undesirable and constitutionally unnecessary in most revocation hearings." Both the U.S. Supreme Court and the

California Supreme Court refused to make the rule in *Morrissey* applicable to parole revocations that occurred before that decision.[64]

THE RIGHT TO CONFRONT WITNESSES: The Court in *Morrissey* said that a parolee facing revocation has "the right to confront and cross-examine adverse witnesses (unless the hearing officer specifically finds good cause for not allowing confrontation)." Lower courts have interpreted this right to be limited, consistent with the concept of "diminished" constitutional rights. In a 1994 case, for example, the Federal Eighth Circuit Court of Appeals decided that a parolee has a limited right to confront and cross-examine witnesses for the government in a parole revocation hearing.[65] It further held that hearsay evidence (statements offered by a witness that are based upon what someone else has told the witness and not upon personal knowledge or observation) may be admitted and considered in a revocation hearing.[66] These rules, the court said, must be properly balanced. Otherwise, due process is violated and the revocation of parole must be reversed. In this case no right to confrontation was given the parolee in either the preliminary or the revocation hearing despite his request to be allowed to question witnesses. Moreover, hearsay evidence was used for revocation, including violation reports, police reports, and a signed statement by the victim. The Eighth Circuit Court acknowledged that the right to confront witnesses is given to a parolee, but this right may be limited by the state if the "hearing officer specifically finds good cause for not allowing confrontation." If the government denies a parolee the right to confrontation, the government has the burden of justifying that denial. Failure to carry that burden means that a parolee's right to due process is violated, hence the revocation is invalid.

The court further said that the parolee must assert the right to confront witnesses at the preliminary hearing. If done then, that right need not be asserted again in the revocation hearing. If the right is asserted, the state must allow the witnesses to be cross-examined unless the parolee waives the right or there is sufficient finding of good cause not to allow confrontation.[67] On the issue of hearsay evidence, the court said that it is admissible in a parole revocation hearing as long as it is reliable. The court suggested questions to establish reliability:

1. Is the information corroborated by the parolee's own statements or other live testimony at the hearing?
2. Does the information fit within one of the many exceptions to the hearsay rule?
3. Does the information have other substantial indicia of reliability?

A "yes" answer to any of these questions signifies that the hearsay is reliable and therefore may be admitted as evidence in court.

EXCLUSIONARY RULE: The decision in *Pennsylvania Board of Probation and Parole v. Scott* addresses the use of the exclusionary rule in parole revocation proceedings. The **exclusionary rule** is a rule of evidence that means to deter police misconduct. The exclusionary rule was initially introduced in 1914 for federal cases in *Weeks v. United States*, to exclude any evidence obtained or seized by the government that was found to be in violation of the Fourth Amendment. The exclusionary rule was later applied to all illegally obtained evidence in state proceedings in the case of *Mapp v. Ohio*. This case further served to protect citizens against illegally seized evidence.

In the case involving parolees, *Pennsylvania Board of Probation and Parole v. Scott*, the court was asked whether the exclusionary rule should apply during parole revocation hearings. The court ruled that the exclusionary rule does not apply to parole revocation hearings.[68] The court ruled in the direction it did in part because

EXCLUSIONARY RULE

A rule of evidence that enforces the Fourth Amendment in which the purpose is to deter police misconduct.

parole officers do not need warrants to conduct a legal search, and the burden of proof is lower in parole revocation hearings than in criminal court prosecutions. A different standard must be met for searches conducted for individuals under parole supervision compared with individuals not under community supervision.[69] Parolees (and probationers) have less expectation of privacy than individuals not under a correctional sentence. The *Scott* ruling was extended the following year to include probation revocation proceedings, in *State v. Pizel*.[70]

DUE PROCESS IF THE BOARD CHANGES ITS MIND BEFORE PAROLE RELEASE: An issue related to parole revocation is whether the parole board must give an inmate due process if it changes its mind after informing the inmate that he or she is to be released on parole. In *Jago v. Van Curen*, the U.S. Supreme Court said that no due process rights are needed if the board changes its mind before inmate release.[71] In that case inmate Van Curen pleaded guilty to a charge of embezzlement and was sentenced to not less than 6 nor more than 100 years in prison. Van Curen was interviewed in 1974 by a panel representing the parole board. The panel recommended that he be paroled "on or after April 23, 1974." The parole board approved the recommendation, and the inmate was notified of this decision. Several days after Van Curen was interviewed, the parole board was informed that he had been truthful neither during the interview nor in the parole plan that he submitted to his parole officers. Van Curen had told the panel that he had embezzled $1 million when in fact he embezzled $6 million. In his parole plan Van Curen stated he would be living with his half-brother if paroled. It was discovered, however, that Van Curen intended to live with his homosexual lover. The parole board withdrew his early parole as a result of these revelations and, at a later meeting, formally denied Van Curen parole. At no time was Van Curen granted a hearing to explain the false statements he had given the parole authorities. He sued the parole authorities, claiming that the withdrawal of his parole without a hearing violated his constitutional right to due process. The Court disagreed and held that the due process clause does not guarantee a hearing in cases of parole withdrawal prior to actual release on parole. The Court said,

> We would severely restrict the necessary flexibility of prison administrators and parole authorities were we to hold that any one of their myriad decisions with respect to individual inmates may . . . give rise to protected "liberty" interests which could not thereafter be impaired without a constitutionally mandated hearing under the Due Process Clause. This decision implies that withdrawal of parole prior to release is not equivalent to parole revocation after the inmate has been released and therefore does not trigger due process guarantees.

CANCELLATION OF PROVISIONAL RELEASE: In a 1997 case, *Lynce v. Mathis*, the U.S. Supreme Court held that a Florida law canceling provisional release credits violates the *ex post facto* (penal legislation that has retroactive application) prohibition of the Constitution.[72] Lynce was convicted of attempted murder in 1986 and sentenced to 22 years in a Florida prison. He was released in 1992 based on the Florida Department of Corrections' determination that he had accumulated five different types of early release credits totaling 5,668 days, 1,860 of which were provisional credits given as a result of prison overcrowding. After the prisoner was released, the state attorney general issued an opinion stating that a 1992 Florida law retroactively canceled all provisional credits awarded to inmates convicted of murder or attempted murder. Lynce was rearrested and returned to prison. He went to court alleging that the retroactive cancellation of his provisional credits violated the *ex post facto* clause of the Constitution. The Court agreed, saying the 1992 Florida law "has unquestionably disadvantaged the petitioner because it resulted in his arrest and prolonged his imprisonment." The Court added that the Florida law "did more than simply remove a mechanism that created an opportunity for early release for a class of prisoners. . . . [R]ather, it made ineligible for early release a class of prisoners who were previously eligible—including some, like petitioner, who had actually been released."

Lynce is significant because it limits the applicability of newly enacted restrictive parole laws to inmates who were benefited by previous liberal laws. Restrictive parole laws can be enacted, but they apply only to inmates who have not yet earned parole credits. It cannot be applied to inmates who were benefited by and had earned release credit under a more advantageous law.

DUE PROCESS RIGHTS OF PRISONERS RELEASED UNDER PREPAROLE: In another 1997 decision, *Young v. Harper*, the U.S. Supreme Court held that Oklahoma's preparole release program was equivalent to parole.[73] Therefore, released prisoners under preparole were entitled to due process rights, similar to those given in *Morrissey*, prior to being brought back to prison because their preparole had been revoked. In this case the state of Oklahoma established a preparole conditional supervision program so that when Oklahoma's prisons become overcrowded the Pardon and Parole Board could conditionally release prisoners before their sentences expired. Upon determination of the board, an inmate could be placed on preparole after serving 15 percent of his or her sentence. An inmate became eligible for regular parole only after one-third of his or her sentence had elapsed.

Preparole program participants and regular parolees were released subject to similar conditions. The board reviewed Harper's criminal record and prison conduct and simultaneously recommended him for parole and released him under the preparole program. At that time he had served 15 years of a life sentence. After five months of preparole release the governor denied Harper's parole, and he was ordered by his parole officer to prison without any type of hearing. The Court held that Oklahoma's preparole release program was similar to parole, and therefore inmates released on preparole were entitled before preparole revocation to the due process rights given in *Morrissey*. In essence, the Court said that any state program for relieving prison congestion that has parole features is considered parole (regardless of what the program is called), so bringing an inmate back to prison requires due process.

Using the same principles as the *Harper* case, another court decision, in *Hawkins v. Freeman*, said that parole boards that commit an error and parole a prisoner before his or her minimum parole eligibility date cannot automatically rescind (take back) parole without first determining whether the parolee's liberty interest has taken shape.[74] In the *Hawkins* case, Hawkins was sentenced to a 50-year term under habitual offender legislation in North Carolina. He was paroled in 1992 by mistake, and the parole board did not realize its error until two years later. The parole board had Hawkins arrested and placed back into custody. Hawkins objected, saying that he was law-abiding for two years and had earned a substantial interest in his liberty while on parole before the parole board realized its mistake. The outcome of the ruling resulted in Hawkins being returned to parole.

PRISON TIME CREDIT FOR TIME SERVED ON PAROLE: In most jurisdictions the parolee whose parole is revoked receives no credit for the time spent on parole. In other jurisdictions the parolee receives credit on the sentence as straight time; that is, without the benefit of good-time credits. In a few states the parolee receives credit on his or her sentence equal to the time spent on parole and also earns reductions for good behavior while on parole. Generally a parolee whose parole has been revoked may be paroled again, but in some cases the revoked parolee must remain in prison for a specified time before becoming eligible for another parole.

THE RIGHT TO APPEAL REVOCATION: The right to appeal revocation was not addressed in *Morrissey* or in any subsequent case decided by the U.S. Supreme Court. In the absence of an authoritative decision, the answer has been "no." One source reports that parolees, presumably by state law or agency policy, are entitled to appeal the revocation decision in 24 states. No such right is given in 26 states.[75]

The court has agreed, however, that the discretionary functions of both the parole board and parole officers qualify them for various levels of legal protection, otherwise known as immunity. There are two types of immunity: absolute and qualified. **Absolute immunity** protects workers from legal action unless they engage in discretion that is intentionally and maliciously wrong. In **qualified immunity,** workers are not liable when their actions are found to be "objectively reasonable."

In *King v. Simpson*, the court ruled that parole board officials have absolute immunity in all decisions to grant, deny, or revoke parole. For parole officers, the level of immunity depends on which function is being performed. Parole officers have absolute immunity when acting in a quasi-judicial or prosecutorial function, such as when initiating parole revocation proceedings and when presenting the case during parole revocation hearings. However, parole officers have only qualified immunity when performing administrative or other discretionary functions.[76]

Parole officer functions are defined differently among jurisdictions. In a case decided in New York, parole officers have only qualified immunity when recommending the issuance of a revocation warrant. Under New York law, issuing a revocation warrant is considered an investigatory, not a prosecutorial, function.[77]

THE TIME IT TAKES TO REVOKE AND OUTCOMES: The time it takes to revoke parole varies from one jurisdiction to another. In a nationwide study of the revocation process, Peggy B. Burke found that the average time it took from the time of violation detection by the officer to disposition by the parole board or the court ranged from 44 to 64 days. Most violators (82 percent) were brought in by warrants, and the remaining answered summons or citations to appear.[78] More jurisdictions are using citations in place of automatic warrants for most probation and parole violators waiting revocation hearing, unless the violation was violent or indications exist that absconding from the area may be a problem. The advantage of this allows the offender to continue working and supporting dependents, while at the same time preparing for a possible entrance or return to jail or prison. Another distinct advantage is that citations save jail space.[79]

Parole revocation hearings usually result in revocation and incarceration for the original term. A study by Rhine, Smith, and Jackson reveals that in 47 states (92.2 percent) the parolee may be returned to custody if parole is revoked. If the hearing shows that the parolee committed the alleged violation, other sanctions are also available to the parole board:

1. No change in the parole status (used in 38 states)
2. Modification of parole conditions (used in 38 states)
3. Serve out-of-state sentence concurrently with or consecutively to the new sentence (used in 22 states)
4. Restoration to parole status, but parole term is extended (used in 21 states)
5. Incarceration for an extended term (used in 18 states)
6. Incarceration for a new term (used in 16 states)[80]

ABSOLUTE IMMUNITY

Protection from legal action or liability unless workers engage in discretion that is intentionally and maliciously wrong.

QUALIFIED IMMUNITY

Protection from liability in decisions or actions that are "objectively reasonable."

As in the case of probation, returning a parolee to prison is usually discretionary with the board even in cases in which the parolee commits a new offense. The only exception is if state law provides for automatic revocation if the parolee commits another crime, particularly a violent offense. In *Richardson v. New York State Executive Department*, the court ruled that parolees who commit a new violent crime while on parole may have their parole revoked and be returned to prison even if the parolee has not yet been convicted on the new violent offense.[81] This is possible because while conviction for a new offense requires guilt beyond reasonable doubt, parole revocation usually requires a lower degree of certainty—either a preponderance of the evidence or reasonable suspicion that the parolee violated the terms of parole.

As states overhaul policies and procedures for responding to violators, responses have become more streamlined and more efficient, thus increasing administrative options and decreasing time spent waiting for revocation hearings and resources spent prosecuting revocations. One example of this is in Illinois, where legislation was created to give authority to probation officers to impose increased sanctions on non-compliant offenders, without having to go back to court each time. Judges of each judicial circuit created a series of administrative sanctions that the probation officer was mandated to follow. This saved time for both the court and the probation officer.[82]

In other states, such as South Carolina, revised revocation policies were found to be "more consistent, more equitable, and more proportional to the seriousness of the violations."[83] A more structured response to revocation decision making includes expanding the intermediate sentencing options for parole (and probation) violators. Some states, such as Georgia, have a parole violator unit. Violators must complete a 90–day prison boot camp program. Other programs include intensive supervision probation or parole, electronic monitoring, house arrest, therapeutic communities, and residential treatment centers.[84] These intermediate sanction programs are discussed in Chapters 12 and 13.

PAROLE EFFECTIVENESS

Parole has been widely criticized as a "revolving door" to prison that reduces the impact of criminal sentences and threatens public safety. Critics claim that studies have failed to provide any assurance that paroled inmates will not continue their criminal activities while under supervision. Some public concerns are valid. For example, one study found that California parole officers "lost track of about one-fifth of the parolees they were assigned to in 1999."[85] However, some parolees (and probationers) do complete their term of supervision successfully.

These facts, however, do not fully answer the question: Is parole effective? Completion of parole without revocation may represent the parole officers' failure to adequately supervise offenders. On the one hand, violations, particularly technical violations, might not come to the attention of an officer who cannot or refuses to supervise closely. On the other hand, closer supervision would probably reveal a larger number of technical violations, which could be reflected in higher recidivism statistics. Yet many of the particular offenders may not be considered failures by their supervising officers or the respective courts.

To illustrate this point, consider the following examples. Which parolees are successful, and which are not?

1. Richard has not been arrested for any offense during the term of his supervision but was cited several times for technical violations, such as failure to report, failure to maintain employment, and excessive use of alcohol.

2. Manuel has no known technical violations but was arrested on two occasions for failure to pay court-ordered child support. A review of the records indicates that he got very far behind while incarcerated but has been paying regularly since being placed under supervision. He has not been able to "catch up" the delinquent balance, however, and his ex-wife regularly files charges of delinquent child support against him.

3. Josephine has no known technical violations but was arrested for driving under the influence of alcohol two months after being placed under supervision. She agreed to enter an alcohol treatment program, and there have been no further reported violations. Her alcohol treatment counselor reports that her progress is favorable.

4. David has no new crimes and no technical violations. However, he has a bad attitude and refuses to cooperate with the parole officer beyond the bare minimum required by his parole agreement.

5. Jean successfully completes five years of supervision with no arrests or technical violations. One year before she is scheduled to be terminated from supervision, she is arrested for a new offense. This is the first time in her adult life that she has gone more than six months without being arrested.

6. Jeffrey is not arrested for any new offenses, and there are no reported technical violations. However, the supervising officer has been advised repeatedly by law enforcement authorities that Jeffrey is heavily involved in narcotics trafficking.

7. Raymond was released from prison a year ago. He is working regularly and has no reported violations. One evening when returning from a movie with his wife he is involved in a minor traffic accident. In the ensuing events he and the other driver exchange blows, and both are arrested. He is charged with simple assault and fined $200.

Which of these probationers and parolees is successful? The question cannot be answered by arrest and conviction statistics only. A strict accounting might conclude that offenders #4 and #6 are successful. A subjective analysis might suggest that offenders #4 and #6 are failures. When examining recidivism studies, pay attention to three factors:

1. How recidivism is defined (by rearrest, conviction, parole revocation, return to prison, or other form of returning to criminal behavior)
2. The duration of time that the subjects were studied (the longer period of time subjects were followed—for example, up to three years—the better)
3. The size of the sample studied (a larger sample, or one that samples from more than one area of the country, is more generalizable)

Recidivism Studies

Many recidivism studies that were conducted between the 1950s and the 1990s are fraught with methodological problems that limit their generalizability. Some of the more methodologically sound research studies have reported mixed findings on the impact that certain factors have on parole success. Some of these factors include:

- Race and ethnicity
- Involvement in prison education programs
- Length of time served in prison
- Behavior while incarcerated
- Current conviction type
- Parolee age

In other words, some studies show that these factors are significant in predicting parole outcome, and other studies show no differences. For example, one study found an inverse relationship between time served in prison and parole success. Don Gottfredson and colleagues found that the less time offenders served in prison, the greater the likelihood of parole success.[86] Meanwhile, a nationwide study yielded no difference in time served behind bars and parole outcome.[87]

Regarding type of crime, studies have consistently found that murderers have a significantly higher parole success rate.[88] However, offenders convicted of other types of crimes have been shown to have more inconsistent rates of recidivism. One study by Allen J. Beck and Bernard E. Shipley measured the rate of rearrest for three years following release. Generally speaking, for state-level offenders, property offenders (for example, burglars) have higher recidivism rates (68 percent) on parole than offenders convicted of violent crimes (59.6 percent), drug offenders (50.4 percent), and public-order offenders (54.6 percent).[89] In a different study of offenders returning to the federal system between 1986 and 1997, offenders convicted of violent crimes (for example, robbery) were more likely to return to federal prison within three years than any other offender type. About 32 percent of violent offenders returned to prison as opposed to only 13 percent of drug offenders.[90]

Some of these differences stem from the different patterns of offending behavior that criminals exhibit. Some criminals begin their "criminal career" at an earlier age, accrue more arrests, and sustain criminal behavior for a long time before decelerating the rate of offending. These criminals are termed "repeat" or "habitual" offenders. Other criminals, such as murderers, do not have criminal careers per se, but they commit a serious offense, for which they get caught and serve time. These criminals are much less likely to recidivate.

Related to this idea of criminal careers and offending patterns is the relationship between age and recidivism. Research that examines this relationship has found that younger parolees, especially those under the age of 25, are more likely to recidivate than older parolees.[91] One recent study of California parolees determined that gang membership should also be taken into consideration when examining different age groups. In this study, Frank P. Williams III and his colleagues found that younger parolees who were not gang members had similar rates of reoffending as older parolees. The researchers conclude:

> In sum, our analyses lead us to believe that the youngest parolees, as a group, are not the worst of the parolee population. There is some evidence that they may be slightly worse than the average in parolee failure, violent and serious reoffending, dangerousness, and consumption of intervention resources. But when gang membership is controlled, much of that trend is called into question. On the other hand, they are not among the best of the parolee population either.[92]

The three variables that have shown more consistent findings in predicting parole outcome are gender, number of prior arrests, and supervision versus no supervision.

GENDER DIFFERENCES: In general, studies have shown that male parolees return to prison at higher rates than women parolees (16 percent compared with 12 percent, respectively).[93] Another research study found that women parolees are more compliant with parole conditions than are male parolees.[94]

NUMBER OF PRIOR ARRESTS: An inverse relationship exists between prior criminal history and parole outcome. Specifically, the lower the number of previous arrests, the greater the likelihood of parole success.[95]

SUPERVISION VERSUS NO SUPERVISION: Howard R. Sacks and Charles H. Logan studied two groups of offenders to determine the effect of parole supervision on recidivism. One group of felony offenders released from prison by a court order had no postrelease supervision whatsoever. They were compared with a similar group of prisoners who had parole supervision. Recidivism was measured by offenders who had a new conviction for any crime (felony or misdemeanor). By the end of three years, most paroled offenders were totally off supervision. Sacks and Logan found that after three years, 85 percent of the group without postrelease supervision recidivated, while 77 percent of the group under parole supervision recidivated. The difference was more pronounced between the two groups after just the first year, indicating that parole supervision slows down the recidivism rate and may assist some offenders in maintaining law-abiding lives.[96] A second, more recent study of federal offenders supports this finding. Of the offenders who recidivated in the federal system, offenders released on some form of community supervision were in the community for an average of 17 months before returning to prison for a new crime. Offenders released without any supervision stayed out for just over 13 months before returning to prison for a new crime.[97]

PAROLE FAILURE RATES: Statistics indicate that most rearrests of parolees occur in the first six months after release from prison. Within three years, two-thirds of all parolees have been rearrested. Joan Petersilia states: "The numbers are so high that parole failures account for a growing proportion of all new prison admissions. In 1980, they constituted 17 percent of all admissions, but they now make up 35 percent."[98]

Another study supports Petersilia's point. Research of 3,995 young parolees in 22 states found that within six years of release from prison, 69 percent were rearrested, 53 percent were convicted of a new offense, and 49 percent were reimprisoned.[99] Although these figures represent a high rate of recidivism—whether it is defined as arrest, conviction, or return to prison—they are misleading. A closer reading reveals that only 37 percent of the sample were rearrested while still on parole. Recidivism rates were the highest during the first two years following release from prison. Consequently, it is difficult to compare these findings with those that measure recidivism within the parole period only. Moreover, there was no comparison group (control group) in this study. In evaluating parole as a release mechanism, parolee recidivism rates should be compared with the rates of persons released to mandatory supervision and those released at expiration of sentence.

AN UPCOMING EVALUATION OF PAROLE: The U.S. Department of Justice is currently sponsoring a research project called The Reentry Partnerships Initiative. This research, headed by Faye Taxman of the University of Maryland, is being conducted by a collaborative team of researchers at eight sites around the country to study restorative justice within the community using parolee prerelease planning, enhanced surveillance, and a variety of community reintegration programs. The project is scheduled for completion sometime in 2002.

THE FUTURE OF PAROLE

Research has continually developed to validate parole prediction tables, recidivism outcome indices, and other instruments that aid parole boards in predicting the future behavior of offenders being considered for parole. Interest in predicting parole success and failure dates back to the 1940s, but today's prediction tables involve more complex and robust statistical techniques. Prediction research into the causes of recidivism and subsequent revocation could be invaluable in equipping the parole officer with the tools necessary for aiding parolees in this area. Most important, research must examine which factors in inmates' backgrounds and present circumstances predict success or failure on parole. Much work needs to be done before that goal is achieved.

Advances in Parole Risk Assessment

The variables included in most assessment instruments are classified as either static "risks" or dynamic "needs." While static characteristics do not change, dynamic parolee characteristics are subject to vary. Examples of static parolee characteristics are prior convictions, age at first arrest, absconding history, and prior revocations. Dynamic factors are, for example, treatment needs, employment status, financial situation, and relationships with family and friends.

The state of California has been involved with researchers in testing a new parole risk assessment instrument that was developed around 1997. This new classification instrument has similar components to previous versions, but the main difference is how the instrument is used in the field for parole management. The computer database is being used to adjust parole agent workload by current classification categories, degree of supervision required, expenditures, or treatment program needs.[100] Frank P. Williams III and his colleagues argue that risk assessments should not only focus on the probability of reoffending, but should also pertain to an offender's perceived threat of reoffending, potential harm to the public, and potential negative consequences for the parole agency brought on by high-profile offenders.

The researchers suggest that field parole officers could use laptop computers to "dial in to intranets and automatically recalculate parolee risk scores." Ultimately, the parole classification system would be linked with other automated parole information, such as program cost for specific types of parolees, and program success rates.[101]

SUMMARY

Parole boards enjoy a wide level of discretion when imposing parole conditions. The extent of authority and the limitations are basically similar to those for probation. Courts will generally uphold conditions that are reasonable but will strike down those that are impossible to meet. Parole conditions may be categorized into standard conditions and special conditions. Standard conditions are imposed on all parolees, while special conditions are tailored to fit the needs of a particular offender. While on parole, parolees enjoy diminished constitutional rights and therefore do not have the exact same rights as nonoffenders.

Revocation is the formal termination of a parolee's conditional freedom, usually (but not always) resulting in a reinstatement of imprisonment. Parole is revoked if a new crime is committed or a series of technical violations occur. Although parole officers do routinely work with offenders who do not meet some of their parole conditions, the question arises: How realistic is it to expect parolees to meet simultaneously the considerable number of conditions they are faced with after leaving an environment in which they are absent of responsibility? Is the system of conditions so rigid and pressure-filled that parolees are destined to fail?

Morrissey v. Brewer, the leading case on parole revocation, holds that prior to revocation parolees must be given five basic rights. However, parolees do not have a constitutional right to counsel at a revocation hearing; this right is given on a case-by-case basis. Two recent U.S. Supreme Court decisions have given parolees more rights. One holds that a state law canceling an inmate's provisional release is unconstitutional if applied to a prisoner who was convicted before the law took effect. Another case decided that prisoners released under preparole are entitled to due process rights, similar to those granted in *Morrissey*, prior to being brought back to prison. Parolees do not have a constitutional right to appeal a revocation, but about half of the states, by law or agency policy, give parolees the right to appeal an adverse revocation decision.

With the advent of computer modeling and risk prediction assessment, for predicting parole release as well as how to respond to parole violators, the future of parole seems to be continually moving in the direction of modifying parole from an art to a science. The effects of this shift remain to be seen.

DISCUSSION QUESTIONS

1   What problems do parolees have when they are released from prison? What ideas do you have that might assist parolees in their reintegration to society?

2   What are the limitations on the power of the parole board to impose conditions of parole?

3   What are the two types of parole conditions? Distinguish one from the other.

4   Is submission to a penile plethysmograph valid as a parole condition? Support your answer.

5   Discuss what this statement means: "Parolees have diminished constitutional rights." Does that statement apply to preferred rights? Explain.

6   What is the general rule on residential searches of a parolee's home by a parole officer? Is a warrant necessary?

7   "All parole officers are given authority to arrest a parolee without a warrant." Is that statement true or false? Support your answer.

8   What is the leading case on parole revocation, and what did that case say?

9   Parolees must be given five basic rights prior to revocation. What are those rights?

10   Does a parolee have a right to counsel at a revocation hearing? Justify your answer.

11   What is hearsay evidence, and is it admissible in a revocation hearing?

12   In 1997 the U.S. Supreme Court decided cases giving parolees more rights. What do these cases say?

13   Imagine that you are the probation or parole officer supervising the seven parolees described in the chapter. In two or three sentences, evaluate each case as a success or as a failure.

14   How might you justify parole for a violent offender who has served eight years of a ten-year sentence?

15   Is parole an effective sanction? Justify your answer with specific examples.

 **WEB SITES**

Missouri Department of Corrections Code of State Regulations
Parole guidelines, conditions on parole, and parole revocation procedures

   http://mosl.sos.state.mo.us/csr/14csr.htm

Article on Parole Absconders

http://www.corrections.com/aca/cortoday/February00/legislative.html

Services Offered to Parolees

http://www.cdc.state.ca.us/program/parole3.htm

Careers in Corrections Database

http://database.corrections.com/career/

Corrections Chat Rooms

www.corrections.com/chatbd/chatbd.html

Please go to the book-specific Web site for Supplemental Readings related to the material in this chapter:
An Innovative Parole Program in Pennsylvania: Transitioning Incarcerated Fathers
http://www.wadsworth.com/product/0-534-559662s

CHAPTER 11 | CASE STUDY EXERCISE
Parole Conditions and Revocation

As indicated in this chapter, the courts have granted a great deal of leeway to paroling authorities in setting parole standard conditions and special conditions for offenders. Court rulings seem to center around whether the condition is reasonable, whether parolees have diminished rights, and whether the condition is related to the convicted criminal behavior.

Conditions pertaining to sex offenders have received added attention in recent years. In some jurisdictions standard conditions for sex offenders include some or all of the following;

- No contact with any minor child (including offender's minor children), if victim of sexual crime was a minor, or no contact with minors at all even if the victim(s) were adult age
- Contact with minor children approved only if parole officer approves another supervising adult to be present at the time of the contact
- No possession of sexually explicit material, written, audio, or visual
- If offense involved use of Internet or computer, not to have a personal computer and cannot work where access to Internet is allowed; or in some jurisdictions no computer access at all even if offense did not involve computer usage
- Notification to neighbors and employers of their sexual offense history and supervision status
- Mandatory participation in sexual offender treatment or aftercare programs
- Mandatory routine polygraph exams as a part of treatment or supervision
- If offense involved filming or pictures of victims, no camera or video equipment access allowed
- Cannot work in any type of employment that would allow access to children or victim aged groups; cannot be self-employed
- Cannot live within certain distance from schools, playgrounds, public parks, or other places where minors congregate

Using Case B from the Chapter 10 Case Study Exercise, what if any of these conditions should be imposed on the offender if paroled? What are some of the advantages, from a parole supervision view, that these conditions present?

Intermediate Sanctions and Special Issues

Burgeoning prison populations and high recidivism rates among felony probationers have prompted the search for alternative sanctions for certain offenders. These are the offenders for whom a sentence of imprisonment is unduly severe and regular probation is too lenient. One study of felony probation in California sounded a clarion call for the development of "intermediate sanctions." In its 1985 report *Granting Felons Probation*, the RAND Corporation stated that the

> current troubles are self-perpetuating. Without alternative sanctions for serious offenders, prison populations will continue to grow and the courts will be forced to consider probation for more and more serious offenders. Probation caseloads will increase, petty offenders will be increasingly "ignored" by the system (possibly creating more career criminals), and recidivism rates will rise. In short, probation appears to be heading toward an impasse, if not a total breakdown, if substantially more funds are not made available to create more prison space. Since that is highly unlikely (and also, we believe, undesirable), alternative "intermediate" punishments must be developed and implemented.

In Part III, these problems will be examined and programs designed to more effectively deal with them will be discussed. Included in the chapters that follow are issues of intermediate sanctions, juvenile justice, and loss and restoration of rights upon conviction.

Intermediate sanctions lie on the continuum between traditional probation and prison incarceration. Chapter 12 examines sanctions in which offenders must live away from home and inside a facility while they are completing their sentence. Residential programs include boot camps, halfway houses, and other specialized residential community corrections facilities. Chapter 13 explores nonresidential community corrections programs in which the offender lives at home, while participating in the program from home or by visiting the program on a periodic basis. Nonresidential programs include intensive supervision probation, house arrest, electronic monitoring, day reporting centers, restitution, community service, and fines.

Recent years have witnessed an increase in both the number of juvenile offenders and in the seriousness of the offenses they commit. These issues and correctional programs to deal with them are discussed in detail and recent court decisions affecting juvenile probation and parole are analyzed in Chapter 14.

Chapter 15 examines the disabilities imposed on convicted offenders that are not directly imposed by the court; that is, losses that attach by the fact of the conviction, such as loss of the right to vote, loss of the ability to hold certain jobs, and loss of the right to own a firearm, among others.

Finally, Chapter 16 considers the mechanisms by which convicted offenders may have some or all of their rights restored.

12

Residential Intermediate Sanctions

Stock Boston

What You Will Learn in This Chapter

In this chapter you will learn about residential intermediate sanctions as alternatives to probation and prison. The practices of boot camps, halfway houses, and therapeutic community programs will be described and evaluated.

INTRODUCTION

Recent years have witnessed the evolution of a range of **intermediate sanctions** to fill the gap between regular probation and prison. In the wake of research showing that traditional probation and parole by themselves were ineffective in controlling crime, many jurisdictions began to develop alternative sentencing options—intermediate sanctions—that stressed closer supervision and holding offenders accountable. Intermediate sanctions are seen as a way to reduce the need for additional prison beds and to provide a continuum of sanctions that allow judges greater latitude in selecting a punishment that more closely fits the circumstances of the crime and the offender.[1]

All of these new sanctions are attempts to provide increased control over offenders within the community. Until the advent of these intermediate punishments, the courts were faced with the polarized choice of either probation or prison. Criminologists Norval Morris and Michael Tonry write,

> Effective and principled punishment of convicted offenders requires the development and application of a range of punishments between prison and probation. Imprisonment is used excessively; probation is used even more excessively; between the two is a near-vacuum of purposive and enforced punishments.[2]

Morris and Tonry argue that the United States has been both too lenient and too severe; that is, too lenient with probationers who need tighter controls and too severe with prisoners who would present no serious threat to public safety if under supervision in the community.[3] They advocate the use of intermediate punishments such as intensive supervision probation (ISP), house arrest, electronic monitoring, restitution, community service orders, and fines. These punishments, they point out, do not exist in isolation. The fine is frequently combined with probation and incarceration. Electronic monitoring is not a sentence in itself. It can be used to enforce parole, house arrest, and curfews. Community service orders are combined with probation or parole. Intermediate sanctions are sometimes combined with brief jail or prison terms.[4] Morris and Tonry maintain,

> For some offenders, a substantial fine may well be combined with an order that the offender make restitution to the victim, pay court costs, and be subject to a protracted period of house arrest, monitored electronically, for which the offender pays the costs. For others, intensive probation involving regular and close supervision by a supervising officer playing a police role and also by a caseworker may be combined with a defined period of residence in a drug treatment facility, followed by regular urinalyses to ensure the offender remains drug-free, and also an obligation to fulfill a set number of hours of community service-all strictly enforced.[5]

In the continuum of sanctions, intermediate sanction programs are situated in the middle between probation and prison. Because intermediate sanctions are, in theory, different punishments than traditional probation and prison, a research team

KEY TERMS

Intermediate sanctions
Widening the net
Shock incarceration
Boot camp
Residential community corrections facilities
Halfway houses
Restitution centers
Residential drug and alcohol treatment centers
Relapse
Work and study release

INTERMEDIATE SANCTIONS

A range of punishments that fall between probation and prison.

from the University of Cincinnati sought to determine whether offenders sentenced to a community corrections sanctions in the state of Ohio were different in practice than prisoners or probationers.

The researchers found that a continuum of sanctions did exist in practice, measured by the risk and needs levels that the offenders posed in all three groups. Offenders in intermediate sanction programs had more severe criminal records than probationers but less severe records than people incarcerated in prison. Furthermore, in comparison with regular probationers, offenders in intermediate sanction programs, particularly those in residential community programs, had more needs that required treatment intervention, such as employment services, education, emotional or mental health needs, financial management, and substance abuse. Because of all their issues, offenders with intermediate community sentences were more likely than probationers and prisoners to acquire technical violations that later led to sentence revocation.[6] Nonetheless, the study found that intermediate sanctions were more costly than probation, but they "produced savings and revenues between $4,500 and $5,000 per offender when compared to imprisonment."[7]

Intermediate sanctions are also intended to allow for more rational allocation of resources and for more equitable sentencing options.[8] The positioning over where a particular sanction lies in the continuum of sanctions often depends on who selects program participants. For example, research shows that if prosecutors and judges are the key decision makers in program selection, they are more likely to choose offenders who should have received probation. This process is called widening the net, and it has received criticism. **Widening the net** means to sentence individuals who should have received probation to a harsher intermediate sanction, only because that sanction is available, not because the offender requires more intensive supervision. Widening the net increases costs, because individuals are receiving more supervision, not less. In addition, prison and jail populations are not reduced because participants are drawn from the wrong population. Intensifying a punishment for probationers thus removes all the positive cost-saving benefits that intermediate sanctions are supposed to attain. In comparison, if prison or correctional administrators are the key decision makers, they can choose program participants from offenders who are already sentenced to prison, thus reducing the institutional population and costs of confinement. This chapter and Chapter 13 will review and evaluate various types of intermediate sanction programs. Some of the evaluation components to bear in mind include whether the intermediate sanction reduced prison beds, whether it produced a cost savings, and whether it reduced recidivism—or a return to criminal behavior.[9]

SHOCK INCARCERATION

Shock incarceration refers to a brief period of imprisonment that precedes a term of supervised probation in hope that the harsh reality of prison will deter future criminal activity. A variety of shock incarceration formats are used, and they go by a number of names—shock probation, shock parole, intermittent incarceration, split sentence, and boot camp. The programs vary somewhat in design and organization, but all feature a short prison term followed by release under supervision. The target population is young offenders with no previous incarcerations in adult prisons.

In shock probation, an offender is sentenced to imprisonment for a short time (the shock) and then released and resentenced to probation. The prison experience is thought to be so distasteful that the offender will fear returning and thereafter avoid criminal behavior. The original shock probation program was established in Ohio in 1965. It was praised for limiting prison time, assisting in reintegration into the com-

WIDENING THE NET

When an individual who should have received probation is sentenced to a harsher intermediate sanction, only because that sanction is available, not because the offender requires more intensive supervision.

SHOCK INCARCERATION

A brief period of incarceration followed by a term of supervised probation. Also called shock probation, shock parole, intermittent imprisonment, or split sentence.

munity, helping the offender to maintain family ties, and reducing prison populations and the costs of corrections.[10] The program's stated purposes were as follows:

- To impress offenders with the seriousness of their actions without a long prison sentence
- To release offenders found by the institutions to be more amenable to community-based treatment than was realized by the courts at the time of sentencing
- To serve as a just compromise between punishment and leniency in appropriate cases
- To provide community-based treatment for offenders while still imposing deterrent sentences where public policy demands it
- To protect the briefly incarcerated offender against absorption into the inmate culture.[11]

Shock probation programs have been evaluated by a number of researchers. Early studies reported success rates between 78 and 91 percent. Programs were praised for limiting prison time, providing a chance for offenders to be reintegrated back into the community quickly, and making offenders more receptive to probation supervision by illustrating the problems they will encounter if they violate the terms of their probation.

However, shock incarceration was not always imposed on those for whom it was intended—young first offenders. Nicolette Parisi, in a study of federal probationers, found that a third of those who had received split sentences had previously been incarcerated on other charges, which negated the value of the "shock." Furthermore, Parisi was unable to find evidence that probationers who had first served a short period of incarceration were more successful than those who had not.[12]

Despite mixed findings on success rates, a recent study shows that the use of shock probation and split sentencing is increasing nationwide. An estimated 10 percent of all adults on probation received a split sentence in 1998, of some combination of incarceration and probation.[13]

Correctional Boot Camps

Since their inception in Georgia in 1983, **boot camp** programs have multiplied as the most common form of shock incarceration. Boot camp programs exist inside state prisons, local jails, within the community, and even as a small part of the Federal Bureau of Prisons.[14] At a minimal level, all boot camps are designed to instill discipline and responsibility through an experience much like that of military basic training with intensive physical training, hard labor, drill and ceremony, and structure. However, most boot camps also provide therapeutic and educational activities, such as drug and alcohol education, individual or group counseling, vocational training, anger management, and academic education. The therapy is provided in concert with military drills and discipline.[15] Ronald W. Moscicki, superintendent of a boot camp program in New York, states the importance of having both military and treatment components:

> Boot camps often seem to begin with the assumption, "If it ain't rough, it ain't right." Most people think that "rough" is sweaty drills, "in your face" and bulging muscles. They never associate "rough" with inmates sitting in a circle in white shirts and ties, with counselors and drill instructors leading a treatment group or academic classes, teaching inmates how to read and write. . . . In truth, the military part is the easiest because it is constant repetition. . . . If all we expect from our inmates is that they follow orders, we will have good inmates. Inmates, even good ones, belong in jail.[16]

BOOT CAMP

A form of shock incarceration that involves a military-style regimen designed to instill discipline in young offenders.

Boot camp participants live in "barracks," wear military-style fatigues, use military titles, and address their drill instructors by "sir" or "ma'am." The whole "platoon" is responsible for the actions of every individual, given that many boot camps use group rewards and punishments to encourage people to work together. A small number of programs even use "brigs" or punishment cells for temporary solitary confinement.

Criteria vary from program to program, but in general, eligible candidates must be first-time felony offenders, convicted of a nonviolent offense, fall within a certain age group, and meet minimum physical requirements. Many eligible offenders have been involved with drugs or alcohol in the past, and most program participants volunteer to participate. After a specified period, typically 90–180 days, the probationer graduates to either probation or parole supervision. Boot camps provide the court with an alternative disposition, stricter and more structured than regular probation, yet with less time than a regular prison sentence.

There are two main types of boot camp programs:

1. Prison Boot Camps. Offenders are chosen to participate from the general prison population. The boot camp is usually within a prison correctional facility, but boot camp participants remain separate from the general population for the program duration. Offenders are paroled upon graduation from boot camp. Time served is significantly less than with a regular prison sentence.
2. Probation/Jail Boot Camps. Offenders are chosen to participate at time of sentencing by judges or by jail authorities. Although the judges are directed to choose offenders who otherwise would have gone to prison, probation boot camps are criticized for widening the net—choosing offenders who otherwise would have been sentenced to probation. These boot camps are located in the community and are supervised by county sheriff departments, probation departments, or a combination of both. Offenders in probation boot camps do not go to prison but remain in a residential community facility. Following boot camp, offenders graduate to intensive supervision probation or regular probation.

Example of Prison Boot Camps

As of January 1, 1999, there were a total of 6,389 inmates in 50 adult boot camp programs in 32 states. Of those offenders, 553 (8.7 percent) were female and 5,836 (91.3 percent) were male. The total number in boot camps in 1999 was a decline of 30 percent since 1995.[17] During 1998, more than 13,000 inmates successfully completed the boot camp programs, which averaged five months in duration. The average cost per day was $58 per offender. The New York prison system is currently the most avid user of boot camp programs within its walls. Georgia, Kansas, and Ohio opened new boot camp programs in 1999.[18]

Illinois, Louisiana, New York, and South Carolina are among the states in which the state Department of Corrections chooses offenders for participation.

NEW YORK STATE BOOT CAMPS: The New York State Department of Correctional Services (DOCS) began a shock incarceration program in 1987 and currently operates four adult facilities with a total capacity of 1,570, including 180 beds for women offenders. New York's boot camps, like almost all others, emphasize strict, military-like discipline, unquestioning obedience to orders, and highly structured days filled with hard work. However, they also focus on providing a total learning environment that fosters involvement, self-direction, and individual responsibility.[19]

TABLE 12.1 *Daily Schedule for Offenders in New York Shock Incarceration Facilities*

Time	Schedule
A.M.	
5:30	Wake up and standing count
5:45–6:30	Calisthenics and drill
6:30–7:00	Run
7:00–8:00	Mandatory breakfast and cleanup
8:15	Standing count and company formation
8:30–11:55	Work and school schedules
P.M.	
12:00–12:30	Mandatory lunch and standing count
12:30–3:30	Afternoon work and school schedule
3:30–4:00	Shower
4:00–4:45	Network community meeting
4:45–5:45	Mandatory dinner, prepare for evening
6:00–9:00	School, group counseling, drug counseling, prerelease counseling, decision-making classes
8:00	Count while in programs
9:15–9:30	Squad bay, prepare for bed
9:30	Standing count, lights out

Source: National Institute of Justice, *Program Focus Shock Incarceration in New York* (Washington, DC: U.S. Department of Justice, National Institute of Justice, August 1994).

The New York program has two legislatively mandated goals:

1. To treat and release selected state prisoners earlier than their court-mandated minimum period of incarceration without endangering public safety
2. To reduce the need for prison bed space[20]

In New York, judges cannot sentence an offender directly to a shock incarceration program. DOCS staff select participants they consider suitable for the program from the inmate population. To qualify for the boot camp program, offenders must be under 35 and eligible for parole within three years of admission to the DOCS. All offenders in the DOCS who are legally qualified for the boot camp program are initially sent to an orientation and screening center. At the center they are informed about the program and allowed to volunteer to participate instead of serving their full term in prison. Those who volunteer are screened for physical and mental problems that would prohibit them from participating. They are then introduced to some of the boot camp programs for a brief period. DOCS officials believe that this brief introduction to the activities of the program has resulted in lower failure rates among those who finally enter the program full time.

Those who are accepted into the program are assigned to one of four minimum security facilities. Male participants work in platoons of 54–60 men and proceed through the 180–day program as a unit. Table 12.1 shows a schedule of the daily activities of participants.

While the inmate is in the facility, 41 percent of his or her time is devoted to treatment and education. Physical training and drill constitute 26 percent of the time, with hard labor on facility and community projects constituting the remaining 33 percent. This schedule with close supervision and strict discipline places severe limitations on inmates' behavior. For most such limits are new and unique. Many cannot conform to the program and drop out. Cherie L. Clark and her associates report that about 37 percent of those who enter shock incarceration do not complete it.

Those who successfully complete the six-month regimen are paroled and enter a six-month postrelease phase of the program known as AfterShock. The goal of AfterShock is to continue the close supervision that began in the institutional phase and to provide opportunities and programs in the community designed to improve the parolee's chances for successful integration. Each participant has two parole officers to allow increased contacts between the officers and parolees for home visits, curfew checks, and drug testing. AfterShock parolees have priority access to community services such as educational and vocational training. After completion of AfterShock, parolees are transferred to regular parole supervision.[21]

The DOCS has found that the shock incarceration program saves money by reducing costs in regular prison programs and by avoiding capital costs for new prison construction. The DOCS estimates that it saves $2 million in prison costs for every 100 shock incarceration graduates. Recidivism rates for graduates 12 months after completion of the program were 10 percent compared with 15 percent for those who were screened but rejected and 17 percent for those who withdrew or were removed from shock incarceration before completion. After 24 months, 30 percent of graduates had returned to prison, compared with 36 percent of the considered inmates and 41 percent of those who failed to complete the program. At 36 months, shock incarceration graduates still returned to prison at lower rates, but the difference was significant only between program graduates and the considered group.[22] Clark and her associates sum up the program:

> DOCS evaluation so far indicates that the program is responding to the legislature's call for reducing prison bed space needs without increasing the public's risk. Even more important, New York's therapeutic approach may point the way for redirecting the lives of a number of young offenders, helping them stay out of the criminal justice system once they have paid their debt to society.[23]

Example of Jail/Probation Boot Camps

Like prison boot camps, jail boot camps also intend to reduce institutional crowding, provide rehabilitation, punish offenders, and reduce recidivism. Ten jail boot camps are operating at a daily cost between $28 and $117 per inmate. Staff to offender ratios is between 1:2 and 1:5.[24] Table 12.2 includes detailed information about adult boot camp programs administered by probation and parole agencies. There are 24 programs, with 8 more in the process of opening. The current total capacity is 3,786 persons for the operating programs, of which 2 percent are female and 98 percent are male. The average program length is the same as prison boot camps (five months), at an average cost of nearly $57 per day per offender. Nearly 7,000 offenders have graduated from these programs.[25]

HARRIS COUNTY, TEXAS, BOOT CAMP CRIPP PROGRAM: In 1991 Harris County (Houston), Texas, implemented a boot camp program for young felony offenders. The CRIPP (Courts Regimented Intensive Probation Program) boot camp program is administered jointly by the Harris County Community Corrections

TABLE 12.2 *Boot Camp Programs Administered by Probation and Parole Agencies*

Program	Use Boot Camps	Boot Camp Programs	Planned Open 1998	First Year Opened	Persons Assigned	Females Assigned	Success Completed	Female Successes	Length of Program (months)	Cost/Day Boot Camp
Probation										
California[a]	X									
Colorado[b]	X	1	8	1993	480	0	407	0	2	$101.00
District of Columbia[c]	X	1	0	1995	25	0	165	0	24	43.10
Georgia[d]	X	2	0	1991	415	0	1,715	0	3	41.81
Kansas	X	1			105	0	72	0	6	57.00
Massachusetts	X				217	22	846	32	3	
Michigan	X	1	0	1985	353	17	740	45	6	38.52
Mississippi	X	3								
New Hampshire	X									
North Carolina[e]	X	3	0	1989	215	13	183	12	2.7	53.00
Tennessee	X	1	0	1991	60	0	264	0	3	58.08
Texas	X	4	0	1991	494	0	1,389	0		
Total or average	**12**	**17**	**8**	**1991**	**2,364**	**52**	**5,781**	**89**	**6**	**$56.07**
Parole										
Louisiana	X	1	0	1987	166	6	221	8	6	
Maryland	X				630					
New York[f]	X	1	0	1987	61	0	263	0	6	$53.00
Tennessee	X			1989					4	
Total or average	**4**	**2**	**0**	**1988**	**857**	**6**	**484**	**8**	**5**	**$53.00**
Probation and parole										
Florida[g]	X	2	0	1987	121	20	315	45	4	$55.30
Minnesota[h]	X									
Virginia[i]	X	1	0	1991	79	0	202	0	4	
Wisconsin	X	2	0	1991	365	0	173	0	6.5	65.96
Total or average	**4**	**5**	**0**	**1990**	**565**	**20**	**690**	**45**	**5**	
Overall total or average	**20**	**24**	**8**	**1989**	**3,786**	**78**	**6,955**	**142**	**5**	**$56.57**

Data Note: Blank cells mean the state agency did not provide complete information.
[a]1997 data. [b]Number of persons assigned is annual. [c]Length of program is one year to three phases. Figure is average of two years. [d]Boot camps are administered by facilities. [e]Eighty-five percent of all persons assigned are successes; 96 percent of all women assigned are successes. Length of program is 81 days. [f]The division supervises release from the Department of Correctional Services' program, the shock incarceration program, which offers reduced sentences to certain nonviolent inmates who participate in a six-month intensive treatment and "boot-camp" style program. Parole provides specialized services to the releases from the shock program on reduced caseloads under enhanced contact requirements. [g]One hundred twenty days is the minimum length of program. [h]Boot camp program is run through the Adult Facility Division. [i]Cost per graduate is $7,915.
Source: Camille Graham Camp and George C. Camp, *The Corrections Yearbook: 1999* (Middletown, CT :Criminal Justice Institute, 1999).

Department (Probation) and the Harris County Sheriff's Department, which provides drill instructors to supervise boot camp participants and provides security and custody staff for the facility.

Unlike most other boot camp programs, offender participation in CRIPP is not voluntary, and judges select the offenders for the program, without any input from the boot camp staff. Furthermore, once an offender is in the program, he or she cannot voluntarily decide to quit the program (this explains the 97 percent completion rate). Offenders who could not complete the program must appear in court before the same judge.

CRIPP is a co-ed program for a maximum of 48 women and 336 men, each grouped together in a cohort of 48 members who stay together for the full 90–120 days of the program. CRIPP participants are engaged in activities for about 15–17 hours every day with a few hours of free time every Saturday.[26] A wide range of services and program opportunities are provided:

- Medical services. Participants undergo an extensive medical examination before arriving at the facility. Probationers with physical limitations are referred back to the sentencing court. Participants are also provided medical counseling services such as AIDS (acquired immune deficiency syndrome) counseling and anonymous, voluntary HIV (human immunodeficiency virus) testing.
- Vocational services. Probationers can participate in vocational skills programs, including basic computer literacy skills.
- Physical training. Physical conditioning, including drill and calisthenics, occupies the largest portion of the participants' time in the CRIPP program.
- Social skills. Participants may choose to participate in drug and alcohol counseling provided by counselors from the county health department and from probation staff.[27]

Upon release participants are transferred to a 90–day superintensive probation program (SIPP). Probationers have daily contact with probation officers for the first 30 days after release, biweekly contact for the next 30 days, and one contact weekly for the following 30 days. The life skills classes that were started in boot camp are continued during SIPP two nights per week. In addition, a licensed counselor runs a boot camp support group one night per week.

Velmer S. Burton and his colleagues evaluated the CRIPP program to determine if it changed offender attitudes (see Box 12.1). The study measured attitudinal change in the areas of coping and self-control, perceptions of boot camp staff, benefits of participating in AIDS and drug and alcohol counseling, attitudes toward the CRIPP program, perceptions of future opportunities, and the quality of relationships with family and friends.[28] They found that the CRIPP program did produce significant positive results, as measured by attitudinal change. Offenders improved their outlook on family life, and many came to realize the influence of their friends on their criminal behavior. CRIPP graduates demonstrated greater self-control and better coping skills than they had when entering the program. In addition, they appeared to be less impulsive and more in control of their personal situations. With the exception of their attitudes regarding AIDS counseling and education, positive effects were noted in all areas.[29]

James F. Anderson and his colleagues conducted a recidivism study in 1996 on CRIPP program graduates at two different times. Two years after release, 22 percent of boot camp graduates had been sentenced to prison. After four years following boot camp, 61.7 percent of graduates had been sentenced to prison (including some recidivists from two years after release).[30] Accurately comparing how CRIPP boot camp graduates fared with regular probationers and parolees is difficult because there was no matched control group.

BOX 12.1 *Boot Camp Study Points to Success*

A little over three months ago, Mark Alvarado thought the drill instructors at the Harris County Boot Camp were his tormenters. He believed the judge who sentenced him to 120 days in the intensive probation program was unfair.

Alvarado, 21, graduates from boot camp in two weeks.

On Thursday, he said, once is enough in the tough, military-style drill program.

At the same time, he said, it has made a difference in his outlook.

"Now, I wouldn't trade it for anything," he said.

Alvarado's experience is typical of Harris County Boot Camp graduates, according to a Sam Houston State University study released this week.

That study found graduates emerge from the demanding probation regimen with better attitudes—the key to staying out of trouble, officials said Thursday.

An improved attitude is "extremely important," said Boot Camp Director Mike Enax.

"I think the attitude that they had when they got here is what got them in trouble in the first place," Enax said.

Bob Wessels, county criminal court manager, who works as a link between judges and probation programs, said reports like the Sam Houston study help the courts know which programs work.

"We begin to match for-real— based on our experience in Harris

County—programs to people," Wessels said.

"One of the things the Sam Houston study shows is you (lower recidivism rates) if you can raise their literacy, improve their job skills, teach them to read, and improve their self-esteem."

The study, by professors Velmer S. Burton Jr., James W. Marquart, Steven J. Cuvelier, Leanne Fiftal Alarid, and Robert J. Hunter, examined attitude changes in 389 probationers who completed the boot camp program.

Boot campers completing the program were more likely to accept criticism and to respect authority figures and drill instructors than when they entered the program, according to the study.

They were also more likely at the end of the program to want to avoid criminal behavior.

The study found that probationers completing boot camp had improved attitudes about drug and alcohol counseling and felt that counseling would help them beat their habits.

In addition, the study found that as boot camp residents spent time in the program, their opinions changed about the positive influence the experience was having on their lives.

Similar results were reported in probationers' attitudes about the quality of the boot camp's educational programs and about their future prospects for returning to school or securing a job.

The study reported probationers emerged with better attitudes about coping skills and self-control and that some developed more positive attitudes about family relationships.

Enax said the results square with statistics compiled by the Harris County Community Supervision and Corrections Department, which found that 85 percent of the over 2,300 men and women completing the program have not committed new crimes.

"When they first get here, they feel like it's been done as a punishment," he said.

"But after a while, they see what everybody's doing for them. Their attitude starts to be that, 'Maybe they put me here so I could learn something and get somewhere.'"

Alvarado, a convicted auto thief who was put on probation only to have it revoked later, agreed.

"When I first came in, I thought that the judge was just being unfair to me," he said.

After four months of strict discipline meted out by the boot camp instructors, Alvarado is making plans to stay out of trouble.

He wants to complete his last year at Houston Community College and begin work toward a teaching certificate at the University of Houston.

"My attitude has improved," he said.

Source: Andrea D. Greene, "Boot Camp Study Points to Success," *Houston Chronicle*, November 5, 1993, pp. 29A, 34A.

Offender Perspectives

Many participants of prison boot camps feel fortunate to have been chosen for the program, because upon boot camp program completion, they obtain release much faster than a traditional prison sentence. For example, Hank, age 23, was sentenced to prison for 18 months and provides his perspective on getting out early from participating in a Massachusetts boot camp:

> I came here to get out of jail in 4 months that is all. I've been in and out of jail for a lot of years. So I know about jail environments. This place is a positive community environment. You don't see anything like this in regular jail. My family tells me how much I've changed. I lost 25 pounds, learned to control my impulses, and learned to not drink. The program and classes are all supportive. I never expected to learn about wellness and parenting. I have a 2-year-old-son and another one just 3 months old. I want to go home and do the right thing. I wanted to quit many times; for a while, every day I thought, "This is the day I quit and get out of here." The staff made me realize that I need to stick it out "one day at a time." I learned how to talk to other people, staff, and other inmates. . . . I was always a follower who got into trouble easily. I learned how to say "no" to my impulses. The first week I hated the DIs [drill instructors] . . . [but] they taught me respect. When I think of it, that was missing in my life. Today, when I leave here, I can hold my head high and be proud of my completion of the program. I also know I need a support system to keep myself from getting into negative situations.[31]

Another male prisoner named Wayne, an 18-year-old Native American convicted of assault and battery, was a perfect candidate for the Massachusetts boot camp. Not only does Wayne have a problem controlling his temper, but he also has a drinking problem. He talks about the changes he has experienced because of boot camp:

> This was a heck of an experience. I've been in several programs and halfway houses, and this is the best program I've ever seen. . . . The 12-step classes are outstanding. They teach you how to stay sober. In addition, they teach you how to be responsible for yourself. This is, mentally, a tough program. When I first got here, I thought this place was crazy, a bunch of cops yelling. I did not know what to expect. I thought about quitting often. I've been impulsive and did what I wanted to do. One day, I was tired and when a DI was yelling at me, I told him I would not give him the pleasure of seeing me quit. I've learned to respect the DI. I can talk to the DI. They're not cops, the enemy. They made me responsible for myself. They taught me to care. . . . When I leave here Friday, I've already got plans to go to A.A. [Alcoholics Anonymous] meetings. . . . There is no negativity here like regular jail. I've tried to think about something negative . . . nope, nothing. Now don't get me wrong. I hate this place. . . . However, I love what the program has done for me. I never had plans or goals in my life. I've learned to suck it up and drive on. Open my ears and shut my mouth, otherwise, you are in the front leaning push-up position a lot. I have not found myself in that position in about a month; that's progress.[32]

Offenders also listed negative effects of boot camp, including no free time, limited visits with family, inmates are not always treated fairly (DIs often "adopt" another inmate), learning experiences are humiliating, and high levels of stress are frequently present.[33]

Criticisms of Boot Camps

One of the primary concerns is that boot camps widen the net, especially for probation boot camps and juvenile boot camps (juvenile boot camps are discussed in Chapter 14). In net widening, the costs increase because offenders who should be on probation are going through a more expensive program.

Another concern is that the confrontational style of the military-style boot camp is antithetical to the goals of therapeutic treatment. Merry Morash and Lila Rucker warned that boot camps hold potential for negative outcomes, because many boot camp environments are characterized by inconsistent standards, contrived stress, and leadership styles that are likely to reduce self-esteem, increase the potential for violence, and encourage the abuse of power.[34] Lutze and Brody even go so far as to suggest that the "harsh correctional environment" in many boot camps may violate the Eighth Amendment prohibition on cruel and unusual punishment. This situation may place boot camps as targets for offender lawsuits.[35]

In another study related to treatment outcomes for women boot camp participants, Doris Layton MacKenzie and a team of researchers conducted site visits and interviews of seven boot camp programs for women (out of thirteen available nationwide). Some of the boot camps were integrated with men, while others were gender-specific. The researchers concluded that women, particularly those who had been previously abused and those who were drug dependent, fared better in gender-specific boot camps than in integrated boot camps designed for men.[36]

Evaluations of Boot Camp Programs

Boot camp effectiveness has been determined in a number of ways: participant attitude or behavioral change, measured decrease in institutional crowding, or reduction in budget costs.

ATTITUDE CHANGE AND ADJUSTMENT: Supporters of the boot camp concept contend that some evidence shows that boot camps may be more positive than incarceration in traditional prisons. Moreover, offenders who have completed such programs describe the experience as difficult, but constructive. One study found that boot camp graduates who were supervised more intensively following boot camp completion had higher positive adjustment scores than offenders in other programs who had less aftercare.[37] When attitudes of boot camp graduates were compared with a matched group of regular prisoners, boot camp had a more positive attitudinal impact than did the deteriorating effects of prison.[38]

Another study that compared boot camp participants with regular probationers found evidence in some jurisdictions that boot camp graduates "appear to be involved in more positive social activities than similar offenders on probation."[39]

BEHAVIORAL CHANGE: Early boot camp studies found that recidivism rates for those who complete boot camp programs are approximately the same as for those who serve longer periods in traditional prisons or on probation.[40] An evaluation of the Regimented Inmate Diversion (RID) jail boot camp program in Los Angeles found that the program did not meet its expectations of cutting costs, reducing jail overcrowding, and reducing recidivism.[41]

EIGHT SITE STUDY: The National Institute of Justice (NIJ) sponsored an evaluation of eight adult boot camp programs nationwide. The boot camp programs differed in a variety of ways, including length of stay, size, location (inside a prison or in a separate facility), emphasis on treatment and therapeutic programming, and the existence and intensity of postrelease supervision.[42]

In five of the states evaluated (Florida, Georgia, Oklahoma, South Carolina, and Texas) the boot camp programs did not reduce recidivism. In the other three states (New York, Illinois, and Louisiana) graduates had lower rates on one measure of recidivism. In the states in which recidivism was reduced, the researchers found a strong focus on postrelease supervision and an emphasis on rehabilitation, voluntary participation, selection from prison-bound offenders, and a longer program duration. Each program had a high dropout rate. The researchers concluded that any or all of these factors "could have had an impact on offenders with or without the boot camp atmosphere."[43] However, the findings suggest that the boot camp experience, by itself, does not seem enough to reduce recidivism.

REDUCTION OF CROWDING AND COSTS: The issue of whether boot camps reduce prison crowding depends on whether the program targets prison-bound offenders. The NIJ study found that programs that allowed the department of corrections to select participants (prison boot camps) were more likely than programs involving judicial selection (probation boot camps) to alleviate prison crowding because they "maximized the probability of selecting offenders who would otherwise have been sentenced to prison."[44] Dale G. Parent suggests other ways boot camps can reduce prison overcrowding:

> Population simulations suggest that to reduce prison crowding boot camps must recruit offenders who otherwise would be imprisoned, offer big reductions in prison terms for completing a boot camp, minimize washout and return to prison rates, and operate on a large scale.[45]

Then, Parent goes on to explain why many boot camps have failed to reduce costs and institutional crowding:

> Many limit eligibility to nonviolent first offenders, select offenders who otherwise would receive probation, and intensively supervise graduates, thus increasing return to prison rates for technical violations. In most jurisdictions, boot camps appear more likely to increase correctional populations and costs rather than reduce them.[46]

Dale Colledge and Jurg Gerber note that each boot camp has its own stated goals, and each program's success or failure should be judged on whether it meets its own goals, not whether and to what degree the program meets standards set by evaluators.[47]

The Future of Shock Incarceration Programs

Evidence at this stage of growth and widespread use of boot camps seem to indicate a small but significant positive effect on recidivism and prison costs for a limited number of programs. Public demand for these programs continues. The Violent Crime Control and Law Enforcement Act of 1994 allowed $2 billion to create and operate more boot camps. For this reason alone boot camps will likely be a part of correctional practice for a longer while.[48]

Part of a successful future of boot camp programs seems to lie in treatment programs during boot camp. Gordon Bazemore and Thomas J. Quinn suggest ways to incorporate a restorative justice model to boot camps by offering victim impact panels and individual victim-offender mediation sessions within the boot camp itself. They also advocate drill instructors taking boot camp participants into the community to perform useful group community service, instead of just digging trenches and carrying logs within the boot camp compound.[49]

In addition, voluntary participation, selection from the prison population, and intensive aftercare provisions should be an integral part of the boot camp experience.

Researchers stress "continuity" during aftercare, or carrying through what was learned in boot camp in the outside world.[50] Without aftercare as an integral part of shock incarceration, any rehabilitative effects could be lost.[51]

RESIDENTIAL COMMUNITY CORRECTIONS FACILITIES

Residential community corrections facilities (RCCFs) are a popular intermediate sanction because they provide more intensive supervision than probation and parole, but they allow offenders to remain in the community and receive more treatment than they otherwise would in prison. RCCFs cost less than jail or prison, in part, because offenders subsidize a portion of the cost provided for by (largely) private agencies. Offenders can continue to work and contribute to their own families, as well as pay back victims for harm done.

RCCFs are the most diverse type of community corrections sanction. Thus, it is difficult to describe an "average" residential facility. Residential community corrections facilities do have the following commonalities:

1. Residents live in the facility (not at home).
2. Residents must be employed (or be working part time and going to school).
3. Residents can leave the facility at any time for work at a verified job.
4. Residents must be preapproved to leave the facility for any other reason, and they are limited to a certain pass duration, purpose, and curfew.[52]

Outside of those similarities, many differences exist, such as facility size, whether the facility is public or private, type of treatment programs offered, and type of clients selected. Halfway houses are one of the oldest types of RCCFs, having been around since the 1830s. But there are other newer adaptations of residential facilities. Edward J. Latessa and Lawrence F. Travis include halfway houses, community corrections centers, prerelease centers, and restitution centers.[53] To this list, we add work release centers and residential drug treatment facilities.

Although traditional halfway houses are still widely used, newer programs, particularly those operated by corrections departments, are closer to "minimum-security prisons than a rehabilitative community."[54] For example, some prerelease centers house several hundred inmates who will be released on parole, while other, more specialized programs accept only a small number of offenders (for example, ten). Restitution centers are for offenders who owe their victims restitution. These offenders are sentenced to a residential facility to make installment payments to their victim while serving time in the community.

After a review of a number of studies, Latessa and Travis found that RCCF residents did have more treatment needs than regular probationers or parolees. These needs were related to program outcome. However, success completion of a RCCF does not translate into automatic success on probation or parole, because the two levels of supervision are vastly different. Some offenders perform better with more structured supervision (such as an RCCF) but do not behave as well under less monitoring.[55]

Number of Facilities

Because of the diversity of RCCFs, it is difficult to estimate the number in the United States. The most recent statistics, which are a conservative estimate, are published by the Criminal Justice Institute in a work by Camille Graham Camp and George C.

RESIDENTIAL COMMUNITY CORRECTIONS FACILITIES

A sanction in the community in which the convicted offender lives at the facility and must be employed, but he or she can leave the facility for a limited purpose and duration if preapproved. Examples include halfway houses, prerelease centers, restitution centers, drug treatment facilities, and work release centers.

Camp. As shown in Table 12.3, by January 1, 1999, there were 628 RCCFs and halfway house facilities operating in the United States, housing nearly 19,500 offenders. Of this number, 55 (8.7 percent) facilities are operated by the department of corrections, while the rest are privately owned and operated. The number of inmates in RCCFs represents 4.4 percent of the total inmate population.[56]

HALFWAY HOUSES

HALFWAY HOUSES

The oldest and most common type of community residential facility for probationers or parolees who require a more structured setting than would be available if living independently.

Halfway houses are residential facilities for probationers, parolees, or those under ISP supervision that requires a more structured setting than would be available from living independently. Halfway houses are staffed 24 hours a day, 7 days a week as a facility for various types of offenders.

"HALFWAY OUT":

a) State-level pre-release offenders who are transferred from the department of corrections (DOC or prison) to the community and anticipate receiving parole within the next 1–2 years

b) Paroled offenders who pose a greater community risk, and need assistance in making the transition from prison to the community.

"HALFWAY-IN":

a) As an intermediate sanction sentence for offenders requiring more structure and control than that provided by probation, ISP, or even house arrest, but for whom prison is too severe a sanction

b) As an increased sanction for probation and parole violators

c) As a diversion program, where upon completion, charges are dismissed

d) For individuals who are waiting trial but are unable to make bail or meet release on recognizance requirements, and are not a threat to the community[57]

History of Halfway Houses in the United States

The halfway house concept has been traced back to the early 1800s in England and Ireland. In the United States, the halfway house idea originated in 1816, at the time when most penitentiaries still practiced the Pennsylvania-style system of solitude and complete silence. Prisoners were locked in their cells all day and were not allowed to interact with each other for fear that they would "contaminate" each other. Interaction would take away from the penance that prisoners must seek for full reformation.[58]

Following a tumultuous riot in a Pennsylvania prison, a commission was appointed to examine the problems with the prison system. One commission recommendation was to create temporary shelters for prisoners to get back on their feet as they were transitioning back to the community. This proposal was not adopted by the legislature because of strong feelings that prisoners, even after release from prison, should not be allowed to interact.

As penitentiaries transitioned from the solitude of the Pennsylvania system to the silent interaction of the Auburn or "congregate" system, prisoners were allowed to work outside of their cells but were not allowed to talk to each other. Because state support for halfway houses was still lacking, private, nonprofit organizations with the goal of prison reform opened halfway houses for the first time to provide a place for prisoners to go after release from prison.

For example, in 1845, the Isaac T. Hopper Home opened for male prisoners in New York City. In 1864, the Temporary Asylum for Discharged Female Prisoners

TABLE 12.3 Adult Correctional Community Treatment Centers on January 1, 1999

State	ADMINISTERED CTCs	ADMINISTERED Inmates	ADMINISTERED Average Per Diem	CONTRACTED CTCs	CONTRACTED Inmates	CONTRACTED Average Per Diem	TOTALS CTCs	TOTALS Inmates	TOTALS Percent of Total Inmates
Alaska				10	604	$54.95	10	604	14.7
California	2	140		30	949	39.88	32	1,089	0.7
Connecticut				37	767	59.08	37	767	4.3
District of Columbia	1	190	$49.00	4	281	43.00	5	471	4.7
Georgia	5	718		0			5	718	1.8
Hawaii				2	84	70.00	2	84	1.7
Iowa[a]	21	1,151		1			22	1,151	14.1
Kansas				2	30	23.79	2	30	0.4
Kentucky				15	500	27.82	15	500	3.3
Louisiana				8	683	18.50	8	683	2.1
Maryland				4	164		4	164	0.7
Minnesota				18	265	41.10	18	265	4.5
Missouri[b]				8	455	45.66	8	455	1.8
Montana[c]	2	85	53.98	4	295	42.92	6	380	13.9
Nevada	2	130	29.39				2	130	1.4
New Hampshire	3	133	25.05				3	133	5.7
New Jersey				24	2,176	56.47	24	2,176	7.0
New Mexico	1	40	37.02	1	133	37.02	2	173	3.4
North Dakota				6	7	40.00	6	7	0.7
Ohio				23	1,575	51.10	23	1,575	3.3
Oklahoma				11	651	35.73	11	651	3.1
Pennsylvania[d]	14	363	43.21	30	285	53.00	44	648	1.8
South Dakota				2	60	28.00	2	60	2.4
Tennessee				2	50		2	50	0.2
Utah	4	330	65.00	0			4	330	6.5
Virginia				10	235	32.00	10	235	0.7
Wisconsin[e]				26	319	60.00	26	319	
Wyoming				4	230	32.45	4	230	14.6
Federal				291	5,412	43.62	291	5,412	4.4
Total	55	3,280		573	16,210		628	19,490	4.4%
Average	5.5	328.0	$43.24	21.2	675	$42.55	21.7	672.1	
Percent of all inmates		1.2			2.5			2.7	

[a]Contracted community treatment center (CTC) is state-owned and privately operated. [b]Capacity in contracted CTCs is shared by the department and institution.
[c]Administered facilities are female and contracted facilities are male. [d]Average per diem is an estimate. [e]Majority of facilities are operated by private entities.
Source: Camille Graham Camp and George C. Camp, *The Corrections Yearbook: 1999* (Middletown, CT: Criminal Justice Institute, 1999).

opened in the Boston area. The Boston halfway house for women received less opposition than facilities for men. The reason for this difference was an underlying belief that, unlike male prisoners, women prisoners did not associate for the purpose of talking about criminal activity. Women prisoners were believed to contribute to their own rehabilitation.[59] At that time, halfway houses merely provided food and shelter to ex-prisoners. They did not provide treatment and services.

By the end of the nineteenth century, private halfway houses opened in eight other states. Criminal justice officials, such as law enforcement officers and corrections administrators, remained opposed to this idea. Funds for halfway houses dwindled, and with the Great Depression of the 1930s, many were forced to close. Only one halfway house, The Parting of the Ways in Pittsburgh, remained open.[60]

In the 1950s, private halfway houses were viewed in a brand-new light. Concern about crime and high parole revocation rates prompted halfway houses to assume a role beyond offering food and shelter. Halfway houses were now providing transition services to prisoners and became involved in both treatment and correctional supervision. In addition to being less expensive than prison, halfway houses protect the community because residents are more heavily monitored than traditional parolees. Those who misbehave can be returned to prison.[61]

In the 1960s, halfway houses became a more visible part of corrections when they received government assistance for the first time. At the urging of then Attorney General Robert F. Kennedy, Congress appropriated funds to open federal-level halfway houses for young offenders. Financial support increased as a direct result of emphasis placed on reintegration by the President's Commission on Crime and Administration of Justice.[62] The Safe Streets Act of 1968 established the source of funding for halfway house expansion throughout the 1970s. In 1964, the first meeting of the International Halfway House Association was held in Chicago. The name of the organization was changed in 1989 to the International Association of Residential and Community Alternatives. This organization currently represents 250 private agencies operating approximately 1,500 programs throughout the world.[63]

Although government funding and support decreased substantially in the early 1980s, private halfway houses in the 21st century have increasingly found a niche in the corrections market to provide alternatives to imprisonment and to create an outlet for prison crowding control.[64] For example, New York offers residential halfway house programs for mentally retarded and developmentally disabled offenders as an intermediate sanction, a diversionary option, or as a prison transition mechanism.[65]

Currently, no one set model exists for the programs provided at halfway houses. Each halfway house is unique in structure, treatment programs offered, and type of clients it accepts.[66] Private halfway houses can choose which clients they wish to accept on a contractual basis. The state or county government pays the facility a specified amount per day per offender, and the offender also pays rent. For example, it costs an average of $43 per day per offender to operate a residential halfway house.[67] Of this amount, the government will pay the halfway house about $32 per day per offender, which is less expensive than incarceration, but more expensive than probation or parole. In addition to what the government pays, each client is charged about 25 percent of the cost, or $11 per day.

The halfway house can offer certain benefits. The following were listed in a survey of 37 halfway house residents:

- Assist in readjustment to living in the free world
- Help them find a better job
- Allow closer family relations than when in prison

Douglas Burrows/Liaison International

Halfway houses are a type of residential community correction facility for probationers, parolees, or clients under ISP supervision. Most halfway houses are privately owned and operated and some are located in the middle of residential neighborhoods.

- Assist in abstaining from drugs and alcohol
- Allow them to financially assist their families[68]

The researchers also found that compared with their arrival at the halfway house, residents who completed the program successfully also experienced an increased internal locus of control and decreased levels of loneliness.[69]

Program Components

Offenders live in the facility, leaving to go to work, attend church, and attend school or participate in rehabilitation activities such as drug treatment. Residents are required to maintain a full-time job or be going to school full time. When not at work, residents maintain the facility through assigned chores, perform court-ordered community service, and attend classes or counseling sessions that their case manager mandates. Most halfway houses require residents to submit to regular drug testing and breathalyzers. Prison systems make extensive use of halfway houses to allow inmates a graduated release—something to fill the gap between total incarceration and absolute freedom. A six-month stay in a halfway house allows the inmate to decompress and adjust to freedom more readily.

LEVELS SYSTEM: A FORM OF BEHAVIOR MODIFICATION: Increased freedom must be earned and is based on good behavior, the amount of time spent in the program, and the client's financial situation. Most halfway house programs have some kind of a behavior modification program called a "levels system." In a levels system, the bottom level is the most restricted and the top level has more freedom away from the halfway house and more privileges. The following example will show the types of privileges a five-level system might contain. New clients start on Level 5, where there is a "hold" placed on them (they cannot leave the facility) until their case manager has completed the intake process. Once intake is complete, clients move to

Level 4, where they remain until they obtain a job and get caught up on their rent. Level 4 clients are allowed passes to attend treatment (Alcoholics Anonymous and Narcotics Anonymous) and one four-hour pass per week to attend church (outside of leaving for work). Each level has its own curfew, which is not applicable to clients who work evenings or nights. In addition to treatment and church passes, Level 3 clients can take one daytime pass of no longer than eight hours, with a curfew of 10:00 P.M. Level 2 clients have Level 3 privileges, with a later curfew of 11:59 P.M. At Level 1, clients must be caught up on all restitution, community service, and rent. They must have $100 in savings. Level 1 clients have a weekday curfew of 11:59 P.M. but can take weekend passes, from Friday to Sunday, to visit preapproved friends and family. Level 1 clients can own an insured car and have driving privileges, while all other clients must depend on someone else for a ride or must take the bus. All clients, regardless of their level, must produce receipts and verification that the requested place was visited. Passes are allowed to a verified pass address of a family member or for four hours at a time to see a movie or to go shopping. Some programs require clients to spend 14 days on each level before advancing to the next level.

Upon program completion of the residential phase, paroled clients are assigned a parole officer in the appropriate jurisdiction. Most successful probation clients are transferred to the "nonresidential" phase of the halfway house program. During the nonresidential phase, clients live at home but come to the halfway house to be tested for drugs, to attend group treatment, or to visit their nonresidential case manager.

Worker Perspectives and Role Orientation

Working at a halfway house involves two different types of staff. One group of staff is primarily involved in activities that are custody-oriented; the other staff (case managers and counselors) takes care of treatment and rehabilitation. The job of the halfway house case manager has been described similarly to that of a probation and parole officer, in the sense that the counselor must be "capable of possessing conflicting goals of rehabilitation and punishment."[70]

Leanne Fiftal Alarid, one of this book's coauthors, worked at a halfway house located in Denver, Colorado. Alarid describes her job responsibilities working both different types of positions:

> I began working as a member of the client management staff, involved in security and physical accountability of over 80 males and females. In this capacity, I conducted population counts, searched people and belongings for contraband, signed clients in and out of the facility, dispensed medications and Antabuse, and conducted Breathalyzers and urine screenings. When an opportunity for working as a case manager became available, I transferred within the facility from the security-oriented job to one orientated around treatment. In this position, I became occupied with treatment, programming, and revocation issues for 20–24 individuals. A case manager is very similar to a parole or probation officer, in that I assessed my client's needs and risks, and I devised individual program plans to meet each of their needs. I assisted my clients with adjustment problems they experienced while in the program, and I supervised their progress. I also taught drug and alcohol treatment classes for new clients, and I prepared prerelease plans and attended monthly parole board hearings.

Another perspective on working in a halfway house comes from Melodye Lehnerer. Lehnerer writes about the different roles she played during her two-year experience conducting ethnographic research data from one halfway house. Lehnerer began as a volunteer, moved to being a "peripheral member," and then became an "active member" as an assistant caseworker. As membership involvement increased, role conflict arose between staff affinity and identification as a researcher. Lehnerer did not particularly like being a caseworker because it was too much of a "social control agent" for her self-identity, and it also made collecting data more difficult.[71] Thus, Lehnerer decided to quit being a case manager and take on more of a "helping agent" role and started teaching general equivalency diploma (GED) classes and life skills to clients. As a teacher and staff member, Lehnerer explains how the clients still viewed her differently as "staff" from when she was a volunteer:

> Quite often residents would approach me after class and apologize for their or someone else's behavior. It was their way of teaching me how the game was played. Given the context, staff members and residents were protagonists. That was just the way it had to be. . . . [I]n the classroom setting there existed a preexisting relationship based upon power differences.[72]

Lehnerer discusses how residents maintained a code of secrecy from staff. She also stressed how residents and staff did not trust each other, and how information control was a valuable resource by both parties: "Lack of trust was directly linked to staff beliefs that residents were concealing information and resident beliefs that staff were using information to further discredit them."[73]

PUNISHMENT AND TREATMENT ROLE ORIENTATIONS: The interplay between punishment and treatment roles has been examined in other correctional settings, such as prisons. However, one study examined the orientation of halfway house counselors toward custody or rehabilitation by administering surveys to 67 counselors in three Texas facilities.[74] This research found that halfway house counselors supported rehabilitation more than custody and punishment, but that role conflict was not present. Workers who supported custody over treatment were less satisfied with their job, but they reported less job stress. The findings of this study make sense, but the reasoning behind the results requires more explanation. The author reasons that "halfway houses are guided by a rehabilitative orientation."[75] We disagree. We believe that worker orientations do not guide facility orientation. It is the other way around. Halfway houses do provide treatment but are guided primarily toward minimizing risk, which is a custody concern. The findings that halfway house counselors support rehabilitation makes sense, but this is because worker ideologies (treatment or custody) are defined not by individual characteristics, but by the expectations and responsibilities of the job and of upper management. The expectations of being a halfway house counselor are to support rehabilitation, but not to ignore the importance of the custody orientation. Counselors who were ideologically more custody-oriented would tend to be less satisfied in their job because the job definition of a counselor, in comparison with the client manager involved solely in security issues, would not match personal philosophy. Alarid explains:

> When I moved from client manager to case manager, my orientation changed to match my new responsibilities. Unlike the client manager who is involved in security issues and running facility operations, the case manager role has two sides: treatment and reprimand. The most effective case managers were the ones who could balance the two sides and who believed in both. But as a case manager, the job required an ideological orientation toward treatment and rehabilitation, whereas the client manager did not. However, some counselors were lopsided, in that they invested heavily in treatment issues but could not bring themselves to put someone in jail that posed a liability risk to the community. I was fully invested in the progress my clients were making. By the same token, once one of my clients committed too many violations or committed a new crime, I arranged the arrest and met with them just prior to them

being transported back to prison. No one ever "likes" sending someone back to prison, but you have to be willing to enforce the rules. The most valuable thing I learned was to treat people with fairness and consistency. I was not concerned like other case managers were with the need to be liked. I knew and accepted that many of my clients did not like me, but I was told that they did respect me.

Examples of Halfway House Programs

Texas established rehabilitation centers (formerly restitution centers) where nonviolent offenders, as a condition of probation, live for up to one year. While there, the residents work at their regular jobs. Their pay is submitted directly to the center director, who deducts the amounts for room and board, support for dependents, supervision fees, and victim restitution. The remainder is returned to the resident after release from the center. During off-work hours the residents are required to perform community service. Preliminary reports indicate that over 80 percent of residents completed their term of residence without violating their probation.

Evaluations of Halfway House Programs

As with other community-based programs, it is difficult to measure the effectiveness of halfway house programs. Wide variation exists in the quality of programs and in the types of offenders admitted. Effectiveness has typically been measured by examining the program success or failure rates or by comparing recidivism rates of halfway house residents with a matched sample of probationers or parolees. The relationship between program success and postrelease recidivism is unclear.[76]

Three studies examined both program completion and recidivism rates for halfway houses. Latessa and Travis found that the only variable that predicted success and lack of recidivism was clients who did not use illegal drugs, while Jennifer D. Hartmann and colleagues found that race and ethnicity (being of Caucasian descent) predicted both behaviors.[77] Eric R. Dowdy found that fewer disciplinary reports (write-ups for misbehavior) predicted both program completion and lower recidivism rates.[78]

One study reported that 65 percent of halfway house residents successfully complete the program.[79] In another study, halfway house clients committed fewer and less severe new crimes in a 12–month period than did a matched group of parolees.[80] However, James L. Beck found no significant difference between rate of rearrest between federal halfway house residents and a comparison group of parolees and probationers. Beck did find that halfway house clients were employed for a longer amount of time and earned more income than parolees and probationers.[81] This was likely related to the rent that halfway houses charge clients and the higher pressure applied on clients to find a job.

In an assessment of 44 recidivism studies, Edward Latessa and Harry E. Allen found that while halfway house residents are generally higher-need, higher-risk, and more likely to recidivate than ordinary parolees, no difference in outcome between the two groups was observed. Halfway house residents generally received more treatment intervention than those did on regular probation or parole. The authors concluded that such program participation might have been the critical difference.[82]

Higher success rates in halfway house programs were significantly related to having past employment skills, a higher education level, and gender (being female).[83] In a second study three years later by the same researchers, a whole new set of significant predictors emerged: age, drug and alcohol use, emotional problems, and community ties. The researchers found that clients who were younger, used drugs and alcohol, had more extensive prior criminal history, and had less community ties were more likely to fail in residential community corrections facilities.[84] Similar predictors were found by C. L. Walsh and S. H. Beck, who also found that individuals convicted of a violent crime were more likely to recidivate than property offenders.[85]

In sum, most halfway house samples have more treatment needs than traditional probationers.[86] The weight of the evidence suggests that probationers and parolees who spent time in a halfway house had similar recidivism rates (in terms of new crimes committed) and similar positive adjustment scores to traditional probationers offenders who did not reside in a halfway house. The strongest predictor of program success is criminal history. Clients with a more extensive criminal history are significantly more likely to fail.[87] The continued use of drugs and alcohol, lack of employment and educational skills, and younger age of the offender were also strong predictors of failure in many studies.[88]

OTHER TYPES OF RESIDENTIAL COMMUNITY CORRECTIONS FACILITIES

Most evaluation research has focused on halfway houses, primarily because they have been around the longest. However, there are other types of residential community corrections facilities: restitution centers, drug and alcohol treatment centers, work and study release, and a specialized residential program for women offenders to live with their children.

Restitution Centers

Restitution centers are a type of residential community facility specifically targeted for property or first-time offenders who owe victim restitution or community service. Restitution centers may provide some outside treatment, but the focus is on stable employment and paying back the victim. Some programs will release the offender when the restitution is paid in full.

MINNESOTA RESTITUTION CENTER: Minnesota provided the prototype for contemporary restitution centers. Established in 1972, the Minnesota Restitution Center (MRC) accepted adult males who had been sentenced to the Minnesota State Prison for two years or less and had served at least four months of their sentences. Recidivists, violent offenders, and professional criminals were not eligible for the program, nor were middle-class persons who could make restitution without the assistance of the center. While in prison, the inmate, with the assistance of an MRC staff member, met with the victim face to face to establish a restitution plan. After the parole board approved the restitution plan, the offender was released on parole to the center, where he lived, secured employment, and fulfilled the terms of the agreement. The offender could also receive additional services there, including group therapy, supervision in the community corrections center, and assistance in obtaining employment. Although the MRC was considered a success, it was closed in 1976 because the number of property offenders being sent to prison was reduced by the implementation of the state's Community Corrections Act.

GEORGIA COMMUNITY DIVERSION CENTER: Georgia based its restitution program on the Minnesota model. Unlike the Minnesota model, however, Georgia residential programs—known as community diversion centers—serve both probationers and parolees. Residential centers located throughout the state house 20 to 40 offenders each for up to five months. During their stay, center residents develop restitution plans, receive individual and group counseling, and are referred for a variety of other services as needed. They may also be required to work at community service projects on weekends and during evening hours. The offenders normally remain at the center until their restitution is completed.

One evaluation of the program revealed that about 85 percent of the participants were rearrested within 18 months after release. Although this does not suggest a great reduction in recidivism, the program's economic benefits are considerable. Belinda Rogers McCarthy and Bernard J. McCarthy Jr. state,

> During a one-year period, the residents earned a total of $128,437 in restitution payments; [and] 8,372 hours of community service were provided. Over $150,000 was paid in state and federal taxes, and over $200,000 was spent in the local communities for clothing, transportation, recreation, and personal items. In addition, the total cost of care per individual has been much less for restitution center residents than prison inmates.[89]

Residential Drug and Alcohol Treatment Centers

While restitution centers focus on employment and restitution, **residential drug and alcohol treatment centers** in the community focus on substance abuse treatment. Employment is of secondary importance. Some programs do not even require offenders to work at all while undergoing treatment, because finding employment takes away from intensive treatment time. The Residential Treatment Center in Greeley, Colorado, is six to nine months long and is specifically designed for clients who failed various Denver-area halfway house programs because of alcohol abuse and illegal substance use. Given only a specified number of beds, candidates were screened for suitability and readiness for treatment. If accepted, offenders with a substance abuse problem did not go back to prison but were given a chance to "kick the habit" without the outside pressures of paying rent and paying for treatment. Clients who graduated from the program went out on probation or parole, depending on their initial status. Clients who continued to use drugs and alcohol while in the drug treatment program were removed and incarcerated for the remainder of their sentence.

Sometimes community residential treatment programs are used as a transition step for clients who graduate from prison-based therapeutic communities or other type of drug treatment programs while behind bars. For example, women in California with drug problems could attend a drug treatment program and then, upon their release, could be transferred to a residential program in the community to deal with issues of relapse and opportunity. An evaluation of these programs indicates that women who completed both the institutional treatment phase and the community residential treatment phase resulted in lower incidences of drug use and higher levels of parole completion. Female drug offenders who participated in the institutional phase but did not enter the community phase did not fare so well. The researchers concluded that there is a shortage of facilities for women drug abusers. Many women applied but were unable to enter the community residential phase of the program because of space shortages. These women did not complete treatment, which left them vulnerable to relapse.[90] **Relapse** is when an offender with a substance abuse problem returns to using alcohol and drugs.

Residential drug and alcohol treatment programs are also used as diversion from prison. For example, Florida has an 18-month Drug Punishment Program, which includes 6 months in a secure facility, 3 months in a community facility, followed by 9 months of intensive supervision probation. Like the Colorado program, candidates are screened for suitability and readiness for treatment. This program targets males and females age 21 and younger. During the early phases, they are diagnosed, an individual treatment plan is developed, and clients receive group counseling.[91]

Another similar program for nonviolent probationers exists in Dallas, Texas. This 300-bed facility provides 200 beds for clients in the first six-month residential phase of the program. Then, clients with adequate support systems enter a six-month aftercare program where they live at home and report to a probation officer. The remaining 100 beds are reserved for clients who do not have strong support systems and need an additional three months to make a successful transition through the "live-in, work-out" program. This is unique, because transition from residential living to community living is seen as a prime opportunity for relapse. Probation officers work with the treatment facility staff to review clients' progress.[92] Unfortunately, few evaluations have been made of the effectiveness of these programs.

Work and Study Release

Work and study release could be considered a type of institutional corrections program, given that offenders reside in a facility (a community facility, jail, or prison) but are released into the community to work or attend education classes or both. Work and study release is much more restrictive than halfway houses, because offenders are not allowed to leave the facility for any other reason except work and school. This type of release is for a specified purpose and for a specific duration. We discuss work and study release here because the offender is out in the community in a form of prerelease program and is preparing for release into the community.

Work or study release would be a useful tool for dealing with first-time offenders. Work release can be imposed as a judicial sentence. In this case, the offender already has a job or is already going to school at the time the crime is committed. The judge orders that offenders must reside in jail and be allowed to continue working to pay restitution or to continue attending school (for example, college classes). This option is sometimes used when restitution centers or halfway houses are not available.

Table 12.4 shows the estimated number of offenders who participated in work and study release programs. Work release is used much more frequently (with nearly 38,000 offenders) than study release (with just over 100 offenders). The frequency of placing offenders on work release has declined steadily since 1994. No available evidence shows that placing offenders on work and study release increases the risk to the community. Two studies conducted between 1991 and 1994 of prison work release programs in Washington show that few inmates committed crimes while on work release, and recidivism rates were similar for work release groups compared with prisoners who were not released for employment.[93] The decline, then, has stemmed mainly from political pressures to dissuade the use of options that place incarcerated offenders in the community temporarily.

An experimental program named CREST combines a prison-based therapeutic community (substance abuse treatment) with work release. Clients entering the program from prison must first progress through a significant amount of drug and alcohol education, counseling, and confrontation before they are eligible for the work release phase in the community. Preliminary evaluation data indicate that CREST participants have significantly lower relapse and lower recidivism rates than a comparison group.[94]

WORK AND STUDY RELEASE

Offenders who reside in a facility (a community facility, jail, or prison) but who are released into the community only to work or attend education classes or both.

TABLE 12.4   Inmates Placed in Work and Study Release and Other Programs During 1998

State	Work Release	Study Release	Diversion	Electronic Monitoring	Day Reporting	Intensive Supervision	Halfway Houses
Alaska	4						3,743
Arizona				231			
Arkansas	526						
California							5,204
Colorado[a]	2,565						
Connecticut				84			1,536
Delaware	479			703			190
District of Columbia	117		8	159	1,458		222
Florida	3,690						
Hawaii	428	5	3,339	251	163		84
Idaho[b]	172						
Illinois	4,394			2,307			
Indiana	528	6					
Iowa[c]	1,212			487	1,410	2,755	
Kansas	436						
Louisiana	1,916						
Maine	460						
Maryland	342			2,279			
Massachusetts	917	29		79			49
Michigan	14		1,043	2,198			3,438
Minnesota	651			275	200	240	500
Mississippi				1,233			
Missouri[b]	1,257			318.5			62.2
Montana				18		182	414
Nebraska	196						
Nevada				178			130
New Hampshire							480
New Jersey	112			1,671			5,646
New Mexico	420	20					
New York	9,085			3,180			
North Dakota	46	2					
Ohio	1,139			1,086			2,621
Oklahoma	380		8		121	91	1,065
Oregon	1						
Pennsylvania[d]	87						3,812
Rhode Island	106			221			
South Carolina	1,052						
South Dakota[e]	223						72
Tennessee	23			379		862	196
Virginia[f]	228		631	2,041	887	1,989	235
Washington	2,788			100	1,000		
West Virginia	230	35					
Wisconsin	1,726			125			
Wyoming		6			34		174
Federal[g]				10,000			20,000
Total	**37,950**	**103**	**5,029**	**24,617**	**10,226**	**6,153**	**49,873**

[a]Work release includes intensive supervision.   [b] Figures are based on monthly average.   [c]These are community corrections programs not run by institutions. Release decisions for work release made by parole board.   [d]Number of inmates placed in halfway houses includes parolees transferred from state correctional institutions to community corrections centers. [e]Number of inmates placed in work release is for fiscal year 1998.   [f]Number of inmates placed under intensive supervision estimated. Number of inmates placed in halfway houses is the ADP (average daily population, defined as the average number of prisoners in an agency on any given day during the calendar year) in halfway houses during fiscal year 1998.   [g]Number placed under electronic monitoring are those placed under home confinement, which may or may not be electronically monitored. Approximately 50 percent of all halfway houses inmates are eventually placed on home confinement.
Source: Camille Graham Camp and George C. Camp, The Corrections Yearbook: 1999 (Middletown, CT: Criminal Justice Institute, 1999).

Women Offenders Living with Children

The last type of residential community corrections facility is strictly for women offenders who have young children. The purpose of this RCCF is for women to live with their children while they are serving a residential community sentence. There are a very small number of these types of facilities, and most are still in the early stages of development. Given that most women in the criminal justice system are mothers (65 percent of women have at least one child under the age of 18), studies indicate that the children of offenders suffer emotionally, developmentally, and economically when their parents go to prison. Children of incarcerated parents stand a greater chance of following in the footsteps of their parents, by becoming involved in the juvenile justice system at an early age. Because the mother is still the primary caretaker in the majority of families, the effect of incarcerating mothers with dependent children is more pronounced.[95] The question then becomes: How can women offenders be punished or sanctioned without punishing their children?

Statistics on convicted women offenders indicate that most women are nonviolent property or drug offenders, and they do not pose a threat to the community.[96] Therefore, most women felons do not require prison sentences and would be ideal candidates for community placement.

JOHN P. CRAINE HOUSE: The John P. Craine House opened in 1993 in Indianapolis, Indiana. The facility is designed specifically for women offenders with preschool-aged children who have been convicted of misdemeanors or nonviolent felony offenses.[97] The Craine House holds a maximum capacity of 6 adults and 8 children at one time and serves between 10 and 17 women and about 20 children each year.

William H. Barton of the Indiana University School of Social Work is conducting research in cooperation with Cheryl Justice, the executive director of the John Craine House. The researchers point out that the Craine House serves a dual role, "both as an alternative to incarceration for the women and as a preventive intervention for their children."[98]

The Craine House resembles a halfway house in the sense that women pay for part of the program cost through the expectation of employment. The needs of each woman are assessed, and an individualized treatment plan is formulated. However, unlike the halfway house, this facility seems to provide much more individualized and specialized attention, not only for the offender's needs, but also for her children. Specific interventions focus on

> parenting skills, substance abuse treatment, job seeking skills, educational and/or job placement in the community, personal budgeting, nutrition information, and advocacy as indicated by individualized assessments. The program arranges for daycare for the children at nearby locations to enable the women to work in the community. The program is staffed around the clock by counselors and family living specialists. . . . Basic goals for the Craine House program are to provide a safe, structured environment; promote the preservation of mother-child relationships; enhance the offenders' abilities to maintain economic and emotional independence while leading responsible, law-abiding lives; and prevent the neglect, abuse and potential delinquency of the offenders' children.[99]

Because of the high level of services offered, it costs the Craine House $80 per person per day. The disadvantage to this is that it costs more than incarceration. However, considering that the program is also providing prevention programs for the children, the cost may be money well spent in the long run. The long-term effects of this program remain to be seen.

Statistics indicate that between 1993 and 1999 the average length of stay in the program was five months (6.5 months for those who complete the program and 2 months for noncompleters). Just over 70 percent (53) of the women have successfully completed the program, while 22 women did not because of a technical violation or the commission of a new crime. The other five women still resided at the Craine House.

Recidivism after successfully completing the program was measured by whether the women had appeared in court on a new charge or crime. As of 1999, out of the 53 women who successfully completed the program, 11 committed a new crime. Most graduates were out for an average of two years before recidivating. Women who recidivated committed either a property or drug crime, but no one committed a violent crime.[100] The recidivism data for the first cohort of women extend six years. As the researchers note, it would be worthwhile to determine the long-term effects of the Craine House as a prevention mechanism for the children who participated.

SUMMARY

With more than 4.4 million people on probation and parole and an additional 2 million in jails and prisons, the criminal justice system must acknowledge the need for intermediate sanctions as alternatives to traditional sentencing options. Boot camps and residential community corrections facilities are examples of intermediate sanctions. Boot camps are a type of shock incarceration program that varies in the degree of treatment programs offered. Boot camps are a popular sanction with the public, but the recidivism rates for boot camps with minimal treatment programs are no different from recidivism for prisoners. A small but significant positive effect has been evident on recidivism and prison costs for a limited number of boot camp programs, particularly those that stress treatment over marching and drills. Voluntary participation, selection from the prison population, and intensive aftercare provisions are an important part of the boot camp experience.

Halfway houses remain the most common type of residential community program for offenders who have needs greater than offenders on regular probation or parole. Halfway houses are a more intensive form of supervision than probation and parole, but they are also valuable as a reentry tool for prisoners coming out of prison. Since the 1970s, many different adaptations of RCCFs have opened that offer internal treatment service for a more specialized offender population. Overall evaluations of halfway houses show that the benefits outweigh the costs, but the effectiveness of other types of RCCFs is yet to be determined.

DISCUSSION QUESTIONS

1. What factor(s) brought about the development of intermediate sanctions?
2. What do Norval Morris and Michael Tonry mean when they say that criminal justice and corrections are both too lenient and too severe?
3. Discuss the evolution and use of boot camps. What are the purposes of shock incarceration?
4. How successful have boot camps been?
5. What are some of the positive and negative aspects associated with boot camps?
6. What are some examples of residential community corrections facilities?

7   What would working in a halfway house be like? What might be some of the problems you would face?

8   What are some of the program components inherent in halfway houses?

9   Do halfway houses work?

10 Compare a therapeutic community environment with a boot camp.

11 What goals does a therapeutic community attempt to achieve?

12 Should more programs such as the John Craine House be expanded?

 **WEB SITES**

International Association of Residential and Community Alternatives

http://www.iccaweb.org/ICCA_Info/icca_info.html

Community Corrections Association of Pennsylvania
Exchanges ideas and information regarding work release programs

http://www.c-cap.org

Please go to the book-specific Web site for Supplemental Readings related to the material in this chapter:
A Boot Camp Teacher's Unforgettable Experience
http://www.wadsworth.com/product/0-534-559662s

Intermediate Sanctions: When Traditional Probation is Not Enough

Intermediate sanctions lie on the punishment continuum between traditional probation and incarceration. All intermediate sanction programs reinforce the importance of taking responsibility and control for one's actions. The degree of accountability, however, varies by type of program. Intermediate sanctions are appropriate if an offender needs more structure than traditional probation provides, or if an offender's prior criminal history disqualifies him or her from probation.

In the following cases, determine what type of intermediate sanction might be appropriate for each offender and justify your choice.

Case A: John is a 29-year-old male who has been twice convicted of fraud by forging checks. His first conviction resulted in a sentence of five years' probation with an order to make restitution in the amount of $320. John made three payments of $30 each before absconding supervision. He turned up again after six months and was reinstated on probation by the court after he promised to faithfully fulfill the terms of his supervision and to complete his restitution obligation. During his supervised release he was in violation of probation conditions regularly and never completed his restitution payments. However, because the state prison was seriously overcrowded, the court did not revoke his probation and he was finally released from supervision.

The current case involves passing a forged check at a local grocery store in the amount of $124. Because of his previous failure on probation, the court is concerned that he is not capable of following court-ordered probation conditions, yet does not want to commit him to the state prison or to a jail term. John has a wife and two small children and is their only source of support. He is currently employed as a house painter.

Case B: Ricardo is a 19-year-old male with a history of minor criminal offenses including car burglary, shoplifting, and several counts of driving under the influence. He is not assaultive and has not been convicted of a felony. His current offense is larceny, involving theft from a customer of his employer, a local carpet laying company. The probation report concludes that Ricardo needs more structure than can be gained from probation or intensive supervision but does not recommend a prison sentence. The probation officer reports that Ricardo needs to learn discipline, good work habits, and respect for the rights of others.

13

Nonresidential Intermediate Sanctions

David Young-Wolff/Photo Edit

What You Will Learn in This Chapter

*I**n this chapter you will learn about the various intermediate sanctions in which offenders complete the conditions of their sentence in the community but sleep in their own house. You will learn that many of the following sanctions are used in some combination with each other: intensive supervision probation, house arrest, electronic monitoring, day reporting center, restitution, community service, and fines. Offenders contribute to these punishments through monetary payments or working without payment. This helps keep the cost of the programs to a minimum. Each program is discussed and evaluated.*

INTRODUCTION

Programs that required offenders to live at a facility during their community-based sentence were discussed in Chapter 12. Each residential program provided some form of nonresidential aftercare, usually in the form of probation or parole. This further aided the transition process. Sanctions and programs that offenders participate in while living at home are examined in this chapter. These programs can be sentences by themselves, or they can be combined with other sanctions. Such combinations include additional sanctions to probation, as a phase of aftercare or following a period of time spent in a residential facility, or additional sanctions to confinement in jail and prison.

INTENSIVE SUPERVISION PROBATION

INTENSIVE SUPERVISION PROBATION

A form of probation that stresses intensive monitoring, close supervision, and offender control.

Intensive supervision probation (ISP) programs developed rapidly around the country since the early 1980s. By 1990, every state had adopted some form of ISP for adult offenders.[1] ISP offenders remain on probation but are subjected to closer surveillance, more conditions, and more exposure to treatment than regular probationers.

Through smaller caseloads, ISP was originally designed to enhance rehabilitation and public safety by affording greater contact between the probation officer and the probationer. The purpose of ISP has been expanded to include three primary goals:

1. Relieve prison overcrowding and the costs of incarceration
2. Keep offenders from committing crimes in the community while they are involved in the program
3. Impose intermediate punishment that is less severe than imprisonment but more severe than regular probation

To accomplish these goals, ISP is designed for high-risk, high-need offenders who are prison-bound. Most ISP programs, though, are considered "probation or parole enhancements" because participants are drawn from the pool of probationers. ISPs are also seen as "socially cost-effective" because they are less likely than incarceration to contribute to the breakup of offenders' families, they allow offenders to remain employed, and they are less stigmatizing than prison.

The programs vary from jurisdiction to jurisdiction, but most of them require contact three to five times per week with probation officers, community service, curfew, random night and weekend visits, unscheduled drug or alcohol testing, and strict enforcement of probation conditions. Many ISP programs also include one or more of the following: payment of probation fees, house arrest, restitution, and some form of electronic surveillance.[2]

ISP Caseloads

Probation officers who supervise ISP clients generally have smaller caseloads than officers with regular probation caseloads. Probation and parole officers first advocated smaller caseloads in the early 1960s, contending that they allow the officers to give more assistance to the probationer in his or her rehabilitation efforts. While smaller caseloads were found to provide greater protection to the community through increased surveillance and control, they did not necessarily enhance rehabilitation or decrease recidivism.[3] Using smaller caseloads for increased surveillance was viewed during the conservative 1980s as a viable alternative to saving prison bed space and decreasing institutional costs. As a result, the ISP movement increased in popularity beginning in 1983.

Most ISP programs mandate specified levels of contact between probationer and probation officer and reduced caseload size. The reduced caseload size is typically accompanied by more focused supervision than regular probation, which may include curfew checks, and more frequent visits to the client's home or place of employment. Whereas the average probation caseload is between 94 and 124 offenders, ISP officers generally supervise about 25–30 offenders. Parole officers averaged 67 cases on regular caseloads and 25 on ISP caseloads.[4] The data show a significant difference between number of contacts on regular probation versus intensive probation. Probation officers average 14 face-to-face contacts per year with probationers on regular supervision and 74 contacts with offenders on intensive supervision probation.[5]

Attitudes toward ISP

Today, ISP programs continue to flourish. The surveillance orientation and punitive properties of ISP appeal to the public's preference that community penalties be demanding. Well over 120,000 offenders are placed on ISP annually.[6]

The success of ISP reaching its goal of enrolling high-risk, high-need offenders depends largely on the understanding and attitudes of criminal justice practitioners. Two studies were conducted on how criminal justice practitioners perceived ISP. Arthur Lurigio conducted the first known study with judges, public defenders, district attorneys, and private attorneys in Chicago. Most respondents believed ISP was useful to have as an option, but ideologies on rate of usage were consistent according to occupation. Public defenders thought ISP should be expanded, while district attorneys thought ISP should be decreased. Judges wanted more clarification regarding selection and operational procedures.[7]

A later study adapted Lurigio's survey instrument to practitioner perceptions of ISP in Kansas City, Kansas. Criminal justice practitioners thought that ISP offenders have been appropriately placed according to risk and needs and that ISP is useful at reducing the number of offenders who would have gone to prison.[8] However, when asked about what the purposes of ISP are and how the public might perceive ISP, practitioner responses were broad and, in some cases, contradictory.[9] The researchers raised the issue that the success of ISP stems in part from effectively communicating the central goals and the importance of assessing risk and needs so that all participants are "on the same page."

Critics of ISP programs point to evidence of a net widening effect. Studies have found that ISP participants are not necessarily chosen from a high-risk, high-need offender pool as originally purported but may only be of medium-risk or have medium-level needs.[10] Critics also maintain that ISP is not designed for the restorative justice philosophy. Victim restitution is mandatory in many ISP programs, but victim needs and wants lie at the peripheral compared with offender needs.[11]

Evaluations of ISP

Early evaluations of ISP programs in Georgia found evidence that ISP was effective in reducing rearrests of probationers. The Georgia program reported that the first 1,000 participants committed only 25 serious offenses while under supervision and that by the sixth year the program had saved the state millions of dollars in correctional costs. However, because of the demanding conditions of ISP coupled with closer contact with probationers, ISP officers discovered more rule violations than regular probation officers. Therefore, the intensive supervision programs had higher failure rates than regular probation even though their rearrest rates were lower. The findings of early ISP evaluations in Georgia and New Jersey have been called into question because the researchers did not use control groups for comparison. Furthermore, other confounding effects, such as incarceration, were not taken into consideration.[12]

RECIDIVISM RATES AND TECHNICAL VIOLATIONS: Later evaluations questioned whether ISP programs were responsible for the reported successful outcomes. A study by the RAND Corporation found that judges used extra caution in sentencing offenders to the ISP programs in the early years because the programs were untested. Many programs limited participation to property offenders with minor criminal records, which undoubtedly helps to explain the lower rearrest rate.[13] When such biasing factors were controlled statistically, the researchers found no significant difference in the rearrest rates of ISP and regular probationers. Furthermore, in two of the three sites studied, no significant difference was evident in the technical violation rates of regular probation and ISP participants. The findings suggest that ISP programs are not effective for high-risk offenders if effectiveness is judged solely by offender recidivism rates.[14]

A study of three different groups of offenders in Arizona confirmed that ISP does not significantly reduce recidivism rates any differently than offenders sentenced to prison or probation. Within three years of sentencing, about one-half of offenders in all three groups in Maricopa County and one-third of offenders in all three groups in Pima County had been arrested for a new crime. A report to Charles E. Schumer, then chairman of the U.S. House of Representatives Subcommittee on Crime and Criminal Justice, equivocally concludes:

> Despite mixed results, intensive supervision has a role to play in the near future of corrections policy. The findings from Arizona are not strong enough to recommend a major expansion of intensive supervision programs. At the same time, however, our findings do contribute to a growing body of research that shows that these programs have some merit. Given the lack of unambiguously successful alternatives, any option that controls crime (even on a transitory basis for a select group of offenders), and that simultaneously offers the promise of dollar savings, deserves serious policy attention.[15]

REDUCTION OF PRISON BEDS: Some observers doubt that ISP reduces prison populations, however. Norval Morris and Michael Tonry suggest that research evidence and experience show that intermediate punishments free up fewer prison beds and save less money than their proponents claim. Just as with boot camps, judges who impose ISP on probation-bound offenders widen the net and produce higher costs.[16] Supporting this contention, Thomas B. Blomberg found that 28 percent of those placed in Florida's prison-alternative ISP program would have received probation if ISP had not been available as a sentencing alternative.[17]

COST-BENEFIT ANALYSES: The costs of ISP programs are definitely greater than regular probation. Earlier evaluation studies produced mixed results. Cost savings were reported in Illinois and New Jersey, while no cost savings was achieved in Massachusetts and Wisconsin.[18] In 1993, the average annual cost per ISP offender was $4,000; while for prisoners, it was $12,000. High violations that sent ISP offenders to prison increased the actual cost of ISP to $7,200. When this cost is compared with violation rates of probationers and parolees on routine supervision, that cost is $4,700 per person per year.[19]

In one study of a Minnesota ISP program designed to divert prison-bound offenders, ISP was used in lieu of prison and regular parole. The annual savings of $5,000 per offender were offset by the increased cost of intensive supervision that was more expensive than regular parole. No cost savings resulted because the money saved in the beginning was made up for the increased cost at the end.[20]

Rigorous cost-benefit analyses of 14 ISP programs demonstrated that none had a cost savings like that reported earlier in Georgia. The reason is that most analyses have inappropriately used average daily costs instead of marginal costs.[21] In other words, savings of 250 beds in a prison facility that holds 2,000 offenders will save on meals, medical care, and other minor supplies provided for 250 offenders. Assuming the 250 beds were not filled with other more serious offenders, the reduction of such a small group (12.5 percent) would not justify changing the number of correctional officers, medical care, or other facilities that must be provided to the remaining 1,750 offenders. The only way that 250 beds would save daily costs is if the facility closed down or a substantial number of staff members were laid off. Staff salaries make up the largest portion of all correctional budgets, so enough beds would have to be emptied to justify closing off portions of a prison unit. That trend is simply not occurring.

TREATMENT PARTICIPATION: The ISP evaluation literature reveals some positive findings. Partial victim restitution rates were paid by more ISP participants (12 percent) than by routine probationers (3 percent).[22] Michael Tonry and Mary Lynch conclude that ISP did succeed at some sites in increasing participants' involvement in counseling and other treatment programs. The drug treatment literature demonstrates that participation can reduce both drug use and crime by drug-using offenders.[23] The relationship between principles of effective intervention and lower recidivism is being advocated by the American Probation and Parole Association as a way to strengthen ISP.[24] Through a more integrated balance between treatment and surveillance, ISP may be able to achieve similar effects as boot camps.

EVALUATION SUMMARY: The weight of the evidence illustrates that ISP programs, as they currently operate, do not produce cost savings, they do not significantly decrease the number of prison beds, and they do not reduce recidivism rates. Technical violation rates are high, and in the case of ISP programs, recidivism measures not individual levels of crime, but measures the system's ability to detect crime and act on it (through arrests). . . . [I]t may be that an ISP offender is committing the same number or fewer crimes than someone on routine supervision who has a lower probability of being arrested for them. The ISP offender, whose behavior is more closely monitored, may be caught in the enforcement net, while the offender on routine probation or parole may escape it.[25]

As a result of the high violation levels, probation and parole enhancement ISP programs may increase the number of jail and prison commitments. No hard evidence is available about the effect of ISP as a prison diversion. Both prison diversion test sites in Oregon and Wisconsin experienced research design problems (which obstructed valid results) related to willingness to expand the eligibility criteria to offenders who should be behind bars.[26] Does this mean that ISP efforts have failed and should be abandoned? We do not think so. Dismissing ISP as having failed is premature until the eligibility standards have changed to reflect the original intent of a prison diversion program or until the goals have changed to reflect the current eligibility standards of ISP as a form of probation enhancement. There seems to be additional potential in offering certain treatment intervention strategies in ISP programs in hopes of lowering recidivism.[27]

HOUSE ARREST

House arrest, or **home confinement,** is an intermediate sanction designed to confine offenders to their homes during the hours when they are not at work, attending a treatment program, or visiting their probation officer. House arrest is typically either a condition of ISP or is a sanction by itself. Florida uses house arrest extensively and has over 14,000 offenders under house arrest, many of whom were electronically monitored.[28]

Purposes of House Arrest

House arrest, or home confinement, is neither a new concept nor a U.S. innovation. Galileo (1564–1642) was placed under house arrest by church authorities for his heretical assertion that the earth revolved around the sun. More recently, Soviet physicist Andrey Sakharov (1921–89) was confined to an apartment in Gorky for "antistate" activities.

House arrest programs proliferated in the 1980s. House arrest serves as an alternative to incarceration and a means of easing prison overcrowding. The purpose of house arrest is not, however, to deter or to reduce recidivism.[29]

Programs vary, but most require that offenders remain within the confines of their home during specified hours—ranging from 24-hour-per-day confinement to imposition of late-night curfews. Most states and the federal system now operate some form of house-arrest program. California, Florida, Georgia, Kentucky, Oklahoma, and Oregon all make extensive use of this option. Florida's "community controllees" (those under house arrest) are required to maintain employment and to participate in self-improvement programs, such as a general equivalency diploma (GED) program to obtain a high school diploma, drug and alcohol counseling, or other "life skills" programs. Many are required to perform community service as well. When they are not participating in work, self-help programs, or community service, they must be at home.

Florida's community control officer caseloads are limited by statute to 20 offenders, and the officers work weekends and holidays. They are required to make a minimum of 28 contacts per month with each offender. Officers' schedules vary from day to day, resulting in regular but random visits with the offenders. If an offender is not where he or she should be at any particular time, a violation of community control is reported to the court. Some house arrest programs randomly call offenders, and a computer verifies the offender's unique voice electronically by computer. If the voice is that of another person or a tape-recorded voice of the offender, the computer will register an unauthorized absence. Too many unauthorized absences may result in a technical violation of probation and time in jail.

Criticisms of House Arrest

The first criticism directed at house arrest is that it does not seem to be a punishment. Staying at home for most people is considered a luxury, and not a negative experience. The courts also recognize that home confinement is not the same as jail or prison confinement. Thus, time spent on home confinement awaiting trial as a pretrial detainee cannot be counted as time served toward the conviction like pretrial detainees in jail obtain.[30] Some house arrest programs for convicted offenders do not apply time served on home confinement if the sentence must be revoked. Thus, if an offender with a one-year sentence to home confinement fails to complete the program, and his home arrest is revoked, he must begin his one-year sentence in jail and serve the full term.

Another argument is that the intrusiveness of house arrest violates a probationer's constitutional right to privacy in the home (which is usually occupied by other family members). Because most programs are voluntary, if the offender does not agree to the conditions, he or she will be resentenced to another sanctioning option. A convicted offender's privacy rights are limited as a result of a felony conviction.

Potential risks with house arrest are that offenders can still commit crimes from their house. For example, one probationer was arrested for selling drugs out of his home. Customers came to him and he never left his house, so there were no violations recorded when he received random calls. If it were not for suspicious neighbors calling the police, the probationer may have been able to continue selling drugs without getting caught for some time.

Another challenge of house arrest is that domestic violence incidents may erupt. Because the offender is home all the time and cannot leave the house to "cool off," some offenders take out their frustrations on other family members in the wrong way. Several community control officers in Florida report that it is not unusual for the spouse of an individual on house arrest to complain that he or she cannot stand another day with the husband or wife at home all day. And according to the officers, several house arrestees have requested that they be sent to prison instead of continue on house arrest. One told his supervising officer, "If I have to spend any more time with my old lady, I'll probably kill her. Send me on down to Raiford [the state prison]."

Joan Petersilia warns that house arrest programs are often inaugurated with unrealistic goals and expectations of success. She points out that because considerable self-discipline is required to comply with house arrest and many offenders are impulsive by nature, many offenders are likely to be unable to sustain the required behavior for long periods.[31]

Effectiveness of House Arrest

Given that house arrest is an enhancement for probation or parole and has more conditions than routine supervision, house arrest suffers from many of the same problems as ISP. Offenders on house arrest are twice as likely as regular parolees to have their parole revoked for a technical violation.[32]

HOUSE ARREST VERSUS RESIDENTIAL COMMUNITY CORRECTIONS FACILITIES: Harjit S. Sandhu and his colleagues conducted a unique program comparison between offenders sentenced to house arrest and another group of offenders sentenced to a residential community treatment center (CTC).[33] The CTC residents had done time in prison and were within six to nine months of being released on parole. CTC residents lived at the facility and paid room and board, while house arrestees lived at home but did not wear electronic monitoring devices. A significantly higher percent of CTC residents (51 percent) were unemployed compared with people on house arrest (17 percent), who most likely never lost their present job. A follow-up period of one year indicated that despite a significantly more serious criminal history, offenders on house arrest had lower recidivism rates (92 percent) than offenders sentenced to the residential community treatment center (74 percent). The authors attribute the differences in success rates to house arrestees having stable employment and living with their family, which may have given them greater motivation to succeed to avoid going to prison.[34] Although the authors state that a high rate of current employment of offenders on house arrest appeared to contribute to their success, many offenders who fail residential community corrections facilities-type programs seem to have unemployment status in common. Offenders who do not remain employed or have a difficult time finding a job out of prison have a greater likelihood of program failure, especially in programs that charge for subsistence.

PRETRIAL DETAINEES: House arrest could be used for defendants awaiting trial who would otherwise be held in jail. Defendants who cannot afford bail and who do not qualify for release on personal recognizance may be considered for house arrest. In Marion, Indiana, house arrest for defendants awaiting trial was instituted to relieve jail overcrowding. Although the program accepted less than 25 percent of those referred for screening, 73 percent of those accepted successfully completed the program. Of those who failed to complete the house arrest program, 13 percent were technical violators and 14 percent absconded.

ELECTRONIC MONITORING

Imagine this scenario: Samson has been in prison for the last three years, convicted of reckless endangerment and possession of a weapon. Samson was paroled from prison on the condition that for at least the first year he wear an electronic device that fits snugly around his ankle. A transmitter in Samson's ankle bracelet sends a continuous signal to his personal receiver, which is attached to the phone at his mother's house. This receiver only transmits to Samson's ankle device and to no other. If the signal is broken for any reason—say if Samson moves beyond the 500 feet of his device—the transmitter automatically records this and calls into a centralized computer. A worker checks to see if the absence is authorized or unauthorized. The absence is authorized if Samson has received prior permission from his parole officer to go out looking for a job or is at work during his scheduled hours. If the absence is unauthorized, his parole officer is automatically notified. Samson has a curfew, and he still must visit his parole officer who checks the device to make sure he has not tried to tamper or remove it in any way.

ELECTRONIC MONITORING

A correctional technology used as a tool in intensive supervision probation or parole or home confinement, in which an intermittent signal transmitted through telephone lines into a transmitter box determines whether the offender is within a certain distance from his or her personal telephone.

Samson's situation is called **electronic monitoring** (EM). EM is a correctional technology used in intensive supervision probation, specialized parole caseloads, and house arrest. EM can also be used for pretrial detainees; that is, suspects who have not yet been convicted but need an elevated level of supervision while out on bail. EM is a technological means of assuring that certain conditions of probation, such as curfew, are met. Like house arrest, EM has the potential to satisfy the goals of imprisonment without the social and financial costs associated with incarceration.

Various manufacturers sell or rent a variety of EM products to correctional facilities and the government. The continuous signal device, worn by Samson in the above example, is the first type of EM to come out on the market and is the least expensive. A second type of transmitter device intercepts signals from local area monitors, similar to the way a cell phone works. The third type emits signals that may also be intercepted by parole or probation officers who have handheld portable receiving units. This type enables officers to drive by an offender's house (or work) randomly to verify where the offender is without seeing him or her in person.

With all three types, the offender must wear the device and cannot tamper or remove the device without sounding an alarm to the central control. Central control agencies typically contract out to the government and other agencies to monitor unauthorized removal or absences. They are responsible for recording, interpreting, and notifying the appropriate corrections officers of the nature of the violation within 24 hours.

Frequency of Use

Electronic monitoring devices emerged in the 1960s, during the deinstitutionalization movement of the mentally ill. When thousands of mentally ill patients were released from mental hospitals, some mental patients were monitored in the community as an alternative to institutionalization.[35] The first official use in criminal justice of EM devices was in 1983 in New Mexico for driving under the influence (DUI) and white-collar offenders.

In 1998, more than 21,400 probationers and parolees were under electronic monitoring in the United States (see Table 13.1). Florida, Michigan, Missouri, North Carolina, Pennsylvania, Wisconsin, and the federal government make the greatest use of electronic monitoring in probation and parole. According to another source, more than 75,000 offenders nationwide were electronically monitored in 1998.[36]

Each EM transmitter and receiver costs about $50,000 each. EM supervision costs nearly $10 per day per offender. Offenders share some of the program costs by paying a monthly fee. Offenders are charged an average of about $26 per month, ranging from $10 in Georgia, Kentucky, Montana, South Dakota, Texas, and Wisconsin to as much as $53 in Louisiana.

Offenders wear an EM bracelet for an average of between 11 and 18 weeks, which is within the optimal range.[37] Research found that success rates decrease after about six months on electronic monitoring.[38]

Criticisms and Problems of Electronic Monitoring

Legal and constitutional issues have been raised with regard to electronic monitoring, but the courts have consistently rejected them. Claims that it constitutes an unconstitutional search and seizure or that it violates the offender's right to privacy have not made much headway. Equal protection and due process arguments have also been raised without success. EM has passed constitutional muster and has become an often-used alternative to imprisonment, primarily because it is cost-effective and keeps the offender in the community.

Various problems of implementation have been noted. Some critics suggest that surveillance by the use of electronic monitoring may constitute unreasonable search and seizure and that, because eligibility for electronic monitoring programs requires a telephone and payment of a fee for electronic surveillance, the program discriminates against those who cannot pay the fee or afford telephone service.[39] Joan Petersilia reports that some jurisdictions have avoided this criticism by basing fees on a sliding scale or providing telephones for those who do not have them.[40]

TABLE 13.1 Use of Electronic Monitoring during 1998

Program	Use Electronic Monitors	Number of Devices	Weeks Worn	Program	Use Electronic Monitors	Number of Devices	Weeks Worn
Probation				Texas[j]	X	1,552	8
Arizona	X	120	18	West Virginia			
California[a]	X			U.S. Parole Commission	X		
Colorado	X			**Total**	**14**	**3,850**	
Connecticut	X			**Average**		**385**	**18**
District of Columbia							
Georgia				**Probation**			
Hawaii	X	14	4	**and parole**			
Illinois	X			Alabama	X	40	
Indiana[b]	X			Alaska			
Kansas	X	165	6	Arkansas	X	233	9
Massachusetts	X		24	Delaware	X		
Maine	X			Florida	X	900	26
Nebraska	X	248	4	NeIdaho	X	151	26
New Jersey	X			Iowa	X	130	12
New York[c]	X			Kentucky[k]	X	100	12
South Dakota				Louisiana	X	200	16
Tennessee	X	250	12	Maryland	X	125	12
Texas	X			Michigan[l]	X	4,400	12
West Virginia[d]	X	0		Minnesota[m]	X	70	6
Federal	X	3,433	12	Mississippi			
Total	**17**	**4,230**		Missouri	X	620	16
Average		**604**	**11**	Montana	X	28	
				Nevada	X		
Parole				New Hampshire	X		26
Arizona[e]	X	140	12	New Mexico	X		
California	X	70	78	North Carolina	X	2,200	12
Colorado	X	545	17	North Dakota[n]	X	8	3
Connecticut	X			Ohio	X		
District of Columbia				Oklahoma			
Georgia	X	582	11	Oregon	X		
Hawaii				Pennsylvania	X	765	
Illinois[f]		365	12	Rhode Island	X		16
Indiana[g]	X		12	South Carolina	X	425	
Kansas	X	60		Utah[o, p]	X	110	8
Massachusetts[h, i]	X		14	Vermont			
Nebraska	X		12	Virginia	X	225	12
New Jersey	X	200	3	Washington	X		4
New York	X	322	20	Wisconsin	X	2,500	12
South Dakota	X			Wyoming	X	94	16
Tennessee	X	14	12	**Total**	**28**	**13,324**	
				Average		**666**	**13**

X = Yes.

[a]This information is from 1997 data. [b]The 1998 figures are not yet available. [c]Monitors are used in select counties. [d]County is responsible to monitor home confinement. [e]Monitors can be worn from 12 to 16 weeks. [f]Monitoring is used for IIP (inmates in prison boot camp) graduates only. [g]Number of devices are contracted with other agency. [h]Parolees pay for their own equipment. [i]Monitors are worn for approximately 12–16 weeks. [j]Monitors are worn for eight weeks in superintensive supervision program and for the duration of supervision. [k]Number of devices is estimated. [l]The weeks worn figure is an average. Probation is for 16 weeks; parole lasts eight weeks. [m]The weeks worn figure is an average. Probation is for four weeks; parole lasts eight weeks. [n]Number of devices figure is combined from the six devices for probation and two for parole. [o]Number of devices figure is combined from 100 devices for parole and 10 for probation. [p]Weeks worn for probation is six; parole, nine.

Source: Camille Graham Camp and George C. Camp, *The Corrections Yearbook: 1999* (Middletown, CT: Criminal Justice Institute, 1999).

Annesley Schmitt directed a study of electronic monitoring and observed that offenders must learn to handle the equipment properly and that their families must adapt to using the telephone sparingly so that computer "calls" can be completed. Poor telephone service, bad wiring, and call-waiting and call-forwarding features on the telephone have caused technical problems. Offenders who live close to FM radio stations or transmitters have had difficulty receiving and sending the required information via the electronic devices. Correctional authorities reported unanticipated costs—for extra telephone lines, special interconnections, underestimated long-distance charges, and supplies.[41] A Texas probation agency reported that its programmed-contact computer malfunctioned and called one probationer more than 300 times in one night.[42] Charles M. Friel and Joseph B. Vaughn reported other problems:

- Large metal objects, such as furnaces and refrigerators, between the transmitter and receiver have interrupted transmissions and caused false alarms.
- False alarms have occurred when offenders curled up while sleeping, positioning their bodies between the receiver and transmitter and blocking the signal.
- Probationers living in mobile homes, constructed largely of metal, have experienced transmission problems.
- Power outages have caused the systems to "crash."
- Batteries in the devices worn by probationers sometimes fail.[43]

Another problem with electronic monitoring devices is that devices made by certain companies can be removed, though it is difficult (see Box 13.1). To counteract the potential for removal, companies that manufacture and sell their products to state and local government have improved the durability of EM devices.

Other critics are concerned that the widespread use of electronic monitoring may result in net widening. Although the program was developed as an alternative to imprisonment, it is sometimes inappropriately used with offenders who would otherwise have been placed under regular probation supervision. Friel and Vaughn caution,

> Using the technology with individuals who would be granted probation anyway is potentially abusive. It has already been pointed out that this application is likely to raise costs without necessarily increasing benefits. In addition, it widens the correctional net needlessly and is an undue invasion of privacy.[44]

Evaluations of Electronic Monitoring Programs

In view of the promise as well as the perils associated with electronic monitoring, careful evaluation studies must be undertaken.[45] J. Robert Lilly and colleagues conducted one such study. The Florida program, developed by Pride Inc., a nonprofit company, began in 1984. The Pride Inc. program was a widely publicized EM program and was a model for many others across the country. Lilly and his associates reviewed five years of cases ($N = 415$). They found that 97 percent of the offenders completed the EM period of their probation successfully and 80 percent completed the entire term of their probation. The researchers noted,

> The EM completion rate is especially impressive in view of the fact that the likelihood of probation violations is highest earliest in the probation period [during which the electronic monitoring occurred]. When one takes into account the fact that the tighter EM control is more likely to provoke trouble because of the offender's resistance to authority and more likely to result in detection of many minor technical violations that would have escaped attention later, the low EM revocation rate is even more impressive.[46]

Electronic house arrest in North Carolina was found to be positively related to rearrest for women, but there was no relationship for men.[47] More recently, an electronic monitoring program in Virginia acted as a protective factor for unmarried offenders against rearrest but had no affect for married offenders.[48]

No large-scale evaluations have been conducted of house arrest and electronic monitoring programs like those of boot camps and ISP. Several small studies and two recent literature reviews stress the scantiness of the research evidence. Michael Tonry and Mary Lynch summarize the research:

> [W]hile a fair amount has been learned about the operation and management of electronic monitoring systems, about technology, and about implementation of new programs . . . the most comprehensive review of the research observes that "we know very little about either home confinement or electronic monitoring."[49]

The Future of Offender Tracking

With the technological advances made in recent times, the potential for offender tracking is limitless. One option is the complete privatization of offender tracking in the community using electronic monitoring devices (called "tagging" in Europe). Geografix Limited and Securicor Custodial Services Limited are independent, private, tagging companies currently operating in the United Kingdom. Geografix designs and manufactures its own tracking devices, installs the devices, and monitors the offenders, including investigating unauthorized absences and taking the offender back to court to be resentenced if necessary. Thus, the company is a fully integrated technical supplier and service supplier. Tagging has been so successful that Sweden, the Netherlands, France, and Ireland are experimenting with the full service provider.[50]

Another avenue that is currently being pursued is the use of a video camera, hooked up to a computer, which is plugged into the Internet. Offenders under this system would be required to step in front of the camera when beeped or called. The video camera allows for interaction (for example, a weekly meeting) between a probation officer and the offender.

A third way to use technology in offender monitoring is satellite tracking. A company out of Palm Harbor, Florida, called Pro Tech Monitoring, developed a system that uses federal government satellites to monitor the geographical restrictions of offenders in large areas. Each offender would be required to wear a device that is preprogrammed with information about where the offender is not allowed. For example, a compulsive gambler would not be allowed to enter any casino without the device sounding an unauthorized area alarm.

A fourth approach would be to surgically implant a monitoring device inside an offender's body. This type of monitoring is the most intrusive and would be a violation of the Fourth Amendment unless it can be shown that the need for the monitoring in this manner outweighs the level of privacy being violated. At this time, no offenders are monitored using this method. But in the future, it may be possible to track offender's whereabouts 24 hours per day by an external computerized patch. The notion that "Big Brother is watching" may become more real sooner than expected.

DAY REPORTING CENTERS

Day reporting centers (DRCs) are a type of nonresidential program typically used for defendants on pretrial release, for convicted offenders on probation or parole, or as an increased sanction for probation or parole violators. DRCs have been popular in England and Wales since the 1970s and began to appear in the United States in 1985. DRCs developed using the "day centre" idea from the British, combined with inspiration from juvenile day treatment centers already established in the United States.[51] Connecticut and Massachusetts were the first states to adopt day reporting centers, to reduce prison crowding and provide a closer level of supervision than traditional probation or parole. DRCs are frequently used to reduce pretrial confinement. This idea has caught on throughout the United States in a short period of time. In 1990, there were only 13 DRCs, but five years later the number swelled to 114 DRCs.[52]

According to a nationwide study of 54 DRCs, these programs are used for a wide variety of clients:

> 87 percent of the DRCs admit probationers
> 73 percent allow probation and parole violators
> 42 percent enroll parolees from prison
> 37 percent of DRCs admit defendants on pretrial release
> 25 percent let in individuals who need to be released early from jail
> 20 percent supervise offenders on furlough or administrative release from prison
> 6 percent of DRCs accept prisoners on work release[53]

While five of the larger DRCs handle more than 300 offenders at one time, most DRCs have a capacity for an average of 85 offenders. The largest DRC in the country is located in Houston, Texas, and can handle up to 2,000 offenders in one day.[54]

DAY REPORTING CENTERS

A type of nonresidential program typically used for defendants on pretrial release, for convicted offenders on probation or parole, or as an increased sanction for probation or parole violators. Services are provided in one central location, and offenders must check in daily.

Purposes of DRCs

Although goals vary from program to program, the three primary purposes of DRCs are to

1. Save space in jail and prison
2. Provide a close level of community supervision
3. Provide offenders with access to services and treatment programs[55]

For example, three DRCs operating in Boston, Springfield, and Worchester, Massachusetts, are used for offenders who would otherwise be incarcerated. These DRCs serve the county jails and admit offenders who are within three months of discharging their jail sentence. These offenders are let out of jail and live at home. They must report every day to the day center, get tested randomly for drugs at least twice per week, and be in touch with program staff by phone at least twice per day. The offenders must either be employed full time, be going to school full time, or a combination of both.[56]

Because some probationers do not take the conditions of their probation seriously, other DRCs serve to provide enforcement or "muscle" for probationers and parolees without sending them to jail or prison. Box 13.2 tells the story of a typical experience at a day reporting center.

The theory behind DRCs is that offenders will stay out of trouble when they are occupied, especially with activities that will improve their chances—for example, by obtaining a GED or finding a job. As of 1998, the state of Connecticut had 17 private (nonprofit) alternative to incarceration centers, which are included as day reporting centers. These centers are popular because they offer cost savings, less bureaucracy, and accountability, and they provide more services to the state using fewer government employees (small government).[57]

Treatment-Oriented versus Supervision-Oriented

Some DRCs are more "treatment-oriented" while others are more "supervision-oriented."[58] Treatment-oriented DRCs provide a wide range of services such as drug abuse education, psychological counseling, life skills training, and classes in job seeking skills. DRCs require unemployed offenders to come to the center during daytime business hours to focus on literacy, GED classes, and getting a job. Employed offenders are required to attend treatment programs at night or on weekends, as well as check in with the DRC and provide the center with a 24-hour itinerary of their schedule. "The itineraries state when clients are to leave home, their destinations, how they will travel (walk, drive, take the bus, or get a ride), when they are to arrive, and when they are to return home."[59] Itineraries are important for two reasons. First, clients learn (some for the first time) how to plan their days in advance. Second, the DRCs can monitor where the clients are when random phone calls are placed via a computer.

Supervision-oriented DRCs ensure that clients are abiding by their terms of probation. The DRC staff will monitor the offender by random phone calls to the offender at home. DRCs are authorized to give out Antabuse, a prescription medication prescribed for alcoholics, that prevents the use of alcohol. Urine screenings and alco-sensor tests ensure that clients have not been using drugs. Many DRCs have a mixture of both supervision and treatment orientations.

Many day centers operate on a levels system, where the initial level involves the most intense contact. Offenders can proceed to less frequent contacts the longer they remain in good standing in the program. Another characteristic of DRCs is that many

BOX 13.2　*Prison without Walls: A Typical Day Reporting Experience*

John, 28 years old and unemployed, is arrested for possession of cocaine. He is sentenced to probation, but during that time he misses several meetings with his probation officer and tests positive for drug use. Rather than punishing John for this probation violation by sending him to the State prison, which is already 10 percent over capacity, the judge assigns him to a nearby DRC [day reporting center]. The DRC, which the State judicial department began operating two years ago, accepts John because, based on his history and offense, he is of small risk to the community and is in need of drug abuse treatment and other services. Furthermore, by keeping John under community supervision, the judge avoids adding to the already high prison population.

John begins the first phase of the three-phase program in June. For the first three weeks, he must report to the DRC five times each week, where he twice is tested for drug use. The program is open from 8 A.M. to 6 P.M. Monday through Friday and from 9 A.M. to

1 P.M. on Saturdays. When he is not at the center, John must remain at home except to do errands that he has already planned on a weekly itinerary, on record at the DRC. Program staff telephone John several times during the day to monitor his whereabouts and ensure that he is abiding by his 8 P.M. curfew. Once a week, staff also make an unannounced visit to his home. John also begins to attend drug abuse education classes, GED [general equivalency diploma] classes, job skills training, and group counseling sessions, conducted on-site by program staff. In addition, twice a week he goes to a drug abuse outpatient clinic, referred by the DRC.

In the middle of his second week, John misses a counseling session and a GED class. Instead of moving to the second, more lenient phase at the end of the third week, John must remain under the more intensive form of supervision for an additional week. Informed that another violation might land him in the State correctional facility, he subsequently commits no other

violations. By the end of June, he is ready to begin the second phase, during which he must continue with his drug abuse treatment and classes but report to the DRC only twice a week. In addition, he joins many of the other 90 offenders in performing several cleanup and construction projects around the city.

After three months without violating any regulations, John begins the third and final phase of the program, during which he reports to the DRC only once a week. With assistance from a job placement agency that offers its services at the DRC, he finds employment with the State parks system. By the end of November, he has been released from the DRC. The cost to the State of his placement in the DRC has been half of what it likely would have been had he been incarcerated, and John seems on his way to making a more productive contribution to society.

Source: Dale Parent, Jim Byrne, Vered Tsarfaty, Laura Valade, and Julie Esselman, *Day Reporting Centers*, vol. 1 (Washington, DC: U.S. Department of Justice, 1995), 23.

---

clients are also on 24-hour electronic monitoring. As the clients remain longer in the program, DRCs may be able to give clients more freedom by removing the electronic monitoring device while still remaining on supervision.[60]

In many ways, DRCs are nonresidential versions of halfway houses because the two programs provide very similar services, except DRC offenders live at home.[61] Like most halfway houses, DRCs are private facilities that contract out to state and local entities, except for a few in Massachusetts and the one in Houston.[62] Furthermore, as much or more contact is made between program staff and offenders in DRCs than with intensive supervision probation. While ISP programs have more field visits (where the officer goes to the home or job site to visit the offender), DRCs have more phone and office visits because the offender comes to the center.[63]

Sentences to DRCs range from 40 days to 9 months in duration.[64] The average daily cost per offender in 1995 was just over $35. This would make the DRC more costly than traditional probation or parole, and even more expensive than ISP. However, DRCs cost less than residential treatment or incarceration in jail or prison.[65]

TABLE 13.2 *Sources of Payment for Day Reporting Center Services*

| | PERCENTAGE OF DRCS IN WHICH | | |
Agency	DRC Pays	Another Agency Pays	Offender Pays (Fees)
Job-seeking skills (*N* = 53)	74	17	4
Drug abuse education (*N* = 52)	73	23	12
Group counseling (*N* = 51)	73	20	8
Job placement services (*N* = 50)	58	30	8
Education (*N* = 49)	53	43	10
Drug treatment (*N* = 48)	50	46	25
Life skills training (*N* = 49)	74	12	2
Individual counseling (*N* = 47)	72	19	13
Transitional housing (*N* = 32)	28	72	6
Recreation and leisure (*N* = 31)	77	10	16

Note: Day reporting centers (DRCs) may have more than one payment source.
Source: Dale Parent, Jim Bryne, Vered Tsarfaty, Laura Valade, and Julie Esselman, *Day Reporting Centers*, vol. 1 (Washington, DC: U.S. Department of Justice, 1995), 15.

Most DRC programs exist in states that do not have ISP as a sentencing option.[66] Much of the treatment program costs are absorbed by the DRC itself or by another agency (see Table 13.2). In one out of every four DRCs, offenders pay for their own drug treatment. Other DRCs will have cost sharing for their services. This helps keep program costs down.

Evaluations of DRCs

Few day reporting center evaluations have been completed. Identified assessments measure day reporting effectiveness using termination and rearrest rates.

TERMINATION RATES: DRC clients who failed in the program were "administratively terminated" and returned to custody.[67] Termination rates for the 54 DRCs surveyed averaged 50 percent and ranged from 14 percent to 86 percent. Termination rates were higher for service-oriented programs than for supervision-oriented DRCs. This was caused, in part, by the type of offender admitted to the program. While work release programs seem to accept lower risk offenders, DRCs tended to accept probation and parole violators and other types of higher risk clients.[68] Another reason contributing to completion rates was that service-oriented DRCs had more rules, and thus more chances that the offender may fail the program.[69]

Evaluations of European DRCs are roughly the same as those for American DRCs. In one British study of more than 600 offenders in 38 DRC programs, 63 percent of offenders were reconvicted of a new crime within two years of being sentenced to a DRC.[70] George Mair comments about this finding:

> On the face of it, this may look high, but the offenders targeted by centers represent a very high risk group in terms of probability of reconviction. Probation centers [DRCs] may be condemning themselves to what appears to be a high reconviction rate by successfully diverting offenders from custody, and this must be taken into consideration when interpreting the overall reconviction rate.[71]

RATE OF REARREST: John J. Larivee reports that the DRCs in Massachusetts have had about 3 percent of participants abscond or commit a new crime, and "none so far for a violent offense."[72] While Massachusetts DRCs recruit offenders from jail, North Carolina DRC offenders are on probation.

In a 12-month follow-up evaluation of 15 DRC programs in North Carolina, Amy Craddock notes that the typical client has a history of prior convictions, suffers with a substance abuse problem, and is on probation for a nonviolent offense. The goals of this DRC are to reduce recidivism, reduce probation revocations, reduce substance abuse relapse, and provide a cost savings.[73] Craddock examined 419 DRC clients on probation with 440 similarly situated probationers (the comparison group). Both groups had similar offense types and prior records. Day center participants were significantly more likely than the comparison group to be unemployed and less likely to have graduated from high school. Furthermore, a higher percentage of females and minorities were participating in the DRC program than in other types of probation. Craddock found that 20.1 percent of DRC participants were rearrested within one year; 24.5 percent of the comparison probation group. However, more DRC clients committed technical violations (25.2 percent) than the other probationers (14.2 percent).

This research also differentiates DRC program completers from noncompleters, something the George Mair and Claire Nee study did not do. The rate of rearrest for DRC participants who completed the program was only 13.0 percent, versus noncompleters at 25.4 percent. Those who did not complete the program were also rearrested in a shorter amount of time than the DRC graduates and regular probationers. Only 11.2 percent of DRC offenders who completed the program accrued technical violations, whereas 34.2 percent of clients who did not complete the program accumulated violations that ultimately led to their removal from the program. The overall findings thus seem to indicate that not only was the DRC program successful at reducing the amount of offenders who were rearrested, but also that DRC participants who completed the program were significantly more likely to have fewer rearrests and fewer technical violations than regular probationers.[74]

In sum, there is no one "right way" to operate a DRC. Each day center has different goals and different clients it accepts. The key is to specifically define the goals of the DRC program (for example, reduce institutional crowding) and then measure whether the program is achieving those goals. Dale Parent, who has been actively involved in DRC research and evaluation, concludes:

> If policymakers want DRCs to reduce prison and jail crowding, they should use day reporting as an early release mechanism and should let corrections officials (not judges at the time of sentencing) select inmates for DRC placement. Among inmates released early, DRCs should be used for those who pose the greatest risk to the public or who have the most serious problems that are likely to impair their adjustment. To reduce total costs, officials should use less structured and less expensive forms of supervision for low-risk, low-need inmates who are granted early release. Future research should focus on DRCs costs and impacts on offenders' adjustments.[75]

RESTITUTION

Restitution is defined as repairing a victim's losses suffered at the hands of the offender through the offender's monetary payment or restoring a crime victim's property. Restitution is two of four main types of restorative justice sanctions. Figure 13. 1 depicts two different beneficiaries (the community and the victim) and two different

FIGURE 13.1 *Typology of Restorative Justice Sanctions*

RECIPIENT

	Victim	Community
Monetary	Monetary Restitution	Fine or Day Fine
Service	Personal Service Restitution	Community Service

FORM OF PAYMENT

Source: Burt Galaway, "Restitution as Innovation or Unfilled Promise?" in *Towards a Critical Victimology*, ed. Ezzat A. Fattah (New York: St. Martin's Press, 1992), 350.

forms of payment (money and working without pay to provide services). Restitution can be payment of money or personal services in which the victim or the victim's family is the beneficiary. Restitution differs from a fine. A fine is paid to the state; restitution, directly to the victim. Restitution is not the same thing as community service, because community service is technically repayment to the community through improving community surroundings. Victim restitution is also different from victim compensation, in that victim compensation money originates from state funds specifically set aside for this purpose.[76]

Restitution is a popular intermediate sanction. It requires an offender to repay the victims of his or her crime for losses directly resulting from the crime. Restitution is an act of atonement for the criminal. The money or services offered by the offender help rehabilitate the victim financially. According to one source, one-third of all probationers are required to pay restitution.[77] Victims typically apply for restitution through the prosecutor's office. To receive the restitution, the victim must press charges and agree to testify if necessary. Restitution is declared as a victim's right in some states, even when the offender has been incarcerated.[78] In states where restitution is defined as offender rehabilitation, restitution is forfeited if the offender goes to prison. In states where restitution is a victim's right, victims are more likely to get reimbursed if the offender is sentenced to a community sanction outside of jail or prison.

Restitution centers are a type of residential facility (see Chapter 12). Residential restitution centers are operating in at least 30 states to enforce the payment of restitution. Restitution can also be commonly ordered as a condition of probation or parole, or it may be used as a diversionary device. Diversion provides offenders the opportunity to avoid having a criminal record altogether. In this situation, a first offender (usually) is ordered to pay monetary restitution during a period when his or her case is "continued" by the court. After the required restitution is satisfied, the court simply dismisses the charges.

Restitution in History

Like house arrest, restitution has a long history. The Old Testament specifies fivefold restitution for stealing and then killing an ox and fourfold restitution for stealing and killing a sheep. Double restitution is mandated for stealing (Exodus 21). Leviticus commands that restitution plus an additional fifth be made by robbers (Leviticus 6). The Code of Hammurabi, developed between 1792 and 1750 B.C., mandates thirtyfold restitution if the victim is a "god" or a "palace" and tenfold restitution if the victim is a "villein" (a low-status laborer).

British philosopher Jeremy Bentham (1748–1833) prescribed restitution as an essential means of making the punishment fit the crime. In the mid-1800s Quaker prison reformer Elizabeth Fry saw restitution as a mechanism of offender rehabilitation, stating that "repayment is the first step toward reformation."

As early as the 1930s, 11 states and the federal probation system imposed restitution as a probation condition, but collection was not well enforced until the early 1970s.[79] One of the earliest proponents of restitution was Stephen Schafer, who in 1960 argued that restitution must be an integral part of the criminal justice system to raise the importance of the victim. Schafer wrote that the criminal justice system has become too centered on the offender and the state's interests, and the role of the crime victim seems to have become lost in the process.[80] Schafer continued to advocate the restitution movement over the next 16 years until his death in 1976.

During the 1960s and 1970s, restitution became more formalized. Various national commissions on criminal justice and the model codes of the era emphasized the value of restitution both as punishment and rehabilitation. The Model Penal Code proposed that an offender placed on probation might be required to "make restitution of the fruits of his crime or to make reparation in an amount he can afford to pay, for the loss or damage caused."[81] The National Advisory Commission on Criminal Justice Standards and Goals in 1973 considered restitution as a factor that might mitigate the imposition of a prison sentence.[82] Both the American Bar Association and the National Council on Crime and Delinquency support the use of restitution as a condition of probation. A detailed account of the relationship between the development of restitution and restorative justice through victim and offender mediation can be found in Andrew R. Klein's book *Alternative Sentencing, Intermediate Sanctions, and Probation.*[83]

Using Restitution in Restorative Justice

Burt Galaway, an early proponent of restitution, strongly believes that restitution can be used not only in probation, but also as a correctional tool in restorative justice. Restorative justice is centered on the victim throughout the whole process (see Chapter 1). Restorative justice emphasizes offender responsibility to repair the injustice and wrong the offender has caused the victim. Galaway states that restitution is a "mechanism for reintegrating victim interest into the justice system, for contributing to the state interest in reforming offenders, and for providing a punishment for the offender."[84] Galaway delineated five purposes of restitution:

1. Restitution provides a less severe and more humane sanction for the offender.
2. Restitution aids the rehabilitation of the offender, and it integrates the punitive and rehabilitative purposes of the criminal law. Because the rationale incorporates the notion that punishment is related to the extent of damages done, it is perceived as just by offenders and allows them a sense of accomplishment as they complete the requirements. Restitution also provides offenders a socially appropriate, concrete way of expressing their guilt and atoning for their offenses.
3. Restitution benefits the criminal justice system by providing an easily administered sanction that reduces demands on the system.
4. Restitution may reduce the need for vengeance in the administration of criminal law because offenders are perceived as responsible persons taking active steps to make amends for their wrongdoing.
5. Restitution provides redress for crime victims.

Galaway suggests, however, that helping crime victims should not be the primary aim of a restitution program. Too many crimes go unsolved, and in many the arrest does not result in a conviction. Even when a conviction is secured, restitution might not be the appropriate sanction. Thus restitution will help only a small number of crime victims. He suggests, instead, a publicly funded victim compensation program.[85]

Losses Available for Compensation

The authority of courts to grant restitution originates entirely from federal statutes. From 1925 to 1982, restitution could only be imposed as a condition of probation, and it was strictly discretionary. The federal Victim Witness Protection Act (VWPA) of 1982 broadened the use of restitution, and it is now the primary restitution statute that authorizes restitution in either federal probation or prison sentences.[86] The scope of the VWPA was restricted in 1990 to victim compensation as a direct result of the offense of conviction, as per the *Hughey v. United States* court decision.[87]

Since the *Hughey* ruling, Congress has made further changes to expand victims rights to restitution. In 1992, Congress passed a mandatory provision for courts to impose restitution for back child support, if the offender has failed to make some or all child support payments. Two years later, Congress passed the Violence against Women Act, which mandated that restitution be ordered in cases of sexual abuse, sexual exploitation of children, domestic violence, and telemarketing fraud. In 1996, Congress passed the Mandatory Victims Restitution Act, which requires that restitution be imposed by the courts for violent crimes and Title 18 property offenses.[88]

As a result of these statutes, some states have broadened the types of losses available for compensation as well as parties eligible to receive restitution. For example, restitution is available for the purpose of physical injuries, financial losses, expenses involving the investigation and prosecution of the case, counseling sessions, sexual assault exams, human immunodeficiency virus (HIV) testing, occupational and rehabilitative therapy, moving expenses, case-related travel and meal expenses, and burial expenses. Eligible parties may include individuals or organizations. Eligible individuals are the victim or the victim's family. Eligible organizations or funding sources are businesses and corporations, the victims' estate, victim service organizations, and private organizations that provide victim assistance.[89] Even the government can receive victim restitution.[90]

Legal Problems Associated with Restitution

Three of the legal problems associated with restitution are indigence of the defendant, determining the restitution amount, and collecting restitution.

INDIGENT OFFENDERS: If the defendant is indigent and cannot pay, courts cannot cite the defendant for contempt or send the defendant to prison. However, indigence at the time of sentencing does not entitle the offender to immunity from restitution, but it is more dependent on the offender's future ability to pay.[91] If the defendant is able to pay but refuses, then incarceration is valid. In the federal system, if an incarcerated federal prisoner has restitution to pay and has the ability to pay, parole release can be contingent upon the prisoner first paying off the entire restitution amount while incarcerated.[92]

DETERMINING THE RESTITUTION AMOUNT: The judge ultimately sets the restitution amount, but in many jurisdictions, probation officers completing presentence investigations can suggest a restitution amount to the judge. Catharine Goodwin of the Administrative Office of the U.S. Courts suggests that probation officers follow the four steps below in sequence for each case to determine a restitution amount that will decrease the chance of being legally challenged by the defendant:

1. Determine whether restitution in the case is discretionary or mandatory (usually defined by offense of conviction).
2. Identify the victims of the offense of conviction.
3. Identify the harms to those victims that were caused by the offense of conviction.
4. Identify the harms that are compensable as restitution.[93]

Victims sometimes overestimate the amount of their losses. Thus, it is often difficult for probation officers and judges to accurately establish a fair restitution amount. The government has the burden of proof to prove, based on preponderance of the evidence, that the victim did suffer harm for which the victim is requesting restitution from the offender.[94] In one case, the Indiana Court of Appeals ruled that the amount of restitution must be based on expenses the victim incurred by the time of sentencing. Restitution may not be ordered for future victim expenses, such as counseling.[95]

The other issue is that the harm has to be as a direct cause from the offense or the offender. However, the Violence against Women Act does not specifically provide a causation standard.[96] Goodwin concludes by saying:

> The message to probation officers making recommendations on restitution is to make every effort to tie the restitution to a specified, compensable harm under the VWPA and/or any applicable specific mandatory restitution statute. When this is done, the order is likely to be upheld, so long as the harm was suffered by a victim of the offense of conviction.[97]

COLLECTING RESTITUTION: The problem of collecting restitution has always been difficult. The mode of collection is left to the probation officer. The probation officer acts as both a finance officer and a collection agent by determining the payment schedule in weekly or monthly installments.[98] Offenders who get too far behind on payments, or who are able to pay but refuse to do so, are reassigned to a formal collection agency.

In 1990 the Pennsylvania Supreme Court further exacerbated the problem by holding that bankruptcy served to discharge a restitution debt.[99] A later court case decided in 1993 disagreed, saying that bankruptcy does not dissolve restitution obligations, although it may affect the rate schedule and payment amounts.[100]

Effectiveness of Restitution

One study assessed recidivism rates using a predefined group of prison inmates who owed restitution on their case. Out of this group, inmates were selected randomly to be released to the Minnesota Restitution Center to take part in paying the restitution. The control group remained in prison and did not pay the restitution. The study found that there was

> no difference in the likelihood of return to prison between the two groups. The restitution group, however, was somewhat more likely to have been returned to prison for technical parole violations, whereas the control group was more likely to have been returned to prison for a new offence.[101]

The same offenders in these two groups were tracked for 16 months after their release. Members of the restitution group had fewer convictions and were employed for more of the time than members of the control group. So it seems that inmates who owe restitution can effectively pay restitution through a restitution center. The benefits are that the victims receive payment, at no more risk to the public.[102] Similar results have been found with experimental studies of youths in restitution and comparison groups.[103]

VICTIM AND PUBLIC VIEWS TOWARD RESTITUTION: Victim-offender reconciliation projects (VORP) are when the victim agrees to meet with the offender, and restitution is made a large part of the incentive for victims to participate. In a two-year study of VORP with juvenile property offenders in Minnesota, the results indicate that 55 percent of victims have agreed to meet with the offender. Out of the VORP sessions, 95 percent of the meetings have resulted in mutual agreement, with a 93 percent completion rate.[104]

In another study, victims and juvenile offenders were asked their perceptions on the "fairness" of restitution as a punishment for juvenile offenders. A vast majority of both offenders and victims reported that paying restitution was fair, and many preferred restitution to other punishments.[105] The general public is also supportive of restitution as a community sanction, especially when informed of the cost of incarceration versus community corrections punishments.[106]

Galaway has been involved in restitution research since the early 1970s. He provides his perspective on what the available research suggests:

> In summary, the experience since 1972 has established that restitution is feasible and can be implemented, strongly suggests that restitution will be perceived as a fair penalty and will have as positive an impact on offender recidivism as other penalties, and indicates public and victim support for substituting restitution for other penalties, including incarceration.[107]

COMMUNITY SERVICE

Community service has been called "the most underused intermediate sanction in the United States."[108] **Community service** is defined as unpaid service to the public to compensate society for harm done by the crime committed. Offenders repay the community they offended by performing service instead of by making monetary reparation. One study estimates that 6 percent of all felons are sentenced to perform community service, usually along with other sanctions.[109] Community service might consist of working for a tax-supported or nonprofit agency such as hospitals, public parks or libraries, a poverty program, or a public works program. It may involve picking up roadside litter, doing landscape maintenance, removing graffiti, or painting buildings. If community service is to be assigned in a particular case, judges typically order between 40 and 1,000 hours of community service for one offender.

History of Community Service

Community service first began in the United States as an organized program in 1966 in Alameda County, California. This initiative was created as a substitute for paying fines for low-income female traffic offenders. The women worked without pay in lieu of their fine and avoided jail for fine nonpayment. Because of the positive attention this program received, hundreds of community service programs were established in the 1970s, especially for juveniles and nonviolent adults. In the United States, community service developed as an alternative to fines or as an additional condition of probation.[110]

THE ENGLISH MODEL: Between 40 and 240 hours of community service sufficed in England and Wales as an acceptable alternative to prison. Special community service officers administer the sanction. The English model became popular in other areas of Europe, such as Scotland and the Netherlands. The United States did not follow the English model, believing instead that community service was not punitive enough to substitute for prison. It is not uncommon to see American judges order between 100 and 1,000 hours of community service in addition to other probation conditions.[111] This difference in American perceptions of community service demonstrates that, in comparison with most other countries in the world, community corrections sanctions are more punitive (and are not just reflected in long prison sentences).

Purpose of Community Service

Like monetary restitution, community service is both punitive and rehabilitative. It is punitive in that the offender's time and freedom are restricted until the work is completed. It is rehabilitative in the sense that it allows offenders to do something constructive, to increase their self-esteem, to reduce their isolation from society, and to benefit society through their efforts. In comparison with restitution, community service requires neither that there be an identifiable victim nor that the victim be cooperative in the prosecution process.

Furthermore, community service provides an alternative sanction for poor offenders who are unable to afford significant monetary sanctions or for those whose financial resources are so great that monetary restitution has no punitive or rehabilitative effect.[112] Community service is a good example of a restorative justice program, and it can also be used to divert offenders from having a formal conviction on their record.

Effectiveness of Community Service

Community service has always had wide public support, but scant attention has been paid to research evaluating the effectiveness of community service. Community service has had positive effects on the federal system in Georgia for offenders and for members of the general public (see Box 13.3). Many nonprofit organizations, such as churches, homeless shelters, libraries, and the U.S. Forest Service, have benefited from the labor provided by offenders. Agencies report that the completion rates vary from 50 percent to a high of 85 percent, depending on how community service is enforced.[113] Some research suggests that without community service programs, the vast majority of offenders who now have community service orders would have simply been placed on regular probation and the victims would have been ignored.

Douglas McDonald evaluated a large community service project funded by the Vera Institute of Justice in New York City. This program was for repeat property offenders who faced between 6 to 12 months of jail time. Half of the participants were drawn from a prison-bound group, while the other half were probationers with less extensive records. McDonald found that community service programs had no significant effect on recidivism. However, the prison diversion goals of the project were met, and the program saved taxpayers money.[114] Tonry and Lynch conclude, "Both American and European research and experience show that community service can

BOX 13.3 *Community Service of Federal Offenders in Georgia*

Carl worked as a mail carrier for the U.S. Post Office. He repeatedly threw away all third-class mail in a dumpster because he deemed it as a nuisance to his customers. When his crime was detected, he was fired and prosecuted for a misdemeanor. He was ordered to pay restitution and to perform 300 hours of community service. The PSI [presentence investigation] indicated that Carl was one quarter short of obtaining a B.A. degree in mathematics, and he was a nonviolent misdemeant. The community service probation officer assigned Carl to work a seven-hour shift once per week at an elementary school for 42 weeks. He was initially assigned to playground and lunchroom duties. But his knowledge and leadership qualities were so impressive that he became assigned as a math tutor for three boys in the third grade. Because part of the learning problem was

lack of parental discipline, Carl met with the parents of the boys to discuss the problem. The boys improved their math grades and overall classroom performance. At the end of his community service, Carl was offered a job as a teacher aide. Although he turned down the offer, Carl felt he had touched the lives of a few kids and had received much more in return. Because of the success of Carl's placement, the courts have expanded community service to four other schools.

Carl's case is one example of the many federal offenders who must complete community service. In a ten-year period, in the Northern District of Georgia, offenders worked 300,000 hours and finished projects valued at over $3 million. The success of community service programs depends on good agency relationships between the probation department and outside community agencies. Success also

depends on the placement skills and monitoring from probation officers. The officers must be attuned to whether the community service is intended by the court to be punitive or rehabilitative. The placement also must match the skills and risk level of the offender.

Richard Maher, a supervising U.S. probation officer of the Northern District of Georgia, reports that over a three-year period, 5 percent of probationers who are sentenced to community service later accept paid jobs with their placement or through contacts established while doing community service work. Community service saves money, provides work for nonprofit agencies, and opportunity for offenders.

Source: Richard J. Maher, "Community Service: A Good Idea That Works," *Federal Probation* 58, no. 2 (1994): 20–23; and Richard J. Maher, "Community Service: A Way for Offenders to Make Amends," *Federal Probation* 61, no. 1 (1997): 26–28.

serve as a meaningful, cost-effective sanction for offenders who would otherwise be imprisoned."[115]

As the search continues for less costly and more effective methods of dealing with offenders, community service has the potential to be a growing trend in U.S. corrections. One difficult problem with evaluating and expanding community service programs is that most do not have clear goals and objectives. In expanding their use, the following must be delineated:

1. Is the purpose of community service to reduce recidivism, to save the system money through diversion, or both? If both goals are desired, how are deterrence and cost savings attained?
2. Should community service be used for only misdemeanor and petty crimes?
3. Should community service be expanded for prison-bound offenders?
4. How is the value of community service work calculated?
5. Should community service be used instead of or in addition to other sanctions?
6. How many hours of community service would be equivalent to (for example, one day in) jail?
7. How many hours of community service equal a fine (for example, $500)?

Fines can be used as a punishment for offenses ranging from traffic violations to serious felony crimes. Fines for serious offenses are typically accompanied by probation or incarceration. Fines tend to be underused because their collection is not well enforced.

There is no easy answer to these questions. The potential for greater use of community service through offender labor as an alternative to jail or prison is limitless, if developed without further increasing community risk.

FINES AND DAY FINES

Fines are routinely imposed for offenses ranging from traffic violations to drug trafficking. A **fine** is defined as a fixed monetary sanction imposed by the judge; the amount depends on the severity of the offense. Most people convicted of misdemeanor or felony crimes receive a fine. The fine can either be in isolation or accompanied by probation, an intermediate sanction, or time in jail or prison.

FINE

A fixed monetary sanction imposed by a judge, depending on the seriousness of the crime.

Fines have been used in the criminal justice system as a sanction for some time. However, fines have been underused and their collection not well enforced. Rethinking the use and collection of fines has thus received considerable attention in the last two decades. The Federal Comprehensive Crime Control Act of 1984 specifies that for every sentence to probation the court must also order the defendant to "pay a fine, make restitution, and/or work in community service."[116] For incarcerated offenders, the federal system mandates that federal prisoners shall not be released on parole or mandatory release until the fine is paid in full.[117]

Morris and Tonry specify some characteristics of fines that make them the "punishment of choice for most crimes."

- Although in current practice fines are generally set in amounts too modest to be calibrated meaningfully in relation to serious crime, in principle fines can vary from small change to economic capital punishment.
- Although in current practice fines are too often haphazardly administered and collected, in principle fines can be collected with vigor and ruthlessness.

- Although in current practice fines seem unfair to the poor and unduly lenient to the rich, in principle fine amounts can be tailored to the offender's assets and income so as to constitute roughly comparable financial burdens.[118]

Judicial Perspectives of Fines

George Cole and his colleagues conducted an extensive study of the use of fines in the United States. Their research estimates that well over $1 billion in fines is collected annually by courts across the country. Many judges did not regard a fine by itself as a meaningful incarceration or probation alternative. However, judges in lower courts were more positively disposed to using fines than were those in higher courts. Fines were used in 86 percent of all misdemeanor and petty offenses; 42 percent of felony cases.[119]

Some judges are reluctant to use fines because of the difficulty of collecting and enforcing them. Other branches of government enforce other penalties imposed by judges, but fines must be enforced directly by the courts, and judges have little incentive to expend their own resources to administer the collection of fines.[120] It is estimated that less than half the fines ordered are ever collected. In two jurisdictions examined, the fine payment rate was only 14 percent in one area and 19 percent in another.[121] A later study of probationers in Illinois, however, found that nearly two-thirds of probationers satisfied their financial obligations in full.[122]

Many judges point out that offenders tend to be poor and may have no means other than additional criminal activity to obtain the funds to pay their fines. Affluent offenders, meanwhile, can "buy their way out" when fines are an integral part of the sentence. A fixed fine amount of $500 may burden a poor person but may be an inconsequential amount to a wealthy offender.

Probationers' Perspectives

G. Frederick Allen and Harvey Treger conducted a study in an Illinois probation department of 82 probationers, asking them their perceptions of monetary sanctions. Fines and monetary restitution were grouped together in the analysis. The researchers asked the probationers to choose how probationers viewed the purpose of monetary sanctions.[123]

Over 70 percent of probationers believed that monetary sanctions were related to punishment, and 45 percent believed fines and restitution promoted justice and reconciliation. One-third believed that rehabilitation of the offender played a part, and one-fourth of probationers believed that monetary sanctions served a deterrent component. Offenders believed the system should emphasize the repayment of the identified victims over punishment.[124] Another improvement suggestion was that individual probation officers should be more consistent in their collection efforts. Offenders commented on how one probation officer placed a high priority on the payment of fines and restitution, while other officers in the same department placed low or no priority on restitution or fine collection.[125]

Day Fines

Because of the problems associated with using regular fines in criminal sentencing, a pilot program began in 1988 to use fines in a different way. A court in Staten Island, New York, initiated a program based on the day fine system used in many European countries. **Day fines,** otherwise known as structured fines, are court fines figured as multiples of the offender's daily income. Thus a school custodian and a stockbroker, both convicted of the same offense, with the same criminal history and identical risk factors, would pay different amounts because they earn different amounts of money. The stockbroker, who makes an annual income of $100,000 per year, would pay more than the custodian, who makes $25,000 per year. Based on a day fine, the stockbroker would be fined, say, $10,000 and the custodian would pay $2,500. Here is how the system works. The two offenders would be fined the same multiple or percent of income, which would be determined by their crime and prior history. In this way, day fines would provide the same percentage of financial hardship to each offender. Using the previous example, in a tariff or conventional fine situation, the stockbroker and custodian may have received the same fine amount. Thus, day fines are expected to overcome many of the shortcomings associated with conventional or tariff fines.

DAY FINES

Fines that are calculated by multiplying a percent of the offender's daily wage by the number of predefined punishment units (the number of punishment units depends on crime seriousness).

Establishing Structured Fine Units

Some U.S. courts are in the process of establishing a day fine system. The day fine structures in Germany and Sweden have provided the United States with two different models on how to translate monetary amounts into "punishment units." One of the difficulties of doing this is deciding what goals day fines are to achieve. In other words, are day fines to be used as alternatives to short-term jail sentences? Are day fines to be used instead of probation? Or are day fines to be accompanied by probation, intermediate sanction, or jail? The German model is seen as more relevant if day fines are intended as a jail alternative; the Swedish model is more applicable when used along with other sanctions.[126]

In establishing punishment unit tables and formulas, the Bureau of Justice Assistance recommends first determining the offender's "net daily income" by figuring gross income and adjusting downward for taxes, subsistence needs, family responsibilities, and number of dependents.[127] Then, the adjusted net daily income can be multiplied by the number of punishment units (for example, 10, 50, 90) depending on offense severity.

Another important part of establishing day fine amounts is determining how to effectively collect monetary sanctions. It is recommended that there be:

- A short time period for payment (three months), which increases the likelihood of full payment
- A convenient location to make payments (police stations, probation departments, night deposit boxes outside the court, payment by mail, and so on)
- A wide variety of payment methods (credit cards, debit cards, cash, personal checks, money orders)
- Discounts for early payment
- Surcharges for late payment
- Overdue payment reminder notices in the mail or by telephone
- Consequences for nonpayment[128]

Evaluation of Day Fines

Fines seem to have a deterrent value. Recent research found that offenders with similar criminal histories and current conviction types had lower recidivism rates when assessed a fine compared with similar offenders who were sentenced to probation or a jail term.[129]

For the purpose of evaluation, goals that day fines may achieve over tariff fines include:

- Increased fairness for offenders of various economic situations
- Effective system for fine collection
- Increasing credibility for monetary sanctions
- More efficient use of court and correctional resources
- Increased total revenue[130]

Douglas C. McDonald, Judith Greene, and Charles Worzella evaluated the use of day fines in two jurisdictions: Staten Island, New York, and Milwaukee, Wisconsin.[131]

STATEN ISLAND, NEW YORK: In Staten Island, day fines were used for only misdemeanor cases, and fines were limited to a maximum of $1,000. Lawyers and judges alike were in full acceptance of this system. The study found that in comparison with fines assessed and collected before the study began, the average fine amount increased, as did the proportion of fines collected. Seventy percent of those assessed day fines paid in full, 13 percent were resentenced to community service or jail sentence averaging 11 days, and 14 percent of offenders absconded. As a result of this study, the New York legislature examined the possibility of removing the cap of $1,000 (which reflected the old tariff system) to make it possible to bring in more revenue under the day fine system (up to 18 percent more revenue). The researchers found that a workable day fine system could be developed for regular use in courts.[132]

MILWAUKEE, WISCONSIN: The Milwaukee project involved the impact of day fines on noncriminal violations. There were two groups (an experimental and a control group), and simultaneous comparisons could be made between regular fines and day fines. The results were somewhat disappointing. The proportions of those who failed to pay in full were 59 percent of the day fine group and 61 percent for the conventional fine group. However, the proportions of those who paid in full were 37 percent for the day fine group and 25 percent of the conventional group. Day fines did seem to benefit the collection of fines from the poorest offenders. Offenders with monthly incomes less than $197 were more likely to pay a day fine (33 percent) than a regular fine (14 percent).[133] Day fines do not seem to deter future criminal conduct any more than a conventional fine. Within nine months after sentencing, the evaluators found no significant difference in recidivism between the experimental group (day fines) and the control group (tariff fines). Furthermore, the county treasury received less total collections overall, which resulted in resistance to further use of day fines. Thus, the project was abandoned.[134]

PHOENIX, ARIZONA: As a result of the earlier studies, other pilot project sites were selected for evaluation in Connecticut, Iowa, and Oregon. At one site in Phoenix, Arizona, day fines were used as a substitute for probation for low-risk offenders who are not in need of formal supervision. Potential candidates of the Financial Assessment Related to Employability (FARE) program are identified by probation officers during the completion of the presentence investigation report. FARE offenders are supervised by a special FARE probation officer, whose primary job is fine collections. FARE is considered a success because a high rate of probationers paid their fines, saving probation officer time.[135]

SUMMARY

Nonresidential intermediate sanctions have been suggested as means of achieving a rational system of corrections and alleviating some of the problems associated with incarceration and probation. The use of intensive supervision programs, electronic monitoring, house arrest, and day reporting centers would be more effective once goals are clarified and target offender populations are more accurately defined to best meet offender needs without unduly compromising public safety.

Day fines and community service seems to hold promise. Because day fines are scaled to the offender's ability to pay, they are likely to be used more often and be a more meaningful sanction. Present patterns in the use of fines still vary widely. Observers predict greater emphasis on fines and day fines in the future, both as a sentence by itself and in conjunction with other sentences.

However, others feel that monetary programs such as restitution and fines are not punitive unless some type of incarceration or intermediate sanction facility residency accompanies them. Restitution and fines might contribute to offenders sinking deeper into poverty, creating a stressful "no-win" situation. Probationers and parolees who cannot afford to pay the installment payments, as well as abide with the other conditions, "fail" their conditions and take a guaranteed trip to prison. Stephen C. Richards and Richard S. Jones called this phenomenon the "perpetual incarceration machine."[136]

However, the importance of community-based correctional programs can best be understood by considering the consequences of imprisonment. Criminologist Harry Allen and Edward Latessa conclude,

> It is hard to identify the benefits inmates gain from prison, but the harm done there is readily seen. If you want to increase the crime problem, incite men to greater evil, and intensify criminal inclinations and proclivities, then lock violators up in prison for long periods, reduce their outside contacts, stigmatize them and block their lawful employment when released, all the while setting them at tutelage under the direction of more skilled and predatory criminals. I know of no better way to gain your ends than these.[137]

DISCUSSION QUESTIONS

1. How does intensive supervision probation differ from regular probation?
2. Discuss the relationship between ISP caseload size and recidivism.
3. What are the advantages and disadvantages of house arrest?
4. How does electronic monitoring support house arrest? What ethical and social criticisms are associated with EM?
5. How do electronic monitoring devices work? What are some of the technical problems associated with them?
6. How are day reporting centers different from ISP?
7. Do day reporting centers accomplish their objectives?
8. How is community service used as a correctional tool?
9. How do monetary restitution and community service differ? How are they alike?
10. Does restitution provide for integration of both offender and victim in the criminal justice system?
11. How can restitution be used in the juvenile justice system?

12 Why don't more judges use fines as intermediate sanctions?
13 What is a day fine, and how does it overcome one of the major problems associated with conventional fines?
14 Which of the intermediate sanctions discussed in this chapter are probation or parole enhancements, and which sanctions are true alternatives to prison?
15 Why should intermediate sanction programs have clear goals and objectives?

 **WEB SITES**

American Correctional Association
List of community corrections publications

http://www.corrections.com/newcorrections/aca/pubs

National Institute of Corrections
List of publications

http://www.bop.gov/nicpg/niccbpub.html

Intermediate Sanctions in Florida

http://www.dos.state.fl.us/fgils/agencies/fcc/reports/intermediate_sanctions

RAND Corporation
Research on reducing crime risk

http://www.rand.org/areas/crim.toc.html

National Victim Center and Restitution Center

http://www.nvc.org

Alternatives to Incarceration

This chapter explored alternatives to incarceration in which the offender lives at home but must maintain sobriety while fulfilling daily employment, treatment, and financial responsibilities. These programs included electronic monitoring, day reporting centers, community service, and restitution. Consider the cases below as if you were the judge and were being asked to decide an appropriate sentence in lieu of incarceration. Think of all the types of intermediate sanctions in this chapter. What kinds of questions would the judge need to have answered to determine what sentence conditions should be imposed?

Case A: Andy is on probation for possession of drugs and simple assault. His probation officer (P.O.) has filed a petition to revoke his probation because of his failure to report regularly, failure to maintain regular employment, and having a positive urinalysis on the last surprise drug testing. Although Andy does not appear to be a hardcore criminal, he does not seem capable of following through on his probation conditions. The probation officer reports that when he is supervised very closely he seems to do well, but because of the large caseloads in the probation department, the P.O. can only make two or three contacts with Andy during the month. The P.O. tells the judge that Andy needs more structure and closer supervision than he can receive on regular probation. The judge agrees but does not think that Andy should be committed to prison. He searches for an appropriate alternative. He is considering the merits of electronic monitoring or a day reporting center.

Case B: Tawanda has been arrested for two charges (vandalism and possession of crack cocaine) but has not yet been convicted. In a jealous rage, Tawanda destroyed $1,000 worth of property belonging to her boyfriend. Tawanda was subsequently arrested for the vandalism when the boyfriend called the police. She was found to have five to seven rocks of crack cocaine in her pocket. The judge notes from the presentence investigation that Tawanda has had two previous convictions for drug-related charges, and she received regular probation supervision. Tawanda does not seem to pose a dangerous community threat but does have a problem with crack and alcohol addiction. Tawanda has never received drug and alcohol treatment. Tawanda has a tenth-grade education but did not have stable employment. If she pleads guilty, the judge is considering sentencing her to a day reporting center. In addition, the judge is contemplating restitution or community service but is unsure of Tawanda's ability to pay.

14

Juvenile Justice, Probation, and Aftercare

Bob Daemmrich/Stock Boston

What You Will Learn in This Chapter

You will learn about the background, the history, and the basics of juvenile justice. The juvenile and adult systems are compared, and an overview of the juvenile justice system is presented. You will learn about parens patriae and the leading cases decided by the U.S. Supreme Court in juvenile law. You will become familiar with two kinds of probation conditions, the profile of probation officers, and the skills required for the job. Probation supervision and revocation are discussed, including the role played by probation officers in these proceedings. You will learn about special programs for juveniles and some current challenges facing juvenile probation. The chapter ends with a look at juvenile justice for the 21st century.

INTRODUCTION

Juvenile crime has been a major problem in the United States for decades. From the late 1980s to the early 1990s the increase in violent crime was alarming. The House Judiciary Committee of the U.S. Congress reports that "between 1965 and 1992, the number of 12-year-olds arrested for violent crimes increased 211 percent; the number of 13- and 14-year-olds rose 301 percent; and the number of 15-year-olds rose 297 percent."[1] In the late 1990s, however, juvenile crime started to decline (see Figure 14.1). The Office of Juvenile Justice and Delinquency Prevention (OJJDP) of the U.S. Department of Justice summarized the juvenile crime figures for 1998 as follows:

- The U.S. murder rate in 1998 was the lowest since 1967
- The juvenile share of the crime problem decreased in 1998
- In 1998, 27 percent of juvenile arrests were arrests of females
- Juvenile arrests disproportionately involved minorities
- Compared with adult violence, a smaller proportion of juvenile violence was directed toward family members
- Juvenile arrests for violence in 1998 were the lowest in a decade
- Few juveniles were arrested for violent crime
- Juvenile arrests for property crimes declined substantially in 1998[2]

Although the rate of violent juvenile crime started to decline in the late 1990s, state and local governments are still seeking legislative solutions to a problem that has alarmed and mobilized the nation. Answers do not come easily, partially because society wrestles with conflicting philosophical approaches. On the one hand, the benevolent *parens patriae* doctrine seeks to do what is best for the juvenile; on the other hand, the theory of just deserts advocates punishing offenses based on the seriousness of the act committed and not on the personal circumstances of the offender. The public has gone through cycles of punitiveness and rehabilitation. The pendulum will likely continue to swing from one side (vengeance) to the other (mercy) as long as the problem of juvenile crime exists. At the start of the 21st century, the public appears to be in a mood for vengeance (see Table 14.1).

FIGURE 14.1 *Juvenile Crime*

Juveniles were involved in about one in five arrests made by law enforcement agencies in 1997, one in six arrests for a violent crime, and one in three arrests for a property offense

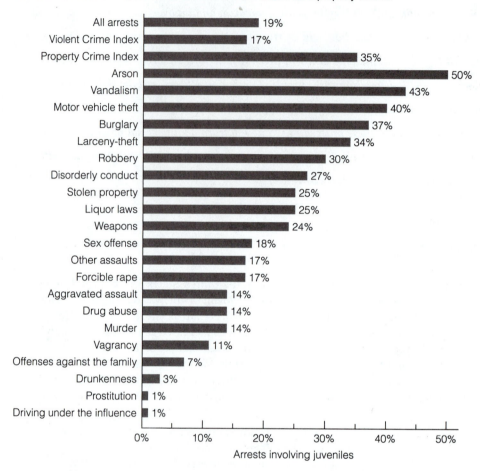

All arrests	19%
Violent Crime Index	17%
Property Crime Index	35%
Arson	50%
Vandalism	43%
Motor vehicle theft	40%
Burglary	37%
Larceny-theft	34%
Robbery	30%
Disorderly conduct	27%
Stolen property	25%
Liquor laws	25%
Weapons	24%
Sex offense	18%
Other assaults	17%
Forcible rape	17%
Aggravated assault	14%
Drug abuse	14%
Murder	14%
Vagrancy	11%
Offenses against the family	7%
Drunkenness	3%
Prostitution	1%
Driving under the influence	1%

Arrests involving juveniles

Note: Running away from home and curfew and loitering violations are not presented in this figure because, by definition, only juveniles can be arrested for these offenses.

Source: *Crime in the United States 1997* (Washington, DC: U.S. Government Printing Office, 1998), table 38, as featured in "Juvenile Arrests 1997," *Juvenile Justice Bulletin* (December 1998); 4.

BACKGROUND AND HISTORY

MENS REA

Latin term for "a guilty mind." Without intent an act is generally not considered criminal.

Criminal liability is based on the concept of ***mens rea,*** which is the Latin term for "a guilty mind."[3] Without intent an act is generally not considered criminal. A guilty mind implies that the actor knows what he or she is doing. Therefore, the act is punishable because the actor intended for the injury to occur. Children below a certain age are presumed by law to be unaware of the full consequences of what they do. Absent *mens rea,* they should not and cannot be punished like adults.

During the latter part of the 18th century children younger than seven were deemed incapable of *mens rea* and were exempt from criminal liability. Those above seven years of age could be prosecuted and sentenced to prison or given the death

TABLE 14.1 *Changes in State Juvenile Justice Systems, 1992–97*

State	Changes in Law or Court Rule			State	Changes in Law or Court Rule		
Alabama	T		C	Montana	T	S	C
Alaska	T		C	Nebraska			
Arizona	T	S	C	Nevada	T	S	C
Arkansas	T	S	C	New Hampshire	T	S	C
California	T		C	New Jersey		S	C
Colorado	T	S	C	New Mexico	T	S	C
Connecticut	T	S	C	New York			
Delaware	T	S	C	North Carolina	T		C
District of Columbia	T	S		North Dakota	T		C
Florida	T	S	C	Ohio	T	S	C
Georgia	T	S	C	Oklahoma	T	S	C
Hawaii	T		C	Oregon	T	S	C
Idaho	T	S	C	Pennsylvania	T		C
Illinois	T	S	C	Rhode Island	T	S	C
Indiana	T	S	C	South Carolina	T		C
Iowa	T	S	C	South Dakota	T		
Kansas	T	S	C	Tennessee	T	S	C
Kentucky	T	S	C	Texas	T	S	C
Louisiana	T	S	C	Utah	T		C
Maine			C	Vermont			
Maryland	T		C	Virginia	T	S	C
Massachusetts	T	S	C	Washington	T		C
Michigan		S	C	West Virginia	T		C
Minnesota	T	S	C	Wisconsin	T	S	C
Mississippi	T		C	Wyoming	T		C
Missouri	T	S	C				

Note: From 1992 through 1997, legislatures in 47 states and the District of Columbia enacted laws that made their juvenile justice systems more punitive. T = transfer provisions; S = sentencing authority; C = confidentiality.
Source: Author's adaptation of Patricia Torbet et al. *State Responses to Serious and Violent Juvenile Crime;* and Patricia Torbet and L. Szymanski *State Legislative Responses to Juvenile Crime: 1996–97 Update,* as featured in Howard N. Snyder and Melissa Sickmund, *Juvenile Offenders and Victims: 1999 National Report* (Washington, DC: National Center for Juvenile Justice, September 1999).

penalty if found guilty.[4] No state in the United States at present punishes juveniles so severely at such an early age, but the minimum age for juveniles to come under the jurisdiction of juvenile courts varies from one state to another.

The philosophy of juvenile courts is heavily influenced by **parens patriae,** a Latin term for the doctrine that "the state is parent" and therefore serves as sovereign and guardian of persons under legal disability, such as juveniles. *Parens patriae* led to the family model of processing juveniles, which treats juveniles like members of one's family. The main concern of the juvenile court is to ensure that legal proceedings are presided over by judges who, acting as wise parents, have the best interest of the child in mind. Constitutional safeguards used to be minimal or nonexistent. Instead, personal attention, love, and care were to be provided.

Over the years pure *parens patriae* declined, paving the way for greater due process, meaning that from having no rights, juveniles now have essentially the same rights as adults, at least during adjudication proceedings. The case that signaled the erosion of *parens patriae* was *In re Gault* (1967).[5] In that case the U.S. Supreme Court

PARENS PATRIAE

Latin term for the doctrine that "the state is parent" and therefore serves as sovereign and guardian of persons under legal disability, such as juveniles.

said that "neither the Fourteenth Amendment nor the Bill of Rights is for adults alone." Since then the Court has decided other cases giving rights to juveniles they previously did not have.

Juvenile proceedings at present are considered by most courts as either civil or administrative in nature. The only constitutional rights denied to juveniles are the right to a jury trial, the right to bail, the right to a public trial, and the right to a grand jury indictment. These rights, however, are usually given to juveniles by state law. As one writer aptly says, the juvenile justice process over the years has become "adultified," at least during the adjudication process.[6]

JUVENILE JUSTICE AND ADULT JUSTICE SYSTEMS COMPARED

The differences between the juvenile justice and adult justice processes may be summarized as follows:[7]

Adult Proceedings
1. Arrested
2. Charged
3. Accused of crime under the penal code
4. Trial
5. Formal, public trial
6. Judge is neutral
7. Found guilty of a criminal offense by an impartial judge or jury
8. Sentenced if found guilty
9. Sent to jail or prison
10. Judge or jury determines length of incarceration
11. Serves sentence for definite term, subject to parole law
12. Purpose is punishment
13. Released on parole, if eligible
14. A criminal case

Juvenile Proceedings
1. Taken into custody by police
2. Prosecutor petitions court
3. Violation comes under the juvenile code or family code
4. Adjudication
5. Usually a private, informal hearing
6. Judge acts as wise parent
7. Found to have engaged in delinquent conduct
8. Disposition
9. Committed to a state facility for juveniles
10. Youth detention authorities determine when to release
11. Committed for an indeterminate amount of time, but usually released upon reaching age of majority
12. Purpose is rehabilitation
13. Released on aftercare
14. A civil or quasi-civil case

These differences, however, are more symbolic than substantive and have minimal impact because the procedures are essentially similar regardless of the term used. For example, in both arrest (for adults) and being taken into custody (for juveniles), the offender is deprived of liberty. Neither is there much difference between the adult suspect being charged and the prosecutor petitioning the court for the juvenile to be adjudicated because both processes lead to hearings. Sentencing and disposition both subject the offender to lawfully prescribed sanctions, which includes incarceration. Nonetheless, society shuns the use of adult criminal law terms in juvenile proceedings and refuses to brand juveniles as criminals in hopes that rehabilitation is better served by not labeling them as such.

JUVENILE COURTS

Juvenile courts, as they are known today, are an American creation. The first U.S. juvenile court was established in Chicago in 1899, with the passage of the Illinois Juvenile Court Act. The court was founded on the belief that a child's behavior was the product of poor family background and surroundings. It operated informally, was civil in nature, and was geared toward rehabilitation.[8]

Some believe that juvenile courts were created so the public could "go easy" on young criminals.[9] This may be an oversimplification. While "some reformers were motivated by a desire to save growing numbers of poor and homeless children from the streets of America's cities," others were "mainly interested in removing the legal obstacles that prevented criminal courts from dealing effectively with young hoodlums."[10] Another scholar says that "the 1899 Illinois Juvenile Court Act was, in part, yet another response to the growing incidence of jury nullification, concern about the dominance of sectarian industrial schools in a Chicago filling with immigrants, and reform-based opposition to confining youth with adults."[11] Whatever the motivation, the idea caught on and spread quickly. By 1925, 46 states, 3 territories, and the District of Columbia had juvenile courts.[12] Juvenile courts have gone a long ways since they were first established more than a century ago. Although they have undergone changes, they are still the core of juvenile justice in the United States.

Juvenile court judges play a central and crucial role in the administration of juvenile justice. This is because of the *parens patriae* approach. The judge ideally plays the role of a wise parent instead of an impartial arbiter, as judges are expected to do in criminal proceedings. In the words of one observer:

> In addition to the traditional judicial capacity, the juvenile court judge has the authority to affect case processing long before and after a formal adjudication hearing. In many jurisdictions, the juvenile court judge is the direct administrator of the juvenile probation department and/or court staff. When operating in this capacity, the juvenile court judge can assure coordination of services between the court and the probation department and may also take on the burden of fiscal management.[13]

Teen Courts

Since the 1990s, two variations of the regular juvenile court have been established: teen courts and drug courts for juveniles. Teen courts are courts that "involve young people in the sentencing of their peers, whether in a school, juvenile justice, or a community setting."[14] They have teens serving as jurors and performing the roles of prosecuting attorney, defense attorney, judge, bailiff, or other officers of the court, but they serve the function of real courts. The number of teen courts has grown from 50 programs in 1991 to around 500 programs in 1998, when approximately 65,000 cases were processed.[15] One scholar states that teen courts use four case processing models:[16]

- Adult Judge Model. An adult serves as judge and rules on legal terminology and courtroom procedure, but teens serve as attorneys, jurors, clerks, bailiffs, and so on (used by 47 percent of teen courts).
- Youth Judge Model. A teen serves as a judge (used by 9 percent of teen courts).
- Tribunal Model. Teen attorneys present the case to a panel of three youth judges, who decide the appropriate disposition for the defendant (used by 10 percent of teen courts).
- Peer Jury Model. Does not use youth attorneys, but a youth or adult presents the case to a youth jury, which then questions the defendant directly (used by 12 percent of teen courts).

Although some teen courts are authorized to determine guilt or innocence, most do not perform that function. Instead, they serve as diversion alternatives and therefore the teen against whom charges are brought must admit to the charges if he or she is to come under the court's jurisdiction. A study shows that teen court sentences commonly include community service, jury duty, restitution, apology, counseling, educational workshops on substance abuse or safe driving essay writing, victim awareness classes, curfew, drug testing, school attendance, and peer discussion groups.[17]

Juvenile Drug Courts

Another variation of the regular juvenile court is juvenile drug courts, which began as a grassroots initiative and has spread throughout the country. These courts focus on drug users and offer such incentives as deferred prosecution for those willing to participate in drug treatment programs. As of 1997, 244 drug courts were in operation or were being planned in the United States, with 25 being dedicated to juveniles. Drug courts involve local teams of judges, prosecutors, attorneys, treatment providers, law enforcement officials, and others whose main concern is forcing abstinence from drugs and altering behavior of offenders with a combination of intensive judicial supervision, escalating sanctions, mandatory drug testing, treatment, and strong aftercare programs.[18] The following features are common to juvenile drug courts, as opposed to the regular juvenile courts:[19]

- Much earlier and much more comprehensive intake assessments
- Much greater focus on the functioning of the juvenile and the family throughout the juvenile court process
- Much closer integration of the information obtained during the assessment process as it relates to the juvenile and the family
- Much greater coordination among the court, the treatment community, the school system, and other community agencies in responding to the needs of the juvenile and the court
- Much more active and continuous judicial supervision of the juvenile's case and treatment process
- Increased use of immediate sanctions for noncompliance and incentives for progress for both the juvenile and the family

Although teen courts and juvenile drug courts started as local initiatives, they have spread nationwide and many are now being financially supported by the government through federal grants. Their effectiveness has yet to be established, but their use is increasing.

Jurisdiction of Juvenile Courts

The kinds of cases that go to juvenile courts are defined by state law, hence juvenile jurisdiction varies from state to state. In general, juvenile court jurisdiction is two-pronged, consisting of the age of the offender and the kinds of acts committed.

The first prong, based on age, has a minimum and a maximum age, as determined by state law (see Figure 14.2). A wide variation exists among states—from a minimum of 7 years old to a maximum of 24. Most states, however, have a minimum age of 7 years and maximum age of 20 years. Juveniles younger than 7 years who commit criminal acts are usually processed informally by the police or placed in the care of

FIGURE 14.2 *Upper Age of State Juvenile Court Jurisdiction*

The upper age of juvenile court jurisdiction in delinquency matters is defined by state statute. In most states the upper age is 17.

Oldest age for original juvenile court jurisdiction in delinquency matters

15	16	17		
Connecticut	Georgia	Alabama	Kansas	Ohio
New York	Illinois	Alaska	Kentucky	Oklahoma
North Carolina	Louisiana	Arizona	Maine	Oregon
	Massachusetts	Arkansas	Maryland	Pennsylvania
	Michigan	California	Minnesota	Rhode Island
	Missouri	Colorado	Mississippi	South Dakota
	South Carolina	Delaware	Montana	Tennessee
	Texas	District of Columbia	Nebraska	Utah
			Nevada	Vermont[a]
		Florida	New Hampshire	Virginia
		Hawaii	New Jersey	Washington
		Idaho	New Mexico	West Virginia
		Indiana	North Dakota	Wisconsin
		Iowa		Wyoming

- Many states have higher upper ages of juvenile court jurisdiction in status offense, abuse, neglect, or dependency matters—often through age 20.
- In many states the juvenile court has jurisdiction over young adults who committed offenses while juveniles.
- Several states also have minimum ages of juvenile court jurisdiction in delinquency matters—ranging from 6 to 12.
- Many states exclude married or otherwise emancipated juveniles form juvenile court jurisdiction.

[a]In Vermont the juvenile and criminal courts have concurrent jurisdiction over all 16- and 17-year-olds.

Source: L. Szymanski, *Upper Age of Juvenile Court Jurisdiction Statutes Analyses: 1994 Update* (1995); and L. Szymanski, *Lower Age of Juvenile Court Jurisdiction: 1994 Update* (1995), as featured in Howard N. Snyder and Melissa Sickmund, *Juvenile Offenders and Victims: A National Report* (Washington, DC: National Center for Juvenile Justice, Office of Juvenile Justice and Delinquency Prevention, August 1995).

state custodial services. Offenders who are beyond the maximum age are processed as adult criminals. The minimum and maximum ages are usually determined at the time the act itself was committed, not when the offender was caught or tried.

The second prong is based on the kinds of acts committed. Juvenile acts that trigger court intervention are generally of two types: **juvenile delinquency** and **conduct in need of supervision (CINS).** Each state, by law, defines the acts that come under each category and therefore vary from state to state. In general, however, juvenile delinquency results from acts committed by juveniles that are punishable as crimes by a state's penal code. Examples are murder, robbery, and burglary. In contrast, CINS (also known in some jurisdictions as CHINS [children in need of supervision], MINS [minors in need of supervision], or JINS [juveniles in need of supervision]) is likely to be a status offense, meaning acts that it would not be punishable if committed by adults. Status offenses include truancy, running away,

JUVENILE DELINQUENCY:

In general, acts committed by juveniles that are punishable as crimes by a state's penal code. Each state, however, defines the specific acts that constitute juvenile delinquency in that state.

CONDUCT IN NEED OF SUPERVISION (CINS)

Likely to be status offenses, meaning acts that would not have been punishable if committed by adults. Like juvenile delinquency, each state defines the specific acts that constitute conduct in need of supervision in that state.

inhalant abuse, curfew violation, and underage drinking. Sanctions imposed for juvenile delinquency are often more severe than those for conduct in need of supervision. In some states, juvenile delinquency can result in being sent to a state institution, while conduct in need of supervision merely results in probation or referral to juvenile programs in the community.

TRANSFER OF JURISDICTION FROM JUVENILE COURT TO ADULT COURT

All states have provisions for the transfer of jurisdiction from juvenile courts to adult courts. These transfer provisions may be classified into three general categories:[20]

- Judicial Waiver. "[T]he juvenile court judge has the authority to waive juvenile court jurisdiction and transfer the case to criminal court." This process is known in some states as certification, remand, or bind over for criminal prosecution. In 1997, judicial waiver was used in 46 states and the District of Columbia.
- Concurrent Jurisdiction. "[O]riginal jurisdiction for certain cases is shared by both criminal and juvenile courts, and the prosecutor has discretion to file such cases in either court." This process is also known in some states as prosecutorial waiver, prosecutor discretion, or direct file. In 1997, **concurrent jurisdiction** was used in 14 states and the District of Columbia.
- Statutory Exclusion. "[S]tate statute excludes certain juvenile offenders from juvenile court jurisdiction." This process is also known in some states as legislative exclusion.

Transfer provisions, generally more punitive, have gained more popularity as the public's response to the problem of violent juvenile crime. Adult sanctions are imposed if a juvenile is tried in adult court, hence much is at stake for the juvenile and the public. Of the three categories, **judicial waiver** is the most commonly used, but the two other approaches are also available in some states. Although judicial waivers are widely available, only a small portion of juvenile cases go through this procedure. One study reports that, in 1997, waivers to criminal court represented "less than 1% (approximately 8,400 cases) of the formally processed delinquency caseload."[21] Wide variation exists among states on judicial waivers, some making waivers mandatory while others consider it discretionary. Twenty-two states and the District of Columbia have at least one provision for transferring juveniles to the criminal court for which no minimum age is specified.[22]

AN OVERVIEW OF THE JUVENILE JUSTICE PROCESS

The juvenile justice process is essentially similar to the adult justice process, but differences do exist. The terms used are different, the proceeding is deemed civil or quasi-civil (some consider it semicriminal, others call it administrative), and the discretion given to a juvenile court judge is more extensive than that given to criminal court judges (see Figure 14.3).

Procedure before Adjudication

The juvenile justice process starts in various ways, and procedures vary from state to state. Juvenile behavior that sets the process in motion may come to the attention of the government through oral or written reports from diverse sources such as the

CONCURRENT JURISDICTION

Original jurisdiction for certain juvenile offenses is shared by both criminal and juvenile courts, and the prosecutor has discretion to file such cases in either court.

JUDICIAL WAIVER

A process whereby a juvenile court judge waives juvenile court jurisdiction and transfers a juvenile case to the regular adult criminal court.

FIGURE 14.3   Stages of Delinquency Case Processing in the Juvenile Justice System

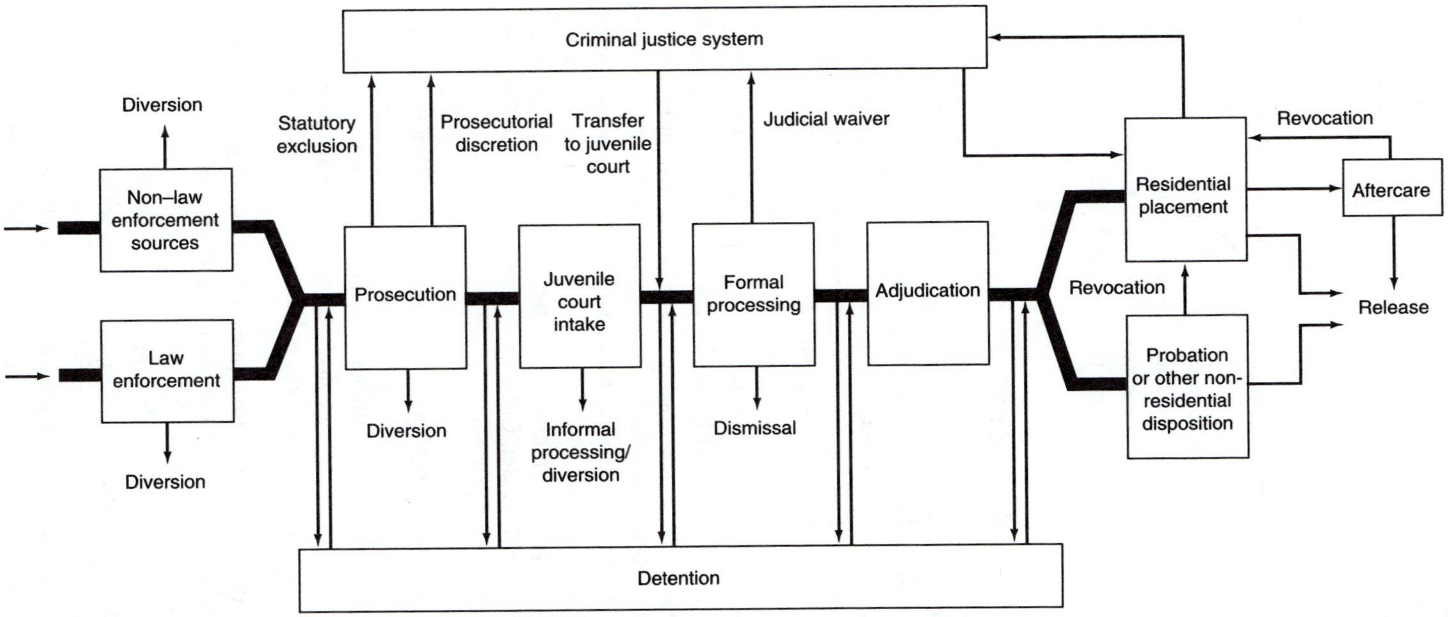

Note: This chart gives a simplified view of caseflow through the juvenile justice system. Procedures vary among jurisdictions. The weights of the lines are not intended to show the actual size of caseloads.

Source: Howard N. Synder and Melissa Sickmund, *Juvenile Offenders and Victims: 1999 National Report* (Washington, DC: National Center for Juvenile Justice, September, 1999).

general public, probation officers, victims, parents, neighbors, school authorities, and the police. The Office of Juvenile Justice and Delinquency Prevention reports that "law enforcement referrals accounted for 85% of all delinquency cases referred to juvenile courts in 1992" and that "the remaining referrals were made by others such as parents, victims, schools, and probation officers."[23]

Contact with the police can lead to a variety of actions such as taking the juvenile into custody for possible prosecution, taking the juvenile into protective custody, referring the juvenile to pertinent agencies, or releasing the juvenile. One publication notes that "most state statutes explicitly direct police officers to release to a parent or refer to court those juveniles who are taken into custody."[24] In practice, police officer dispositions can include such informal procedures as outright release, warning, referral to community agency for services, referral to a "citizen hearing board," or referral to court intake.

FORMAL VERSUS INFORMAL PROCESSING: Juvenile cases are handled formally or informally. Formal handling means that the case involves a formal charge, a hearing, and a disposition. Informal processing means that the case is handled outside the regular procedures and with an eye toward diversion from the system. The number of cases handled informally has increased over the years. A study shows that 44 percent of state delinquency cases in 1987 were handled informally; this increased to 53 percent in 1996,[25] then further increased to 57 percent in 1997.[26]

THE INTAKE STAGE: A juvenile taken into custody by the police usually goes through the **intake** process, considered by some to be "one of the most crucial case processing points in the juvenile justice system."[27] *Intake* is a term unique to juvenile justice, but its meaning varies from state to state. In general it refers to a process whereby a juvenile is screened to determine if the case should be processed further by the juvenile justice system or whether other alternatives are better suited for the juvenile. It is usually done by a probation officer or other individuals designated by the court or the prosecutor. Arnold Binder, Gilbert Geis, and Dickson D. Bruce Jr. summarize the functions of the intake process as follows:[28]

- Determine whether the circumstances of the case bring it within the jurisdiction of the juvenile court
- Determine whether the evidence is sufficient to warrant a court hearing
- Decide whether the case is serious enough to require a court hearing
- Arrange for a process of informal supervision if that alternative seems desirable

Intake may also involve detention screening, presentence investigation, crisis intervention, or other procedures mandated by the court. It does what state law or court policy intends for the process to accomplish.

A juvenile may be detained by the police, but only for a limited time. State law usually requires that a detained juvenile be given a hearing within 24 hours after the child is placed in detention.[29] Federal rules provide that juveniles be separated from adult offenders by "sight and sound." This assures that juveniles are detained in facilities separate from those used for adults. In the case of *Schall v. Martin* (1984), however, the U.S. Supreme Court held that preventive detention of juveniles (where a juvenile is detained because of the likelihood that he or she will commit other offenses) is constitutional, subject to limitations.[30]

If the intake officer decides to refer the case to court, the prosecutor petitions the court for the juvenile to be adjudicated. Summons are issued directing the juvenile to appear before the court at a specified time and place for an initial appearance on the

---

INTAKE

Process whereby a juvenile is screened to determine if the case should be processed further by the juvenile justice system or whether other alternatives are better suited for the juvenile. It is usually done by a probation officer or other individuals designated by the court or the prosecutor.

FIGURE 14.4 *Adjudicated Delinquency Cases, 1988–97*

There has been a substantial increase in the number of cases in which the youth was placed on probation or ordered to a residential facility between 1988 and 1997.

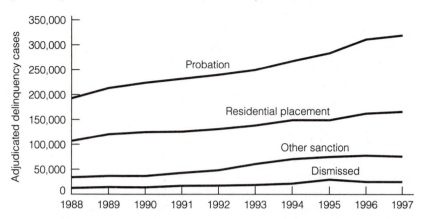

Source: Howard N. Snyder and Melissa Sickmund, *Juvenile Offenders and Victims: 1999 National Report* (Washington, DC: National Center for Juvenile Justice, September 1999.)

petition. An arraignment is then held, and the juvenile is given the opportunity to admit or deny the allegations.[31]

The Adjudication Stage

Adjudication is the equivalent of a trial in adult criminal cases. However, it is less formal, and the judge takes a more active part in the hearing—including asking questions of juveniles, their parents or guardians, and witnesses. Juvenile courts were designed to be different from adult courts. Originally no lawyers were allowed, formal rules of evidence were waived, and the juvenile enjoyed no legal or constitutional protections. This led some critics to label them "kangaroo courts." That has changed considerably. Now the features of the original juvenile courts are barely recognizable. In the words of Peter Greenwood,

> The informality is largely gone. Juveniles sit with their lawyers like adult defendants. Juvenile hearings or trials proceed along the same lines as criminal trials. The rules of evidence and rights of the parties are about the same, except that juveniles still do not have the right to a jury trial or to bail.[32]

In addition to not having the right to a jury trial or to bail, juveniles are denied the constitutional right to a public trial and a grand jury indictment in states that use them. These rights, however, may be given by state law or agency policy.

The Disposition Stage

If a juvenile is found to have engaged in the conduct alleged in the petition, the disposition stage follows. **Disposition** is the equivalent of sentencing in adult cases, but the juvenile court judge wields greater discretion than in adult criminal trials. Because most states consider rehabilitation an integral part of juvenile corrections, the judge typically has a wide choice of available dispositions ranging from a mild reprimand to confinement in a state institution (see Figure 14.4). Institutionalization (also known as residential commitment) is usually the most severe disposition in

ADJUDICATION

Juvenile justice equivalent of a trial in adult criminal cases.

DISPOSITION

Juvenile justice equivalent of sentencing in adult cases

juvenile cases and is imposed primarily in juvenile delinquency cases. Status offenders are typically placed on probation as the maximum sanction. If probation is revoked, however, the juvenile may then be classified as a delinquent because of a violation of a court order, and he or she may be dispatched to a state institution.

Once the juvenile is confined in a state institution, release is left to the discretion of institutional officials. Many states provide for aftercare (the equivalent of parole) for juveniles who are fit for release before serving the maximum amount of time set by state law. If released on aftercare, the juvenile is supervised, but supervision usually ceases after the juvenile reaches the age of majority—generally 18. If the provisions of aftercare are breached, the juvenile is sent back to a state juvenile institution instead of to a state prison, after a hearing where the breach is established.

Despite the growing similarity between juvenile and adult criminal proceedings, some differences persist, the most notable being the role played by the juvenile court judge, who acts as a wise parent instead of an impartial arbiter. Therefore, the judge is more likely to take an active part in the proceedings, such as in questioning the alleged offender, cross-examining witnesses, and bringing up a juvenile's background. A second difference is in the imposition of the death penalty as a sanction. In *Thompson v. Oklahoma* (1988), the U.S. Supreme Court held that it is unconstitutional to sentence a juvenile to death if he or she was 15 years of age or younger at the time of the commission of the act, regardless of its nature.[33] A year later, however, in *Stanford v. Kentucky*, the Court held that it is constitutional for a state to impose the death penalty on a juvenile who was at least 16 years old at the time the crime was committed.[34] Together the *Thompson* and *Stanford* cases hold that juveniles cannot constitutionally be given the death penalty if the crime was committed at 15 years of age, but the death penalty may be administered if the crime was committed when the juvenile was 16 years old. Thus a bright-line rule has been drawn in death penalty cases involving juveniles. The actual age at which a juvenile may be given the death penalty is, however, determined by state law. The United States executed ten juvenile offenders in the decade of the 1990s. As of the year 2000, 25 states (out of the 38 that have the death penalty) allowed the execution of juveniles whose crimes were committed at ages 16 and 17.

> Juvenile courts usually do not try cases involving the death penalty. Those cases are tried instead in the regular criminal courts after waiver proceedings or upon authorization from special state laws providing severe penalties, including death, for juveniles who commit serious crimes.[35]

MAJOR U.S. SUPREME COURT CASES IN JUVENILE JUSTICE

For a long time, the U.S. Supreme Court did not decide any case involving juveniles on the issue of constitutional rights to which they are entitled in the course of a juvenile proceeding. In essence, the Court adopted a hands-off policy on juvenile cases, preferring the full *parens patriae* approach that deprived juveniles of basic constitutional rights because they were to be treated as members of the family. All that ended in the 1960s when the Court decided the *In re Gault* and *Kent v. United States* cases.

The leading and most important case in juvenile justice is *In re Gault* (1967).[36] In that case a 15-year-old boy and a friend were taken into custody in Arizona as a result of a complaint that they had made lewd telephone calls. Gault's parents were not informed that he was in custody, and they were not shown the complaint that was filed against their son. The complainant never appeared at any hearing, and no written record was made of the hearing that was held. Gault was committed to a state institution as a delinquent until he reached the age of majority—a total of six years from the date of the hearing. The maximum punishment for the offense, had it been committed by an adult, was a fine of from $5 to $60 or imprisonment for a maximum of two months. Gault appealed the conviction, saying he was denied his rights during the hearing. The U.S. Supreme Court agreed.

Gault provides that juveniles must be given four basic due process rights in adjudication proceedings that can result in confinement in an institution in which their freedom would be curtailed. These rights are:

1. Reasonable notice of the charges
2. Counsel, appointed by the state if the juvenile is indigent
3. The ability to confront and cross-examine witnesses
4. The privilege against self-incrimination

In re Gault is significant because it was the first case decided by the U.S. Supreme Court that gave due process rights to juveniles, thus initiating the erosion of the pure *parens patriae* approach. *Parens patriae* is still alive in juvenile justice, but its purity has been sapped by a gradual process of "adultification" through judicial intervention.

A year before *Gault,* the Court decided *Kent v. United States* (1966).[37] It held that a juvenile must be given due process rights before being certified or transferred from a juvenile to an adult court. In that case, a 16-year-old was arrested and charged with housebreaking, robbery, and rape. After a "full investigation," the juvenile was transferred to an adult court for criminal trial. The judge gave no reason for the waiver. Kent was convicted in criminal court on six counts of housebreaking and robbery. On appeal, the Court said that a transfer of jurisdiction from a juvenile to an adult court is a "critically important stage" in the juvenile process and therefore required the following due process rights:

1. A hearing
2. Representation by counsel at such hearing
3. Access to records considered by the juvenile court
4. A statement of the reasons in support of the waiver order

In re Winship, decided in 1970, followed the pattern of *parens patriae* decline by holding that proof beyond a reasonable doubt, not simply a preponderance of the evidence, is required in juvenile adjudication hearings in cases in which the act would have been a crime if committed by an adult.[38] In that case, a New York family court judge found that a 12-year-old boy had entered a locker and stolen $112 from a woman's purse. The petition, which charged the juvenile with delinquency, alleged that his act, if done by an adult, would constitute the crime of larceny. The judge then acknowledged that guilt might not have been established beyond a reasonable doubt, but the New York Family Court Act required that the verdict need only be based on a preponderance of the evidence, hence the juvenile was ordered to be placed in a training school. On appeal, the U.S. Supreme Court held that the due process clause of the Constitution requires proof beyond a reasonable doubt in a juvenile adjudication hearing, so the commitment to a training school based on preponderance of the evidence was unconstitutional. Preponderance of the evidence simply means more than 50 percent certainty that the offender committed the offense. Guilt beyond reasonable doubt requires a much higher degree of certainty, roughly 95 percent certainty.

In *Breed v. Jones* (1975), the Court further placed juveniles in the same category as adults, holding that juveniles are entitled to the constitutional right against double jeopardy in juvenile proceedings.[39] In that case, a petition was filed in the Los Angeles County juvenile court, alleging that a 17-year-old committed acts that, if committed by an adult, would constitute robbery with a deadly weapon. A detention hearing was held and the juvenile was ordered detained pending a hearing on the petition. During the adjudicatory hearing, the court found the allegations against the juvenile to be true and ordered further detention. At the dispositional hearing (the equivalent in adult trial of sentencing), the juvenile court found that that the offender was unfit for treatment as a juvenile and therefore ordered that he be prosecuted as an adult. The juvenile was subsequently found guilty of robbery by the adult criminal court. On appeal, Court said that a juvenile who has undergone adjudication proceedings in juvenile court cannot be tried on the same charge as an adult in a criminal court because such would constitute double jeopardy. The Court reasoned that "in terms of potential consequences, there is little to distinguish an adjudicatory hearing, such as was held in this case, from a traditional criminal prosecution," hence the prohibition against double jeopardy applies.

Despite these decisions, which granted constitutional rights, the Court has refused to extend all constitutional rights to juveniles. For example, in *McKeiver v. Pennsylvania* (1971), the Court decided that juveniles have no constitutional right to trial by jury, even in juvenile delinquency (as opposed to status offense where the penalty is usually lower) proceedings.[40] The Court said, "The imposition of the jury trial on the juvenile court system would not strengthen greatly, if at all, the fact finding function, and would, contrarily, provide an attrition of the juvenile court's assumed ability to function in a unique manner." Then in *Davis v. Alaska* (1974), the Court said that despite state confidentiality laws, the probation of a juvenile witness may be brought out by the opposing lawyer on cross-examination in cases in which a juvenile is on the witness stand.[41] In *Fare v. Michael C.* (1979), the Court decided that a request by a juvenile to see his probation officer is not equivalent to asking for a lawyer. As a result, there is no lawyer-client privilege to confidential information. Then in *New Jersey v. T.L.O.* (1985), the Court concluded that public school officials need only have "reasonable grounds" to search students; they do not need a warrant or probable cause.[42]

The above cases show a roller-coaster ride for juveniles in the U.S. Supreme Court. On the whole, however, Court decisions have dealt a serious blow to the pure *parens patriae* approach and has criminalized juvenile proceedings—at least in cases involving delinquency when placement in a juvenile institution is a possible sanction. While juvenile proceedings are still civil in nature, at least on paper, Supreme Court decisions strongly imply that they are treated as criminal proceedings and therefore basic constitutional rights apply.

What led to the gradual erosion of pure *parens patriae*? The answer may be found in the footnote in the *Gault* case. Quoting the decision in *Kent v. United States*, the Court said, "There is evidence . . . that there may be grounds for concern that the child receives the worst of both worlds; that he gets neither the protections accorded to adults nor the solicitous care and regenerative treatment postulated for children."[43] Given this concern about the juvenile receiving "the worst of both worlds," the Court infused due process into juvenile proceedings, thus eroding the pure *parens patriae* concept that had been the hallmark of juvenile justice from its inception.

JUVENILE PROBATION AND AFTERCARE

As is true with adults, probation is the disposition most often used by judges when formally adjudicating juvenile delinquency cases. The second most popular disposition is residential placement. In 1997, around 320,000 juveniles were placed on probation, and around 160,000 were placed in residential treatment programs.[44]

Origin

The origin of juvenile probation is traced to John Augustus, the Boston shoemaker who in 1847 persuaded judges in Massachusetts to place wayward youth under his care. Since then juvenile probation has grown in popularity. More than one-third of juvenile delinquents disposed of by American juvenile courts in 1990 were placed on probation. Moreover, 43 percent of all petitioner cases and 28 percent of cases handled informally were placed on probation.[45] One study reports that in 1993 nearly 1.5 million delinquency cases were handled by juvenile courts and that "virtually every one of those cases had contact with a probation officer at some point."[46] And in 1996, juvenile probation handled 1.76 million delinquency cases.[47] Clearly, juvenile probation is an integral and significant part of juvenile justice.

Structure and Administration

Juvenile probation and aftercare practices have much in common with their adult counterparts. Differences exist, however, in structure, philosophy, and programs. Hunter Hurst IV and Patricia McFall Torbet of the National Center for Juvenile Justice classify the structure and administration of juvenile probation and aftercare as follows:[48]

Juvenile Probation—Administration and Organization

Local and judicial	16 states and Washington, D.C.
State and judicial	7 states
Local and executive	3 states
State and executive	10 states
Combination	14 states

Juvenile Aftercare—Administration and Organization

Local and judicial	2 states
State and judicial	2 states
Local and executive	Washington, D.C.
State and executive	37 states
Combination	9 states

The structure of juvenile probation and aftercare vary greatly in administration and organization. Differences exist on the issues of whether juvenile probation and aftercare are administered locally or statewide, whether the department is under judicial or executive control, whether juvenile probation is combined with adult probation, and whether juvenile probation and aftercare are combined or separate departments.

Some probation departments are administered by the local government, others are administered by the state (see Figure 14.5). Some are under the executive branch, others are under the judicial branch. Most have separate juvenile and adult probation and aftercare departments, but in some jurisdictions, particularly in smaller counties,

FIGURE 14.5 *Organization and Administration of State Juvenile Services*

Probation supervision tends to be administered by local juvenile courts or by a state executive branch agency

State administration		Local administration	
Judicial branch	**Executive branch**	**Judicial branch**	**Executive branch**
Connecticut	Alaska	Alabama	California
Hawaii	Arkansas	Arizona	Oregon
Iowa	Delaware	Arkansas	Idaho
Kentucky	District of Columbia	California	Kentucky
Nebraska	Florida	Colorado	Minnesota
North Carolina	Georgia	Georgia	Mississippi
North Dakota	Idaho	Illinois	New York
South Dakota	Kentucky	Indiana	Washington
Utah	Louisiana	Kansas	Wisconsin
West Virginia	Maine	Kentucky	
	Maryland	Louisiana	
	Minnesota	Massachusetts	
	Mississippi	Michigan	
	New Hampshire	Minnesota	
	New Mexico	Missouri	
	North Dakota	Montana	
	Oklahoma	Nevada	
	Rhode Island	New Jersey	
	South Carolina	Ohio	
	Tennessee	Oklahoma	
	Vermont	**Pennsylvania**	
	Virginia	Tennessee	
	West Virginia	**Texas**	
	Wyoming	Virginia	
		Washington	
		Wisconsin	
		Wyoming	

Note: In states in bold, probation is provided by a combination of agencies. Often larger, urban counties operate local probation departments while in smaller counties probation is state operated.

Source: H. Hurst and P. Torbet, *Organization and Administration of Juvenile Services: Probation, Aftercare, and State Institutions for delinquent youth* (1993).

State institutions for delinquents are administered by executive branch agencies—most often by a social services agency

Human services		Adult corrections	Juvenile corrections	Children and families
Alaska	Missouri	Colorado	Alabama	Delaware
Arkansas	Nevada	Illinois	Arizona	Montana
DC	New Hampshire	Indiana	California	Rhode Island
Florida	North Carolina	Louisiana	Connecticut	New Mexico
Hawaii	Oklahoma	Maine	Georgia	Virginia
Idaho	Oregon	Minnesota	Maryland	Wyoming
Iowa	Pennsylvania	Nebraska	New York	
Kansas	Utah	New Jersey	Ohio	
Kentucky	Vermont	North Dakota	South Carolina	
Massachusetts	Washington	South Dakota	Tennessee	
Michigan	Wisconsin	West Virginia	Texas	
Mississippi				

Note: Agencies were grouped as follows: broad-based social services/welfare agencies, adult corrections, juvenile corrections, and children and family services and protective services.

Source: H. Hurst and P. Torbet, *Organization and Administration of Juvenile Services: Probation, Aftercare, and State Institutions for Delinquent Youth* (1993), as featured in Howard N. Snyder and Melissa Sickmund, *Juvenile Offenders and Victims: A National Report* (Washington, DC: National Center for Juvenile Justice/Office of Juvenile Justice and Delinquency, August 1995), 90.

they are combined. In some states probation and aftercare are combined and staffed by the same officers; in other states they are separate agencies that barely interact with each other. Some states contract out aftercare services to private agencies or to local probation departments. Structural differences in juvenile probation are more pervasive than in adult probation.

Juvenile Probation Officers

Probation officers are the crucial players in juvenile probation. Theirs is an interesting job made more challenging by changing philosophies, innovative programs, and an increasingly high-risk clientele. A 1996 publication reports the following data and demographics about juvenile probation officers:

> There are an estimated 18,000 juvenile probation professionals impacting the lives of juveniles in the United States. Eighty-five percent of these professionals are involved in the delivery of basic intake, investigation, and supervision services at the line officer level; the remaining 15 percent are involved in the administration of probation offices or the management of probation staff.[49]

The same publication states that juvenile probation officers are generally college-educated white males, 30–49 years of age, with five to ten years of field experience. In 1993 they typically earned $20,000–$39,000 per year and had an average caseload of 41 juveniles. Most had arrest powers, but they normally did not carry weapons.[50]

Probation officers are usually appointed and also terminated by the juvenile court judge. The following provision from the state of Indiana typifies the legal provisions in most jurisdictions.

> The judge of the juvenile court shall appoint a chief probation officer, and may appoint other probation officers, and an appropriate number of other employees to assist the probation department. The salaries of the probation officers and other juvenile court employees shall be fixed by the judge and paid by the county, subject to the approval of the county council. In addition to their annual salary, probation officers shall be reimbursed for any necessary travel expenses incurred in the performance of their duties in accord with the law governing state officers and employees.[51]

> The *Desktop Guide to Good Juvenile Probation Practice* (hereinafter referred to as the *Desktop Guide*), published by the National Center for Juvenile Justice, recommends the following skills for juvenile probation officers:[52]

Basic knowledge of pertinent law
Skill in oral and written communication
Ability to plan and implement investigative or supervision services
Ability to analyze social, psychological, and criminological information objectively and accurately
Basic knowledge of criminological, psychological, and economic theories of human behavior
Ability to use authority effectively and constructively

Juvenile probation officers play a multifaceted role, a function often more demanding than that performed by adult probation officers. As the *Desktop Guide* observes, "The probation officer is expected to fulfill many different roles, often 'taking up the slack' after judges, attorneys, social agencies, parents, and so on have met what they see as their own clearly defined responsibilities in the case and have expressed an unwillingness to extend themselves beyond these limits."[53] In many cases, the juvenile probation officer is the last hope of rehabilitation for the juvenile. The *Desktop Guide* states that a juvenile probation officer is expected, among other things, to be a cop, a prosecutor, a confessor, a rat, a teacher, a friend, a problem solver, a crisis manager, a hand, holder, a community resource specialist, and so on. It is a challenging task.

Informal Juvenile Probation

About one-half of all cases referred to juvenile court intake are handled informally.[54] This includes a process called **informal probation,** which is authorized in almost every juvenile code and is commonly used in probation agencies across the country. Informal probation differs from regular probation in that informal probation is used early in the juvenile justice process before the juvenile is adjudicated. It can take place during the intake process or just before adjudication.

INFORMAL PROBATION

A form of probation in which a juvenile is placed on probation before he or she is formally adjudicated.

Informal probation is criticized as presuming a juvenile's guilt prior to adjudication. Such criticism is muted, however, by the fact that informal probation is voluntary and entered into by the parties with the knowledge that adjudication is always an option for the juvenile. Therefore, any possible coercive effect of informal probation is minimized.

CONDITIONS OF PROBATION AND AFTERCARE

Juvenile court judges have considerable discretion when imposing probation conditions. Hardly any state specifies the conditions that should be imposed. The setting of conditions is left to the sound discretion of the juvenile court, usually upon recommendation of the probation officer. Similarly, aftercare conditions are left to the discretion of juvenile institutional officers who are authorized to release the juvenile. Typically conditions include provisions designed to control as well as rehabilitate the juvenile.[55] These dual goals make the imposition of conditions more challenging for the court, particularly because the approaches to control and rehabilitation may be inconsistent.

Kinds of Conditions

Juvenile probation or aftercare conditions are usually of two kinds: mandatory and discretionary. Both may be specified by law or left to the discretion of the juvenile court judge or the releasing authority in the case of aftercare. Only a few states impose mandatory conditions, and where imposed, they vary from one jurisdiction to another. Mandatory conditions usually provide the following:[56]

- Probationers may not commit a new local, state, or federal delinquent act.
- Probationers must report as directed to their probation officers.
- Probationers must obey all court orders.

Discretionary conditions also vary from one jurisdiction to another. As an example, the New Jersey juvenile statutes list the following discretionary conditions:[57]

- Pay a fine.
- Make restitution.
- Perform community service.
- Participate in a work program.
- Participate in programs emphasizing self-reliance.
- Participate in a program of academic or vocational education or counseling.
- Be placed in a suitable residential or nonresidential program for the treatment of alcohol or narcotic abuse.

- Be placed in a nonresidential program operated by a public or private agency, providing intensive services to juveniles for specified hours.
- Be placed in any private group home with which the Department of Correction has entered into a purchase of service contract.

SUPERVISION

Supervision has been called the "essence of juvenile probation."[58] The *Desktop Guide* states that "the common thread that runs through all approaches to supervision is utility; that is, that juvenile justice intervention must be designed to guide and correct the naturally changing behavior patterns of youth."[59] It adds, "Unlike adult probation, juvenile supervision views a young offender as a developing person, as one who has not yet achieved a firm commitment to a particular set of values, goals, behavior patterns, or lifestyle. As such, juvenile justice supervision is in the hopeful position of influencing that development and thereby reducing criminal behavior."[60]

Standards and Goals

As in all corrections agencies (such as jails, prisons, and parole), standards have been set by the American Correctional Association and other organizations for juvenile probation and aftercare. None of these standards, however, has been enacted into law by any state or imposed upon any juvenile probation department by court order. Therefore, they aim merely to persuade and remain as ideals to aspire for. The *Desktop Guide* notes that the reason for nonadoption is that "there are no universally accepted probation standards because there is more than one way to provide probation services that observe the legal rights of minors and meet the needs for rehabilitation and safety."[61] Differences pervade in the treatment of juveniles.

The *Desktop Guide* recommends that probation departments "consider the converging interests of the juvenile offender, the victim, and the community at large in developing individualized case plans for probation supervision."[62] To reconcile conflicting goals (such as rehabilitation versus punishment, treatment versus control, and public safety versus youth development), the same publication states that probation "must endeavor to not only protect the public and hold the juvenile offender accountable, it must also attempt to meet his needs."[63] Thus the ideal form of juvenile probation supervision aims more at rehabilitation than merely meting out punishment. Standards proposed by several organizations recommend that before a juvenile is placed on probation, a needs assessment should be conducted and a service plan developed.[64] These standards further suggest that the probation officer, in conjunction with the juvenile and family, assess needs in the following areas: medical problems, proximity of the program to the youth, the capacity of the youth to benefit from the program, and the availability of placements.[65] In addition, the standards place strong emphasis on the "availability of supplemental services to facilitate the youth's participation in a community-based program."

Intensive Probation

Intensive probation is a type of supervision used in both juvenile and adult probation. It is defined as a program of intensive surveillance of and contact with an offender and aimed at reducing criminal conduct by limiting opportunities to engage in it. Intensive supervision strategies vary from state to state, but one scholar identifies the following common features in intensive supervision for juveniles:[66]

1. A greater reliance is placed on unannounced spot checks. These may occur in a variety of settings including home, school, known hangouts, and job sites.
2. Considerable attention is directed at increasing the number and kinds of collateral contacts made by staff, including family members, friends, staff from other agencies, and concerned residents in the community.
3. Greater use is made of curfew, including both more rigid enforcement and lowering the hour at which curfew goes into effect.
4. Surveillance is expanded to ensure 7-day-a-week, 24-hour-a-day coverage.

Contrary to popular belief, intensive probation is usually not designed to deal with violent juvenile offenders. The majority of juveniles placed on intensive supervision are "serious and/or chronic offenders who would otherwise be committed to a correctional facility but who, through an objective system of diagnosis and classification, have been identified as amenable to community placement."[67]

Fare v. Michael C.—An Important Case in Juvenile Probation Supervision

The only case ever to be decided by the U.S. Supreme Court on juvenile probation supervision is *Fare v. Michael C.* (1979).[68] This important California case helps define the relationship between a probation officer and a probationer during probation supervision.

Michael C., a juvenile, was taken into police custody because he was suspected of having committed a murder. He was advised of his *Miranda v. Arizona* rights (anything he said could be used against him, and he could have a lawyer). When asked if he wanted to waive his right to have an attorney present during questioning, he responded by asking for his probation officer. He was informed by the police that the probation officer would be contacted later, but that he could talk to the police if he wanted.

Michael C. agreed to talk and during questioning made statements and drew sketches that incriminated himself. When charged with murder in juvenile court, Michael C. moved to suppress the incriminating evidence, alleging it was obtained in violation of his *Miranda* rights. He said that his request to see his probation officer was, in effect, equivalent to asking for a lawyer. However, the evidence was admitted at trial, and Michael C. was convicted.

On appeal the U.S. Supreme Court affirmed the conviction, holding that the request by a juvenile probationer during police questioning to see his or her probation officer, after having received the *Miranda* warnings, is not equivalent to asking for a lawyer and is not considered an assertion of the right to remain silent. Evidence voluntarily given by the juvenile probationer after asking to see his probation officer is therefore admissible in court in a subsequent criminal trial.

The *Michael C.* case is significant because the Supreme Court laid out two principles that help define the supervisory role of a juvenile probation officer. First, the Court stated that communications of the accused with the probation officer are not shielded by the lawyer-client privilege. This means that information given by a probationer to the probation officer may be disclosed in court, unlike the information given to a lawyer by a client—which cannot be revealed to anyone unless the right to confidentiality is waived by both the client and the lawyer. Said the Court:

> A probation officer is not in the same posture [as a lawyer] with regard to either the accused or the system of justice as a whole. Often he is not trained in the law, and so is not in a position to advise the accused as to his legal rights. Neither is he a trained advocate, skilled in the representation of the interests of his client before police and courts. He does not assume the power to act on behalf of his client by virtue of his sta-

tus as advisor, nor are the communications of the accused to the probation officer shielded by the lawyer-client privilege.

Fare v. Michael C. shows that despite *parens patriae*—a doctrine based on a parent-child relationship—confidentiality of communication between the probation officer and a probationer does not exist. Confidentiality of juvenile records exists in most jurisdictions, but it stems from state law or agency policy prohibiting disclosure.

Second, the Court made it clear in *Fare v. Michael C.* that a probation officer's loyalty and obligation is to the state, despite any obligation owed to the probationer. The Court said,

> Moreover, the probation officer is the employee of the State which seeks to prosecute the alleged offender. He is a peace officer, and as such is allied, to a greater or lesser extent, with his fellow peace officers. He owes an obligation to the State notwithstanding the obligation he may also owe the juvenile under his supervision. In most cases, the probation officer is duty bound to report wrongdoing by the juvenile when it comes to his attention, even if by communication from the juvenile himself.

This statement defines where a probation officer's loyalty lies. Professionalism requires that the officer's loyalty be with the state and not with the probationer.

REVOCATION

Violation of probation conditions leads to revocation. As in adult probation, revocation for conditions violation is largely discretionary with the juvenile court. The only exception is if revocation is mandated by law for certain serious violations, which seldom happens.

Initiation of Revocation

Revocation of juvenile probation is usually initiated by the juvenile probation officer or the agency. In many jurisdictions the motion to revoke is filed in court by the prosecutor. A warrant is then issued for the juvenile's arrest. In most states the warrant is served by law enforcement officers. Some states, however, authorize juvenile probation officers to make an arrest and conduct searches and seizures. Once arrested, the juvenile is held in custody in a juvenile facility pending a revocation hearing.

Few Rights during Revocation

Unlike adult revocation cases, in which the rights during revocation proceedings are clearly laid out in the case of *Gagnon v. Scarpelli* (1973), the U.S. Supreme Court has not specified the rights to which juveniles are entitled during revocation.[69] Not many lower courts have addressed this issue, but a Michigan appellate court has decided that the juvenile revocation hearing "requires only that a certain procedural format be followed. . . . [T]he hearing is conducted only to determine whether the probation has been violated; the hearing does not result in a conviction of the underlying crime." The Michigan appellate court then held that "only a dispositional hearing was required before revoking appellant's probation; furthermore, we find that such a procedure is not violative of appellant's due process rights."

Despite the absence of constitutional rights guarantees during revocation, at least one state appeals court has reversed revocation that was based on the "unsworn testimony of the child's probation officer, where the juvenile was given no opportunity to review any written data, reports, or records from which the probation officer testified, and where no opportunity was given the juvenile to rebut the testimony" because "the juvenile was not given the essentials of due process and fair treatment."[70] Thus, although a juvenile may not be entitled to the same rights as adults during revocation, fair treatment is required.

No Standards for Revocation

The judge has considerable discretion to revoke or not to revoke juvenile probation. These decisions are usually final and not appealable, the rationale being that the judge knows what is best for the juvenile and therefore should not be second-guessed by an appellate court. The judge has various options ranging from keeping the juvenile on probation without any change of conditions whatsoever, to imposing more severe conditions or changing treatment, to revoking probation and sending the juvenile to an institution. Judges usually rely on the recommendations of the probation officer to determine the proper action to be taken. The *Desktop Guide* says that the probation officer's recommendation "should not, and need not, be all or nothing," urging instead that the officer "should recommend just what is needed to produce the juvenile's compliance with his probation and no more." The implication is that revocation should be used as a last resort and not as a first option. The *Desktop Guide* then adds that ordering the juvenile to perform community work or adding curfew restriction as a condition may suffice to convince the juvenile that the effects of violation are serious.[71] Restraint, not quick revocation, is recommended.

Result of Revocation

Revocation sends the probationer to an institution for juveniles. The effect of revocation is similar to a finding of juvenile delinquency in that the juvenile may now be given the same sanctions as a juvenile delinquent, which includes being deprived of freedom and confinement in a juvenile institution. Unlike adult probationers who must serve the jail or prison term originally imposed (subject to parole law), juveniles are kept in state institutions only until they reach the age of majority (adulthood). The release of a juvenile on aftercare prior to reaching the age of majority is usually determined by the juvenile authorities who run the state institution, not by the judge. In some cases, certain types of juveniles are kept beyond the age of majority by special laws that mandate harsher sanctions. However, most youth in state juvenile correctional custody are released to parole or aftercare.[72] In 1992, 69 percent of juveniles were released to parole or aftercare and therefore remained under the jurisdiction of the juvenile department. Only 15 percent were discharged without further supervision.[73]

SPECIAL PROGRAMS

Special programs are developed by juvenile probation departments to meet the needs of juveniles. They often include developing vocational skills, providing educational opportunities, and treating the mentally impaired. As is true of adult probation, juvenile programs vary between states and within a state—limited only by what local communities are willing to undertake. Variations are caused by funding levels and community receptiveness to a variety of treatment programs.

Schooner's is a public fast food restaurant that is solely operated by staff and residents from Excell Center, a residential treatment program in California for at-risk boys, ages 11–17. The program is designed to train youths to seek and retain employment as one part of the overall program that includes school and counseling services.

Anonymous

Family Counseling

A state survey reveals that the most common program offered to juvenile probationers is family counseling.[74] This type of counseling is important because juvenile delinquency is often traceable to bad parenting and a criminogenic home environment. Juvenile offenders disproportionately come from dysfunctional families where there is little awareness of the causes of delinquency. Consequently, family members might expect the courts to provide a panacea and "fix" the child, not realizing that family relationships and conditions are at the root of the problem. Often no amount of judicial threat or homily can make a difference; only total family commitment can. To encourage this, states authorize juvenile courts to require the family to undergo counseling and require other family members to participate in the rehabilitation process. This approach reflects the growing realization that rehabilitation efforts are doomed unless the family environment is changed.

Curfew

Curfews are used in many jurisdictions to control the problem of juvenile crime. A California-based policy institute study concludes that, although popular, "youth curfews do nothing to reduce juvenile crime and may even lead to worse relationships between minors and law-enforcement officers," and it labels curfews as "just another dead end."[75] The study by this private group further concludes that curfew arrest rates throughout California from 1978 to 1996 show that "there was no category of crime which declined significantly as a result of curfews." The results of this study have been challenged, but it proves that a program that is intuitively perceived by the public to be effective might fail to produce desired results.

Punishing Parents for What Their Children Do

Parental responsibility laws impose sanctions on parents for what their children do. In 1997, at least 37 states had such laws, with 17 states holding parents criminally liable for offenses committed by their children.[76] Some local governments have also passed ordinances imposing punishment on parents of erring children, particularly those who do not attend school. The assumption behind these laws is that children become wayward or delinquent because of poor parenting and that parents become responsible if faced with possible sanction for negligence. Punishments range from fines and probation to incarceration. As one report says: "Parents across the country have spent a night or two in jail for failing to get their children to school. Some have had to pay the costs of their children's detentions. And in states such as Louisiana and California, parents can wind up in jail if their children associate with gangs or drug dealers."[77] In the words of one former juvenile court judge: "I've got a jaded attitude towards some parents. I saw a lot of kids go down the toilet all because in most cases, the parents did not put forth enough effort. Those are the parents you'd love to throw in jail."[78]

Punishing parents, however, is a controversial solution to juvenile waywardness and its effectiveness has yet to be established. It can be unfair to parents who, despite their efforts, somehow cannot control their children. Its constitutionality is also doubtful. How far the government can go to punish parents for what their children do has not been authoritatively addressed by the courts. Requiring parents to pay fines, court costs, and restitution is often held valid, but criminal penalties for parents are likely to run afoul of the due process clause as being fundamentally unfair, particularly if the criminal penalty is severe.

Juvenile Boot Camps

One scholar characterizes boot camps as "facilities that emphasize military drill, physical training, and hard labor."[79] **Boot camps** are hard to define with precision because structure and goals vary from one jurisdiction to another. One publication, however, identifies the following characteristics of boot camps:[80]

- Participation by nonviolent offenders only (to free up space in traditional facilities for violent felony offenders, meaning those who have used dangerous weapons against another person, caused death or serious bodily injury, or committed serious sex offenses)
- A residential phase of 6 months or less
- A regimented schedule stressing discipline, physical training, and work
- Participation by inmates in appropriate education opportunities, job training, and substance abuse counseling or treatment
- Provision of aftercare services that are coordinated with the program provided during the period of confinement

In 1999, there were 52 boot camps housing 4,500 juveniles across the country.[81] Boot camps strike a responsive cord with the public and are popular because they are perceived to be more effective and less expensive than incarceration. Their effectiveness as a rehabilitative tool, however, is debatable. A 1999 Koch Crime Institute study revealed that the recidivism rates for juveniles from boot camps ranged from 64 percent to 75 percent; from detention, from 63 to 71 percent.[82] Moreover, boot camps have become controversial because of reported abuses that have taken place. One critic summarizes the controversy as follows: "The boot camp is a model that lends itself to abuses. . . . There is no evidence that the camps do any good."[83] Despite critics, however, boot camps continue to thrive and appear to enjoy public support.

SOME CHALLENGES TO JUVENILE PROBATION

The face of juvenile probation has changed over the years. *Parens patriae* is still alive, but its focus has changed and the philosophical foundation for community corrections is being reexamined. These changes will continue in forthcoming years, driven by the ebb and flow of public opinion and the judicial desire to achieve due process and equal protection in juvenile justice.

More Dangerous Caseloads

The Office of Juvenile Justice and Delinquency Prevention identifies two basic challenges facing juvenile probation. The first is increasing and more dangerous caseloads, and the second is a changing philosophical approach to dealing with juveniles.[84] Because more juveniles have been brought into the system, probation caseloads have increased and the type of juveniles under probation has changed. Juveniles who would otherwise have been sent to institutions are now being placed on probation because of space limitations. As a result, officer on-the-job safety has become a problem. The same publication states that almost one-third of the respondents in a survey reported that "they had been assaulted on the job at some point in their careers." Asked whether they were ever concerned about their personal safety while performing their duties, "42 percent of the respondents reported that they were usually or always concerned."[85] Thus, says the publication, balancing juvenile probation officers' safety and the safety of the public with probationers' needs is a major challenge.

One response to the problem has been to allow juvenile probation officers to carry firearms. While this may reassure some officers, others argue that carrying firearms changes the focus of juvenile probation from rehabilitation to surveillance. That in turn may attract probation officers who are police-oriented instead of rehabilitation-oriented. Moreover, probation departments may not want to deal with legal liability issues that arise from allowing officers to carry firearms. To minimize legal liability, an officer should be allowed to carry firearms only if that officer is trained like police officers and required to enroll in continuing education programs. This is more than many juvenile departments want to do or can afford.

The Need for a New Paradigm

The second challenge identified by the Office of Juvenile Justice and Delinquency Prevention is whether juvenile probation should adopt a new paradigm (meaning a new way of looking at juvenile justice). This new paradigm suggests a way of looking at juvenile justice that goes beyond the traditional approaches of just deserts and treatment. The more current buzz phrases in the juvenile justice vocabulary are *balanced approach* and *restorative justice.* The balanced approach "espouses the potential value of any case applying, to some degree, an entire set of principles along with individualized assessment." These are the principles of community protection, accountability, competence development, and treatment. Restorative justice "promotes maximum involvement of the victim, offender, and the community in the justice process." A combination of these two concepts results in the new **balanced and restorative justice model,** which suggests that "justice is best served when the community, victim, and youth received balanced attention, and all gain tangible benefits from their interactions with the juvenile justice system."[86] The Office of Juvenile Justice and Delinquency Prevention illustrates this new paradigm this way: "Programs that require young offenders to engage in meaningful, productive work and service in their communities (competency development) during free time under structured adult supervision (community protection) can also provide a source of funding for repayment of victims as well as opportunities for community service (accountability)."[87]

This new balanced and restorative justice model suggests an innovative approach at a time when the public is grasping for solutions that combine the elements of retribution, rehabilitation, and fairness. Whether this new approach will work or not remains to be seen. Like other concepts that have come and gone, the balanced and restorative model is easier proposed than implemented. It is much easier to articulate than to translate into an effective working reality (see Chapter 1 and Figure 14.6).

Systemic Racial and Ethnic Discrimination

A third major challenge is racial and ethnic discrimination. As one report says: "While 'Equal Justice Under Law' is the foundation of our legal system, and is carved on the front of the U.S. Supreme Court, the juvenile justice system is anything but equal."[88] A recent OJJDP study finds that "blacks are overrepresented at all stages of the juvenile justice system, compared with their proportion in the population."[89] The administrator's message that precedes the report summarizes the findings as follows:

> The most recent statistics available reveal significant racial and ethnic disparity in the confinement of juvenile offenders. In 1997, minorities made up about one-third of the juvenile population nationwide but accounted for nearly two-thirds of the detained and committed population in secure juvenile facilities. For black juveniles, the disparities were most evident. While black juveniles ages 10–17 made up about 15% of the juvenile population, they accounted for 26% of juveniles arrested and 45% of delinquency cases involving detention. About one-third of adjudicated cases involved black youth, yet 40% of juveniles in secure residential placements were black.[90]

The report does not discuss the more complex problem of identifying causes for the disparity. It concludes, however, with this observation that hints at a possible solution: "Disproportionate minority confinement sends a signal that we need to take a closer look at how our society treats minority children, not just those who become offenders. Providing all youth with equal opportunity to learn, thrive, and achieve at every stage of their lives is the best guarantee of a safe and prosperous future for our Nation."

Youth Gangs

Gangs are a national problem and a challenge to juvenile probation. Although gangs may include adults, their members are usually teens and juveniles. In a 1995 nationwide survey by the Office of Juvenile Justice and Delinquency Prevention, "2007 law enforcement agencies reported gang activity in their jurisdictions, a total of 23,388

FIGURE 14.6 *Retributive and Restorative Assumptions*

Retributive Justice	Restorative Justice
Crime is an act against the State, a violation of a law, an abstract idea.	Crime is an act against another person or the community.
The criminal justice system controls crime.	Crime control lies primarily in the community.
Offender accountability defined as taking punishment.	Accountability defined as assuming responsibility and taking action to repair harm.
Crime is an individual act with individual responsibility.	Crime has both individual and social dimensions of responsibility.
Punishment is effective. a. Threat of punishment deters crime. b. Punishment changes behavior.	Punishment alone is not effective in changing behavior and is disruptive to community harmony and good relationships.
Victims are peripheral to the process.	Victims are central to the process of resolving a crime.
The offender is defined by deficits.	The offender is defined by capacity to make reparation.
Focus on establishing blame, on guilt, on past (did he/she do it?).	Focus on problem solving, on liabilities/obligations, on future (what should be done?).
Emphasis on adversarial relationship.	Emphasis on dialog and negotiation.
Imposition of pain to punish and deter/prevent.	Restitution as a means of restoring both parties; goal of reconciliation/restoration.
Community on sideline, represented abstractly by State.	Community as facilitator in restorative process.
Response focused on offender's past behavior.	Response focused on harmful consequences of offender's behavior; emphasis on the future.
Dependence upon proxy professionals.	Direct involvement by participants.

Source: Adapted from Zehr (1990) as featured in *Balanced and Restorative Justice Program Summary* (Washington, DC: National Center for Juvenile Justice, Office of Juvenile Justice and Delinquency Prevention), 7.

gangs, and 664,906 gang members." Moreover, 49 percent of the agencies surveyed described their gang activity as getting worse.[91] They are of immediate concern in juvenile justice and law enforcement. The national response to the gang problem has been intense, but hardly any consensus has been reached on what approaches work. Various federal and state agencies have funded projects that seek to remedy the gang problem, but agreement on an effective solution is lacking. The Office of Juvenile Justice and Delinquency Prevention, which funds several projects relating to the gang problem, states that several common elements appear to be associated with programs aimed at sustained reduction of the gang problem. In summary, these elements are:[92]

- Community leaders must recognize the presence of gangs and seek to understand the nature and extent of the local gang problem through a comprehensive and systematic assessment of the gang problem.
- The combined leadership of the justice system and the community must focus on the mobilization of institutional and community resources to address gang problems.
- Those in principal roles must develop a consensus on definitions (for example, for *gang, gang incident*); specific targets of agency and interagency efforts; and interrelated strategies based on problem assessment, not assumptions.

- Any approach must be guided by concern not only for safeguarding the community against youth gang activities but also for providing support and supervision to present and potential gang member in a way that contributes to their prosocial development.

Many of these elements have been adopted by probation departments across the country as their response to the prevalent gang problem. As best as can be determined, however, no concerted national approach has been taken by probation or aftercare agencies, perhaps because no single approach works every time. Probation is burdened by the gang problem in that it makes supervision more difficult and revocation more likely. Gang members are inevitably prohibited by probation conditions from associating with former friends or engaging in gang-related activities. This is often said than done, however, and has led to more intense collaboration between probation officers and the police. This collaboration, in turn, raises a host of legal issues: Can the requirements of probable cause and a warrant be bypassed when the police work with juvenile probation officers? Is entry by the police into a house always valid if accompanied by a probation officer? Is evidence obtained by the police when accompanying a probation officer admissible as evidence in a revocation hearing and in a criminal trial? Do probation officers have to give the *Miranda* warnings when questioning a suspect in the presence of the police? These issues have yet to be clearly resolved by the courts.

A JUVENILE JUSTICE SYSTEM FOR THE 21ST CENTURY

Juvenile justice courts have just celebrated their century of existence. Over the years much has changed with juvenile justice, perhaps the most notable being the erosion of pure *parens patriae* in favor a model that is partly due process-oriented. This means that juveniles now enjoy more rights in the process, but certain rights are still denied them.

The public's mood toward juveniles is like a pendulum that swings from treatment to retribution. The public mood in the last decade or so has moved toward retribution. That mood will likely last for a while before the pendulum swings back again. At the end of the 20th century, the National Center for Juvenile Justice identified five themes and trends in state laws targeting violent and other serious crimes committed by juveniles.[93]

1. Diminution of jurisdictional authority of juvenile courts. More serious and violent juvenile offenders are being removed from the juvenile justice system in favor of criminal court prosecution.
2. Expansion of judicial disposition and sentencing authority. More state legislatures are experimenting with new disposition and sentencing options.
3. New correctional programming. Correctional administrators are under pressure to develop programs as a result of new transfer and sentencing laws.
4. Less confidentiality of juvenile court records and proceedings. Traditional confidentiality provisions are being revised in favor of more open proceedings and records.
5. Participation of victims of juvenile crime. Victims of juvenile crime are being included as active participants in the juvenile justice process.

As the 21st century begins, the juvenile justice system faces even more challenges. In a monograph entitled *A Juvenile Justice System for the 21st Century,* the Office of Juvenile Justice and Delinquency Prevention concludes that "an effective juvenile justice system must meet three objectives: (1) hold the juvenile offender accountable; (2) enable the juvenile to become a capable, productive, and responsible citizen; and (3) ensure the safety of the community."[94] The monograph adds that "these objectives are best met when a community's key leaders, including representatives from the juvenile justice system, health and mental health systems, schools, law enforcement, social services, and other systems, are jointly engaged in the planning, development, and operation of the juvenile justice system." It then asserts: "OJJDP's intensive review of juvenile justice programs that work, coupled with the findings of 30 years of studies by premier researchers . . . points the way towards understanding the crucial elements for success in State juvenile justice systems." The monograph's author concludes that "a carefully conceived, properly implemented, and adequately funded juvenile justice system in the 21st century can be expected to bring about the following: (1) Increased juvenile justice system responsiveness; (2) increased accountability; (3) increased community involvement; (4) decreased costs of juvenile corrections; and (5) increased program effectiveness."

Most scholars and field practitioners would likely agree that "the most effective long-term response to the problem of juvenile delinquency and violence lies in improving the juvenile justice system and working to prevent delinquency before it occurs."[95] These are twin goals that must be addressed but primarily by different sectors. Improving the juvenile justice system calls for strong government leadership and involvement. Preventing delinquency primarily begins at home with good parenting. Achieving these goals is easier said than done in a democratic society that values privacy and rejects excessive governmental intrusion into family life.

SUMMARY

Juvenile justice has its roots in the concepts of *mens rea* and *parens patriae. Mens rea* denotes that only actors with guilty minds should be punished; *parens patriae* holds that the state acts as a wise parent to the child and therefore juveniles should be treated like a member of the family. Differences exist between the way the criminal justice system processes juveniles and adults, but those differences are perhaps more symbolic than substantive.

Juvenile courts are an American creation and were founded on the belief that rehabilitation, concern, and care should be at the core of juvenile proceedings. Later, however, due process guarantees were infused into these proceedings through a series of court decisions, the most notable of which is *In re Gault.* Two types of juvenile acts trigger judicial intervention: juvenile delinquency and conduct in need of supervision. Juvenile delinquents are minors who commit acts punishable by the state's criminal laws. Conduct in need of supervision usually consists of status offenses, meaning acts that would not be punishable if committed by adults. Juvenile adjudication can result in probation. Crucial actors in juvenile probation are probation officers, who act as extensions of judicial authority and who are usually appointed and terminated by the judge. Informal probation and intensive probation are used in many juvenile jurisdictions to divert and control juveniles.

If a juvenile violates the conditions of probation, revocation ensues. Revocation is discretionary with the judge and is recommended as a last resort. Juvenile probation features many special programs, among them family counseling, boot camps, and programs designed to provide education and vocational skills. Although widely used, none of these programs has proved to be a silver bullet for the problem of juvenile crime.

Juvenile justice, in general, and juvenile probation, in particular, are beset with problems. Among them are more dangerous caseloads, a changing philosophy, fragmentation, and systemic discrimination. To be effective, the juvenile justice system for the 21st century must hold the offender accountable, enable the offender to become a capable and responsible citizen, and ensure the safety of the community. Improving the juvenile justice system and preventing delinquency are long-range solutions to the juvenile problem, but they are easier identified than accomplished.

DISCUSSION QUESTIONS

1. What is the concept of *mens rea* and how does it affect the way society deals with juveniles?
2. What is *parens patriae* and what is its implication for juvenile justice?
3. Give five distinctions between adult proceedings and juvenile proceedings.
4. What are teen courts? Are they a good idea? Justify your answer.
5. Jurisdiction of juvenile courts is based on two prongs. What are they? Discuss each.
6. Transfer of jurisdiction from juvenile court to adult court may be classified into three categories. What are those categories? Explain how one differs from the other. Are you in favor of or against transfers of jurisdiction? Justify your response.
7. Outline the juvenile justice process, identifying the major procedures from the time the juvenile is taken into custody up to release from the juvenile justice system.
8. *In re Gault* is the most important case ever to be decided by the U.S. Supreme Court in juvenile justice. What did that case say and why is it important?
9. "Juveniles now have the same constitutional rights as adults." Is that statement true or false? Support your answer.
10. There are differences in the structure and administration of juvenile probation and aftercare. Discuss those variations.
11. What did the U.S. Supreme Court say in the case of *Fare v. Michael C.*? Why is that case important for juvenile probation officers?
12. Assume that the state of Illinois passes a law stating that parents, after trial wherein they are found guilty, are to pay a fine not to exceed $500 and face incarceration not to exceed six months, if their children are found delinquent by the court. Is that law constitutional? Aside from the issue of constitutionality, are you in favor of or against that law? Support your answer.
13. Identify three challenges to juvenile probation and discuss each.
14. What are the features of the balanced and restorative justice model? Do you think it will work? Justify your answer.
15. Assume you have all the power in the world to be able to establish an "ideal juvenile justice system" for the 21st century. Identify four main features of your system and state why it is better than the existing one.

WEB SITES

American Bar Association Juvenile Justice Center

http://www.abanet.org/crimjust/juvjus/home.html

Juvenile Justice Clearinghouse

http://www.fsu.edu/~crimdo/jjclearinghouse

National Council on Crime and Delinquency

http://www.nccd.com

Texas Youth Commission

http://www.tyc.state.tx.us/catalog.html

A Bibliography of Gangs

http://www-lib.usc.edu/~anthonya/gang.htm

National Youth Gang Center

http://www.iir.com/nygc

Federal Gang Violence Act

http://www.senate.gov/member/ca/feinstein/general/gangs.html

CHAPTER 14

CASE STUDY EXERCISE

Sentencing in the Juvenile Justice System

In each case below, you are the judge or probation officer. What would you do? Justify your decision.

Case A: The subject, Brian Andrews, is a 13-year-old male who has come to the attention of the court for the offense of vandalism. He and a friend "tagged" a school building with graffiti and broke several windows in the school gymnasium. The school principal estimated the total damage and cleanup costs to be approximately $1,300. Brian resides with both natural parents and two younger siblings. The family income is $65,000 annually. Brian admits the offense but refuses to identify his co-offender to authorities. The family has agreed to pay complete restitution. Brian has no prior juvenile record, although he has been disciplined several times in school in the past year for minor violations of school rules. His grades, which were formally A's and B's, have fallen off to C's and D's.

Case B: Quint is a 17-year-old male who has been referred to the Court for aggravated robbery. Quint is accused of robbing a convenience store and assaulting the clerk. Quint is a high school dropout with a lengthy history of arrests including robbery, burglary, car theft, and larceny. He was adjudicated delinquent for burglary ten months before the current offense and placed on probation. His probation officer reports that he has been uncooperative and hostile toward supervision. He lives off and on with his mother and three younger siblings. His mother reports that she has little control over his behavior and that he spends many nights away from home. She suspects that he is using drugs.

Case C: Carlos is a 15-year-old male who was referred to the court for truancy. Carlos has missed 34 school days in the past 90 days. He is failing in all his classes. His parents report that they send him to school every day but he never stays. Even when they take him to the front door of the school, he leaves immediately after they do. Carlos is of average intelligence and relates well to his peers. He has no other involvement with illegal activity and, until this past school year, did well in school and attended regularly. His parents have no explanation for the change in his behavior.

Case D: Cathy is a 14-year-old female who has been referred to the court for runaway. Cathy's parents report that she is a chronic runaway, having left home on more than ten occasions since age 12. She is in the seventh grade. She had been "left back" twice and is thus two grade levels behind her peers. Cathy was diagnosed with attention deficit disorder at age seven. She is currently taking Ritalin under a physician's supervision. The parents have attempted to get help for Cathy on many occasions, but nothing seems to be effective. Cathy is sexually active and was treated last year for a sexually transmitted disease. She has been referred once for shoplifting, three times for truancy, and three times previously for runaway.

15

Direct and Collateral Consequences of Conviction

Have you been convicted of a crime in the past ten years other than mis-demeanors and summary offenses?

Yes ☐   No ☐

If yes, explain circumstances and disposition of matter below.

What You Will Learn in This Chapter

Conviction brings both direct and collateral consequences. Direct consequences include fines, probation, imprisonment, and other sanctions. Collateral consequences include disabilities that are not directly imposed by the court but attach to the individual from the fact of the conviction. Examples of collateral consequences are the loss of the right to vote, loss of citizenship, loss of the ability to hold certain jobs, and loss of the right to own a firearm. In this chapter you will learn about these collateral consequences of conviction.

INTRODUCTION

The distinction between the direct and collateral consequences of conviction deserves consideration. Conviction is usually followed by the imposition of both criminal penalties and civil disabilities. What usually comes to mind is only the direct sanctions—a fine, commitment to a penal or correctional institution, commitment to an institution or program for specialized treatment, probation, or some combination of these—but the imposed sanctions also include collateral consequences.

Collateral consequences are disabilities that accompany convictions that are not directly imposed by the sentencing authority. They stem from the fact of conviction and are imposed by operation of law, the decisions of licensing or other administrative bodies, and private individuals, such as when an employer refuses to hire an ex-convict. Most such adverse decisions of licensing bodies and private individuals result from the perception that a convicted offender lacks "good moral character." Because benefits under licensing laws are customarily restricted to persons of good moral character, this is one of the most damaging effects of conviction.

Collateral consequences also include certain incidental criminal and quasi-criminal sanctions that may follow a conviction. Examples of these restrictions include but are not limited to

- Voting
- Sitting on a jury
- Firearm possession or ownership
- Holding a public office
- Parental rights
- Grounds for divorce
- Dishonorable discharge from the armed forces
- Registration with local law enforcement
- Revocation of occupational licenses
- Loss of pension rights
- Loss of benefits under some insurance policies
- Impeachment as a witness
- Preclusion from being bonded
- Prohibition from serving as a notary public

Although collateral consequences are normally considered as the loss of civil rights or the imposition of civil disabilities, they may involve effects that have a crim-

COLLATERAL CONSEQUENCES

Disabilities that follow a conviction that are not directly imposed by a sentencing court—such as loss of the right to vote, serve on a jury, practice certain occupations, or own a firearm.

inal nature or that are closely related to the criminal realm. Law professor Richard Singer has observed that "for many criminals—particularly for the 50 percent of convicted persons who are never imprisoned—[these consequences] are anything but collateral; they are, in fact, the most persistent punishments that are inflicted for crime."[1] Moreover, the number of convicted persons suffering from collateral consequences is substantial. Based on 1987 estimates, 14 million people were affected by collateral consequences.[2] The current number is estimated to be more than 20 million people.

The overall effects of a conviction on an offender—direct and collateral consequences—are the criminal and civil disabilities or penalties that the person suffers. This "real" sentence results from

- Fixed legislative penalties
- The sentence imposed by the sentencing authority
- The operation of good-time statutes
- Suspended sentence and probation and parole laws
- The disabilities that result from decisions of licensing bodies
- The actions of private individuals, including the disabilities that result from loss of good moral character

Civil and Political Rights Defined

A **civil right** is a right that belongs to a person by virtue of citizenship. **Political rights** relate to the establishment, support, or management of government. Civil rights usually include political rights, but sometimes the two kinds of rights are distinguished. For example, a resident alien may not exercise political rights, such as the right to vote or to hold political office, but has full enjoyment of civil rights.

In common usage, and in some statutes, the word *citizenship* is sometimes used to mean "civil rights." It is sometimes stated that conviction deprives the offender of citizenship, or that a pardon restores the convicted person to citizenship. This is an unfortunate use of words, for a conviction does not deprive a natural-born citizen of citizenship. A convicted illegal immigrant, however, may face deportation or some adverse-related immigration restriction.[3]

In the 1958 case *Trop v. Dulles*, the accused, convicted of desertion in time of war, was deprived of his United States citizenship. The Supreme Court declared that to deprive a man of his citizenship and thus condemn him to "statelessness" is "a penalty more cruel and punitive than torture, for it involves a total destruction of the individual's status in organized society."[4] In a later case, a statute that attempted to remove citizenship from persons who leave the United States to avoid the draft was likewise declared unconstitutional.[5]

Although a person cannot be deprived of citizenship as a result of conviction, that person can and does lose civil and political rights and suffers from certain civil disabilities. The civil penalties and disabilities are seldom mentioned in a court's sentence, but the offender experiences them as a collateral consequence of conviction.

History of Civil Disabilities

Civil disabilities as a consequence of crime have been traced back to ancient Greece.[6] The Greeks called the disability *infamy*, a word that found its way into Anglo-American criminal law in the term *infamous crimes*. Infamous crimes carried severe penalties as well as the additional sanctions of outlawry and attainder. **Outlawry** deemed a person outside the protection and aid of the law. In effect it established a

CIVIL RIGHTS

Rights that belong to a person by virtue of citizenship.

POLITICAL RIGHTS

Rights related to the establishment, support, or management of government.

OUTLAWRY

In old Anglo-Saxon law, the process by which a criminal was declared an outlaw and placed outside the protection and aid of the law.

kind of open season on the offender, who could be hunted down and killed by any citizen. This person, who was "attaint," lost all civil rights and forfeited all property to the Crown through **attainder.** The individual's entire family was declared corrupt, which made them unworthy to inherit his or her property. The theory behind both outlawry and attainder was that because the offender had declared war on the community by committing an infamous crime, the community had the right to retaliation and retribution against the offender.

The Constitution of the United States forbids "bills of attainder," and similar provisions against attainder or its effects are found in the constitutions and statutes of various states.[7] Although the outlaw was a familiar figure in pioneer society, particularly in the West, outlawry as a form of punishment was expressly forbidden.

CIVIL DISABILITIES TODAY

In spite of constitutional and statutory provisions against outlawry and certain aspects of attainder, every state has enacted civil disability laws that affect the convicted offender. Many disabilities are imposed by state law, instead of by federal law, even for federal convictions. There are many state-by-state differences in the way civil rights are removed and restricted.

Issues of Variance in Rights Lost

The loss of rights and the civil disabilities that result from such laws vary from state to state and crime to crime.[8] They range from statutes that deprive the criminal of all or almost all civil rights while he or she is serving a prison sentence.[9]

WHEN IS A PERSON CONVICTED?   Some rights are automatically lost upon conviction of specified felonies, and some may be imposed for certain misdemeanors. This brings up the following issue: At what point is a person considered convicted? Is it when entering a guilty plea, or during sentencing? What if appeals are pending? What if a person does not plead guilty, but (in states that allow it) enters a plea of nolo contendre (no contest), which technically requires no admission of guilt? There is no easy answer, because the point at which a person is considered convicted varies from state to state.[10]

WHAT IF AN OFFENDER RELOCATES?   In some cases conviction results in the loss of rights only within a particular state. In other cases the loss extends to other states, even when the offender relocates.[11] What happens, though, when the state that the offender was convicted in differs from the new state that the offender relocated to? Some states define a felony by an offense punishable by incarceration of one year or more, while other state legislatures designate a crime as a felony or a misdemeanor, without regard to amount of time. For example, Jeff was convicted of a misdemeanor theft and served the maximum sentence of 18 months in a county jail. The conviction state has deemed this theft a misdemeanor, but Jeff moved across the state line into a state that defines any criminal act over 12 months a felony. Does Jeff lose his civil rights?

MILITARY CRIMES: How are they treated? Another issue is in regard to military offenses. Because military crimes are not classified as either felonies or misdemeanors, and some military crimes do not constitute a crime under civilian law, do people convicted of a military crime lose all their rights as a civilian? Susan M. Kuzma, of the Office of the United States Pardon Attorney, discusses both the relocation issue and the resolution of military crimes by saying:

> Some states' laws permit resolution of such interpretational problems by providing that the disability applies only when the conduct would constitute a felony under the law of the state imposing the disability (the state of residence).[12]

OTHER DIFFERENCES: Other differences exist as well. For example, some rights can be lost according to judicial or administrative discretion, and private employers may deny some rights. According to some statutes, a conviction must be followed by incarceration for a specified period before rights are lost. In such cases the right is not lost if conviction is followed by probation or if the sentence to probation is not considered a conviction. Other statutes provide that conviction alone leads to forfeiture. Some rights are permanently lost and cannot be restored. Others are automatically restored upon completion of the sentence or may be restored by action of the executive or a court. To determine the status of a particular convicted offender's rights, one must examine the statutory provisions, judicial decisions, administrative rulings and practices, and actions of individuals in both the state of conviction and the state in which a particular right is sought to be enforced.[13]

Extent of Loss of Rights

The civil penalty may amount to a complete denial of a right, or it may merely impose restrictions and conditions upon its exercise. In some jurisdictions, for example, the right to vote and the right to hold public office are denied for life unless they are restored by pardon or special proceeding. However, a conviction (except a conviction for perjury) generally does not completely disqualify the offender from serving as a witness—the effect is to permit the proof of the conviction to be shown in impeachment of the individual's testimony. Statutes concerning marital status may automatically give the spouse grounds for divorce, or they may give the spouse grounds for divorce only if the conviction is accompanied by imprisonment for a specified length of time. Generally in the matter of civil disabilities, the particular right must be considered to determine the extent of the loss.

Loss of Rights during Probation Period

The rights of the probationer during the probation period are determined basically by whether the probationer has been convicted. If the probated offender is convicted, he or she loses those rights that any convicted person in that jurisdiction loses. However, special statutory provisions for expunging the conviction and restoring those rights may exist. If probation has been ordered before the imposition of sentence, application of the narrow definition of *conviction* in particular situations may protect the probationer from the loss of civil rights. In a state where the court may grant probation in either of two ways—by suspending imposition of sentence or by imposing a sentence and thereafter suspending its execution—some probationers lose their civil rights while others do not. Some states impose loss of rights only if the convicted person is imprisoned. In some states and the federal government, probation is a sentence in itself and is regarded as a conviction, no matter how stated.

Justification for Imposing Civil Disabilities

In her years of experience with the Office of the United States Pardon Attorney, Susan Kuzma offers the following insight:

> Laws imposing disabilities reflect a struggle between the competing interests of clarity and flexibility, punishment and rehabilitation, and protection of the community and reintegration of the offender into society. . . . [This] raises questions about the ability of an offender to comply with the laws, the ability of society to enforce those laws, and the impact of the laws on the goal of reintegrating the offender into a law-abiding society.[14]

Many deprivations during imprisonment can be justified in that they are appropriate to the punitive aims of imprisonment. For example, holding public office and serving as a juror are incompatible with the nature of imprisonment. In addition, certain deprivations are useful as independent sanctions for criminal behavior. For example, suspending or revoking a driver's license for a conviction involving driving while intoxicated or restricting firearm possession for a violent felon is appropriate. These restrictions are likely to be an effective deterrent, and they propose to protect society from the particular kind of danger that person poses. Few of the present laws regarding loss of civil rights upon conviction can be so justified. The laws have not been rationally designed to accommodate the varied interests of society and the individual convicted person.[15]

Such consideration prompted the American Bar Association to suggest in its *Standards Relating to Probation* that most civil rights be retained by the probationer. It stated: "Every jurisdiction should have a method by which the collateral effects of a criminal record can be avoided or mitigated following the successful completion of a term of probation and during its service."[16] At the very least, the statutes that authorize a sentence of probation should also address the problem of collateral disabilities and provide a method by which their effect can be individualized to the particular case.[17]

CIVIL AND POLITICAL RIGHTS AFFECTED BY CONVICTION

Many privileges and rights are restricted or removed following conviction of a crime. Eight of these restricted rights are:

1. The right to claim good moral character
2. The right to hold public office
3. The right to vote
4. The right to serve on a jury
5. The right to be a witness
6. Employment-related rights, such as the right to an occupational license, to public employment, to private sector employment, and to be bonded
7. The right to own a firearm
8. The registration and community notification of sex offenders

Loss of Good Character

GOOD MORAL CHARACTER

The totality of virtues that forms the basis of one's reputation in the community.

One of the most inclusive and damaging consequences of a conviction is the loss of **good moral character.** Because good character is not a civil or political right, loss of good character is not customarily included in a list of rights lost upon conviction. In

Under some state laws, ex-convicts are disqualified from voting. Former inmates like J. C. Townes, shown here, are attempting to have their voting rights reinstated.

practical effect, however, this loss constitutes the basis for statutes and practices that deny the offender licenses and other employment benefits. The loss is serious, because there is considerable doubt that pardon or other proceedings to expunge a conviction restore the person's good character.

The Right to Hold Public Office

The laws of the federal government and of many states and municipalities disqualify all convicted persons or persons convicted of certain crimes from holding public office. A public office has been defined as an "agency for the state, the duties of which involve in their performance the exercise of some portion of the sovereign power, great or small."[18]

State prohibitions take two forms:

1. Most states' statutes expressly bar persons convicted of felonies, infamous offenses, or specified offenses from holding public office.
2. Some states indirectly bar convicted felons from holding public office by requiring that a holder of public office be a qualified voter. Most states disqualify convicted felons as voters, which precludes them from holding public office.[19]

Federal statutes and the U.S. Constitution also contain provisions that exclude certain offenders from holding certain positions in the government of the United States. With the limited exception of Section 3 of the Fourteenth Amendment, the Constitution does not bar offenders from holding any position in the federal government.[20] Congress, however, may bar ex-felons from holding any nonconstitutional public office.[21] The U.S. pardon attorney notes that Congress has passed statutes that exclude persons convicted of specified offenses from holding any nonconstitutionally created federal office. These offenses include falsifying, destroying, or removing public records or documents; receiving compensation in matters affecting the government; rebellion; and treason.[22] Conviction for treason disqualifies the defendant from holding "any office under the United States."

Every state except Alaska and Vermont imposes restrictions on holding public office after a conviction. Some states permanently restrict the right to hold public office after a felony conviction unless the convicted person receives a pardon or is otherwise restored to full franchisement. Some states return the right to hold public office after discharge from probation, parole, or prison. A few states permit probationers to hold public office while still on probation.[23]

The thrust of the National Advisory Commission on Criminal Justice Standards and Goals would seem to prohibit holding public office only during a period of confinement and presumably would permit the holding of a public office during a period of probation that did not involve confinement.[24]

The Right to Vote

Although the right to vote is considered a fundamental right of citizenship, it is generally held that it can be denied to convicted felons. The provisions of constitutions and laws of 50 states and the District of Columbia that remove or limit (disenfranchise) the convicted offender's right to vote vary widely. Disenfranchisement may follow convictions of a felony, an infamous crime, a crime involving moral turpitude, and specified other offenses.[25]

The California Supreme Court, in 1973, declared that the provisions of the California constitution and statutes that deprived the convicted felon of the right to vote violated the equal protection clause of the U.S. Constitution.[26] The decision was overruled by the U.S. Supreme Court in the case of *Richardson v. Ramirez,* which held that a state may strip ex-felons who have fully paid their debt to society of their fundamental right to vote without running afoul of the Fourteenth Amendment.[27]

Nothing in *Richardson v. Ramirez* requires a state to deny the vote to the person on probation or parole or to the convicted felon, however. Thus some states disqualify persons only during a period of imprisonment, which may result in preserving the right of a person on probation to vote. Currently the right to vote is lost in all but four states (Maine, Massachusetts, Texas, and Vermont). Utah restricts the right to vote only for defendants convicted of election crimes or treason. A minority of states permanently denies convicted felons the right to vote unless they are pardoned. The other jurisdictions vary widely in their handling of convicted persons' voting rights. About half of the remaining jurisdictions deny the vote only while the felon is under correctional supervision (prison, probation, or parole).[28] Some states mandate that ex-felons wait for a period of time after the sentence is served—five years in Pennsylvania, for example.[29]

As of 1998, nearly 4 million convicted felons were permanently unable to vote. Out of this number, 1.4 million of them were African American men.[30] Recently, the right to vote issue has been revived, after a 1998 study by Human Rights Watch indicated that the voting voice of the black community is being increasingly silenced, because a disproportionate number of African American men go to prison.[31] Some states, such as Texas, have shown their sensitivity to the problem by restoring this right back to ex-felons who have completed their sentence. Texas House Bill 1001, passed in 2000, removed the two-year voting restriction.[32]

The Right to Serve on a Jury

The exclusion of convicted persons from jury service has its origin in common law. Most states have enacted the common law rule and exclude persons from jury duty if they have been convicted of felonies, infamous crimes, crimes involving moral turpitude, or certain specified crimes.[33] The right to serve on a jury is deprived in all but five states (Colorado, Illinois, Iowa, Maine, and New Hampshire). Some states permit felons to serve on juries after they have fully completed their sentences. Others suspend the right only until the offender is released from incarceration. In some others, the right may be restored by pardon.[34] The federal rule is that citizens are not competent to serve on a federal grand or petit (trial) jury if they have been convicted of a crime punishable by imprisonment for more than one year.[35] A statute that says only citizens having good character can serve on a jury also disqualifies the person with a criminal record. If the law requires that only persons who are qualified electors can serve on a jury, loss of the right to vote following a conviction carries with it loss of the right to serve on a jury.

The Right to Be a Witness

Common law disqualified as a witness any citizen convicted of treason, felony, or crimes involving fraud or deceit. This absolute disqualification extends today in a few states to persons convicted of perjury or subornation of perjury.[36] The usual situation, however, is that a person who has been convicted of a crime is permitted to testify, but the fact of the conviction may be shown to impeach (discredit) his or her testimony. The theory behind both absolute disqualification and impeachment is that a person who has been convicted of a crime cannot be trusted to give truthful testimony. Thus, the court and the jury are entitled to take the conviction into account. The witness can be asked if he or she has been convicted of a felony or other crime and must answer truthfully. Opposing counsel is then at liberty to argue that because the witness is a convicted offender the testimony should not be believed. This does not mean that the jury (or the court) will disbelieve the witness. The jury or the judge may decide that the convicted offender is telling the truth and give the individual's testimony the weight accorded to the testimony of any other witness.

The Supreme Court in *Davis v. Alaska* placed the constitutional right of confrontation by a defendant in a criminal case above any considerations that might protect the offender on probation against impeachment.[37] At issue in the case was whether an adjudication of delinquency could be shown against a prosecution witness, although the statutes of Alaska, like those of many states, provide that an adjudication of delinquency is not a conviction. The Court held that the right of the defendant to confront the witness and to inquire into all circumstances that might affect the witness's credibility was paramount over the statutory policy against permitting the use of an adjudication of delinquency for impeachment purposes.[38]

TABLE 15.1   *Occupations That Require a License in Many Jurisdictions*

Embalmer	Minnow dealer	Motor car dealer
Junk dealer	Fur dealer	Manufacturer of narcotics
Midwife	Sewage work operator	Seller of hearing aids
Liquor dealer	Florist	Operator of driver training
Taxicab operator	Photographer	school
Solicitor and canvasser	Seller of lightning rods	Hospital administrator
Vocational nurse	Weigh master	Threshing machine
Watchmaker	Fish and game guide	operator and dealer
Guide dog trainer	Surveyor	Tile layer
Tourist camp operator	Manicurist	Yacht salesperson
Inhalation therapist	Milk dealer	Tree surgeon
Dental hygienist	Operator of hotel, lodge,	Pest controller
Massage parlor operator	or home for the aged	Well digger
Water well contractor	Anthracite coal mine	Potato grower
Operator of a "public cart"	inspector	Hypertrichologist
Psychiatric technician	Mine foreman	(hair remover)
Trading stamp dealer	Police officer	Dealer in scrap tobacco
Night clerk	Oil and gas inspector	Landscape architect
Practical nurse	Forester	Billiard hall owner and
Seller of horse meat	Money lender	operator

Source: D. Rudenstine, *The Rights of Ex-Offenders* (New York: Avon, 1979).

The Right to an Occupational License

Federal, state, and local governments throughout the United States restrict entry into more than 350 occupations and professions through licensing requirements (see Table 15.1 for some of these occupations).[39] For example, the states of California and Florida require automobile mechanics to be licensed.

Some states do not allow employers to deny ex-convicts a job or occupational licensing unless the conviction is somehow related to the occupation. The restriction may not apply to all felons, but only to offenders convicted of certain types of offenses.

Restrictions can also vary by local licensing regulations. Disqualification may result from the express words in general statutes—as for example in the business or professional code—or from the licensing acts governing the particular trade or profession. A criminal record affects both the renewal and initial granting of a license, and power to revoke an existing license is granted to the licensing agency as well as to the courts. Even without express words, statutory or even administrative requirements that a license may be issued only to persons of good moral character effectively exclude the convicted person.[40]

The exact provisions of licensing statutes vary from state to state, from occupation to occupation, and even within occupations. The criminal record that disqualifies may be a felony, a misdemeanor, a felony with moral turpitude, a crime with moral turpitude, or an infamous crime. The conviction that disqualifies may be interpreted according to the narrow or the broad definition of *conviction*.

Unfortunately rehabilitation—whether evidenced by a pardon, successful completion of probation, certificate of good conduct, expungement proceedings, sealing of the record of conviction, or otherwise—does not effectively open the door to professional and occupational licenses. This is true not only in the imprisoning state, but it is also inevitable if the offender moves to a different state. The lack of uniformity in the laws and practices of the various states and localities makes it almost impossible for persons with criminal records to determine where they might be allowed to apply their training and skills, whether they acquired them in or out of prison. The ironic part of this situation is that ex-offenders are expected to remain out of prison and in legitimate jobs, but then they are limited in the kinds of jobs they can obtain and society wonders why offenders do not remain in stable employment.

THE REQUIREMENT OF GOOD CHARACTER: The most serious obstacle to the offender who seeks to enter a licensed occupation arises from the fact that many licensing statutes require that the licensee possess good character. It is almost universally assumed that a person who has been convicted of a criminal offense is not of good character. The obstacles created by the provisions and assumptions about good character are all the more serious because a convicted person has hardly any way to restore his or her good character. Although pardon and other forms of wiping out convictions may remove particular civil disabilities and, for example, permit the convicted person to vote or serve on a jury, such a pardon or expungement proceeding does not necessarily, or even by implication, restore good character.[41]

Most, if not all, professions require that the applicant for licensing prove good character. This requirement is usually statutory, but even when the provision is not expressed, courts have found that the licensing authority has the implied power to bar persons who are "morally unfit" from being licensed.[42] Conviction of a crime is generally held to be evidence that the offender lacks the requisite character for the professional license.[43] In some instances, however, the rule is that the fact of conviction is evidence only of loss of good character, and additional inquiry is made to determine if the offense involved **moral turpitude**—conduct that is offensive to society.

Because the public's moral standards vary with place and time, it is impossible to know which crimes involve moral turpitude. The terms *good moral character* and *good character* are also susceptible to changing meanings. Thus, as a practical matter, licenses are refused or revoked according to the meanings licensing agencies place on such terms. In general, however, a licensing agency regards a conviction as conclusive evidence of bad character, and the courts seldom overrule such decisions.[44]

The Right to Public Employment

The term *public employment* is often used interchangeably with the term *public office*, although certain technical distinctions can be made between the two. Elective positions in federal, state, and municipal governments as well as some appointive positions are generally regarded as **public offices.** A public office may not be compensated, as for example positions on a school board or even positions on a municipal council. **Public employment** is paid employment with some type of governmental agency. The vast majority of government jobs are considered public employment.

Most state statutes permit public employment for persons convicted of a felony. Some statutes allow employment after completion of sentence. Others allow convicted felons public employment, but they give the hiring agency or the civil service commissioner the right to deny public employment to a convicted offender on the sole basis of his or her felony conviction. In a few states a felony conviction may not be the sole grounds for denial of public employment unless the offense bears a direct relationship to the position sought. In addition, a small number of states apply a direct relationship test and consider other factors such as rehabilitation, the time lapse since offense, the offender's age at the time of conviction, and the nature and seriousness of the offense. Most jurisdictions, however, permit public employment

MORAL TURPITUDE

An act of baseness, vileness, or depravity in the private and social duties a person owes to other humans or to society in general that is contrary to the accepted, customary rule of right and duty between persons. A grave infringement of the moral sentiment of the community. A felony or a misdemeanor that is contrary to the public's moral standards.

PUBLIC OFFICES

Uncompensated, elected or appointed government positions.

PUBLIC EMPLOYMENT

Paid employment at any level of government.

after final completion of sentence because civil rights are restored at this time. No statutory restrictions are placed on public employment of convicted persons in the District of Columbia, Maine, Utah, or Vermont.[45]

Private Employment

A job applicant with a criminal record faces almost insurmountable barriers to private employment. It is difficult to identify the nature and extent of these barriers because of the complexity and diversity of private employment and because of the reluctance of some private employers to admit that they discriminate against ex-convicts. Discrimination based on age, sex, or race is unlawful, and it has been held that a private employer's refusal to hire a job applicant because of his or her arrest record violates the applicant's civil rights.[46] This protection does not extend to persons who have been convicted of a criminal offense, however. The distinction between conviction and criminal offense is left almost completely to the private employer's discretion. The probationer, regardless of his or her technical legal status, is a convicted person as far as the general public is concerned.

Some business and trade organizations and private employers make a point of providing jobs to convicted offenders. The Solution to Employment Problems (STEP) program of the National Association of Manufacturers is one such effort.[47] In this and similar programs, employers provide equipment and instructors to train offenders while they are in prison and then guarantee them jobs upon their release.

The Right to Be Bonded

Jobs in which employees handle money or merchandise may require the employee to be bonded. For example, banks, warehouses, truck driving companies, collection agencies, bookkeepers, ticket-takers, and vendors may require a bond before the employee will be allowed to work. The purpose of a bond is to protect the employer or the company from losses sustained from dishonest employees. The employee who is bonded is known as the principal.

The principal signs and pays the fee to obtain a simple bond. A **surety bond** is signed by the principal and by one or more third parties, known as sureties, who promise to pay money in the event that the assured, the party in whose favor the bond is written, suffers damage because the principal failed to perform as agreed.

Private individuals are sometimes sureties on bonds for friends or relatives, but insurance and bonding companies that are in the business of writing bonds write most surety bonds. No bonding company is required by law to furnish a bond to all applicants. The decision to write or deny a bond is with the surety. The company carefully investigates all persons who request bonds and refuses to bond persons it considers poor risks. Because they refuse to bond poor risks, the saying goes that "bonding companies bond only those who don't need it." The loss of the right to be bonded that follows a criminal conviction is not so much a loss of the right to be bonded as it is the loss of the ability to get a bond. This is because almost without exception, a person with a criminal record, particularly one that is violent, is considered a poor risk. Irrespective of any other obstacle, this inability to be bonded may constitute the final barrier to employment.

The U.S. Department of Labor, through the Employment and Training Administration, offers fidelity bonding coverage for job applicants. The coverage is available to persons who cannot obtain suitable employment because they have police, credit, or other records that prevent their being covered by the usual commercial bonds. Ex-

SURETY BOND

A certificate signed by the principal and a third party, promising to pay in the event the assured suffers damages or losses because the employee fails to perform as agreed.

offenders are eligible for the bonds if they are qualified and suitable for the particular position and they are not commercially bondable under ordinary circumstances. The applicant applies for the bond through a state employment office, and the bond becomes effective when the applicant has begun work and the manager of the local employment service office or other authorized representative of the state agency has certified the bond.[48]

Unfortunately, few ex-offenders seek to take advantage of this program. Both employers and prospective employees seem to lack information about the bonding that is available through state employment agencies. It is a sad fact that ex-offenders generally refrain from applying for jobs that require bonding.

The Right to Own a Firearm

The right to own a firearm continues to be the most restrictive of all civil disabilities lost by conviction. Federal law independently restricts convicted felons from possessing any firearms, yet every state except Vermont (which relies on federal law) has additional statutory restrictions.[49] As Velmer S. Burton Jr., Francis T. Cullen, and Lawrence F. Travis point out, "The rationale behind this restriction, of course, is to keep weapons out of the hands of dangerous individuals and to protect an unsuspecting public."[50] Thirty-six states restrict firearm ownership for persons convicted of any felony. Others restrict the possession of firearms to those convicted of violent or drug-related crimes.[51] Some states vary on the type of firearm possessed—whether it is a handgun, a rifle, or both types of weapons.

Changes in federal firearms laws are not just limited to convicted felons anymore. The most recent expansion of this law has been to prohibit anyone convicted of a misdemeanor crime involving domestic violence. This includes people who have ever been convicted of domestic violence, even before the law went into effect, as well as law enforcement personnel who must be able to carry a firearm to perform their job. The expansion of the federal firearms law has had a substantial impact on thousands of law enforcement officers at all levels of government. Many have chosen to keep their jobs by seeking formal restoration of their right to carry a firearm or other alternatives (see Chapter 16).

Critics of the expanded firearms law say that it may be unconstitutional because it should not apply to any convictions before the law went into effect. Others are opposed to the law enforcement officers who are seeking to restore their right to carry a firearm (and thus their job) through pardons and expungement processes. Because of this, legislation has been introduced (not yet passed) that would abolish federally funded programs that allow convicted felons to have the gun-ownership right restored.[52]

Sex Offender Registration Laws

Sex offender registration statutes (otherwise known as Megan's Law) were initially enacted with the goals of enabling parents to protect their children's safety and to improve the ability of police to investigate sex crimes. Registration with the local police is listed as a loss of civil rights because 49 states also make the information a matter of public record, and this has a great impact on where offenders on community supervision and ex-offenders are able to live and work without fear of community retaliation.[53]

All 50 states require that sex offenders both on and off supervision register with the local authorities. The most common time frame is within one month following release or completion of sentence. Washington was the first state to require registration of all sex offenders in 1990. Other states, such as New Jersey, developed three

TABLE 15.2 *Principal Features of Seven Sex Offender Notification Statutes*

State	Year Statue Went into Effect	How Long Offenders Remain Subject to Notification	Notification Mandatory or Discretionary	Notification Proactive or Only in Response to Request
Alaska	1994	For life: 2 or more convictions; 15 years: 1 conviction	Mandatory by administrative regulation	Upon request
Connecticut	1996	10 years after end of probation or parole	Discretionary	Proactive
Louisiana	1992	10 years after release	Mandatory	Proactive
New Jersey	1994	Indefinitely, but may petition for relief 15 years after release	Mandatory	Proactive
Oregon	1993, 1995	For life; may petition for waiver after 10 years	Varies[a]	Proactive and upon request
Tennessee	1995	10 years minimum; then may petition for relief	Discretionary	Proactive
Washington	1990	For life, 15 years or 10 years depending on seriousness of offense	Discretionary	Proactive and upon request

[a] Mandatory if under supervision; discretionary if not.

tiers of risk, and each tier has its own set of notification procedures (see Table 15.2). An offender is judged to fit into one of those three tiers, because the belief is that sex offenders pose different levels of risk to the community, depending on the nature and prevalence of their crimes as well as their choice of victim. Of the 32 states that have notification statutes, 21 permit or require proactive dissemination (knocking on doors, flyers, and so on) and the other 11 permit information dissemination only in response to individuals who first contact their local police department.[54]

Most states require sex offenders to register annually for a period of ten years, and some are for the duration of the offender's life. Information typically requested includes name, address, date of birth, Social Security number, vehicle registration, place of employment, fingerprints, and recent photo. Some states also collect blood or DNA (deoxyribonucleic acid) samples or both.[55]

Some states have expanded the sex offender registration law to include convicted misdemeanor sex offenders. In Missouri, the expansion of the law took effect in 2000 and includes convicted misdemeanant sex offenders who have pled guilty since July 1, 1979. Failure to register is a Class A misdemeanor, which is punishable by a $1,000 fine and up to one year in jail.[56]

Even though every state has thousands of offenders convicted of past sex crimes, isolated cases arise, particularly in smaller communities, in which a sex offender is ostracized from his home community. For example, in 1994, Carl DeFlumer was run

Sex Offenses Covered by Statute	Implementing Agency	Immunity Explicitly Provided to Implementers	Who May Be Notified	Retroactivity	Information That May Be Disseminated
All offenses	State Department of Public Safety	Provided	Anyone	Retroactive	Limited by statute
Selected offenses	Probation	Not provided	Anyone	Not retroactive	Unrestricted
All offenses	Offenders supervised by probation	Provided	Limited by statute	Retroactive to June 1992	Limited by statute
Selected offenses	Prosecutor and police	Provided	People likely to encounter the offender	Retroactive	Not specified
Selected offenses	Probation and police	Not provided	Anyone	Retroactive	Unrestricted
All offenses	Tennessee Bureau of Investigation	Provided	Not specified	Retroactive	"Relevant" information
All offenses	Police	Provided	Not specified	Retroactive	Not specified

Source: Peter Finn, *Sex Offender Community Notification* (Washington, DC: U.S. Department of Justice, February 1997), 4.

out of his community in Bethlehem, New York, after he was released from prison. DeFlumer was incarcerated for killing one boy and sodomizing another boy.[57] High-profile sex offenders, such as DeFlumer, seem to be more successful relocating to a large city. This example shows how difficult it is to balance public safety and fear of sex offenders with the due process rights of ex-convicts seeking a place to live. One way to help integrate sex offenders into the community along with providing public notification about a sex offender's whereabouts is a public education program.

One study has empirically examined whether community notification of sex offenders reduces recidivism and whether the program aids law enforcement in offender apprehension. The study used a treatment and a matched control group and found after 54 months no statistically significant difference between the two groups on the rate of arrest. However, the offenders who participated in the notification program were arrested more quickly than members of the control group.[58]

Another study, conducted by Richard G. Zevitz and Mary Ann Farkas, investigated the impact of community notification on the workloads of Wisconsin probation and parole officers who supervise sex offenders. Because Wisconsin is a state that has authorized proactive information dissemination, the researchers found much effort went into dealing with the community itself. Overall results indicated that sex offender supervision takes an extraordinary amount of training, time, and resources to find suitable housing, conduct home and employment visits, and monitor sex offenders to the rising community expectations.[59] The full impact of Megan's Law is yet to be determined as more studies are conducted.

SOCIAL STIGMATIZATION OF EX-OFFENDERS

Stigmatization and loss of social status are probably the most severe of the collateral consequences of a felony conviction. The status degradation that follows a person with a court record extends beyond the offender's discharge from the correctional process. This is particularly true when the person is committed to a state or federal correctional institution after conviction. One study found through a mail survey of 281 respondents that an inverse relationship exists between the degree of ex-convict stigmatization and the degree to which the respondents thought prisons were effective. In other words, as belief in the effectiveness of prisons decreases, the level of stigmatization of ex-felons increases.[60]

A kind of circular effect can be observed in the assignment of such a status. Ex-offenders suffer from civil disabilities that bar them from jobs and entry into professions. Society thus limits their occupational choices to jobs considered menial. The public then views all ex-offenders as holding menial jobs and characterizes them as members of a lower stratum of society. Membership in the lower strata of society forecloses opportunities for more prestigious jobs, and the possibility of movement into the upper levels of society is restricted. The result is the creation of a permanent class of outcasts who can never be assimilated into the mainstream of community life.[61]

In some rare cases, ex-offenders are appointed to or gain high-profile positions that receive media attention. For example, in 1998, the board chairman for the National Association for the Advancement of Colored People (NAACP) appointed a convicted embezzler to a key post within the NAACP organization. Some NAACP members called for the chairman to rescind the appointment.[62] This exceptional example demonstrates the inability for the majority of society, even within the NAACP itself, to fully embrace ex-offenders as worthy of such a high-profile appointment.

Whether the removal of continuing civil disabilities would change community attitudes toward the offender remains an open question. On the one hand, rehabilitated ex-offenders have a right to start their lives over with the tools that they have been given through treatment efforts. On the other hand, attention must also be paid to the proposition that the public has a right to know of the previous criminal record to protect itself against the recidivist offender. Susan Kuzma, of the Office of the United States Pardon Attorney, points out the importance of achieving some kind of balance within competing perspectives:

> [Restrictions] . . . require careful consideration and reflection about whether the rigidity and severity of such an approach is justified by identifiable societal gains in protecting the community. . . . It's a tough issue for society as a whole to resolve. When has an offender paid his debt to society? The price for crime can't be too cheap, lest no one follow the law. Yet, do we achieve another bad result by making it impossible to stop paying for having committed a crime?[63]

Removal of civil disabilities may not in itself change the public attitude toward the offender, but distinctions must be made. The imposition of civil disabilities should bear some rational relationship to the offense committed and to the function to be performed. Different treatment must be accorded the hard-core recidivist offender and the rehabilitated offender, and a way must be found to distinguish one from the other. Procedures for removing disabilities must be simplified and provide for a restoration of good character when circumstances warrant. Most important of all, affirmative education efforts must involve the public in corrections and in the welfare of the ex-offender. Professionals in law enforcement and corrections and the leaders of the bench and bar must concern themselves with removing the inconsistencies and inequities that characterize the consequences of conviction today.

SUMMARY

Conviction is followed by both direct and collateral consequences. Direct consequences include fines, probation, imprisonment, and other sanctions imposed by the court. Collateral consequences are disabilities that follow a conviction that are not directly imposed by a court, such as loss of civil and political rights and loss of good moral character. The overall effects of a conviction are thus direct and collateral sanctions.

The particular rights lost by conviction depend on the crime for which the offender was convicted and the jurisdiction in which the conviction occurred. Little agreement exists among states as to which rights are lost by conviction or the manner by which the rights may be restored, if they may be restored at all.

Apart from the loss of rights by operation of law or from interpretations by administrative bodies and licensing agencies, the convicted individual also loses social status and suffers social stigmatization. He or she is usually thought to have lost good moral character, a loss that often results in further collateral sanctions— such as the loss of employment opportunities. Procedures for removing disabilities should be simplified and should provide for restoration of good moral character when circumstances warrant.

DISCUSSION QUESTIONS

1. Distinguish between civil and political rights.
2. What were the facts and the holding in *Trop v. Dulles*?
3. Compare and contrast the concepts of outlawry and attainder.
4. What is the general trend with regard to loss of civil rights upon conviction? Why do you think this is so?
5. Discuss the loss of rights during community supervision. What are the issues?
6. What are the justifications for imposing civil disabilities on convicted persons?
7. What is the current status of loss of the right to vote as a civil disability upon conviction? How have the courts ruled on this issue?
8. Assuming that ex-offenders want to obtain honest work, how do laws that restrict employment and licensing affect recidivism?
9. What do you see are the pros and cons of Megan's Law?
10. Should ex-felons be allowed to possess a firearm? If so, under what circumstances?
11. Should police officers convicted of a misdemeanor for domestic violence receive a pardon or lose their jobs because they cannot possess a firearm?
12. In what respects is social stigma a civil disability?

 **WEB SITES**

Civil Disabilities of Convicted Felons

> *www.corrections.com/news/justin/index.html*
> *www.corrections.com/aca/cortoday/august98/kuzma.html*

Sex Offender Registry and Community Notification[64]

State	Web Site
Alabama	*http://www.gsiweb.net*
Alaska	*http://www.dps.state.ak.us/sorcr/*
Connecticut	*http://www.state.ct.us/dps*
Delaware	*http://www.state.de.us/dsp/sexoff/index.htm*
Florida	*http://www.fdle.state.fl.us*
Georgia	*http://www.ganet.org/gbi/disclaim.html*
Indiana	*http://www.state.in.us/cji/registry/index.html*
Kansas	*http://www.ink.org/public/kbi/kbisexpage.html*
Michigan	*http://www.mipsor.state.mi.us*
New York	*http://www.criminaljustice.state.ny.us*
North Carolina	*http://sbi.jus.state.nc.us/sor*
South Carolina	*http://www.scattorneygeneral.com/public/registry.html*
Tennessee	*http://www.ticic.state.tn.us/sexoffender.htm*
Texas	*http://records.txdps.state.tx.us/dps/default.htm*
Utah	*http://www.cr.ex.state.ut.us/soreg/info_soreg.htm*
Vermont	*http://www.dps.state.vt.us/cjs/s_registry.htm*
Virginia	*http://www.vsp.state.va.us*
West Virginia	*http://www.wvstatepolice.com*

Please go to the book-specific Web site for the Supplemental Reading related to the material in this chapter:
Summary of State Law Firearms Disabilities Imposed upon Conviction
http://www.wadsworth.com/product/0534559662s

16

Pardon and Restoration of Rights

Corbis

Pardon

Commutation

Full pardon

Conditional pardon

Automatic restoration of rights

Certificate of discharge

Expungement

Sealing

Good moral character

What You Will Learn in This Chapter

*I*n this chapter you will learn the history and philosophy of pardons. You will also learn the various types of pardons, how they are obtained, and the legal consequences of a pardon. Alternative ways by which a conviction might be set aside—automatic restoration of rights, expungement, and sealing—are examined. And court decisions on the issue of restoring good moral character are reviewed. Finally, an overview of the status of restoration of civil rights after conviction is provided.

INTRODUCTION

A conviction for a criminal offense or an adjudication of delinquency is followed by both a direct consequence in the form of criminal sanctions and collateral consequences in the form of loss of civil rights. The rights affected by a conviction include voting rights, the right to hold public office, employment opportunities, and judicial rights such as the rights to sue, execute legal instruments, serve on a jury, and testify without impeachment. Certain marital and parental rights also may be lost, and some rights relating to property—including insurance, workers' compensation, and pension benefits—may be impaired.

The direct consequences of conviction—the criminal sanctions—end with the completion of the sentence. Generally a sentence is completed on the day the offender is released from an institution or discharged from probation or parole supervision. In contrast, the collateral effects of a conviction or adjudication (the loss of one or more civil rights) generally continues for the offender's lifetime or until some affirmative act occurs that by law prevents the continuance of the civil disabilities or serves to reduce or even erase them completely. These affirmative acts are of limited value—some because they are not intended to completely reduce or wipe out the conviction, others because they cannot reach some occupational licensing practices or the private employer. Almost all procedures for restoring civil rights have the additional weakness of not wiping out a criminal conviction or adjudication of delinquency. In other words, they do not restore "good character."

The methods of removing the collateral consequences of a conviction or adjudication include pardon, automatic restoration of rights upon application, expungement, sealing, court decisions, governors' executive orders, and legislative acts. Unfortunately, the methods in use do not seal, expunge, nullify, or restore in any practical, effective way.

PARDON

PARDON

An executive act that mitigates or sets aside punishment for a crime. The power to pardon is generally vested in state governors, but the president has the power to pardon for federal offenses. Pardons are either conditional or absolute (full).

Operating as a distinct subsystem of the criminal justice process, a **pardon** fulfills a necessary function. Yet despite its importance to a well-balanced system of justice, it has received little scholarly attention. This lack of study has led to its misapplication and to confusion about its nature and function.

Even the courts have been misled into ambiguous and insupportable holdings. Some jurisdictions have held that a pardon wipes out the crime as though it never happened. Other jurisdictions have held that for some purposes a pardon does not wipe out the fact of a conviction. Thus the recipient of a pardon is regarded not as a "new person" but as a convicted criminal. This is true, for example, when the pardoned criminal takes the stand as a witness in a trial. His or her testimony may be impeached by the fact of the previous conviction even though a pardon has been granted.

Ideally the pardon's effect should reflect the grounds for which it is granted. A pardon that is granted because later evidence shows the convicted person to be innocent should wipe out the crime for all purposes, whereas a pardon granted because a prisoner helped stop a prison riot probably should not.

The Power to Pardon

Historically the power to pardon belonged to the king or sovereign. Because a crime was considered to be an offense against the king, he was deemed to have the power to forgive it. In early American law, however, the power to pardon was generally given to the legislature. When it was granted to the executive, it was severely restricted. By the time the U.S. Constitution was written, the older rule was again followed. The president was given the power of pardon in all federal cases except that of impeachment.[1] In most states today the power to pardon state felony cases is given to the governor, acting either alone or in conjunction with some official or board.[2]

When granted to the governor, the power may be either restricted or without limitation. In a number of states the governor's power to pardon does not extend to treason and impeachment. When the governor's power is restricted in this manner, these excepted crimes may usually be pardoned by the legislature. Normally the power to pardon does not extend to violations of municipal ordinances; it extends only to offenses against the state. In some states, the power to pardon permits a pardon at any time after charge or indictment. In other states, the power can be exercised only after conviction. Other states forbid pardon until the minimum sentence or a certain length of sentence has been served or until after a specific number of years of successful parole. Where state law so provides, both absolute and conditional pardons may be issued.

Objectives of Pardons

The pardoning power was originally seen as a method of righting legal wrongs and of freeing the innocent. Later a commutation of sentence, or a pardon, became an acceptable way to correct unduly severe sentences or to recognize mitigating circumstances that were not taken into consideration at the trial. The divergent views concerning the death penalty have often been expressed in the use of the power of executive clemency to reduce the sentence to life imprisonment. Prisoners who are old, infirm, or have a fatal illness are often pardoned for humanitarian reasons or given an emergency medical reprieve. Escaped prisoners who have rehabilitated themselves are occasionally pardoned in recognition of their exemplary lives during the period of freedom. The pardoning power is sometimes used to prevent deportation of an alien and sometimes—in the form of amnesties or general pardons—to achieve political purposes.[3]

The pardoning power, used either alone or in connection with special statutory proceedings, is now frequently used to remove the civil disabilities that are a collateral consequence of a conviction. Its use for this purpose of restoring civil rights is the chief concern in this chapter.

Kinds of Pardons

Pardons generally are either full (absolute) or conditional. A **full pardon** freely and unconditionally absolves an individual from the legal consequences of his or her crime and conviction. A **conditional pardon** does not become operative until certain conditions are met or after the occurrence of a specified event. A conditional pardon generally does not restore the full civil rights of the offender unless express language to that effect is stated in its proclamation.

Delivery and Acceptance of Pardons

A pardon is not effective until it is delivered, and until delivered, it may be revoked. An absolute pardon need not be accepted by the prisoner.[4] A conditional pardon, however, must be accepted, because a prisoner may prefer to serve out his or her sentence rather than accept the conditions attached to the pardon.

Revocation

A full pardon, once delivered, cannot be revoked. A conditional pardon may be revoked for violation of the conditions imposed. Some courts have attempted to restrict the right of the governor to revoke a conditional pardon by prohibiting revocation without some sort of determination that the person pardoned has violated the conditions.

Procedure for Obtaining a Pardon

The procedure for obtaining a pardon is fixed by statute or by regulations of the pardoning authority. Generally the convicted person must apply for a pardon, and some time must elapse after release from confinement or discharge on parole before the offender may apply.[5] When the offender makes application he or she is required to notify certain persons, typically the prosecuting attorney, the sheriff, and the court of conviction. Posting—publication of a public notice—may be required. There may be limitations on repeated applications for pardon, such as a minimum time interval between applications. In most cases the pardoning authority conducts an investigation. A hearing on the application may be held, which is open to the public in some states.[6]

A controversial pardon of recent times was President Bill Clinton's decision to pardon Marc Rich the night before Clinton left office. The question was whether Rich's pardon was linked to the merits of his case or to a $450,000 contribution Rich's former wife made to the Clinton presidential library. Many argued that Rich was not a viable candidate to be pardoned. As of March 2001, the United States attorney's office was investigating potential improprieties in some of Clinton's pardon decisions.[7]

Legal Effects of a Pardon

The most important question the offender asks about a pardon is: What rights are restored by a pardon? The general answer is that a pardon restores certain civil rights that were lost upon conviction. To determine the precise legal effects of a pardon, one must examine both statutory and case law in the jurisdiction where the pardon is granted.

There are two points of view as to whether a pardon wipes out guilt. The classic view, which represents the minority position today, was expressed by the U.S. Supreme Court over a century ago:

A pardon reaches both the punishment prescribed for the offense and the guilt of the offender; and when the pardon is full, it releases the punishment and blots out the existence of the guilt, so that in the eyes of the law the offender is as innocent as if he had never committed the offense. If granted before conviction, it prevents any of the penalties and disabilities consequent upon conviction from attaching; if granted after conviction, it removes the penalties and disabilities and restores him to all his civil rights; it makes him, as it were, a new man, and gives him new credit and capacity.[8]

The opposite and majority view, stated in *Burdick v. United States*, is that a pardon is an implied expression of guilt and that the conviction is not obliterated.[9] Depending on which view prevails in a given state, the relevant statutory or constitutional provisions, and the reasons for the granting of a pardon in a particular case, a number of consequences follow.

ENHANCEMENT OF PUNISHMENT: Depending on the statutory provisions and court interpretations, an offense for which the offender has been pardoned may or may not be counted in enhancement-of-punishment procedures for declaring the offender a "habitual offender." The minority position is that if the pardon is held to have wiped out the offender's guilt, or if it was issued on the basis of a finding or belief that the offender was in fact innocent of the offense, then it will probably not be used for enhancement. The majority position, however, is that inasmuch as the pardon does not wipe out guilt for the underlying offense but implies guilt, the conviction remains and may serve to enhance punishment at the trial of a subsequent offense.[10]

RIGHTS TO VOTE, SERVE ON A JURY, HOLD PUBLIC OFFICE, AND BE A WITNESS: A full pardon generally restores the ordinary rights of citizenship, such as the rights to vote and hold public office. The effect of the pardon may be set out in the state constitution or statutes or in the regulations of the pardoning authority. Pardon restores eligibility for public office, but it will not restore a person to any public office he or she held at the time of conviction. A **commutation** or a conditional pardon, however, does not restore rights or remove disqualifications for office.[11] Generally, a conviction for which a witness has been conditionally pardoned can also be used to impeach him or her. Some states bar the showing of a conviction that has been pardoned, however, and even those that do not will allow the fact of the pardon to be offered in rebuttal.

LICENSING LAWS: Generally, where an occupational licensing law disqualifies persons convicted of crime, a pardon does not remove the disqualification. It also does not automatically restore a license that has been revoked on the grounds of a criminal conviction. Some decisions have indicated that although loss of a professional license is a penalty, the proceedings to revoke a license are not penal.[12] The revocation of professional license is thus not a conviction for which the executive has the power to pardon. The California statute provides generally that a pardon shall "operate to restore to the convicted person all the rights, privileges, and franchises of which he has been deprived in consequence of said conviction or by reason of any matter involved therein." However, the statute also states,

> [N]othing in this article shall affect any of the provisions of the Medical Practices Act, or the power or authority conferred by law on the Board of Medical Examiners therein, or the power or authority conferred by law upon any board which permits any person or persons to apply his or their art or profession on the person of another.[13]

COMMUTATION

Changing a punishment to one that is less severe, as from execution to life imprisonment.

AUTOMATIC RESTORATION OF RIGHTS

AUTOMATIC RESTORATION OF RIGHTS

Reinstatement of some or all civil rights upon completion of sentence. The extent of restoration varies by state and may vary by offense type.

CERTIFICATE OF DISCHARGE

Official written documentation signifying an offender has completed his or her sentence.

In 1996 the Office of the United States Pardon Attorney published a state-by-state survey entitled *Civil Disabilities of Convicted Felons*. The study reported that 33 states have laws for **automatic restoration of rights** upon completion of sentence. The remaining states require some affirmative action on the part of the offender.[14]

For example, the New Hampshire statute, which provides automatic restoration by virtue of a **certificate of discharge,** reads, in part,

> the order, certificate, or other instrument of discharge, given to a person sentenced for a felony upon his discharge after completion of service of his sentence or after service under probation or parole, shall state that the defendant's rights to vote and to hold any future public office of which he was deprived by this chapter are thereby restored and that he suffers no other disability by virtue of his conviction and sentence except as otherwise provided by this chapter.[15]

The laws of the other states that grant automatic restoration of rights are basically similar, but the provisions differ somewhat. The Illinois Unified Code of Corrections, for example, contains this language:

> On completion of sentence of imprisonment or on a petition of a person not sentenced to imprisonment, all license rights and privileges granted under the authority of this State which have been revoked or suspended because of conviction of an offense shall be restored unless the authority having jurisdiction of such license rights finds after investigation and hearing that restoration is not in the public interest.[16]

The Wisconsin statute is one of the oldest and most comprehensive statutes providing that every person who has been convicted of a crime obtains a restoration of his or her civil rights by serving out the term of imprisonment or otherwise satisfying the sentence. The statute reads, in part, "Civil rights restored to convicted persons satisfying sentence. Every person who is convicted of crime obtains a restoration of his civil rights by serving out his term of imprisonment or otherwise satisfying his sentence."[17]

Most courts consider the effect of automatic restoration of rights to be equivalent to that of a pardon. Typically the conviction can be considered in any subsequent criminal action and under the enhancement statutes. The ex-offender is not restored to eligibility to receive an occupational or professional license and must report the conviction on job application forms.

EXPUNGEMENT

EXPUNGEMENT

An erasure. Process by which the record of a criminal conviction (or juvenile adjudication) is destroyed or sealed after expiration of time.

The word *expunge* means "erase." Thus the purpose of **expungement** statutes is to allow the record of a crime to be erased as if it never happened.

The typical expungement statute does not specify automatic restoration of rights because it requires affirmative action by the offender. Expungement differs from the issuance of "certificates of relief of good conduct" (as in New York) in that the issuance of the certificates restores rights without attempting to wipe out the criminal record. A study of expungement statutes reported in 1988 that 28 states have some method of judicial restoration of civil rights.[18] Eligibility for expungement, however, varies widely. In some states expungement statutes apply only to probationers. Other states expunge records only for nonviolent offenses or low-grade felonies. Some others allow expungement of felony offenses only for first offenders. California permits the conviction for a felony to be set aside and issues a certificate of rehabilitation.[19]

Expungement after Successful Completion of Probation

Adult probation laws of many states contain procedures that permit the probationer, either after completion of probation or after a specified period on probation, to apply for an order that terminates the probation and wipes out the conviction. Texas statutes, for instance, provide that at any time after the defendant has satisfactorily completed one-third of the original probationary period or two years of probation, whichever is less, the court may reduce or terminate the period of probation.[20]

The American Bar Association recommends that "Every jurisdiction should have a method by which the collateral effects of a criminal record can be avoided or mitigated following the successful completion of a term on probation and during its service."[21]

Two approaches are taken by present statutes on the subject:

1. Deferring formal adjudication of guilt through the period of probation and discharging the defendant following successful service without ever declaring the defendant guilty.
2. Permitting withdrawal of a guilty plea and dismissal of the charges following the successful service of all or part of the probation term.

The American Bar Association advisory committee on standards regarding sentencing alternatives and procedures cites with approval the Maryland procedures that permit placing a consenting defendant on probation after the determination of guilt but before a formal entry of judgment. Such a provision allows the offender—upon successful completion of probation—to avoid the disabilities that attach to a felony conviction.[22]

All of these statutes, model codes, and standards serve at least a limited purpose of mitigating the effects of a conviction, but they apply only to probationers. Some states, such as California, have enacted statutes that also extend opportunities for expungement to offenders who have not been placed on probation.

SEALING

Sealing statutes have the same objective as expungement statutes in that they seek to erase the record of a conviction. However, they go further; they attempt to conceal the fact of conviction. Typically these statutes relate to juveniles or to persons who were under the age of 21 when they committed a crime. Sealing statutes are defended on the basis of public policy, which demands that certain documents and records be treated as confidential and therefore not be open to indiscriminate inspection even though they are in custody of a public officer or board and are of a public nature. Examples of such documents include those kept on file in public institutions concerning the condition, care, and treatment of inmates and those in offices charged with the execution of laws relating to the apprehension, prosecution, and punishment of crimes. Nevertheless, only a few states have sealing statutes. The statutes that exist tend to be limited in scope, and the procedures for sealing cumbersome.

Sealing provisions in juvenile court statutes must be read with reference to other provisions in those statutes that restrict access to juvenile records to persons with a

SEALING

The legal concealment of a person's criminal (or juvenile) record such that it cannot be opened except by order of the court.

legitimate interest in the protection, welfare, or treatment of the child and that provide for the destruction of fingerprints. Also related are the juvenile code provisions that specifically state that neither an adjudication of delinquency nor a commitment is a conviction and the statutes that give the juvenile court the authority to dismiss a petition and set aside findings. The sealing statutes operate to provide additional protection.

RESTORATION OF RIGHTS UPON APPLICATION

Some states provide by statute for procedures the offender can initiate to remove the disabilities that follow a conviction. These procedures differ from expungement procedures in that they do not attempt to wipe out the conviction. They are more or less straightforward attempts to remove the disabilities that are collateral consequences of conviction. Typically the certificate or other document that is furnished upon completion of the proceedings specifies the rights that are restored.

An ex-offender must possess one of these certificates to apply for a job or license barred by virtue of a criminal conviction. California provides a certificate of rehabilitation to all offenders who complete their sentence. The purpose of the certificate is to facilitate employment opportunities and to assist in occupational or professional licensing.

These certificates and the order of the court usually restore the ex-offender to such political rights as the right to vote and provide him or her with a document that is some evidence of his or her good conduct since release from custody. Nonetheless, they do not prevent a prospective employer or a licensing agency from taking the conviction into account in deciding whether to give the offender a job or a license.

COURT DECISIONS

In many cases in which the broad definition of the term *conviction* was adopted (that is, where sentencing constitutes a conviction), the purpose and the effect of the decision were to protect the defendant's right to practice his or her profession or engage in other licensed occupation.[23] As one scholar has noted, the difference between two burglars on probation in California can be dramatic. Whereas the sentenced burglar (broad definition) has lost all civil rights, the unsentenced burglar (narrow definition) is a provisional or conditional felon and, as such, retains his or her civil rights and is subject to no disabilities except those prescribed in the terms of probation.[24]

Similar attempts to minimize the effects of a conviction can be seen in cases that narrow the definition of *moral turpitude* or *infamous crime*.[25] Some of these cases are forerunners of the "reasonable relationship" statutes, which require that a reasonable relationship exist between conviction and the rights or privileges the convicted person is deprived of. In the *Otsuka v. Hite* case, the issue was the right to vote. The court limited the meaning of *infamous crime* to offenses in which the elements of the crime are such that the person who committed it may reasonably be deemed to pose a threat to the integrity of the elective process.[26]

An important Supreme Court case decided the issue of whether an ex-convict can possess good moral character as generally required in licensing statutes. In the case of *Schware v. Board of Bar Examiners*, the evidence showed that the applicant for the New Mexico bar examination had used several aliases in the 20 years prior to his application, had been arrested but never tried or convicted, and had been a member of the Communist Party 17 years earlier.[27] The State Board of Bar Examiners refused to permit him to take the bar exam on the ground that he had not shown good moral character. The Court reversed the decision of the board, stating that a state cannot exclude a person from the practice of law or from any other occupation in a manner or for reasons that contravene the due process or equal protection clause of the Fourteenth Amendment. The Court emphasized that the applicant had done nothing in the 15 years preceding the application to reflect adversely on his character.[28]

A significant decision was handed down by the District of Columbia Court of Appeals in the case of *Miller v. District of Columbia*.[29] The agency involved had denied a vendor's license to an applicant, a former offender, because it found that he was not rehabilitated. Reversing the agency and finding that the applicant was rehabilitated, the court not only ordered the agency to grant the applicant a license but also went on to express "serious concern" about the agency's lack of standards. The court said, in part,

> Unless there are some standards relating the prior conduct of an applicant to the particular business activity for which he seeks a license, the power to deny a license inevitably becomes an arbitrary, and therefore, unlawful, exercise of judgment by one official, a graphic example of which is so clearly revealed by the record in this case.

RESTORING GOOD MORAL CHARACTER

None of the methods and procedures for removing or reducing the collateral consequences of a criminal conviction examined in this chapter restores **good moral character** to the ex-offender. They all suffer from this overriding deficiency. Because licensing statutes almost universally require that the holders of a professional or occupational license be of good character, and many private employers of nonlicensed workers impose the same requirement, the effect is "to close the door of hope to a person once sentenced for a crime, frustrating his chances for rehabilitation in a useful occupation for which he is trained."[30]

One of the problems in applying the standard of good moral character is the vagueness of the term. The Supreme Court in *Konigsberg v. State Bar* noted that

GOOD MORAL CHARACTER

The totality of moral virtues that forms the basis of one's reputation in the community.

> the term [good moral character] by itself is unusually ambiguous. It can be defined in an almost unlimited number of ways, for any definition will necessarily reflect the attitudes, experiences, and prejudices of the definer. Such a vague qualification, which is easily adapted to fit personal views and predilections, can be a dangerous instrument for arbitrary and discriminatory denial of the right to practice law.[31]

Yet the rule remains as it was when announced by the Supreme Court in 1898:

> [The state] may require both qualifications of learning and of good character, and if it deems that one who has violated the criminal laws of the state is not possessed of sufficient good character, it can deny to such a one a right to practice medicine, and further, it may make the record of a conviction conclusive evidence of the fact of the violation of the criminal law and of the absence of the requisite good character.[32]

This rule has been generally observed in subsequent legislation and court decisions.[33]

Bad Character

The early law on restoring good moral character developed in the law of pardons. The general rule there seemed to be that all disqualifications that are imposed solely because of bad character—which may be incidentally evidenced by a conviction for a crime—are unaffected by a pardon. According to this rule a pardoned felon was thus restored the rights to vote, serve on a jury, receive a pension, and testify in court because the individual had not lost these rights simply because of bad moral character. When the exercise of a right is associated with a character requirement, however, the result is different. In that case the conviction may be evidence, even conclusive evidence, of bad character, unaffected by the pardon, and by extension of the same reasoning unaffected by certificates of rehabilitation and similar procedures.[34]

Thus when a qualification of good moral character is written into a licensing statute or into a statute prescribing qualifications for public office, it has been held to be within the power of the legislature to require that weight be given to the fact of a criminal conviction as evidence of bad character. An Ohio court stated,

> Whatever the theory of the law may be with regard to a pardon, it cannot work such moral changes as to warrant the assertion that a pardoned convict is just as reliable as one who has constantly maintained the character of a good citizen.[35]

The Direct Relationship Test

Although the authority of legislatures to impose civil disabilities on offenders and of licensing authorities to consider convictions in determining good character has not been seriously eroded, the trend is to impose what is becoming known as the direct relationship test. In a case in which the California Supreme Court declared that several convictions for participating in civil rights demonstrations did not determine an applicant unfit to admission to the bar, the court stated the fundamentals of this test:

> The nature of these acts, moreover, does not bear a direct relationship to petitioner's fitness to practice law. Virtually all of the admission and disciplinary cases in which we have upheld decisions of the State Bar to refuse to admit applicants or to disbar, suspend, or otherwise censure members of the bar, have involved acts which bear upon the individual's manifest dishonesty and thereby provide a reasonable basis for the conclusion that the applicant or attorney cannot be relied upon to fulfill the moral obligations incumbent upon members of the legal profession.[36]

THE STATUS OF CIVIL DISABILITIES TODAY

Civil disability statutes in general, and licensing statutes in particular, are being attacked in the courts on several grounds. The authors of "The Collateral Consequences of a Criminal Conviction" effectively summarized the problems and proposed solutions.[37] They argued as follows:

1. Civil disability laws are overbroad in that the laws of most jurisdictions provide for the blanket imposition of disabilities upon a criminal conviction.
2. The laws are inconsistent.

3. Although most jurisdictions provide for the eventual restoration of convicted criminals' rights, these procedures are of limited effectiveness. As a result, many ex-convicts suffer disabilities long after deprivation is justifiable.
4. Among the disabilities suffered, the loss of employment opportunity is one of the most onerous. This is increasingly true as the number of licensed occupations continues to increase. Under existing laws, discrimination against convicted criminals by private employers is legal.
5. Although regulations of many public and licensed occupations are necessary, many of the regulations are unreasonable, and procedures with respect to denial and revocation of licenses are not fair.

Attacks on the constitutionality of civil disability laws are being made on the following grounds:

- Civil disability laws are bills of attainder.
- Imposition of civil disabilities is cruel and unusual punishment.
- Procedures with reference to the imposition and application of civil disability laws violate due process.
- Civil disability laws deny equal protection.

In addition, these laws achieve none of the objectives of modern correctional theory and impede offenders' rehabilitation, both within the correctional institution and in the community. Recommendations to ameliorate these situations include:

- Elimination of unnecessary restrictions
- Reasonable application of necessary restrictions
- Adoption of the direct relationship test
- Greater participation by the sentencing court in determining the civil disabilities to be imposed on the individual defendant
- Automatic restoration of rights and privileges five years after the convict's release into the community

SUMMARY

Although the direct consequences of a conviction end with the completion of the sentence, most of the collateral consequences continue for the lifetime of the offender—unless some affirmative act takes place to prevent the civil disabilities from attaching or reduce them. The methods used to restore rights include pardons, automatic restoration of rights, expungement, sealing, and restoration of rights upon application. None of these, however, has the effect of restoring good moral character, a requirement of all professional and occupational licensing boards and many private employers. This has the effect of denying employment to many ex-offenders and thereby frustrates their chances for rehabilitation in a meaningful occupation.

Civil disability laws achieve none of the goals of modern corrections. Although reasonable restrictions on some ex-offenders are justified—where there is a direct relationship between the crime committed and the functions and responsibilities of the licensed business or profession—the arbitrary barring of convicted persons from most licensed occupations serves no realistic public purpose and may have negative consequences for society.

DISCUSSION QUESTIONS

1. Compare and contrast the two types of pardons.
2. Who has the power to pardon, and under what circumstances may a pardon be granted?
3. What are the legal effects of a full pardon? Does a pardon wipe out guilt? What are the two major positions on this issue?
4. How does a pardon affect the right to vote? The right to serve on a jury? The right to hold public office? The right to serve as a witness?
5. Does a pardon restore a person's license to practice a profession? Explain.
6. How do various states deal with the issue of automatic restoration of rights upon completion of sentence? What is the trend?
7. What is expungement, and how do the various states handle this issue? What is the American Bar Association position?
8. How are sealing and expungement alike and different?
9. Discuss sealing in juvenile court.
10. How do various jurisdictions address the issue of restoration of rights following a conviction?
11. What is your position on whether rights should be restored to ex-convicts?
12. Which rights and privileges would you be most likely to restore?

 WEB SITES

Alaska Board of Parole Clemency Handbook of Definitions

http://www.correct.state.ak.us/Corrections/Parole/clembk/clembk8.htm

Impact of a Criminal Record

http://www.intelcities.com/lee_avenue/record/

Legally Speaking: Be Careful What You Ask for When Advocating Enforcement
Article by Karen L. MacNutt, published in *Gun Week,* a magazine advocating the right to bear arms

http://www.tyksnews.com/Depts/2nd_Amend/legally_speaking.htm

Office of the Pardon Attorney
Presidential pardons, 1945–2001

http://www.nytimes.com/images/2001/01/29/national/010129_nat_PARDONch.html

The Pardon Resource Center
Twelve steps to a federal pardon

http://www.silicon-valley.com/pardonme/index.html

Firearms Owners' Protection Act: A Historical and Legal Perspective
Article by David T. Hardy, published in *Cumberland Law Review* 17 (1986): 585–682

http://www.2ndlawlib.org/journals/hardfopa.html

Endnotes

Chapter 1

1. U.S. Department of Justice, Bureau of Justice Statistics, *Probation and Parole in the United States, 1999* (Washington, DC: U.S. Department of Justice, July 2000); and U.S. Department of Justice, *Sourcebook of Criminal Justice Statistics 1999* (Washington, DC: U.S. Department of Justice, forthcoming), www.albany.edu/sourcebook/1995/pdf/section6.pdf.

2. Allen J. Beck, *Prisoners in 1999* (Washington, DC: U.S. Department of Justice, Bureau of Justice Statistics, August 2000), 1.

3. Beck, *Prisoners in 1999*, 10–12.

4. Brian Forst, "Prosecution and Sentencing," in *Crime*, ed. J. Q. Wilson and J. Petersilia (San Francisco, CA: Institute for Contemporary Studies, 1995), 363–86.

5. Michael Tonry, *Intermediate Sanctions in Sentencing Guidelines* (Washington, DC: U.S. Department of Justice, National Institute of Justice, May 1997), xii.

6. Forst, "Prosecution and Sentencing," 376.

7. Michael Tonry, "Parochialism in U.S. Sentencing Policy," *Crime and Delinquency* 45, no. 1 (1999): 48–65.

8. Tamasak Wicharaya, *Simple Theory, Hard Reality: The Impact of Sentencing Reforms on Courts, Prisons, and Crime* (New York: State University of New York Press, 1995).

9. Karen Lutjen, "Culpability and Sentencing Under Mandatory Minimums and the Federal Sentencing Guidelines: The Punishment No Longer Fits the Criminal," *Notre Dame Journal of Law, Ethics, and Public Policy* 10, no. 1 (1996): 389–466.

10. 28 U.S.C. 991–998 (1988).

11. Lutjen, "Culpability and Sentencing Under Mandatory Minimums and the Federal Sentencing Guidelines."

12. Dale Parent, Terence Dunworth, Douglas McDonald, and William Rhodes, *Key Legislative Issues in Criminal Justice: The Impact of Sentencing Guidelines* (Washington, DC: U.S. Department of Justice, National Institute of Justice, November 1996).

13. Parent et al., *Key Legislative Issues in Criminal Justice*, 5.

14. Tonry, "Intermediate Sanctions in Sentencing Guidelines," xii–xv.

15. David M. Altschuler, "Trends and Issues in the Adultification of Juvenile Justice," in *Research to Results: Effective Community Corrections*, ed. Patricia M. Harris (Lanham, MD: American Correctional Association, 1999), 233–71, especially 234.

16. Altschuler, "Trends and Issues in the Adultification of Juvenile Justice," 257–62.

17. Todd R. Clear and Ronald P. Corbett, "Community Corrections of Place" (1997): 2, http://www.corrections.com/njaca/Fact_Sheets/Fact_sheets_start.htm.

18. Mark Mauer, "The International Use of Incarceration," *Prison Journal* 75 (1995): 113–23.

19. Camille Graham Camp and George M. Camp, *The Corrections Yearbook: 1999* (Middletown, CT: Criminal Justice Institute, 1999), 85.

20. Combined parole and probation departments had smaller budgets, averaging $48.8 million. Camp and Camp, *The Corrections Yearbook*, 185.

21. Samuel Walker, *Sense and Nonsense about Crime and Drugs*, 5th ed. (Belmont, CA: Wadsworth, 2001), 11.

22. Matthew Silberman, *A World of Violence* (Belmont, CA: Wadsworth, 1995).

23. James Austin and John Irwin, *It's about Time: America's Imprisonment Binge*, 3rd ed. (Belmont, CA: Wadsworth, 2001), 236.

24. Joan Petersilia, "Debating Crime and Imprisonment in California," *Evaluation and Program Planning* 17, no. 2 (1994): 165–77.

25. Hubert G. Locke, "Closing Comments," in *Successful Community Sanctions and Services for Special Offenders*, ed. B. J. Auerbach and T. C. Castellano (Lanham, MD: American Correctional Association, 1998), 253–59.

26. James M. Byrne and Faye S. Taxman, "Crime Control Policy and Community Corrections Practice," *Evaluation and Program Planning* 17 (1994): 227–33.

27. Norval Morris and Michael Tonry, *Between Prison and Probation: Intermediate Punishments in a Rational Sentencing System* (New York: Oxford University Press, 1990).

28. Stanton E. Samenow, *Inside the Criminal Mind* (New York: Times Books, 1984), 211–44, 251–52.

29. William M. DiMascio, *Seeking Justice: Crime and Punishment in America* (New York: Edna McConnell Clark Foundation, 1997), 41.

30. Paul Gendreau, "Keynote Speech: What Works in Community Corrections: Promising Approaches in Reducing Criminal Behavior," in *Successful Community Sanctions and Services for Special Offenders*, ed. B. J. Auerbach and T. C. Castellano (Lanham, MD: American Correctional Association, 1998), 59–74.

31. Gendreau, "Keynote Speech," 68.

32. Ted Palmer, *The Re-emergence of Correctional Intervention* (Newbury Park, CA: Sage, 1992).

33. President's Commission on Law Enforcement and Administration of Justice, *The Challenge of Crime in a Free Society* (Washington, DC: U.S. Government Printing Office, 1967), 169.

34. President's Commission on Law Enforcement and Administration of Justice, *The Challenge of Crime in a Free Society*, 165.

35. Edward J. Latessa and Harry E. Allen, *Corrections in the Community* (Cincinnati, OH: Anderson, 1997), 28.

36. Belinda McCarthy, Bernard McCarthy, and Matthew C. Leone, *Community-Based Corrections*, 4th ed. (Belmont, CA: Wadsworth, 2001), 4–5.

37. David R. Karp, *Community Justice: An Emerging Field* (Lanham, MD: Rowman and Littlefield, 1998); Daniel Van Ness and Karen Strong, *Restoring Justice* (Cincinnati, OH: Anderson Publishing, 1997); and Martin Wright, *Justice for Victims and Offenders: A Restorative Response to Crime*, 2nd ed. (Winchester, England: Waterside Press, 1996).

38. Mark S. Umbreit, "Restorative Justice: What Works," in *Research to Results: Effective Community Corrections*, ed. Patricia M. Harris (Lanham, MD: American Correctional Association, 1999), 276.

39. Umbreit, "Restorative Justice," 284.

40. Malcolm M. Feeley and Sam Kamin, "The Effect of 'Three Strikes and You're Out' on the Courts," in *Three Strikes and You're Out: Vengeance as Public Policy*, ed. David Shichor and Dale K. Sechrest (Thousand Oaks, CA: Sage, 1996), 150.

41. U.S. Department of Justice, Bureau of Justice Assistance, *Critical Elements in the Planning, Development, and Implementation of Successful Correctional Options* (Washington, DC: U.S. Department of Justice, February 1998), 30.

42. Joan Petersilia, Susan Turner, James Kahan, and Joyce Peterson, *Granting Felons Probation: Public Risks and Alternatives* (Santa Monica, CA: RAND, 1985), 24.

43. DiMascio, *Seeking Justice*, 24.

44. DiMascio, *Seeking Justice*, 24.

45. Camp and Camp, *The Corrections Yearbook*, 176.

46. Tonry, *Intermediate Sanctions in Sentencing Guidelines*, 11.

47. 18 U.S.C. 3563 (a) (2).

48. George F. Cole, Barry Mahoney, Mariene Thornton, and Roger A. Hanson, *The Practices and Attitudes of Trial Court Judges regarding Fines as a Criminal Sanction* (Washington, DC: U.S. Department of Justice, National Institute of Justice, 1987).

49. Tonry, *Intermediate Sanctions in Sentencing Guidelines*, 13.

50. Robert N. Altman and Robert E. Murray, "Home Confinement: A '90s Approach to Community Supervision," *Federal Probation* 61, no. 1 (1997): 30–32; and Charles Rose, "Electronic Monitoring of Offenders: A New Dimension in Community Sentencing or a Needless Diversion?" *International Review of Law, Computers, and Technology* 11, no. 1 (1997): 147–53.

51. Altman and Murray, "Home Confinement," 30–32; Rose, "Electronic Monitoring of Offenders," 147–53.

52. Doris Layton MacKenzie, Robert Brame, David McDowell, and Claire Souryal, "Boot Camp Prisons and Recidivism in Eight States," *Criminology* 33, no. 3 (1995): 328–57.

53. Merry Morash and Lila Rucker, "A Critical Look at the Idea of Boot Camp as a Correctional Reform," *Crime and Delinquency* 36 (1990): 204–22.

54. Robert Martinson, "What Works? Questions and Answers about Prison Reform," *Public Interest* (Spring 1974), 25.

55. Douglas Lipton, Robert Martinson, and Judith Wilks, *The Effectiveness of Correctional Treatment* (New York: Praeger, 1975), 627.

56. Ted Palmer, *A Profile of Correctional Effectiveness and New Direction for Research* (Albany, NY: State University of New York Press, 1994), xxi.

57. Hubert G. Locke, "Closing Comments," in *Successful Community Sanctions and Services for Special Offenders*, ed. B. J. Auerbach and T. C. Castellano (Lanham, MD: American Correctional Association, 1998), 257.

58. Locke, "Closing Comments," 254.

59. Tonry, *Intermediate Sanctions in Sentencing Guidelines*, 6.

60. Petersilia et al., *Granting Felons Probation*. 20.

61. Joan Petersilia, "Probation in the United States," *National Institute of Justice Journal* (Washington, DC: U.S. Department of Justice, September 1977), 4.

62. Petersilia, "Probation in the United States," 5.

63. Michael Tonry and Mary Lynch, "Intermediate Sanctions," in *Crime and Justice: A Review of Research*, vol. 20, ed. Michael Tonry (Chicago: University of Chicago Press, 1996), 127.

64. DiMascio, *Seeking Justice*, 41.

65. DiMascio, *Seeking Justice*, 41.

Chapter 2

1. Edgardo Rotman, "The Failure of Reform," in *The Oxford History of the Prison*, ed. Norval Morris and David Rothman (New York: Oxford University Press, 1995), 71–197.

2. Sol Rubin, Henry Weihofen, George Edwards, and Simon Rosenzweig, *The Law of Criminal Correction* (St. Paul, MN: West, 1963), 16. They cite Sir Fitzjames Stephens, *A History of the Criminal Law of England* (London, England: Macmillan, 1883), 491–92.

3. Rubin et al., *The Law of Criminal Correction*.
4. *Commonwealth v. Chase*, in *Thacher's Criminal Cases*, 267 (1831), recorded in vol. 11 of the *Records of the Old Municipal Court of Boston*, 199.
5. Sol Rubin advocated a greater use of suspended sentence without probation, arguing that this would provide an additional sentencing alternative of particular value in situations in which apprehension and conviction have so thorough a corrective impact on the offender that supervision by probation is unnecessary. Sol Rubin, *The Law of Criminal Correction*, 2nd ed. (St. Paul, MN: West, 1973), 197–200.
6. *Mempa v. Rhay*, 389 U.S. 128, 88 S. Ct. 254, 19 L. Ed. 2d 336 (1967); *Morrissey v. Brewer*, 408 U.S. 471, 92 S. Ct. 2593, 33 L. Ed. 2d 484 (1972); and *Gagnon v. Scarpelli*, 411 U.S. 778, 93 S. Ct. 1756, 36 L. Ed. 2d 656 (1973).
7. *Commonwealth v. Chase*.
8. *Ex parte United States*, 242 U.S. 27, 37 S. Ct. 72, 61 L. Ed. 129 (1916).
9. *Ex parte United States*.
10. *Ex parte United States*.
11. *People ex rel. Forsyth v. Court of Sessions*, 141 N.Y. 288, 36 N.E. 386 (1894).
12. American Bar Association, *Standards Relating to Probation*, approved draft (New York: Institute of Judicial Administration, 1970), sec. 1.1(b) reads: "In this report, the term *probation* means a sentence not involving confinement which imposes conditions and retains authority in the sentencing court to modify the conditions of the sentence or to resentence the offender if he violates the conditions. Such a sentence should not involve or require suspension of the imposition or the execution of any other sentence."
13. 18 U.S.C.A. sec. 3561.
14. Paul Tappan, *Crime, Justice, and Correction* (New York: McGraw-Hill, 1960), 542.
15. Tappan, *Crime, Justice, and Correction*, 542.
16. Tappan, *Crime, Justice, and Correction*, 542.
17. See John Augustus, *A Report of the Labors of John Augustus, for the Last Ten Years, in Aid of the Unfortunate* (Boston, MA: Wright and Hasty, 1852), reprinted as John Augustus, *First Probation Officer* (New York: National Probation Association, 1939).
18. Augustus, *First Probation Officer*.
19. Augustus, *First Probation Officer*.
20. Augustus, *First Probation Officer*, 34.
21. Augustus, *First Probation Officer*, 96.
22. Augustus, *First Probation Officer*, 23.
23. Augustus, *First Probation Officer*, 78–79.
24. Augustus, *First Probation Officer*, 78–79.
25. U.S. Department of Justice, *The Attorney General's Survey of Release Procedures* (Washington, DC: U.S. Government Printing Office, 1939).
26. *Ex parte United States*.
27. *Ex parte United States*.
28. Millard Earl Moon, "An Assessment of Federal Probation Officers' Perceptions regarding Certain Selected Factors Related to Job Performance." Ph.D. dissertation, University of Alabama, 1990, 21.
29. Moon, "An Assessment of Federal Probation Officers' Perceptions regarding Certain Selected Factors Related to Job Performance," 23–24.
30. *United States v. Murray*, 275 U.S. 347, 48 S. Ct. 146, 72 L. Ed. 309 (1928).
31. Frederic L. Faust and Paul J. Brantingham, *Juvenile Justice Philosophy* (St. Paul, MN: West, 1974), 44.
32. Faust and Brantingham, *Juvenile Justice Philosophy*, 45.
33. Faust and Brantingham, *Juvenile Justice Philosophy*, 62.
34. Faust and Brantingham, *Juvenile Justice Philosophy*, 63.
35. Julian W. Mack, "The Juvenile Court," *Harvard Law Review* 23 (1909): 102, as quoted in Faust and Brantingham, *Juvenile Justice Philosophy*, 159–69.
36. Mack, "The Juvenile Court," 162.
37. Mack, "The Juvenile Court," 163.

Chapter 3

1. Edna McConnell Clark Foundation, *Seeking Justice: Crime and Punishment in America* (New York, 1997).
2. Edna McConnell Clark Foundation, *Seeking Justice*, 2.
3. Edna McConnell Clark Foundation, *Seeking Justice*, 2.
4. Joan Petersilia, "A Crime Control Rationale for Reinvesting in Community Corrections," *Prison Journal* 75, no. 4 (December 1995).
5. U.S. Department of Justice, Bureau of Justice Statistics, *Probation and Parole Statistics* (Washington, DC: U.S. Department of Justice, June 28, 2000).
6. Edna McConnell Clark Foundation, *Seeking Justice*, 35.
7. Petersilia, "A Crime Control Rationale for Reinvesting in Community Corrections."
8. Rolando del Carmen, Betsy Witt, Thomas Caywood, and Sally Layland, *Probation Law and Practice in Texas* (Sam Houston State University, Criminal Justice Center, 1989), 29–35.
9. Joan Petersilia, Susan Turner, James Kahan, and Joyce Peterson, *Granting Felons Probation: Public Risks and Alternatives* (Santa Monica, CA: RAND, January 1985).
10. Joan Petersilia, *Expanding Options for Criminal Sentencing* (Santa Monica, CA: RAND, November 1987).
11. Del Carmen et al., *Probation Law and Practice in Texas*, 35.
12. *United States v. Wiley*, 267 F. 2d 453 (7th Cir.1959), on remand 184 F. Supp. 679 (N.D. Ill. E.D. 1960).
13. *Burns v. United States*, 287 U.S. 216, 53 S. Ct. 154, 77 L. Ed. 266 (1953).
14. Patrick A. Langan and Mark Cunniff, *Recidivism of Felons on Probation, 1986–1989*, special report (U.S. Department of Justice, Bureau of Justice Statistics, February 1992).
15. Larry Siegel, *Criminology*, 5th ed. (St. Paul, MN: West, 1995).

16. Lynn S. Branham, "The Model Adult Community Corrections Act," *Community Corrections Report* 1, no. 3 (February 1994): 4.
17. California Penal Code, sec. 1203 (West).
18. New York Penal Law, sec. 65.00–1 (McKinney).
19. Edward J. Latessa and Harry E. Allen, *Corrections in the Community* (Cincinnati, OH: Anderson, 1997), 268.
20. Thomas P. Bonczar and Lauren F. Glaze, *Probation and Parole in the United States, 1998* (Washington, DC: U.S. Department of Justice, Bureau of Justice Statistics, 1999).
21. Branham, "The Model Adult Community Corrections Act."
22. James Stanfiel, "Criminal Justice Decision Making: Discretion vs. Equity," *Federal Probation* (June 1983).

Chapter 4

1. Administrative Office of the U.S. Courts, *The Presentence Investigation Report*, publication 107 (Washington, DC: Administrative Office of the U.S. Courts, 1992).
2. A. Bolster, "Adult Probation, Parole, and Suspended Sentence," *Journal of Criminal Law* 444 (1910).
3. G. Ferris, "The Case History in Probation Service," in *Probation and Criminology*, ed. S. Glueck (1933).
4. Administrative Office of the U.S. Courts, *The Presentence Investigation Report*, monograph no. 103 (Washington, DC: Administrative Office of the U.S. Courts, 1965).
5. These categories were excerpted from Administrative Office of the U.S. Courts, *The Presentence Investigation Report*, monograph no. 105 (Washington, DC: Administrative Office of the U.S. Courts, 1978).
6. Richard Singer, "Sentencing," *Crime File* (Washington, DC: U.S. Department of Justice, n.d.), 1.
7. Administrative Office of the U.S. Courts, *The Presentence Investigation Report* (1978), 6.
8. *Presentence Investigation Reports under the Sentencing Reform Act of 1984*, publication 107 (Washington, DC: Administrative Office of the U.S. Courts, Division of Probation, 1992).
9. *Federal Sentencing Guidelines Handbook: Text, Analysis, Case Digests* (Shepard's/McGraw-Hill, 1990), 5.
10. Andrew E. Doom, Connie M. Roerich, and Thomas H. Zoey, "Sentencing Guidelines in Minnesota: The View from the Trenches," *Federal Probation* 52 (1988), 34–38.
11. *Presentence Investigation Reports under the Sentencing Reform Act of 1984*, n. 7.
12. Administrative Office of the U.S. Courts, *The Presentence Investigation Report* (1978), 6, n. 5.
13. 28 U.S.C. 235(a)(1)(B)(ii)(IV) of Public Law 98–473 provided that the amendment made by Public Law 98–473 is effective October 12, 1984.
14. 28 U.S.C. 235(a)(1)(B)(ii)(IV), 21–22.
15. *Presentence Investigation Reports under the Sentencing Reform Act of 1984*, 6, n. 7.
16. American Bar Association, *Standards Relating to Sentencing Alternatives and Problems* (Chicago: American Bar Association, n.d.).
17. *Presentence Investigation Report Program* (Sacramento, CA: American Justice Institute, 1981).
18. Rodney Kingsnorth and Louis Rizzo, "Decision Making in the Criminal Court: Continuities and Discontinuities," *Criminology* 17 (May 1979).
19. Eugene Czajkoski, "Exposing the Quasi-Judicial Role of the Probation Officer," *Federal Probation* 37 (September 1973).
20. Czajkoski, "Exposing the Quasi-Judicial Role of the Probation Officer," 120.
21. *United States v. Trevino*, 89 f.3d 187, U.S. [4th Cir. July 1996].
22. *Williams v. Oklahoma*, 358 U.S. 576 (1959); and *Williams v. New York*, 337 U.S. 241 (1949).
23. American Bar Association, *Standards Relating to Sentencing Alternatives and Procedures*, secs. 4.3 and 4.4.
24. Model Penal Code, sec. 7.07 (5).
25. *United States v. Rivera*, 96 F.3rd 41 [2nd cir. September 1996]; and *United States v. Lockhart*, 58 F.3d 86 [4th Cir. June 1995].
26. *United States v. Lasky*, 592 F.2d 5670 [9thCir. 1979]; and *Moore v. United States*, 571 F.2d 179 [3rd Cir. 1978].
27. *Miranda v. Arizona*, 384 U.S. 436 [1966].
28. *United States v. Allen*, 13 F.3d 105 [U.S. 4th Cir. December 1993]; and *United States v. Washington*, 11 F.3d 1510 [U.S. 10th Cir. November 1993].
29. *United States v. Gordon*, 4 F.3d 1567 [U.S. 10th Cir. September 1993]; and *United States v. Washington*.

Chapter 5

1. *Houston Chronicle*, July 30, 1996, p. 11A.
2. *Dallas Morning News*, March 9, 1996, p. 1.
3. *People v. Howland*, 108 AD 2d 1019 (Sup. Ct. App. Div. 1985).
4. *Rich v. State*, 640 P2d 159 (Alaska Ct. App. 1982).
5. *Huff v. State*, 554 So. 2d 616 (Fla. Dist. Ct. App. 1989).
6. *Almond v. State*, 350 So. 2d 810 (Fla. 4th DCA 1977).
7. *Norris v. State*, 383 So. 2d 691 (Fla. Dist. Ct. App. 1980).
8. *Panko v. McCauley*, 473 F. Supp. 325 (C.D. Wisc. 1979).
9. *Sobell v. Reed*, 327 F. Supp. 1294 (S.D. N.Y. 1971).
10. *Huff v. State*, 554 So. 2d 616 (Fla. Dist. Ct. App. Dec. 1989).
11. *State v. Labure*, 427 S. 2d 855 (La. 1983).
12. James J. Gobert and Neil P. Cohen, *The Law of Probation and Parole*, 189.
13. *United States v. Thurlow*, 44 F. 3d 46 (U.S. 1st Cir. 1995).
14. *United States v. Porotsky*, 105 F. 2d 69 (U.S. 2nd Cir. 1997).
15. *United States v. Edgin*, 92 F. 3d 1044 (U.S. 10th Cir. 1996).
16. *Goldschmitt v. State*, 490 So. 2d 123 (Fla. Dist. Ct. App. 1986). See also *Lindsay v. State*, 606 So.2d 652 (Fla. App. 4th Dist. 1992).
17. *Ballenger v. State*, 436 S. E. 2d 793 (Ga. App. 1993).
18. *People v. Heckler*, 16 Cal. Rptr. 2d 681, 13 C. A. 4th 1049 (1993).
19. *People v. Meyer*, 176 Ill. 2d 372, 680 N. E. 315 (1997).

20. *People v. Letterlough*, 655 N. E. 2d 146, (N.Y. 1995).
21. *Jones v. Commonwealth*, 185 Va. 335 (1946).
22. *Owens v. Kelly*, 681 F. 2d 1362 (11th Cir. 1982).
23. *Warner v. Orange County Department of Probation*, 870 F. Supp. 69 (S.D.N.Y. 1994).
24. Rolando V. del Carmen, *Potential Liabilities of Probation and Parole Officers* (Cincinnati, OH: Anderson, 1985), 1102.
25. *People v. Dominquez*, 64 Cal. Rptr. 290 (1967).
26. *Rodriguez v. State*, 378 So. 2d 7 (Fla. Dist. Ct. App. 1979).
27. *People v. Mason*, 488 P. 2d 630 (1971).
28. *United States v. Scott*, 678 F. 2d 32 (5th Cir. 1982).
29. *Griffin v. Wisconsin*, 483 U.S. 868 (1987).
30. *State v. Cate*, 683 A. 2d 1010 (Vt. Sup. 1996).
31. *Montana v. Imlay*, 813 P. 2d 979 (1991).
32. *State v. Gonzalez*, 853 P. 2d 526 (Alaska, 1993).
33. Camille Graham Camp and George M. Camp, *The Corrections Yearbook: 1999* (Middletown, CT: Criminal Justice Institute, 1999), 189.
34. Model Penal Code, sec. 301.2.
35. American Bar Association, *Standards Relating to Probation* (Chicago: American Bar Association, n.d.), sec. 1.1(d); and American Bar Association, *Standards, Sentencing Alternatives, and Procedures* (Chicago: American Bar Association, n.d.), sec. 2.4.
36. American Bar Association, *Standards Relating to Probation*, sec. 5.1(b).
37. American Bar Association, *Standards Relating to Probation*, sec. 3.1.
38. *Gagnon v. Scarpelli*, 411 U.S. 778 (1973).
39. *Costa v. State*, 58 Md. App. 474 (1984).
40. Texas Code of Criminal Procedure, Art. 42.12, Sec. 20.
41. Federal Rules of Criminal Procedure, Art. 3564.
42. 18 U.S.C.A., Sec. 3563 (b) (11); and Federal Sentencing Guidelines Handbook: Text, Analysis, Case Digests.
43. Bureau of Justice Statistics, July 2000, NCH 183508.
44. American Bar Association, *Standards Relating to Sentencing Alternatives and Procedures*, sec. 2.4(a)iii.
45. Camp and Camp, *The Corrections Yearbook*, 186.
46. Camp and Camp, *The Corrections Yearbook*, 188.
47. *Black's Law Dictionary*, 5th ed. (St. Paul, MN: West, 1979), 568.
48. *Federal Sentencing Guidelines Handbook*, 335.
49. *Bearden v. Georgia*, 461 U.S. 660 (1983).
50. *United States v. Wolff*, 90 F. 3d 191 (7th Cir. 1996).
51. *Black's Law Dictionary*, 118.
52. John Ortiz Smykla, *Probation and Parole: Crime Control in the Community* (New York: MacMillan, 1984), 222.
53. Douglas C. McDonald, *Restitution and Community Service* (Washington, DC: National Institute of Justice, 1992), 192.
54. Patrick A. Langan and Mark Cunniff, "Recidivism of Felons on Probation, 1986–1989," special report (Washington, DC: U.S. Department of Justice, Bureau of Justice Statistics, February 1992).
55. Rolando V. del Carmen, Jeffrey D. Dailey, and Lance Emerson, *Community Supervision: Law and Practice in Texas* (Huntsville, TX: SHSU Press, 1996), 106.
56. Larry Siegel, *Criminology*, 4th ed. (St. Paul, MN: West, 1992), 561.
57. *Todd v. State*, 911 S.W. 2d 807 (Tex. App. 1995).
58. *State v. Toups*, 499 S. 2d 1149 (La. Ct. App. 1987).
59. Langdan and Cunniff, "Recidivism of Felons on Probation," 7.
60. Del Carmen, Dailey, and Emerson, *Community Supervision*, 105.
61. Texas Code of Criminal Procedure, Art. 42.12 Sec. 22(a)(1).
62. *Higdon v. U. S.*, 627 F. 2d 893 (9th Cir. 1980).
63. Del Carmen, Dailey, and Emerson, *Community Supervision*, 103.
64. *United States v. Duff*, 831 F. 2d 176 (9th Cir. 1987).
65. For a collection of cases on the legality of drug testing as a condition of probation, see *Drug Testing Guidelines and Practices for Adult Probation and Parole Agencies*, monograph (Washington, DC: Bureau of Justice Assistance, July 1991), 87–108.

Chapter 6

1. U.S.C.A. 3651.
2. Cited in Howard Abadinsky, *Probation and Parole: Theory and Practice*, 7th ed. (Upper Saddle River, NJ: Prentice Hall, 2000), 102.
3. U.S. Department of Justice, *Attorney General's Survey of Release Procedures* (New York: Arno, 1974), 24.
4. U.S. Department of Justice, *Attorney General's Survey of Release Procedures*, 22–23, n. 75.
5. U.S. Department of Justice, *Attorney General's Survey of Release Procedures*, 25.
6. U.S. Department of Justice, *Attorney General's Survey of Release Procedures*, 105–06.
7. U.S. Department of Justice, *Attorney General's Survey of Release Procedures*, 299–300.
8. U.S. Department of Justice, *Attorney General's Survey of Release Procedures*, 2.
9. U.S. Department of Justice, *Attorney General's Survey of Release Procedures*, 7.
10. U.S. Department of Justice, *Attorney General's Survey of Release Procedures*.
11. Paraphrased from the National Advisory Commission on Criminal Justice Standards and Goals, *Report on Corrections* (Washington, DC: U.S. Government Printing Office, 1973), 315–16.
12. Mitchell Silverman, "Ethical Issues in the Field of Probation," *International Journal of Offender Therapy and Comparative Criminology* 37 no. 1 (1993): 85–94.
13. National Advisory Commission on Criminal Justice Standards and Goals, *Report on Corrections*, 315–16.
14. Jim Scott, "Deconsolidation: Design for the Future Stolen from the Past," *Journal of the Texas Probation Association*

9, no. 1 (January 1997): 1.

15. National Council on Crime and Delinquency, Standard Probation and Parole Act, secs. 3.3 and 7.7; and American Bar Association, *Standards Relating to Probation* (New York: Institute of Judicial Administration, 1970), 75–76.

16. National Advisory Commission on Criminal Justice Standards and Goals, *Report on Corrections.*

17. John Ortiz Symkla, *Probation and Parole: Crime Control in the Community* (New York: Macmillan, 1984), 90.

18. M. Kay Harris, "Key Differences among Community Corrections Acts in the United States: An Overview," *Prison Journal* 76, no. 2 (1996):192–238.

19. Patrick D. McManus and Lynn Zeller Barclay, *Community Corrections Act: Technical Assistance Manual* (College Park, MD: American Correctional Association, 1994).

20. Harris, "Key Differences among Community Corrections Acts in the United States," 202.

21. Community Corrections Act, Oregon Revised Statutes 423.505. Oregon Laws 1995.

22. The states that passed community corrections acts are Alabama, Arizona, California, Colorado, Connecticut, Florida, Illinois, Indiana, Iowa, Kansas, Kentucky, Maine, Maryland, Michigan, Minnesota, Missouri, Montana, Nebraska, New Mexico, North Carolina, Ohio, Oregon, Pennsylvania, South Dakota, Tennessee, Texas, Virginia, and Wyoming.

23. Edward J. Latessa, Lawrence F. Travis, and Alexander Holsinger, *Evaluation of Ohio's Community Corrections Act Programs and Community Based Correctional Facilities* (Cincinnati, OH: University of Cincinnati, Department of Criminal Justice, February 1997).

24. Gregory B. Cole, "Communication within Parole and Probation," master's thesis, University of Baltimore, 1999, 136.

25. E. Kim Nelson, Howard Ohmart, and Nora Harlow, *Promising Strategies in Probation and Parole* (Washington, DC: U.S. Government Printing Office, 1978).

26. Cole, "Communication within Parole and Probation," 137.

27. Joan M. Petersilia, "Probation in the United States, Part 1," *Perspectives* 22 (Spring 1998): 30–41.

28. Norval Morris and Michael Tonry, *Between Prison and Probation: Intermediate Punishments in a Rational Sentencing System* (New York: Oxford University Press, 1990).

29. Morris and Tonry, *Between Prison and Probation*, 230–31.

30. Abadinsky, *Probation and Parole*, 330.

31. The selection is, however, subject to the approval of the chief U.S. district judge of the judicial district, who officially appoints all U.S. probation officers.

32. Cole, "Communication within Parole and Probation," 25–26.

33. The U.S. Parole Commission was abolished by the Comprehensive Crime Control Act of 1984. Although the commission was scheduled to be phased out by 1992, it was extended for an additional five years.

34. This is the situation in Texas. See Tex. Fam. Code Ann., sec. 51.04 (Vernon).

35. Abadinsky, *Probation and Parole*, 330.

36. Abadinsky, *Probation and Parole*, 330.

37. American Correctional Association, *Standards for Adult Probation and Parole Field Services* (Rockville, MD: American Correctional Association, Commission on Accreditation for Corrections, 1981).

38. National Advisory Commission on Criminal Justice Standards and Goals, *Report on Corrections*, 12.

39. National Advisory Commission on Criminal Justice Standards and Goals, *Report on Corrections.*

40. Janette Logan, "HIV/AIDS-Core Competencies for Practice: A Framework for the Education and Training of Social Workers," *Social Work Education* 11, no. 3 (1992): 22–35.

41. Millard Earl Moon, "An Assessment of Federal Probation Officers' Perceptions regarding Certain Selected Factors Related to Job Performance," Ph.D. dissertation, University of Alabama, 1990, 45.

42. Meryl Aldridge and Tina Eadie, "Manufacturing an Issue: The Case of Probation Officer Training," *Critical Social Policy* 17, no. 1 (1997): 111–24; and Brian Williams, "Probation Training: The Defence of Professionalism," *Social Work Education* 15, no. 3 (1996): 5–19.

43. Moon, "An Assessment of Federal Probation Officers' Perceptions regarding Certain Selected Factors Related to Job Performance," 44.

44. LIS Inc., *State and Local Probation Systems in the United States* (Longmont, CO: LIS Inc., 1995).

45. John P. Crank, "The Construction of Meaning during Training for Probation and Parole," *Justice Quarterly* 13, no. 2 (1996):265–90.

46. Michael Lee Stowe, "Professional Orientation of Probation Officers: Ideology and Personality," Ph.D. dissertation, University of Pittsburgh, 1994, 154.

47. Charles T. Ruby, "Defusing the Hostile Ex-Offender: Rational Behavior Training," *Emotional First Aid: A Journal of Crisis Intervention* 1, no. 1 (Spring 1984): 17–22.

48. James Rainey, "Probation Cadets See Job from Behind Bars," *Los Angeles Times*, February 8, 2000, p. A3.

49. Camille Graham Camp and George M. Camp, *The Corrections Yearbook: 1999* (Middletown, CT: Criminal Justice Institute, 1999), 206.

50. Robert C. Cushman and Dale Sechrest, "Variations in the Administration of Probation Supervision," *Federal Probation* 56, no. 3 (1992): 19–29.

51. Camp and Camp, *The Corrections Yearbook*, 207.

52. Richard D. Sluder, Robert A. Shearer, and Dennis W. Potts, "Probation Officers' Role Perceptions and Attitudes toward Firearms," *Federal Probation* 55 (1991): 3–11.

53. Phillip J. Bigger, "Officers in Danger: Results of the Federal Probation and Pretrial Services Association's National Study on Serious Assaults," *APPA Perspectives* 17 (1987): 14–20.

54. Reported in Dean Champion, *Probation, Parole, and Community Corrections*, 2nd ed. (Englewood Cliffs, NJ: Prentice-Hall, 1996), 429–30.

55. Probation officers are peace officers in Arizona, California, Colorado, Connecticut, Georgia, Illinois, Iowa, Nebraska, New Mexico, New York, Oregon, Utah, and the federal system. Parole officers are peace officers in California, Colorado, Georgia, Illinois, Kansas, Massachusetts, New Mexico, New York, and Utah. Probation and parole officers are peace officers in Alabama, Alaska, Delaware, Kentucky, Louisiana, Mississippi, Nevada, New Hampshire, North Dakota, Oklahoma, Pennsylvania, South Carolina, and Washington. All information about peace officer status was cited in Camp and Camp, *The Corrections Yearbook*, 205. Under Missouri Senate Bill 367 passed in 1997, Missouri probation and parole officers are also authorized to carry firearms.

56. Missouri Department of Corrections, "1997 Legislative Session: Summary of Legislation Passed of Interest to Corrections," *The Horizon* 11, no. 4 (October 1997): 19–20.

57. American Probation and Parole Association, "APPA Position Statement: Weapons," approved 1994.

58. American Probation and Parole Association, "APPA Position Statement."

59. American Probation and Parole Association, "APPA Position Statement."

60. See, for example, Interstate Parole Reciprocal Agreement, III., Ann. Stat. Ch. 38, secs. 123–25, 123–26 (Smith-Hurd).

61. California Interstate Compact on Juveniles, Cal. Welf. and Inst. Code, secs. 1300–1308 (West).

62. Camp and Camp, *The Corrections Yearbook*, 173–75.

63. Cindy Loose, "Waiting for the Champ's Return: Homeless Men Disappointed as Tyson Shifts His Service," *Washington Post*, July 18, 1999, p. A14.

64. Cushman and Sechrest, "Variations in the Administration of Probation Supervision," 25.

Chapter 7

1. U.S. Department of Justice, *Attorney General's Survey of Release Procedures* (Washington, DC: U.S. Department of Justice, 1939), 261.

2. National Advisory Commission on Criminal Justice Standards and Goals, *Report on Corrections* (Washington, DC: U.S. Department of Justice, 1973), cited in George Killinger and Paul Cromwell, eds., *Corrections in the Community*, 2nd ed. (St Paul, MN: West, 1978), 108.

3. Helen D. Pidgeon, *Probation and Parole in Theory and Practice* (New York: National Probation and Parole Association, 1942), 105.

4. National Advisory Commission on Criminal Justice Standards and Goals, *Report on Corrections*.

5. National Advisory Commission on Criminal Justice Standards and Goals, *Report on Corrections*, 107–08.

6. National Advisory Commission on Criminal Justice Standards and Goals, *Report on Corrections*, 115.

7. Robert Gemignani, "Rethinking Probation," *Change* 5, no. 4 (1983).

8. Gemignani, "Rethinking Probation," 2.

9. Gemignani, "Rethinking Probation," 2

10. Gemignani, "Rethinking Probation," 3.

11. Gemignani, "Rethinking Probation," 3.

12. *Supervision of Federal Offenders*, monograph no. 109 (Washington, DC: Administrative Office of the U.S. Courts, 1991). 2.

13. See Robert G. Culbertson and Thomas Ellsworth, "Treatment Innovations in Probation and Parole," in *Probation, Parole, and Community Corrections*, ed. Lawrence W. Travis III (Prospect Heights, IL: Waveland Press, 1985).

14. D. Lipton, Robert Martinson, and Judith Wilks, *The Effectiveness of Correctional Treatment: A Survey of Treatment Evaluation Studies* (New York: Praeger, 1975).

15. Willard Gaylin and David Rothman, "Introduction," in Andrew von Hirsch, *Doing Justice: The Choice of Punishments* (New York: Hill and Wang, 1976), xxi–xli.

16. Michael R. Gottfredson and Travis Hirschi, *A General Theory of Crime* (Stanford, CA: Stanford University Press, 1990), xv.

17. Gottfredson and Hirschi, *A General Theory of Crime*, 95.

18. *Webster's Third New International Dictionary* (Springfield, MA: Merriam-Webster, 1986).

19. *Supervision of Federal Offenders*, 2.

20. *The Supervision Process* (Washington, DC: U.S. Probation Service, n.d.). Materials in this section rely heavily on the "Systematic Approach to Supervision Responsibilities" in this manual.

21. Joy Davidoff-Kroop, *An Initial Assessment of the Division of Parole's Employment Services* (Albany: New York State Division of Parole, 1983), 1.

22. U.S. Department of Justice, National Institute of Justice, *Drug Use Forecasting—1996* (Washington, DC: U.S. Department of Justice, 1997).

23. Culbertson and Ellsworth, "Treatment Innovations in Probation and Parole," 29.

24. Culbertson and Ellsworth, "Treatment Innovations in Probation and Parole," 32.

25. Carl B. Klockars Jr., "A Theory of Probation Supervision," *Journal of Criminal Law, Criminology and Police Science* 63, no. 4 (1974).

26. *Supervision of Federal Offenders*.

27. This discussion relies heavily on the federal probation manual, *Supervision of Federal Offenders*.

28. *Supervision of Federal Offenders*.

29. *Supervision of Federal Offenders*, 18.

30. *Supervision of Federal Offenders*.

31. George M. Camp and Camille G. Camp, *The Corrections Yearbook: 1999* (Middletown, CT: Criminal Justice Institute, 1999).

32. Camp and Camp, *The Corrections Yearbook*, 24.

33. American Probation and Parole Association, "Position Statement: Caseload Standards."

34. American Probation and Parole Association, "Position Statement."

35. American Probation and Parole Association, "Position Statement."

36. See Howard Abadinsky, *Probation and Parole: Theory and Practice*, 7th ed. (Englewood Cliffs, NJ: Prentice-Hall, 2000).

37. Edward E. Rhine, William R. Smith, and Ronald W. Jackson, *Paroling Authorities: Recent History and Current Practice* (Laurel, MD: American Correctional Association, 1991), 112.

38. American Bar Association, *Standards for Criminal Justice: Standards Relating to Probation* (Chicago: American Bar Association, n.d.).

Chapter 8

1. See http://www.ojp.usdoj.gov/bjs/pub/press/pp99pr.pr.

2. Patrick Langan, "Between Prison and Probation: Intermediate Sanctions," *Science* (1994), 791–93, as cited in Joan Petersilia, "Probation in the United States: Practices and Challenges," *National Institute of Justice Journal* (September 1997), 4.

3. Rolando V. del Carmen, Jeffrey D. Dailey, and Lance Emerson, *Community Supervision: Law and Practice in Texas* (Huntsville, TX: SHSU Press, 1996), 108.

4. See http://www.supreme.state.az.us/asd/outcome.htm.

5. Authority to grant probation lies with the court having jurisdiction to try the offense. See 18 U.S.C.A. sec. 3561 and 18 U.S.C. sec. 3563. State statutes often have similar provisions.

6. *Federal Code and Rules*, Title 18, Ch. 227, Rule 3565(a).

7. *Federal Code and Rules*, Title 18, Ch. 227, Rule 35651(b).

8. The traditional officer's attitude toward revocation decisions reflects the rehabilitative, not the punitive, focus of the probation and parole systems. For example, here is a quote from *Gagnon v. Scarpelli*, 411 U.S. 778 (1973): "Revocation is, . . . if anything, commonly treated as a failure of supervision. While presumably it would be inappropriate for a field agent never to revoke, the whole thrust of the probation/parole movement is to keep [individuals] in the community, working with adjustment problems there, and using revocation only as a last resort where treatment has failed or is about to fail."

9. *Statistical Summary Fiscal Year 1999* (Texas Department of Criminal Justice Executive Services, February 2000), 2.

10. *Texas Code of Criminal Procedure*, Article 42.12, sec. 11(1).

11. *1995 Federal Guidelines Manual* (Washington, DC, 1996), sec. 7B1.1.

12. Langan, "Between Prison and Probation," 72.

13. *People v. King*, 267 Cal. App. 2d 814 (1968).

14. *People v. McClean*, 130 Cal. App. 2d 439 (1955).

15. *Olivas v. State*, 168 Tex. Crim. 437 (1959).

16. *House v. State*, 166 Tex. Crim. 41 (1958).

17. *Rinto v. State*, 628 S.W.2d. 159 (1982).

18. *United States v. Furukawa*, 596 F.2d. 921 (9th Cir. 1979).

19. *Baker v. State*, 428 S.W.2d 684 (Fla. Dist. Ct. App. 1983).

20. *Supervision of Federal Offenders*, monograph no. 109 (Washington, DC: Administrative Office of the U.S. Courts, Probation and Pretrial Services Division, 1991), 39–40. The guidelines require mandatory revocation for possession of a firearm or controlled substances.

21. Langan, "Between Prison and Probation," 791–93.

22. Peggy D. Burke, *Policy-Driven Responses to Probation and Parole Violations* (National Institute of Corrections, March 1997), 12.

23. *Federal Criminal Code and Rules*, 1995, chap. 229, sec. 3603.

24. *Bruggeman v. State*, 681 So.2d. 822 (1996).

25. *1995 Federal Guidelines Manual*, sec. 7B1.5.

26. *Gagnon v. Scarpelli*.

27. *Mempa v. Rhay*, 389 U.S. 128 (1967).

28. *Kuenstler v. State*, 486 S.W.2d. 367 (Tex. 1972).

29. *Burkett v. State*, 485 S.W.2d. 578 (Tex. 1972).

30. *Morrissey v. Brewer*, 408 U.S. 471 (1972).

31. *People v. Sweeden*, 116 Cal. App. 2d. 891 (1953).

32. *Soliz v. State*, 171 Tex. Crim. 376 (1961).

33. *People v. Price*, 24 Ill. App. 2d. 364 (1960).

34. *Dickerson v. State*, 136 Ga. App. 885 (1975); and *Cooper v. State*, 599 P. 2d. 419 (Okla. Crim. App. 1979).

35. *Smith v. State*, 932 S.W.2d. 279 (Tex. App. 1996).

36. *United States v. McCormick*, 54 F. 3d 214 (U.S. 5th Cir. 1995).

37. Rolando V. del Carmen, *Potential Liabilities of Probation and Parole Officers* (Washington, DC: National Institute of Corrections, August 1995), 144.

38. *State v. Varnado*, 384 So. 440 (LA. 1980).

39. *Herrington v. State*, 534 S.W.2d. 311 (Tex. Crim. App. 1976).

40. *Meyer v. State*, 596 P.2d. 1270 (Okla. Crim. App. 1979).

41. *State v. Dement*, 42 N.C. App. 254 (1979).

42. *Gilbert v. State*, 150 Ga. App. 339 (1979).

43. Rolando V. del Carmen, *Criminal Procedure: Law and Practice* (Belmont, CA: Wadsworth, 1998).

44. *State v. Turner*, 873 P. 2d. 208 (Kansas App. 1994).

45. Del Carmen, *Potential Liabilities of Probation and Parole Officers*, 147.

46. *Pennsylvania Board of Probation and Parole v. Scott*, 524 U.S. 357 (1998).

47. *Pennsylvania Board of Probation and Parole v. Scott*.

48. *Bearden v. Georgia*, 461 U.S. 660 (1983).

49. *Black v. Romano*, 471 U.S. 606 (1985).

50. Del Carmen, *Potential Liabilities of Probation and Parole Officers*, 152.

51. *Jones v. State*, 916 S.W.2d. 766 (Ark. App. 1996).

52. *Federal Criminal Code and Rules*, 1995, Ch. 227, sec. 3565.

53. III. Unified Code of Corrections sec. 1005–6–5(2).

54. *Supervision of Federal Offenders*, 39–40.

55. Carl B. Klockars, "A Theory of Probation Supervision," *Journal of Criminal Law, Criminology, and Police Science* 63, no. 4 (1974).

56. *Gagnon v. Sarpelli*.

57. Ralph W. England, "A Study of Postprobation Recidivism among Five Hundred Federal Offenders," *Federal Probation* 19 (1955), 10–16.

58. Patrick A. Langan and Mark A. Cuniff, "Recidivism of Felons on Probation, 1986–1989," special report (Washington, DC: U.S. Department of Justice, Bureau of Justice Statistics, February 1992).

59. Harry Allen, Eric Carlson, and Evalyn Parks, *Critical Issues in Adult Probation: A Summary* (Washington, DC: National Institute of Law Enforcement and Criminal Justice, 1979).

60. Allen, Carlson, and Parks, *Critical Issues in Adult Probation*, 36.

61. Allen, Carlson, and Parks, *Critical Issues in Adult Probation*, 37.

62. Joan Petersilia, Susan Turner, James Kahan, and Joyce Peterson, *Granting Felons Probation: Public Risks and Alternatives* (Santa Monica, CA: RAND, 1985), p. vii.

63. Petersilia et al., *Granting Felons Probation*, 52.

64. Petersilia et al., *Granting Felons Probation*, 52–56.

65. Petersilia et al., *Granting Felons Probation*, 53.

66. Petersilia et al., *Granting Felons Probation*, viii.

67. Petersilia et al., *Granting Felons Probation*, 53.

68. Petersilia et al., *Granting Felons Probation*, 65.

69. Petersilia et al., *Granting Felons Probation*, 65.

Chapter 9

1. Joan Petersilia, "When Prisoners Return to the Community: Political, Economic, and Social Consequences," *Sentencing and Corrections: Issues for the 21st Century* (Washington, DC: U.S. Department of Justice, November 2000), 1–3.

2. 18 U.S.C. 3583 (e) (3).

3. Claire Wilcox, *Theory of Parole* (1927), 20, quoted in U.S. Department of Justice, *Attorney General's Survey of Release Procedures: Parole*, vol. 4 (Washington, DC: U.S. Department of Justice, 1939).

4. Warren F. Spaulding, *Proceedings of the Annual Congress of the American Prison Association* (Indianapolis, IN: W. B. Burford, 1916), 548.

5. Justin Miller, "Evils of Confusion between Pardon and Parole," Proceedings of the Annual Congress of the American Prison Association (Indianapolis, IN: W. B. Burford, 1932).

6. U.S. Department of Justice, *Attorney General's Survey of Release Procedures*, 6.

7. Quoted in Fredrick H. Wines, *Punishment and Reformation: A Study of the Penitentiary System* (New York: T. Y. Crowell, 1919), 219.

8. Wines, *Punishment and Reformation*, 194.

9. Wines, *Punishment and Reformation*, 195.

10. William C. Parker, *Parole: Origins, Development, Current Practices, and Statutes* (College Park, MD: American Correctional Association, 1975).

11. The historical discussions in this chapter rely on U.S. Department of Justice, *Attorney General's Survey of Release Procedures*; Charles L. Whitehead, "Adult Parole in Texas," M.A. thesis, Sam Houston State University, May 1975; and Robert Hughes, *The Fatal Shore: The Epic of Australia's Founding* (New York: Vintage, 1986).

12. Howard Abadinsky, "Parole History: An Economic Perspective," *Offender Rehabilitation* 2, no. 3 (1978): 275–78.

13. Donald R. Walker, *Penology for Profit* (College Station, TX: Texas A&M University Press, 1988).

14. Walker, *Penology for Profit*.

15. Peter Hoffman, "History of the Federal Parole System: Part I (1910–1972)," *Federal Probation* 61, no. 3 (1997): 23–31.

16. Hoffman, "History of the Federal Parole System."

17. Francis T. Cullen and Karen E. Gilbert, *Reaffirming Rehabilitation* (Cincinnati, OH: Anderson, 1982), 76.

18. Warren F. Spaulding, "The Treatment of Crime—Past, Present, and Future," *Journal of the American Institute of Criminal Law and Criminology* 3 (May 1912): 378.

19. Cited in Edwin H. Sutherland, Donald R. Cressey, and David F. Luckenbill, *Principles of Criminology*, 11th ed. (Dix Hills, NJ: General Hall, 1992), 560.

20. Lawrence F. Travis III and Vincent O'Leary, *Changes in Sentencing and Parole Decision Making, 1976–1978* (Washington, DC: National Institute of Corrections, 1979), a publication of the National Parole Institutes and Parole Policy Seminars.

21. Travis and O'Leary, *Changes in Sentencing and Parole*, 6.

22. U.S. Department of Justice, *Attorney General's Survey of Release Procedures*.

23. Sanford Bates, "The Next Hundred Years," speech delivered at the 35th Annual Conference of the National Probation Association, Atlantic City, New Jersey, 1941. Sanford Bates, then commissioner for parole for the state of New York, became the director of the U.S. Bureau of Prisons. Bates reorganized the Bureau of Prisons, introduced psychologists and psychiatrists into the system, and is often recognized as the father of "the new prison."

24. Bates, "The Next Hundred Years."

25. "Harris Poll," *Los Angeles Times*, August 14, 1967.

26. National Advisory Commission on Criminal Justice Standards and Goals, *A National Strategy to Reduce Crime* (Washington, DC: Law Enforcement Assistance Administration, 1973).

27. National Advisory Commission on Criminal Justice Standards and Goals, *A National Strategy to Reduce Crime*.

28. Petersilia, "When Prisoners Return to the Community," 2.

29. Robert Martinson, "What Works? Questions and Answers about Prison Reform," *Public Interest* (Spring 1974): 25.

30. Cullen and Gilbert, *Reaffirming Rehabilitation*, xxvii.

31. David B. Griswold and Michael D. Wiatrowski, "The Emergence of Determinate Sentencing," *Federal Probation* (June 1983): 28–35.

32. Reported in Michael S. Serrill, "Determinate Sentencing: The History, the Theory, the Debate," *Corrections Maga-*

zine 3 (September 1977): 3–13. Much of the material on the history of the determinate sentencing movement drew liberally from this excellent paper.

33. American Friends Service Committee, *Struggle for Justice* (New York: Hill and Wang, 1971).

34. Andrew von Hirsch, *Doing Justice: The Choice of Punishments* (New York: Hill and Wang, 1976).

35. David Fogel, ". . . *We Are the Living Proof . . .": The Justice Model for Corrections*, 2nd ed. (Cincinnati, OH: Anderson, 1979).

36. Fogel, ". . . *We Are the Living Proof . . ."*

37. Cited in Edward R. Rhine, William Smith, and Ronald W. Jackson, *Paroling Authorities: Recent History and Current Practice* (Laurel, MD: American Correctional Association, 1991), 25.

38. Stephen Gettinger Smith, "Conference Takes a Hard Look at Proposals," *Corrections Magazine* 3 (September 1977): 64–68.

39. Jeremy Travis, "But They All Come Back: Rethinking Prisoner Reentry," *Sentencing and Corrections: Issues for the 21st Century* (Washington, DC: U.S. Department of Justice, May 2000), 2–3.

40. Petersilia, "When Prisoners Return to the Community," 5.

41. Michael Tonry, "Reconsidering Indeterminate and Structured Sentencing," *Sentencing and Corrections: Issues for the 21st Century* (Washington, DC: U.S. Department of Justice, 1999).

42. These states were California, Colorado, Illinois, Indiana, Maine, and New Mexico between 1976 and 1979; Connecticut, Florida, Minnesota, North Carolina, and Washington between 1980 and 1984; and Delaware in 1990.

43. Petersilia, "When Prisoners Return to the Community," 5.

44. Peggy B. Burke, *Abolishing Parole: Why the Emperor Has No Clothes* (Lexington, KY: American Probation and Parole Association, and California, MO: Association of Paroling Authorities, International, 1995).

45. Kevin Krajick, "Abolishing Parole: An Idea Whose Time Has Passed," *Corrections Magazine* 9 (June 1983): 32–40.

46. U.S. Department of Justice, Bureau of Justice Statistics, *Probation and Parole in 1999* (Washington, DC: U.S. Department of Justice, July 2000), 5.

47. Camille Graham Camp and George M. Camp, *The Corrections Yearbook: 1999* (Middletown, CT: Criminal Justice Institute, 1999), 167.

48. Frank P. Williams III, Marilyn D. McShane, and H. Michael Dolny, "Developing a Parole Classification Instrument for Use as a Management Tool," *Corrections Management Quarterly* 4, no. 4 (2000): 45–59.

49. A. Keith Bottomley, "Parole in Transition: A Comparative Study of Origins, Developments, and Prospects for the 1990s," in *Crime and Justice: View of Research*, vol. 12, ed. Michael Tonry and Norval Morris (Chicago: University of Chicago Press, 1990), 342.

50. Burke, *Abolishing Parole*, 16.

51. Bottomley, "Parole in Transition," 27.

52. Rhine, Smith, and Jackson, *Paroling Authorities*, 96. Reporting on the American Correctional Association Parole Task Force survey, they stated, "Regardless of the pressure to release, most parole board chairs surveyed by the Task Force do not believe that the management of prison population levels should be an important responsibility of parole boards."

53. Cited in Rhine, Smith, and Jackson, *Paroling Authorities*, 97–98.

54. Theodore M. Hammett, Lynne Harrold, Michael Gross, and Joel Epstein, *1992 Update: HIV/AIDS in Correctional Facilities* (Washington, DC: U.S. Department of Justice, 1994).

55. Newton E. Kendig, Barbara Boyle, and Anthony Swetz, "The Maryland Division of Correction Medical-Parole Program: A Four-Year Experience, 1991 to 1994," *AIDS & Public Policy Journal* 11, no. 1 (1996): 21–27.

56. The description and procedure of evaluation was borrowed closely from Kendig, Boyle, and Swetz, "The Maryland Division of Correction Medical-Parole Program," 22–24.

57. Kendig, Boyle, and Swetz, "The Maryland Division of Correction Medical-Parole Program," 22.

58. Kendig, Boyle, and Swetz, "The Maryland Division of Correction Medical-Parole Program," 22.

59. Kendig, Boyle, and Swetz, "The Maryland Division of Correction Medical-Parole Program," 25.

Chapter 10

1. American Correctional Association, *Manual for Adult Parole Authorities*, 2nd ed. (Washington, DC: American Correctional Association, 1980).

2. Information on eligibility dates, time sheets, and good time is taken from Leanne Fiftal Alarid's work experience as a correctional case manager.

3. Jon L. Proctor, "The New Parole: An Analysis of Parole Board Decision Making as a Function of Eligibility," *Journal of Crime and Justice* 22, no. 2 (1999): 193–217.

4. Joan Petersilia, "When Prisoners Return to the Community: Political, Economic, and Social Consequences," *Sentencing and Corrections: Issues for the 21st Century* (Washington, DC: U.S. Department of Justice, November 2000), 3.

5. Edward E. Rhine, William R. Smith, and Ronald W. Jackson, *Paroling Authorities: Recent History and Current Practice* (Laurel, MD: American Correctional Association, 1991), 51. Connecticut, Delaware, Hawaii, Minnesota, and Mississippi have full-time chairs and members who serve part time. In Iowa and Utah, the chair and at least one member are full time, and other members serve part time.

6. Camille Graham Camp and George M. Camp, *The Corrections Yearbook: 1999* (Middletown, CT: Criminal Justice Institute, 1999), 209.

7. Camp and Camp, *The Corrections Yearbook 1999*, 209.

8. Individuals or a board within the department of corrections appoints parole board members in Idaho, Michigan, Minnesota, Texas, and Utah. In Maryland, appointment takes place by the secretary of the Department of Public Safety, and Ohio chooses candidates from a civil service list. On some occasions, having the governor name parole board members has resulted in appointments on the basis of political affiliation instead of qualifications for making parole decisions.

9. Rhine, Smith, and Jackson, *Paroling Authorities*, 51.

10. American Correctional Association, *Manual of Correctional Standards* (College Park, MD: American Correctional Association, June 1980), 117, 118.

11. Rhine, Smith, and Jackson, *Paroling Authorities*, 36.

12. American Correctional Association, *Manual for Adult Parole Authorities*, 124.

13. David T. Stanley, *Prisoners among Us* (Washington, DC: Brookings Institution, 1976).

14. Proctor, "The New Parole," 197.

15. William J. Genego, Peter D. Goldberger, and Vicki C. Jackson, "Parole Release Decision Making and the Sentencing Process," *Yale Law Journal* 84 (1975): 810.

16. Petersilia, "When Prisoners Return to the Community," 5.

17. William H. Parsonage, Frances P. Bernat, and Jacqueline Helfgott, "Victim Impact Testimony and Pennsylvania's Parole Decision Making Process: A Pilot Study," *Criminal Justice Policy Review* 6, no. 3 (1994): 187–206.

18. Frances P. Bernat, William H. Parsonage, and Jacqueline Helfgott, "Victim Impact Laws and the Parole Process in the United States: Balancing Victim and Inmate Rights and Interests," *International Review of Victimology* 3, no. 1/2 (1994): 121.

19. Bernat, Parsonage, and Helfgott, "Victim Impact Laws and the Parole Process in the United States," 128.

20. Bernat, Parsonage, and Helfgott, "Victim Impact Laws and the Parole Process in the United States," 131–33.

21. Parsonage, Bernat, and Helfgott, "Victim Impact Testimony and Pennsylvania's Parole Decision Making Process."

22. Parsonage, Bernat, and Helfgott, "Victim Impact Testimony and Pennsylvania's Parole Decision Making Process."

23. Brent L. Smith, Erin Watkins, and Kathryn Morgan, "The Effect of Victim Participation on Parole Decisions: Results from a Southeastern State," *Criminal Justice Policy Review* 8, no. 1 (1997): 57–74.

24. Elizabeth L. Taylor, "In Search of Equity: The Oregon Parole Matrix," unpublished monograph, 1981. In 1974 the U.S. Court of Appeals for the Seventh Circuit held that an inmate must be provided written notice of the reason for denial of parole. See *King v. United States*, 492 F. 2d 1337 (7th Cir. 1974).

25. Genego, Goldberger, and Jackson, "Parole Release Decision Making and the Sentencing Process," 820.

26. *Menechino v. Oswald*, 430 F. 2d 403, 407–408 (2d Cir. 1970), cert. denied, 400 U.S. 1023, 91 S. Ct. 588, 27 L. Ed. 2d 635 (1971).

27. National Advisory Commission on Criminal Justice Standards and Goals, *Corrections* (Washington, DC: National Advisory Commission on Criminal Justice Standards and Goals, 1973), 397.

28. American Correctional Association, *Manual for Adult Parole Authorities*, 22.

29. David J. Rothman, *Conscience and Convenience: The Asylum and Its Alternatives in Progressive America* (Boston: Little, Brown, 1980), 173.

30. Rothman, *Conscience and Convenience*, 174.

31. Later called the U.S. Parole Commission, it was to be phased out by the Comprehensive Crime Control Act of 1984 but was subsequently given until 2002 before final abolition.

32. Peter B. Hoffman, "Twenty Years of Operational Use of a Risk Prediction Instrument: The United States Parole Commission's Salient Factor Score," *Journal of Criminal Justice* 22, no. 6 (1994): 477–94.

33. Hoffman, "Twenty Years of Operational Use of a Risk Prediction Instrument."

34. Hoffman, "Twenty Years of Operational Use of a Risk Prediction Instrument."

35. Hoffman, "Twenty Years of Operational Use of a Risk Prediction Instrument," 485.

36. Joan Petersilia and Susan Turner, "Guideline-Based Justice: Prediction and Racial Minorities," in *Prediction and Classification*, ed. D. Gottfredson and M. Tonry (Chicago: University of Chicago Press, 1987), 151–81.

37. Proctor, "The New Parole."

38. Victoria J. Palacios, "Go and Sin No More: Rationality and Release Decisions by Parole Boards," *South Carolina Law Review* 45 (1994): 613.

39. John Irwin, "Adaptation to Being Corrected: Corrections from the Convict's Perspective," in *Handbook of Criminology*, ed. Daniel Glaser (Chicago: Rand McNally College Publishing, 1974), 983.

40. James Cole and Charles Logan, "Parole: The Consumer's Perspective," *Criminal Justice Review* 2 (1977): 71–80.

41. James L. Beck, "Offender Perceptions of Parole Decision Making," unpublished monograph, 1981.

42. From the files of Paul F. Cromwell, one of this book's coauthors.

43. Mika'il A. Muhammad, "Prisoners' Perspectives on Strategies for Release," *Journal of Offender Rehabilitation* 23 (1996): 131–52, especially 136.

44. Muhammad, "Prisoners' Perspectives on Strategies for Release," 137, 145.

45. Muhammad, "Prisoners' Perspectives on Strategies for Release," 137.

46. Muhammad, "Prisoners' Perspectives on Strategies for Release," 146.

47. Walter T. Haesler, "The Released Prisoner and His Difficulties to Be Accepted Again as a 'Normal' Citizen," *Euro-Criminology* 4 (1992): 61–68.
48. Palacios, "Go and Sin No More."
49. Palacios, "Go and Sin No More."
50. *French v. Ciccone*, 308 F. Supp. 256, 257 (W. D. Mo. 1969).
51. *Anderson v. Corall*, 263 U.S. 193, 44 S. Ct. 43, 68 L. Ed. 247 (1923).
52. *Scarpa v. United States Board of Parole*, 477 F. 2d 278, 281 (5th Cir. 1972), vacated as moot; 414 U.S. 809, 94 S. Ct. 79, 38 L. Ed. 2d 44 (1973); and *Menechino v. Oswald*, 430 F. 2d 403, 407 (2d Cir. 1970), cert. denied, 400 U.S. 1023, 91 S. Ct. 588, 27 L. Ed. 2d 635 (1971).
53. *Scarpa v. United States Board of Parole*, 281.
54. Genego, Goldberger, and Jackson, "Parole Release Decision Making and the Sentencing Process," 843.
55. *Menechino v. Oswald*.
56. *Menechino v. Oswald*.
57. See United States ex rel. *Campbell v. Pate*, 401 F. 2d 55 (7th Cir. 1968); Palermo v. Rockefeller, 323 F. Supp. 478 (S.D.N.Y. 1971); and *Monks v. New Jersey State Parole Board*, 55 N.J. 238, 277 A. 2d 193 (1971).
58. 442 U.S. 1, 60 L. Ed. 2d 668, 99 S. Ct. 2100 (1979).
59. *Greenholtz v. Inmates of the Nebraska Penal and Correctional Complex*, 442 U.S. 1, 14, 99 S. Ct. 2100, 2107, 60 L. Ed. 2d 668 (1979).
60. *Greenholtz v. Inmates of the Nebraska Penal and Correctional Complex*.
61. *Greenholtz v. Inmates of the Nebraska Penal and Correctional Complex, 16*.
62. *Greenholtz v. Inmates of the Nebraska Penal and Correctional Complex, 9–10*.
63. 482 U.S. 369 (1987).
64. *Williams v. Missouri Board of Probation and Parole*, 661 F.2d 698 (8th Cir. 1981), cert. denied, 455 U.S. 993 (1982).
65. American Correctional Association, *Standards for Adult Parole Authorities*, 242–48.
66. Palacios, "Go and Sin No More," 613.
67. In Texas, the parole board is an independent and autonomous agency that decides whether to parole an inmate. Once paroled, the parolee is under the custody and supervision of the Parole Division, which is an agency under the Texas Department of Criminal Justice.
68. Rhine, Smith, and Jackson, *Paroling Authorities*, 32–33.
69. American Correctional Association, *Manual of Correctional Standards*, 500. See also Justice William O. Douglas's separate opinion in *Morrissey v. Brewer*.

Chapter 11

1. Frank P. Williams III, Marilyn D. McShane, and H. Michael Dolny, "Developing a Parole Classification Instrument for Use as a Management Tool," *Corrections Management Quarterly* 4, no. 4 (2000): 45–59.
2. Camille Graham Camp and George C. Camp, *The Corrections Yearbook: 1999* (Middletown, CT: Criminal Justice Institute, 1999).
3. Craig Hemmens, "Life in the Joint and Beyond: An Examination of Inmate Attitudes and Perceptions of Prison, Parole, and Self at the Time of Release," Ph.D. dissertation, Sam Houston State University, 1998, 172.
4. Hemmens, "Life in the Joint and Beyond," 173–74.
5. Daniel Glaser, *The Effectiveness of Prison and Parole Systems* (Indianapolis, IN: Bobbs-Merrill, 1969); John Irwin, *The Felon*, (Englewood Cliffs, NJ: Prentice-Hall, 1970); and E. Studt, "Reintegration from the Parolee's Perspective," paper presented at the National Symposium on Law Enforcement Science and Technology, U.S. National Institute of Law Enforcement and Criminal Justice, Washington, DC, 1973.
6. Robert M. Grooms, "Recidivist," *Crime and Delinquency* 28 (1982): 541–45.
7. Grooms, "Recidivist," 543.
8. Grooms, "Recidivist," 545.
9. Rosemary J. Erickson, Wayman J. Crow, Louis A. Zurcher, and Archie V. Connett, *Paroled But Not Free* (New York: Behavioral Publications, 1973).
10. Erickson et al., *Paroled But Not Free*, 96–97.
11. Erickson et al., *Paroled But Not Free*, 16–17.
12. Erickson et al., *Paroled But Not Free*, 27–29.
13. Erickson et al., *Paroled But Not Free*, 98.
14. Stephen C. Richards and Richard S. Jones, "Perpetual Incarceration Machine: Structural Impediments to Postprison Success," *Journal of Contemporary Criminal Justice* 13, no. 1 (1997): 4–22.
15. Richards and Jones, "Perpetual Incarceration Machine," 13–14.
16. Richards and Jones, "Perpetual Incarceration Machine," 14.
17. Joan Petersilia, "When Prisoners Return to the Community: Political, Economic, and Social Consequences," *Sentencing and Corrections: Issues for the 21st Century*, paper 9 from the Executive Sessions on Sentencing and Corrections (Washington DC: U.S. Department of Justice, November 2000).
18. Mona Lynch, "Waste Managers? The New Penology, Crime Fighting, and Parole Agent Identity," *Law and Society Review* 32, no. 4 (1998): 839–69.
19. Lynch, "Waste Managers?" 855.
20. Edward E. Rhine, William R. Smith, and Ronald W. Jackson, *Paroling Authorities: Recent History and Current Practice* (Laurel, MD: American Correctional Association, 1991).
21. Douglas M. Anglin and Hser Yih-Ing, "Treatment of Drug Abuse," in *Drugs and Crime; Crime and Justice: A Review of Research*, vol. 13, ed. Michael Tonry and James Q. Wilson (Chicago: University of Chicago Press, 1990).
22. Norman Holt, "The Current State of Parole in America," in *Community Corrections: Probation, Parole, and Interme-*

diate Sanctions, ed. Joan Petersilia (New York: Oxford University Press, 1998), 36.

23. *Boling v. Romer,* 101 F. 3d 1336 (10th Cir. 1996).

24. *Rise v. Oregon,* 59 F. 3d 1556 (9th Cir. 1995); and *Jones v. Murray,* 962 F. 2d 302 (4th Cir. 1992).

25. *Walrath v. Getty,* 71 F. 3d 679 (7th Cir. 1995).

26. American Correctional Association, *Standards for Adult Parole Authorities,* 2nd ed. (College Park, MD: American Correctional Association, 1980), 28.

27. *United States v. Turner,* 44 F. 3d 900 (10th Cir. 1995).

28. *People v. Randazzo,* 15 N.Y. 2d 526 (1964). A California case reached the same result—*People v. Denne,* 141 Cal. App.2d 499 (1956).

29. *People v. Langella,* 244 N.Y.S. 2d 802 (1963). See also *DiMarco v. Greene* 385 F. 2d 556 (6th Cir. 1967).

30. *Commonwealth v. Pickron,* 535 Pa. 241 (1993).

31. *Commonwealth v. Walter,* 655 A. 2d 554 (Pa. 1995).

32. *Commonwealth v. Williams,* 1997 Pa. LEXIS 786 (1997), as cited in Neil P. Cohen and James J. Gobert, *The Law of Probation and Parole* (Colorado Springs, CO: Shepard's/McGraw-Hill, 1993, supplement 1997), 315.

33. Cohen and Gobert, *The Law of Probation and Parole,* 380. See also *Correctional Law Reporter* (October 1994), 36.

34. 18 U.S.C.A. sec. 3606.

35. Howard Abadinsky, *Probation and Parole: Theory and Practice,* 7th ed. (Upper Saddle River, NJ: Prentice Hall, 2000), 254.

36. Although an emergency warrant may be issued on telephoned request from a parole officer, the board has traditionally limited the issuance of such warrants to situations that absolutely require immediate arrest and detention.

37. Shawn Schwaner, "They Can Run, But Can They Hide? A Profile of Parole Violators at Large," *Journal of Crime and Justice* 20, no. 2 (1997): 19–32; and Frank P. Williams, Marilyn D. McShane, and H. Michael Dolny, "Predicting Parole Absconders," *Prison Journal* 80, no. 1 (2000): 24–38.

38. Dale G. Parent et al., *Responding to Probation and Parole Violations* (Washington, DC: U.S. Department of Justice, 1994), 25.

39. Dale G. Parent, "Structuring Policies to Address Sanctions for Absconders and Violators," in *Reclaiming Offender Accountability: Intermediate Sanctions for Probation and Parole Violators,* ed. Edward E. Rhine (Laurel, MD: American Correctional Association, 1993), 10.

40. Parent et al., *Responding to Probation and Parole Violations,* 25–26.

41. Parent et al., *Responding to Probation and Parole Violations,* 27, 33.

42. Schwaner, "They Can Run, But Can They Hide?"

43. Schwaner, "They Can Run, But Can They Hide?"

44. Williams, McShane, and Dolny, "Predicting Parole Absconders."

45. Williams, McShane, and Dolny, "Predicting Parole Absconders," 31–36.

46. Parent et al., *Responding to Probation and Parole Violations,* 28–34.

47. In *Lay v. Louisiana Parole Board,* 741 So.2d 80 (La. Ct. App. 1st Cir. 1999), the court decided that a preliminary parole revocation hearing is not necessary when state law mandates revocation after conviction for a new crime.

48. Hee-Jong Joo, Sheldon Ekland-Olson, and William R. Kelly, "Recidivism among Paroled Property Offenders Released during a Period of Prison Reform," *Criminology* 33, no. 3 (1995): 389–410.

49. U.S. Department of Justice, Bureau of Justice Statistics, *Correctional Populations in the United States, 1995* (Washington, DC: U.S. Department of Justice, 1997), 130, Table 6.5.

50. William J. Sabol, William P. Adams, Barbara Parthasarathy, and Yan Yuan, "Offenders Returning to Federal Prison, 1986–1997," special report (Washington, DC: U.S. Department of Justice, Bureau of Justice Statistics, September 2000), 1.

51. Jeremy Travis, "But They All Come Back: Rethinking Prisoner Reentry," *Sentencing and Corrections: Issues for the 21st Century,* paper 7 in Executive Sessions on Sentencing and Corrections (Washington, DC: U.S. Department of Justice, May 2000), 3.

52. Allen J. Beck, "Prisoners in 1999," *Bureau of Justice Statistics Bulletin* (August 2000), 11.

53. Sabol et al., "Offenders Returning to Federal Prison," 1.

54. Parent et al., *Responding to Probation and Parole Violations,* 3–4.

55. Parent et al., *Responding to Probation and Parole Violations,* 4–5.

56. Parent et al., *Responding to Probation and Parole Violations,* 10.

57. Parent et al., *Responding to Probation and Parole Violations,* 10.

58. 408 U.S. 471 (1972).

59. Rhine, Smith, and Jackson, *Paroling Authorities,* 128.

60. Rhine, Smith, and Jackson, *Paroling Authorities,* 129.

61. Rhine, Smith, and Jackson, *Paroling Authorities,* 128.

62. 397 U.S. 254 (1970).

63. 411 U.S. 778 (1973).

64. *In re Prewitt,* 8 Cal. 3d 470 (1972).

65. *Belk v. Purkett,* 15 F. 3d 803 (8th Cir. 1994).

66. Wesley Gilmer, *The Law Dictionary,* 6th ed. (Cincinnati, OH: Anderson, 1986), 160.

67. See *Correctional Law Reporter* (October 1994), 35.

68. *Pennsylvania Board of Probation and Parole v. Scott,* 118 S. Ct. 2014 (1998).

69. Craig T. Hemmens, Kathryn Bennett, and Rolando del Carmen, "The Exclusionary Rule Does Not Apply to Parole Revocation Hearings: An Analysis of *Pennsylvania Board of Probation and Parole v. Scott,*" *Criminal Law Bulletin* 35, no. 4 (1998): 388–409.

70. *State v. Pizel,* 987 P.2d 1288 (Utah Ct. App. 1999).

71. 454 U.S. 14 (1981).

72. No. 95–7452 (1997).

73. No. 95–1598 (1997).
74. *Hawkins v. Freeman,* 166 F.3d 267 (1999).
75. Rhine, Smith, and Jackson, *Paroling Authorities,* 129.
76. *King v. Simpson,* 189 F.3d 284 (2d Cir. 1999).
77. *Best v. State,* 264 A.D.2d 404, 694 N.Y.S.2d 689 (2d Dep't 1999).
78. Peggy B. Burke, *Policy-Driven Responses to Probation and Parole Violations* (Washington, DC: U.S. Department of Justice, National Institute of Corrections, March 1997), 12.
79. Burke, *Policy-Driven Responses to Probation and Parole Violations,* 18.
80. Rhine, Smith, and Jackson, *Paroling Authorities,* 131.
81. *Richardson v. New York State Executive Department,* 602 N.Y.S.2d 443 (1993).
82. Burke, *Policy-Driven Responses to Probation and Parole Violations,* 18.
83. Parent et al., *Responding to Probation and Parole Violations,* 10.
84. John P. Prevost, Edward E. Rhine, and Ronald W. Jackson, "The Parole Violations Process in Georgia," in *Reclaiming Offender Accountability: Intermediate Sanctions for Probation and Parole Violators,* ed. Edward E. Rhine (Laurel, MD: American Correctional Association, 1993).
85. Joan Petersilia, "When Prisoners Return to the Community." 3.
86. Don Gottfredson, Michael Gottfredson, and James Garofalo, "Time Served in Prison and Parolee Outcomes among Parolee Risk Categories," *Journal of Criminal Justice* 5 (1997): 1–12.
87. Allen J. Beck and Bernard E. Shipley, *Recidivism of Prisoners Released in 1983,* special report (Washington, DC: U.S. Department of Justice, Bureau of Justice Statistics, April 1989).
88. Gennaro Vito, D. G. Wilson, and Edward J. Latessa, "Comparison of the Dead: Attributes and Outcomes of Furman-Commuted Death Row Inmates in Kentucky and Ohio," in *The Death Penalty in America: Current Research,* ed. Robert M. Bohm (Cincinnati, OH: Anderson Publishing, 1991), 101–11.
89. Beck and Shipley, *Recidivism of Prisoners Released in 1983,* 2.
90. Sabol et al., "Offenders Returning to Federal Prison," 3.
91. Joo, Ekland-Olson, and Kelly, "Recidivism among Paroled Property Offenders Released during a Period of Prison Reform."
92. Frank P. Williams III, Marilyn D. McShane, Lorraine Samuels, and H. Michael Dolny, "The Youngest Adult Parolees: Do They Have Different Parole Experiences?" paper presented at the annual meeting of the American Society of Criminology, San Francisco, CA, November 14–17, 2000.
93. Sabol et al., "Offenders Returning to Federal Prison," 3.
94. Leslie Acoca and James Austin, *The Crisis: The Woman Offender Sentencing Study and Alternative Sentencing Recommendations Project: Women in Prison* (Washington, DC: National Council on Crime and Delinquency, 1996).
95. Beck and Shipley, *Recidivism of Prisoners Released in 1983,* 2.
96. Howard R. Sacks and Charles H. Logan, "Does Parole Make a (Lasting) Difference?" in George F. Cole, *Criminal Justice: Law and Politics,* 4th ed. (Pacific Grove, CA: Brooks/Cole, 1984), 362–78.
97. Sabol et al., "Offenders Returning to Federal Prison," 6.
98. Petersilia, "When Prisoners Return to the Community," 3.
99. Allen J. Beck and Bernard E. Shipley, *Recidivism of Young Parolees,* special report (Washington, DC: U.S. Department of Justice, Bureau of Justice Statistics, 1987).
100. Williams, McShane, and Dolny, "Developing a Parole Classification Instrument for Use as a Management Tool."
101. Williams, McShane, and Dolny, "Developing a Parole Classification Instrument for Use as a Management Tool."

Chapter 12

1. William M. DiMascio, *Seeking Justice: Crime and Punishment in America* (New York: Edna McConnell Clark Foundation, 1997).
2. Norval Morris and Michael Tonry, *Between Prison and Probation: Intermediate Punishments in a Rational Sentencing System* (New York: Oxford University Press, 1990), 3.
3. Morris and Tonry, *Between Prison and Probation.*
4. Morris and Tonry, *Between Prison and Probation,* 7.
5. Morris and Tonry, *Between Prison and Probation,* 8.
6. Edward J. Latessa, Lawrence F. Travis, and Alexander Holsinger, "Evaluation of Ohio's Community Corrections Act Programs and Community Based Correctional Facilities," unpublished agency report, University of Cincinnati, Division of Criminal Justice, 1997.
7. Latessa, Travis, and Holsinger, "Evaluation of Ohio's Community Corrections Act Programs and Community Based Correctional Facilities," 69.
8. Dale Parent, Terence Dunworth, Douglas McDonald, and William Rhodes, *Key Legislative Issues in Criminal Justice: Intermediate Sanctions* (Washington, DC: U.S. Department of Justice, January 1997), 1.
9. Michael Tonry, *Intermediate Sanctions in Sentencing Guidelines* (Washington, DC: U.S. Department of Justice, 1997), 6–7.
10. Gennaro Vito and Harry Allen, "Shock Probation in Ohio: A Comparison of Outcomes," *International Journal of Offender Therapy and Comparative Criminology* 25 (1981): 70–76.
11. Vito and Allen, "Shock Probation in Ohio," 71.
12. Nicolette Parisi, "A Taste of the Bars," *Journal of Criminal Law and Criminology* 72 (1981): 1109–23.
13. Thomas P. Bonczar and Lauren E. Glaze, "Probation and Parole in the United States, 1998," *Bureau of Justice Statistics Bulletin* (1999), 4.

14. Doris L. MacKenzie and Eugene E. Hebert, eds., *Correctional Boot Camps: A Tough Intermediate Sanction* (Washington, DC: U.S. Department of Justice, 1996), viii.

15. Ernest L. Cowles and Thomas C. Castellano, "Substance Abuse Programming in Adult Correctional Boot Camps: A National Overview," in *Correctional Boot Camps: A Tough Intermediate Sanction*, ed. Doris L. MacKenzie and Eugene E. Hebert (Washington, DC: U.S. Department of Justice, 1996), 207–32.

16. Ronald W. Moscicki, "If You Don't Take Responsibility, You Take Orders," in American Correctional Association, *Juvenile and Adult Boot Camps* (Lanham, MD: American Correctional Association, 1996), 287–88.

17. Camille Graham Camp and George M. Camp, *The Corrections Yearbook: 1999* (Middletown, CT: Criminal Justice Institute, 1999), 120–21.

18. Camp and Camp, *The Corrections Yearbook*, 121–23.

19. Cherie L. Clark, David W. Aziz, and Doris L. MacKenzie, *Shock Incarceration in New York: Focus on Treatment* (Washington, DC: National Institute of Justice, August 1994).

20. Clark, Aziz, and MacKenzie, *Shock Incarceration in New York*, 2. New York law permits shock incarceration graduates to be paroled before they have served the mandatory minimum prison term that would otherwise apply.

21. Blair B. Bourque, Mei Han, and Sarah M. Hill, "A National Survey of Aftercare Provisions for Boot Camp Graduates," *National Institute of Justice Research in Brief* (Washington, DC: U.S. Department of Justice, 1996), 6.

22. Clark, Aziz, and MacKenzie, *Shock Incarceration in New York*, 9.

23. Clark, Aziz, and MacKenzie, *Shock Incarceration in New York*, 11.

24. James Austin, Michael Jones, and Melissa Bolyard, "A Survey of Jail-Operated Boot Camps and Guidelines for Their Implementation," in *Correctional Boot Camps: A Tough Intermediate Sanction*, ed. Doris L. MacKenzie and Eugene E. Hebert (Washington, DC: U.S. Department of Justice, 1996), 119–34.

25. Camp and Camp, *The Corrections Yearbook*, 197.

26. Austin, Jones, and Bolyard, "A Survey of Jail-Operated Boot Camps and Guidelines for Their Implementation," 122–28.

27. Velmer S. Burton, James W. Marquart, Steven J. Cuvelier, Leanne Fiftal Alarid, and Robert J. Hunter, "A Study of Attitudinal Change among Boot Camp Participants," *Federal Probation* 57, no. 3 (1993): 46–52.

28. Burton et al., "A Study of Attitudinal Change among Boot Camp Participants," 46–52.

29. Burton et al., "A Study of Attitudinal Change among Boot Camp Participants," 51.

30. James F. Anderson, Laronistine Dyson, and Jerald C. Burns, *Boot Camps: An Intermediate Sanction* (Lanham, NY: University Press of America, 1999), 80, 88–89.

31. George Ransom and Mary Ellen Mastrorilli, "The Massachusetts Boot Camp: Inmate Anecdotes," *Prison Journal* 73, no. 3/4 (1993): 307–18, especially 309–10.

32. Ransom and Mastrorilli, "The Massachusetts Boot Camp," 313–14.

33. Ransom and Mastrorilli, "The Massachusetts Boot Camp," 316.

34. Merry Morash and Lila Rucker, "A Critical Look at the Idea of Boot Camp as a Correctional Reform," *Crime and Delinquency* (April 1990): 204–22.

35. Faith E. Lutze and David C. Brody, "Mental Abuse as Cruel and Unusual Punishment: Do Boot Camp Prisons Violate the Eighth Amendment?" *Crime and Delinquency* 45, no. 2 (1999): 242–55.

36. Doris Layton MacKenzie, Lori A. Elis, Sally S. Simpson, and Stacy B. Skroban, "Boot Camps as an Alternative for Women," in *Correctional Boot Camps: A Tough Intermediate Sanction*, ed. Doris L. MacKenzie and Eugene E. Hebert (Washington, DC: U.S. Department of Justice, 1996), 233–44.

37. Robert Brame and Doris Layton MacKenzie, "Shock Incarceration and Positive Adjustment during Community Supervision: A Multisite Evaluation," in *Correctional Boot Camps: A Tough Intermediate Sanction*, ed. Doris L. MacKenzie and Eugene E. Hebert (Washington, DC: U.S. Department of Justice, 1996), 282.

38. Doris Layton MacKenzie and Claire Souryal, "Inmates' Attitude Change during Incarceration: A Comparison of Boot Camp with Traditional Prison," *Justice Quarterly* 12, no. 2 (1995): 325–54.

39. Doris Layton MacKenzie and James W. Shaw, "The Impact of Shock Incarceration on Technical Violations and New Criminal Activities," *Justice Quarterly* 10 (1993): 465.

40. Doris Layton MacKenzie, "Boot Camp Programs Grow in Number and Scope," *NIJ Reports* (November/December 1990).

41. James Austin, Michael Jones, and Melissa Bolyard, "A Survey of Jail-Operated Boot Camps and Guidelines for Their Implementation," 131.

42. Doris Layton MacKenzie, Robert Brame, David McDowall, and Claire Souryal, "Boot Camp Prisons and Recidivism in Eight States," *Criminology* 33, no. 3 (1995): 327–57.

43. MacKenzie et al., "Boot Camp Prisons and Recidivism in Eight States."

44. MacKenzie et al., "Boot Camp Prisons and Recidivism in Eight States."

45. Dale G. Parent, "Boot Camps and Prison Crowding," in *Correctional Boot Camps: A Tough Intermediate Sanction*, ed. Doris L. MacKenzie and Eugene E. Hebert (Washington, DC: U.S. Department of Justice, 1996), 263.

46. Parent, "Boot Camps and Prison Crowding," 263.

47. Dale Colledge and Jurg Gerber, "Rethinking the Assumptions about Boot Camps," *Federal Probation* 62, no. 1 (1998): 54–61.

48. James F. Anderson, Jerald C. Burns, and Laronistine Dyson, "Effective Aftercare Provisions Could Hold the Key to the Rehabilitative Effects of Shock Incarceration Programs," *Journal of Offender Monitoring* 10, no. 3 (1997): 10–17, especially 15.

49. Gordon Bazemore and Thomas J. Quinn, "Boot Camps, Work Camps, and Community Needs: A Restorative Justice Perspective on Correctional Objectives," in American Correctional Association, *Juvenile and Adult Boot Camps* (Lanham, MD: American Correctional Association, 1996), 219–32.

50. Blair B. Bourque, Mei Han, and Sarah M. Hill, "A National Survey of Aftercare Provisions for Boot Camp Graduates," *National Institute of Justice Research in Brief* (Washington, DC: U.S. Department of Justice, 1996), 10.

51. Anderson, Burns, and Dyson, "Effective Aftercare Provisions Could Hold the Key to the Rehabilitative Effects of Shock Incarceration Programs," 16.

52. Edward J. Latessa and Lawrence F. Travis, "Residential Community Correctional Programs," in *Smart Sentencing: The Emergence of Intermediate Sanctions*, ed. J. M Byrne, A. J. Lurigio, and J. Petersilia (Newbury Park, CA: Sage, 1992), 170.

53. Latessa and Travis, "Residential Community Correctional Programs," 167.

54. Latessa and Travis, "Residential Community Correctional Programs," 170.

55. Latessa and Travis, "Residential Community Correctional Programs," 175–76.

56. Camp and Camp, *The Corrections Yearbook*, 124.

57. Terry L. Wells, "Halfway House Counselors: An Empirical Assessment of Job Orientation," Ph.D. dissertation, Sam Houston State University, 1997, 10–12.

58. Ronald L. Goldfarb and L. R. Singer, *After Conviction* (New York: Simon and Schuster, 1973).

59. Wells, "Halfway House Counselors," 3–4.

60. Oliver J. Keller and Benedict S. Alper, *Halfway Houses: Community-Centered Correction and Treatment* (Lexington, MA: D. C. Heath and Company, 1970).

61. Daniel Glaser, *Preparing Convicts for Law-Abiding Lives: The Pioneering Penology of Richard A. McGee* (Albany, NY: State University of New York Press, 1995), 106–07.

62. Latessa and Travis, "Residential Community Correctional Programs."

63. International Community Corrections Association, web site at http://www.iccaweb.org/icca_info/icca_info.html, accessed on January 15, 2001.

64. Latessa and Travis, "Residential Community Correctional Programs."

65. Joan Petersilia, "Justice for All? Offenders with Mental Retardation and the California Corrections System," *Prison Journal* 77, no. 4 (1997): 358–80.

66. C. L. Walsh and S. H. Beck, "Predictors of Recidivism among Halfway House Residents," *American Journal of Criminal Justice* 15, no. 1 (1990):137–56.

67. Camp and Camp, *The Corrections Yearbook: 1999*, 124.

68. Sarah E. Twill, Larry Nackerud, Edwin A. Risler, Jeffrey A. Bernat, and David Taylor, "Changes in Measured Loneliness, Control, and Social Support among Parolees in a Halfway House," *Journal of Offender Rehabilitation* 27, no. 3/4 (1998): 77–92, especially 86.

69. Twill et al., "Changes in Measured Loneliness," 87–88.

70. Wells, "Halfway House Counselors," 27.

71. Melodye Lehnerer, "Becoming Involved: Field Research at a Halfway House for Ex-Offenders," Ph.D. dissertation, York University, 1992, 180.

72. Lehnerer, "Becoming Involved," 156.

73. Lehnerer, "Becoming Involved," 228.

74. Wells, "Halfway House Counselors."

75. Wells, "Halfway House Counselors," 107.

76. Jennifer D. Hartmann, Paul C. Friday, and Kevin I. Minor, "Residential Probation: A Seven Year Follow-Up Study of Halfway House Discharges," *Journal of Criminal Justice* 22, no. 6 (1998): 503–15.

77. Edward J. Latessa and Lawrence F. Travis, "Halfway House or Probation: A Comparison of Alternative Dispositions," *Journal of Crime and Delinquency* 14, no. 1 (1991): 53–75; and Hartmann et al., "Residential Probation."

78. Eric R. Dowdy, "Inside the Black Box of Community Corrections: An Examination of the Influence of Halfway House Experiences on Program Success and Post-Release Recidivism," Ph.D. dissertation, Colorado State University, 1997, 130–31.

79. P. G. Donnelly and B. Forschner, "Client Success or Failure in a Halfway House," *Federal Probation* 48 (1984): 38–44.

80. Harry E. Allen and Richard P. Seiter, "The Effectiveness of Halfway Houses: A Reappraisal of a Reappraisal," *Chitty's Law Journal* 24, no. 6 (1976): 196–200.

81. James L. Beck, "An Evaluation of Federal Community Treatment Centers," *Federal Probation* 43 (1979): 36–40.

82. Edward Latessa and Harry E. Allen, "Halfway Houses and Parole: A National Assessment," *Journal of Criminal Justice* 10, no. 2 (1982): 153–63.

83. Donnelly and Forschner, "Client Success or Failure in a Halfway House."

84. P. G. Donnelly and B. E. Forschner, "Predictors of Success in a Co-Correctional Halfway House: A Discriminant Analysis," *Journal of Crime and Justice* 10 (1987): 1–22.

85. Walsh and Beck, "Predictors of Recidivism among Halfway House Residents."

86. Latessa and Travis, "Halfway House or Probation."

87. Kim K. English and M. J. Mande, "Empirical Support for Intervention Strategies in Community Corrections," *Journal of Contemporary Criminal Justice* 7 (1991): 95–106; Hartmann et al., "Residential Probation"; Latessa and Travis, "Halfway House or Probation"; and K. Moczydlowski, "Predictors of Success in a Correctional Halfway House for Youthful and Adult Offenders," *Corrective and Social Psychiatry and Journal of Behavior Technology, Methods, and Therapy* 26 (1980): 59–72.

88. Latessa and Travis, "Halfway House or Probation"; Hartmann et al., "Residential Probation"; Donnelly and Forschner, "Client Success or Failure in a Halfway House"; and Donnelly and Forschner, "Predictors of Success in a Co-Correctional Halfway House."

89. Belinda Rogers McCarthy and Bernard J. McCarthy Jr., *Community-Based Corrections,* 2nd ed. (Belmont, CA: Brooks/Cole, 1990), 154.

90. Michael L. Prendergast, Jean Wellisch, and Mamie Mee Wong, "Residential Treatment for Women Parolees Following Prison-Based Drug Treatment: Treatment Experiences, Needs and Service, Outcomes," *Prison Journal* 76, no. 3 (1996): 253–74.

91. U.S. Department of Justice, Bureau of Justice Assistance, *Critical Elements in the Planning, Development, and Implementation of Successful Correctional Options* (Washington, DC: U.S. Department of Justice, February 1998), 40–41.

92. Andrea G. Barthwell, Peter Bokos, John Bailey, Miriam Nisenbaum, Julien Devereux, and Edward C. Senay, "Interventions/Wilmer: A Continuum of Care for Substance Abusers in the Criminal Justice System," *Journal of Psychoactive Drugs* 27, no. 1 (1995): 39–47.

93. Susan Turner and Joan Petersilia, "Work Release in Washington: Effects on Recidivism and Correctional Costs," *Prison Journal* 76, no. 2 (1996): 138–64.

94. Amie L. Nielsen, Frank R. Scarpitti, and James A. Inciardi, "Integrating the Therapeutic Community and Work Release for Drug-Involved Offenders: The CREST Program," *Journal of Substance Abuse Treatment* 13, no. 4 (1996): 349–58.

95. C. J. Mumola, *Incarcerated Parents and Their Children* (Washington, DC: U.S. Department of Justice, Bureau of Justice Statistics, 2000).

96. Joycelyn M. Pollock, *Criminal Women* (Cincinnati, OH: Anderson, 1999).

97. William H. Barton and Cheryl Justice, "The John P. Craine House: A Community Residential Program for Female Offenders and Their Children," paper presented at the annual meeting of the American Society of Criminology, San Francisco, CA, November 14–17, 2000.

98. Barton and Justice, "The John P. Craine House," 7.

99. Barton and Justice, "The John P. Craine House," 7–8.

100. Barton and Justice, "The John P. Craine House," 9–10.

Chapter 13

1. Joan Petersilia and Susan Turner, *Evaluating Intensive Supervised Probation/Parole: Results of a Nationwide Experiment,* NCJ 141637 (Washington, DC: U.S. Department of Justice, National Institute of Justice, 1993), 2.

2. William DiMascio, *Seeking Justice: Crime and Punishment in America* (New York: Edna McConnell Clark Foundation, 1997), 36.

3. See Roger J. Lauen, *Community-Managed Corrections* (Laurel, MD: American Correctional Association, 1988); Stuart Adams, *Evaluation Research in Corrections* (Washington, DC: U.S. Government Printing Office, 1975); Robert M. Carter, Daniel Glaser, and Leslie Wilkins, *Probation, Parole, and Community Corrections,* 3rd ed. (New York: Wiley, 1984); and Edward E. Rhine, William R. Smith, Ronald W. Jackson, *Paroling Authorities: Recent History and Current Practice* (Laurel, MD: American Correctional Association, 1991).

4. Camille Graham Camp and George M. Camp, *The Corrections Yearbook: 1999* (Middletown, CT: Criminal Justice Institute, 1999), 176.

5. Camp and Camp, *The Corrections Yearbook.*

6. Paul Gendreau, Francis Cullen, and James Bonta, "Intensive Rehabilitation Supervision: The Next Generation in Community Corrections," *Federal Probation* 58 (1994): 72–78.

7. Arthur Lurigio, "The Perception and Attitudes of Judges and Attorneys toward Intensive Probation Supervision," *Federal Probation* 51 (1987): 16–24.

8. Gerald J. Bayens, Michael W. Manske, and John Ortiz Smykla, "The Attitudes of Criminal Justice Workgroups toward Intensive Supervised Probation," *American Journal of Criminal Justice* 22, no. 2 (1998): 189–206, especially 198.

9. Bayens, Manske, and Smykla, "The Attitudes of Criminal Justice Workgroups toward Intensive Supervised Probation," 203–04.

10. Philip Reichel and Billie D. Sudbrack, "Differences among Eligibles: Who Gets an ISP Sentence?" *Federal Probation* 58, no. 4 (1994): 51–58.

11. Bayens, Manske, and Smykla, "The Attitudes of Criminal Justice Workgroups toward Intensive Supervised Probation," 203–04; and Mark Jones, "Predictors of Success and Failure on Intensive Probation Supervision," *American Journal of Criminal Justice* 19 (1995): 239–54.

12. James Byrne, Arthur Lurigio, and Christopher Baird, "The Effectiveness of the New Intensive Supervision Programs," *Research in Corrections* 2 (1989): 1–48; and Petersilia and Turner, *Evaluating Intensive Supervised Probation/Parole,* 2.

13. Joan Petersilia and Susan Turner, *Intensive Supervision for High-Risk Probationers: Findings from Three California Studies* (Santa Monica, CA: RAND Corporation, November 1990).

14. Petersilia and Turner, *Intensive Supervision for High-Risk Probationers,* 5.

15. U.S. General Accounting Office, *Intensive Probation Supervision: Crime-Control and Cost-Saving Effectiveness,* GAO/PEMD 93-23 (Washington, DC: U.S. General Accounting Office, 1993), 8.

16. Norval Morris and Michael Tonry, "Between Prison and Probation: Intermediate Punishments in a Rational Sentencing System," *NIJ Reports* (January/February 1990), 9.

17. Personal communication between Paul F. Cromwell, one of this book's coauthors, and Thomas G. Blomberg, professor of criminology, Florida State University, August 1992.

18. Petersilia and Turner, *Evaluating Intensive Supervised Probation/Parole*, 2.

19. Petersilia and Turner, *Evaluating Intensive Supervised Probation/Parole*, 7.

20. Elizabeth Piper Deschenes, Susan Turner, and Joan Petersilia, "A Dual Experiment in Intensive Community Supervision: Minnesota's Prison Diversion and Enhanced Supervised Release Programs," *Prison Journal* 75, no. 3 (1995): 330–56.

21. Joan Petersilia and Susan Turner, "Intensive Probation and Parole," in *Crime and Justice: A Review of Research*, vol. 17 , ed. Michael Tonry (Chicago: University of Chicago Press, 1993).

22. Petersilia and Turner, *Evaluating Intensive Supervised Probation/Parole*, 8.

23. Michael Tonry and Mary Lynch, "Intermediate Sanctions," in *Crime and Justice: A Review of Research*, vol. 20, ed. Michael Tonry (Chicago: University of Chicago Press, 1996), 116.

24. Betsy Fulton, Edward J. Latessa, Amy Stichman, and Lawrence F. Travis, "The State of ISP: Research and Policy Implications," *Federal Probation* 61, no. 4 (1997): 65–75.

25. Petersilia and Turner, *Evaluating Intensive Supervised Probation/Parole*, 5.

26. Petersilia and Turner, *Evaluating Intensive Supervised Probation/Parole*. 7.

27. Fulton et al., "The State of ISP," 72.

28. DiMascio, *Seeking Justice*, 40.

29. Mark Jones and Darrell L. Ross, "Electronic House Arrest and Boot Camp in North Carolina," *Criminal Justice Policy Review* 8 (1998): 383–403.

30. *People v. Ramos*, 48 CrL 1057 (Ill.S.Ct.) (1990).

31. Joan Petersilia, *Expanding Options for Criminal Sentencing* (Santa Monica, CA: RAND Corporation, 1987).

32. Dennis J. Palumbo, Mary Clifford, and Joann K. Snyder-Joy, "From Net-Widening to Intermediate Sanctions: The Transformation of Alternatives to Incarceration from Benevolence to Malevolence," in *Smart Sentencing: The Emergence of Intermediate Sanctions*, ed. James M. Byrne, Arthur J. Lurigio, and Joan Petersilia (Newbury Park, CA: Sage, 1992).

33. Harjit S. Sandhu, Richard A. Dodder, and Minu Mathur, "House Arrest: Success and Failure Rates in Residential and Nonresidential Community-Based Programs," *Journal of Offender Rehabilitation* 19, no. 1/2 (1993): 131–44.

34. Sandhu, Dodder, and Mathur, "House Arrest," 136–42.

35. Sudipto Roy, "Five Years of Electronic Monitoring of Adults and Juveniles in Lake County, Indiana: A Comparative Study on Factors Related to Failure," *Journal of Crime and Justice* 20 (1997): 141–60.

36. Kathleen Maguire and Ann L. Pastore, *Bureau of Justice Statistics Sourcebook of Criminal Justice Statistics, 1997* (Albany, NY: State University of New York at Albany, 1999).

37. Camp and Camp, *The Corrections Yearbook: 1999*, 191.

38. Sudipto Roy, "Adult Offenders in an Electronic Home Detention Program: Factors Related to Failure," *Journal of Offender Monitoring* 7 (1994): 17–21.

39. Elise Kalfayan, ed., *RAND Checklist* (Santa Monica, CA: RAND Corporation, January 1989), 2.

40. Petersilia, *Expanding Options for Criminal Sentencing*.

41. Petersilia, *Expanding Options for Criminal Sentencing*.

42. Personal communication with Paul F. Cromwell, one of this book's coauthors.

43. Charles M. Friel and Joseph B. Vaughn, "A Consumer's Guide to Electronic Monitoring," *Federal Probation* 50, no. 3 (September 1986): 3–14.

44. Friel and Vaughn, "A Consumer's Guide to Electronic Monitoring," 12.

45. J. Robert Lilly, Richard A. Ball, G. David Curry, and Richard C. Smith, "The Pride, Inc., Program: An Evaluation of 5 Years of Electronic Monitoring," *Federal Probation* (December 1992): 42–47.

46. Lilly et al., "The Pride, Inc., Program," 45.

47. Mark Jones and Barbara Sims, "Recidivism of Offenders Released from Prison in North Carolina: A Gender Comparison," *Prison Journal* 77 (1997): 335–48.

48. Randy R. Gainey, Brian K. Payne, and Mike O'Toole, "The Relationships between Time in Jail, Time on Electronic Monitoring, and Recidivism: An Event History Analysis of a Jail-Based Program," *Justice Quarterly* 17, no. 4 (2000): 733–52.

49. Tonry and Lynch, "Intermediate Sanctions," 122.

50. Charles Rose, "Electronic Monitoring of Offenders: A New Dimension in Community Sentencing or a Needless Diversion?" *International Review of Law, Computers, and Technology* 11, no. 1 (1997): 147–53.

51. Dale G. Parent, "Day Reporting Centers," in *Intermediate Sanctions in Overcrowded Times*, ed. Michael Tonry and Kate Hamilton (Boston, MA: Northeastern University Press, 1995), 125.

52. Dale Parent, Jim Byrne, Vered Tsarfaty, Laura Valade, and Julie Esselman, *Day Reporting Centers*, vol. 1 (Washington, DC: U.S. Department of Justice, National Institute of Justice, 1995).

53. Parent et al., *Day Reporting Centers*, 18.

54. Parent et al., *Day Reporting Centers*, 18.

55. David W. Diggs and Stephen L. Pieper, "Using Day Reporting Centers as an Alternative to Jail," *Federal Probation* 58 (1994): 9–12.

56. John J. Larivee, "Day Reporting in Massachusetts," in *Intermediate Sanctions in Overcrowded Times*, ed. Michael Tonry and Kate Hamilton (Boston, MA: Northeastern University Press, 1995), 128–30.

57. Patrick J. Coleman, Jeffrey Felten-Green, and Geroma Oliver, *Connecticut's Alternative Sanctions Program: $619 Million Saved in Estimated Capital and Operating Costs* (Washington, DC: Bureau of Justice Assistance Practitioner Perspectives, October 1998), 6.

58. David C. Anderson, *Sensible Justice: Alternatives to Prison* (New York: New Press, 1998), 56.

59. Anderson, *Sensible Justice*, 63.
60. Jack McDevitt and Robyn Miliano, "Day Reporting Centers: An Innovative Concept in Intermediate Sanctions," in *Smart Sentencing: The Emergence of Intermediate Sanctions*, ed. James M. Byrne, Arthur J. Lurigio, and Joan Petersilia (Newbury Park, CA: Sage Publications 1992), 160–61.
61. Charles Bahn and James R. Davis, "Day Reporting Centers as an Alternative to Incarceration," *Journal of Offender Rehabilitation* 27 (1998): 139–50.
62. Parent, "Day Reporting Centers," 126.
63. Parent, "Day Reporting Centers," 126.
64. Parent, "Day Reporting Centers," 126.
65. Parent et al., *Day Reporting Centers*, 18.
66. Parent, "Day Reporting Centers," 126.
67. McDevitt and Miliano, "Day Reporting Centers," 161.
68. Parent, "Day Reporting Centers," 127.
69. Parent et al., *Day Reporting Centers*, 22–23.
70. George Mair and Claire Nee, "Day Centre Reconviction Rates," *British Journal of Criminology* 32 (1992): 329–39.
71. George Mair, "Day Centers in England and Wales," in *Intermediate Sanctions in Overcrowded Times*, ed. Michael Tonry and Kate Hamilton (Boston, MA: Northeastern University Press, 1995), 137.
72. John J. Larivee, "Day Reporting in Massachusetts," 131.
73. Amy Craddock, "Quasi-Experimental Examination of Outcomes of Community Corrections Programs Established under North Carolina's Structured Sentencing Law," paper presented at the annual meeting of the American Society of Criminology, San Francisco, November 2000.
74. Craddock, "Quasi-Experimental Examination of Outcomes of Community Corrections Programs Established under North Carolina's Structured Sentencing Law."
75. Parent, "Day Reporting Centers," 127–28.
76. Rolando del Carmen, *Criminal Procedure: Law and Practice*, 3rd ed. (Belmont, CA: Wadsworth, 1995), 436.
77. Thomas P. Bonczar, *Characteristics of Adults on Probation* (Washington, DC: U.S. Department of Justice, 1997), 7.
78. Examples of applicable states include Alaska, Arizona, Florida, Hawaii, Maryland, Maine, Mississippi, Nebraska, New Jersey, New York, Ohio, Oregon, South Dakota, and Vermont.
79. Andrew R. Klein, *Alternative Sentencing, Intermediate Sanctions, and Probation*, 2nd ed. (Cincinnati, OH: Anderson, 1997), 157.
80. Stephen Schafer, *Restitution to Victims of Crime* (London, England: Stevens and Sons, 1960).
81. American Bar Association, Commission on Correctional Facilities and Services and Council of State Governments, *Compendium of Model Correctional Legislation and Standards*, 2nd ed. (Washington, DC: American Bar Association, 1975), III–48.
82. American Bar Association, *Compendium of Model Correctional Legislation and Standards*, III–58.
83. Klein, *Alternative Sentencing*.
84. Burt Galaway, "Restitution as Innovation or Unfilled Promise?" in *Towards a Critical Victimology*, ed. Ezzat A. Fattah (New York: St. Martin's Press, 1992), 347–71, especially 348.
85. Burt Galaway, "The Use of Restitution," *Crime and Delinquency* 23, no. 1 (1977): 57–71.
86. Catharine M. Goodwin, "The Imposition of Restitution in Federal Criminal Cases," *Federal Probation* 62, no. 2 (1998): 95–108, especially 95.
87. *Hughey v. United States*, 495 U.S. 411, 413 (1990).
88. Goodwin, "The Imposition of Restitution in Federal Criminal Cases," 96.
89. Office for the Victims of Crime, *New Directions from the Field: Victims' Rights and Services for the 21st Century*, NCJ#172812 (Washington, DC: U.S. Department of Justice, Office for Victims of Crime, 1998), 13.
90. Goodwin, "The Imposition of Restitution in Federal Criminal Cases," 98.
91. *United States v. Bachsian*, 4 F.3rd 288 (1993).
92. U.S. Parole Commission, *Rules and Procedures Manual* (Washington, DC: U.S. Parole Commission, 1997), sec. 2.7.
93. Goodwin, "The Imposition of Restitution in Federal Criminal Cases," 96.
94. Goodwin, "The Imposition of Restitution in Federal Criminal Cases," 97.
95. *Carswell v. State*, 721 N.E.2d 1255 (Ind. Ct. App. 1999).
96. Goodwin, "The Imposition of Restitution in Federal Criminal Cases," 100.
97. Goodwin, "The Imposition of Restitution in Federal Criminal Cases," 102.
98. Rolando del Carmen, *Criminal Procedure*, 437.
99. *Pennsylvania Department of Public Welfare v. Davenport*, 110 S. Ct. 2126 (1990).
100. *Baker v. State*, 616 So.2d 571 (1993); and *State v. Hayes*, 437 S.E.2d 717 (N.C. App.Dec.) (1993).
101. Galaway, "Restitution as Innovation or Unfilled Promise?" 357.
102. J. Heinz, Burt Galaway, and J. Hudson, "Restitution or Parole: A Follow-Up Study of Adult Offenders," *Social Service Review* 50, no. 1 (1976): 148–56.
103. Anne Schneider, "Restitution and Recidivism Rates of Juvenile Offenders: Four Experimental Studies," *Criminology* 24, no. 3 (1986): 533–52.
104. Galaway, "Restitution as Innovation or Unfilled Promise?" 354.
105. S. Novack, B. Galaway, and J. Hudson, "Victim Offender Perceptions of the Fairness of Restitution and Community Service Sanctions," in *Victims, Offenders, and Alternative Sanctions*, ed. J. Hudson and B. Galaway (Lexington, MA: D. C. Heath/Lexington Books, 1980), 63–69.
106. Galaway, "Restitution as Innovation or Unfilled Promise?" 362.
107. Galaway, "Restitution as Innovation or Unfilled Promise?" 363.

108. Michael Tonry, "Evaluating Intermediate Sanction Programs," in *Community Corrections: Probation, Parole and Intermediate Sanctions*, ed. Joan Petersilia (New York: Oxford University Press, 1998), 89.

109. DiMascio, *Seeking Justice*, 37.

110. Michael Tonry, "Parochialism in U.S. Sentencing Policy," *Crime and Delinquency* 45, no. 1 (1999): 48–65, especially 56–57.

111. Tonry, "Parochialism in U.S. Sentencing Policy," 57–58.

112. Rolando del Carmen, Betsy Witt, Thomas Caywood, and Sally Layland, *Probation Law and Practice in Texas* (Huntsville, TX: Sam Houston State University, Criminal Justice Center, 1989), 4.

113. Anderson, *Sensible Justice*, 25–35.

114. Douglas McDonald, *Punishment without Walls* (New Brunswick, NJ: Rutgers University Press, 1986).

115. Tonry and Lynch, "Intermediate Sanctions," 127.

116. 18 U.S.C. 3563(a)(2).

117. U.S. Parole Commission, *Rules and Procedures Manual*, sec. 2.7.

118. Morris and Tonry, *Between Prison and Probation*, 114.

119. George Cole, Barry Mahoney, Marlene Thornton, and Roger A. Hanson, *The Practices and Attitudes of Trial Court Judges regarding Fines as a Criminal Sanction* (Washington, DC: U.S. Department of Justice, 1987).

120. Cole et al., *The Practices and Attitudes of Trial Court Judges regarding Fines as a Criminal Sanction*.

121. Dale Parent, *Day Reporting Centers for Criminal Offenders: A Descriptive Analysis of Existing Programs* (Washington, DC: U.S. Department of Justice, National Institute of Justice, 1990).

122. G. Frederick Allen and Harvey Treger, "Fines and Restitution Orders: Probationers' Perceptions," *Federal Probation* 58, no. 2 (1994): 34–40.

123. Allen and Treger, "Fines and Restitution Orders," 34–35.

124. Allen and Treger, "Fines and Restitution Orders," 35–36.

125. Allen and Treger, "Fines and Restitution Orders," 39.

126. Bureau of Justice Assistance, *How to Use Structured Fines (Day Fines) as an Intermediate Sanction* (Washington, DC: Bureau of Justice Assistance, 1996), 17–18.

127. Bureau of Justice Assistance, *How to Use Structured Fines (Day Fines) as an Intermediate Sanction*, 18–19.

128. Bureau of Justice Assistance, *How to Use Structured Fines (Day Fines) as an Intermediate Sanction*, 29–33.

129. Sally T. Hillsman, "Day Fines," in *Intermediate Sanctions in Overcrowded Times*, ed. Michael Tonry and Kate Hamilton (Boston, MA: Northeastern University Press, 1995), 19.

130. Bureau of Justice Assistance, *How to Use Structured Fines (Day Fines) as an Intermediate Sanction*, 10–11.

131. Douglas C. McDonald, Judith Greene, and Charles Worzella, *Day Fines in American Courts: The Staten Island and Milwaukee Experiments* (Washington, DC: U.S. Department of Justice, National Institute of Justice, 1992).

132. Hillsman, "Day Fines," 25.

133. McDonald, Greene, and Worzella, *Day Fines in American Courts*, 6–7.

134. McDonald, Greene, and Worzella, *Day Fines in American Courts*, 6–7.

135. Susan Turner and Joan Petersilia, *Day Fines in Four Jurisdictions* (Santa Monica, CA: RAND Corporation, 1996).

136. Stephen C. Richards and Richard S. Jones, "Perpetual Incarceration Machine: Structural Impediments to Post-Prison Success," *Journal of Contemporary Criminal Justice* 13, no. 1 (1987): 4–22.

137. Edward Latessa and Harry Allen, *Corrections in the Community* (Cincinnati, OH: Anderson, 1999), 1.

Chapter 14

1. "Putting a Sterner Face on Juvenile Justice," *Christian Science Monitor*, May 9, 1997.

2. *OJJDP Juvenile Justice Bulletin* (December 1999): 1.

3. *Black's Law Dictionary*, 5th ed. (St. Paul, MN: West, 1979), 889.

4. Howard Snyder and Melissa Sickmund, *Juvenile Offenders and Victims: A National Report* (Washington, DC: National Center for Juvenile Justice, Office of Juvenile Justice and Delinquency Prevention, August 1995), 70.

5. *In re Gault*, 387 U.S. 1 (1967)

6. Cindy S. Lederman, "The Juvenile Court: Putting Research to Work for Prevention," in *Juvenile Justice: An Evolving Juvenile Court, 100th Anniversary of the Juvenile Court 1899–1999* (Washington, DC: National Center for Juvenile Justice, Office of Juvenile Justice and Delinquency Prevention), 24.

7. Rolando V. del Carmen, Mary Parker, and Francis P. Reddington, *Briefs of Leading Cases in Juvenile Justice* (Cincinnati, OH: Anderson Publishing Company, 1998), 9.

8. Del Carmen, Parker, and Reddington, *Briefs of Leading Cases in Juvenile Justice*.

9. Jeffrey A. Butts and Adele V. Harrell, "Delinquents or Criminals: Policy Options for Young Offenders," Urban Institute, *http://www.urban.org/crime/delinq.htm1*.

10. Butts and Harrell, "Delinquents or Criminals," 4.

11. Robert E. Shepherd Jr., "The Juvenile Court at 100 Years: A Look Back," in *Juvenile Justice: An Evolving Juvenile Court, 100th Anniversary of the Juvenile Court, 1899–1999* (Washington, DC: National Center for Juvenile Justice, Office of Juvenile Justice and Delinquency Prevention), 16.

12. Shepherd, "The Juvenile Court at 100 Years," 16.

13. Megan Kurlychek, Patricia Torbet, and Melanie Bozynski, "Focus on Accountability: Best Practices for Juvenile Court and Probation," *JAIBG Bulletin* (August 1999), 2.

14. Paula A. Nessel, "Teen Court: A National Movement," *Technical Assistance Bulletin*, no. 17, 1.

15. Jeffrey Butts, Dean Hoffman, and Janeen Buck, "Teen Courts in the United States: A Profile of Current Programs," OJJDP Fact Sheet (October 1999), 1.

16. Butts, Hoffman, and Buck, "Teen Courts in the United States."
17. Nessel, "Teen Court," 1.
18. Marilyn Robers, Jennifer Brophy, and Caroline Cooper, "The Juvenile Drug Court Movement," OJJDP Fact Sheet #59 (March 1997), 1.
19. Robers, Brophy, and Cooper, "The Juvenile Drug Court Movement," 2.
20. "Juvenile Justice: A Century of Change," 1999 National Report Series, *OJJDP Juvenile Justice Bulletin* (1999): 13.
21. Charles M. Puzzanchera, "Delinquency Cases Waived to Criminal Court: 1988–1997," OJJDP Fact Sheet (February 2000), 1.
22. "OJJDP Statistical Briefing Book," http://www.ojjdp.ncjrs.org/ojstatbb/qa086,htm1.
23. Snyder and Sickmund, *Juvenile Offenders and Victims: A National Report*, 76–79.
24. *Desktop Guide to Good Juvenile Probation Practice*, Juvenile Probation Officer Initiative Working Group (Washington, DC: National Center for Juvenile Justice, Office of Juvenile Justice and Delinquency Prevention, 1993), 32. Hereinafter referred to as *Desktop Guide.*
25. "Trends in Juvenile Violent Crime," Case Highlights: Examining the Work of State Courts, February 2000, 1.
26. Puzzanchera, "Delinquency Cases Waived to Criminal Court."
27. *Desktop Guide*, 32.
28. Arnold Binder, Gilbert Geis, and Dickson D. Bruce Jr., *Juvenile Delinquency*, 2nd ed. (Cincinnati, OH: Anderson Publishing Company, 1997), 260.
29. Snyder and Sickmune, *Juvenile Offenders and Victims: A National Report*, 70.
30. *Schall v. Martin*, 104 S. Ct. 2403 (1984).
31. *Desktop Guide*, 40.
32. Peter Greenwood, "Juvenile Offenders," National Institute of Justice, Crime File Study Guide (Washington, DC: National Institute of Justice, 1985), 1.
33. *Thompson v. Oklahoma*, 487 U.S. 815 (1988).
34. *Stanford v. Kentucky*, 109 S.Ct. 2969 (1989).
35. *Boston Globe*, November 11, 1999, http://www.boston.com.
36. *In re Gault.*
37. *Kent v. United States*, 383 U.S. 541 (1966).
38. *In re Winship*, 397 U.S. 358 (1970).
39. *Breed v. Jones*, 421 U.S. 517 (1975).
40. *McKeiver v. Pennsylvania*, 403 U.S. 528 (1971).
41. *Davis v. Alaska*, 415 U.S. 308 (1974).
42. *New Jersey v. T.L.O.*, 469 U.S. 325 (1985).
43. *Kent v. United States.*
44. Howard Snyder and Melissa Sickmund, *Juvenile Offenders and Victims: 1999 National Report* (Washington, DC: National Center for Juvenile Justice, September 1999), 1.
45. *Desktop Guide*, 43.
46. *Juvenile Probation: The Workhorse of the Juvenile Justice System* (Washington, DC: National Center for Juvenile

Justice, Office of Juvenile Justice and Delinquency Prevention, 1996).
47. "Focus on Accountability: Best Practices for Juvenile Court and Probation," Office of Juvenile Justice and Delinquency Prevention, http://ojjdp.ncjrs.org/pubs/jaibgbulletin/contents.htm1.
48. Hunter Hurst IV and Patricia McFall Torbet, *Organization and Administration of Juvenile Services: Probation, Aftercare, and State Institutions for Delinquent Youth* (Washington, DC: National Center for Juvenile Justice).
49. *Juvenile Probation*, 4.
50. *Juvenile Probation*, 2–3.
51. Indiana Code Title 31, Article 6, Chapter 9, Section 31–6–9–4(a).
52. *Desktop Guide*, 120.
53. *Desktop Guide*, 119–120.
54. Snyder and Sickmund, *Juvenile Offenders and Victims: 1999 National Report*, 1.
55. Snyder and Sickmund, *Juvenile Offenders and Victims: 1999 National Report.*
56. *Desktop Guide*, 16.
57. New Jersey juvenile statutes, 2A and 4A–B, as cited in supra note 24, 17.
58. *Desktop Guide*, 79.
59. *Desktop Guide*, 70.
60. *Desktop Guide*, 79.
61. *Desktop Guide*, 32.
62. *Desktop Guide.*
63. *Desktop Guide*, 79.
64. *Desktop Guide*, 44.
65. *Desktop Guide.*
66. *Desktop Guide*, 87.
67. *Desktop Guide.*
68. *Fare v. Michael C.*, 442 U.S. 707 (1985).
69. *Gagnon v. Scarpelli*, 411 U.S. 788 (1973).
70. *Matter of J.B.S.*, 696 S.W.2d. 223 (Tex. App. 1985).
71. *Desktop Guide*, 19.
72. *Desktop Guide*, 177.
73. *Desktop Guide.*
74. Rolando V. del Carmen, Wendy Hume, Elmer Polk, Frances Reddington, and Betsy Witt, *Texas Juvenile Law and Practice* (Sam Houston State University, Criminal Justice Center, 1991), 180.
75. *Houston Chronicle*, June 5, 1998, p. 7A.
76. *Dallas Morning News*, January 26, 1997, p. 1A.
77. *Dallas Morning News*, p. 24A.
78. *Dallas Morning News*, p. 25A.
79. Clare A. Cripe, *Legal Aspects of Corrections Management* (Gaithersburg, MD: Aspen Publishing, 1997), 371.
80. *Boot Camps for Juvenile Offenders: A Program Summary* (Washington, DC: Office of Juvenile Justice and Delinquency Prevention, 1997), 3.
81. *New York Times*, December 19, 1999, p. 42.
82. *New York Times.*
83. *New York Times.*
84. *Juvenile Probation*, 7.

85. *Juvenile Probation.*
86. *Juvenile Probation*, 8–9.
87. *Balance and Restorative Justice: Program Summary* (Washington, DC: National Center for Juvenile Justice, Office of Juvenile Justice and Delinquency Prevention), 8.
88. National Council on Crime and Delinquency report on racial disparities in juvenile justice, as quoted in *Criminal Justice Newsletter* 30, no. 20, 1.
89. "Minorities in the Juvenile Justice System," 1999 National Report Series, *OJJDP Juvenile Justice Bulletin* (December 1999): 2.
90. "Minorities in the Juvenile Justice System."
91. James H. Burch II and Betty M. Chemers, "A Comprehensive Response to America's Youth Gang Problem," *OJJDP* Fact Sheet #40 (March 1997), 1.
92. Burch and Chemers, "A Comprehensive Response to America's Youth Gang Problem."
93. Patricia Torbet et al., *Executive Summary of State Responses to Serious and Violent Juvenile Crime: Research Report* (Washington, DC: National Center for Juvenile Justice), xi.
94. Shay Bilchik, "A Juvenile Justice System for the 21st Century," *OJJDP Juvenile Justice Bulletin* (May 1998): 1.
95. Bilchik, "A Juvenile Justice System for the 21st Century."

Chapter 15

1. Richard Singer, "Conviction: Civil Disabilities," in *Encyclopedia of Crime and Justice*, ed. Stanford Kadish (New York: Free Press, 1983), 243–48.
2. Velmer S. Burton Jr., Francis T. Cullen, and Lawrence F. Travis III, "The Collateral Consequences of a Felony Conviction: A National Study of State Statutes," *Federal Probation* (September 1987): 52.
3. Susan M. Kuzma, "Civil Disabilities of Convicted Felons," *Corrections Today* (August 1998): 68–72.
4. *Trop v. Dulles*, 356 U.S. 86, 78 S. Ct. 590, 2 L. Ed. 2d 630 (1958).
5. *Kennedy v. Mendoza-Martinez*, 372 U.S. 144, 83 S. Ct. 554, 9 L. Ed. 2d 644 (1963).
6. R. Damaska, "Adverse Legal Consequences of Conviction and Their Removal: A Comparative Study," *Journal of Criminal Law, Criminology and Police Science* 59 (1968): 347 .
7. U.S. Constitution, Article 1.
8. Much of the material on the current status of civil disabilities of convicted persons for this chapter was obtained from the following sources: Office of the Pardon Attorney, *Civil Disabilities of Convicted Felons: A State-by-State Survey* (Washington, DC: U.S. Department of Justice, Office of the Pardon Attorney, 1996); Burton, Cullen, and Travis, "The Collateral Consequences of a Felony Conviction"; and Velmer S. Burton Jr., Lawrence F. Travis III, and Francis T. Cullen, "Reducing the Legal Consequences of a Felony Conviction: A National Survey of State Statutes,"
9. *International Journal of Comparative and Applied Criminal Justice* 12, no. 1 (Spring 1988): 101–09.
10. Joseph G. Cook, *Constitutional Rights of the Accused*, 2nd ed. (San Francisco: Bancroft-Whitney, 1986); Burton, Cullen, and Travis, "The Collateral Consequences of a Felony Conviction"; and Burton, Travis, and Cullen, "Reducing the Legal Consequences of a Felony Conviction."
11. Kuzma, "Civil Disabilities of Convicted Felons," 70.
12. Kuzma, "Civil Disabilities of Convicted Felons," 69.
13. Kuzma, "Civil Disabilities of Convicted Felons," 72.
14. The most complete and current listing with which we are familiar is Office of the Pardon Attorney, *Civil Disabilities of Convicted Felons*.
15. Kuzma, "Civil Disabilities of Convicted Felons," 72.
16. Burton, Cullen, and Travis, "The Collateral Consequences of a Felony Conviction."
17. American Bar Association, *American Bar Association Standards for Criminal Justice*, 2nd ed. (Boston, MA: Little, Brown, 1980), sec. 4.3.
18. American Bar Association, *American Bar Association Standards for Criminal Justice*, 54–65.
19. *Yaselli v. Goff*, 12 F. 2d 396 (2d Cir. 1926).
20. David Rudenstine, *The Rights of Ex-Offenders* (New York: Avon, 1979).
21. The U.S. Constitution, Fourteenth Amendment states: "No person shall be a Senator or Representative in Congress, or elector of President or Vice President, or hold any office, civil or military, under the United States, or under any state, who, after having previously taken an oath of a member of Congress, or as any officer of the United States, or as a member of any state legislature, or as an executive or judicial officer of any state, to support the Constitution of the United States, shall have engaged in insurrection or rebellion against the same, or given aid or comfort to the enemies thereof. But Congress may by a vote of two-thirds of each house, remove such disability."
22. Ironically, the Constitution would not disqualify a convicted felon from serving as president, vice president, or in either house of Congress. However, the Constitution (Article 2, Section 4) does provide that the "President, Vice President and all civil officers of the United States, shall be removed from Office on Impeachment for, and Conviction of, Treason, Bribery, or other high Crimes or Misdemeanors." The Constitution (Article 1, Section 3) further provides that a judgment in the case of impeachment may include removal from office and "disqualification to hold and enjoy any Office of honor, Trust or Profit under the United States."
23. Office of the Pardon Attorney, *Civil Disabilities of Convicted Felons*, 7.
24. Office of the Pardon Attorney, *Civil Disabilities of Convicted Felons*.
25. National Advisory Commission on Criminal Justice Standards and Goals, *A National Strategy to Reduce Crime*

(Washington, DC: Law Enforcement Assistance Administration, 1973), Standard 16.17.

25. Office of the Pardon Attorney, *Civil Disabilities of Convicted Felons*.
26. *Ramirez v. Brown*, 9 Cal. 3d 199, 107 Cal. Rptr. 137, 507 P. 2d 1345 (1973).
27. *Richardson v. Ramirez*, 418 U.S. 24, 94 S. Ct. 2655, 41 L. Ed. 2d 551 (1974).
28. Office of the Pardon Attorney, *Civil Disabilities of Convicted Felons*.
29. Richard Willing, "Ex-Convicts Hope to Regain the Right to Vote," *USA Today*, March 6, 2000, p. 3A.
30. Joan Petersilia, "When Prisoners Return to the Community: Political, Economic, and Social Consequences," *Sentencing and Corrections: Issues for the 21st Century* (Washington, DC: U.S. Department of Justice, November 2000), 5.
31. Petersilia, "When Prisoners Return to the Community," 5.
32. Salatheia Bryant, "A Drive to Register Ex-Felons to Vote: Houston Legislator Is Getting Word Out on Texas Law That Restores Their Right," *Houston Chronicle*, September 11, 2000, p. A13.
33. Rudenstine, *The Rights of Ex-Offenders*, 120, 121.
34. Office of the Pardon Attorney, *Civil Disabilities of Convicted Felons*, Appendix A.
35. 28 U.S.C.A. sec. 1865 (b) (5).
36. Subornation of perjury means to procure or induce another to commit perjury.
37. *Davis v. Alaska*, 415 U.S. 308, 94 S. Ct. 1105, 39 L. Ed. 2d 347 (1974).
38. *Davis v. Alaska*.
39. Rudenstine, *The Rights of Ex-Offenders*, 82–83.
40. Rudenstine, *The Rights of Ex-Offenders*, 83–85.
41. New York issues a certificate of good conduct to convicted persons after five years of good conduct. A few New York licensing statutes require recognition of the certificate.
42. *Dorf v. Fielding*, 20 Misc. 2d 66, 18,197 N.Y.S. 2d 280 (1948). A person convicted for running a house of prostitution was denied a license to sell secondhand goods.
43. *Application of Brooks*, 57 Wash. 2d 66, 355 P. 2d 840 (1960), cert. den. 365 U.S. 813, 81 S. Ct. 694, 5 L. Ed. 2d 692 (1961).
44. Some decisions require a hearing before denial of license, particularly if the criminal record is remote. *Peterson v. State Liquor Authority*, 42 A.D. 2d 195, 345 N.Y.S. 2d 780 (1973).
45. The current status of restrictions on public employment was obtained from Burton, Cullen, and Travis, "The Collateral Consequences of a Felony Conviction," 56.
46. *Gregory v. Litton Systems Inc.*, 316 F. Supp. 401 (C.D. Cal. 1970). An employer was enjoined from denying a job to a black applicant because of his arrest record on the ground that blacks are arrested more frequently than whites.
47. The National Association of Manufacturers operates Solutions to Employment Problems (STEP) in correctional institutions as part of work release programs in certain federal institutions.
48. U.S. Department of Labor, *Guidebook for Operation of the Federal Bonding Program* (Washington, DC: U.S. Government Printing Office, November 1990).
49. Office of the Pardon Attorney, *Civil Disabilities of Convicted Felons*, Appendix B.
50. Burton, Cullen, and Travis, "The Collateral Consequences of a Felony Conviction," 58.
51. Office of the Pardon Attorney, *Civil Disabilities of Convicted Felons*, Appendix B.
52. Michael Kilian, "Simon, Durbin Bills Fight Felon Gun Rights," *Chicago Tribune*, August 13, 1995, p. 2C.
53. Peter Finn, *Sex Offender Community Notification* (Washington DC: National Institute of Justice, 1997), 2.
54. Finn, *Sex Offender Community Notification*, 2–3.
55. Finn, *Sex Offender Community Notification*, 2.
56. Christine Vendel, "Misdemeanors Added to Sex Offender Registry," *Kansas City Star*, September 24, 2000, pp. B1–B2.
57. Janny Scott, "Sex Offender Due for Parole, But No Place Will Have Him," *New York Times*, September 19, 1994, p. A1.
58. Finn, *Sex Offender Community Notification*, 11.
59. Richard G. Zevitz and Mary Ann Farkas, "The Impact of Sex-Offender Community Notification on Probation/Parole in Wisconsin," *International Journal of Offender Therapy and Comparative Criminology* 44, no. 1 (2000): 8–21.
60. Richard S. Bobys, "Perceived Effectiveness of Prisons and Mental Hospitals and Its Influence on Stigmatization," *Free Inquiry in Creative Sociology* 20, no. 1 (1992): 87–89.
61. E. Sutherland and D. Cressey, *Principles of Criminology* (Philadelphia: Lippincott, 1966).
62. Larry Bivins, "NAACP Chief Names Ex-Felon to Key Post: Critics Label Move Political Payoff by Bond," *Detroit News*, March 5, 1998, p. A5.
63. Kuzma, "Civil Disabilities of Convicted Felons," 72.
64. The web sites on sex offender registry and community notification were taken from Devon B. Adams, *Summary of State Sex Offender Registry Dissemination Procedures* (Washington, DC: U.S. Department of Justice, Bureau of Justice Statistics, 1999), 3–8. Web sites are provided for 18 states that had them available at the time of source publication. States not listed are either in the process of developing web sites or access is restricted to law enforcement only.

Chapter 16

1. U.S. Constitution, Article II, Section 2, Clause 1 states: "[The president] shall have the power to grant reprieves and pardons for offenses against the United States except in cases of impeachment." The president has no power to pardon a state offender. *In re Bocchiaro*, 49 F. Supp. 37 (W.D.N.Y. 1943).

2. In California, by virtue of its constitution, the general authority to grant reprieves, pardons, and commutations of sentence is with the governor. Calif. Const. art. V, sec. 8, Cal. Penal Code sec. 4800, et seq. The Board of Prison Terms has replaced the Advisory Pardon Board as the investigative and advising agency. Cal. Penal Code sec 4801. In New York the power to pardon lies with the governor by constitutional provision. N.Y. Const. art. IV, sec. 4. In Texas the application for pardon is directed to the Board of Pardons and Paroles, and the governor may not grant a pardon unless it has been recommended by the board. However, the governor may refuse to grant a recommended pardon. Tex. Const. Art. IV, sec. 11. Texas Admin. Code, Title 37, sec. 143.1.

3. David Rudenstine, *The Rights of Ex-Offenders* (New York: Avon Books, 1979), 141–42.

4. In *Biddle v. Perovich*, 274 U.S. 480, 47 S. Ct. 664, 71 L. Ed. 1161 (1927), the Supreme Court, in a case in which the president had commuted a death sentence to life imprisonment, held that an acceptance of the pardon was not necessary. The Court held that a pardon is not an act of grace but a tool for the public good. Justice Oliver Wendell Holmes Jr. wrote that a pardon is not an act of grace but a "determination of the ultimate authority that the public welfare will be better served" by a pardon.

5. In Texas, for example, an applicant must show a minimum of one year of good behavior after release from prison and completion of his or her sentence before an application can be made. A pardon will not be considered for an inmate still in prison unless his or her innocence has been established beyond a reasonable doubt. Furthermore, a pardon will not be issued to a dead person.

6. The hearings are open in New York and closed in California. No hearings are provided for in Texas.

7. David Johnson, "U.S. Attorney in New York Will Coordinate Inquiry on Pardons," *New York Times*, March 14, 2001, p. 4B.

8. *Ex parte Garland*, 71 U.S. 333, 18 L. Ed. 366 (1867).

9. *Burdick v. United States*, 236 U.S. 79, 59 L. Ed. 476 (1915).

10. *State v. Walker*, 432 So. 2d 1057 (La. Ct. App. 1983); and *Durham v. Wyrick*, 665 F. 2d 185 (8th Cir. 1981).

11. *Ex parte Lefors*, 303 S.W. 2d 394 (Tex. Crim. App. 1957).

12. *Marlo v. State Board of Medical Examiners*, 112 Cal. App. 2d 276, 246 P. 2d 69 (1952); and *Murrill v. State Board of Accountancy*, 97 Cal. App. 2d 709, 218 P. 2d 569 (1950).

13. Cal. Penal Code sec. 4853 (West).

14. Office of the Pardon Attorney, *Civil Disabilities of Convicted Offenders* (Washington, DC: U.S. Department of Justice, 1996).

15. N.H. Rev. Stat. Ann. sec. 607–A:5.

16. Illinois Unified Code of Corrections, sec. 1005–5–5(d).

17. Wis. Stat. Ann. sec. 57.078.

18. Velmer S. Burton Jr., Lawrence F. Travis III, and Francis T. Cullen, "Reducing the Legal Consequences of a Felony Conviction: A National Survey of State Statutes," *International Journal of Comparative and Applied Criminal Justice* 12, no. 1 (Spring 1988): 101–09.

19. Burton, Travis, and Cullen, in "Reducing the Legal Consequences of a Felony Conviction," report that the certificates are generally granted after completion of the sentence to facilitate employment or licensing. New York has a similar procedure.

20. Tex. Code Crim. Proc. Ann. art. 42.12, sec. 7 (Vernon).

21. American Bar Association, *American Bar Association Standards for Criminal Justice,* 2nd ed. (Boston, MA: Little, Brown, 1980), sec. 4.3.

22. American Bar Association, Special Committee on Minimum Standards for the Administration of Justice, *Standards Relating to Sentencing Alternative and Procedures* (New York: Institute of Judicial Administration, 1968), 68–69.

23. *State Medical Board v. Rodgers*, 190 Ark. 266, 79 S.W. 2d 83 (9135).

24. "The Effect of Expungement on a Criminal Conviction," *Southern California Law Review* 40 (1967):127–47.

25. *Otsuka v. Hite*, 51 Cal. Rptr. 284, 414 P. 2d 412 (1966). The court held that a burglar no longer would be considered as convicted of an infamous crime for purposes of disfranchisement.

26. *Otsuka v. Hite.*

27. *Schware v. Board of Bar Examiners*, 353 U.S. 232, 77 S. Ct. 752, 1 L. Ed. 2d 796 (1957).

28. *Schware v. Board of Bar Examiners.* See also *Mindel v. United States Civil Service Commission*, 312 F. Supp. 485 (N.D. Cal. 1970); and *Morrison v. State Board of Education*, 82 Cal. Rptr. 175, 461 P. 2d 375 (1969).

29. *Miller v. District of Columbia*, 294 A. 2d 365 (D.C. App. 1972).

30. "Note: Entrance and Disciplinary Requirements for Occupational License in California," *Stanford Law Review* 18 (1962): 533–50 (1962).

31. *Konigsberg v. State Bar*, 353 U.S. 252, 77 S. Ct. 722, 1 L. Ed. 2d 810 (1957).

32. *Hawker v. New York*, 170 U.S. 189, 18 S. Ct. 573, 42 L. Ed. 1002 (1898).

33. In 1960 the Supreme Court refused to overturn a civil disability law. *De Veau v. Braisted*, 363 U.S. 144, 80 S. Ct. 1146, 4 L. Ed. 2d 1109 (1960).

34. See, generally, "Note, Constitutional Law—Power of Legislature to Exclude a Pardoned Felon from a Civil Service Position," *Iowa Law Review* 27 (1942): 305–09.

35. State ex rel. *Attorney General v. Hawkins*, 44 Ohio St. 98, 5 N.E. 228 (1886).

36. *Hallinan v. Committee of Bar Examiners*, 65 Cal. 2d 447, 55 Cal. Rptr. 228, 421 P. 2d 76 (1966).

37. This summary relied heavily on the definitive study of loss and restoration of civil rights by convicted offenders, Walter Matthews Grant, John LeCornu, John Andrew Pickens, Dean Hill Rivkin, and C. Roger Vinson, "The Collateral Consequences of a Criminal Conviction," *Vanderbilt Law Review* 23, no. 5 (1970): 929–1241.

Glossary

abjuration   An oath to forsake the realm forever taken by an accused person who claimed sanctuary.

absconder   An offender under community supervision who, without prior permission, escapes or flees the jurisdiction he or she is required to stay within.

absolute immunity   Protection from legal action or liability unless workers engage in discretion that is intentionally and maliciously wrong.

adjudication   Juvenile justice equivalent of a trial in adult criminal cases.

amercement   A monetary penalty imposed upon a person for some offense, he or she being in mercy for his or her conduct. It was imposed arbitrarily at the discretion of the court or the person's lord. *Black's Law Dictionary* distinguishes between fines and amercements in that fines are certain, are created by some statute, and can be assessed only by courts of record; amercements are arbitrarily imposed.

attainder   At common law, the extinction of civil rights and capacities that occurred when a person received a sentence of death or outlawry for treason or another felony. The person's estate was forfeited to the Crown.

John Augustus   The "father of probation."

automatic restoration of rights   Reinstatement of some or all civil rights upon completion of sentence. The extent of restoration varies by state and may vary by offense type.

autonomous model   An organizational pattern in which parole decisions are made by an autonomous body not affiliated with other agencies of the criminal justice system. The most common pattern for adult paroling authorities.

balanced and restorative justice model   A model for juvenile justice suggesting that justice is best served when the community, victim, and youth receive balanced attention, and all gain tangible benefits from their interactions with the juvenile justice system.

benefit of clergy   An exemption for members of the clergy that allowed them to avoid being subject to the jurisdiction of secular courts.

boot camp   A form of shock incarceration that involves a military-style regimen designed to instill discipline in young offenders.

Zebulon R. Brockway   The American prison reformer who introduced modern correctional methods, including parole, to the Elmira Reformatory in New York in 1876.

brokerage of services   Supervision that involves identifying the needs of probationers or parolees and referring them to an appropriate community agency.

casework model   Supervision oriented toward providing services to probationers or parolees to help them live productively in the community.

certificate of discharge   Official written documentation signifying an offender has completed his or her sentence.

civil rights   Rights that belong to a person by virtue of citizenship.

classification   A procedure consisting of assessing the risks posed by the offender, identifying the supervision issues, and selecting the appropriate supervision strategy.

clear conditions   Conditions that are sufficiently explicit so as to inform a reasonable person of the conduct that is required or prohibited.

collateral consequences   Disabilities that follow a conviction that are not directly imposed by a sentencing court—such as loss of the right to vote, serve on a jury, practice certain occupations, or own a firearm.

community corrections   A nonincarcerative sanction in which offenders serve all or a portion of their sentence in the community.

Community Corrections Act   A statewide mechanism through which funds are granted to local units of government to plan, develop, and deliver correctional sanctions and services. The overall purpose of this mechanism is to provide local sentencing options in lieu of imprisonment in state institutions.

community resource management team (CRMT) model   A supervision model in which probation or parole officers develop skills and linkages with community agencies in one or two areas only. Supervision under this model is a team effort, each officer utilizing his or her skills and linkages to assist the offender.

community service Unpaid service to the public to compensate society for harm done by the offense of conviction.

commutation Changing a punishment to one that is less severe, as from execution to life imprisonment.

concurrent jurisdiction Original jurisdiction for certain juvenile offenses is shared by both criminal and juvenile courts, and the prosecutor has discretion to file such cases in either court.

conditional pardon A pardon that becomes operative when the grantee has performed some specific act(s) or that becomes void when some specific act(s) transpires.

conduct in need of supervision (CINS) Likely to be status offenses, meaning acts that would not have been punishable if committed by adults. Like juvenile delinquency, each state defines the specific acts that constitute conduct in need of supervision in that state.

consolidation model An organizational pattern in which parole decisions are made by a central authority that has independent powers but is organizationally situated in the department of corrections.

continuing custody theory The view that the parolee remains in custody of either the parole authorities or the prison and that his or her constitutional rights are limited. Release on parole is merely a change in the degree of custody.

court of general jurisdiction A court having unlimited trial jurisdiction, both civil and criminal, though its judgments and decrees are subject to appellate review.

court of limited jurisdiction A criminal court in which the trial jurisdiction is restricted to hearing misdemeanor and petty cases.

court of record A court that is required to make a record of its proceedings and that may fine or imprison.

Sir Walter Crofton An Irish prison reformer who established an early system of parole based on Alexander Maconochie's experiments with the mark system on Norfolk Island.

day fines Fines that are calculated by multiplying a percent of the offender's daily wage by the number of predefined punishment units (the number of punishment units depends on crime seriousness).

day reporting centers A type of nonresidential program typically used for defendants on pretrial release, for convicted offenders on probation or parole, or as an increased sanction for probation or parole violators. Services are provided in one central location, and offenders must check in daily.

determinate sentencing A sentencing philosophy that focuses on certainty and severity for the crime committed and incorporates an exact amount of time or narrow sentencing range of time to be served in prison or in the community. Amount of time served depends on the legislative statutes or the sentenc-

ing guidelines, which mandate how much time is to be served before the offender is eligible (if at all) for early release.

diminished constitutional rights Constitutional rights enjoyed by an offender on parole that are not as highly protected by the courts as the rights of nonoffenders.

disclosure The right of a defendant to read the presentence investigation report prior to sentencing.

disposition Juvenile justice equivalent of sentencing in adult cases.

due process Laws applied in a fair and equal manner. Fundamental fairness.

early termination Termination of probation at any time during the probation period or after some time has been served.

electronic monitoring A correctional technology used as a tool in intensive supervision probation or parole or home confinement, in which an intermittent signal transmitted through telephone lines into a transmitter box determines whether the offender is within a certain distance from his or her personal telephone.

exclusionary rule Evidence that is obtained in violation of the Fourth Amendment guarantee against unreasonable searches and seizures is not admissible in a criminal prosecution to prove the defendant's guilt.

expungement An erasure. Process by which the record of a criminal conviction (or juvenile adjudication) is destroyed or sealed after expiration of time.

filing A procedure under which an indictment was "laid on file," or held in abeyance, without either dismissal or final judgment in cases in which justice did not require an immediate sentence.

fine A fixed monetary sanction imposed by a judge, depending on the seriousness of the crime.

full pardon A pardon that frees the criminal without any condition whatever. It reaches both the punishment prescribed for the offense and the guilt of the offender.

good moral character The totality of moral virtues that forms the basis of one's reputation in the community.

good time Reduction in sentence for institutional good conduct.

grace or privilege theory The view that parole is a privilege and a matter of grace (mercy) by the executive. Under this theory parole confers no particular rights on the recipient and is subject to withdrawal at any time.

grievous loss Revoking parole is a grievous loss because it involves being sent back to prison.

halfway houses The oldest and most common type of community residential facility for probationers or parolees who require a more structured setting than would be available if living independently.

hearsay evidence Information offered as a truthful assertion that does not come from the personal knowledge of the person giving the information, but from knowledge that person received from another.

Matthew Davenport Hill   As recorder of Birmingham (England), he established probation-like practices with young offenders.

house arrest, home confinement   A community-based sanction in which offenders serve their sentence at home. Offenders have curfews and may not leave their home except for employment and correctional treatment purposes.

Illinois Juvenile Court Act of 1899   Established the first juvenile court in the United States.

indeterminate sentencing   A sentencing philosophy that focuses on treatment and incorporates a broad sentencing range or undetermined amount of time served in prison or in the community, where release is reliant on offender rehabilitation or readiness to function prosocially.

informal probation   A form of probation in which a juvenile is placed on probation before he or she is formally adjudicated.

institutional corrections   An incarcerative sanction in which offenders serve their sentence away from the community in a jail or prison institution.

institutional model   An organizational pattern in which parole release decisions are made primarily within the institution. Advocates of the institutional model believe that because institutional staff are most familiar with the offender and his or her response to institutional programs, they are most sensitive to the optimal time for release. Most commonly used in the juvenile field.

intake   Process whereby a juvenile is screened to determine if the case should be processed further by the juvenile justice system or whether other alternatives are better suited for the juvenile. It is usually done by a probation officer or other individuals designated by the court or the prosecutor.

intermediate sanctions   Community corrections strategies that vary in terms of their supervision level and treatment capacity, ranging between probation and incarceration.

indeterminate sentence   A sentence to imprisonment in which the duration is not fixed by the court but is left to be determined by some other authority (typically a parole board or other agency) after some minimum period is served. The basis of parole.

integrated model   A supervision model that integrates a concern for control with a concern for treatment.

intensive supervision probation   A form of probation that stresses intensive monitoring, close supervision, and offender control.

Interstate Compact for the Supervision of Parolees and Probationers   An agreement signed by all 50 states that allows for the supervision of parolees and probationers in a state other than the state of conviction.

the Irish system   Developed in Ireland by Sir Walter Crofton, the Irish system involved graduated levels of institutional control leading up to release under conditions similar to modern parole. The American reforms at Elmira Reformatory were partially based on the Irish system.

judicial reprieve   Withdrawal of a sentence for an interval of time during which the offender was at liberty and imposition of other sanctions was postponed.

judicial waiver   A process whereby a juvenile court judge waives juvenile court jurisdiction and transfers a juvenile case to the regular adult criminal court.

just deserts   The concept that the goal of corrections should be to punish offenders because they deserve to be punished and that punishment should be commensurate with the seriousness of the offense.

justice model   The correctional practice based on the concept of just deserts. The justice model calls for fairness in criminal sentencing, in that all persons convicted of a like offense will receive a like sentence. Prisons are viewed as places of even-handed punishment, not rehabilitation. This model of corrections relies on determinate sentencing and abolition of parole.

juvenile delinquency   In general, acts committed by juveniles that are punishable as crimes by a state's penal code. Each state, however, defines the specific acts that constitute juvenile delinquency in that state.

law violations   Violations of probation or parole conditions that involve the commission of a crime.

liberty interest   Any interest recognized or protected by the due process clauses of state or federal constitutions.

Alexander Maconochie   A British naval captain who served as governor of the penal colony on Norfolk Island, who instituted a system of early release that was the forerunner of modern parole. Maconochie is known as the "father of parole."

mandatory release   Conditional release to the community that is automatic at the expiration of the maximum term of sentence minus any credited time off for good behavior.

mark system   Credits for good behavior and hard work. In Alexander Maconochie's mark system on Norfolk Island, convicts could use the credits or marks to purchase either goods or time (reduction in sentence). In this system the prisoner progressed through stages from strict imprisonment, through conditional release, to final and complete restoration of liberty, with promotion being based on the marks accredited. One of the historical foundations of parole.

maximum eligibility date   The longest amount of time that can be served before the inmate must be released by law.

medical model   The concept that given proper care and treatment, criminals can be changed into productive, law-abiding citizens. This approach suggests that people commit crimes because of influences beyond their control, such as poverty, injustice, and racism. Also called the rehabilitation model.

medical parole   The conditional release from prison to the community for prisoners with a terminal illness who do not pose an undue risk to public safety.

Mens rea Latin term for "a guilty mind." Without intent an act is generally not considered criminal.

minimum eligibility date The shortest amount of time defined by statute, minus good time earned, that must be served before the offender can go before the parole board.

moral turpitude An act of baseness, vileness, or depravity in the private and social duties a person owes to other humans or to society in general that is contrary to the accepted, customary rule of right and duty between persons. A grave infringement of the moral sentiment of the community. A felony or a misdemeanor that is contrary to the public's moral standards.

motion to quash An oral or written request that the court repeal, nullify, or overturn a decision, usually made during or after the trial.

net widening Using an intermediate sanction as a stiffer punishment for offenders who would have ordinarily been sentenced to probation or other lesser sanction.

nolo contendere A plea option, available in a small number of states, that literally means "I do not wish to contend the charges."

Norfolk Island The notorious British penal colony 1,000 miles off the coast of Australia.

Offender-based presentence report A presentence investigation report that seeks to understand the offender and the circumstances of the offense and to evaluate the offender's potential as a law-abiding, productive citizen.

Offense-based presentence report A presentence investigation report that focuses primarily on the offense committed, the offender's culpability, and the offender's criminal history.

Outlawry In old Anglo-Saxon law, the process by which a criminal was declared an outlaw and placed outside the protection and aid of the law.

pardon An executive act of clemency that absolves an individual from the legal consequences of a crime and conviction. A pardon is an act of grace or a remission of guilt. A full pardon freely and unconditionally absolves the party from the consequences of the crime and conviction. A conditional pardon becomes operative when the grantee has performed some specified act, or it becomes void after the occurrence of some specified event, or it remits only a portion of the penalties that are the legal consequences of a crime and conviction.

parens patriae Latin for "parent of the country"; refers to the traditional role of the state as guardian of persons under legal disability, such as juveniles, the insane, and incarcerated persons. The assumption is that the state acts in the best interest of those over whom the *parens patriae* relationship exists.

parole Conditional release, by an administrative act, of a convicted offender from a penal or correctional institution, under the continual custody of the state, to serve the remainder of his or her sentence in the community under supervision.

parole board An administrative body (usually 3–18 members) empowered to decide whether inmates shall be conditionally released from prison before the completion of their sentence, to revoke parole, and to discharge from parole those who have satisfactorily completed their terms.

parole conditions The rules under which a paroling authority releases an offender to community supervision.

parole d'honneur French for "word of honor," from which the English word *parole* is derived.

parole eligibility date The point in a prisoner's sentence at which he or she becomes eligible to be considered for parole. If the offender is denied parole, a new parole eligibility date is scheduled in the future.

parole guidelines Guidelines to be followed in making parole release decisions. Most guidelines prescribe a presumptive term for each class of convicted inmate depending on both offense and offender characteristics.

political rights Rights related to the establishment, support, or management of government.

preferred rights Rights more highly protected than other constitutional rights.

preliminary hearing An inquiry conducted at or reasonably near the place of the alleged parole violation or arrest to determine if there is probable cause to believe that the parolee committed a parole violation.

presentence investigation An investigation undertaken by a probation officer at the request of the court for the purpose of obtaining information about the defendant that may assist the court in arriving at a rational, fair sentence.

presentence investigation (PSI) report A report prepared from the presentence investigation and provided to the court before sentencing that serves a number of purposes.

presumptive sentence A statutorily determined sentence convicted offenders will presumably receive if convicted. Offenders convicted in a jurisdiction with presumptive sentences will be assessed this sentence unless mitigating or aggravating circumstances are found to exist.

public employment Paid employment at any level of government.

public offices Uncompensated, elected or appointed government positions.

qualified immunity Protection from liability in decisions or actions that are "objectively reasonable."

reasonable conditions Probation conditions that can be reasonably complied with by the offender.

receiving state Under the interstate compact, the state that undertakes the supervision.

recidivism The repetition of or return to criminal behavior, variously defined in one of three ways: rearrest, reconviction, or reincarceration.

recognizance Originally a device of preventive justice that obliged persons suspected of future misbehavior to stipulate with and give full assurance to the court and the public that the apprehended offense would not occur. Recognizance was later used with convicted or arraigned offenders with conditions of release set. Recognizance was usually entered into for a specified period.

relapse   When an offender with a substance abuse problem returns to using alcohol or drugs.

residential community corrections facilities   A sanction in the community in which the convicted offender lives at the facility and must be employed, but he or she can leave the facility for a limited purpose and duration if preapproved. Examples include halfway houses, prerelease centers, restitution centers, drug treatment facilities, and work release centers.

residential drug and alcohol treatment centers   A type of residential community facility specifically targeted for drug offenders or offenders with a substance abuse problem who are amenable to treatment.

restitution   Repairing victim's losses suffered at the hands of the offender through the offender's monetary payment or restoring a crime victim's property through individual service.

restitution centers   A type of residential community facility specifically targeted for property or first-time offenders who owe victim restitution or community service.

restorative justice   The philosophy and sanction of allowing the offender to remain in the community with the responsibility of restoring the victim's losses.

revocation   The formal termination of a parolee's conditional freedom and the reinstatement of imprisonment.

revocation hearing   A due process hearing that must be conducted before parole can be revoked.

risk assessment   A procedure that provides a measure of the offender's propensity to further criminal activity and indicates the level of officer intervention that will be required.

Salient Factor Score   The parole guidelines developed and used by the U.S. Parole Commission for making parole release decisions. Served as the model for parole guidelines developed in many other jurisdictions.

sanctuary   In old English law, a consecrated place, such as a church or abbey, where offenders took refuge because they could not be arrested there.

sealing   The legal concealment of a person's criminal (or juvenile) record such that it cannot be opened except by order of the court.

security for good behavior   A recognizance or bond given the court by a defendant before or after conviction conditioned on his or her being "on good behavior" or keeping the peace for a prescribed period.

sending state   Under the interstate compact, the state of conviction.

shock incarceration   A brief period of incarceration followed by a term of supervised probation. Also called shock probation, shock parole, intermittent imprisonment, or split sentence.

shock probation   A period of incaceration imposed as a condition of probation.

special conditions   Conditions tailored to fit the needs of an offender.

split sentence   A term of jail or imprisonment followed by a period of probation.

standard conditions   Conditions imposed on all parolees or probationers in a jurisdiction.

stigmatization   Loss of social status and respect as a result of having a felony conviction.

supervision   The oversight that a probation or parole officer exercises over those in his or her custody.

surety bond   A certificate signed by the principal and a third party, promising to pay in the event the assured suffers damages or losses because the employee fails to perform as agreed.

suspended sentence   An order of the court after a verdict, finding, or plea of guilty that suspends or postpones the imposition or execution of sentence during a period of good behavior.

technical violations   Violations of the conditions of probation that do not involve law violations.

Peter Oxenbridge Thacher   Massachusetts judge who introduced probation-like practices in the early 19th century.

ticket-of-leave   A license or permit given to a convict as a reward for good conduct, which allowed him to go at large and labor for himself before his sentence expired, subject to certain restrictions and revocable upon subsequent misconduct. A forerunner of parole.

ticket-of-leave man   A convict who has obtained a ticket-of-leave.

transportation   The forced exile of convicted criminals. England transported convicted criminals to the American colonies until the Revolutionary War and afterward to Australia. The foundations of the transportation system are found in the law of 1597, 39 Eliz. c.4, "An Acte for Punyshment of Rogues, Vagabonds, and Sturdy Beggars." The act declared that obdurate idlers "shall . . be banished out of this Realm . . . and shall be conveyed to such parts beyond the seas as shall be . . . assigned by the Privy Council."

victim impact statement A written account by the victim(s) as to how the crime has taken a toll physically, emotionally, financially, or psychologically on the victim and the victim's family. Victim impact statements are considered by many states at time of sentencing and at parole board hearings.

widening the net   When an individual who should have received probation is sentenced to a harsher intermediate sanction, only because that sanction is available, not because the offender requires more intensive supervision.

work and study release   Offenders who reside in a facility (a community facility, jail, or prison) but who are released into the community only to work or attend education classes or both.

Table of Cases

Name Index

Subject Index

New York State Department of Corrections Services (DOCS), shock incarceration program, 246–248, 37920
Ninth Amendment, right to privacy, 79
Nolo contendere, **41**
Norfolk Island, **165**

O

Occupational licenses. *See* Licenses, occupational
Offender-based presentence reports, 57–**58**
Offenders
    boot camps as viewed by, 252
    drug, 3, 119–120
    first, as shock incarceration population, 244, 245, 246
    sex, 217, 347–350, 352, 387n64
Offender tracking, 282–283
    See also Electronic monitoring (EM)
Offense-based presentence reports, **59**–61
Offenses, status, 309–310
Office of Juvenile Justice and Delinquency Prevention (OJJDP)
    discrimination in juvenile justice system, 328
    juvenile crime figures, 303
    juvenile probation caseloads, 327
    juvenile probation paradigm, 327–328
    objectives of juvenile justice system, 330–331
    referrals to juvenile courts, 312
    youth gangs, 328–330
Office of the United States Pardon Attorney, 358
Outlawry, **337**, 338

P

Pardons, **162**, **354**–357
    bad character, 362
    delivery and acceptance of, 356, 388n4
    kinds of, 356, 357
    legal effects of, 356–357
    objectives of, 355
    parole vs., 162
    power to grant, 355, 387n1, 388n2
    procedure for obtaining, 356, 388nn5-6
    revocation of, 356
Parens patriae, **305**–306, 307
    case signaling decline of, 305–306, 314–315, 316

parole viewed as, **202**
Parental responsibility laws, 326
Parole, 14, **14**, 157–240, **159**
    abolition of, 175–176, 177–178, 374n42
    average length of, 211
    boot camp programs, 249
    budget for, 7, 39, 365n20
    discretionary, 159–160, 161, 174–176
    effectiveness of, 233–236
    eligibility for, 188–189
    federal, 33, 168–169
    functions of, 176–183, 374n52
    future of, 236–237
    good-time policies, 181–182
    history of, 162–168
    in justice model, 173–174
    medical, **182**–183
    in medical model, 169–171
    number of adults on, 3, 4, 39, 160–161, 176
    organizational models, 187–188
    pardon vs., 162
    parolees' views of, 211–214
    prerelease preparation within institution, 189–190
    prisoners' perceptions of selection for, 200–202
    prison population levels regulated by, 5, 178–181, 374n52
    prison time credit for time served on, 231–232
    probation vs., 160–161
    theoretical views of, 202
Parole absconders, **220**–223
Parole boards, **187**
    abolition of, 174, 177–178
    change of decision by, 230
    characteristics of, 190, 192–193, 374n5, 375n8
    functions of, 187
    members of, 190–191
    parole conditions imposed by, 205
    parole release decision by, 194–200, 375n24
Parole conditions, **211**, 215–220
    consequences of violating, 224
    imposed by parole board, 205
    legal issues, 217
    special, **215**, 216
    standard, **215**–216
Parole decisions
    avoiding arbitrary, 204–205
    before 1970s, 194–195

    lack of written reasons for, 194, 375n24
    parole guidelines for making, 195–200
    parole release risk instruments, 199, 200
    prisoners' perceptions of, 200–202
    Salient Factor Score, 196, 197
    See also Parole hearings
Parole d'honneur, **162**
Parole eligibility date, **189**
Parolees
    committing new crimes, 224, 377n47
    constitutional rights of, 218–219, 228–233
    female, risk prediction instruments for, 200
    parole absconders, 220–223
    power to arrest, 219–220, 377n36
    predicting behavior of, 221–223, 237
    studies of recidivism by, 234–236
    studies of view of, 211–214
    supervision of, 113, 205, 376n67
Parole guidelines, **195**–200
Parole hearings, 191–194
    deferral of release decision, 194
    due process during, 202–205, 226–227
    victim participation in, 192–194
    See also Parole decisions; Parole revocation hearings
Parole officers
    appointment of, 102
    assaults against, 108
    caseloads, 128–130, 214
    education and experience, 103, 104–105, 214–215
    firearms for, 107–109, 371n55
    functions of, 214
    job pressure management by, 215
    power to arrest parolees, 219–220
    qualifications of, 214
    salaries, 105–107
    training requirements, 103–105
    See also Probation officers
Parole revocation, 182, **223**–226
    due process, 226–228, 230, 231
    exclusionary rule, 147–148, 229–230
    leading case on, 226, 228
    public attitudes toward, 226
    rates of, 224–226
    right to appeal, 232
    right to counsel, 228–229

Sanctions
    continuum of, 16–17
    intermediate, 14–15, 19–20, 47
Sanctuary, **26**–27
"Scarlet letter" conditions, 77–78
Sealing, **359**–360
Securicor Custodial Services Limited, 282
Security for good behavior, **27**
Self-control, as basis for theory of crime, 117
Self-incrimination, privilege against, 81
Sending states, **109**
Sentences, **42**
    determinate, **59**, **172**
    indeterminate, 58–**59**, 167, **168**
    presumptive, **173**
    recommended by probation officers, 64
    revocation of, due to PSI report inaccuracies, 66
    split, **176**, 245
    suspended, **28**–30, 94, 367n5
    types of, imposed by courts, 42–43
    See also Sentencing
Sentencing, **42**
    considerations in deciding on probation in, 44–52
    continuum of sanctions, 16–17
    determinate, **5**–6, 172, 187
    goals of, met by probation, 9
    indeterminate, **3**–5, 187
    legal issues, 43–44
    methods of developing information for, 47–49
    "truth in sentencing" laws, 5
    See also Sentences
Sentencing guidelines, 5, 50–52, 59
    See also Determinate sentences
Sentencing Reform Act (1984)
    abolished parole as option to control prison crowding, 5
    created supervised release, 159
    sentence suspension vs. probation, 30
Sentencing Reform Act, Sentencing Guidelines, and Parole, 81–82
Sex offenders
    parole for, 217
    registration of, 347–350, 352, 387n64
Shaming conditions, 77–78
Shock incarceration, 84–85, **244**–255
    See also Boot camps
Shock parole. *See* Shock incarceration
Shock probation, **84**–85

See also Shock incarceration
Sixth Amendment, 68
Social history report, 48
Solution to Employment Problems (STEP), 346, 387n47
Special conditions
    of parole, **215**, 216
    of probation, **73**, 74–75
Split sentences, **176**, 245
    See also Shock incarceration
Standard conditions
    of parole, **215**–216
    of probation, **73**, 74
Standards for Adult Parole Authorities (American Correctional Association), 217
Standards Relating to Probation (American Bar Association), 81, 340, 367n12
Standards Relating to Sentencing Alternatives and Procedures (American Bar Association), 61, 65–66, 85
States
    abolishing parole/parole boards, 174, 175–176, 177–178, 374n42
    administration of probation by, 96–98, 100, 101
    adults on parole, 160–161, 178–181
    adults on probation, 46, 48–49
    automatic restoration of rights statutes, 358
    boot camp programs, 246–251
    caseloads of probation/parole officers, 128, 129
    with Community Corrections Acts, 370n22
    early probation legislation, 95
    education and training requirements for probation officers, 103–105
    electronic monitoring use, 280
    evidence/proof in revocation proceedings, 146–147
    extent of community corrections, 40
    firearms for probation and parole officers, 108, 371n55
    fugitive units, 221, 222
    good-time policies, 182
    imposing death penalty, 43
    interstate compacts on probation, 109–110
    juvenile court jurisdiction, 309
    juvenile crime laws, 305, 330
    juvenile probation and aftercare, 318

parole board characteristics, 190, 192–193, 374n5, 375n8
parole guidelines, 196–200
probation conditions, criteria and eligibility, 44, 45, 73
receiving vs. sending, **109**
residential community corrections facilities, 257, 266
salaries of probation and parole officers, 105–107
sentencing guidelines, 5, 50–52
sex offender registration laws, 347–349
using parole to regulate prison population levels, 179–180
victim participation in parole hearings, 192–194
Status offenses, 309–310
Stigmatization of ex-offenders, **350**–351
Struggle for Justice (American Friends Service Committee), 172
Substance abuse treatment. *See* Drug and alcohol treatment
Supervised release, 102, 169
Supervision, **113**, 117, 159
    caseloads and workloads, 128–130
    case plan development, 126
    classification step, 122–128
    juvenile probation, 321–323
    levels of, contact requirements, 126–127
    models of, 113–121
    number of adults under, 3, 4
    parole, responsibility for, 205, 376n67
    and parolee recidivism, 236
    parole vs. probation, 113
    planning, federal model of, 123–126
    shift of emphasis in, 100
    surveillance function, 118
    treatment function, 119–121
    types of, in community-based corrections, 7–8
    See also Intensive supervision probation (ISP)
Supervision of Federal Offenders, 116, 123
The Supervision Process, 120
Surety bond, **346**
Surveillance, 100, **118**
Suspended sentences, **28**–30, 367n5
Suspension of execution of sentence (SES), 94
Suspension of imposition of sentence (SIS), 94

T

Technical violations, **138**, 139–141, 274
Teen courts, 307–308
Ticket-of-leave, **164**
    English system, 166
    Irish system, 167
Ticket-of-leave men, **165**, 167
"Tough on crime." *See* "Get tough" approach
Training, of probation and parole officers, 103–105
Transportation, **164**–165
Treatment
    in boot camps, 245, 254
    in day reporting centers, 284–286
    drug and alcohol, 16, 119–121, 216, 264–265, 265
    identifying needs for, 126
    with intensive supervision probation, 275
    in supervision, 119–121
"Truth in sentencing" laws, 5

U

U.S. Board of Parole, 195, 375n31
    See also U.S. Parole Commission
U.S. Congress, House Judiciary Committee report on juvenile crime, 303
U.S. Constitution
    bills of attainder forbidden by, 338
    ex post facto clause, 230–231
    offenders excluded from certain government positions, 342, 386nn20, 21

power to pardon, 387n1
First Amendment, 78–79, 218
Fourth Amendment, 67, 79, 80–81, 147–148, 218, 219, 283
Fifth Amendment, 79, 81
Sixth Amendment, 68
Eighth Amendment, 43, 78, 85, 253
Ninth Amendment, 79
Fourteenth Amendment, 86, 217, 226, 342, 386n20
    See also Constitutional rights
U.S. Department of Justice
    Drug Use Monitoring program, 120
    juvenile crime figures, 303
    The Reentry Partnerships Initiative, 236
U.S. Department of Labor, Employment and Training Administration
    fidelity bonding coverage, 346–347
U.S. Parole Commission, 102, 169, 178, 370n33, 375n31
U.S. Sentencing Commission, 169

V

Vermont
    probation organizational pattern, 95
    Reparative Probation Program, 13
Victim impact statements, **60**, **192**
    in parole hearings, 192–194
    sample, 61
Victim-offender reconciliation projects (VORPs), 292
Victim Witness Protection Act (VWPA), 290

Violations
    law, **138**, 139
    resulting in motion to revoke, 142
    technical, **138**, 139–141, 274
Violence against Women Act, 290, 291
Violent Crime Control and Law Enforcement Act (1994), 254
Vote, right to, 342–343, 357

W

Weapons. *See* Firearms
". . . *We Are the Living Proof. . .": The Justice Model for Corrections* (Fogel), 173
Widening the net, **244**
Witnesses
    right to be, 343, 357
    right to confront, 229
Women
    boot camp programs, 249, 253
    parole risk instruments, 200
    See also Gender
Women offenders living with children, 267–268
Workloads, for probation and parole officers, 128
Work and study release, **265**–266

Y

Youth gangs, 328–330

Photo Credits